Ways of War

From the first interactions between European and native peoples to the recent conflicts in Afghanistan and Iraq, military issues have always played an important role in American history. Now in its updated second edition, *Ways of War* comprehensively explains the place of the military within the wider context of the history of the United States, showing its centrality to American culture, economics, and politics. The fifteen chapters provide a complete survey of the American military's evolution that is designed for semester-length courses.

Features of the revised and fully updated second edition include:

- Chronological and comprehensive coverage of North American conflicts in the seventeenth century and all wars undertaken by the United States;
- New or expanded sections on Non-English Colonization in Northeast North America, the Beaver Wars, Pontiac's War, causes of the American Revolution, borderlands conflicts from 1848 to 1865, causes of the American Civil War, Reconstruction, the Meuse-Argonne Campaign, Barack Obama's second term as president, the Syrian Civil War, and the rise of the Islamic State;
- 50 revised maps, 20 new images, chapter timelines identifying key events, and text boxes providing biographical information and first-person accounts;
- A companion website featuring a testbank of essay and multiple-choice questions for instructors, as well as student study resources such as an interactive timeline, chapter summaries, annotated further readings, links to online resources, flashcards, and a glossary of key terms.

Extensively illustrated and written by experienced instructors, the second edition of *Ways of War* remains essential reading for all students of American Military History.

Matthew S. Muehlbauer is currently an Assistant Professor with the Department of History at the United States Military Academy.

David J. Ulbrich is currently the Program Director of the Master of Arts in History and Military History degrees at Norwich University.

Ways of War

American Military History from the Colonial Era to the Twenty-First Century

2nd Edition

Matthew S. Muehlbauer
David J. Ulbrich

Routledge
Taylor & Francis Group

NEW YORK AND LONDON

Second edition published 2018
by Routledge
711 Third Avenue, New York, NY 10017

and by Routledge
2 Park Square, Milton Park, Abingdon, Oxon, OX14 4RN

Routledge is an imprint of the Taylor & Francis Group, an informa business

First edition published by Routledge 2014

Library of Congress Cataloging-in-Publication Data
Names: Muehlbauer, Matthew S., author. | Ulbrich, David J., author.
Title: Ways of war : American military history from the colonial era to the twenty-first
  century / by Matthew S. Muehlbauer and David J. Ulbrich.
Description: Second edition. | New York : Routledge, 2018. | Includes bibliographical
  references and index.
Identifiers: LCCN 2017020613 (print) | LCCN 2017021140 (ebook) |
  ISBN 9781315545691 (ebook) | ISBN 9781138681613 (alk. paper)
Subjects: LCSH: United States—History, Military—Textbooks. | United States—Armed
  Forces—History—Textbooks.
Classification: LCC E181 (ebook) | LCC E181 .M92 2018 (print) | DDC
  355.00973—dc23
LC record available at https://lccn.loc.gov/2017020613

ISBN: 978-1-138-68161-3 (hbk)
ISBN: 978-1-138-68162-0 (pbk)
ISBN: 978-1-315-54569-1 (ebk)

Typeset in Bembo
by Apex CoVantage, LLC

Visit the companion website: www.routledge.com/cw/muehlbauer

The views expressed in this work do not necessarily reflect the official policies or
positions of the U.S. Army, the U.S. Department of Defense, or the U.S. Government.

In Memory of Professor Russell F. Weigley, 1930–2004.
Respected Teacher, Scholar, Mentor

Contents

11 Mobilizing for the Second World War, 1941–1943 330

12 Winning the Second World War, 1943–1945 362

Acknowledgments

In the fall of 2009, when Matthew Muehlbauer was working in the Department of History at the United States Military Academy, some editors from Routledge gave a presentation to the faculty about how they evaluate monograph proposals. A chance remark by one of them led to the first edition of *Ways of War* being published in 2014. David Ulbrich had joined this project in 2010 and wrote the chapters on the twentieth and twenty-first centuries for that first edition.

The first edition picked up numerous course adoptions, including at the U.S. Air Force Academy. In addition, our book garnered constructive reviews from Jeremy Black, Wayne Lee, Mark Grimsley, and Richard Stewart. Then Routledge commissioned a second edition of *Ways of War*. Matt revised his chapters extending from the seventeenth century through 1902, and Dave updated the chapters covering 1902 to 2017.

We must thank Eve Mayer and several of her colleagues at Routledge and its parent firm Taylor & Francis: Genevieve Aoki, Margo Irvin, Chelsea Pengal, Staci Custus, Rebecca Shillabeer, Sarah Collins, Theodore Meyer, and Mark Whiting. They showed great flexibility and enthusiasm in bringing this project to fruition. Numerous people also assisted us in the essential tasks of copyediting, cartography, proofreading, providing illustrations, and creating additional content for this volume's accompanying website. Of these, Eric Gillespie and Ian Brown deserve recognition.

In addition to those people helping to produce the book, many people played instrumental roles in helping us develop the second edition. Among these colleagues are Bobby Wintermute, Daniel Krebs, Ellen Tillman, Paul Thomsen, Joseph Henrotin, Jerry Sweeney, Brigadier General Peter "Duke" Deluca (USA, Ret.), and faculty of the U.S. Air Force Academy's Department of History, including Lieutenant Colonel Grant Weller (Ret.), Robert Wetteman, and Lieutenant Colonel Mark Grotelueschen. Other instructors also assigned *Ways of War* in their courses and later offered useful critiques that helped make the second edition a better teaching tool.

Special mention should also be made of Gregory J. W. Urwin, our common advisor who guided us through our doctoral studies at Temple University, and the late Russell F. Weigley, who continued to teach graduate courses until his unexpected passing in 2004. Many readers will recognize that the title of this volume is in part an homage to Professor Weigley's seminal study *The American Way of War*. This work has defined the parameters of scholarly treatments of U.S. military history ever since its publication in 1973.

Lastly, the greatest appreciation must go to our families, who shared more of their time with the second edition: Elizabeth Schoetz for her enduring patience, good humor, and support; Samantha and Jacob Muehlbauer for occasionally getting their father away from the computer and providing perspective; and Tom and Pat Ulbrich for always being there with good advice and enjoyable vacations.

Matthew S. Muehlbauer
New City, New York

David J. Ulbrich
Barre, Vermont

August 2017

Figures

Maps

Introduction

The definition of military history has changed over time. For centuries, it was primarily the conduct of armed forces, particularly how they fight, which is sometimes called "drum and bugle" history. More recently, scholars have examined why wars are fought and their broader consequences, examining political, social, cultural, economic, and other factors. This approach is known as the "new military history" or "war and society." *Ways of War* combines both approaches to demonstrate the complexities of American military history over several centuries.

Military forces can pursue many missions, including peacekeeping, nation-building, and humanitarian assistance functions. But their distinguishing characteristic is that they are armed and have the capacity to fight. Military historians use various terms and concepts to discuss war. This section presents a brief overview of the more common and important ones that will help readers understand American military history. These terms and concepts will appear throughout this textbook.

What Is War?

A war is a state of belligerency. The term does not refer to a specific event or action, such as a battle. A war occurs when adversaries attempt to use military force against one another, and expect enemies to do the same. Rulers or governments might openly declare a war. If not, it begins when one side mobilizes armed forces, precipitating the other to do likewise, and produces combat actions. A war ends when both sides agree to stop fighting, and usually involves signing a treaty or otherwise agreeing to terms of surrender or truce. Although a war may involve little combat, the status of belligerency exists so long as both sides expect each other to fight.

Using armed forces, war entails both the potential risk and the actual infliction of death and destruction. Its purpose is to induce the opponent to stop fighting and negotiate a peace, or force terms upon a foe. The devastation caused by war can be focused narrowly upon enemy combatants but may also target civilians. Even when a government attempts to limit the scope of violence, war always has broader effects. It requires resources and sacrifices, and hence can have a great impact upon societies in the form of military spending, government regulation, taxes, and demands upon the population to perform military service. Armed forces also disrupt areas in which they operate, destroying buildings and other structures, as well as economic and transportation networks. Civilians in or near a combat zone face dangers such as the destruction of property and homes, the onset of starvation and illness, and the possibility of death or maiming. Both the demands war places upon a society and the impact of military operations on noncombatants affect a belligerent's ability and willingness to continue fighting.

Combat Actions

Various terms describe specific incidents of combat, which can be broadly called "engagements."

Smaller engagements involve dozens, hundreds, or perhaps a few thousand combatants. These include ambushes, raids, and skirmishes. In an ambush, one force waits in hiding to surprise another, usually to destroy it or inflict high casualties. In a raid, combatants attack a specific location—not to capture it but to inflict casualties, seize goods and equipment, or test local defenses. A skirmish is similar to a battle (see below) but occurs between relatively small forces. Smaller engagements often occur prior to a large battle, or during a siege.

A battle involves larger numbers of combatants. Small ones may involve hundreds, whereas large ones might involve many thousands or (in the case of the World Wars) millions. A battle occurs when two opposing armies or fleets are near each other and are looking to fight, though each tries to surprise the other or acquire some advantage. In a battle, each side seeks either to destroy or cripple the enemy, or drive the enemy away from the battlefield.

Like a battle, a siege involves many combatants. But a siege seeks to capture a specific place such as a city or fortress. To "besiege" a target, an attacker first surrounds it. The besiegers may then wait until the defenders' supplies run out and they surrender. (Troops assigned to defend a fort or city are usually called its "garrison.") If time is an issue, the attackers may bombard the target with artillery, or assault or "storm" it with infantry, to try to capture it quickly. The naval equivalent of a siege is a blockade, which can be extended along a coastline to deprive the enemy of trade, supplies, and reinforcements.

Types of War

People describe wars in different ways. Some terms refer to the types of combat and combatants prevalent in certain conflicts. Other terms describe the reasons for a war, or the nature of the belligerents.

Wars Described by Types of Combat

What are called "high-intensity" wars have also been known as "conventional" or "regular" wars. These feature armies that seek to dominate territory, and which are prepared to fight battles and conduct sieges to do so. Similarly, navies try to control sea lanes and access to ports. Such conflicts as the American Civil War and the Second World War are considered "high-intensity" because of the large number of combatants involved and resources and equipment needed to supply and arm them. They are also called "conventional" or "regular" because, after the Middle Ages, European nations came to view them as the "usual" type of warfare (addressed in Chapter 1). Similarly, combatants that fight in such wars are often called "conventional forces" or "regulars."

What are called "low-intensity" wars have also been known as "guerrilla," "partisan," or "irregular" wars, or *petit guerre* (French for "little war"). Irregulars do not necessarily attempt to control an area. They seek instead to hurt, harass, demoralize, or destroy enemy units, and to capture resources. When not attacking, they avoid combat. Irregulars rely upon speed, stealth, and terrain to avoid detection and prepare their own assaults. Such warfare is called "low-intensity" partly because it frequently consists of smaller engagements with fewer combatants compared to conventional war. Similarly, irregulars usually are not as well armed as regulars, and do not consume the same quantities of supplies. Whereas conventional armies usually store and transport provisions and arms to troops, irregulars are more likely to find what they need from the surrounding countryside.

Many wars contain both high- and low-intensity warfare. In fact, low-intensity combat often accompanies high-intensity fighting. Prior to a large battle, for example, troops advancing between the main field armies might conduct raids, ambushes, and skirmishes with opposing forces. If irregular combat occurs mostly as an adjunct to regular fighting, or is not as prevalent, then the war is usually regarded as a conventional conflict. Other wars, however, are more mixed, in that low-intensity combat occurs frequently and is separate and distinct from the operations of regular armies. An example of such a "hybrid" war is the American Revolution. Another possibility is "asymmetrical warfare." This term describes a conflict in which an army trained and prepared to wage high-intensity warfare fights an irregular foe instead, as happened in phases of the Philippine-American War, the Vietnam War, and the Global War on Terror. In such asymmetrical conflicts, regulars face irregulars who avoid combat except when fighting is to their advantage.

Wars Described by the Nature of Belligerents

The term "war," without any qualification, usually refers to a conflict between two independent, autonomous political entities such as empires, countries, states, or city-states. But wars also occur within political communities. In general, the terms "revolt" or "rebellion" describe attempts to overthrow an established government or regime from within. These only generate wars if they lead to an ongoing state of belligerency. For example, a revolt that is immediately crushed by armed forces, or that produces a rapid change in government leadership (a *coup d'etat*), will not create a war. But an ongoing rebellion can produce different types of wars.

The term "guerrilla war" can simply mean the predominance of low-intensity combat, as often occurs in areas behind an invading army. Guerrillas, though, can also be rebels trying to overthrow an established regime but who lack the resources to fight in a conventional manner. Conflicts in which rebels can raise conventional forces are often described as civil wars—and can feature both regular and irregular combat. An insurgency is closer to a guerrilla war than a civil war in that insurgents do not usually mount conventional operations. But they often employ intimidation and terror to both obtain aid and compliance from local populations, and to undermine support for the established regime. Guerrillas do so as well if their goal is rebellion as opposed to harassing an invader.

Military Service

Traditionally, soldiers have been men. Women began entering armed forces (beyond the medical service) during the twentieth century. Often, they have been restricted from combat duties, though such constraints are being lifted in the U.S. military as of this writing. People join military forces in different ways. Some volunteer. If not enough do so, as might occur in a large conventional conflict such as the American Civil War, a government might impose conscription or call a draft, compelling some people to serve. A draft occurs to raise manpower for a conflict, or to address a threat during a specific time. A country utilizing conscription regularly requires some adults (generally young men) to provide military service. Conscripts and draftees usually serve for limited terms, a few years or perhaps the duration of a war. Depending on circumstances, volunteers might enlist for a short or a long period, or reenlist when a term of service expires.

In a conventional army, service is more than a full-time occupation. It requires volunteers, draftees, and conscripts to leave civilian society and live in an environment defined by military needs and responsibilities. In other types of armed forces, the distinction between civilian and military worlds is not as stark. Militia units, for example, require their members to report only occasionally for training. In a war or similar emergency, a government might mobilize a militia unit for full-time service, or expect militiamen to join conventional forces as volunteers or draftees.

This book identifies three distinct periods of military service in American military history: the "militia" era, running from the 1600s to the early twentieth century; the "conscription" era, starting in 1917 during the First World War and ending in 1973 with the conclusion of the Vietnam War; and the "volunteer" era from 1973 to the present. These periods describe, broadly speaking, the predominant type of military service in particular eras—though not the only type. Volunteers have been important in all the nation's wars, for example. Individual colonies imposed the first drafts in American history, with the first national drafts occurring during the Civil War.

Levels of Warfare

Military professionals and historians often use the following terms to distinguish war's different scales and effects when employing armed forces on land, at sea, or in the air.

- *Strategy:* In general parlance, the term "strategy" has come to mean a plan of action. In military affairs, it has more specific meaning. Strategy is the broadest use of armed forces to achieve specific goals. These goals will vary depending upon circumstances, and can include acquiring or retaining territory, shaping economic and diplomatic relationships, or winning or suppressing a people's political independence or rights. Whatever the specific goals, military or civilian leaders must deduce how armed forces can achieve them. It might entail invading and occupying a foreign country (often a particular region), blockading a coastline, or destroying or disabling an enemy's military forces. "Strategy" often means just the use of armed forces, whereas "grand strategy" encompasses military, economic, and diplomatic means to achieve war objectives. Sometimes the term "national strategy" identifies the policies of a specific country when it is part of a coalition of allies.

- *Operations:* After a strategy has been decided, military commanders implement it with an "operation" or multiple "operations." The term has become prominent since World War II, but an older expression still used is "campaign." An operation or campaign involves the movement of military forces to achieve a strategic goal. Such goals can be the capture or defense of a major city or fortress, the occupation or protection of an important region, or maneuvering units to cripple enemy forces in a battle. A "field army" is a conventional force engaged in a particular campaign, though multiple campaigns might be launched in pursuit of the same strategic goal.

- *Tactics:* Operational movements produce combat actions. How soldiers fight them is the province of tactics. More than just weapons, tactics describe how soldiers move, coordinate, and employ arms while under fire to defeat or drive off an enemy force. They will vary according to combat actions (battles, sieges, skirmishes, etc.). Many other factors also influence tactics, including technological changes, the structure and organization of armed forces, and cultural and social ideas about warfare.

A given combat action may have minimal or great consequences, or varying effects at different levels of warfare. One minor skirmish, for example, is unlikely to impact larger military operations. In a battle, though, one side will drive away the other and win a tactical victory. That tactical outcome, in turn, will have operational effects: It might allow an invading force to continue a campaign, or conversely, delay or even stop it. In the latter case, a defending army that suffers a tactical defeat might still gain an operational victory. A battle or siege can have even larger consequences if it allows one side to achieve a strategic goal, or even convinces a belligerent to cease hostilities and negotiate a peace.

War and Society

For centuries, military history consisted primarily of narratives of wars, campaigns, and battles, and decisions made by top commanders. Starting in the late twentieth century, such works as Peter Karsten's anthology *The Military in America* (1980) began giving attention to the interaction between war and broader society. These have examined how social and cultural ideas shape the organization and employment of armed forces. Others, such as Peter Kindsvatter's *American Soldiers* (2003) and John McManus' *Grunts* (2010), have scrutinized how men experienced war and its consequences. As this is a survey text, the following chapters consist mostly of narratives to introduce readers to historical events and developments. Nevertheless, some sections will explore "war and society" issues, particularly regarding the formation and development of U.S. military institutions and organizations.

Ways of War

The term "way of war" has often been used to describe how armed forces of a particular nation prepare for and conduct warfare—the German way of war, for example. Such descriptions emphasize characteristics that make a national "way of war" distinctive from others and might highlight traits such as reliance on firepower, influence of ideological beliefs, emphasis on soldiers' morale, or effects of geographical features. These models and traits can be useful for discussing a given nation's military forces in a limited historical period (sometimes just a specific war). But they tend to break down when military institutions are examined over longer periods of time.

In 1973, the late Russell F. Weigley published his seminal volume *The American Way of War*. Drawing upon the writings of Carl von Clausewitz and Hans Delbrück from the nineteenth century, Weigley argued that Americans preferred strategies that sought to "annihilate" their opponents in decisive, short conflicts. He pointed to the American Civil War and the Second World War as his chief examples, noting that prior to the former conflict, the United States lacked adequate resources for such a strategy. During these periods of relative weakness, the U.S. military employed a strategy of "attrition" to wear down enemies over time. Weigley wrote *The American Way of War* because he puzzled over why the American military, with its preference for annihilation and preponderance of power, could fail to achieve victory in the Vietnam War. His thesis became quite popular because it described an approach to war that seemed predominant in the United States for much of the twentieth century.

Brian Linn started the process of challenging, if not supplanting, Weigley's thesis in his 2002 article, "*The American Way of War* Revisited." Linn noted that the United States has not always sought to overwhelm enemies, even in conflicts fought between the Civil War and the Second World War. Looking specifically at the U.S. Army, Linn's more recent book, *The Echo of Battle*, argues that competing groups within that service have shaped and modified its approach to war over time. He finds three typologies of Army leader: the guardian, the warrior, and the manager. Generals could sometimes combine two of them. Regardless, in each conflict or era of American military history, the typologies competed with each or complemented one another. The results could mean victory in the Second World War, but other conflicts like Vietnam showed the wrong typology could lose wars.

Other books have also explored alternative ways to understand American perspectives on war. John Grenier's *The First American Way of War* (2005) focuses on the colonial era, in which British settlers and soldiers adopted a particularly brutal form of warfare against native peoples. Grenier labels this "extirpative warfare," and he finds no continuity of Weigley's thesis to war-making before and after the American War for Independence. In his *The American Culture of War* (2008), Adrian Lewis examines the effects of civilian policy decisions, military strategies, technological innovations, and public perceptions on American war-making from 1945 through the Global War on Terror. He finds, for example, that the culture of the American military and society changed substantially when the conscripted force changed to the All-Volunteer Force in 1973.

Most recently in *Reconsidering the American Way of War* (2014), Antulio Echevarria asserts that Weigley's thesis has become obsolete in practice and unsuitable in analysis. The U.S. military, according to Echevarria, has never completely nor consistently employed strategies of annihilation or attrition. Instead, he finds the uses of American force to be fluid, situational, and adaptable. Wearing down the British over time (not from battle casualties) in the Revolutionary War differed from the use of graduated pressure in the Mexican War, which in turn did not resemble the trial-and-error experiments in the World Wars or the blind American faith in firepower and technology in the Vietnam War. Taken as a whole, however, Echevarria's book points to multiple American ways, styles, and concepts of war. His book stands as the best synthetic study to date.

Although frequently challenged and critiqued since its publication in 1973, it cannot be denied that Russell Weigley's argument in *The American Way of War* did break new ground because he set conditions for ongoing debates about patterns of American war-making. The styles, strategies, and practices of war have evolved in response to shifting historical factors and events—points this textbook illustrates in the process of introducing students to American military history. Ultimately, readers will not find any unified style and single type of war that can fit every conflict in American history. There have instead been many complex, always changing, and sometimes contradictory *ways* of American war, as reflected in this textbook's title.

Short Bibliography

Echevarria, Antulio J., II. *Reconsidering the American Way of War: U.S. Military Practice from the Revolution to Afghanistan*. Washington: Georgetown University Press, 2014.

Grenier, John. *The First American Way of War: American War Making on the Frontier*. New York: Cambridge University Press, 2005.

Karsten, Peter, ed. *The Military in America: From the Colonial Era to the Present*. Rev. ed. New York: Free Press, 1986.

Kindsvatter, Peter S. *American Soldiers: Ground Combat in the World Wars, Korea, and Vietnam*. Lawrence: University Press of Kansas, 2003.

Lewis, Adrian R. *The American Culture of War: A History of U.S. Military Force from World War II to Operation Enduring Freedom*. 2nd ed. New York: Routledge, 2012.

Linn, Brian McAllister. "The *American Way of War* Revisited." *Journal of Military History* 66 (2002): 501–30.

———. *The Echo of Battle: The Army's Way of War*. Cambridge: Harvard University Press, 2009.

Mahnken, Thomas. *Technology and the American Way of War since 1945*. New York: Columbia University Press, 2010.

McManus, John C. *Grunts: Inside the American Infantry Combat Experience: World War II through Iraq*. New York: New American Library, 2010.

Trauschweizer, Ingo. "American Ways of War since 1945." *International Bibliography of Military History* 32 (Summer 2012): 28–50.

Ulbrich, David J. "Review of *Reconsidering the American War of War*. By Antulio J. Echevarria II." *On Point: The Journal of Army History* 21 (Winter 2016): 60.

Weigley, Russell F. *The American Way of War: A History of United States Military Strategy and Policy*. Bloomington: Indiana University Press, 1973.

1609–14	1622–32	1636–38	1640s	1644–46
First Anglo-Powhatan War	Second Anglo-Powhatan War	Pequot War	Beaver Wars begin (end in 1701)	Third Anglo-Powhatan War

TIMELINE

Chapter 1

Early Colonization and Conflict, 1607–1689

In the seventeenth century, colonization brought people from widely disparate cultures and societies into close proximity in North America. In a few cases, colonial and native groups coexisted peacefully and adapted to one another, establishing mutually beneficial relationships. American Indian peoples often tried to cultivate relations with settlers to gain potential allies against native rivals and access to trade goods. In other cases, competition over land and trade fueled violence. Moreover, Europeans regarded their Western culture and Christian faith as vastly superior to Indian lifestyles and beliefs, which prevented settlers from appreciating native perspectives and concerns.

Prior to colonization, Native Americans and Europeans had each developed distinctive approaches to warfare. But over the course of the seventeenth century, as settlers and Indians interacted, both fought against and with each other, and their military styles were altered. Colonists developed tactics and operations to fight a foe that did not engage in European-style pitched battles, often doing so by employing native allies. Indian tactical and operational practices did not change as much but became married to Western technology, particularly muskets. Assisted by such weapons, warriors at times inflicted levels of killing and destruction beyond what had been typical for native warfare, spurred in part by settlers' examples.

Colonists came to North America from a number of European countries, including France, Spain, and the Netherlands. Because the experiences of English settlers had the greatest bearing upon later U.S. military institutions, this chapter will focus primarily on the Chesapeake and New England colonies, with some attention to non-English settlements in the northeastern part of the continent. (Students wanting to learn about military experiences in what became Spanish America can visit the companion website to this volume at www.routledge.com/cw/muehlbauer). Whatever their national origin, though, up until the late seventeenth century colonists fought wars of their own volition, with negligible direction or assistance from their mother countries. The next chapter will address North American wars from the late 1600s until the mid-eighteenth century, in which European states took a greater interest.

In this chapter, students will learn about:

- Native American and European approaches to warfare prior to colonization.
- How military practices changed as a result of cross-cultural contact.
- Military experiences and conflict involving French Canada and early Dutch settlements.
- Military experiences and conflict in the seventeenth-century Chesapeake.
- Military experiences and conflict in seventeenth-century New England up through King Philip's War (1675–76).

Native American Societies and Warfare

A wide disparity of native peoples and cultures inhabited North America in the millennium before European colonization. In the forested eastern half of the continent, most lived in semi-sedentary societies, occupying a few locations over the course of a year to pursue different sustenance activities such as farming, hunting, and fishing, depending upon terrain and ecological conditions. Different autonomous bands and nations often spoke similar dialects within a common language group and shared common cultural practices and folklore. In eastern North America, the two predominant language groups were Algonquian and Iroquoian.

These Indian societies also lacked the social stratification of European ones. Gender and age contributed much more to defining one's role within an indigenous community. Men, for example, engaged in hunting and fishing for sustenance but also participated in warfare. Women generally maintained households, fields, and gardens. Older people generally held greater responsibility: women, over the disposition of household and community resources; men, over interactions with other native groups, including diplomacy and military decisions. These relatively egalitarian societies also lacked means of coercion. European rulers, for example, had officials and troops to enforce law and suppress revolts against authority. In Native America, however, leaders could persuade, but not force, their peoples to accept their decisions. When an Indian community was seriously divided over an issue, many of its members might leave and either join another native group or establish their own autonomous band.

Various reasons caused warfare between native groups. Often, the issue was access to territory desired for hunting, fishing, or planting. If a people believed that its members had been victimized by another, and diplomacy failed to produce redress, warriors might launch revenge attacks. In the northeast, Daniel Richter has demonstrated that the Five Nations of the Iroquois practiced "mourning war": When many people died in a community, they dispatched war parties to capture prisoners who they would then adopt. (The Five Nations

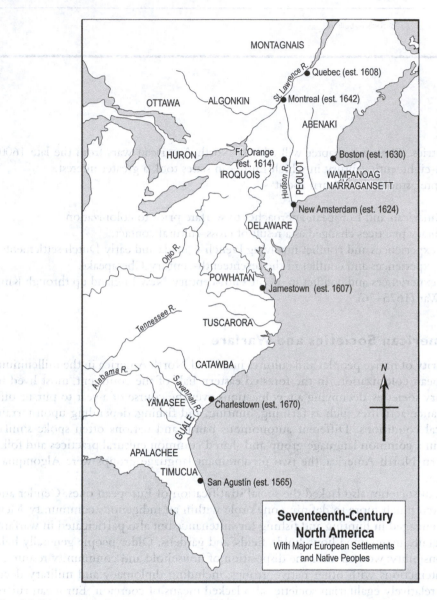

Map 1.1 Seventeenth-Century North America

comprised only some of the bands within the Iroquoian language group.) Seasonal constraints affected warfare, for at certain times of year warriors needed to hunt, fish, or perform other sustenance activities.

In the centuries prior to European contact, the intensity of native warfare oscillated. Archeological evidence indicates that, in some places, massacres of large numbers of men, women, and children occurred. The frequency of such incidents, relative to raids and ambushes that produced fewer casualties, cannot be determined with great accuracy. By the period of colonization, however, native peoples generally engaged in combat that was not very lethal, at least by Western standards.

All young men were expected to learn hunting and military skills. Males who had previously proven their courage or ability provided leadership. Although war parties often initiated combat according to a common plan, each warrior acted on his own volition, without waiting for direction from another (such as an officer in European armies). For native men, the capture of loot, plunder, and captives brought success and respect. Warriors killed, and in the seventeenth century adopted the practice of scalping their opponents so they could return home with evidence of their lethality (a practice later mimicked by colonists). But they preferred to take live captives who could then be adopted into one's home community or released for a ransom (though at times adult male prisoners might be ritually executed).

Tactically, native bands engaged in what is today called "low-intensity warfare," particularly raids, ambushes, and skirmishes. They generally attacked only when they held the advantage and used stealth and knowledge of local terrain to surprise enemies. Conversely, Indians retreated if attacked themselves, and many native villages had palisades in the seventeenth century to protect inhabitants from marauders. A battle between two prepared and ready forces occurred rarely and usually ended after one side suffered a few casualties. In the Native American context, operations consisted of dispatching war parties to enemy areas where they would raid settlements and camps and launch ambushes. Strategy entailed harming and harassing an enemy people enough that its leaders would concede or compromise on whatever issues had sparked hostilities.

Western Europe and the Military Revolution

In contrast to North American Indians in this era, European society was very hierarchical. During the Middle Ages, rural peasants had labored on lands controlled by a small aristocracy, with limited numbers of merchants, artisans, and craftsmen dwelling in town and villages. In the early modern period, more people moved to urban locations, and the "middle classes" began to grow. The abolition of serfdom in Western Europe allowed peasants to migrate, and commerce expanded, including overseas trade with Africa and Asia. These changes made a significant impact by the seventeenth century, creating some social mobility. But opportunities to acquire enhanced status were limited, and European society remained stratified.

Both the broader changes affecting Europe and its hierarchical nature shaped evolving military forces. From the late fifteenth to the eighteenth centuries, European states grew in size, became fewer in number, and created large, permanent armies and navies. In the Middle Ages standing forces were small, if they existed at all. Monarchs and princes required military service of their nobles in times of war. The latter traditionally served as armored horsemen, and to pay for their expensive arms and equipment aristocrats received control of lands. Nobles often had castles to protect and dominate the nearby countryside. In addition, locals often served in militias to defend their communities. By the sixteenth century, this system was breaking down. Some nobles exploited commercial opportunities to make money and offered rulers funds in lieu of military service. Moreover, technological and organizational changes had already undermined the military dominance of heavy cavalry and traditional fortifications (addressed in the next section).

These and other developments prompted rulers to create large, standing, infantry-based armies. But doing so required other changes: greater taxation and other means to generate public income; larger bureaucracies and administrative capabilities to collect revenues and oversee expenditures; and systems to recruit, train, and lead soldiers. The men who became officers in these expanded military establishments generally had noble backgrounds, and hence the armies replicated the hierarchical structure of traditional Western society. As a result of these developments, the impact of war (and preparations for it) upon European society increased dramatically, particularly in how states—in order to maintain larger armed forces—themselves became more powerful. Some historians call this trend the "military revolution."

The relevance of the military revolution for early American history is mixed. Colonists did not have the resources or organization needed to maintain large permanent military establishments, and their mother countries only sent small numbers of regular troops to North America before the mid-eighteenth century. The military revolution, however, established what is now called "high-intensity conflict" as the normative form of Western war. Low-intensity hostilities (also called "*petit guerre*") composed of raids, ambushes, and skirmishes still occurred in Europe, and in some regions were the dominant form of conflict. But high-intensity battles and sieges were not just distinct, dramatic episodes involving large numbers of trained, full-time soldiers. Their outcomes could have great effects, even determine the outcome of an entire war. As Western states acquired the resources to field large armies capable of fighting big battles and pursuing large operations, Europeans came to see high-intensity conflict as "normal." Though colonists could not maintain standing forces, this bias often shaped how they approached warfare.

Technological Developments in Early Modern Europe

The Chinese had used gunpowder for centuries, primarily in fireworks, by the time it became known in the West by the early 1300s. Europeans quickly realized the military possibilities for gunpowder, particularly for attacking people sheltering behind castle or town walls, and later for destroying fortifications themselves. But it took a long time to develop cannons that were both strong enough to withstand internal gunpowder explosions and small enough that they could be transported. By the end of the 1400s, such capabilities were realized with the advent of cast bronze guns. A few decades later, cast iron cannons offered another alternative. These were actually heavier than similarly sized cast bronze guns and more prone to corrosion. But iron guns were much cheaper and allowed the English, in particular, to mount large numbers on their oceangoing ships.

By the late fifteenth century, cannons were small enough that they could be placed on carriages and moved by teams of horses. Monarchs could assemble and move groups of artillery, called "batteries," which would quickly destroy medieval-style castles. However, engineers responded to these artillery threats by designing a new type of fortress called a *trace italienne* (originating in Italy). These had low, thick walls that could better withstand bombardment. To guard against infantry assaults that threatened to scale walls, these fortresses also had projections called "bastions" that enabled defenders to fire into the flanks of approaching soldiers (also called "enfilade fire").

Gunpowder also changed infantry weapons. Muskets became the preferred military long arm in the sixteenth century. (Pistols are smaller, shorter-range weapons.) Their barrels were smooth on the inside, making them easier and faster to load but limiting their accuracy and range. Rifles, in contrast, were more accurate with greater range because they had grooves that imparted a spin to a bullet. But these weapons took a long time to load, as projectiles had to be hammered down the barrel, and armies made limited use of them. Both weapons were loaded from the muzzle, or the open end of the weapon where the bullet exited. As with most artillery, these weapons had touchholes drilled into the bottom or back end of the barrels. After powder and bullet were secured down the muzzle, some powder was placed down the touchhole and in a pan on the outside of the barrel next to the hole. A firing mechanism then ignited the powder in the pan, which then spread though the touchhole into the firing chamber, causing the explosion that would propel the bullet out the muzzle.

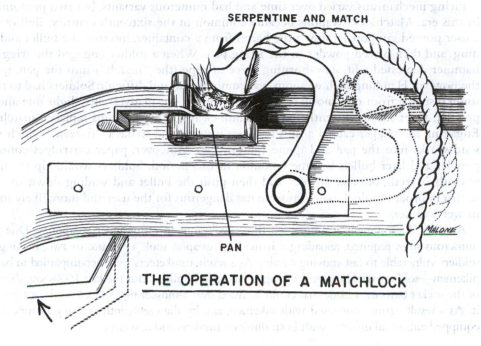

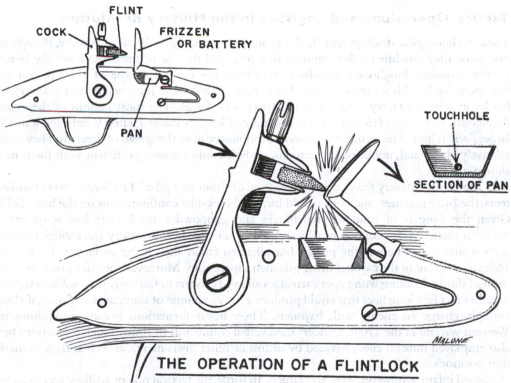

Figure 1.1 Matchlock and Flintlock Firing Mechanisms

Illustration by P. D. Malone and Patrick Malone

Firing mechanisms varied over time and had numerous variants, but two predominated in this era. Matchlock weapons became common in the sixteenth century. Before firing, a user poured gunpowder down the barrel from a container, inserted the bullet and wadding, and then placed powder in the firing pan. When a soldier engaged the trigger, the hammer depressed a lit, slow-burning piece of rope (the "match") into the pan, igniting the powder. Handling such weapons was cumbersome and difficult: Soldiers had to remain some distance from one another to ensure they did not inadvertently light one another's powder. Over the seventeenth century, flintlock firing mechanisms replaced matchlocks. Engaging the trigger caused a flint to move forward and strike a "frizzen," which would send sparks into the pan and ignite the powder. Moreover, paper cartridges containing powder and later bullets became common in this period. Soldiers would rip them open with their teeth, pour in powder and then push the bullet and wading down the barrel with a ramrod. Flintlock weapons were less dangerous for the user and more likely to work in wet weather.

Another development accompanied these evolutions in gunpowder weaponry. Due to the numerous steps required, reloading a matchlock weapon took a minute or two, making these soldiers vulnerable to fast-moving cavalry. As a result, musketeers were accompanied in battle by pikemen—soldiers wielding long, strong spears called "pikes." But the late 1600s saw the advent of the socket bayonet, a blade that could be fitted over a musket that still allowed a soldier to fire it. As a result, armies dispensed with pikemen, and by the eighteenth century, European states equipped almost all infantry with both flintlock muskets and bayonets.

Tactics, Operations, and Logistics in the Military Revolution

These technological developments had a profound impact upon Western warfare, though in one sense they amplified a development that preceded the use of firearms. Tactically, heavy cavalry (armored knights on horseback) had been the dominant type of combat unit on European battlefields for most of the Middle Ages. But the late medieval period saw various battles in which infantry armies prevailed over such forces. The most famous of these was Agincourt, where in 1415 archers and dismounted knights under Henry V defeated a much larger French host. This trend became more pronounced after the spread of firearms: They were relatively cheap and, unlike other weapons, soldiers could become proficient with them in a short time.

In the 1500s, infantry forces usually consisted of "shot and pike." The former were musketeers, the latter pikemen, and both would form in block-like configurations on the battlefield. Given the dangers of handling matchlocks and gunpowder, musketeers had some space between them, while pikemen usually formed closer together. If cavalry threatened, musketeers would retreat behind the pikes—but pikemen could also charge an enemy. In the late 1600s, the advent of the bayonet made pikemen superfluous. Moreover, the safer firing mechanism of flintlocks along with paper cartridges allowed officers to tactically mass soldiers tightly together in a few long lines that could produce a heavy volume of simultaneous fire or, if close enough, charge an enemy with bayonets. These linear formations became ubiquitous in Western warfare in the 1700s. Officers used verbal commands to control such formations but also employed musical cues provided by drums or other instruments, as well as flags to mark unit positions.

Massed infantry, however, were also targets. In battle, the tactical role of artillery was to break up such forces or use counterbattery fire to prevent enemy cannon from firing upon friendly units. Heavy cavalry still attacked, but only after artillery or infantry fire had broken up enemy forces. In contrast, light cavalry had mostly operational functions, engaging in reconnaissance and patrolling before and after large battles. Infantry also participated in such missions, which involved low-intensity conflict such as skirmishes, raids, and ambushes.

The tactical firepower of early modern armies came at a cost. These growing armies required ever-increasing amounts of weapons, ammunition, supplies, and equipment—as well as incredible numbers of horses and wagons to move them. An early expedient to get men into the field quickly was for rulers to hire mercenaries. But their captains' desire to preserve their forces was often at odds with the military objectives of their employers. Moreover, if payment was slow or in arrears (which happened frequently), mercenaries had a habit of taking what they wanted from the local population.

To exert greater control over military forces, states created standing, permanent armies and bureaucracies needed to support them—defining aspects of the military revolution. Governments created magazines or depots where they stockpiled supplies and equipment for future campaigns, which were usually located inside major fortresses. In war, moving supplies to a field army took time and slowed the troops down, and protecting supply lines back to the army's magazine limited operational options. In fact, partly because of the logistical importance of fortresses and their magazines, sieges became more common in European warfare than field battles from the sixteenth to the early eighteenth centuries.

Another reason for the use of sieges was that a well-planned and organized one was much more likely to result in success than a battle. For early modern commanders, tactical victories were highly uncertain, but battle was certain to generate significant casualties. In contrast, by the eighteenth century, military engineers had developed a tactical approach for sieges that involved digging a systematic network of trenches to shelter attacking forces while they advanced enough artillery to blast into enemy fortresses (or threaten them). These operations took a long time—months, and occasionally years—but were usually successful if besieging forces were large enough to isolate a fort and beat off attempts by enemy armies to drive them away.

As European states imposed more control over military forces, civilian society suffered less. By the eighteenth century, European armies generally observed common laws and practices with respect to the treatment of prisoners of war, the treatment of noncombatants in war zones, and the conduct of sieges (the latter encouraged defenders to surrender and avoid bloody assaults). Governments preferred not to have regions—either those they ruled or hoped to acquire—devastated by soldiers, as had happened in the sixteenth and early seventeenth centuries when they relied more upon mercenary forces and when religious differences had contributed to many wars. But these limitations took time to develop, and as some scholars have noted, relied upon shared aspects of Western culture such as Christian theology and Roman law—bonds that did not exist between European settlers and American Indians.

The Military Revolution in America

Colonists had problems replicating Western approaches to warfare in North America. As already noted, they lacked the numbers, resources, and organization to launch campaigns on a European scale. But in addition to specific socioeconomic and political factors, Western warfare also reflected a particular topographical context. The tactical formations developed by Western armies assumed large battles would occur in the open spaces common in cultivated Europe, which also had a robust road network to keep military forces well supplied. Such features were not prevalent in North America. Instead, its forests, hills, and mountains were ideal for the low-intensity combat fought by American Indians.

Colonists did benefit from Western technology and military practices. For example, they built forts. These were much smaller than the huge fortresses European states constructed to defend their borders and house magazines, and (like palisades surrounding native towns) were constructed from wood, not stone. Settlers, though, often included bastions on their fortifications. Colonists also had access to firearms and cannons, but this advantage was not as great as some suggest. Indians quickly acquired access to firearms through trade. Moreover, scholars such as Patrick Malone argue that—in the case of seventeenth-century New England—natives were quicker to appreciate the advantages of flintlocks over matchlocks. Warriors regularly employed weapons for hunting, which few settlers engaged in. But native peoples could not manufacture gunpowder, for which they were dependent upon colonial traders or officials. Neither did Indians have artillery, though early settlers rarely had any in significant numbers, and they were difficult to move over local terrain. Warriors, however, appreciated Western technology other than muskets: Metal axes, for example, were stronger than traditional stone ones.

Colonists, from a culture where conventional, high-intensity warfare was becoming the norm, had to adjust their approach to account for native foes and local conditions. Western technology helped, but it did not offer settlers a panacea for confronting Indian enemies. They would instead have to find tactical and operational means to better cope with low-intensity conflict. But the bias toward high-intensity conflict did not vanish and shaped American warfare in later conflicts, particularly when facing a Western foe. Moreover, English settlers brought with them particular practices and experiences that shaped their colonial armed forces and, later, the development of U.S. military institutions.

The next two sections will examine developments in parts of northeastern America that involved non-English European settlers and the Indian peoples with which they interacted. Conflicts between English colonists and native peoples will be discussed subsequently.

Non-English Colonization in the Northeast

After the Spanish founded San Agustín or St. Augustine in 1565 (see www.routledge.com/cw/muehlbauer for more on the Spanish in North America), Europeans did not establish permanent colonies on the Atlantic seaboard until the seventeenth century. But natives and Westerners still interacted. In some areas Europeans established temporary and seasonal settlements, particularly fishermen from various European countries who came to the Grand Banks throughout the sixteenth century. They often came ashore to dry fish and trade with local natives, and especially valued beaver pelts.

These pelts became so popular that Europeans, particularly the French, set up seasonal or temporary trading posts around the gulf of the St. Lawrence River. In 1608 explorer and trader Samuel de Champlain established Quebec, the first permanent French settlement in Canada, or the colony of New France, with subsequent communities founded farther up the St. Lawrence River at Trois-Rivières (1634) and Montreal (1642). Simultaneously, the Dutch pursued permanent posts to facilitate the fur trade to the south. In 1609 Henry Hudson sailed up the river that now bears his name, establishing contacts with native peoples. In 1614, the Dutch established the trading post of Fort Nassau, later replaced by Fort Orange, upriver at what is today Albany. About a decade later, to guard the Hudson River's mouth and provide supplies to Fort Orange and additional settlements, they founded New Amsterdam (now the city of New York).

Trade helped foster amicable relations between colonists and natives, especially in the French case. But New France never possessed a large population—roughly 3,000 in 1663—and its officials sought Indian groups as allies. Missionary efforts were also respectful of native customs, as French Jesuits first sought to learn about indigenous societies and spiritual beliefs to better facilitate the introduction of Catholicism to local peoples. As with other Europeans, the French did not regard natives as cultural equals. But in other cases colonizers sought to impose author-ity and beliefs on indigenous peoples, whereas circumstances motivated the Canadian French to treat local peoples in a way where both contributed relatively equally to their interactions, a development historian Richard White calls the creation of a "middle ground."

The Dutch case is more mixed. At Fort Orange, colonists generally maintained good relations with native groups. But further south, a number of wars erupted prior to the English conquest of New Netherland in 1664. In the lower Hudson River valley, trade with natives was negli-gible, and colonial officials focused on enticing immigrants to the colony to cultivate land and provide manpower for local defense. Dutch demands for tribute and efforts to extend their authority had generated tensions with local Wappinger peoples for years before Governor Willem Kieft ordered an attack on an unsuspecting native group in 1643. The resulting con-flict—Kieft's War—engulfed New Amsterdam and its environs until 1645. Kieft was replaced in 1647 by the more competent Pieter Stuyvesant, yet wars erupted with Indians in the lower Hudson in 1655, 1659–60, and 1663–64.

These latter hostilities were similar to those that early English colonies would experience. But cross-cultural trade gave rise to a much larger series of conflicts that spanned both the bulk of the seventeenth century and a large swath of the North American interior known as the Beaver Wars. The key belligerents in all of these wars were Five Nations of the Iroquois (com-prised of the Seneca, Cayuga, Onondaga, Oneida, and the Mohawk), a large confederation of peoples located in what is now central and western New York State. The central issue was trade with Europeans, who offered many goods greatly valued by indigenous peoples, including cloth, alcohol, metal tools, and firearms. Indian nations able to control distribution of such items (and deny such to native competitors) would greatly enhance their status and influence.

The Beaver Wars

When the French first settled the St. Lawrence River valley, they established relationships with nearby Abenaki groups as well as the Huron confederacy further west in the Great Lakes region north of Lakes Ontario and Erie. The Huron acquired pelts through barter with indigenous bands living further in the continental interior and then exchanged them with the French in return for manufactured items. This trade threatened the status of the Iroquois nations. After the Dutch established their trading posts on the upper Hudson, the Five Nations had their own source of Western goods. But to obtain pelts for trade, they needed access to Indian bands further west and north.

The Beaver Wars began in the 1640s between the Iroquois and the Huron. Hostilities first consisted of Five Nations warriors raiding and ambushing Huron parties traveling down the St. Lawrence to trade with the French. But the Iroquois dramatically escalated the intensity and lethality of their operations by the end of the decade, culminating in 1648–49 with campaigns that involved hundreds to over 1,000 warriors and that destroyed large Huron towns. These assaults also disrupted Huron cycles of planting and harvesting, producing food shortages. As a result, hundreds died and the Huron confederacy was effectively destroyed, though most individuals survived: The Iroquois captured and adopted a few thousand into Iroquois com-munities, and the rest dispersed to join other native bands or establish communities further north, west, and south of their traditional homelands.

These campaigns featured many Iroquois innovations. They not only involved unprece-dented numbers of warriors but also winter operations and night assaults, traditionally avoided by native peoples. Huron towns possessed palisades, or tall wooden walls, to defend their inhab-itants. To counter them, scholar Craig Keener observes that the Iroquois developed new assault tactics that took advantage of European technology, including both firearms and metal axes that were superior to indigenous stone ones. While some warriors fired guns to engage the defenders' attention, others would advance to chop holes in the palisades and enter into the town. These assault tactics proved short-lived, for the Iroquois later came across native foes who had adopted another European innovation—the *bastion*. A bastion is a projection from a wall that allows defenders to fire down its length into any enemy engaged in close assault (such fire into an enemy's side or flank is also called "enfilade fire" or "enfilading fire"). When Iroquois warriors encountered towns whose palisades had bastions in the mid–1600s, they reverted back to ambush and raiding tactics.

Figure 1.2 Depiction of an Iroquois Assault of an Erie Town in 1655

Note the attackers' use of large shields, or "mantlets," which provided protection as they approached the palisade, where they would use iron axes to hack through the wall. Also note a warrior shooting his gun at the top of the palisade, providing fire that helped protect warriors advancing to the wall.

From Craig S. Keener, "An Ethnohistorical Analysis of Iroquois Assault Tactics used against Fortified Settlements in Northeast in the Seventeenth Century." *Ethnohistory* 46 (1999): p. 794.

The Beaver Wars did not end with the destruction of the Huron confederacy. As scholars such as Daniel Richter note, trade with Europeans became an additional motivation for war between native groups. For the Five Nations, traditional incentives for war included access to hunting grounds, extending their influence over other groups, and pursuing mourning wars to replace those who had died in wars or epidemics. All these reasons enticed the Five Nations to fight numerous other indigenous peoples over the next few decades, such as the Erie and Neutrals to the west, the Susquehannocks to the south, and various Algonquian-speaking bands and groups (including the Abenaki) to the east and north.

Moreover, direct conflict between the Five Nations and New France also intensified. As early as 1609 Samuel de Champlain assisted Algonquian allies against Iroquois warriors (the first time natives of either side had seen the use of a firearm), and Five Nations war parties occasionally raided French settlements and outposts. But in the late 1600s New France mounted large invasions of Iroquoia, with numbers totaling a few hundred to up to 2,000 regular troops, Canadian militiamen, and native allies. Mohawk homelands were invaded in 1666 and 1693, Seneca in 1687, and Onondaga in 1696; most inhabitants fled from these advances, but the French always destroyed Iroquois homes and fields.

The last of the Beaver Wars coincided with King William's War (1689–97) between England and France, addressed in the next chapter. By that time, decades of warfare had exhausted the Iroquois. Whereas the Five Nations numbered perhaps more than 20,000 in the early 1660s, casualties and prisoners lost in war as well as epidemics had reduced that to under 10,000 by century's end—despite the fact that the Iroquois continued to practice mourning war to replace their numbers. As a result, the Five Nations and New France agreed to end hostilities and established peace with the Grand Settlement of 1701. The Iroquois did not completely eschew war, though. They generally remained neutral in the eighteenth-century imperial wars between the French and the British but fought indigenous peoples such as the Catawba and other groups in the continent's southeast.

The Beaver Wars demonstrate how the mere presence of European colonies made native warfare more lethal and destructive. Part of this development stemmed from Western technology. Muskets were much more lethal than bows and arrows, yet even simple iron hatchets enabled Iroquois to more effectively attack enemy palisades. Beyond weapons per se, access to European trade goods and beaver pelts created powerful incentives to fight. These interacted with traditional incentives for war to create a series of native conflicts unprecedented in scale. Moreover, the Beaver Wars did not just exhaust the Iroquois and destroy the Huron confederacy; it produced a seventeenth-century exodus. To escape the ravages of the Five Nations, Indian peoples originally residing around the eastern Great Lakes and Ohio River valley migrated west, most stopping on the far side of Lake Michigan. There they intermingled, creating new nations. Most remained friendly with the French and would play an important role in the imperial conflicts of the mid-eighteenth century.

Overview: Early Modern England, Its Wars, and Military Service

England did not create standing, peacetime military forces until well into the 1600s. But men from Britain participated in a wide variety of conflicts in the sixteenth and seventeenth centuries. Of particular interest were efforts to extend English control over Ireland in the late 1500s. These hostilities primarily consisted of low-intensity skirmishes and raids, but were brutal and victimized Irish noncombatants, involving the destruction of homes and property, and the killing of women and children. Scholars such as Nicholas Canny claim prejudice contributed to the violence. English and Scottish volunteers, being both Protestant and from sedentary, agricultural societies, regarded native Gaelic populations—who practiced Catholicism and a seminomadic, grazing lifestyle—as inferior, dubbing them "wild Irish." Canny argues that strife in Ireland set a precedent for later violence inflicted upon American Indians, who colonists also regarded as inferior to Christian, "civilized" Englishmen.

The English monarchy also raised and sent forces to the Netherlands, which as a result of the Eighty Years War (also known as the Dutch Revolt) of 1568–1648, won its independence from Spain. There, English soldiers learned and fought in the conventional warfare becoming prevalent in continental Europe. Some, like John Smith and Myles Standish, later played significant roles in the early colonies. On the seas, English privateers (privately owned ships with licenses from the monarchy to attack enemy targets) raided Spanish shipping and colonies in the Americas from the late 1500s to the early 1600s, and naval forces defeated the Spanish Armada that attempted to invade England in 1588.

The British Isles themselves were ravaged by the Civil Wars of 1638–51, encompassing Scotland and Ireland as well as England. Both Parliament and King Charles I raised forces that fought major battles and conducted sieges (as well as low-intensity conflict) in the British Civil Wars. Parliament prevailed on the victories of the New Model Army commanded by Oliver Cromwell, which included the capture and subsequent execution of the king. In the 1650s, this army enabled Cromwell to rule England as a *de facto* dictator, a period known as the Interregnum. In 1660, not long after his death, Parliament restored the monarchy and placed Charles I's son, Charles II, on the throne, and the New Model Army dissolved. For years thereafter, Englishmen were wary of standing forces, but after the Glorious Revolution of 1688–89, Parliament began raising armies and navies to participate in wars against France, addressed in the next chapter.

Ironically, given their common Protestant religion and cooperation against the Spanish in the Eighty Years War, the English and the Dutch fought three commercial conflicts in the seventeenth century (1652–54, 1664–67, and 1672–74). The Anglo-Dutch Wars were mostly naval conflicts, but in North America, they resulted in English forces conquering New Netherland in 1664 with almost no resistance. After a brief Dutch occupation in the third war, New York remained part of the British Empire.

Though England did not possess standing peacetime forces prior to the late seventeenth century, it still had institutions and systems for raising military manpower. When the Crown needed soldiers (and Parliament, in the British Civil Wars), it issued "commissions" to men who recruited volunteers from towns and the countryside for new units they would then command, appointing the junior officers. To this day, when someone becomes a military officer, they receive a commission, or are commissioned. The system relied upon nobles' and local leaders' ability to attract volunteers, along with promises of pay, booty, or adventure, though some men joined to avoid problems with the law.

In the sixteenth century, England revived another military institution, the militia. Traditionally, these consisted of men in a particular region who would rally together if danger threatened their communities. With the threat of Spanish invasion in the late 1500s, Queen Elizabeth's government sought to resuscitate the militia but was concerned about high costs and wary of arming common peasants. Hence relatively few men, and ones from more prosperous backgrounds, were organized into trained bands, or "trainbands." In England's American colonies, militia service would be much more widespread among the adult male population and would provide the basic training in arms and drill that enabled colonial authorities to raise volunteer units for campaigns.

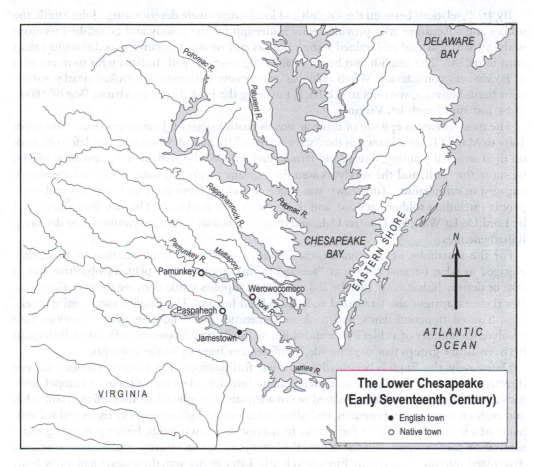

Map 1.2 The Lower Chesapeake (Early Seventeenth Century)

Early Virginia and the First Anglo-Powhatan War, 1609–14

In 1607, the Virginia Company of London founded Jamestown, the first permanent English settlement in America. The colonists have often been derided for establishing it in a swamp about 40 miles up the James River from the Chesapeake Bay, for many died from diseases prevalent in the marshy terrain. But the Jamestown site offered military advantages. The swamp would hamper any assault on the small colony, and the location well upriver helped conceal it from Spanish raiders. The Virginia Company hoped these settlers would find riches or commercially exploitable resources and that natives could be used as a local labor source.

Numerous indigenous bands and groups inhabited the Chesapeake region. Most of these were affiliated with the confederacy headed by the chief Powhatan, totaling about 14,000 people. Powhatan initially had tributary groups welcome the newcomers, providing gifts and food. But he also apparently arranged for other bands to test English defensive capabilities, including an assault on the Jamestown fort as it was being constructed. The English accepted the gifts and food, and began trading with local peoples. Both Powhatan and English leaders tried to establish themselves as the dominant partner in their interactions, and each expressed this intent symbolically through rituals and ceremonies.

By 1609, relations between the English and local natives were deteriorating. John Smith, the soldier and adventurer who provided early leadership for the colony and established relations with Powhatan, armed and trained some colonists and went on putative expeditions to extort corn as tribute. The English also began establishing contacts with Indians who were enemies of Powhatan's confederacy. When colonists at two new settlements provoked nearby natives with harsh behavior, warriors struck back, initiating the First Anglo-Powhatan War of 1609–1614, just after Smith left Virginia.

The most infamous episode of this war was the native siege of Jamestown from November 1609 to May 1610, also known as the "starving time." By its end, when warriors left to embark on their seasonal planting, disease and famine had reduced the settlement's population of 200 by more than half, and the survivors were in a greatly weakened state; a few had reportedly engaged in cannibalism. Jamestown was almost abandoned, but then fresh supplies and more people (including soldiers) arrived, and the colony's new leader, Sir Thomas West (succeeded by Lord De La Warr, Sir Thomas Dale, and then Sir Thomas Gates), committed it to defeating Indian enemies.

For the remainder of the conflict, the English held the initiative. Starting in 1610, they engaged in what became known as "feedfights," operations whose primary objective was to take or destroy Indian corn, thereby acquiring food supplies while denying them to their foes. But these campaigns also terrorized and intimidated Indians. The English razed native dwellings, harmed noncombatants, and took or sometimes killed hostages (one notorious case involved the murder of a chief's wife and children). Such expeditions often failed to distinguish between native groups that were hostile, indifferent, or friendly to the colonists.

Defensively, the English benefited from their fortifications. Powhatan's warriors did not directly assault these during the war, preferring to lure defenders out of them or compel colonists to abandon posts that were isolated or not adequately supplied. Indians preferred ambushes and raids on unsuspecting enemies, including firing upon English vessels in rivers and streams. Such attacks made it difficult for settlers to harvest their own fields, hence generating more motivation for feedfights. But the danger the latter posed to native crops and homes sometimes galvanized warriors to meet the English in battle. Later in the war, the colony had a few hundred experienced troops (veterans of warfare in the Low Countries) armed with muskets and equipped with metal armor, making engagements a one-sided affair against natives mostly armed with bows and arrows.

The war also militarized the small colony. Discipline and direction were sorely lacking before John Smith took effective control of Jamestown and after he left. Starting in 1610, Lord De La Warr assigned all male colonists to 50-man companies, each commanded by a veteran soldier, to receive military training. He also began to impose a strict and coercive legal code entitled *Lawes Divine, Morall and Martiale*, modeled after similar codes used for troops in Europe, though its full implementation did not occur until the following year. These rules instituted a range of punishments, from fines to whippings to death, for numerous offenses.

After 1611, operations and combat decreased, though the English established some new fortifications and settlements in the face of native resistance. By 1614, the previous capture of Powhatan's daughter, Pocahontas, provided the English with an opportunity for the warring sides to negotiate an end to mutually enervating hostilities, a peace symbolized by her marriage to the Englishman John Rolfe. The war took a few hundred lives on either side, including men, women, and children, and wrought large devastation on indigenous and English settlements. The colony's military regime was dismantled, including the requirement to train and participate in militia companies. The next few years brought hope that the brutality of the conflict might be forgotten as colonists and natives resumed trade, established domiciles close to one another, and some English pursued efforts to introduce Christianity to local peoples.

King Powhatan *comands* C. Smith *to be flayne his*
daughter Pokahontas *beggs his life his thankfullnes*
and how he Subiecled 39 of their kings readely histor

Figure 1.3 "King Powhatan Comands C. Smith to be Slayne"

In John Smith, *The Generall Historie of Virginia, New-England, and the Summer Isles.* London, 1624

The most famous story to come out of the early colonization of Virginia is that of the young Pocahontas saving John Smith from execution by her father Powhatan. Scholars now believe the event was a case of political theater, that Pocahontas was playing a role to provide her father with an excuse for sparing Smith after the chief had first demonstrated his power. Powhatan apparently wanted the English as allies but to also dominate the relationship. Not understanding native customs, this meaning was lost on Smith. Moreover, shortly thereafter the colonists attempted a similar ritual, staging a ceremony to crown Powhatan and place him under the authority of King James I. The native chief supposedly would not bow to accept the crown. This image is found in John Smith's book about his experiences in the New World.

Bettmann/Getty Images

The Second and Third Anglo-Powhatan Wars, 1622–32 and 1644–46

Hopes of enduring peace were soon dashed. As tobacco cultivation expanded, the increasing English population and its need for land pressured local Indians. But diplomatic tensions, colonial efforts to remove muskets from native hands, and prominent murders of an English trader and a popular Powhatan war chief helped spark the next round of hostilities. Opechancanough, brother and successor of the now-deceased Powhatan, organized a surprise attack, hoping it would induce the English to abandon the region. On March 22, 1622, natives visited English homes and farms throughout Virginia on apparently peaceful business but then struck down their hosts. Over 300 settlers lost their lives, including women and children—people who, previous to this attack, Powhatan warriors had usually spared. More than 25% of the colony's population of 1,240 died, and the remainder fled to a few settlements along the James River, which were harassed by warriors for weeks.

Following the shock of the 1622 Massacre, and as with the previous war, the English again pursued feedfight campaigns. Indians usually fled with what they could carry and destroyed the rest ahead of the approaching English. Colonists then took steps to increase the chances of capturing native supplies, such as waiting until grain was harvested or using truces to induce local bands to reoccupy communities. Only one pitched battle occurred during the war, in July 1624 when English troops attacked Opechancanough's town of Pamunkey. Sixty soldiers with muskets and body armor repelled assaults from hundreds of warriors over two days, suffering 16 wounded and none killed, and then proceeded to cut down and remove corn after the Indians had exhausted themselves.

By late 1622, colonists were beginning to reoccupy their homesteads. Their need to work their farms hampered the colony's ability to raise manpower for military expeditions. Scholars such as William Shea note the solution to the problem permanently established the militia system in Virginia. In 1624 (when the Virginia Company lost its charter and the colony came under royal authority), the governor and legislative assembly—the House of Burgesses—decreed that the neighbors of any colonist serving on a campaign had to provide labor to maintain that settler's fields. Moreover, anyone injured or maimed while providing military service would be supported by the colony, permanently if need be. Later, the colonial government decreed that, except for newly arrived settlers and those present since 1612, all males aged 16 to 60 were liable for military service and could be taxed according to their means to support the war effort. Local authorities also mandated regular military training and started distributing firearms, for few settlers owned such weapons prior to 1622.

As with the first war, there were occasional truces and periods of minimal military activity during the Second Anglo-Powhatan War of 1622–32. The colony, for example, sometimes ran out of gunpowder. But by the end of the war, Virginia was well organized for ongoing military operations. The government divided the colony into four districts, with local commanders directed to mount regular operations against nearby native groups, and granted discretion to raise militiamen for launching such campaigns as opportunities arose. Colonists also built fortifications. Most were to protect individual farmsteads, but as the war ended in 1632, the colony was completing a palisade (including blockhouses) between the York and the James Rivers across the peninsula that contained the bulk of colonial settlement.

The reasons for the war's end in 1632 are not clear. Native raids had decreased over time, though the English had had earlier opportunities to negotiate a peace. Violent incidents occasionally happened afterward, and tensions between colonists and Indians again grew. These climaxed on April 18, 1644, when Opechancanough, now about 100 years old, launched another surprise attack, beginning the Third Anglo-Powhatan War (1644–46). The second massacre killed more than the first, over 500, but proportionally these casualties were smaller, for the colony's population had greatly increased by then to over 10,000.

In response, the colony mustered 300 militiamen, armed them with muskets and armor, and dispatched them to attack Opechancanough's town of Pamunkey. The English also pursued campaigns against natives on the south bank of the James and in the region west of the palisade. By 1645, these operations had cleared Indians from areas inhabited by colonists north of the James, and the colony decided to build more forts to block native attempts to raid settlements on the main peninsula.

Previous fortifications had been close to colonial homes and communities. The new ones were at a greater distance and could not be easily manned by part-time militia with short terms of service. Hence, authorities recruited and paid volunteers to garrison the forts for up to one year. Virginia also recruited a force of rangers or scouts to patrol areas south of the James along similar lines. This practice of raising and paying volunteers for full-time service was repeated later and in other colonies, particularly for campaigns against distant enemies (militiamen generally stayed close to home).

With the building of these forts, the English reduced the expeditions sent against indigenous foes. One group of militiamen, however, in 1646 tracked down the elusive Opechancanough, who had survived the earlier assault against Pamunkey. Governor Sir William Berkeley with some cavalry then overtook a group of Pamunkeys bearing the aged chief on a litter. Captured, Openchancanough was brought to Jamestown, where he was murdered by a guard. The Powhatan peoples then agreed to peace. Surrendering land, "negroes and guns," they were subsequently limited in where they could live and trade, and agreed to pay tribute and become English subjects and allies.

With the final destruction of the Powhatan confederacy in 1646, Virginia colonists dominated the Chesapeake. But other threats required the maintenance and occasional mustering of the militia. A few violent encounters with native peoples, for example, accompanied the continuing expansion of English settlement. During the Second and Third Anglo-Dutch Wars (1664–67 and 1672–74), raiders appeared in the Chesapeake and destroyed some English vessels. Berkeley's government had militia garrison coastal forts to repel Dutch landing parties. It also modified militia organization and service over time. For example, fines were instituted for unexcused training absences, and tobacco was offered as compensation for militia service.

Virginia was not the only English colony in the region. Maryland was established in 1632 north of the Potomac River and around the head of Chesapeake Bay, initially as a refuge for English Catholics. This colony had problems with native peoples in the 1640s, particularly the Susquehannocks. Later, though, the two allied in the face of conflict with the Five Nations of the Iroquois. When the latter inflicted various defeats on the Susquehannocks in the late 1660s, Maryland allowed them to occupy the colony's Fort Piscataway on the Potomac—which helped precipitate Virginia's greatest crisis in the late seventeenth century.

Bacon's Rebellion, 1676

By 1675, Virginia's population included about 38,000 white colonists, 2,500 African slaves, and 3,500 Indians. Until then, tobacco planters had usually imported white indentured servants to meet their labor needs. Indentures generally lasted a few years, and when freed, a servant received some combination of tools, goods, and money to acquire his own land or pursue a trade. But up until mid-century, high mortality rates meant most servants died during their servitude or shortly thereafter. In the mid-1600s, however, incidents of fatal diseases fell and the lifespan of new arrivals to the colony increased.

As more servants survived their indentures and became freemen, they discovered that a small group of large planters owned the best land, particularly areas along rivers or streams where tobacco crops could be easily loaded onto boats. Poor freemen could only afford land farther inland, which meant large transportation costs. They would also be closer to any potentially hostile Indians. Proportionally, small landholders also paid a greater share of the colony's taxes than the large plantation owners. The resulting resentments exploded into rebellion when the government's response to frontier violence appeared to promise higher taxes for poor freemen without enhancing their safety.

In July 1675, violence erupted between Doeg Indians and some Virginia settlers. Two militia captains then led an attack on a Doeg village and a nearby cabin across the Potomac, killing about two dozen Indians. But the cabin was occupied by Susquehannocks, and their warriors responded with raids on English settlements in Virginia and Maryland. In September, two other Virginia militia officers mobilized 500 militiamen and joined with 250 Maryland soldiers to besiege Fort Piscataway. After a few weeks, the inhabitants broke through the English cordon and escaped. For months thereafter, Susquehannocks raided the Virginia frontier. When they seemed to withdraw in early 1676, other Indian marauders terrorized settlers.

Governor Berkeley and the colonial assembly decided to build nine forts along the outskirts of the colony, raise men to garrison them, and create a unit of dragoons (mounted soldiers) to patrol the regions between the forts. For the governor, the emphasis on defensive measures rather than offensive operations likely reflected distrust of local militia officers, as the actions of a few had escalated the crisis and provoked Susquehannock attacks. Moreover, many settlers could not or would not distinguish between hostile and friendly native groups. The plan also resembled the approach used to defeat the Powhatans in the Third Anglo-Powhatan War.

But the government's proposal infuriated poor freemen living on Virginia's frontiers. Its cost would greatly increase their already-large tax burden but could not prevent raids on colonial homesteads. In the Third Anglo-Powhatan War, most English settlement was on the peninsula between the James and York Rivers, and a few forts could impede movement to the area. By the 1670s, however, colonists had spread out west and north, and native raiding parties could easily bypass forts and patrols to attack other parts of the colony.

Berkeley also infuriated frontier freemen by denying requests to march against native groups. Responding to their anger, in April 1676 Nathaniel Bacon, a young nobleman and recent immigrant to the colony, organized such an expedition without authorization. His force came across and attacked some Occaneechee, a native band friendly to the English. Maltreatment of friendly natives was of no concern to frontier colonists, however, who now regarded Bacon as their champion.

Over the next few months, a complex series of events unfolded that precipitated the collapse of the colonial government. At one point Berkeley declared Bacon a rebel, arrested him, and then released him. Later, the colonial assembly agreed to stop building the new forts and raise 1,000 militiamen only to have Bacon arrive in Jamestown with 500 armed supporters who coerced a commission from Berkeley to lead troops against Indians. The governor again declared Bacon a rebel but fled to the Eastern Shore (the peninsula between the Atlantic Ocean and the Chesapeake Bay) after failing to organize his own army.

Over the summer, Bacon led another expedition against friendly Pamunkeys. In September, he marched to Jamestown after hearing Berkeley had returned with troops. Outnumbered, Bacon's forces constructed fortifications outside the town. They repelled an attack by Berkeley's men and then bombarded Jamestown's defenses with two cannon. When Bacon paraded relatives of Berkeley's supporters and some captured Pamunkeys in front of his positions, morale in the governor's army collapsed. Berkeley's men deserted, and he again retreated to the Eastern Shore.

On October 19, the victors burned Jamestown to the ground. Bacon died a week later, and without his leadership, the rebellion floundered. At the end of 1676, Berkeley's loyalists launched operations along the coast and rivers, and the last rebel stronghold surrendered by the end of January 1677. Berkeley had little opportunity to exact revenge, though, for royal commissioners with 1,000 regular English troops arrived and took control of the colony. Ironically, native depredations on the frontier had continued throughout the rebellion, and a few would occur even after the colony made peace with local peoples in the spring of 1677.

Bacon's Rebellion stemmed from settlers' frustration over their colony's apparent unwillingness to protect them. Bacon himself likely did not wish to overthrow Berkeley's government and instead sought to have Berkeley address settlers' security needs. His raising of large forces without official sanction, however, led the governor to treat him as a rebel. Berkeley understood that unauthorized operations by local militia officers had exacerbated tensions in 1675, and the fort proposal had sought to minimize reliance upon militia that could provoke further hostilities. Conversely, poor settlers saw all Indians as threats, and by the spring of 1676 preexisting social resentments and ongoing native raids made them willing to follow any leader who seemed concerned for their safety, regardless of official authorization.

The revolt had a profound impact on Virginia's development. Big planters thereafter became more sensitive to the concerns of small ones. For labor, large landowners began to rely more upon black slaves, who remained in bondage for life, than on white indentured servants who would ultimately become freemen. The colony also reduced the size of its militia and started relying more upon mounted forces composed of men who were generally more well-to-do and supportive of the colonial regime. (By this time Indians and Africans had been barred from militia service.) The militia system would work well for the immediate future, for the colony faced no grave threats until late in the next century.

Early New England

The desire to establish communities that could pursue religious practices beyond the oversight of the Anglican Church played a great role in New England's colonization. Europeans had been visiting the region for many years before the founding of the first permanent colony at Plymouth in 1620. Previous encounters included positive interactions with local Indians but also some violence, including some kidnappings (usually to teach Indians English for future visits). Of greater import were epidemics in 1616–19 and the early 1630s that decimated the indigenous populations of southeastern New England—which helps explain why colonization did not initially produce the same degree of tensions with native peoples as in the Chesapeake.

The first Plymouth colonists brought with them one fully equipped professional soldier, Myles Standish, and an assortment of guns, swords, and pieces of armor. Wary of natives, they built a fort, organized militia companies, and constructed a palisade around the entire settlement. The colony soon established a long-lasting friendship with Massasoit, leader of the nearby Wampanoag nation. Massasoit regarded the English as potential allies against other native rivals such as the Narragansetts (who lived west of Narragansett Bay in what is today Rhode Island), and Plymouth at times sent soldiers to support him or to fight against perceived mutual enemies, such as in 1622 when Standish led troops against Massachusetts Indians.

Plymouth's entire population was perhaps a few hundred when the "great migration" began in 1630. Over the following decade about 10,000 English Puritans arrived in Massachusetts Bay. Acquiring land for the new colony from local Indians was not problematic in its early years. Settlers established amicable relations with local Massachusetts Indians and with the

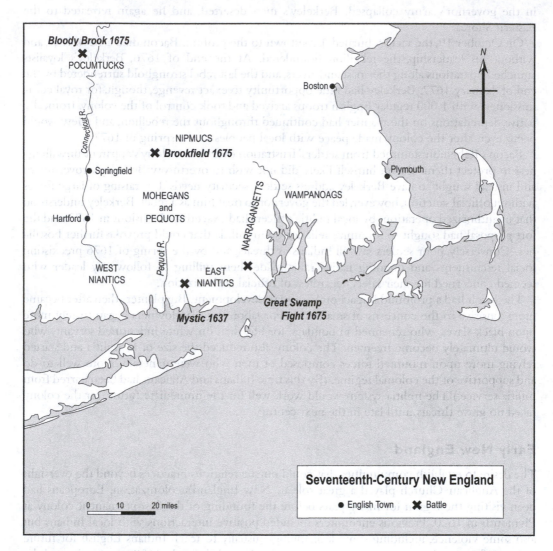

Map 1.3 Seventeenth-Century New England

Narragansetts to the southwest. In 1634, a delegation of Pequots from what is now southeastern Connecticut arrived at Massachusetts Bay and negotiated a treaty—which helped spark the region's first war between colonists and native peoples. The Narragansetts and Pequots were the most populous native groups in southern New England and were rivals in the wampum trade. Wampum consisted of strings of polished seashells, which were popular among indigenous peoples in the continent's interior. In the early 1600s, the Dutch developed the wampum trade, procuring it from coastal groups around Long Island Sound such as the Narragansetts and Pequots and then exchanging it with inland Indians for beaver pelts.

By 1634, hostilities had erupted between the Narragansetts and the Pequots, and the latter approached Massachusetts Bay for help negotiating a settlement. A problem existed, however, for earlier that year Pequots had killed English sea captain John Stone on the Connecticut River. Their envoys said it was an accident, that a Dutch captain had recently killed some of their nation, and warriors seeking revenge did not realize Stone was English. Colonial leaders initially accepted the story and agreed talk to the Narragansetts on the Pequots' behalf. In exchange, the Pequots would send to Massachusetts Bay a large gift of wampum and goods (some of which would be given to the Narragansetts), grant rights for the English to settle on the Connecticut River, and agree to deliver John Stone's murderers to colonial authorities.

English-Pequot relations thereafter deteriorated. Pequot leaders apparently decided not to approve the treaty, and Massachusetts Bay received neither the stipulated gift nor Stone's murderers. In 1635, Bay colonists did establish three new settlements on the Connecticut River (Windsor, Wethersfield, and Hartford), while a group out of England established Fort Saybrook at the river's mouth. But by the summer of 1636, rumors stemming from a trading house on the Connecticut River warned that Stone's killers remained at large and that Pequots were planning attacks on English ships. An emissary dispatched by the Bay colony did not receive adequate reassurances. That same summer, John Oldham, another English captain, was discovered killed in waters off Rhode Island. The English initially suspected the Narragansetts, who denied any involvement and blamed one of their tributary bands, the natives residing on Block Island in Long Island Sound.

In late August 1636, Massachusetts Bay organized an expedition of 90 men led by John Endecott. Its first mission was to go to Block Island to "do justice" for Oldham's murder, whereby they would "put to death the men" but spare the women and children, removing them from the island. The expedition would then visit the Pequots to demand Stone's killers and obtain fines in the form of wampum and children as hostages for future good behavior. Endecott was authorized by colonial officials to use force if necessary. When Endecott's force arrived at Block Island, the English received a hail of arrows but then could find no Indians, and instead of carrying out its mission burned wigwams and corn.

The Pequot War, 1636–38

The expedition arrived at the Pequot River (now the Thames) in September. Endecott tried to negotiate but was frustrated when the Pequots said their chiefs were absent and had to be found. After waiting many hours, he saw native women and children leaving and became more suspicious when Pequots asked the English to disarm prior to a parley. Instead he prepared his men for a pitched battle in the European tradition, forming them in close order and marching onto a field with flags flying and drums beating in anticipation of meeting the enemy. In response the Pequots, as described by the English officer John Underhill, "standing remotely off did laugh at us for our patience." Refused a battle, Endecott's men destroyed dwellings and corn, and then left the next day for Boston.

Thus began the Pequot War of 1636–38. Sparked by Endecott's frustrations and suspicions, its genesis lay in English insecurities about Pequot intents fostered by the absence of any meaningful diplomacy between the two peoples after 1634. Yet having started the war, Massachusetts Bay took no further action until the following spring. In the interim, Pequot warriors harassed Fort Saybrook and any unwary English caught in its environs, who risked torture and death. But the Pequots wondered about their foes, particularly what limits they observed in war. In early 1637 during a parley with Lion Gardiner, the commander of Fort Saybrook, natives inquired if the English killed women and children. As with indigenous peoples in other parts of North America, New England natives generally did not harm women and children in their conflicts. Gardiner answered that "they should see that hereafter." In response, he was told: "We are Pequots, and have killed Englishmen, and can kill them as mosquitoes, and we will go to Connecticut and kill men, women, and children, and we will take away the horses, cows, and hogs."

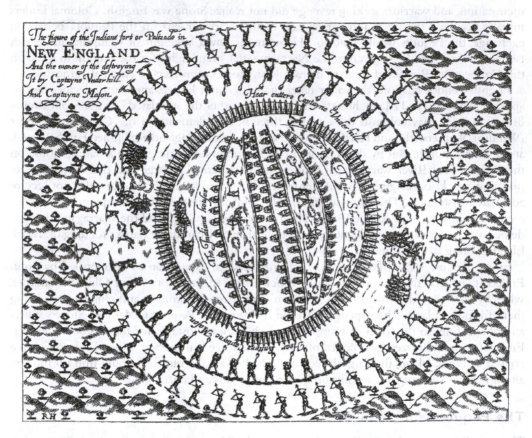

Figure 1.4 Drawing of the Mystic Assault

From John Underhill's *Good Newes from America*, 1638

This drawing from John Underhill's 1638 pamphlet depicts the assault on Mystic village. English troops comprise the inner ring of attackers, with native allies on the outside. At the time, the two entrances in the palisade were obstructed with trees and other debris, and the soldiers had to break through to enter the town. The image also depicts the native dwellings arranged along streets, and the English both firing the initial volley into the town from the outside as well as fighting Pequots within the town. Electronic transcriptions of accounts of the Pequot War, including Underhill's *Good Newes from America*, John Mason's *A Brief History of the Pequot War*, and Lion Gardiner's *A Relation of the Pequot Warres*, are available at http://digitalcommons.unl.edu.

Underhill, John and Paul Royster, editor, "Newes from America; Or, A New and Experimentall Discoverie of New England; Containing, A Trve Relation of Their War-like Proceedings These Two Yeares Last Past, with a Figure of the Indian Fort, or Palizado" (1638). Electronic Texts in American Studies. Paper 37. http://digitalcommons.unl.edu/etas/37

Not long afterward, in late April 1637, the Pequots raided Wethersfield, killing six men and three women, capturing two young "maids," and slaughtering a herd of cattle. Though hostilities had begun months earlier, the three upriver English settlements apparently did not feel threatened by the Pequots prior to this attack. Their reaction, though, was resolute. In May, the General Court of Connecticut colony declared "offensive war" against the Pequots and raised and armed a force of 90 men (out of the total male population between the three towns of a few hundred) commanded by John Mason to go against them.

Mason sailed his force, including the native leader Uncas and his band of Mohegans, downriver to Fort Saybrook. Taking a roundabout route, they continued east past the Pequot lands to Narragansett Bay and then marched west. Mason's intent was to surprise the Pequots, approaching from an unexpected direction rather than sail directly to their main settlement on the Pequot River. At dawn on May 26, Mason led his force against a smaller Pequot settlement on the Mystic River. English soldiers surrounded the town, fired a musket volley into the palisade, and then launched an assault through the two entrances. The troops engaged Pequot warriors in hand-to-hand combat and then withdrew, but set the town on fire. The vast majority of Mystic's population—a few hundred men, women, and children—died in the fire or trying to escape, as the English killed all but a handful who fled. After the attack, as Mason's men marched to rendezvous with their ships in the Pequot River, their native allies fended off attacks by warriors from the larger Pequot town nearby.

The assault on Mystic is one of the most infamous episodes in American colonial history. The slaying of an entire village was destruction well beyond what New England's Indians conceived as appropriate in war. Some native allies declared to John Underhill, "[M]ach it, mach it; that is, it is naught, it is naught, because it is too furious, and slays too many men." Such carnage was reminiscent of the brutality used in extending English control over Ireland in the sixteenth century and also occurred amid the Thirty Years War (1618–48) that ravaged central Europe.

Hostilities did not end at Mystic, however. Shortly thereafter, 120 Massachusetts troops commanded by Israel Stoughton arrived in the region. They joined Connecticut soldiers led by Mason and native allies such as the Mohegans to track down bands of Pequots fleeing across southern New England. The largest resulting action occurred that July in western Connecticut, when colonial forces confronted numerous Pequots in a swamp. After some combat and a parley, and about 180 Pequot women, children, and old men surrendered to the English. The warriors did not, though, and most broke through the English cordon and escaped the following night. In August 1637, colonists learned that the chief Pequot leaders had been killed, and recalled their forces. Hostilities formally ended the following year with the Treaty of Hartford.

The Pequot War illustrates how English colonies mobilized manpower. Militia companies were administrative and training organizations but not combat units per se. In New England, adult men were supposed to be members of their local militia company. These would muster at regular times where militiamen would drill and practice using arms. But colonies did not send militia companies to war. To raise manpower for a campaign, a colony would instead determine how many men were needed and establish quotas, with each town obligated to provide a stated number of men as well as equip and supply them. Ideally, enough men in these communities would volunteer to fulfill the stated quota. If not, local authorities chose who would go on the campaign, although individuals of means could often avoid service by paying a fine or hiring a substitute. Those who did not volunteer were said to have been "pressed" into military service. But whether volunteers or pressed, all men on a campaign should have had a basic familiarity with arms and drill from their militia duty.

English conduct during the war also demonstrates how colonists relied upon native allies, in this case Uncas and his Mohegans. They accompanied Mason's forces from the beginning of the Mystic campaign, serving as guides and providing reconnaissance in addition to fighting Pequot warriors. Narragansett warriors also provided assistance to the English, but many of them had quickly abandoned Mason's expedition when they learned that he intended to attack a palisaded Pequot town (which to them seemed a reckless endeavor, based on their traditional style of warfare). As such, the English developed close relations with the Mohegans after the war but soon became wary of the Narragansetts.

A Tense Period of Peace

The disposition of the Pequots exacerbated Narragansett–Mohegan tensions. After Mystic, Pequot groups scattered, seeking shelter and protection with other indigenous peoples. This was a traditional native response to danger but one usually pursued by bands that lacked the Pequots' prewar size and status. Most joined the Narragansetts or the Mohegans, which was confirmed by the 1638 Treaty of Hartford. The document stipulated that the refugees would "no more be called Pequots" but would adopt their hosts' identity. (One band of Pequots later reestablished a community in their old territory under English jurisdiction, and still exists.) But competition at the end of the Pequot War to absorb Pequots into their communities created a new rivalry between the Mohegans and the Narragansetts.

Various rumors circulated in New England during the 1640s about supposed Narragansett "plots" against the English. At one point, the Mohegans and Narragansetts fought a battle in which Uncas captured the chief Narragansett leader Miantinomi. Later, with English concurrence, the Mohegan chief executed him. Tensions between the two groups continued, and the New England colonies almost went to war with the Narragansetts in 1645. The latter agreed to a punitive treaty, but English suspicions continued and focused on a Narragansett ally: Ninigret, leader of the Niantics.

After the First Anglo–Dutch War broke out in 1652, fears that the Dutch would collude with Ninigret and other native groups to attack them led some New Englanders to advocate an invasion of New Netherland. Though Massachusetts refused, representatives from other colonies obtained approval from Oliver Cromwell's government for such a campaign, which they were organizing when the war ended in 1654. The Second and Third Anglo–Dutch Wars caused some alarms but no serious threat to the New England colonists. Other developments, though, were moving the region to the biggest conflagration in its history.

Migration from England decreased greatly after 1640, but New England's colonists found their new environment quite healthy and raised large families. Their settlements spread throughout the 1600s, advancing farther up the Connecticut River, along other rivers and around Long Island Sound, deeper into the interior from Massachusetts Bay, and around Narragansett Bay. This expansion increased pressure on natives to sell land and disrupted the animal migration and ecological patterns indigenous peoples required for their traditional lifestyles. Indians faced additional challenges in this period with missionary activity and the creation of praying towns.

To induce Indians to adopt their culture and learn Christianity, colonists set aside land for natives to establish towns similar to their own, where they would adopt English agricultural practices and lifestyles and attend church. Whatever attraction Western faith and culture held for indigenous peoples, an additional benefit was that praying towns offered a means for them to maintain possession of land in areas where it was being bought up by settlers. In the 1650s and 1660s English colonists created about a dozen praying towns. Their decision, however, posed complications for Indians who were trying to preserve their traditional lifestyles, as the migration of some to praying towns weakened the communities they left behind.

These tensions exploded into war in the summer of 1675, precipitated by a group that had long been friendly to the English—the Wampanoags. By 1662, Massasoit had died, and his son Metacom, known as King Philip to the English, became their chief. Plymouth posed numerous challenges to Metacom, particularly when colonists founded Swansea, a new settlement near Wampanoag lands, and a praying town on Cape Cod. He tried to avoid selling land and opposed missionary activities among his people. The colony also sought to impose its authority over the Wampanoags. Following the visit of armed warriors to a town in 1671, its leaders confronted Metacom, made him sign a putative treaty, and confiscated his warriors' guns. Finally, in early 1675, a Christian Indian named John Sassamon was discovered murdered shortly after he had warned Plymouth's governor of a possible native conspiracy. When three Wampanoags were tried and executed for his murder in June, warriors began harassing English settlements around Swansea, precipitating what became known as King Philip's War.

King Philip's War, 1675–76

The name of the conflict is misleading in that it implies Metacom had significant control over the war. As with any native leader, he could not prevent angry warriors from marauding Swansea, lacking any means to restrain them. After Wampanoags initiated hostilities, other Indian groups took up arms against the English, though not all. Of the region's approximate native population of 12,000, about half became belligerent. Others, including inhabitants of praying towns, stayed out of the conflict or helped the New England colonists, who numbered about 50,000.

Swansea's inhabitants soon fled, and Plymouth and Massachusetts dispatched militia to the area. In July the English attacked the Wampanoags at Mt. Hope (the latter's main town on a peninsula that jutted into Narragansett Bay) but discovered the area abandoned. Colonial forces attempted pursuit and fought some skirmishes in swampy areas beyond Narragansett Bay, but Metacom and the Wampanoags escaped to the northwest. Later that summer, groups such as the Nipmucks and Pocumtucks, in what is now central and western Massachusetts, joined the hostilities and assaulted English settlements.

The first occurred in early August at Brookfield, about 20 miles east of the Connecticut River. This engagement was unique in that warriors built a crude siege engine to set a building on fire where they had besieged colonists. Timely rainfall thwarted the attempt, and then a cavalry unit arrived, dispersing the attackers, but colonists then abandoned the town. In September, warriors raided Massachusetts settlements along the Connecticut River. They also ambushed English convoys sent to evacuate two towns. In one incident—known as Bloody Brook—over 60 of 80 soldiers were killed. In October, Indians assaulted and destroyed much of Springfield. Perhaps a third of the town lost their homes and possessions, though only one settler died.

Native attacks ebbed as autumn progressed. That winter, the English mounted their largest operation of the war against the Narragansetts, who were not yet fighting the colonists. In fact, Massachusetts Bay had compelled Narragansett leaders to sign an agreement pledging their fidelity. Some scholars argue the colonies coveted Narragansett lands and pursued the campaign in order to establish claims based on conquest. But this nation remained the largest in New England, and memories of tensions and disputes with the Narragansetts after the Pequot War likely influenced the decision to attack them. By the end of 1675, colonial leaders were expressing suspicions of the Narragansetts and were listening to rumors that they were helping enemies of the English and preparing for war.

In December, the New England colonies gathered almost 1,000 men, including 150 Mohegan and Pequot warriors. A winter offensive was unusual, and while English forces hoped to surprise the Narragansetts, they had difficulty obtaining supplies. Suspecting the colonies' intent, the Narragansetts had retreated to a fort with a palisade and blockhouses in the middle of a large swamp. Marching out on December 18 amid a snowstorm, the attackers found and assaulted an incomplete section of the fortifications. As at Mystic, the English concluded the Great Swamp Fight by burning the fort and dwellings inside, killing many Narragansetts. Many of the perhaps 1,000 Narragansett men, women, and children fled but now had to confront winter without shelter or supplies. As for the colonial army, it suffered over 200 casualties; perhaps 80 men died in combat during the snowy march back to their base or later from their wounds.

Thereafter, hostilities subsided until February. Warriors now including Narragansetts launched numerous attacks on colonial towns. These included Massachusetts settlements on

Figure 1.5 "Attack on Brookfield"

In *The History of Our Country: From the Landing of the Norsemen to the Present Time* (New York: Niglustsch, 1900)

This picture portrays the siege of Brookfield. Unfortunately, the depictions of individual Indians reflect stereotypes and biases prominent among late nineteenth-century white Americans, and hence should not be taken as historically accurate. But the image does demonstrate an innovative Nipmuck effort to burn and destroy a garrison house. Warriors constructed a siege engine using a wagon piled with flammable material set alight and added additional planking to protect Indians pushing it from the defenders' fire. Rain helped thwart this attempt before English reinforcements arrived.

Picture Collection, The New York Public Library, Astor, Lenox, and Tilden Foundations

the Connecticut River, some in Plymouth, and even assaults on Providence in the colony of Rhode Island, which had been friendly with local native groups. But the most alarming attacks were on towns around Massachusetts Bay itself, some less than 20 miles from Boston. By April, five of these towns had been abandoned by their residents, contributing to a significant refugee problem as they sought support and assistance in other communities. English forces seemed helpless, for their native foes moved seemingly undetected through wilderness areas, attacked their targets, and retreated before local forces could engage them.

Box 1.1   Attack on a Garrison House

Mary Rowlandson, a minister's wife and mother in Lancaster, Massachusetts, was captured during an attack on February 10, 1676, when the garrison house where she was shelter-ing was destroyed. She spent about three months as an Indian captive. A few years after the war, she described her experiences in a book entitled *The Sovereignty and Goodness of God*, which established a new literary genre: the Indian captivity narrative. The following excerpt describes the attack when she was captured:

> The house stood upon the edge of a hill; some of the Indians got behind the hill, oth-ers into the barn, and others behind anything that could shelter them; from all which places they shot against the house, so that the bullets seemed to fly like hail; and quickly they wounded one man among us, then another, and then a third. About two hours . . . they had been about the house before they prevailed to fire it (which they did with flax and hemp, which they brought out of the barn, and there being no defense about the house, only two flankers [bastions] at two opposite corners and one of them not finished); they fired it once and one ventured out and quenched it, but they quickly fired it again, and that took . . . . No sooner were we out of the house, but my brother-in-law (being before wounded, in defending the house, in or near the throat) fell down dead, whereat the Indians scornfully shouted, and hallowed, and were presently upon him, stripping off his clothes, the bullets flying thick, one went through my side, and the same (as would seem) through the bowels and hand of my dear child in my arms . . . [T]he Indians laid hold of us, pulling me one way, and the children another, and said, "Come go along with us"; I told them they would kill me: they answered, if I were willing to go along with them, they would not hurt me.
>
> (Mary Rowlandson, *The Sovereignty and Goodness of God . . . and Related Documents*, ed. Neal Salisbury, Boston: Bedford Books, 1997, pp. 68–70).

For the colonies, however, the worst was over. In the late spring and summer of 1676 a combination of sustenance problems, the intervention of the Mohawks, and better English tactical effectiveness turned the hunters into the hunted and ended the war. As English forces and their native allies captured and killed more belligerent Indians, more voluntarily surren-dered. Metacom himself was tracked down and killed in August, and the war ended shortly thereafter (though hostilities continued in what is now Maine).

Thus ended the most devastating conflict in New England's history. King Philip's War left a dozen English towns completely destroyed and abandoned and others with extensive damage. About 800 to 1,000 colonists died in the war. Among settlers known for religious observance, the war caused a crisis of faith: What had they done to deserve such suffering? Yet the Indians suffered more. Of New England's total indigenous population of 12,000, about 3,000 died.

Hundreds, perhaps more than 1,000 natives, were sold into slavery in the West Indies, including many who had surrendered. King Philip's War destroyed what little autonomy native peoples had retained, as the English now confined them to reservations or other areas and placed them under colonial authority—even friendly groups such as the Mohegans.

King Philip's War: Assessment

Operationally and tactically, raiding towns and ambushing enemies comprised traditional Indian approaches to warfare. What was different in King Philip's War was their scale, number, and lethality, for warriors inflicted far more devastation than in prior conflicts. As various scholars note, Mystic had revealed the carnage that the English were prepared to wreak in warfare, and Indians reciprocated in 1675–76. They used relatively simple expedients to do so, such as fire arrows or applying torches to English homes and farms. Furthermore, by the 1670s, flintlock muskets were ubiquitous among New England warriors. When employed in conjunction with their typical skirmishing and ambush tactics, these weapons were very lethal.

King Philip's War also illustrates a New England variant on the problem of tactical defense. In New England, groups of settlers had founded towns together, with families maintaining fields on the outskirts of town, and buildings in the center. In many towns, colonists built some of the larger homes with additional planking for thicker walls and often cut slits or gun ports into doors, window shutters, or walls. These were called "garrison houses." When Indians attacked, settlers fled to them, with men grabbing arms to defend a house until help could arrive. Those inside usually survived unmolested, for warriors risked high casualties if they stormed garrison houses (which were occasionally assaulted anyway). Conversely, settlers caught outside these shelters during a raid were likely to be killed or captured. Indians also burned farms and houses abandoned in the attack and stole or slaughtered livestock. When militia officers learned a nearby settlement was under assault, they usually mustered what men they could find to go to the town's aid. Usually the attack was over by the time they arrived, in which case they tried to pursue the assailants, generally unsuccessfully. Sometimes warriors anticipated this reaction and laid ambushes for troops racing to the relief of a town.

Tactically, English forces became more adept late in the war, due in large part to reliance upon native allies. Given how the war began, colonists in Massachusetts Bay and Plymouth were highly suspicious of native peoples—even ones that professed friendship and lived in praying towns. Many English would have been happy to see all native people killed or expelled. As it happened, during 1675 colonial authorities moved praying Indians to Deer Island in Boston Harbor. There they suffered greatly from lack of shelter and supplies the following winter, and some died. The one exception to this situation was Connecticut. The colony retained a strong bond to Uncas (still alive) and his nation of Mohegans. As a result, Connecticut suffered few attacks and made use of its native friends fairly early in the war. For example, it was the colony's Indian allies that assisted the English in the Great Swamp Fight.

The attacks of early 1676 prompted Massachusetts Bay and Plymouth to seek Indian help, which allowed colonists to better locate and engage enemy groups. The most famous such incident happened that August, when a mixed force of English and Indians led by Benjamin Church tracked down and killed Metacom near the Wampanoag homeland of Mt. Hope. But this was just one of many operations pursued throughout the late spring and summer of 1676 by similar units. As noted above, these units had help, for by then Mohawks were also tracking down and attacking the colonists' Indian enemies from the west.

Logistics were also important for the English victory in King Philip's War. New England's native societies were not used to conducting warfare throughout the year. Though they had survived the winter in part from captured English supplies, by late spring subsistence issues undermined warriors' ability to maintain combat operations. Colonists exploited this problem, such as a case in May when local forces surprised and killed numerous natives around a fishing hole in the Connecticut River valley.

But the war also stretched the English to their limits, particularly with respect to manpower. Colonies raised men for numerous operations, including the July 1675 campaign against the Wampanoags, the Great Swamp Fight, and the defense of towns on the Connecticut River and, later, the western environs of the Bay area. As the war continued, more towns had difficulty meeting manpower quotas, as militiamen became more concerned about defending their own homes and communities rather than those elsewhere. This problem was especially acute in Massachusetts Bay and Plymouth during the native assaults of early 1676. Ultimately, though, the New England colonies were able to field forces longer than their Wampanoag, Nipmuck, Pocumtuck, and Narragansett opponents.

Conclusion

In seventeenth-century North America, peoples from two different cultures met, interacted, and fought. Indians married Western technology to their traditional low-intensity combat. Stymied by native tactics, European colonists built fortifications, used indigenous allies, and pursued operations that wreaked destruction unheard of in indigenous warfare—and which warriors pursued themselves in King Philip's War. John Grenier describes the colonists' emphasis on harming noncombatants as "extirpative war," which—combined with borrowing tactics from native combat—he identifies as part of a distinctive "first" American way of war. Settlers certainly adapted to American conditions and inflicted great destruction on Indian peoples (though some would object to calling colonists the "first" Americans). But neither low-intensity warfare nor excessive violence against civilian populations were unknown in Europe, as demonstrated in sixteenth-century Ireland. What Grenier calls the first way of war was also only applied with any consistency against American Indian foes. As the next chapter will demonstrate, when facing Western opponents, colonists adopted more conventional approaches to warfare.

Short Bibliography

Canny, Nicholas P. "The Ideology of English Colonization: From Ireland to America." *William and Mary Quarterly* 3rd series, 30 (1973): 575–98.

Cave, Alfred A. *The Pequot War.* Amherst: University of Massachusetts Press, 1996.

Gleach, Frederic W. *Powhatan's World and Colonial Virginia: A Conflict of Cultures.* Lincoln: University of Nebraska Press, 1997.

Hirsch, Adam J. "The Collision of Military Cultures in Seventeenth-Century New England." *Journal of American History* 74 (1988): 1187–212.

Karr, Ronald Dale. "'Why Should You Be So Furious?' The Violence of the Pequot War." *Journal of American History* 85 (1998): 876–909.

Keener, Craig S. "An Ethnohistorical Analysis of Iroquois Assault Tactics Used against Fortified Settlements of the Northeast in the Seventeenth Century." *Ethnohistory* 46 (1999): 777–807.

Malone, Patrick M. *The Skulking Way of War: Technology and Tactics among the New England Indians.* Baltimore: Johns Hopkins University Press, 1991.

Mandell, Daniel R. *King Philip's War: Colonial Expansion, Native Resistance, and the End of Indian Sovereignty.* Baltimore: Johns Hopkins University Press, 2010.

Parker, Geoffrey. *The Military Revolution: Military Innovation and the Rise of the West, 1500–1800.* 2nd ed. New York: Cambridge University Press, 1996.

Richter, Daniel K. *The Ordeal of the Longhouse: The Peoples of the Iroquois League in the Era of European Colonization.* Chapel Hill: University of North Carolina Press, 1992.

Shea, William L. *The Virginia Militia in the Seventeenth Century.* Baton Rouge: Louisiana State University Press, 1983.

Steele, Ian K. *Warpaths: Invasions of North America.* New York: Oxford University Press, 1994.

Zelner, Kyle. *A Rabble in Arms: Massachusetts Towns and Militiamen during King Philip's War.* New York: New York University Press, 2009.

1688–89	1689–97	1701	1702–13	1704	1739–48
Glorious Revolution	King William's War	The Grand Settlement ends the Beaver Wars (began in 1640s)	Queen Anne's War	Deerfield Raid	War of Jenkins' Ear

TIMELINE

Chapter 2

Wars Imperial and Regional, 1689–1763

In seventeenth-century North America, natives and colonists fought numerous conflicts that stemmed from regional tensions. Starting in 1689, wars spilled across the Atlantic. Hostilities between Western European states precipitated wars between their American colonies—and this direction reversed in some mid-eighteenth-century conflicts. These imperial contests pitted New France against New York and New England, and southern British colonies against Spanish Florida. The last of these wars, the Seven Years War or the French and Indian War, ended in 1763 with Great Britain dominating the continent.

Amid these broader struggles, local tensions provoked regional hostilities between Indians and colonists, and imperial wars in North America often became a number of simultaneous conflicts prosecuted in different areas. Native groups played crucial roles in all these campaigns, and low-intensity conflict in the form of raids and ambushes typical of earlier seventeenth-century hostilities was common. However, both Britain and France dispatched sizable regular forces across the Atlantic during the French and Indian War. As a result, conventional, high-intensity operations played a much greater role in this conflict, and British victories in these campaigns ultimately led France to abandon its colonies in mainland North America.

In this chapter, students will learn about:

- Late seventeenth-century developments that led to wars between European states and their American colonies from 1689 to 1763.
- Imperial wars in which New France fought against northern British colonies.
- Imperial wars in which Spanish Florida fought against southern British colonies.
- Regional conflicts between particular native peoples and colonies.
- The changing proportion of low-intensity to high-intensity warfare in North America, and the roles played by Indian warriors, colonial forces, and regular European troops.

The Glorious Revolution of 1688–89

In 1688, for the second time in the seventeenth century, relations between the English King and Parliament devolved into a political crisis. The first episode produced the British Civil Wars, leading to the defeat and execution of Charles I and the dictatorship of Oliver Cromwell. After Cromwell died, Parliament placed Charles II on the throne in 1660. One of the new king's policies was to maintain cordial relations with France's Louis XIV. Having already fought the Dutch in two previous wars, Charles II joined the French in warring with the Netherlands in 1672. Parliament ended England's participation in 1674, though the conflict continued until 1678; in the resulting peace treaty, the Dutch, who had recaptured New York, agreed to return it and accept its status as an English colony.

As England was an overwhelmingly Protestant country, Charles II's relationship with Catholic Louis XIV irked many of his subjects. Religion was a passionate matter in early modern Europe, and many Englishmen viewed the Catholic Church as a dire threat to Protestantism. Charles II was not Catholic, but his younger brother James was. When Charles II died in 1685, many Englishmen were already wary of their new king. James II further angered his subjects by trying to exclude Parliament from his efforts to collect and spend tax revenues. Political tensions peaked in 1688 after news spread that James' wife, Queen Mary, had given birth to a son, raising the prospect that Protestant England might be ruled by a succession of Catholic kings.

Soon thereafter, some members of Parliament asked William, Prince of Orange of the Netherlands—both Protestant and married to James II's eldest daughter, Mary—to take the English throne. When William arrived with Dutch troops in November, political leaders and army officers abandoned their allegiance to James II, who fled England. James raised troops in Ireland to reestablish his rule but was defeated at the Battle of Boyne in 1690. Louis XIV then gave him refuge in France. Meanwhile, William and Mary became joint monarchs of England—William III and Mary II—in 1689, though William made executive decisions. He accepted the new English Bill of Rights that limited the monarch's authority, including mandating Parliament's approval for the collection of new taxes and for the raising or maintenance of an army in peacetime.

This political result, known as the Glorious Revolution, set important precedents for American colonists forming a new government at the end of the eighteenth century. More immediately, though, the Glorious Revolution had great political ramifications in the American colonies. In New England there was elation, for James had tried to impose greater royal control over the region, and settlers expelled his appointed governor. Other areas endured political strife in which local militias played key roles. In Maryland, Protestant settlers had long been disgruntled with colonial authorities partial to the colony's Catholic founders. In 1689, following news of James II's overthrow, Protestant militiamen ousted the local government, an action later condoned by William III. Tensions also existed in New York between Dutch and English settlers of modest circumstances and the colony's well-to-do. Again in 1689, news of the Glorious

Revolution incited the militia to rise up against the government. A merchant and German immigrant named Jacob Leisler took leadership of the revolt—known as Leisler's Rebellion—and effectively ruled New York until 1691. Although he sought approval from William III, the king appointed Henry Sloughter as the colony's governor. Leisler surrendered after an initial standoff between his supporters and troops who accompanied Sloughter, only to be later tried and executed for treason.

Overview of Imperial Wars in North America

These crises had run their course by the mid-1690s. By that time, however, the colonies were coping with larger ramifications of the Glorious Revolution. By 1688, the Dutch had fought two wars against Louis XIV's France and were becoming involved in another. William III wished to help his native country, and his new English subjects needed little encouragement, particularly when Louis provided ships and troops for James II's attempt to reclaim the English throne. England joined the War of the League of Augsburg in 1689, which ended with the Treaty of Ryswick in 1697. But Europe had only a short respite before becoming embroiled the War of Spanish Succession (1701–14). Louis XIV died shortly thereafter, and peace lasted for about a quarter century before the two large wars of the mid-eighteenth century. In contrast to prior wars, hostilities erupted in the Western Hemisphere just before the War of the Austrian Succession (1740–48) and the Seven Years War (1756–63).

The timing and the names of these wars differed on the American side of the Atlantic, as indicated below:

European Wars	North American Wars
War of the League of Augsburg (1688–97)	King William's War (1689–97)
War of the Spanish Succession (1701–14)	Queen Anne's War (1702–13)
War of the Austrian Succession (1740–48)	War of Jenkins' Ear (1739–48)
	King George's War (1744–48)
Seven Years War (1756–63)	French and Indian War (1754–63)

With the exception of the War of Jenkins' Ear, all these imperial wars pitted Britain against France, generating conflict in northeastern North America between New France, and New England and New York. Spain was an ally of England during King William's War, but an enemy in Queen Anne's War, pitting Spanish Florida against British Carolina. The War of Jenkins' Ear brought conflict back to the southern Atlantic seaboard, but hostilities died down by the time the French and British faced each other again in King George's War. Spain entered the Seven Years War late, and although Britain attacked many of its overseas holdings, its colonies on the North American mainland remained quiet.

Both New France and Spanish Florida had militia systems and sometimes regular troops. But their small populations relative to the English colonies made them highly dependent upon native allies in wartime. The French used forces comprised of Indians and militia to raid New England's frontiers and distract English colonists from launching campaigns against key Canadian cities—an example of offensive operations serving the goal of strategic defense. King William's War also coincided with the end of the Beaver Wars, a series of conflicts that set the Five Nations of the Iroquois against numerous native allies of the French during the 1600s, and later against New France itself. In 1701, the Iroquois and the Canadian French made peace, and the Five Nations remained mostly neutral in North America's remaining imperial wars. Moreover, since the Iroquois resided between Canada and New York, conflict between the two thereafter was limited until the French and Indian War.

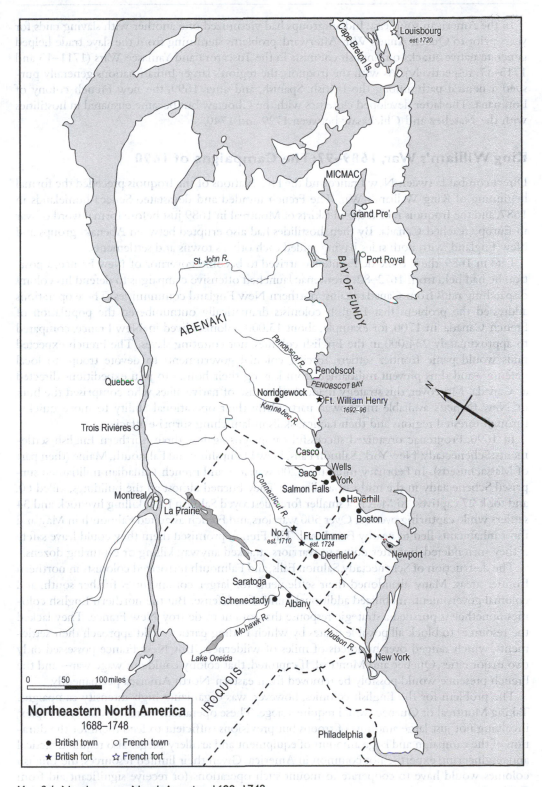

Map 2.1 Northeastern North America, 1688–1748

Northeastern North America
1688–1748

● British town   ○ French town
★ British fort   ☆ French fort

0   50   100 miles

Louisbourg
est. 1720

Cape Breton Is.

MICMAC

Grand Pre'

Port Royal

BAY OF FUNDY

St. John R.

ABENAKI

Penobscot R.

Penobscot
PENOBSCOT BAY

Quebec

Norridgewock

Ft. William Henry
1692–96

Kennebec R.

Trois Rivieres

Casco

Wells

Saco

York

Salmon Falls

Haverhill

Connecticut R.

Montreal

La Prairie

Boston

No. 4
est. 1710

Ft. Dummer
est. 1724

Deerfield

Newport

Saratoga

Schenectady

Albany

Mohawk R.

Hudson R.

Lake Oneida

New York

IROQUOIS

Philadelphia

In the American southeast, Indian groups had victimized one another with slaving raids for years prior to Queen Anne's War. Afterward, problems stemming from the slave trade helped generate native attacks on English colonists in the Tuscarora and Yamasee Wars (1711–13 and 1715–17, respectively). As with the Iroquois, the region's larger Indian nations generally pursued a neutral path among the British, Spanish, and after 1699, the new French colony of Louisiana. The latter developed close ties with the Choctaw but became ensnared in hostilities with the Natchez and Chickasaw between 1729 and 1740.

King William's War, 1689–97: The Campaigns of 1690

Direct combat between New France and the Five Nations of the Iroquois preceded the formal beginning of King William's War. The French invaded and devastated Seneca homelands in 1687, and the Iroquois raided the outskirts of Montreal in 1689 just before formal word of war in Europe reached Canada. By then, hostilities had also erupted between Abenaki groups and New England, with both sides having raided each other's towns and settlements.

Late in 1689, the Comte de Frontenac arrived to become governor of New France, a position he had held from 1672–82. Frontenac launched offensive campaigns to defend his colony, dispatching raids from Canada against northern New England communities. These operations addressed the problem that English colonists dramatically outnumbered the population of French Canada: In 1700, for example, about 15,000 colonists lived in New France, compared to approximately 234,000 in the English colonies, not counting slaves. The French expected raids would panic frontier settlers, forcing colonial governments to devote troops to local defense—and thus prevent militiamen from leaving their homes to join expeditions directed at Canada. Moreover, this strategy made the best use of native allies who comprised the bulk of New France's available manpower, particularly their operational ability to move quickly through forested regions and their tactical skills in launching surprise attacks.

In 1690, Frontenac organized successful campaigns against three northern English settlements: Schenectady, New York; Salmon Falls, New Hampshire; and Falmouth, Maine (then part of Massachusetts). In February, more than 200 warriors and French Canadian militiamen surprised Schenectady in the midst of a blizzard. They burned almost all the buildings, killed 60, and took 27 captives. In March, a smaller force destroyed Salmon Falls, killing livestock and 34 settlers while capturing over 50. Over 500 warriors and French assaulted Falmouth in May, and most inhabitants fled to nearby Fort Loyal. The French promised them they could leave safely if they surrendered, but after doing so warriors attacked anyway, killing or capturing dozens.

The destruction of Schenectady, Salmon Falls, and Falmouth terrorized colonists in northern frontier areas. Many abandoned their settlements for larger communities further south, and colonial governments mobilized additional militia for defense. But the northern English colonies nonetheless pursued a strategic response that sought to destroy New France. They lacked the resources to block all possible routes by which raiding parties could approach their settlements, which ranged over hundreds of miles of wilderness. But New France possessed only two major cities, Quebec and Montreal. If captured, that colony could not wage war—and the French presence would possibly be removed from eastern North America permanently.

The problem for the English colonies, however, was organizing high-intensity campaigns. Taking Montreal or Quebec would require a siege. These operations were logistically complex, involving not just large amounts of troops but provisions sufficient to feed them for the duration of the campaign and large amounts of equipment and artillery. Sieges also required tactical and engineering expertise not common in America. Given their limited resources, the English colonies would have to cooperate to mount such operations (or receive significant aid from England).

In the spring of 1690, officials from various colonies met in New York at the behest of Jacob Leisler, acting as governor as a result of Leisler's Rebellion. They agreed to two campaigns. One would be organized at Albany with troops from many colonies, and Leisler asserted the Iroquois would contribute 1,800 warriors. This force would travel overland and via Lake Champlain to attack Montreal. Massachusetts Bay would mount the other operation, a seaborne expedition to sail to and besiege Quebec. The campaign against Montreal was a fiasco. Only Connecticut and New York sent troops to Albany, totaling less than 300 soldiers. Smallpox sickened many of these men and reduced the Iroquois contingent to a few hundred warriors. The army lacked supplies and canoes when it moved out in July. Its sole accomplishment before disbanding was a raid of La Prairie, a few miles from Montreal. Afterward Governor Frontenac dispatched additional reinforcements to Quebec.

That campaign also failed. Massachusetts Bay appointed Sir William Phips commander, who had just led an expedition around the Bay of Fundy to sack Port Royal in French Acadia (today Nova Scotia). Phips departed Boston on August 21, 1690, with more than 2,000 men on 34 ships. Due to bad weather and unfamiliarity with the St. Lawrence, this force took two months to reach Quebec. By that time, the troops had consumed much of their supplies and faced about 3,000 defenders. Phips landed about 1,200 troops on the north bank of the St. Lawrence, east of Quebec, in order to move behind the city. Harassed by Canadian forces in surrounding swamps and forests, they were stymied when attempting to cross another river and ran out of food and ammunition. Artillery pieces that landed with them sunk in the mud. Phips' ships bombarded Quebec, accomplishing little beyond using up their ammunition and suffering some damage from the cities' batteries. Facing supply shortages and an outbreak of smallpox, the expedition sailed home, having suffered a few hundred casualties, mostly from disease and accidents.

King William's War: Later Campaigns

The failure of the English campaigns in 1690 ended efforts at intercolonial cooperation to invade Canada. The New England colonies limited their efforts to fighting French-allied Abenaki peoples in Maine. The next few years saw each side launching operations against the other's settlements or forts, interspersed with periods of peace or limited violence. For example, in late 1691, Benjamin Church, hero of King Philip's War, led 300 militiamen in a campaign that destroyed native forts. In early 1692, a few hundred Abenaki warriors and Canadian militia raided York, burning most of the town, killing dozens, and capturing over 70; a similar force assaulted nearby Wells later. That August, 150 militiamen with Church and Phips (now Massachusetts governor) constructed Fort William Henry at Casco for future campaigns against the Abenaki. Hostilities relaxed in 1693, but in July 1694 about 250 warriors assaulted Oyster Bay (now Durham), New Hampshire, killing or capturing 90, and then harassed additional settlements, with occasional raids the following year. In 1696, French and Indian forces captured and demolished Fort William Henry, and Church led a retaliatory campaign around the Bay of Fundy that destroyed abandoned native towns. Abenaki raids on English settlements continued, only ceasing in 1699.

New York's participation in the war was complicated by the end of Leisler's Rebellion. In 1691, Leisler was captured, tried, and executed by the man William III appointed as governor, William Sloughter. Responding to Iroquois complaints about inadequate English participation in the war, he organized an expedition of a few hundred New York militia and native warriors, whose singular success was once again an attack on La Prairie. Then Sloughter died. After reviewing war expenses, his replacement, Benjamin Fletcher, limited New York's military exertions to encouraging the Five Nations to raid the French.

This policy fell far short of Iroquois expectations. In the 1670s, after the Third Anglo–Dutch War had ended and New York returned to English control, then-governor Sir Edmund Andros entered into a series of treaties with the Five Nations called "the Covenant Chain." Afterward the colony was a reliable trade partner, but with the outbreak of King William's War, the Iroquois hoped for substantial military assistance in their ongoing wars with New France and its native allies. They were sorely disappointed with English military exertions in 1690 and 1691. Moreover, the Five Nations then suffered the brunt of French operations.

In February 1693, more than 600 French regulars, Canadian militia, and native allies surprised the three main towns of the Mohawks, destroying them and their food supplies as well as taking 300 captives. About 250 New York militiamen joined with Iroquois warriors, caught up to the French forces, and freed most of the captives. Governor Fletcher later arrived in Albany with more troops but too late to make a difference. He offered food, arms, and ammunition to the Iroquois but no further military action. Over the following two years, Five Nations' leaders explored possibilities for peace with New France. But by the summer of 1696, prolonged talks had made Frontenac suspicious and impatient. He dispatched another invasion force of 2,000 French and native fighters that attacked the principal Onondaga town, destroyed local crops, and then razed a nearby Oneida settlement.

The Treaty of Ryswick ended King William's War in 1697. But only the English and French colonies were at peace with each other. As noted above, fighting between New England forces and the Abenaki in Maine did not cease until 1699. Further west, the Beaver Wars continued, with the Iroquois suffering debilitating attacks from French-allied Indians. Exhausted, the Five Nations finally negotiated a peace with the French, called "the Grand Settlement," in 1701. Except for a few pro-English (primarily Mohawk) or pro-French bands, the Iroquois stayed neutral in later imperial wars between France and Britain until the end of the French and Indian War, only pursuing hostilities against distant native foes.

Queen Anne's War, 1702–13: New England and Frontier Warfare

The Treaty of Ryswick settled little, and the belligerents returned territories captured during the war. A new conflict began in Europe in 1701, with Britain now fighting both France and Spain, and reached America the following year. In the northern colonies, Queen Anne's War was similar to King William's War. French and Indian war parties again raided the northern New England frontier, though not New York, in part because the now neutral Iroquois served as a buffer. New Englanders responded with operations against hostile native peoples. As in the previous war, the British tried to mount conventional campaigns to capture Canada's major cities, which again failed.

In August 1703, over 500 warriors and French Canadians struck Maine coastal towns such as Wells and Saco, killing or capturing over 100 settlers. Hostilities then subsided until February 29, 1704, when over 200 native warriors and about 50 Frenchmen raided Deerfield, Massachusetts. About 40 settlers died, and more than 100 men, women, and children—over a third of the town's population—were captured. Massachusetts responded in May by embarking over 500 men on ships, led by Benjamin Church, to assault Abenaki settlements in Acadia and around the Bay of Fundy. They returned to Boston with over 100 captives. Hostilities then ebbed as New England and Canadian officials pursued prisoner exchanges and explored peace options. In 1707, New Englanders raised more than 1,500 men for two unsuccessful attempts to take Port Royal. The following year, the inhabitants of Haverhill, Massachusetts, repelled a French and Indian raid with help from nearby towns.

The 1704 Deerfield raid became especially prominent in histories of the colonial wars. Among those taken was Reverend John Williams, who recorded the captives' experiences. His

Figure 2.1 "Attack on Deerfield"
From the website 1704.deerfield.history.museum
Francis Back for the Pocumtuck Valley Memorial Association/Memorial Hall Museum

The Redeemed Captive Returning to Zion, reprinted many times, dramatically depicted the dangers settlers faced in frontier warfare. Particularly harrowing was Williams' accounts of how raiders killed some English too wounded to travel in order to avoid capture by pursuing militia. The attackers then split into multiple groups, breaking up families in the process, each making its own way back to Canada. Captives had to endure an arduous journey of hundreds of miles through the wilderness in the depths of winter.

Though unique in the number of captives taken, and in how well their travails were recorded by Williams, the Deerfield raid demonstrated the nexus of French and native interests in raiding English frontier towns during the imperial wars. Indians acquired booty and prisoners, helping their communities (and enhancing the reputations of successful warriors). Some captives were adopted by native communities, and others were ransomed back to New England—with the help of French officials who contacted English colonies and negotiated prices. For New France, these raids sowed terror in New England, whose officials initially directed more military efforts to frontier defense and operations against hostile Indian peoples than to planning a large campaign to capture Quebec and Montreal.

Over the course of the imperial wars, English colonial—also known as "provincial"—forces employed a blend of European and native military practices on the frontier. Colonies used fortifications to help defend frontier communities, both garrison houses in towns themselves and larger forts along common invasion routes. New England soldiers patrolled around frontier communities, and also conducted "scouts" beyond English settlements. If they detected a hostile force, and circumstances allowed, troops prepared an ambush, as Indian warriors would. Colonies also launched campaigns to raid native towns, similar to earlier American wars between native people and settlers, such as the Virginia "feedfights." As in those earlier operations, Indians often fled towns before provincial troops arrived, but the latter nonetheless inflicted great devastation by destroying crops and fields.

Box 2.1   Frontier Warfare: Account of an Ambush

Steven C. Eames notes that both Indian warriors and provincial soldiers, if they success-fully ambushed an enemy party, would often charge into it after firing their weapons. In addition, he asserts that New England soldiers would also charge the enemy *if ambushed themselves* to try and break up such an assault. Sometimes this tactic worked, and—as demonstrated from the following excerpt from a provincial officer's journal—sometimes it did not.

. . . we began our march before sunrise, and travelled till about half after 9 o clock; being by the side of the river several of the company desired to stop to refresh themselves, being faint and weary, whereupon we halted and began to take off our packs, and some were set down, and in about half a minute after our halting, the enemy arose from behind a log and several trees about 20 feet or 30 at farthest distant, and fired about 12 guns at us . . . whereupon I called to the men to face the enemy and run up the bank, which I did my self, and several others attemted but the enemy were so thick, they could not. I was no sooner jumpt up the bank but the enemy were just upon me. I discharged my gun at one of them . . . who I see fall,—and about the same time that I discharged my gun the enemy fired about 20 guns at us, and kill'd 4 men . . . The men which were left alive most of them fired immediately on the enemy . . . but seeing the enemy numer-ous and their guns being discharged, they retreated. Several ran across the river . . . . For my own part . . . being beset by the enemy with guns, hatchets and knives . . . I ran down the river, and two Indians followed me, and ran almost side by side with me, calling to me, 'Come Captain, Now Captain,' but upon my presenting my gun towards them (though not charged) they fell a little back and I ran cross the river . . .

("Journal of Capt. Eleazer Melvin," *Collections of the New Hampshire Historical Society*, vol. 5, 1837; also appears in Eames' *Rustic Warriors*, p. 213)

The New England colonies, especially Massachusetts and New Hampshire, raised forces to meet these military needs. All male colonists were ostensibly militiamen. But local militia com-panies were training and administrative organizations. They provided basic drill in arms and enabled officers of militia committees to update rolls of available manpower. Militiamen per se only saw combat if their communities were attacked. Colonies created units to conduct military operations, whether garrisoning forts or frontier towns, patrolling, raiding, or mounting a con-ventional campaign against Quebec or Montreal. They did so by issuing commissions for officers to raise troops, and quotas of manpower that local militia committees had to provide.

Militia committees had the authority to draft, or "press," men if needed, and even those individuals could usually pay fines to hire substitutes in their place. But most men in provincial units were volunteers. The officers who recruited and then commanded them were usually prominent within their communities and often had reputations as good soldiers. In wartime, men in the northern New England colonies generally regarded military service as a civic obli-gation, as a means of protecting their homes and towns. Moreover, most joined these companies with people they knew: friends, relatives, and neighbors. Their terms of service were generally limited to a few weeks or months, after which they would return to their civilian lives.

These methods of creating armed forces varied significantly from those of Europe. There, by the eighteenth century, states had created standing armies of long-serving soldiers who made military service a career, enduring harsh discipline from aristocratic commanders. British officers of this period denigrated provincial soldiers. The latter did not master the close-order tactics required for the high-intensity battles that had become the epitome of Western warfare, and exhibited a familiarity with their officers that was anathema to blue-blooded British commanders. But European states had highly hierarchical societies and ample resources to maintain permanent, professional armies. Moreover, the population density and large number of cities and cultivated areas in Western Europe enhanced the rewards of successful conventional warfare.

North America was mostly wilderness, its colonies too poor to afford standing armies, and soldiers mostly concerned with operations and tactics that would best protect their communities. In this regard, New England troops incorporated native military techniques to better cope with Indian attacks. But as first recognized in King William's War, colonial leaders realized that the best way to protect the frontier would be to conquer Canada, and that war parties could not terrorize English communities without French support, supplies, and arms. That task, though, required a conventional campaign against Montreal or Quebec, and in Queen Anne's War, such efforts produced no greater success than in the prior conflict.

Queen Anne's War: Campaigns Against New France, 1709–11

Remembering the failed campaigns of King William's War, colonists sought British help to capture the major Canadian cities, and in 1709 they received a royal promise of troops and ships. As in 1690, colonial leaders envisioned simultaneous campaigns, one against Montreal, the other a seaborne venture to take Quebec. New York—actively participating in the war for the first time—joined the New England colonies to raise over 1,000 men each at Albany and Boston in the summer of 1709. But colonists learned in October that the Crown had canceled anticipated military operations in America. Disappointed, New England officials again approached England for help. In the summer of 1710, hundreds of marines and numerous Royal Navy ships arrived in Boston. Joined by a few thousand New Englanders, they sailed in September for Port Royal, where the next month the French surrendered and relinquished control of Acadia.

In 1711, Queen Anne's government provided even more assistance for a campaign against Quebec—a fleet with over a dozen warships, scores of transports, and over 5,000 regular troops under the command of the British admiral Sir Hovenden Walker. A few thousand New England militiamen joined this force, while over 2,000 other provincial troops gathered at Albany, once again to advance against Montreal. Walker's expedition reached the mouth of the St. Lawrence in August, but like Phips' expedition in 1690, also lacked knowledgeable pilots. Soon, eight transports ran aground amid poor weather, killing 900–1,000 men. Already pessimistic and worried about the onset of winter, Walker canceled the operation. He sailed directly back to England with the regular troops, while the New Englanders returned to Boston. When word reached the army moving north from Albany, they also returned and disbanded.

The Americas had never before seen the manpower mobilized for the 1711 campaigns—12,000 in the Walker expedition alone, including troops, sailors, and native allies. Their failure, coming shortly after the broken promises of 1709, engendered colonial bitterness toward Britain. But Walker's debacle helped push the British government toward peace with France and Spain, resulting in the Treaty of Utrecht of 1713. The agreement settled important European political issues, such as questions regarding the Spanish throne, and Louis XIV agreed to respect the succession of Protestant English monarchs that began with the Glorious Revolution of 1688. In North America, the French surrendered territories in Acadia, Newfoundland, and Hudson

Bay (and the Caribbean island of St. Kitts) to the British. But France retained control over Cape Breton Island, which controlled access to the St. Lawrence River. Later, it built a large naval base there at Louisbourg, indicating an enhanced commitment to defend the approaches to New France in future wars.

The Indian Slave Trade and Queen Anne's War in the American Southeast

In 1670, a group of English colonists began a new settlement on the southern portion of North America's Atlantic seaboard, called "Charles Town" in honor of their reigning monarch (later Charleston). One of the assumptions underlying this new venture was that it would produce goods such as cattle and timber needed to maintain plantations in the West Indies. As white indentured servants and African slaves cleared fields and cut trees, settlers also established trade relationships with native peoples. Local groups offered deerskins, which English traders valued—but not as much as Indian slaves. Carolina settlers could use them on their own farms, but native slaves tended to run away; the English profited more by selling them to West Indies plantations. This development produced a situation similar to that on the African coast: Native peoples felt compelled to raid others to acquire slaves and participate in the trade with the English rather than risk becoming targets themselves.

Some groups who were initially slavers were later devastated by slave raids themselves. In the 1670s, for example, the Carolina colony established ties with the Westo, who raided Guale and Mocama peoples on what is now the Georgia and northern Florida seacoast. By the end of the decade, though, the English favored the Savannah, who helped destroy the Westo. In the 1680s, the Yamasee became the most powerful group close to Carolina, and launched slaving expeditions against natives dwelling on Spanish missions; after 1700, the English also cultivated relations with a loosely affiliated group of native peoples they dubbed the Creek.

Queen Anne's War expanded the scope of slave raids but also introduced conventional operations into the region, as each imperial belligerent attempted to capture the other's primary settlement: Spanish St. Augustine and British Charlestown. As with New France, capturing these cities held the promise of eradicating an enemy's power and influence from the region—and as in prior attempts, these campaigns proved too difficult for colonial officials to prosecute successfully.

When Queen Anne's War began in 1702, Carolina's governor, James Moore, mounted an expedition to capture St. Augustine. The inhabitants retreated into the fortress of the Castillo de San Marcos, and English forces began siege operations—firing artillery at the wall and digging trenches toward the walls. But they accomplished very little before Spanish warships and reinforcements arrived some weeks later. Moore, whose forces had mostly arrived by boat, destroyed his own vessels and retreated overland. But in the interim, the English and hundreds of native allies, including many Yamasees, wreaked destruction beyond the fortress and took numerous captives. Scholars such as Alan Gallay note that these developments induced the Creek to cultivate stronger relations with Carolina. The colony reciprocated, worried about the threat posed by the recently established French colony of Louisiana (1699) and the Spanish fort at Pensacola (1698).

This alliance underlay large-scale attacks on Spanish-allied Floridian peoples from 1704–06. The English with Creek, Yamasee, and other native allies destroyed about a dozen missions, devastating the Apalachee in particular—perhaps 2,000 to 4,000 were enslaved. The carnage wrought in Florida helped prompt a joint Franco-Spanish campaign to capture Charlestown in 1706. As with the earlier English effort against St. Augustine, this one also failed. Carolina militiamen and Indian warriors defeated Franco-Spanish raiding parties, and English ships drove the French fleet out of the harbor.

Southeastern North America
1700–1748

- British town   ○ French, Spanish, or Native town
- ★ British fort   ☆ French or Spanish fort

Map 2.2 Southeastern North America, 1700–1748

After the Charlestown expedition, European forces only confronted each other directly at Pensacola before the war ended. British troops and Creeks attacked the fort in 1707 and 1711, which the Spanish repelled with the assistance of the French and native allies. In the meantime, slaving raids targeted the Choctaw, allies of the Louisiana French. Though not as destructive as the assaults on the Apalachee, they still enslaved probably more than 1,000 Indians. Such slaving operations benefited British traders but brought warfare directly to English settlements in the Carolinas.

The Tuscarora and Yamasee Wars, 1711–13 and 1715–17

Dwelling in what became North Carolina (Carolina was split into two colonies by 1719), the Tuscarora struggled with both slaving raids and land demands from growing numbers of colonists. Though not all took up arms against the English, the Tuscarora War from 1711–13 began with native raids of white settlements and featured two invasions organized by the colonial government in Charlestown against fortified Indian towns. British allies, such as the Catawba, Cherokee, and Yamasee, comprised most of the attacking forces. One siege ended in a truce, and the other saw attackers burning and bombarding the native fort until it was destroyed. The war enslaved about 1,000 Tuscarora and killed perhaps 1,400. Afterward 1,000–2,000 migrated north to New York, where they became the Sixth Nation of the Iroquois. Some remained in North Carolina, where they were restricted to a reservation, while others relocated to South Carolina.

After decades of encouraging native allies to attack other Indian groups, South Carolina's policies came back to haunt it in the Yamasee War of 1715–17. The Yamasee were a longtime ally of the colony, but by then their relationship with the English had deteriorated, as many had accumulated substantial debts to British traders. Though they benefited from the Tuscarora War, other opportunities to capture slaves for trade were dwindling, and English settlers coveted Yamasee lands. On April 15, 1715—similar to the Powhatan attacks of 1622 and 1644— Yamasee attacked unsuspecting English throughout South Carolina's backcountry, especially traders and colonial representatives. Soon, other Indian peoples such as the Catawaba and some Creeks joined in hostilities against the colonists. As with the Second Anglo-Powhatan War and King Philip's War, the English abandoned many outlying settlements, with the refugees converging on Charlestown. Raids characterized most of the war's operations: The Yamasee and their allies targeted Port Royal and other coastal locales, whereas colonial troops marched inland to find enemies. In the resulting engagements, English forces were sometimes ambushed and defeated, but at other times they managed to hunt down fleeing foes or prevail in battles.

The Yamasee War was the most serious threat to South Carolina in its early history. Allies and diplomacy helped the colony prevail. In early 1716, the Cherokee agreed to help South Carolina and attack the Creek. Virginia sent arms and troops, and terminated all trade with the Yamasees. This latter development surprised native groups, for Virginia and Carolina traders had competed fiercely with each other prior to the war, leading native peoples to assume the two colonies would not help each other. By the end of 1717, the English had negotiated peace with the Creek and other hostile Indians, the big exception being the Yamasees themselves. The latter moved south and, establishing solid relations with the Spanish in Florida, sporadically raided South Carolina's frontiers into the 1720s.

The war had large repercussions for the region. It ended the Indian slave trade, for native groups now refused to raid each other for captives to sell into bondage. As with Virginia, the colony's original proprietors soon lost their claims, and both Carolinas became directly administered by the Crown. Excepting the Catawba, most native groups left South Carolina. Though many former and potential allies thus abandoned the English, it also eased the resettlement of areas abandoned by colonists during the war and subsequent expansion.

A Quarter Century of "Peace"

The 1713 Treaty of Utrecht, along with the 1714 Treaties of Rastatt and Baden between France and Austria, ended the War of the Spanish Succession. For 25 years thereafter, no major wars ravaged Europe. But as the Yamasee War demonstrates, conflicts still occurred between Indian peoples and settlers in North America. In the northeast, for example, a conflict called "Dummer's War" (for the Massachusetts governor) began in 1722 between the eastern Abenaki and New England colonists. The western Abenaki leader Grey Lock then launched hostilities with raids on towns in the upper Connecticut River valley. The colonists and eastern Abenaki concluded a peace in 1727, after which hostilities died out further west as well.

The French also had difficulties in this period, with New France assisting its Indian allies against the Fox people in sporadic hostilities that lasted from 1712 to 1737. More grave for Louisiana was the Natchez War of 1729–33, in which hundreds of white settlers and black slaves were killed or captured. Helped by their Choctaw allies, the French prevailed, but because many Natchez fled to the Chickasaw, another conflict erupted between that nation and the French and Choctaw in 1736. That war ended in 1740, though sporadic conflict continued between the Choctaw and Chickasaw for many years.

Though no prolonged wars ravaged Europe, some limited conflicts occurred that brought hostilities to North America. For example, during the War of the Quadruple Alliance (1718–1720), where France and Britain opposed Spain, the fort at Pensacola exchanged hands a number of times. On the southern Atlantic seaboard, Spanish authorities in Florida encouraged Yamasee warriors to raid South Carolina in the years after the Yamasee War. During the Anglo-Spanish War of 1727–29, the British colony dispatched an expedition that raided and burned Yamasee villages around St. Augustine.

Also significant for the American southeast was the founding of Georgia. In 1732 James Oglethorpe, a former British army officer, helped establish it just north of Spanish Florida. The colony was to provide economic opportunities for debtors and poor English families, but it was also explicitly created to provide a buffer for South Carolina against incursions from the south. Oglethorpe's early accomplishments in Georgia encompassed founding Savannah, constructing numerous forts in the colony's interior and along the coast, and establishing amicable relations with the Creek. By the time the next major war began in North America, he had acquired command of British forces in Georgia and South Carolina, including a regiment of regular soldiers and a unit of Scottish Highlanders (Oglethorpe used the latter as rangers, light troops who took advantage of terrain and fought unconventionally).

The War of Jenkins' Ear, 1739–48

In the Treaty of Utrecht that ended Queen Anne's War, British merchants acquired a monopoly over importing slaves to Spanish colonies—called the *asiento*—and the right to deliver a limited amount of other merchandise. But tensions arose between British shippers and Spanish naval patrols (called *guardacostas*) over imported trade goods. In 1738, British Captain Robert Jenkins appeared before Parliament, telling of how years before, Spaniards had boarded his ship and sliced off his ear. Popular furor followed, and the British government declared war against Spain in 1739, called "the War of Jenkins' Ear." The next year, hostilities began in Europe, though France remained at peace with Britain until 1744. At that point, conflict between Britain and Spain had diminished in the American southeast (though attacks on shipping continued), whereas fighting erupted between New France and the northern British colonies, called "King George's War." All European belligerents stopped fighting with the 1748 Treaty of Aix-la-Chapelle.

Box 2.2   Slaves and the Anglo-Spanish Frontier

In the 1730s, authorities in St. Augustine declared that any slave who successfully fled to Spanish Florida would be granted freedom, subject to service in the colony's militia and conversion to Catholicism. The Spanish also built Fort Mose just north of St. Augustine, the first community in North America specifically for free African Americans, which was destroyed by a British raid in 1740. Efforts by slaves to reach Spanish Florida from South Carolina produced one of the few slave revolts on the North American mainland: the Stono Rebellion of September 1739, where more than 60 slaves and about 20 colonists died. The War of Jenkins' Ear erupted the following month, and rumors of the impending conflict may have encouraged some slaves to risk the journey south.

As with Queen Anne's War, both sides pursued high-intensity, conventional campaigns—the Spanish and British each tried and failed to capture the other's major city in the American southeast—and low-intensity, irregular operations. At the end of 1739, after learning the two countries were at war, Oglethorpe led native warriors and Scottish rangers on a quick raid along the St. John's River, one of the approaches to St. Augustine. His men captured and destroyed some smaller forts but lacked the strength and equipment to take the town's main fortress, the Castillo de San Marcos. Oglethorpe returned in May 1740 with an army of 1,200–1,800 men—consisting of Indians (including many Cherokees), South Carolina provincial troops, and British regulars and Scottish highlanders—who were accompanied by Royal Navy warships. His assault suffered from poor coordination and planning, such as taking artillery too small to damage the Castillo and discovering that he could not bring warships close enough to bombard it with their guns. Soon after deciding to starve out St. Augustine's defenders with a siege, Spanish ships delivered supplies to the garrison. With his troops suffering from disease, Oglethorpe abandoned the campaign in July.

The war's one Spanish campaign against Georgia and South Carolina also failed. In June 1742 Florida's governor, Manuel de Montiano, sailed with a fleet of 1,800–2,000 native warriors, Spanish regulars, and free black volunteers up the Atlantic coast. The expedition sought to raid British coastal settlements, cultivate support for the Spanish among the region's Indians, and (encouraged by the Stono Rebellion of September 1739) incite black slaves to revolt. But first Montiano's forces had to capture British forts on St. Simons Island. After landing, the invaders moved north against Fort Frederica. British forces stymied this advance with many fierce skirmishes, the most dramatic of which featured an ambush by Scottish Highlanders and Indians. Frustrated, Montiano's army returned to St. Augustine—whose environs Oglethorpe raided again in March 1743.

These were the only major operations of the North American mainland. But for the first time, the British recruited American colonists for campaigns elsewhere. Early in the war, Admiral Edward Vernon raided Porto Bello, the Spanish port on the Isthmus of Panama that shipped South American gold and silver to Europe. The dramatic destruction of its fort and many warships, and the capture of a great amount of plunder, bred enthusiasm for an operation against Cartagena, another port that served Spanish treasure fleets. In the fall of 1740, British authorities recruited 3,500–3,600 American colonists, many poor young men, to serve in a regular regiment. Arriving outside Cartegena in early March 1741, the invasion force left the next month, its troops so ravaged by disease they could not mount a siege. Perhaps 600 of the original American volunteers returned home, with tropical diseases accounting for the vast majority of the casualties. The fiasco further damaged colonists' confidence in British military competence.

Louisbourg, 1745

Except for attacks on shipping and a raid of Beaufort, North Carolina, hostilities between the Spanish and the British dissipated after 1743, while a new conflict began between Britain and France. King George's War (1744–48) resembled previous conflicts between the British colonies and New France, but it contained one unique and memorable event: the capture of Louisbourg by New England soldiers. After Queen Anne's War, France had constructed a large, modern fortress on Cape Breton Island to defend against approaches to the St. Lawrence River. When the war began in 1744, the French governor of Cape Breton Island also used Louisbourg to dispatch expeditions against British posts on Acadia (which Britain had acquired via the 1713 Treaty of Utrecht), while French privateers used it as a base to prey on English commerce. New Englanders armed their vessels to counter such attacks but became increasingly alarmed.

Initially, the Massachusetts General Court was hesitant about any campaign against the fortress. But a British officer named James Bradstreet, who had been captured and briefly held at

Figure 2.2 View of the English Landing on the Island of Cape Breton to Attack the Fortress of Louisbourg, 1745

By F. Stephen, 1747

Library and Archives Canada, acc. no. R13133–262

Louisbourg before his release, revealed that the garrison was undermanned and had low morale. The French also lacked enough artillery for all the batteries, and though the fort's defenses were well designed to repel a seaborne assault, they were poorly constructed to defend against over-land attacks. Thus in early 1745 the New England colonies mobilized 3,000–4,000 volunteers who rendezvoused with some Royal Navy warships to capture Louisbourg.

These forces landed on Cape Breton Island in early May. Some troops reconnoitering the "grand battery" on the north shore of the harbor found it abandoned. Though the French had disabled the cannons there, the British repaired and used them to bombard the main fortress to the west. New England soldiers built another position to bombard an island that guarded the harbor's entrance and drive away the defenders. Most of the invasion force encamped northwest of Louisbourg, where it plundered the local countryside and besieged the main fortress, while Royal Navy warships patrolled and intercepted shipping en route to the French base. In June, facing an imminent assault by land and sea, the French commander surrendered.

The Remainder of King George's War, 1744–48

This victory was celebrated throughout British America. Few had thought it possible with colonial forces. Though English colonies had organized conventional campaigns in earlier wars, these had failed from a lack of logistical, operational, and tactical expertise needed to capture fortresses and fortified cities. At Louisbourg though, New England troops exploited French tactical mistakes and induced the commander to surrender. Subsequent events, however, soon tempered this success. The invaders became occupiers, and quickly grew surly. The surrender terms had prevented them from plundering the base, which had been previously offered as an enticement for volunteers, and troops wanted to go home. Moreover, disease killed many New Englanders, and raids on the northern frontier by native warriors and Canadian militia started *after* its capture.

Despite the cost of the Louisbourg expedition, Massachusetts built new forts between the Connecticut River and New York to supplement preexisting ones and raised hundreds of men to serve in garrisons. Some French and Indian forces targeted forts, deflecting violence from settlements further south. But raiding parties nonetheless attacked many towns and lay numerous ambushes between the summers of 1745 and 1748. Areas that suffered the most from these operations were the part of New York encompassing Saratoga and the upper Hudson and Mohawk River valleys, the upper Connecticut River valley, Maine, and Acadia.

Louisbourg's capture once again raised hopes of a campaign against Canada, and in 1746, King George II's government agreed to support the venture. But as in 1709, after the northern colonies had mobilized thousands of men, the British canceled the operation. For its part, in 1747 the Royal Navy turned back a fleet Louis XV had dispatched to recapture Louisbourg. Yet by the war's end, British naval officers had provoked intense enmity from New England colonists. In November 1747, Commodore Charles Knowles, whose five-ship squadron was then in Boston harbor, sent parties ashore to press sailors for service upon his vessels—that is, forcibly compel them to join his crews. This practice was more common in England's sea towns, and enabled the Royal Navy to replenish undermanned crews by essentially conscripting a portion of Britain's maritime labor force, the largest in the world. But Massachusetts' colonists were outraged. The incident sparked a three-day riot, which ended with Knowles releasing the seamen and sailing away with his ships.

The most grievous insult to American colonists, however, came with the Treaty of Aix-la-Chapelle that ended the war in 1748. In North America, the treaty restored the *status quo ante bellum*—all territories returned to their original owners, including Louisbourg and Cape Breton to France. British Americans were infuriated. They had captured France's major naval base in North America with only the help of a few Royal Navy vessels and eliminated a serious threat. The Treaty of Aix-la-Chapelle revived that threat by returning the fortress to French control. Along with the canceled expedition against Canada in 1746 and the Boston impressment riot of 1747, colonists lost confidence that the British government could contribute to their future security.

The French and Indian War, 1754–63: Introduction and the Global Context

The trend of Great Britain's minimal and ineffective commitment of regular forces to North America reversed in the French and Indian War, part of a much larger conflict known as the Seven Years War. In Europe, fighting began when Prussia invaded the small country of Saxony in 1756, precipitating war with Austria, France, and Russia—Britain was its only major ally. By that time, the war in America was already two years old. But fighting extended beyond North America and Europe to Africa, India, and the East and West Indies. Some historians regard the Seven Years War as the first "world" war.

These widespread areas of conflict posed strategic dilemmas for the British, though the central one was not new: whether to commit forces to fighting in Europe, or elsewhere. In prior wars, Europe had often dominated Britain's strategic calculus, an example being when Queen

Anne's government sent an army to the Low Countries during the War of the Spanish Succession. At the beginning of the French and Indian/Seven Years War, the British government had some difficulty determining its priorities. But by 1758, minister William Pitt had firmly established his leadership and made the destruction of New France Britain's chief goal. He did not abandon the fight in Europe, though. Instead, his ministry provided subsidies to keep Prussia in the war and helped maintain an army in the northwest of the continent. As for France, it also dispatched regular troops to America but remained more focused on the European war.

The deployment of large numbers of regular troops gave the French and Indian War a unique character relative to previous American conflicts, encompassing significant amounts of both conventional and unconventional fighting. Initially, New France pursued both effectively. But eighteenth-century conventional Western warfare reflected a set of cultural norms significantly different from those of American Indians. That difference alienated native allies of the French at a time when British conventional operations—which mostly produced failure early in the war—were about to become better organized and more effective.

War Begins in America

By the middle of the eighteenth century, tensions were growing over the Ohio River valley. British settlement was on the verge of expanding west past the Appalachian Mountains, and traders were already venturing farther to trade with Indians who had previously only interacted with the French. Moreover, indigenous peoples who had abandoned the Ohio River valley in the seventeenth century due to the Beaver Wars had started to return. New France cultivated relations with these groups to try to check British expansion into the American interior. But the Iroquois also endeavored to exert their influence in the region.

In 1753, French officials visited peoples in the area, and built a series of forts along the Allegheny River. These developments alarmed both British colonists and King George II's cabinet in London. Virginia's governor, Robert Dinwiddie, dispatched a mission to order the French out of the region; they refused. Dinwiddie then persuaded the colony's House of Burgesses to build a fort where the Allegheny and Monongahela Rivers merge and form the Ohio River—the Forks of the Ohio. To raise manpower, guide it into the Forks, and protect that location, Dunwiddie selected the same young man who had recently returned from the mission to the Allegheny, George Washington. Only 22 years old at the time, Washington came from Virginia's plantation society and held a major's rank in the colony's militia. He raised a regiment of volunteers and marched it out in April 1754.

The campaign went poorly. En route, he learned that French troops had expelled British engineers from the Forks and built their own fortification: Fort Duquesne. Hoping to oust the French, Washington continued, pausing to build a small fort to store supplies called "Fort Necessity." Shortly thereafter, a party of militia and natives he was leading discovered a group of Frenchmen. A firefight erupted, and the opposing commander asked for a truce. While explaining his mission, a native chief walked up and killed the French officer with an ax. Washington then learned a large enemy force was approaching and retreated the Virginia regiment back to Fort Necessity. Placed at the bottom of a valley, and too small to shelter more than a fraction of the troops (about 400), most manned trenches outside the walls. In early July about 700 French soldiers and Indians arrived and fired from the hillsides while a downpour flooded the defenders' positions. Morale and discipline broke down, and when offered the chance to surrender, Washington accepted.

As part of the capitulation agreement, Washington signed documents whereby he admitted—unknowingly, because he did not read French—that his forces had killed a diplomatic envoy.

The French later used that admission as justification for war. George Washington did play a key role in the events that led to the French and Indian War. But his decisions were not its underlying cause, which stemmed from competition and rivalries between the British, French, and native peoples over the Ohio River valley. These experiences though, along with others in the French and Indian War, shaped Washington's attitudes toward command and warfare, which would be of note in a later conflict.

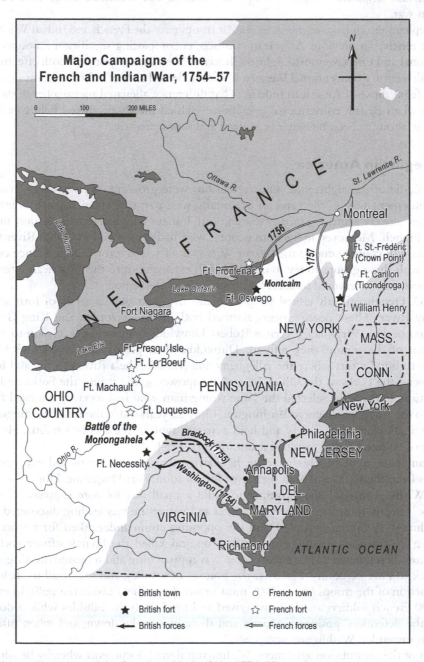

Map 2.3 Major Campaigns of the French and Indian War, 1754–57

The Battle of the Monongahela and Early British Campaigns, 1755

News reached London of the French occupation of the Forks of the Ohio and Washington's defeat in September 1754. The British cabinet, headed by the Duke of Newcastle, responded by sending a major general, Edward Braddock, to take command of all British forces in the American colonies. He was accompanied by two regiments of Irish regular troops and was given authority to form others in America. Colonists were to provide up to 3,000 men for these units, and organize additional forces as well. The colonial governments were also to create a fund for Braddock to pay expenses, as well as provide supplies and housing (or quarters) for his forces. In 1755, British and colonial troops would embark on four separate campaigns to capture Fort Duquesne at the Forks of the Ohio, Fort Niagara at the head of Lake Ontario, Fort St. Frederick on Lake Champlain, and two forts that controlled the neck of land that joined Nova Scotia to the mainland.

This response demonstrated both the Crown's commitment to its American colonies and a coordinated, strategic plan, unlike previous imperial wars. But historian Fred Anderson notes these operations were too ambitious and failed to appreciate the difficulties the American wilderness posed for campaigning armies—not to mention the political and economic challenges of obtaining the colonists' support. Braddock further compounded these problems. In April 1755, he convened a meeting of colonial governors in Alexandria, Virginia. There he presented his campaign plans and the monetary and logistical demands he expected the governors to fulfill. He was uninterested in the legal difficulties in creating a common fund and refused to consider altering his plans when informed, for example, that any campaign against Fort. Duquesne should be delayed until after Fort Niagara—which supplied it—was captured.

Braddock then took personal command of the expedition against Fort Duquesne and quickly discovered the difficulty of moving troops in the forested and mountainous American backcountry. Whereas the previous year Washington had led a few hundred lightly armed troops along the same route, Braddock set out with 2,400 British and colonial soldiers, a few hundred civilians in support roles, and numerous wagons with food and ammunition. To get the wagons through, his troops had to widen the track through the woods. Frustrated, after a week he detached half his force as a "flying column" that moved more rapidly toward Fort. Duquesne, while the other half continued building the road and accompanied the bulk of the supplies, wagons, and much of the artillery.

Braddock lacked Indian allies. In fact, he was so confident of victory that he spurned native assistance. Braddock failed to understand the importance of irregular combat when operating in the American wilderness. Eighteenth-century European conventional forces were designed to fight in flat and open terrain, where officers would maneuver closely packed groups of soldiers in long linear formations and shoot coordinated volleys of musket fire at the enemy. But North America's woods and mountains offered few such spaces. Instead, Indian warfare—emulated by the Canadian French and New England provincial troops—emphasized raids and ambushes rather than battles. Stealth and surprise were crucial, and though Indians coordinated their attacks, they fired and moved individually, without direction from officers as in European armies.

This discrepancy came into stark relief on July 9, 1755, at the Battle of the Monongahela. Braddock's flying column advanced past the Monongahela River to within a few miles of Fort.Duquesne. About midday, these 1,400 troops encountered approximately 600 Indian warriors with French Canadian militia and some French regulars, around 900 in total. The result was a stunning defeat for the British. An advance guard encountered the native and French force and provided some warning, but it retreated into and became intermixed with Braddock's other troops. This development hampered the British regulars as the battle began, as they were trying to deploy from marching order into formations that could deliver musket volleys in the constrained space of the forest track. But their volleys did little damage, as warriors and Canadian militia used terrain for cover. Instead, Indians advanced through the forest to attack the flanks and rear of Braddock's column. The closely packed British regular troops (the provincials also took cover) presented excellent targets for native and French marksmen. Braddock's forces fought well until he was shot and fell off his horse. His men then retreated back to the Monongahela, where they broke and fled.

The French and Indians lost about 40, whereas about two-thirds of Braddock's flying column were killed or wounded. The British survivors fled to the other half of their army. Panicking, they destroyed arms, equipment, and supplies before retreating to their original debarkation point of Fort Cumberland, Maryland (Braddock died of his wounds, and was buried en route). The Battle of the Monongahela thus ensured the French retained control of Fort. Duquesne. Moreover, French-allied Indians subsequently raided the frontier settlements of Pennsylvania, Maryland, and Virginia, areas previously untouched by the imperial wars. Although the situation changed after the British captured Fort Duquesne in 1758, in the interim, thousands of frontier settlers were killed or captured by native attacks. Even more colonists abandoned these areas—perhaps one-third to one-half of the population, depending upon the county—creating refugee problems further east. Part of the problem stemmed from the poor state of the militias in these colonies. Pennsylvania, where nonviolent Quakers dominated the legislature, actually had no colony-wide militia organization. Though it eventually raised some money for frontier defense, these efforts were ineffective.

The two 1755 British campaigns in New York also failed. Supply problems forced the troops marching to Fort Niagara to stop at Fort Oswego, and they suffered during the following winter. The provincial soldiers and Mohawk warriors sent to Lake Champlain never got beyond the foot of Lake George. They fought a battle there on September 8 which—like the Battle of the Monongahela—began with an ambush by French militia, regulars, and allied Indians. British colonials and Mohawks then retreated to a fortified camp by the lake and repulsed a charge by regulars with artillery fire; French forces then retreated. Though the Battle of Lake George was a tactical victory for the British, operationally the French had stopped the campaign against Fort St. Frederick. Afterward, both sides built new forts: the British, Fort William Henry at the southern end of Lake George; the French, Fort Carillon to the north, where the waters of Lake George flow into Lake Champlain. Of all British operations in 1755, the Nova Scotia campaign had the greatest success. In June, colonial troops and British regulars took the two French forts that blocked movement between the peninsula and the rest of the American mainland. But low-intensity, irregular warfare continued in Nova Scotia for years thereafter.

Tensions Civilian-Military, Imperial-Colonial, 1756–57

Braddock's death temporarily elevated William Shirley, governor of Massachusetts, to command of all British forces in America. Shirley had promoted the Louisbourg campaign in 1745, and was appointed a major general and Braddock's second-in-command at the Alexandria meeting in April 1755. He actually had minimal military experience, which became apparent when he tried to command the Niagara expedition the following summer. But as a successful politician, Shirley appreciated factors that were vital for colonial support for the war yet incomprehensible to British army commanders. For example, colonial governors could not simply be ordered to produce men and supplies. Legislative assemblies had to approve the required funds. The expectation of aristocratic British officers that money, housing, supplies, and manpower should be produced upon command was naïve and offensive to colonial leaders, and seemed contrary to the political rights of English subjects.

Shirley also understood important differences between Britain and its American colonies regarding military service. The former maintained permanent standing forces comprised of long-serving regulars subjected to harsh discipline. Colonial men were liable for militia service, which entailed training obligations and the need to defend local communities in case of attack. But campaigns into enemy territory required colonies to recruit volunteers, for which they provided contracts that specified payment, provision of food and equipment, and other conditions of service (sometimes including guarantees that men would serve only in units commanded by particular officers). Such terms were unheard of in the British Army. These differences did not in themselves present problems, except that recent rulings by King George II's government stated that provincial soldiers serving with British troops would be subject to the authority of, and be disciplined by, British regular officers. Moreover, colonial officers—who helped raise the units they commanded—would be considered junior to any and all British officers, regardless of rank.

During his brief period as overall commander, Shirley sidestepped these problems. He proposed two major expeditions for 1756, one to capture Fort Frontenac, where Lake Ontario empties into the St. Lawrence (thereby cutting off supplies to forts further in the American interior), and the other to take the French forts guarding Lake Champlain, St. Frederic and Carillon. The latter campaign was politically popular in New England: Many hoped a successful Lake Champlain campaign would lead to a later invasion of New France. Furthermore, Shirley organized this expedition solely with colonial troops, thereby bypassing the potential problems of mixing provincial and British regular soldiers in the same army. But while preparing these campaigns, Shirley was relieved of command. That summer a lieutenant general, John Campbell, Fourth Earl of Loudoun—or Lord Loudoun—debarked in New York City with eight regiments of regular soldiers. The British government gave him even more authority than it had Braddock, including the right to give orders to civilian colonial officials. As an aristocrat and a senior officer in the British Army, Loudoun took these powers at face value, and was perplexed and irritated when colonists did not.

Box 2.3   American Rangers in the French and Indian War

Lacking significant numbers of Native American allies or other troops proficient in irregular warfare and forest combat, the British army formed various units to address this need in the French and Indian War. New Hampshire militia officer Robert Rogers formed the best known of these, called "Rogers' Rangers" and known for their distinctive green coats. The combat record of the unit was mixed, including a successful raid of the Abenaki village of St. Francis in October 1759 and the Battle on Snowshoes, a failed attempt to ambush a native and French force outside Fort Carillon in March 1758 where Rogers' own men were instead lured into a trap and suffered over 50% casualties.

For example, Loudoun encountered problems with the New England troops gathered at Fort William Henry for the Lake Champlain campaign. Provincial officers made it clear that—on the basis of enlistment contracts—neither they nor their soldiers would serve with regular troops or subject themselves to the command of regular British officers. New England soldiers would instead desert, and their officers resign. This problem at least preceded Loudoun's arrival, and the following year he recruited fewer colonial troops and made clear they would serve under British officers. But he created great ill will regarding quartering. Shirley had paid market rates for housing, at significant expense, but Loudoun expected colonists to quarter the soldiers dispatched for their defense more cheaply. When officials in various towns complained about the illegality of requiring people to accept soldiers into their homes, Loudoun threatened to do so forcibly, at which point colonial legislatures begrudgingly agreed to build barracks. The British commander wanted colonists to demonstrate greater sacrifice for the common good; the colonists thought Loudoun should exhibit more respect for their rights and institutions.

Battlefield victories might have improved his relations with the colonists. But the French captured and destroyed Fort Oswego shortly after Loudoun arrived (described below), and he canceled both British campaigns for 1756. The major effort for 1757 was another joint army–navy expedition to recapture Louisbourg. But bad weather delayed the rendezvous of transports and Royal Navy warships, and when a French squadron arrived at the base, Loudoun recalled the expedition. Meanwhile, tensions between Loudoun and colonial officials festered, exacerbated by his decision to stop trade from all British North American ports in the months before the Louisbourg venture.

Thus, colonists were not dismayed when Loudoun lost his command in early 1758, part of a larger change implemented by William Pitt, British Secretary of State for the Southern Colonies. A highly skilled politician, Pitt had become a minister in King George II's government as a result of Britain's military and naval failures early in the war, including the loss of its major base in the Mediterranean. By 1758, he had taken control of strategy. While continuing to support German allies in continental Europe and employing the Royal Navy to contain the French fleet and raid enemy shipping, Pitt made capturing France's North American territories Britain's primary objective.

Pitt realized that to pursue this strategy, he needed the support of American colonists. He did not just simply recall the unpopular Loudoun but also informed colonial legislatures that the Crown would reimburse them for all war expenses. To resolve the sticky issue of rank and precedence between colonial and British Army officers, Pitt decreed that the former would only be considered junior to regular Army officers of similar or higher rank. The colonies responded enthusiastically, with assemblies voting to raise tens of thousands of troops and the supplies and equipment needed to outfit them. These changes soon altered the course of a war that, until then, had produced mostly French victories.

French Campaigns and Cultural Strains, 1755–57

In earlier wars, New France had pursued a strategic defense with offensive raids on British colonies. The 1755 victory near the Monongahela River meant Canada's leaders could pursue and expand upon that strategy: Fort Duquesne was now used as a staging point for raids directed at the Pennsylvania, Maryland, and Virginia frontiers. Moreover, news of Braddock's defeat enticed more Indians to fight for the French. New France had long benefited from alliances with the Abenaki, Micmac, and other peoples near the St. Lawrence River valley. On the Monongahela, French forces fought with Shawnee, Mingo, and Delaware peoples dwelling in the Ohio River valley. But in 1756 and 1757, Indians from deeper in the American interior, such as the Pottawatomie, Ottawa, and Wyandot peoples of the Great Lakes region, traveled east to fight against the British.

The governor-general of New France, the Marquis de Vaudreuil, had spent most of his life in Canada and favored a strategy of frontier raids. But after the 1755 campaigns in New York, he also pursued operations to hamper subsequent British attempts to invade New France from that colony. In 1756 Vaudreuil organized an army of about 3,000 French regulars, Canadian militia, and Indian allies to destroy Fort Oswego, and gave command to the Marquis de Montcalm. Arriving in August, the garrison surrendered after only a few days, spoiling British plans to advance on Fort Frontenac later that year. Fort Oswego's fall also prevented the campaign against Fort Carillon and spread panic throughout New York.

Though victorious, in one sense Montcalm was appalled. Recently arrived in America, he was typical of most eighteenth-century European officers in that he was of noble birth and trained to command troops who would act on his orders without question. As with many Europeans, Montcalm regarded Indians as "savages" and did not understand their beliefs and cultural norms. His first exposure to native warfare came at Fort Oswego. After the British surrender, warriors broke into the hospital, killing many of the sick and wounded for scalps, and looted and took prisoners elsewhere in the fort. Scalps, prisoners, and booty were the rewards of combat for native men, demonstrating their prowess as warriors and benefiting their communities as well. Vaudreuil and other Canadian French leaders accepted such conduct as necessary to maintain Indian alliances. But Montcalm was shocked: By the customs of eighteenth-century Western warfare, captors were expected to protect those who surrendered.

Montcalm paid Indians ransoms for the British prisoners taken at Oswego. But the same problem occurred a year later. As with Braddock's defeat, news of Oswego prompted more warriors to join French forces the following summer. In 1757, the main French effort was a campaign to capture Fort William Henry at the base of Lake George, again to disrupt British efforts to launch conventional campaigns at Canada. This campaign was also a French success. In July an army of close to 8,000, composed of about 1,800 native warriors as well as French regulars and Canadian militia, congregated at French Fort Carillon. They arrived at Fort William Henry on August 3 and began a siege.

French conventional and unconventional forces worked well together. Native warriors and militia swarmed through the area behind the fort, disrupting its communications with British forces further south, and used muskets to harass defenders on the walls. Meanwhile, regular troops pursued classic European siege tactics: digging trenches to shelter the movement of cannons and troops toward the fort, with artillery fire increasing as they got closer. By August 9, French bombardment had destroyed or disabled most of the British guns and subjected the garrison of 1,100 (and about 150 civilians) to intense shelling. Moreover, guns were being positioned at point-blank range to blow a breach in the fort's walls.

Learning he could expect no reinforcements, the British commander called for a truce. The final surrender agreement provided fair treatment to the defeated forces according to European military customs of the era. Montcalm allowed the British to leave with their arms, personal belongings, and regimental flags if they pledged in return that they would not fight in the war for at least 18 months. He also promised the French would care for the sick and wounded. The only problem was that the arrangement took no account of the Indians who had accompanied Montcalm's campaign: They were not happy to learn they should return home with nothing to show for their efforts.

What happened next became known as the "Massacre of Fort William Henry," immortalized in the novel *The Last of the Mohicans* and its film adaptations. As British troops and civilians marched away, some Indians confronted them in search of booty. Violence erupted, with more warriors joining the fracas and forcibly taking goods as well as captives. Montcalm and his officers intervened, but by the time they had restored order perhaps 185 people were dead and hundreds had been taken into captivity. The French ultimately located 200 captives and paid ransoms to release them. But the incident sparked outrage throughout British America. Thereafter, British officers regarded French promises with suspicion and sometimes denied prisoners the courtesies of European military customs. Moreover, Indian enthusiasm for New France declined, and fewer warriors would fight on its behalf thereafter.

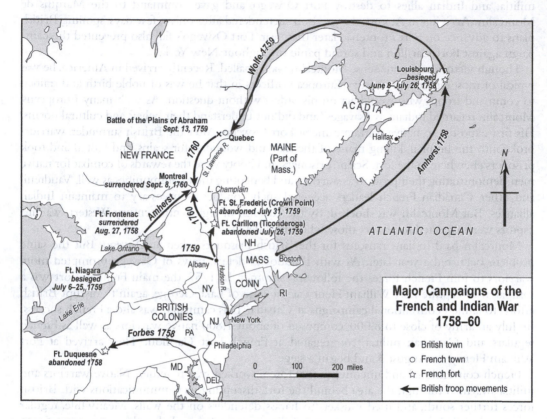

Map 2.4 Major Campaigns of the French and Indian War, 1758–60

The Tide Turns: British Campaigns in North America, 1758–59

Fewer native allies weakened the French ability to pursue irregular warfare. Simultaneously, the British capacity to mount conventional operational operations reached its peak. As in 1755 and 1756, the British planned multiple campaigns against New France in 1758 and 1759. The difference was that William Pitt's leadership now produced cooperation between British and colonial officials along with a commitment of resources never seen before in imperial-colonial relations. Pitt also appointed younger, talented army officers to lead some of these campaigns.

One was Jeffrey Amherst, who led an expedition of up to 14,000 men to capture Louisbourg in June 1758. After a six-week siege, the French surrendered. His success contrasted dramatically with the campaign led by James Abercromby, an older officer who became commander of all British forces in North America when Loudoun was recalled. By early July, he had concentrated about 16,000 British and provincial troops at the former site of Fort William Henry. The expedition's objective was to travel up Lake George, march overland to capture Fort Carillon (later named Fort Ticonderoga) at the head of Lake Champlain, and then continue on to Canada.

After losing his second-in-command in a skirmish (Viscount Howe, another young, talented officer appointed by Pitt), Abercromby moved slowly. Montcalm, who had recently arrived at Fort Carillon, thus had time to prepare defenses. The French hastily erected a fortification of felled trees (abatis) in front of trenches on the hill just in front of Fort Carillon. On July 8 Abercromby, failing to reconnoiter for other alternatives, ordered attacks on these fortifications. The French defenders (less than 4,000) easily repelled the numerous, ill-coordinated charges. British infantry, lacking artillery support and moving uphill, became ensnared in the abatis and suffered almost 2,000 casualties. When Abercromby ordered a retreat that night, the exhausted troops fled in panic, fearing an imminent French attack that never came.

Abercromby's defeat was almost as ignominious as Braddock's three years earlier. But his army survived as a fighting force, and he soon approved a more successful expedition. He permitted John Bradstreet (known for the 1745 Louisbourg campaign) to take a few thousand provincial soldiers, British regulars, and Iroquois warriors to attack Fort Frontenac. Located where Lake Ontario empties into the St. Lawrence River, this post was crucial for supplying French forts deeper in the American interior, such as Fort Duquesne. Arriving on August 25, the garrison of about 100 troops surrendered two days later. The British allowed everyone inside to leave with their possessions, seized a great amount of goods and provisions as plunder, and then destroyed what they could not take.

Another British achievement in late 1758 was the capture of Fort Duquesne at the Forks of the Ohio, which had played a crucial role in instigating the war. This task, along with pacifying the Pennsylvania frontier, had been given to another young promising officer, John Forbes. But unlike Braddock, Forbes respected Indians. He helped arrange a conference that October where hostile native peoples agreed to peace: the Treaty of Easton. Meanwhile, Forbes' troops were building a road west toward Fort Duquesne. Though warriors had defeated a force of about 700 British regulars near the fort in September, fewer Indians had arrived there that year to help the French. Supply problems meant officers had fewer goods to trade with them, and many native groups were considering peace by the time of the Easton conference. Afterward, Fort Duquesne's commander had only 300 troops and militia to face the imminent arrival of thousands of British soldiers. In November, he abandoned Fort Duquesne.

The following year produced the war's most dramatic and decisive British victory in North America: the capture of Quebec. At the end of June 1759, ships landed James Wolfe and his army of about 22,000 men below the city. Although this force outnumbered the 15,000 men commanded by Montcalm, it was not enough to take Quebec by storm or maintain a tight siege. The city remained in communication with and obtained supplies from Montreal and other upriver settlements.

This situation suited Montcalm. The King of France had recently given him command of all French forces in Canada, and he promptly abandoned the raiding strategy and reliance upon native allies. Instead, he withdrew forces from frontier posts to concentrate on a conventional defense of the key settlements on the St. Lawrence River. He had men improve Quebec's defenses, building more trenches and fortifying the walls. Montcalm's strategy was to have Wolfe's men exhaust themselves in attempts to take the city. He expected they would fail and withdraw before winter, and then anticipated a diplomatic solution would end the war before the British launched subsequent campaigns against Canada.

Conversely, Wolfe sought ways to provoke Montcalm to fight outside the city walls, where his core of British regular soldiers would give him the advantage. He shelled the interior of city with his ships, and sent troops to ravage the countryside, destroying homes and churches. But civilian suffering did not provoke Montcalm (though it upset some of Wolfe's officers), and he kept his men within their defenses. At one point Wolfe tested the latter, attacking a line of fortifications just below the city only to have his men repelled. By September, he was running out of time and would soon have to abandon the campaign before bad weather arrived.

The Plains of Abraham and Last British Campaigns in America, 1759–60

Wolfe gambled. As noted earlier, the city sat atop high cliffs above the St. Lawrence and had formidable defenses. But just behind and upriver of the city was an open area called "the Plains of Abraham," ideal for a conventional battle. To get there, though, Wolfe would either have to sail his ships far upriver, where another French force waited, or debark his men at the foot of the cliffs and have them make their way up, during which time they would be vulnerable and easily repulsed if discovered. Wolfe chose the latter. His troops ascended quickly and defeated the small French detachment guarding the area. Montcalm never expected the British to scale the cliffs, and was surprised when on the morning of September 13, he saw Wolfe's regulars deployed in conventional battle array just west of Quebec.

Montcalm then gave Wolfe the fight he wanted—the Battle of the Plains of Abraham. He was worried that the city's walls facing the Plains were fairly weak. Montcalm also faced the prospect of being cut off from other French settlements, and Quebec was low on supplies. Although there were 2,000 French troops upriver, it would take hours for them to arrive. In these circumstances, Montcalm risked battle to forestall a British assault on the city, but he did not have the proper types of forces. Each side deployed about 4,500 men, but almost all of the British troops were regular soldiers. About half of Montcalm's forces were militia who were

Figure 2.3 "A View of the Taking of Quebec, 13 September 1759"

1797 engraving of a sketch by Hervey Smyth

Based on a sketch by one of Wolfe's aides, this picture depicts both the British ascent up the cliffs upriver of Quebec and the Battle of the Plains of Abraham that followed.

Library and Archives Canada, Acc. No. R9266–2102 Peter Winkworth Collection of Canadiana

skilled at raids and forest combat, but not in close-order tactics. Furthermore, as he had not expected to fight a conventional battle, Montcalm had not trained his militiamen in these tactics, using them instead to improve and maintain the city's defenses.

When Montcalm moved his men toward the British, they advanced unevenly. The French regulars maintained an even pace but some militia raced forward while others lagged behind. After stopping and firing their first shots, order broke down when militiamen looked for cover rather than to preserve the cohesion of their units, as the regular troops did. In contrast, the British redcoats maintained discipline, firing and advancing calmly according to their officers' orders. When they got close enough, Wolfe's lines charged, destroying what was left of French resistance. Montcalm's soldiers fled, and the British captured Quebec. Both he and Wolfe were mortally wounded.

Quebec's capture did not immediately end fighting in Canada, for French forces remained further up the St. Lawrence, especially around Montreal. In theory, the other two British campaigns of 1759 were supposed to reach that city. That summer, Amherst, who had succeeded Abercromby as both overall British commander in North America and of the army at Lake George, advanced and captured Forts Carillon and Crown Point on Lake Champlain. Montcalm had evacuated these posts to redeploy forces along the St. Lawrence, but suspicious of a trap, Amherst hesitated until the onset of winter prevented further advances north that year. Another expedition captured Fort Niagara at the head of Lake Ontario—further undermining the French ability to supply forts deeper in the continental interior—but was unable to reach Montreal that year. This campaign was also notable because the Six Nations of the Iroquois, which had generally remained neutral to this point, now joined with the British and convinced native peoples around Niagara to abandon the French.

Yet the British capture of Quebec all but settled the issue of who would prevail in America. The rest of Canada was now cut off from supplies and reinforcements from France. The British had mobilized tens of thousands of regulars and colonial soldiers, and the entrance of the Iroquois into the war further eroded native support for the French. In the summer of 1760, British forces under Amherst's command approached Montreal from three directions. They encountered minimal resistance, and on September 8 French forces in North America surrendered, ending the fighting on the continent.

The War Beyond North America and the Peace of Paris

In other parts of the world, the Seven Years War raged on. British troops defeated the French in India and consolidated control over the subcontinent. After Canada surrendered, Crown forces captured numerous French islands in the Caribbean (valuable for sugar production), and soon engaged a new enemy: Spain. Previously neutral, King Charles II was increasingly worried about Britain's growing power during the war and sought to strengthen ties to France. King George's government reacted by declaring war in early 1762 and proceeded to capture important Spanish colonial possessions such as Havana in Cuba, and Manila in the Philippines.

One of Britain's great advantages in this global war was the Royal Navy. Though France possessed the world's second-largest fleet, Britain's was both larger and its officers and sailors generally better skilled. Although it lost its Mediterranean base early in the war, the Royal Navy increasingly asserted its dominance on the seas, blockading enemy warships in their bases and raiding the French coastline. In November 1759, a squadron commanded by William Hawke won one of Britain's most dramatic naval victories, Quiberon Bay, effectively destroying the only French fleet that could then challenge British control of the seas.

Moreover, afterward France could no longer send troops or supplies to America. With Wolfe's capture of Quebec two months earlier, Quiberon Bay made the British conquest of New France certain.

By February 1763, Britain, France, and Spain had all ratified the Peace of Paris, ending the war. France reacquired its Caribbean possessions but lost everything on the American mainland. Britain acquired all French territory east of the Mississippi. Spain received New Orleans and French territory west of the Mississippi (Louisiana) but had to surrender Florida to Britain. Unlike the previous imperial wars since 1689, the French and Indian War produced a spectacular British victory, forcing its principal rival out of continental North America. Britain made other impressive gains to its colonial empire elsewhere, such as in India. In British America, colonists rejoiced at the destruction of New France, and anticipated great opportunities for westward settlement.

Conclusion

After the Glorious Revolution, conflicts on one side of the Atlantic sparked hostilities on the other. In North America, most of these wars resembled earlier ones, with the predominance of Indian warriors raiding British frontier settlements. New France relied heavily upon native allies, sending Canadian militia to join them in low-intensity offensive operations that sought to enhance the strategic defense of the colony. British colonists responded with similar tactics and directed campaigns against hostile Indian peoples. Their leaders understood that destroying New France would preempt frontier raids, but the British colonies lacked the resources and expertise needed to capture key Canadian cities. The few times when the Crown dispatched regular troops and ships for operations in North America usually ended in failure.

These trends changed with the French and Indian War, part of the broader Seven Years War. Britain made an early commitment to its North American colonies, an effort that encountered early difficulties from military defeats and tensions between British commanders and colonial leaders. But William Pitt overcame these problems and made North America Britain's strategic priority, guaranteeing the resources needed for imperial-colonial cooperation. These produced the conventional campaigns that captured Quebec and Montreal, and conquered New France.

This success, however, contained the seeds of future conflict. Britain had incurred great debt to deploy large numbers of troops and warships around the world. Though New France was gone, the Indians remained. As white settlers and native groups had often clashed over the past 150 years, maintaining peace and security was a concern in London. When the British government pursued solutions to these problems after the French and Indian War, they produced alarm and consternation among its colonists, ultimately leading to the American Revolution.

Short Bibliography

Anderson, Fred. *A People's Army: Massachusetts Soldiers & Society in the Seven Years' War.* Chapel Hill: University of North Carolina Press, 1984.

———. *The War That Made America: A Short History of the French & Indian War.* New York: Penguin Books, 2005.

Eames, Steven C. *Rustic Warriors: Warfare and the Provincial Soldier on the New England Frontier, 1689–48.* New York: New York University Press, 2011.

Gallay, Alan. *The Indian Slave Trade: The Rise of the English Empire in the American South, 1670–1717.* New Haven, CT: Yale University Press, 2002.

Grenier, John. *The First Way of War: American War Making on the Frontier.* New York: Cambridge University Press, 2005.

Haefeli, Evan, and Kevin Sweeney. *Captors and Captives: The 1704 French and Indian Raid on Deerfield.* Amherst: University of Massachusetts Press, 2003.

Ivers, Larry E. *This Torrent of Indians: War on the Southern Frontier, 1715–1728.* Columbia: University of South Carolina Press, 2016.

Leach, Douglas Edward. *Arms for Empire: A Military History of the British Colonies in North America, 1607–1763.* New York: Macmillan, 1973.

Starkey, Armstrong. *European and Native American Warfare, 1675–1815.* Norman: University of Oklahoma Press, 1998.

Steele, Ian K. *Betrayals: Fort William Henry and the "Massacre".* New York: Oxford University Press, 1990.

1763	1775–83	April 19, 1775	June 17, 1775	July 4, 1776	August 27, 1776	December 26, 1776 and January 2–3, 1777
Pontiac's War	War of the American Revolution	Battles of Lexington and Concord	Battle of Breed's (Bunker) Hill	Declaration of Independence	Battle of Long Island	Battles of Trenton and Princeton

TIMELINE

Chapter 3

The American Revolution, 1763–1783

In early 1763, many people regarded Great Britain as the most powerful country in the world. It had mustered astonishingly large military forces in the Seven Years War and deployed them around the world in successful campaigns, including the conquest of Canada. With the ratification of the Peace of Paris, Great Britain ruled all of North America east of the Mississippi River. But afterward, the British government struggled to cope with the enormous debt created during the war and faced challenges in the American backcountry. Native peoples had had no say in the deliberations that ended the French and Indian War, and their territories and traditional lifestyles faced growing pressure from settlers migrating westward. These tensions erupted in Pontiac's Rebellion of 1763, which demonstrated to officials in London the need for security in the colonies. But they imposed their policies in a heavy-handed manner that contravened the traditional light touch applied to British America prior to the Seven Years War. The result was an imperial crisis that ultimately produced a new, independent country.

In this chapter, students will learn about:

- Factors that led to conflict between Great Britain and its North American colonies.
- British and American strategy in the War of the American Revolution.
- The major campaigns, battles, and commanders.
- How diplomatic, political, and logistical factors affected military operations and were in turn impacted by the outcomes of battles and campaigns.
- The different types of combatants and how they fought.

Native Peoples and Pontiac's War

British officials and settlers' relations with native peoples were often strained during the French and Indian War. One case involved the Cherokee, longtime allies of South Carolina. In 1758, colonists attacked warriors returning from Pennsylvania, while Carolina settlers poached game in Cherokee hunting grounds. In 1759, warriors retaliated by killing some frontiersmen. The South Carolina governor stopped all trade with the Cherokee and took chiefs hostage who had journeyed to Charleston to negotiate. In 1760 Cherokees raided backwoods settlements and forts. A British expedition to attack Cherokee towns that summer faced fierce resistance in the mountainous terrain and withdrew, but a larger, better organized campaign devastated Cherokee towns in 1761. Facing disease, starvation, and raids from other native peoples, the Cherokee sued for peace.

In the aftermath of the Cherokee War, the British commander in North America, Jeffrey Amherst, instituted new polices. He ended the practice of bestowing gifts upon native leaders, restricted trade, banned the sale of alcohol, and curtailed how much ammunition warriors could purchase. These developments angered native groups, for the French had long provided gifts to facilitate diplomatic cooperation, and ammunition was crucial for hunting. Moreover, traders could no longer journey to native villages; Indians would have to bring their goods to British forts to trade.

Another problem was expanding white settlement. During the French and Indian War, British officials told Indians their lands would be protected, and that the purpose of any forts would be to facilitate trade. But after Forbes captured Fort Duquesne in 1758, the British built an even larger Fort Pitt on the site and allowed white farmers to settle around it. After the fall of Montreal, British troops replaced French ones at posts throughout the Trans-Appalachian region north of the Ohio River, with hundreds garrisoning larger forts such as Pitt, Detroit, and Niagara. These developments seemed to belie British promises.

A native spiritual movement also began at this time. The Delaware prophet Neolin urged Indians to stop dealing with whites, spurn manufactured goods (including alcohol), and return to native ways and customs. Neolin did not explicitly call for violence against white settlers, though some of his followers did. One was the Ottawa chief Pontiac, who in May 1763 led warriors from numerous native peoples in a siege of Fort Detroit. This act encouraged other Indians to attack more British forts in the region, and some Shawnee and Delaware raided the Pennsylvania and Virginia backcountry—reviving the terror that had afflicted the region from 1755–58.

Warriors often used ruses to fool garrisons and capture forts. The most infamous incident occurred at Fort Michilimackinac, in northern Michigan. Ojibwa warriors began a game of lacrosse just outside the fort, while women entered with concealed weapons. When the ball flew into the fort, the men chased after it. When inside, they grabbed tomahawks and short-barreled guns from the women and attacked the British troops, killing 15. Most of the captured outposts were deceived in similar (if less elaborate) ways, though two fell to native assaults. The largest British forts withstood the uprising. Fort Pitt withstood a brief siege during the summer before the Delaware, Shawnee, Mingo, Ottawa, and Seneca warriors left to attack a supply convoy. The British won the resulting Battle of Bushy Run by feigning a retreat and then counterattacking. Indians then abandoned further attempts against Fort Pitt, though they continued to raid back-country settlements into autumn and skirmished sporadically around Fort Niagara.

The siege at Fort Detroit involved ongoing sniping between warriors and the garrison, and the occasional larger engagements such as the Battle of Bloody Brook, where warriors repelled a column advancing against Pontiac's main camp. The biggest problem for the British was keeping the garrison provisioned, as warriors attacked boats and ships coming across Lake Erie and up the Detroit River. But supply was also an issue for the hundreds of besieging warriors. They dispersed in October for their annual winter hunts.

In 1764 William Johnson, the British official in charge of Indian affairs for the northern colonies, convened a peace conference at Fort Niagara, where native attendees agreed to resume trade and return captives. Two British expeditions to western areas also helped facilitate peace, though Pontiac remained at large until 1765. Native peoples had certainly failed to expel the British from the Ohio country, but if their intent was to convince the British to treat indigenous groups with more respect, they were successful. Royal officials, having been surprised by the uprising, made concessions and used diplomacy to diffuse the crisis.

Prelude to Revolution: Rising Tensions in the Imperial-Colonial Relationship

Meanwhile, officials in London developed policies that altered the relationship between Britain and her American colonies. Until the mid-eighteenth century, the latter had generally been left to govern their own affairs. Although the King appointed governors for most of the colonies, colonial assemblies usually voted for and approved their salaries, curtailing their capacity to pursue independent policies.

Since the mid-seventeenth century, the American colonies had been subject to the Navigation Acts, Parliamentary laws that defined terms and conditions of trade within Britain's empire. For example, goods destined for British ports could only be transported in British-owned vessels. Furthermore, many items produced in the American colonies had to be shipped directly to Great Britain—referred to as "enumerated" products. Though restrictive, American colonists benefited from these laws by obtaining preferred access to British vessels and, as the King's subjects, could participate in the shipping trade itself, which became very large in New England. Moreover, tariffs on goods imported from outside Britain's empire were poorly enforced.

This relative autonomy changed starting in 1763, as British ministers sought to have the American colonies contribute more to the King's coffers. But it was Parliament's unprecedented attempt to levy taxes on American colonists that alarmed the colonists. Their concern was expressed in the phrase "no taxation without representation." Colonists were used to paying taxes levied by their own assemblies, to which they sent their own representatives. But they had no representatives in Parliament. The same anxiety fed opposition to new customs duties: American shippers had long accepted Parliament's authority to impose tariffs to regulate trade but objected to any designed to raise revenue. Driving these developments were efforts to pay down Britain's enormous debt from the Seven Years War and provide for continuing expenses, including maintaining troops for North American security. Moreover, whereas Britons had been heavily taxed by the Parliament, American colonists had not. Yet this situation might not have precipitated rebellion had British officials possessed greater appreciation of the colonists' perspectives.

George Grenville's ministry made the initial attempt to revamp the imperial-colonial relationship. After news of Pontiac's Rebellion reached England, the government issued a royal proclamation forbidding colonists from migrating west of the Appalachian Mountains, reserving those lands for native peoples; the boundary was called "the Proclamation Line of 1763." But settlers were already moving into the region, and generally ignored the decree. In 1764

Parliament passed the Sugar Act: This law actually reduced the customs charges for imported sugar but established more rigorous enforcement to combat smuggling, with cases to be tried in admiralty courts with judges appointed by the Crown—not local colonial courts. The Sugar Act also added new products to the list of "enumerated" items and was followed by passage of the Currency Act, which forbade the use of paper money.

Though the Sugar Act generated some protest, it was the Stamp Act of 1765 that sparked widespread outrage in British America. Colonists would have to purchase official stamps in order to use wills and deeds, newspapers, calendars, playing cards, and similar items. Although stamps had previously been used by colonial and local governments, they had never been imposed by Parliament, and never in such an extensive and intrusive manner. Most colonial assemblies not only condemned the law but sent delegates to a Stamp Act Congress in New York to coordinate opposition to it. Pamphlets such as Daniel Dulany's *Considerations on the Propriety of Imposing Taxes* denied Parliament had any right to so tax American colonists. Crowds formed in cities and ports to protest the act, with riots erupting in Boston. A more peaceful form of popular protest consisted of non-importation agreements, whereby a community agreed to boycott goods imported from Britain until the Stamp Act was repealed.

Confronted with this uproar, Parliament quickly rescinded the Stamp Act. But in the Declaratory Act of 1766, it explicitly asserted the right to impose laws (and hence taxes) upon the colonies. A year later it tested that right with the passage of the Townshend Duties, named for the Chancellor of the Exchequer, Charles Townshend. He believed a new set of customs duties would generate few objections in the colonies, as opposed to the direct taxes of the Stamp Act. But colonists saw the new tariffs as another Parliamentary attempt to tax them. Colonial defiance again included denunciations in assemblies, critical essays such as John Dickinson's *Letters from a Farmer in Pennsylvania*, non-importation agreements, and street protests.

Smaller groups provided crucial leadership for popular demonstrations against the Stamp Act and Townshend Duties. In larger colonial ports, for example, men who called themselves "the Sons of Liberty" mobilized and coordinated responses to British policies. In Boston protests were particularly effective, as demonstrated by a mob that chased away customs officials who had seized the sloop *Liberty* on suspicion of smuggling (owned by the town's largest merchant, John Hancock). The British subsequently dispatched troops to keep order in the city, which was particularly alarming for colonists fearful for their rights.

Rising tensions between British troops and Boston residents erupted on March 5, 1770, when soldiers fired on a crowd that was taunting them. Champions of American rights, now known as "Whigs" or "Patriots," called the incident "the Boston Massacre" and quickly dispatched news of it to rally support. Ironically, that same day the British government decided to repeal the Townshend Duties—except for the one on tea. The soldiers involved in the shooting were tried (only two were convicted), but all other troops left Boston. Tensions then eased, but Patriot groups did not relax: Starting in Massachusetts, communities formed "committees of correspondence" to share information and opinions with other towns and cities.

This development was particularly important for the last round of imperial-colonial confrontation before the war. In 1773 Parliament passed the Tea Act, which would have reduced the price of tea. But it eliminated colonial merchants from the trade, as tea would now be purchased directly from the East India Company. Patriot activists and committees of correspondence denounced the law as yet another illegitimate Parliamentary attempt to tax the colonies—rather than an effort to save the East India Company, whose investors included a number of prominent Britons. In many American ports, crowds prevented ships from unloading the tea, which then left. But in Boston the royal governor would not let these vessels leave.

Figure 3.1 Paul Revere's "The Bloody Massacre in King-Street, March 5, 1770"
Boston, 1770
Library of Congress Prints and Photographs Division (LC-DIG-ppmsca-01657).

The resulting standoff was resolved in December 1773 when dozens of Sons of Liberty, dressed as Indians, boarded the ships and tossed the tea overboard, since known as the Boston Tea Party.

When news reached Britain, Parliament was furious. In early 1774 they passed laws known as the Coercive Acts to punish Massachusetts. The Boston Port Act, for example, closed the port until colonists paid for the destroyed tea; other legislation gave the royal governor enhanced powers and restricted town meetings. Committees of correspondence quickly spread news of the Coercive Acts throughout the American colonies. In numerous towns Patriots condemned the Acts and organized support for New England. Colonial legislatures did so as well, even though in many cases royal governors legally forbade them from convening.

Working through the committees of correspondence, the assemblies organized what became the First Continental Congress. Representatives from all the colonies except Georgia convened in Philadelphia in September 1774. In its Declaration of Rights and Grievances, the Congress denied Parliament's authority to tax the colonies, claiming its capacity to impose tariffs was limited to sole purpose of regulating trade. It also called for a coordinated, intercolonial non-importation agreement—called the Continental Association—until Parliament rescinded the Coercive Acts. Before disbanding, the Congress agreed to reconvene the next year, in May 1775, if needed.

In New England, Patriot leaders quickly organized boycotts of British goods, and crowds prevented judges and officials from enforcing British laws. They also began preparing for armed confrontation. Patriots revived the militia system, which had deteriorated, and started collecting weapons and ammunition (some men, called "minutemen," trained to react to emergencies on a few moments' notice). It was a British operation to check such efforts that actually sparked the rebellion and ultimately led to American independence.

War Erupts: Lexington and Concord, 1775

Thomas Gage was commander of British forces in America and, in 1774, also became military governor of Massachusetts. He felt he had too few troops to confront the Patriot radicals, and feared provoking an outright rebellion. For example, in September 1774 he sent soldiers to confiscate caches of arms and ammunition just outside Boston. Afterward about 4,000 Massachusetts militiamen congregated around the city. They soon dispersed, but Gage requested more troops from the King, having only few thousand in Boston. By April 1775, officials in London had grown weary of Gage's apparent timidity and wanted more forceful action.

Gage dispatched soldiers to seize another reported store of arms in Concord, 20 miles from Boston. When about 700 British soldiers rowed from Boston Neck to the mainland during the night of April 18, two lanterns were hung on the steeple of Boston's North Church, precipitating Paul Revere's famous ride warning towns in the countryside. About 70 militiamen had assembled on Lexington's town green by the time the redcoats (so called because of their uniforms) arrived early in the morning of April 19. Outnumbered, they were dispersing when a shot rang out, prompting British soldiers to fire, then charge. Eighteen colonists fell, and the redcoats continued their march.

When they arrived at Concord, British forces destroyed supplies but did not find large stocks of arms. Leaving about noon, they encountered thousands of militiamen as they marched back to Boston. The resulting combat was not a pitched battle, but rather a running fight: As the British regulars moved along the road militia used skirmish tactics, sniping from cover including trees, rocks, and buildings. Redcoats returned fire and occasionally detached groups to engage the militia off the road. At Lexington, 1,000 reinforcements joined the British. By the time they returned to Boston, they had suffered 73 dead and 200 wounded or missing; the Americans, 49 dead and 43 wounded.

But the militia did not disperse, and about 17,000–20,000 soon converged upon the city. They lacked the artillery, equipment, and training needed to conduct a conventional siege, but they trapped Gage's troops inside Boston. Meanwhile, the Second Continental Congress convened in Philadelphia and faced the challenge of leading a revolt that had now become the War of the American Revolution.

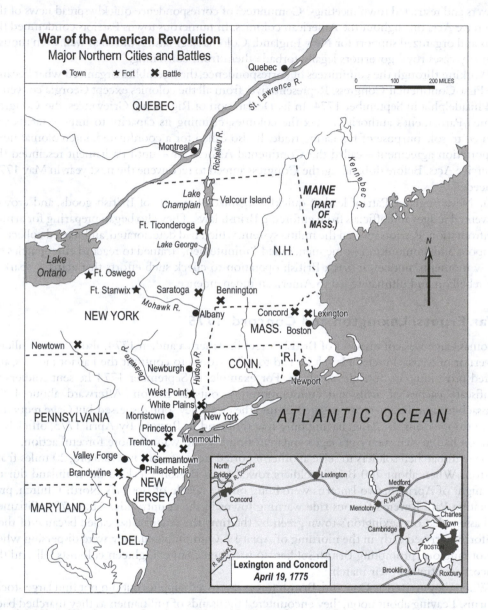

Map 3.1 War of the American Revolution, Major Northern Cities and Battles

British Versus Americans: A Comparison

In 1775, the British Empire spanned the globe, with possessions in the Americas and Asia. Its trade generated great wealth that allowed Great Britain to maintain the world's biggest navy. The fleet in turn helped protect trade and project power—making the Atlantic seaboard, for example, vulnerable to raids or invasions by British troops. Tax revenues and a large government bureaucracy also enabled Britain to sustain a large standing army and enhance it during the war by hiring German mercenaries (called "Hessians" by colonists). To many, the idea that 13 fractious colonies could resist British power seemed absurd.

Yet Britain's strengths were not as overwhelming as they appeared, and the Americans had important advantages. Perhaps the greatest was the rebels' political strength. Most American colonists were not active Patriots. Many, called "Tories" or "Loyalists," remained loyal to the Crown, though perhaps the largest group was indifferent and would have preferred to avoid any conflict. But the Patriots were very well organized after a decade of confronting British authority, as demonstrated by the Sons of Liberty and the committees of correspondence. When the war erupted, rebels took over many local governments. They did so through groups often called "committees of public safety," though names varied. These committees and the local governments they controlled organized and supported Patriot militias, while arresting loyalists and seizing their property to cow opposition.

Such organization was not decisive in and of itself, for in several areas rebel control was weak. At times, militiamen stayed home to protect homes and families rather than answer muster calls. In some localities, Loyalists formed their own militias to counter Patriots. Moreover, before the rebellion, colonists had no permanent institution for setting and enforcing intercolonial (later interstate) policies. During the war, the Second Continental Congress served this function, but it was weak. Lacking the authority to tax or raise troops of its own volition, it depended upon colonies/states to raise troops and supplies for the war effort. The Congress created an administration to acquire supplies, but it functioned poorly. The King's government, in comparison, had a well-established bureaucracy, though it was plagued by administrative rivalries and officials appointed on the basis of personal loyalty rather than ability.

Over the course of the war, local rebel control combined with other factors to undermine Britain's advantages. Its North American colonies encompassed an area of hundreds of thousands of square miles: from Maine to Georgia, and the Atlantic coast to the Appalachian Mountains. Though thousands of British and German mercenary troops crossed the Atlantic, they could only directly control areas where they were physically present; Patriots ruled in other areas. This circumstance, in turn, hampered the logistical and operational capacity of British forces. Though they could obtain provisions from local merchants or receive shipments from Great Britain, their needs often surpassed what either could provide. British and German troops sought additional supplies by foraging, a long-standing practice whereby soldiers dispersed into the countryside to collect (often coerce) goods from inhabitants. But during the Revolutionary War, when foraging troops ventured into Patriot-controlled areas, rebel militias often ambushed or skirmished with such parties (or collected supplies themselves beforehand). Lastly—though they frequently bickered and argued—local Patriot leaders effectively coordinated with state and Continental officials during the war, whereas the relationship between British officers and American Loyalists was often troubled.

Again, these circumstances did not dictate the war's outcome but affected decisions made by leaders on both sides, producing a series of results that culminated in American victory. For Britain, the objective was to end colonial resistance to its authority. But determining *how* to do so was difficult. British leaders changed strategy during the war, and indecision and poor coordination plagued operations. Conversely, the American rebels sought to defy King George III's government, initially in support of rights they claimed as British subjects and then, after July 4, 1776, to achieve political independence. Here too, the larger question was how to maintain such resistance, and in 1775, the Second Continental Congress decided that the answer entailed the creation of a standing army.

Breed's Hill, 1775

By that time, years of confrontations with British authority had made Americans wary of regular troops. Patriots viewed them as the tool of tyrannical rule and a threat to individual liberties. For most rebels, militia was the ideal military force, as it was generally comprised of citizens with ties to the community. Militiamen with their own lives and livelihoods were not dependent upon the government for long-term pay and upkeep in the way regular troops were—a dependence that isolated soldiers from larger society and could make them a more compliant tool for repression. Moreover, Lexington and Concord seemed to demonstrate that militia could be employed effectively against conventional forces, a view bolstered by another battle that occurred shortly thereafter.

Gage received reinforcements by mid-June 1775. These included officers who later became top British commanders: John Burgoyne, Henry Clinton, and William Howe. With his army still trapped on Boston Neck, Gage planned to capture the undefended Dorchester Heights to the south, which overlooked the city. But word of these plans leaked, and American troops preempted the British by taking the heights on Charlestown Neck, north of the city. Militia units arriving on June 16 had orders to fortify and hold Bunker Hill, the highest ground, but local commanders decided to entrench upon Breed's Hill instead, which was closer to Boston. The subsequent fight occurred there, though it erroneously remains known as the Battle of Bunker Hill.

The British spotted the American positions on June 17, and in the early afternoon, redcoats commanded by William Howe landed on the northeastern corner of the Charlestown peninsula. His primary attack sought to advance west and then sweep behind the American positions on Breed's Hill from the north while other units engaged the attention of the defenders. Howe did not expect resistance to his western movement, as the area had not been defended in the early morning. But by the time of the battle, the Patriot commander on the scene had placed troops to defend a fence that ran north from Breed's Hill to the beach. When Howe sent his 2,200 troops to assault the roughly 1,000 New England militiamen in and around Breed's Hill, they were repulsed. Howe ordered a second assault that also failed, and after receiving about 400 reinforcements, a third. By that time the Americans were almost out of ammunition, and they abandoned their positions.

Breed's Hill was a tactical victory for the British, who drove away the American defenders. But over 1,000 of 2,600 redcoats became casualties, including over 200 dead. Over 400 defenders fell, including 140 killed. But the fact that militiamen had successfully repelled two charges and inflicted large casualties greatly bolstered American spirits and support for the rebellion. Operationally, though the British now occupied Charlestown Neck, militia forces still blocked access to the mainland, hence the broader situation had not changed.

After the war, when Americans debated what types of military forces the new republic should maintain, champions of the militia would cite the examples of Lexington, Concord, and Bunker Hill to argue against the need for a standing army. But at the time, having learned of the battle, the Continental Congress nonetheless continued efforts to create a regular force. Militia forces were fine for tasks such as ambushes and skirmishing, reconnaissance, and internal security. But tactically they lacked the training and discipline needed to take and hold ground in pitched battles, whereas the habitual and monotonous drill of regular soldiers prepared them for such a mission. For example, though militia inflicted significant casualties on British forces returning to Boston on April 19, 1775, they had failed to prevent the redcoats from reaching Concord. At Breed's Hill, though Americans bloodied their foe, they fought from behind prepared fortifications, whereas the British advanced over open ground—and despite appalling losses, the attackers eventually drove the rebels from their defensive positions.

After Bunker Hill, Gage's troops remained trapped in Boston, outnumbered by surrounding militia forces. But what if the British landed another army elsewhere? Militia forces served for only short periods of time (about 90 days) and usually within a specific region, which significantly limited their operational capabilities. The Continental Congress realized that it needed a regular force that could remain in the field indefinitely, move to different areas as needed to

Figure 3.2 "View of the Attack on Bunker's Hill, With the Burning of Charles Town, June 17, 1775"

In *The New, Comprehensive, and Complete History of England* ... (London, 1783)

An eighteenth-century drawing of the Battle of (Bunker) Breed's Hill

Library of Congress, Prints and Photographs Division, LC-USZ62–8624

confront British forces, and fight effectively in pitched battles—and it had to find a man who could build such an army from scratch.

George Washington and the Continental Army

On June 14, 1775, the Second Continental Congress created the Continental Army. It initially adopted the militia companies around Boston as its own but also called for the colonies to raise volunteers. A day later Congress appointed George Washington as commander of all Continental troops. Now a plantation owner and prominent politician who was part of Virginia's Congressional delegation, Washington was among a select group of men with significant military experience from the French and Indian War. But most were from New England. One of Congress' goals in 1775 was to demonstrate the commitment of all of the colonies to safeguarding American liberties, not just those whose militias were already confronting the British at Boston. Of the possible candidates who resided beyond New England, Washington was the best known.

Moreover, unlike most others, Washington did not seek the appointment, which assuaged those in Congress concerned about how an army commander might employ his authority and influence. Moreover, his belief that military forces should be subordinated to civilian control and deference to Congressional authority bolstered confidence that the Continental Army would be used to protect American liberties, not threaten them. Washington also possessed a combination of patience, intelligence, perseverance, and tact essential for success. He needed to interact not just with members of Congress but with a variety of colony/state and local officials on issues such as acquiring supplies and manpower, and coordinating with local militia forces. Many of these officials were jealous of their prerogatives or wary of army demands, and Washington's successful interactions with them rested much more upon persuasion than coercion.

Washington intended to mold the Continental Army along British lines to create a force that could fight pitched battles. But the men he found outside Boston in the summer of 1775 had no training, drill experience, or familiarity with conventional operations. Discipline among militia troops was lax, and many units did not have uniforms. Soldiers lacked camp knowledge such as security measures and where to place latrines. Washington quickly became absorbed in instructing troops, officers, and aides in their basic duties, instilling discipline, and establishing supply arrangements. He also had to cope with high turnover, for service obligations of previously mustered militia units were expiring in the summer and fall of 1775 as newly organized ones arrived.

The Continental Army ultimately acquired the battlefield proficiency that Washington intended. But it took years, and his fundamental challenge in that time was to keep it in existence, confronting threats from British forces, poor logistical arrangements, and flagging morale. Complicating Washington's responsibilities was the fact that he was both commander of all Continental forces and of a field army in a particular theater. Other generals led troops in other areas, and were subordinate to him. For example, in June 1775 Congress appointed Philip Schuyler command of the New York Department, later the Northern Department. His forces launched the first and one of the few American offensive campaigns of the war: the invasion of Canada. Some Congressmen hoped French Canadians might support the rebellion, but others believed American forces could capture it easily, hampering future British operations as well as attempts to recruit Native American groups against the colonists.

As Schuyler suffered from poor health, Richard Montgomery was his army's field commander. By November, this small force (perhaps 2,000) occupied Montreal. Meanwhile, George Washington ordered Benedict Arnold to take roughly 1,100 troops through the Maine wilderness to Quebec. This journey became infamous, for Arnold's men trekked over hundreds of miles of rugged wilderness in cold and wet conditions, and ran out of supplies; hundreds deserted. In December, forces led by Arnold and Montgomery rendezvoused outside Quebec. With the enlistments of many soldiers about to expire, they assaulted the city on December 31, and were repulsed: Of about 1,200 attackers, 400 were captured and about 100 killed or wounded, while the British defenders suffered about 20 casualties. Montgomery died in the attack and Arnold, wounded, besieged the city with his remaining forces. But when British reinforcements arrived in May 1776, he retreated.

The Strategic Situation in 1776

By then, the British Army had evacuated Boston. In February 1776, Washington's army acquired heavy artillery from Fort Ticonderoga, which American militia had surprised and captured the previous spring. Washington and his advisors decided to place them on Dorchester Heights, where the guns could fire down on the British fleet in the harbor. On March 5, Continental soldiers took this ground and Major General William Howe—now the top British commander in America after Gage's dismissal the prior October—decided he could no longer remain in Boston. By month's end the British had abandoned the city, sailing to their base at Halifax, Nova Scotia.

But Washington and American leaders knew they would return. In fact, Howe had already decided to leave Boston when the Americans took Dorchester Heights, though it prompted him to withdraw earlier than anticipated. The initial British strategy of crushing Patriot resistance in New England had clearly failed, and King George III, colonial secretary Lord George Germain, and other officials now turned to greater use of conventional forces to cope with the rebellion.

This strategy sought to isolate New England from the rest of the American colonies. Howe would capture New York City and advance troops north up the Hudson River valley, while another British army would push the Americans out of Canada and then move south down Lake Champlain. If successful, these campaigns would preserve the King's authority in the remainder of the colonies and subsequently allow British troops to "reduce" New England to submission.

This strategy shaped British operations for the next two years and focused the war's major campaigns and battles in the northern colonies/states in 1776 and 1777. It failed for various reasons, including the assumption that outside of New England, Loyalism was strong and support for the Patriot cause weak. The British made one limited attempt to support Loyalists in early 1776, dispatching Henry Clinton and some troops to North Carolina to link up with local Tory militias. But in February, Patriot militia defeated Loyalists at the Battle of Moore's Creek Bridge. Clinton's forces diverted to Charlestown instead, but withdrew after failing to capture some harbor defenses. For the next few years, southern Tories were effectively left to fend for themselves and were suppressed by rebels in many areas.

But Britain's biggest problem with its strategy of 1776–77 was arguably that no one official was responsible for enforcing it. Howe pursued Washington's field army at the expense of larger strategic plans. Ironically, he has also been criticized for forgoing opportunities to destroy enemy forces, apparently in hopes of facilitating reconciliation between Britain and the colonists. Other royal officials, such as Germain, bore some responsibility for synchronizing British operations. Whatever their role, British strategic coordination broke down in these years, setting the stage for a great American victory in October 1777.

For Washington, strategy was fairly simple: Preserve the Continental Army. It was the political expression of the colonies' defiance of Great Britain, and its existence maintained support for the rebellion. Yet British forces surpassed the Continentals in numbers, training, arms, and equipment, and could be transported up and down the Atlantic coast by the Royal Navy. Any rash commitment to battle threatened great losses or potentially the destruction of American forces, with grave political consequences. Hence, Washington chose a defensive strategy, confronting the British when necessary and limiting risks. Where possible, he enhanced his army's defensive strength by constructing fortifications and prepared positions—often called "a war of posts." But Washington did not completely eschew offensive operations. He sought instead situations that maximized his chances for success and undermined British advantages. Finding such opportunities, though, required great patience and at times Washington felt compelled to offer battle in adverse circumstances.

The New York–New Jersey Campaign, 1776

The Battle of Long Island was one such engagement. In April 1776, after the British evacuated Boston, Washington moved his army to New York City, one of the most important ports on the Atlantic seaboard. He knew that, if captured, the British could split the colonies, impede colonial trade, and possess an excellent base to maintain their armies. Moreover, the loss of New York City would be a serious political blow to the American rebellion, and Washington could not simply allow the British to occupy it uncontested.

But defending the city was a daunting proposition. High unit turnover continued to plague Washington's army, complicating issues such as training and administration. Moreover, New York harbor lies between Staten Island, Manhattan Island, and Long Island, and all three were vulnerable to landings and assaults by the Royal Navy. Before leaving Boston, Washington dispatched his second-in-command Charles Lee—a former British officer with significant experience—to begin defensive preparations. As the Americans lacked warships, Lee created a series of strongpoints to resist British naval movements. He had troops construct forts on both sides of the Hudson, at the upper tip of Manhattan and directly across in New Jersey. They also fortified Brooklyn Heights on Long Island, across the East River from New York City proper. Americans built numerous positions in the area, many of which were not completed or poorly constructed.

In early July, roughly 130 British ships arrived off Staten Island, landing about 9,000 troops. More soldiers arrived in subsequent weeks, totaling 32,000 by late August—larger than any army Great Britain had previously sent overseas. By that time, Washington had about 20,000 soldiers, about half Continentals and half militia, in and around New York City. While waiting for troops to arrive, Howe and his brother Richard, Lord Howe, the British naval commander, attempted to negotiate with American leaders. But their timing could not have been worse, as the Continental Congress had signed the Declaration of Independence on July 4, 1776. The Howes sought to end the rebellion peacefully and keep the colonies under British authority, an option the Americans would no longer consider.

On August 22, on the southwestern edge of Long Island, 15,000 British and German troops landed. General Howe started north toward Brooklyn Heights: If captured, the British could mount artillery there to bombard New York City and force American troops to withdraw. Washington had around 7,000 men on Long Island, roughly half in the fortifications on Brooklyn Heights and the rest scattered along a wooded ridgeline to the south called "Guana Heights." Though occupying this terrain was tactically astute, he had too few troops for the task. Washington did not know the terrain himself, and he switched local commanders twice in the days before the battle when his original choice, Nathanael Greene, fell ill.

Reconnoitering the area, the British discovered American soldiers occupied a number of passes in the ridgeline, though the Jamaica Pass to the east was weakly held. Henry Clinton, back from his failed southern mission, proposed feints on the other passes while the main British force assaulted Jamaica Pass. Once taken, these redcoats would then march west to attack the remaining American positions in the flank. Howe approved, and the British moved out on the night of August 26–27. The plan worked: Most American positions collapsed, though Continental units along the Gowanus Road fought well and long enough to allow soldiers retreating from the east to reach Brooklyn Heights.

At this point, Howe made a controversial decision. With the enemy routed and confused, British troops had a good chance to successfully storm the positions at Brooklyn Heights and destroy remaining American forces on Long Island. But Howe held back. Some historians claim he did so in reaction to Breed's Hill, where his assaults were repulsed with heavy losses. Others such as Ira Gruber argue he did not wish to destroy the Continental Army outright but expected that merely defeating it would destroy the colonists' will to resist without shedding excessive amounts of blood (and thus make a hoped-for political reconciliation with the colonists easier). Whatever Howe's reasoning, he stopped his forces and prepared to besiege the American fortifications. Washington and his officers withdrew their men back to Manhattan on the night of August 29–30.

Over the next few months, operations consisted of Howe's troops chasing the Americans to bring them to battle. Washington countered by withdrawing, preserving his army, and using fortified positions where possible to help protect its movements ("the war of posts"). On September 16, Howe landed troops at Kip's Bay on the eastern shore of Manhattan Island. Had they moved quickly, the British might have cut off thousands of American troops stationed in New York City to the south. But Howe was cautious, and Continental forces successfully escaped north to fortifications at Harlem Heights. Here, the two armies faced each other until October 12, when Howe used another flanking maneuver. Washington soon discovered British forces had landed on the mainland, to the north and east at Throg's Neck. He retreated, helped by Continentals who resisted another British landing at Pell's Point. The British then chased Washington's forces north, catching up with them at White Plains on October 28. After another battlefield defeat, the Americans fell back to North Castle.

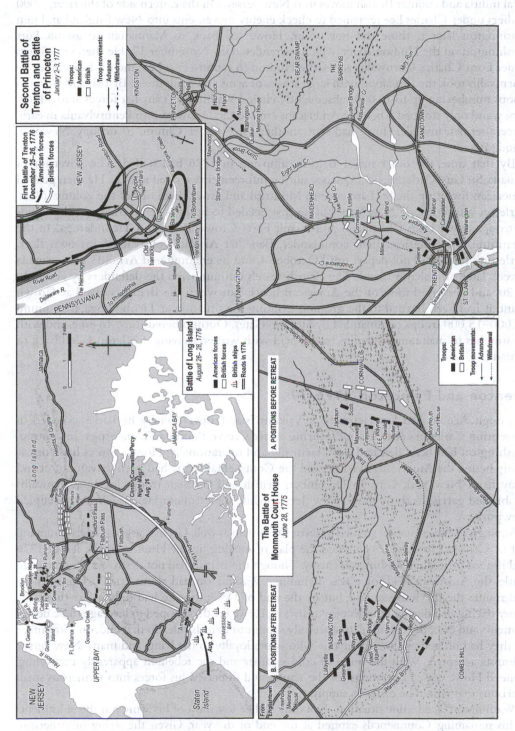

Map 3.2 Tactical Maps of Some of George Washington's Battles: The Battles of Long Island, Trenton, Princeton, and Monmouth Courthouse

Washington then split his forces. He took about 2,000 troops across the Hudson to join local militia and counter British moves into New Jersey. On the eastern side of the river, 7,000 soldiers under Charles Lee remained to check enemy movements into New England and join Washington later if those did not occur. Howe fell back to Manhattan to assault Fort Washington on the Hudson River, which surrendered on November 17. He then sent forces under Lord Charles Cornwallis across the Hudson to capture Fort Lee, and on November 20 Cornwallis took the fort along with large stocks of arms and equipment. British and German troops numbering up to 10,000 subsequently chased Washington's smaller forces across New Jersey, and only stopped when the Americans crossed the Delaware into Pennsylvania in early December. Meanwhile, Howe had sent another force under Clinton to occupy Newport, Rhode Island.

By that time, the other major British campaign in 1776 had stalled. The governor of Canada, Sir Guy Carleton, held Quebec until reinforcements arrived in May. He then pushed American forces up the St. Lawrence to Montreal and drove them out of the colony. Next, Carleton was to invade New York but he first needed to build boats to transport thousands of troops down Lake Champlain and assault Forts Crown Point and Ticonderoga. In the meantime, the American field commander, Benedict Arnold, constructed his own fleet. Carleton's forces did not depart until October 4, and he encountered Arnold's little armada a week later off Valcour Island. The British vessels outnumbered the defenders by about 40 to 20, and destroyed most of the American boats. But when the British arrived at Crown Point, it had been burned to the ground; scouting the situation at Ticonderoga, they found 12,000–15,000 troops commanded by Horatio Gates. Outnumbered three-to-one, and with no supplies to maintain his troops in the field with winter arriving, Carleton sailed back to Canada.

Trenton and Princeton, 1776–77

Although Arnold had lost tactically at Valcour Island, operationally he had succeeded in preventing Carleton's army from capturing either Crown Point or Ticonderoga. In contrast, Washington had been defeated both tactically and operationally: Howe's forces had consistently bested the Americans in battle, and the Continental Army had been driven out of and away from New York City. In December, British and German troops led by Cornwallis established garrisons throughout New Jersey, while forces under Henry Clinton occupied Newport.

Strategically, the situation seemed to favor the British as well. Given Carleton's delays moving out of Canada, Howe had abandoned the plan of moving up the Hudson in the fall of 1776 and instead fixated on Washington's army. Though the British had not destroyed it outright in battle, the American field force was dwindling: Washington had about 20,000 Continentals and militia the previous summer, but by the end of December, he had only a few thousand, many having fled during months of retreat. The Howe brothers hoped to leverage these developments and coax the colonists to peacefully submit to British rule. To that end, on November 30 they had offered pardons to anyone who swore loyalty to the King, and many New Jersey colonists accepted. With the onset of cold weather and the rebellion apparently unraveling, General Howe ceased operations for the winter and dispersed his forces into numerous small garrisons that would be easier to supply.

Washington faced a dire situation. Not only had he lost most of his army, but the enlistments of his remaining Continentals expired at the end of the year. Given the string of American defeats, it was unlikely many men would join up or reenlist in 1777. His solution was to attack, exploiting Howe's decision to scatter his forces in southern New Jersey. Moreover, British and

German troops soon alienated colonists by abusing civilians when they went into the countryside to forage. Both New Jersey and Pennsylvania militia began skirmishing with enemy patrols and convoys, and they provided Washington with intelligence about one garrison of 1,500 German mercenaries at Trenton, just across the Delaware River from American camps.

Washington planned to attack with three different forces. But debarking on Christmas night 1776, only the 2,400 Continentals under his direct command successfully navigated the icy Delaware River to reach the New Jersey shore. Shortly before arriving at Trenton, he sent one group to assault the town from the north and another from the south. The Germans were not prepared for the attack that began about 8 a.m. on December 26. Artillery fired into the streets and Continental infantry attacks overwhelmed their defensive responses. Combat ended after about an hour, with Washington's troops capturing about 800–900 men while killing or wounding over 100; roughly 500 escaped. Only four Americans were wounded, and two died from exposure to the cold.

Trenton was a dramatic victory for American forces. But Washington was not finished. Returning to Pennsylvania, he and his officers prepared another strike into New Jersey, but bad weather delayed their crossing. On December 31, confronted with about 2,000 Continentals whose enlistments were expiring, Washington and his officers convinced about half to remain with appeals and cash offers to those who would serve another six weeks. Meanwhile, Cornwallis concentrated about 8,000 German and British troops at Princeton. Washington and his 5,000 men, mostly Continentals, then met up with about 1,800 militia at Trenton, and he dispatched about 1,000 soldiers up the road to harass British movements.

When Cornwallis' forces advanced on January 2, 1777, American skirmishers slowed their progress. Arriving outside Trenton, they found Washington's men defending high ground behind a swollen creek. For the rest of the day and into the night, Cornwallis launched furious assaults at these positions, which were all repulsed. The next day the Americans had vanished—Washington had abandoned these positions during the night. But rather than fall back, his army marched north to attack the Princeton garrison before Cornwallis could react. Though unexpected, British troops encountered advance elements of Washington's army just outside Princeton, hence the surprise was not as complete as at the First Battle of Trenton. The Americans inflicted heavy casualties, though most of the garrison escaped. In both the engagements of January 2 and 3, the British suffered about 950 casualties, the Americans around 200.

In these battles, the Americans had prevailed over the British tactically, as both attackers and defenders. Operationally, Washington had demonstrated the ability to move quickly and surprise his opponents, and to hold off an attacker and disengage on his terms. But Trenton and Princeton are remembered for their strategic consequences. Observers both then and now have credited Washington with nothing less than saving the American Revolution. These victories provided much-needed hope that the Americans could continue resisting the British. Patriot confidence and morale rose, as did hope that other countries might lend assistance to their cause. Washington kept his army in being, and acquired the reenlistments and new recruits needed for the campaigns of 1777.

These battles also undermined the Howes' strategic approach of sapping colonial support for the rebellion by grinding down the Continental Army in a series of relatively low-casualty defeats. Moreover, those inclined toward Loyalism in New Jersey stopped coming forward to take oaths to the King lest they become targets of Patriot supporters. Operationally, William Howe realized he could not risk keeping his army in many dispersed garrisons and had Cornwallis withdraw troops from southern New Jersey. For the rest of the winter, British and German soldiers quartered in New Brunswick and Amboy, while Washington took his army into winter quarters in Morristown, about 20 miles to the north.

Figure 3.3 George Washington Crossing the Delaware.

By Henry Mosler, 1912–13

George Washington lands on the New Jersey Shore, December 26, 1776.

Library of Congress, Prints and Photographs Division, LC-USZCN4–159

Who Fought?

The Continental Army changed after Trenton and Princeton. To that point, enlistments were short, usually up to a year and generally attracted enthusiastic young men who wished to support the American cause, who wanted to drive out the British, or who sought adventure or glory. Within its ranks, one could find soldiers from all classes of colonial society. But as Washington and others argued, short enlistments prevented the accumulation of training and experience needed to create a conventional force that could stand up to British regular soldiers in battle. After Washington's defeat at the Battle of Long Island, the Continental Congress both increased the size of the Continental Army and lengthened terms of enlistments, generally for three years or the duration of the war.

The latter change tended to draw men from poorer segments of colonial society. One reason was the use of financial incentives to stimulate recruitment, such as cash bounties upon enlistment or promises of land after the war. But other factors contributed as well. Congress lacked the authority to raise troops directly and relied upon individual states to create regiments to join the Continental Army. State officials turned to conscription during the war to meet quotas set by Congress, but a draft notice did not necessarily mean compulsory service. Men had the option of hiring substitutes, who were often poor. Yet these trends did not mean that monetary rewards became the sole motivation of Continental soldiers. Such incentives, for example, cannot fully explain why most of Washington's troops endured hunger, illness, and freezing temperatures rather than deserting (though some did) during the harsh winters at Valley Forge and Morristown later in the war. Other factors motivated Continentals to cope with such conditions, which included a belief in American liberty but also pride in their own units and a willingness to fight to support their comrades in arms.

As with the enlisted ranks, the men who served as officers in the Continental line became more homogenous over time. Of varied backgrounds early in the conflict, later they come more from the upper classes. Wealth was a significant factor because as the conflict continued, usually only officers with significant assets could continue to serve, as pay was low and often late. Those who lacked such means would often have to return home to support their families.

In some ways, Continental soldiers were like British ones. The latter have often been depicted as the "dregs" of society, and during the war, royal officials did occasionally scour jails and poorhouses for able-bodied men. But the majority of British troops came from modest but respectable backgrounds, usually from farming or artisan families, and they often volunteered for the army because of lack of employment. Their service was about 8–10 years which, while providing units with a large reservoir of experience, also isolated them from the civilian world. Redcoats also endured discipline harsher than anything Americans would have tolerated. Another difference was that British officers were aristocrats who had to purchase their commissions. They did not undergo formal training but learned while serving. Some read and wrote about military affairs, while others believed only personal qualities of courage and valor mattered for success. Intriguingly, there may not have been a huge disparity in combat experience between British and American officers, for the last war in which either had served was the Seven Years War. A great difference between these armies, though, was ideological, as Americans fought for defense of homes and political rights, unlike British forces.

Most Continental troops and officers were white colonists. But recruiters also approached immigrants, including indentured servants who might serve in place of their masters or to escape servitude. Many foreigners from Europe volunteered for the American cause, though they often arrived with the expectations of serving as officers and commanding troops. Some, such as the Marquis de Lafayette, Friedrich Steuben, and Thaddeus Kosciuszko, made valuable contributions to the war effort.

Although initially banned by Congress in 1775, African Americans served in the Continental Army later in the war. States with large slave populations worried about arming blacks. But over time, difficulties in raising manpower allowed free blacks and slaves into the ranks, often serving as substitutes or (if slaves) receiving promises of freedom after their service. Though a minority among American soldiers, they were found in many units, even those from southern states. Some historians estimate that out of roughly 100,000 men who fought at some point for the American cause during the war, 5,000 may have been African American. Blacks also fought for the British, often in hopes of gaining their freedom from American masters. In this regard, African Americans posed a thorny problem for royal officials. For example, in 1775, Virginia's governor Lord Dunmore issued a proclamation that granted freedom to slaves who fought for the King—and in doing so, dramatically undermined Loyalist support among Virginia's white population, which lived in fear of slave revolts. By the war's end, commanders like Cornwallis allowed blacks into their camps and used their labor to support British forces.

In contrast to the Continental Army, militia forces generally came from the middle strata of colonial society. Being men who owned modest amounts of property, they preferred militia to Continental service as it was limited to relatively short periods, and usually they did not journey too far from home. Moreover, they often served with friends, relatives, and neighbors, which provided cohesion to their units. Some men fought early in the war with Continental forces and later with

Figure 3.4 "Soldiers in Uniform"

By Jean Baptiste Antoine De Verger, 1781–84

The above image depicts various American soldiers encountered by the artist, a French officer during the War of the American Revolution. The black soldier on the left was likely a member of the First Rhode Island Regiment, a unit unusual in that it was mostly comprised of African-American troops. Most blacks who fought for the Americans did so in units where white soldiers predominated. African-American men also fought with Loyalists, and German "Hessian" units recruited black soldiers as well. In addition, escaped slaves assisted British forces as guides or with their labor, and Cornwallis used thousands to help build fortifications around Yorktown in the summer of 1781.

Anne S. K. Brown Military Collection, Brown University Library

their state militias. As Patriots controlled many areas, some scholars argue that rebel leaders could pressure or coerce men to serve in local militia units. Yet mustering militiamen could be difficult.

The early months of 1777 demonstrate the disparate effectiveness of militia forces. In New Jersey, for example, fighting did not cease after the Battle of Princeton but continued with numerous small engagements. British and German garrisons needed to collect food and supplies. Foraging parties increasingly fell into ambushes and skirmished with New Jersey and Pennsylvania militia, producing casualties and undermining morale. Moreover, as historian Mark Kwasny notes, George Washington coordinated and directed many of these operations with local militia leaders and often sent Continental troops to assist.

Militia forces performed other missions during the war, including providing internal security against Loyalist activities and responding to sudden British movements into a given region. For example, in early 1777, Howe sent raids up the Hudson River valley and against Danbury, Connecticut. The Connecticut militia responded to the latter incursion, but could not stop British troops from reaching Danbury and retreating back to the coast. In New York, officials had difficulty even mustering militia units, as many men preferred to stay home to protect families and property. Such uneven performance was frustrating, but manpower limitations required that American commanders use militia in most operations, and many—including Washington—came to realize that, properly employed, they could make significant contributions to the Patriot cause.

Combat was the province of men, and the few female soldiers in the ranks disguised their sex. The largest contribution American women made to the war was managing farms and businesses when spouses and male relatives left to fight. Yet some directly supported troops in the field as "camp followers." These were common to eighteenth-century armies, and while containing some men as traders and merchants, most were women who took care of their soldier spouses, performing tasks such as dressing wounds and food preparation. But sometimes they were exposed to combat and on rare occasions joined in the fighting, as with the legend of "Molly Pitcher." It is difficult to confirm the details of that story, but a verified case occurred during the defense of Fort Washington in November 1776: When Margaret Corbin's husband was killed, she helped operate a cannon until wounded herself. Debilitated because of her injuries, the Continental Congress later granted her a military pension because of her bravery and service.

More British Strategic Breakdown

The original British strategy for 1776 envisioned campaigns up the Hudson from New York City and down Lake Champlain from Canada to isolate New England. But it fell victim to Carleton's slow movements and William Howe's fixation on Washington's army. In late 1776, Howe began sending plans to Lord Germain for major operations in 1777. At first, these accorded with the initial strategic vision: British troops would advance north from New York City and south from Canada to rendezvous at Albany, though additional forces would also move toward Philadelphia as a diversion and invade New England from Newport, Rhode Island. Later plans, however, were simpler and scrapped major campaigns into New England or up the Hudson: Howe's main objective now became Philadelphia, though he referred to movements of an army out of Canada and indicated that forces left to garrison New York City could move north to assist them.

Planning for 1777 also reflected the arrival of John Burgoyne in London. An ambitious officer who had just served with Carleton, he lobbied the King for command of the British army in Canada. He criticized Carleton's lack of aggression and argued that a drive south from Montreal should be assisted by an advance down the Mohawk River valley from Lake Ontario. These operations would converge on Albany, along with a campaign up the Hudson.

The plan approved by Germain's ministry that spring amalgamated these schemes. Burgoyne received command of the Canadian army and would launch operations down Lake Champlain and the Mohawk River targeting Albany. Howe would go to Philadelphia but after capturing it would move his army back north up the Hudson River to link up with Burgoyne's forces. Such expectations failed to account for the distances Howe's troops had to travel or how American resistance might impede its success. But arguably the greatest problem was failing to ensure that the primary field commanders understood the plan and coordinated with one another. Burgoyne expected Howe to make a major effort north to Albany; Howe's chief objective was Philadelphia, and he relegated any movements up the Hudson to whatever forces the New York City garrison could spare.

Admittedly, communicating such plans was exceedingly difficult for the British, given that messages sent across the Atlantic took weeks to arrive, and was not helped by Howe's changes of mind. His later plans arrived in London after Burgoyne had returned to Canada and Germain had dispatched orders for the upcoming campaigning season. Moreover, Howe ignored messages or reminders that the ministry expected him to cooperate with the Canadian army, whereas before sailing, Burgoyne dismissed Howe's warnings that he would provide little help. These problems produced two large, uncoordinated British campaigns in 1777, one of which ended in a defeat that changed the entire nature of the war.

Howe's Pennsylvania Campaign, 1777

Various motivations drove Howe to Philadelphia. As the seat of the Continental Congress, he thought its capture would deal a harsh blow to the rebellion. Moreover, Howe believed that many Loyalists resided in Pennsylvania, and moving his army there would bring them out to support the King's cause and fight the Patriots. Lastly, after Trenton and Princeton, Howe sought to crush Washington's army, not just defeat it.

In May, Washington led his army out of winter quarters. Howe failed to bring it to battle, and by July his troops were back in New York City. American forces followed and took up positions in the nearby Hudson Highlands. Not long thereafter, expecting Howe would move north, Washington was instead surprised when British and German troops put to sea on July 23, 1776. When the ships were spotted near the Delaware River, he realized they were heading for Philadelphia. By August 25, the Continental Army was at Wilmington, Delaware, while the British had landed at Head-of-Elk at the top of Chesapeake Bay. Howe had used British naval capacity to get around Washington. But the sea journey in cramped quarters with poor food was much longer than anticipated, and his troops arrived exhausted. Meanwhile, few Loyalists met them, and most residents of the area fled.

After stopping to collect supplies and allow his troops to rest, Howe marched them toward Philadelphia. As with New York City, Washington felt compelled to resist the enemy's advance. He moved his army to block Howe's at Brandywine Creek, at a crossing called "Chadd's Ford." But Loyalists informed the British of another crossing farther up the creek. Howe then devised a plan reminiscent of Long Island: He sent part of his force to engage the center of the American positions on the other side of the creek, while another crossed upstream to get around and smash Washington's right flank. When the Battle of Brandywine Creek unfolded on September 11, both armies numbered about 15,000–16,000. Washington received contradictory reports about British movements and shifted forces from flank to center only to reverse himself. A furious fight occurred when the British hit the American right. Washington's forces held for a while before pulling back, and forces under Nathanael Greene kept the redcoats at bay while the Americans retreated.

Bad weather prevented the two armies from engaging again before Howe entered Philadelphia on September 26. Members of the Continental Congress had already fled to Lancaster, Pennsylvania. The British were disappointed with the modest crowds that greeted them, which boded ill for expectations of significant Tory support. Immediately after capturing Philadelphia,

Howe stationed many men in nearby Germantown. Washington sensed an opportunity, and apparently hoped to repeat his prior year's success at Trenton.

At the First Battle of Trenton, Washington split his 2,400 men into two forces to attack the town from different directions. On October 4, 1777, 11,000 Continentals and militia advanced 16 miles toward Germantown in four separate columns. Fog limited visibility and undermined this complex plan: Washington's forces arrived at different times, with columns bumping into each other and falling prey to friendly fire. At first, British troops retreated, but when some occupied a large stone building called "the Chew House," they successfully held up the American advance. Meanwhile, other units launched counterattacks that drove Washington's men back.

At Brandywine Creek and Germantown, Howe's forces prevailed tactically, suffering about 1,000 casualties to the Americans' approximate 2,300. Operationally, Howe had also succeeded in occupying Philadelphia. But anticipated Loyalist support was illusory. Though defeated, Washington's army remained in the field—and Howe suspended efforts to engage it. Rebel leaders had previously built fortifications on the lower Delaware River to guard against possible British advances from the sea. Howe had avoided these by sailing up Chesapeake Bay and then marching overland. But to supply his army in Philadelphia, he needed to reduce these fortifications and open up the river to shipping, which now became the focus of British operations. Moreover, occupying Philadelphia did not significantly hurt support for the American cause, which instead greatly benefited from events farther north.

The Saratoga Campaign, 1777

At the end of May 1777 John Burgoyne, with more than 8,000 troops, moved south down Lake Champlain with an initial objective of Fort Ticonderoga. His men were mostly regular troops, both Germans and British, but included Canadian militia, American Loyalists, and Iroquois warriors. They reached the fort at the end of June. By July 6, outnumbered American forces under Arthur St. Clair were abandoning Ticonderoga. His officers had assumed enemy troops could not move artillery onto the mountains overlooking the fort and were surprised when the British did so.

St. Clair sent supplies, the sick, and artillery south down the lake via boats, while healthy troops marched out in the night. Artillery shelled enemy positions to prevent the British from noticing the withdrawal. At daylight, Burgoyne ordered a pursuit. Some forces chased American boats down Lake Champlain to Skenesboro, others caught up with the rearguard of St. Clair's forces on July 7 at Hubbardton. British and Germans troops won the subsequent battle, but the Americans escaped, and Burgoyne's men were too exhausted to pursue further.

Burgoyne had intended to move down Lake George to Fort George, just a few miles from Fort Edward and the Hudson River. But after the Battle of Hubbardton, he decided to concentrate his army instead at Skenesboro and advance from there to Fort Edward. That route was farther overland than the one from Fort George, but Burgoyne believed marching forces from Hubbardton back to Lake Champlain and then traveling down Lake George would take too long and worried retreating would undermine his troops' morale. His decision, however, had serious operational consequences, as his campaign slowed to a crawl.

Burgoyne had a big supply train, including cannons, ammunition, supplies, and numerous camp followers, including many officers' servants and dependents. (Baron von Riedesel, commander of the German troops, brought along his wife and three daughters.) In Europe, the developed road network made such logistical burdens easier to handle. But Burgoyne was moving his army through the American wilderness. One narrow road ran from Skenesboro to Fort Edward. But Philip Schuyler, Continental commander of the Northern Department, sent parties to block it, who felled trees and destroyed bridges. Soon Burgoyne's army was only advancing about a mile a day.

It arrived at Fort Edward on July 30, finding it destroyed by the Americans. Burgoyne then received confirmation that Howe was going to Pennsylvania and would not be helping him. Lacking supplies and transport animals, Burgoyne now had to choose where to cross the Hudson River: His army was east of it, and Albany was on the west bank. He selected a point a few miles downstream, before the river widened. But first his men scoured the countryside for supplies, and a large expedition of 700–800 German troops went to raid an American supply depot at Bennington. They were not expecting serious resistance when, on August 16, more than 2,000 New England militia and Indians ambushed and defeated them outside the town. The Americans then attacked another unit of 600–700 German troops coming to assist. About 900 Germans were killed, wounded, or captured in total.

Burgoyne had lost a significant percentage of his combat strength and still lacked needed supplies. Between the Battles of Hubbardton and Bennington, as well as detaching men to garrison Ticonderoga and other posts, his army had shrunk by roughly 2,000 men. Conversely, American numbers were increasing. Burgoyne's slow advance gave Continental units from Washington's army, and militia from nearby states, time to reach Albany as reinforcements. Meanwhile, Congress dismissed Philip Schuyler from command of the Northern Department. His efforts had delayed Burgoyne's advance and had provided time for the Americans to react, but many doubted his martial abilities: Schuyler had rarely taken the field with an army, Ticonderoga had fallen without a fight, and his forces were retreating rather than engaging the enemy. Horatio Gates replaced him in August.

From September 13–15, Burgoyne crossed the Hudson at Saratoga with approximately 6,000 troops. Exhausted and low on supplies, they continued along the river, harassed by American militia. Meanwhile, Gates concentrated about 7,000 troops on Bemis Heights a few miles to the south. This high ground dominated both the Hudson River and the road that ran along it and had steep and wooded slopes; Gates and his Polish engineer, Thaddeus Kosciuszko, fortified positions there with artillery. To the west, however, was other high ground that overlooked Bemis Heights. Advancing his army in three columns on September 19, Burgoyne apparently hoped to capture it. After a delay, Gates dispatched forces to block the British advance. Commanded by Benedict Arnold, American troops encountered Burgoyne's in a broad clearing known as "Freeman's Farm." With some pauses, intense fighting occurred there over the next few hours, with each side driving off the other at times. At day's end, the British possessed Freeman's Farm, giving them a tactical victory, but Arnold's men had stopped Burgoyne's movement, thus giving the Americans operational success.

Combat subsided after the Battle of Freeman's Farm, or "the First Battle of Saratoga." Both sides were exhausted, Burgoyne having lost 500–600 men, the Americans about 300. Shortly after the battle, the British general received a letter from Henry Clinton, commanding the New York City garrison. Clinton wrote he was moving some forces up the Hudson but would retreat if they were threatened. The letter gave Burgoyne hope enough to order his forces to dig in, fortify their positions, and repel American attacks while he waited for help.

But days turned into weeks with no further word from Clinton. Meanwhile, Gates' army grew to about 11,000 men. With the approach of winter, the British supply situation was becoming dire; in early October, Burgoyne cut his army's rations by a third. He gambled on one more attack, again hoping to get to the high ground that would force the Americans to abandon Bemis Heights.

On October 7, again moving out three columns, British and German soldiers reached Barber's wheat field a mile west of Freeman's Farm when American forces assaulted them. Using the cover of adjacent woods, the attackers advanced around the enemy left flank toward the rear, precipitating a British retreat. Benedict Arnold, though relieved of command following a dispute with Gates, rode into the fray. He led American forces against the British right flank until they stormed and captured some fortifications called "Breymann's Redoubt." Arnold fell wounded, and the attack soon petered out. But the Americans had defeated the British at the Second Battle of Saratoga, also known as "the Battle of Bemis Heights."

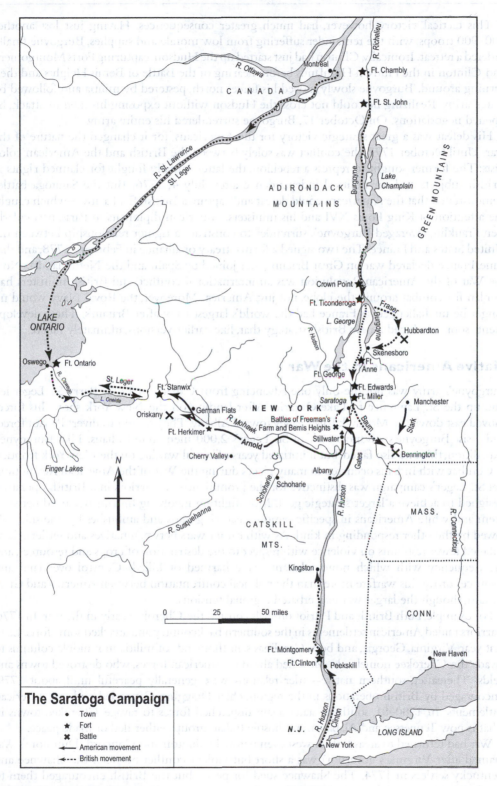

The following labels appear on the map:

R. Ottawa
Montreal
CANADA
R. Richelieu
Ft. Chambly
Ft. St. John
R. St. Lawrence
St. Leger
Lake Champlain
Burgoyne
ADIRONDACK MOUNTAINS
GREEN MOUNTAINS
Crown Point
Ft. Ticonderoga
Fraser
Burgoyne
L. George
Hubbardton
Skenesboro
LAKE ONTARIO
Ft. Anne
Ft. George
Oswego
Ft. Ontario
R. Oswego
St. Leger
L. Oneida
Ft. Stanwix
Oriskany
German Flats
R. Mohawk
Ft. Herkimer
Arnold
NEW YORK
Battles of Freeman's Farm and Bemis Heights
Baum
Saratoga
Ft. Edwards
Ft. Miller
Manchester
Stark
Stillwater
Bennington
Gates
Finger Lakes
Cherry Valley
Schoharie Cr.
Albany
MASS.
N
Schoharie
R. Susquehanna
CATSKILL MTS.
R. Hudson
R. Connecticut
Kingston
0   25   50 miles
CONN.
Ft. Montgomery
Ft. Clinton
Peekskill
New Haven
N.J.
R. Hudson
Clinton
LONG ISLAND
N.Y.
New York

The Saratoga Campaign

• Town
★ Fort
✕ Battle
→ American movement
⇢ British movement

Map 3.3 The Saratoga Campaign

This tactical victory, however, had much greater consequences. Having just lost another 800–900 troops, with the remainder suffering from low morale and supplies, Burgoyne finally ordered a retreat. Ironically, Clinton had just started up the Hudson, capturing Forts Montgomery and Clinton in the Hudson Highlands before hearing of the Battle of Bemis Heights and then turning around. Burgoyne slowly moved his forces north, pestered by militia and followed by Gates' army. Realizing he could not cross the Hudson without exposing his men to attack, he opened negotiations. On October 17, Burgoyne surrendered his entire army.

His defeat was a great strategic victory for the Americans, for it changed the nature of the war. Until October 1777, the conflict was solely between the British and the American colonists: The former sought to repress a rebellion, the latter initially fought for claimed rights as British subjects and for political independence after July 4, 1776. But the Saratoga battles demonstrated that the Americans could defeat and capture a British field army—which caught the attention of King Louis XVI and his ministers. American diplomats in Paris, particularly Ben Franklin, leveraged Burgoyne's surrender to construct a tighter relationship between the United States and France. The two signed a formal treaty of alliance in February 1778, and that June, France declared war on Great Britain (later joined by Spain and the Netherlands). Now the War of the American Revolution was an international conflict, and British ministers had to plan for combat around the globe, not just America. Moreover, the Royal Navy would no longer be unchallenged, as France had the world's largest navy after Britain's. These developments soon produced a new British strategy that, like earlier versions, ultimately failed.

Native Americans in the War

Burgoyne's army was not the only one advancing from Canada in 1777. Barry St. Leger led one up the St. Lawrence to Lake Ontario. After landing on the New York shore, his forces moved east down the Mohawk River valley toward Albany. They sought to divert Patriot forces and assist Burgoyne's advance. Half of St. Leger's 2,000 men were Indians. Like Burgoyne's expedition, this one also failed, but it initiated years of brutal warfare on the New York frontier.

Combat with Indians occurred in many places during the War of the American Revolution. Yet St. Leger's campaign was distinctive for the prominence of warriors in a British operation designed to achieve a larger strategic goal. Most fighting involving Indians occurred between them and white Americans in specific regions, featuring raids and ambushes by one side, followed by the other responding in kind. As with earlier wars between natives and settlers, these entailed fewer restraints on violence with respect to the destruction of crops and resources, and the frequency with which noncombatants were harmed or killed. Control over land and resources drove this warfare more than the political confrontation between America and Great Britain, though the larger war exacerbated regional tensions.

For example, both British and Patriot officials courted the Cherokee early in the war. In 1776, warriors raided American settlements in the southern backcountry and attacked some forts. Later that year, Virginia, Georgia, and both Carolinas sent thousands of militia in multiple columns to invade the Cherokee homelands. Most fled ahead of American forces, who destroyed towns and fields. Thereafter, southern native-settler relations were generally peaceful until about 1779. Encouraged by British operations in the region, chief Dragging Canoe led raids on American settlements. In 1780–81, southern states again dispatched forces to ravage Cherokee towns in what is now Tennessee and Alabama, and hostile Indian groups either fled or made peace.

War had returned to areas farther west even before Lexington and Concord. Dunmore's War (named after Virginia's governor) was a short but violent conflict between the Shawnee and Kentucky settlers in 1774. The Shawnee sued for peace, but the British encouraged them to attack American settlements in 1777. Thereafter, some part of the west was in turmoil for the remainder of the Revolutionary War. George Rogers Clark became famous for leading frontiersmen on a long trek in 1778–79 through the Illinois territory, capturing the ethnically French but British-ruled towns of Kaskaskia and Vincennes. Western hostilities included some atrocities, the most infamous being the massacre of friendly Christian Delaware Indians at the Moravian mission at Gnadenhutten by American soldiers.

In the north, the Six Nations of the Iroquois remained neutral early in the American Revolutionary War. But in 1777, the Cayuga, Seneca, Onondaga, and Mohawk joined the British while the Oneida and Tuscarora allied with the colonists. St. Leger's was the first large British expedition that employed Iroquois warriors. After reaching and beginning a siege of Fort Stanwix in August, they ambushed American militia forces coming to assist the garrison at the Battle of Oriskany. The resulting fight was bloody, and dismayed warriors did not like having to besiege the fort. They soon abandoned St. Leger, who lacked enough forces to continue to Albany.

The following year, groups of Loyalists and Iroquois warriors terrorized frontier settlements. In the summer and fall of 1778, large raids targeted Pennsylvania's Wyoming Valley and the New York towns of German Flats and Cherry Valley. The resulting outcry was so great that in 1779 Washington sent a few thousand Continental troops against Seneca homelands, in what is today western New York State. After winning a battle at Newtown, American troops invaded and devastated Seneca towns and fields. But the Sullivan Expedition (named for commander John Sullivan) did not cow the Iroquois, who continued to raid the Mohawk River valley with Tory allies in 1780.

Figure 3.5 "Joseph Brant (Thayendanegea), 1776"

By George Romney

Thayendanegea, also known as Joseph Brant, was a Mohawk chief. Many Iroquois fought with the British during the American Revolution, hoping to protect traditional homelands. But Thayendanegea journeyed to England to consult with British leaders, and became infamous for leading Indian and Loyalist raids on the New York and Pennsylvania frontiers during 1778–80. After the war, he moved his people to Ontario.

National Gallery of Canada

Native groups were sorely disappointed at war's end. British diplomats took no account of Indian concerns in negotiating the Peace of Paris. While peoples living in western areas still had some time to address the problem of expanding white settlement, the war destroyed the Iroquois Confederacy: Those who had supported the British migrated from their traditional homelands into Canada, whereas allies of the American Patriots stayed but would be pressured to sell their land in years to come.

France's Entry Into the War

Even before 1778, France was helping the Americans. Under the Navigation Acts, Britain had curtailed the development of manufacturing in the colonies, and Louis XIV's government was a source of vital arms and equipment. The French also provided money. The Continental Congress lacked the authority to impose its own taxes, and contributions from individual states fell short. Inflation, driven by weak paper currencies and increasing demand for scarce supplies, became a big problem during the war. France had also allowed American ships to use its ports—whether to pick up supplies, engage in trade, or use as bases for commerce raiding.

But when France committed its own military forces to the war in 1778, it radically changed Britain's strategic calculus. No longer was the goal merely suppressing a colonial rebellion. Great Britain now needed to find more men, arms, and ships to defend regions around the world, including the possibility of a French effort against the English coast. The West Indies, however, posed the most immediate concern, as its sugar and other exports generated great wealth for the British Empire and was an enticing target for French military and naval ventures. While addressing these dangers, London still had to prevail against the American Patriots.

For King George's officials, the answer was the American South, where they believed large numbers of Loyalists resided. The British assumed if they committed troops there, Tories would come out and reestablish royal authority. Moreover, Loyalists would provide manpower for armies to defeat Patriot forces further north, and free redcoats for operations beyond American shores. The British needed time to pursue the new strategy, though. Operations in the American South were limited before 1780, as Britain diverted men and ships to protect the Caribbean. Neither did fighting in the north cease, though for most of the next few years the opposing field armies became effectively stalemated around New York City.

Valley Forge and the Northern Field Armies to 1781

The immediate impact of this strategic shift was the British abandonment of Philadelphia. By June 1778, Henry Clinton replaced William Howe as British Army commander and ordered his men back to New York City. Consolidating his forces, he was expected to provide some for deployment elsewhere, such as the West Indies. For Washington, however, this retreat offered an opportunity that, while misfiring, demonstrated significant changes in his army.

Washington's strategy was to preserve his army and await opportunities to strike the British. The first goal was difficult even without the enemy: The winter of 1777–78 was the infamous one spent at Valley Forge. More than 2,000 Continental soldiers died, and others suffered illness, hunger, and cold. Myriad factors contributed to supply shortages: a chaotic administrative system created by Congress; incompetent supply officers; merchants and farmers who preferred selling to British forces that paid higher prices in hard currency; fraud and corruption; and Loyalists who, emboldened by the British presence in Philadelphia, raided convoys destined for Valley Forge. To address the crisis, Nathanael Greene (one of Washington's most trusted officers) became the army's quartermaster general, while officials scoured New Jersey and New York for supplies and

Washington dispatched foraging expeditions. But Valley Forge was not simply misery. In late winter and spring, Continental officers began a revamped training program. Overseen by recently arrived Prussian officer Friedrich Steuben, it helped improve the Continental Army's facility with conventional tactics, as demonstrated at the Battle of Monmouth Courthouse.

Washington struck Clinton's army on June 28, 1778, as it marched across New Jersey. Possessing slightly larger forces (about 12,000 to 10,000), his plan was apparently to destroy the British rearguard. Washington placed Charles Lee, recently returned from captivity after a prisoner exchange, in charge of the assault force. After initial contact, Lee's forces retreated, and a furious Washington rode up and relieved him of command. For the rest of the day, American troops, utilizing terrain and artillery, beat back British assaults. Having suffered about 360 casualties compared to roughly 500 British, Washington intended to attack again the next day. But Clinton withdrew and continued unimpeded to New York City. Yet despite confusion among their higher command, Continental soldiers and officers fought very well against British regulars throughout a day that included extremely hot temperatures.

Box 3.1   Account of the Battle of Monmouth Courthouse

A teenager at the time, Joseph Plumb Martin became a soldier in 1775 and fought in George Washington's armies for the length of the war. In the following excerpt from his memoir, he describes some of his commander's tactical decisions after the initial retreat of American forces during the Battle of Monmouth Courthouse.

> We had not retreated far before we came to a defile, a muddy, sloughy brook; while the Artillery was passing this place, we sat down by the roadside;- in a few minutes the Commander in Chief and suit[e] crossed the road just where we were sitting . . . . After passing us, he rode on to the plain field and took an observation of the advancing enemy; he remained there some time upon his old English charger, while the shot from the British Artillery were rending up the earth all around him. After he had taken a view of the enemy, he returned and ordered the two Connecticut Brigades to make a stand at a fence, in order to keep the enemy in check while the Artillery and other troops crossed the before-mentioned defile. . . . When we had secured our retreat, the Artillery formed a line of pieces upon a long piece of elevated ground. Our detachment formed directly in front of the Artillery, as a covering party, so far below on the declivity of the hill, that the pieces could play over our heads. And here we waited the approach of the enemy, should he see fit to attack us.
>
> (Joseph Plumb Martin, *A Narrative of a Revolutionary Soldier*, New York: Signet Classics, 2001, pp. 110–111)

Ironically, after Monmouth Courthouse, Washington's field army did not fight another pitched battle for over three years. It occupied positions in the Hudson Highlands and New Jersey while Clinton's army remained based in Manhattan (Morristown became the Continentals' winter camp). Both commanders eyed the other's forces, each refusing to attack the enemy's prepared defenses but watching for opportunities to strike the other. Part of Clinton's caution came from limited prospects for reinforcements and pressures from London to detach men for operations in other theaters. But while major conventional operations ceased, low-intensity fighting continued. For instance, opposing militia units raided and scoured areas between the two field armies, such as Westchester County, New York, which became a "no man's land." Regular forces also embarked on smaller operations. In 1779, British forces seized Stony Point, on the west bank of the Hudson. A few weeks later, a few hundred Continentals commanded by Anthony Wayne recaptured the post in a dramatic nighttime infantry assault.

Shortly after the British returned to New York, a French squadron commanded by Count d'Estaing arrived in nearby waters, the first tangible indication of France's new military alliance with the Americans. Though a great boon for the Patriot cause, coordinating with a coalition partner presented new operational challenges for Washington. Soon after arriving, for example, he and d'Estaing agreed on a campaign to capture Newport, which remained in British hands. When the French fleet arrived in late July, however, the local American commander was still scrounging for troops. By the time he was ready two weeks later, a British squadron had arrived to challenge d'Estaing. Then a hurricane swept through the area, and the French withdrew to Boston to repair their ships. Like the British, the French had interests in multiple regions, and to Washington's frustration d'Estaing soon left to pursue operations farther south.

The Naval War

When the war began, Britain had the world's greatest navy, and the American colonists had none. But this disparity was not as overwhelming as it might appear. The Royal Navy was designed to engage and defeat other European fleets in battles and provide security for shipping lanes. Its best use in the suppression of the American rebellion, however, was not clear, and the British dissipated their naval strength among various priorities. Conversely, though they possessed no navy, Americans had become a vital part of the British Empire as merchants, sailors, and ship builders (roughly one-third of British ships were built in the Americas). Colonial ships produced before and during the war were generally smaller vessels that could patrol coastlines or raid British shipping (the latter called a *guerre de course*). Americans lacked the big warships that could engage in large fleet actions—but the French had them, as did other countries that later joined the war against Britain, such as Spain.

Various American authorities constructed or commissioned warships during the war. In 1775, during the siege of Boston, George Washington gave commissions to New England ship captains to raid British shipping in regional waters (these captains became "privateers"). They took dozens of vessels in subsequent months whose cargoes helped support the American army. Individual colonies, later states, also maintained their own navies, usually for local defense. Pennsylvania's navy, for example, helped defend forts on the Delaware River in 1777. In addition, states also gave commissions to ship captains to raid British commerce.

In late 1775, the Continental Congress began to create its own navy, allocating money to buy preexisting ships, construct 13 new frigates, and establish marine units. It ultimately numbered fewer than 60 smaller vessels that had been purchased, loaned from France, or captured from the British. Perhaps half of the new frigates were completed, as shortages of materials, labor, and funding, as well as a poor purchasing system, plagued ship construction. Continental Navy ships were most successful at commerce raiding, though Congress commissioned many private vessels to also attack British seaborne commerce. Perhaps a few thousand ships served as privateers under authorization of Congress or the states during the war. The most famous American raider was John Paul Jones. In 1778 and 1779, he first prowled British waters in the sloop *Ranger*, and then led a small squadron while in command of the *Bonhomme Richard*, a voyage that culminated in his defeat of the frigate HMS *Serapis*. But numerous American ships raided shipping around the British Isles, the West Indies, and other regions, with estimates of captured vessels ranging into the thousands.

In 1775, the Royal Navy was not what it had been. No new vessels had been built since the Seven Years War, and many existing ones had been poorly maintained. Britain still had scores of warships available but not enough for all its needs. Many supported land operations: In 1776, for example, Royal Navy vessels participated in the relief of Quebec, the aborted assault on Charlestown, and the invasion of New York. Britain also needed warships to escort convoys, prey on American merchant shipping, and maintain a blockade. Allocating perhaps a few dozen vessels at most to patrol the entire Atlantic coastline, the Royal Navy likely stopped a mere fraction of ships going to and from the colonies. The Howe brothers eschewed punitive raids on the American coast, though ships landed troops to destroy American magazines, such as the operation against Danbury, Connecticut, in 1777. Henry Clinton, however, did not oppose punitive expeditions and authorized one in the Chesapeake Bay in 1779, for example.

France's entry into the conflict changed the war at sea. Starting in 1778, Britain had to worry about enemy fleets containing "ships of the line" (the battleships of the sailing era, each possessing at least 74 cannon) threatening its shipping lanes, its colonies, and the English coast itself. Spain and the Netherlands compounded this problem when they joined the war in 1779 and 1780, respectively. The struggling Royal Navy was thus stretched further, though its fleets prevailed in large engagements, such as the Battle of Cape St. Vincent in 1780 and the Battle of the Saints in 1782. But the British did not win every such contest, and one crucial naval defeat set the stage for the battle that finally secured American independence.

The British Southern Campaigns

In late 1778, Clinton dispatched Archibald Campbell with about 3,500 men to Georgia. Landing shortly before Christmas, within a week Campbell captured Savannah. Soon another 2,000 British troops led by Augustine Prevost arrived from Florida. In January 1779, Campbell advanced inland and took Augusta with about 1,000 men, expecting Loyalists would turn out to help occupy the town and secure the countryside. But Patriot militias remained active in the region, cowing local Tories. When British agents recruited a group of a few hundred Loyalists in the Carolina backcountry, partisans ambushed it at the Battle of Kettle Creek in February. The defeat suppressed Loyalist support even further, and unable to muster additional manpower, Campbell abandoned Augusta.

Over the remainder of 1779, British agents raised Loyalist units totaling perhaps 1,000–2,000 Georgians and Carolinians. In the spring, Prevost began and abandoned a campaign to capture Charlestown. In early September, Admiral d'Estaing's fleet arrived off Savannah with 3,500 French and American troops (including some free black volunteers), having spent the past nine months in the Caribbean after the failed Newport venture. His forces began siege operations, digging trenches to approach the fort. But in early October d'Estaing worried he would be found by either a British fleet or a hurricane. Following a failed assault, his forces withdrew.

For most of the year, Henry Clinton had worried about Washington's army and maintaining his troop strength. But at the end of 1779 he initiated a major southern campaign, although he first abandoned Newport so those troops could augment the New York City garrison. In December, Clinton embarked with almost 9,000 men to capture Charlestown. He landed troops nearby in February 1780, building up magazines before advancing toward the city. In March, Royal Navy warships entered the harbor. Charlestown sat on a neck of land formed by two rivers, and by the beginning of April, Clinton's forces had crossed the Ashley River, cutting off land access. For the rest of the month British forces besieged the city. As they dug trenches and slowly moved closer to Charlestown's defenses, both sides exchanged cannon fire. American soldiers raided enemy trenches but failed to impede the British advance. Commander Benjamin Lincoln was outnumbered two to one even after receiving reinforcements of 1,400

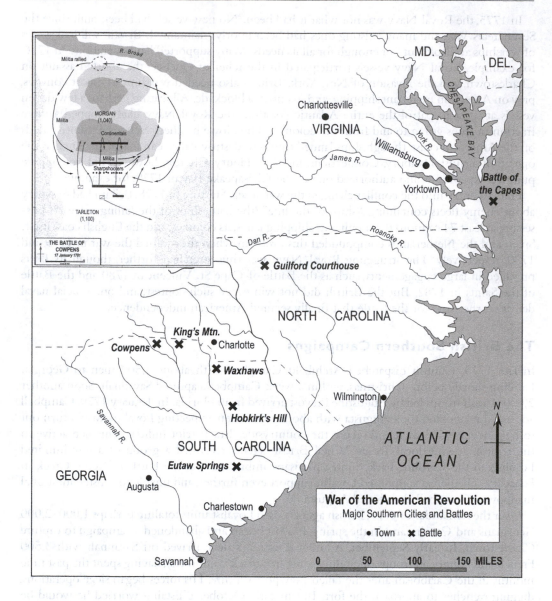

Map 3.4 War of the American Revolution, Major Southern Cities and Battles, With Inset of the Battle of Cowpens

Virginian Continentals. Yet he was apparently torn between pleas to defend Charlestown and abandoning the city to save his men. In the end, the British removed the latter option, and Lincoln surrendered the city and his army on May 11, 1780.

Carolina in Flames

The loss of the south's biggest city and a major port—not to mention an entire field army—was a grave American defeat. But Charlestown was merely the beginning of the campaign. Clinton's men moved inland and established numerous garrisons, expecting Tories to rally, secure the South Carolina countryside, and provide manpower for British forces. Initially the plan worked, as hundreds of Loyalists came out to fight for the King. At the end of May, a Tory cavalry unit led by British officer Banastre Tarleton defeated the one remaining Continental unit in the area at the Battle of Waxhaws. Clinton was so pleased that he returned to New York with many troops in June, leaving Cornwallis with over 6,000 men (including Loyalists) to finish securing South Carolina and then begin operations to the north.

But Clinton's satisfaction was premature, for over the summer more and more men rallied to the Patriot cause. After years of chafing under rebel control, Loyalists now asserted authority. Some were vengeful, arresting enemies and confiscating or destroying their property. Even before the war, tensions had existed between upcountry Carolina farmers and lowland plantation owners: The latter had controlled colonial governments, and many of the former became Patriots in hopes of reducing the political influence of large landholders. Clinton also contributed to political animosities when—having agreed to free Carolina militiamen when he accepted Lincoln's surrender at Charlestown—he then required they first swear oaths to the King. The Battle of Waxhaws also inflamed hatreds: In the midst of the fighting, Continental soldiers tried to surrender (they asked for "quarter"), but Tarleton's Loyalists initially refused. Over 25% of the 300 Continentals were killed (and many more wounded), a very high figure for Revolutionary War battles. Afterward, the phrase "Tarleton's Quarter" came to express the belief that Patriot troops could expect no mercy from their enemies.

As a result of growing Patriot support, the summer of 1780 saw not the consolidation of British rule in South Carolina but the outbreak of civil war in its interior. Patriot and Loyalist groups hunted each other, raided and plundered homes and farmsteads, abused noncombatants, and fought dozens of skirmishes. This guerilla fighting was also very mobile, as combatants were usually mounted. Andrew Pickens, Francis Marion ("the Swamp Fox"), and Thomas Sumter ("the Carolina Gamecock") were the most famous Patriot militia leaders, but there were others. Though they usually fought Loyalist groups, they had a severe impact on British logistics, for they also attacked supply convoys for Cornwallis' garrisons and denuded areas of provisions that could otherwise be foraged by his troops.

Meanwhile, to check British momentum in the south, the Continental Congress turned to the victor of Saratoga, Horatio Gates. By late July, he was leading a few thousand Continentals and militia into South Carolina. Gates hoped to destroy dispersed British units piecemeal, but Cornwallis learned of his approach and concentrated his troops. When the two armies engaged each other at Camden on August 15, American forces actually outnumbered the British. But Gates chose a poor tactical deployment: placing the militia on the left part of his line of battle, directly across the field from redcoats, not the British light infantry and Loyalist units. When the regulars advanced calmly under fire, the American militia panicked and fled. The Continentals on the right (with some North Carolina militia) initially prevailed in their sector only to be overwhelmed after units on their left ran off. Just three months after Charlestown, the British had vanquished another American field army.

In September, Cornwallis advanced into North Carolina. This campaign was supposed to start after securing South Carolina, but Cornwallis thought it would help pacify areas to the south. In his view, North Carolina rebels were providing crucial support for South Carolina Patriots. Leaving most British forces in South Carolina to maintain garrisons and suppress rebel activity, he reached Charlotte with about 2,000 men by month's end. But defeat elsewhere terminated the operation.

Cornwallis had previously dispatched Patrick Ferguson, who recruited about 1,000 men, to raise a force of backcountry Loyalists. But doing so alarmed other colonists, particularly in Tennessee, who felt menaced when Ferguson threatened retribution upon those who would not support the King. Patriots organized an even larger force to hunt down this Loyalist band before it joined with Cornwallis' men. In early October, Ferguson made a stand at King's

Mountain, where his men were surrounded and assaulted. When the Tories asked for mercy, many rebels—remembering Waxhaws—refused. Although more than 300 were killed (including Ferguson) or wounded, most Loyalists were captured. After months of brutal partisan warfare, news of the Battle of King's Mountain chilled Loyalist fervor in the south, and support for the British plummeted. Hearing of this defeat, Cornwallis retreated back to South Carolina.

Nathanael Greene Goes South

To replace Gates, the Continental Congress accepted Washington's recommendation of Nathanael Greene for American commander in the south. Having spent some years as the quartermaster general for the Continental Army, Greene had recently assumed command of the garrison at West Point, New York. By early December, he was at the main American camp at Charlotte, North Carolina. The roughly 1,400 dispirited men there lacked both clothing and prospects for obtaining sufficient supplies.

Greene divided his army. He placed not quite half of his forces under the command of Daniel Morgan and sent them west past the Catawba River; he took the remainder east and south to the Pee Dee River. This choice seemed to fly in the face of conventional wisdom, as he was well outnumbered by Cornwallis' troops and risked having each smaller force defeated separately. But Greene realized that his men could more easily find provisions if they foraged in different areas. He also recognized that operationally, the British were struggling to maintain control of South Carolina. Hence Cornwallis would have to divide his own troops and follow each Patriot army; if not, then whichever American force went unchallenged would harass British outposts and supply lines. Greene also coordinated with partisan leaders, such as Sumter, Marion, and Pickens, to have rebel militia join with and supplement each group.

Greene's plan worked, though it was Morgan who first enjoyed success. Cornwallis did split his forces, sending Banastre Tarleton and about 1,200 men after Morgan while moving north to prevent the two Patriot forces from recombining. Morgan delayed a confrontation, keeping his forces on the move to tire his pursuers and acquire reinforcements. By the time he made his stand on January 16, 1781, his army almost equaled Tarleton's in size. But it was his tactical decisions that produced victory.

Morgan's men confronted Tarleton's at a place called "the Cowpens," used for grazing. A relatively clear area, the ground rose gently to a knoll at its northern end, with a small ridge behind that. Morgan deployed his men into three groups: skirmishers in front of the hill to harass the British as they advanced, a line of militia on the slope, and a line of Continentals toward the top. As Gates had discovered, militia generally did not perform well when placed in a conventional battle line. But Morgan, a former militiaman himself, understood their strengths and weaknesses. He instructed these men to only fire 2–3 volleys, after which they would retreat.

When Tarleton's army arrived, skirmishers fired at its lead elements and fell back. The militia fired their volleys and then retreated around the American left flank. As they did so, Tarleton's cavalry attacked, but Morgan's horsemen, commanded by William Washington, engaged them and beat off the assault. The British infantry continued to advance up the hill, engaging the Continentals. When the American line was in danger of being outflanked, it retreated up beyond the crest of the hill. Assuming Morgan's forces were now fleeing, Tarleton's men raced after them. But the Continentals had reformed beyond the crest, and after firing a volley at close range, charged the British with bayonets. About this same time, both the militia and the cavalry returned to the battle: The militia, having moved all the way around the hill, now attacked Tarleton's left flank while the horsemen attacked the right. The result was a rout. Tarleton escaped with a few hundred men, but most were captured. Not only had Morgan defeated a despised enemy, thereby greatly boosting morale, but he had found a way to success-fully coordinate regular troops with militia in a pitched battle.

Furious, Cornwallis pursued Morgan himself, while Greene combined his two small armies in North Carolina. The opposing forces then engaged in the "Race to the Dan," as the British struggled to catch up to the retreating Americans after the Battle of Cowpens. Greene led them over hundreds of miles of hilly, forested country with poor roads, and across swollen, chilly rivers. At one point, Cornwallis ordered his men to burn all unnecessary baggage and equip-ment, and he put them on whatever mounts he could find. A few times he almost caught his quarry, but by February 15, 1781, all Greene's forces had crossed the Dan River into Virginia. The British were exhausted, and had lost 10% of their men during the trek. Far from his supply bases in South Carolina, and realizing he could not force Greene to give battle, Cornwallis retreated back to Hillsborough, North Carolina.

But Greene was not finished. He now sent forces back into North Carolina to harass the British. Again, Cornwallis came out after Greene, who confronted him at Guilford Courthouse. The British force of almost 2,000 was still worn out from its recent marches. Greene's men were also tired, but had received reinforcements of both Continentals and militia, and by March 15, 1781, outnumbered Cornwallis' forces two to one. That day Greene tried to repeat Morgan's tactical success at Cowpens, using skirmishers, a line of militia, and behind that a line of Continentals. But most of the militiamen, after firing some initial volleys and retiring, never returned to the battle. The fight became a tough slog between regulars, and in the end Greene's men retreated.

Though a tactical loss for the Americans, they reaped the operational and strategic benefits from the Battle of Guilford Courthouse. Cornwallis' smaller force had taken higher casualties. His army spent, he moved it to Wilmington, North Carolina, where it could rest and obtain supplies by sea. Greene moved back into South Carolina, recognizing that if Cornwallis' troops did not follow, he would have the initiative. Thousands of British troops remained in that state, but they were dispersed in multiple, scattered garrisons with tenuous supply lines. Greene had about 1,400 Continentals and knew his numbers would be supplemented by partisan bands, while Loyalist support for the British had all but evaporated.

For the rest of 1781, Patriot forces isolated and harassed enemy posts in South Carolina's interior. Some surrendered after brief sieges, and others were abandoned by the British. Greene himself commanded troops in two more battles, Hobkirk's Hill and Eutaw Springs, and lost both. But by autumn, the British presence in South Carolina and Georgia had been reduced to garrisons in Charlestown and Savannah. Though he never won a field engagement, Greene's operations thwarted the British strategy of gaining control of the southern states. Part of that failure, however, lay with Cornwallis and Clinton, who now contributed to Britain's ultimate defeat in the war.

Yorktown: The Final Campaign, 1781

Instead of following Greene, Cornwallis went north to Virginia. During the war, this state had seen limited bloodshed, though violence had increased in recent years. In May 1779, a British fleet had raided around Chesapeake Bay, plundering and wreaking destruction. In the fall of 1780, about 2,000 British troops under Alexander Leslie arrived with a similar mission, hoping it would help British efforts in the Carolinas. Leslie and his men soon left to join Cornwallis, but were replaced in January 1781 with another force commanded by now–American-traitor and British general Benedict Arnold.

Having failed to pacify the Carolinas, Cornwallis now believed that only operations in Virginia could produce an eventual British victory in the American South. Arriving in late

May 1781 and taking command of British troops already there, for the next few weeks his forces raided and plundered southeastern Virginia. In early June, Governor Thomas Jefferson barely escaped Banastre Tarleton's troops as they dashed into Charlottesville, the seat of the state's government. American forces led by Friedrich Steuben and the Marquis de Lafayette, outnumbered and outmaneuvered by rapid British movements, caused Cornwallis little distress.

Cornwallis' Virginia campaign reflected his frustrations with British strategy. He had too few men to occupy and stabilize the Carolinas and had failed to understand the problems posed by local political conditions. But moving his theater of operations north further undermined the strategy, as he effectively abandoned British and Loyalist forces to the south. His superior, Henry Clinton, compounded these mistakes. Historians have struggled to find a consistent logic or rationale behind his decisions. In 1781, Clinton vacillated between confronting Washington around New York and pursuing operations in Pennsylvania, and his letters to Cornwallis contained confusing instructions. One ordered Cornwallis to move his army to a coastal location on the Chesapeake and establish a naval base to both facilitate the departure of his troops and assist the Royal Navy. In August, an exasperated Cornwallis complied with this directive, occupying Yorktown on the peninsula between the York and James Rivers.

Meanwhile, Washington had struggled to preserve his army. Recent winters at Morristown had been just as debilitating as that at Valley Forge. Acknowledging its failings, the Continental Congress tried to have individual states take more responsibility for maintaining the units they recruited, which failed to help. In early 1781, circumstances were so bad that some Continental soldiers mutinied over delayed pay and because they thought they would be discharged after three years' service (Congress had specified three years or the duration of the war). A combination of negotiation and harsh reprisals resolved these crises, which occurred just months after the betrayal of Benedict Arnold. Commanding at West Point, New York, in 1780, he had tried to sell plans of its fortifications to the British. When the officer carrying them was captured, Arnold fled and entered the King's service. One ray of hope was the arrival in July 1780 of a new French fleet commanded by the Comte de Rochambeau, with about 6,000 soldiers. He established a base at Newport, Rhode Island, and agreed to serve under Washington's command.

Though Washington's priority remained New York City, in early 1781 he sent some reinforcements to the Chesapeake—which were turned back by a British naval squadron. That summer, Rochambeau's troops marched to join the Continentals outside White Plains, New York. While Washington prepared to attack New York City, word arrived that the Comte de Grasse, commanding France's Caribbean fleet and 3,000 soldiers, was sailing to Virginia and would remain there until mid-October. With 29 ships of the line, it could challenge British naval supremacy in North American waters. But Washington had to act quickly to exploit the opportunity, as his army was hundreds of miles away. His men first marched north to cross the Hudson and then down into New Jersey, a route designed to make Clinton think they might attack Manhattan. Instead, they marched south across New Jersey and sailed down Chesapeake Bay. At the end of September, Washington had 17,000–18,000 French and American troops around Williamsburg, west of Yorktown, and had trapped Cornwallis' men on the peninsula.

By then, the French had won the greatest naval victory of the war. De Grasse's fleet arrived off the mouth of Chesapeake Bay in late August. The British squadron that discovered it had only 19 ships of the line. Not only did de Grasse's warships prevail at the Battle of the Virginia Capes in early September but during the fight other French vessels from Newport sailed into the Chesapeake, bringing equipment and supplies to Washington's army and naval reinforcements for de Grasse. The British fleet sailed back to New York, leaving Cornwallis cut off from any support.

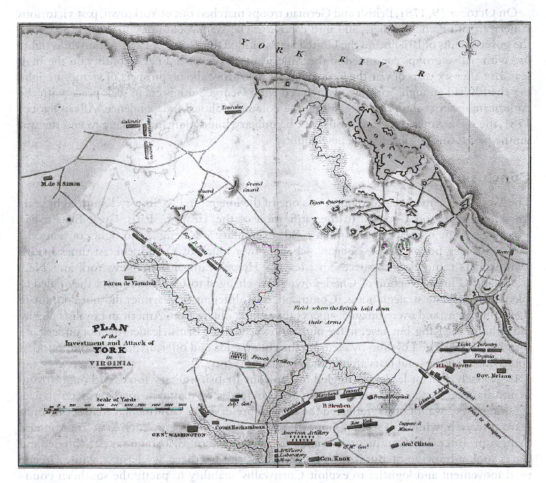

Figure 3.6 "Plan of the Investment and Attack of York in Virginia"

In *The Life of George Washington* (Philadelphia, 1804–07)

A nineteenth-century illustration of the siege of Yorktown.

The Lionel Pincus and Princess Firyal Map Division, The New York Public Library, Astor, Lenox and Tilden Foundations

Why Cornwallis did not take more steps to save his army is a mystery. He had known about the presence of the French fleet for weeks, could see the concentration of American and French forces on the peninsula, and had been urged by his subordinates to act. Whatever the reason, Cornwallis did not block Washington's efforts to besiege his army but had his troops prepare defenses, digging a trench line around the town that included artillery batteries and redoubts (small forts). Additional redoubts and strongpoints were built beyond the main line.

Washington, for the first time in the war, fought from a position of strength. His opponent was surrounded and outnumbered (Cornwallis' army had about 8,000–9,000 men). Moreover, his French allies were arguably the best practitioners of conventional European siege warfare. Troops began digging trenches on the evening of October 6, steadily progressing toward the enemy line. The British responded with artillery fire, but the French and Americans pummeled the defenses after moving their own cannons in range. On the night of October 14, the French and American soldiers captured two British redoubts. Cornwallis lost his will to fight, and asked for surrender terms.

On October 19, 1781, British and German troops marched out of Yorktown, past victorious American and French soldiers, and into captivity. The war would not end until 1783, when the governments of Britain and the United States ratified the Treaty of Paris. Meanwhile, fighting with native groups continued in the American interior, as did naval conflict on the high seas. But after six years of war, the loss of another field army, and no prospect of victory in sight, the British had enough. Yorktown convinced King George's ministers to seek peace with the Americans, even at the price of granting the colonies political independence. After October 1781, the main American effort would not be military, but diplomatic, seeking to end the war on the best terms possible for the new country.

Conclusion

The War of the American Revolution was one of the longest in U.S. history, lasting eight years from Lexington and Concord to the ratification of the Treaty of Paris. Great Britain had advantages in men, weapons, and money. But its military was designed to fight conventional Western forces, not a "people in arms" rebelling over much of a continent. At times British commanders came close to success, particularly Howe's campaign in New York and New Jersey, and Clinton's capture of Charlestown (later changed to Charleston). But they failed to adequately execute strategic ideas. Commanders of different field armies did not coordinate their campaigns, and overestimated support they could obtain from American Loyalists. Tories did fight for the King, but never in the numbers expected, for British leaders did not understand they had to cultivate Loyalism by securing the countryside and offering political solutions that could quell tensions and fears among the population.

Conversely, Patriot leaders struggled to confront British military force. Although strong in militia, they recognized the need for regular forces to maintain long-term resistance. Washington's "war of posts" reflected the need to preserve the Continental Army as he built it from scratch, while still seeking opportunities to hurt the enemy such as at Trenton and Princeton. But other Continental commanders also acted on British mistakes: Schuyler and Gates took advantage of Burgoyne's ignorance of the northern wilderness, while Greene used movement and logistics to exploit Cornwallis' inability to pacify the southern countryside. The War of the American Revolution, though, was not just about Americans. The legacy of the Saratoga campaign was France's entry into the conflict, which fundamentally changed the war. Thereafter the British had to fight around the world and had to change strategy in America to conserve manpower. Washington's victory at Yorktown, following the frustration of the southern campaigns, marked the clear failure of that policy and drove Britain to seek peace.

Short Bibliography

Dowd, Gregory Evans. *War under Heaven: Pontiac, the Indian Nations, and the British Empire.* Baltimore: Johns Hopkins University Press, 2002.

Ferling, John. *Almost a Miracle: The American Victory in the War of Independence.* New York: Oxford University Press, 2007.

Fischer, David Hackett. *Washington's Crossing.* New York: Oxford University Press, 2004.

Gross, Robert A. *The Minutemen and Their World.* New York: Hill and Wang, 1976.

Gruber, Ira D. *The Howe Brothers and the American Revolution.* New York: Atheneum, 1972.

Ketchum, Richard M. *Saratoga: The Turning Point of America's Revolutionary War.* New York: Henry Holt, 1997.

Kwasny, Mark V. *Washington's Partisan War, 1775–1783.* Kent, OH: Kent State University Press, 1998.

Mayer, Holly A. *Belonging to the Army: Camp Followers and Community during the American Revolution.* Columbia: University of South Carolina Press, 1996.

Pancake, John S. *This Destructive War: The British Campaign in the Carolinas, 1780–1782*. Tuscaloosa, AL: University of Alabama Press, 1985.

Piecuch, Jim. *Three Peoples, One King: Loyalists, Indians, and Slaves in the American Revolutionary South, 1775–1782*. Columbia: University of South Carolina Press, 2008.

Shy, John. *A People Numerous and Armed: Reflections on the Military Struggle for American Independence*. Rev. ed. Ann Arbor: University of Michigan Press, 1990.

Taylor, Alan. *The Divided Ground: Indians, Settlers, and the Northern Borderland of the American Revolution*. New York: Random House, 2006.

Wood, Gordon S. *The American Revolution: A History*. New York: The Modern Library, 2002.

1783	1786	1788	1790–95	1794	1798–1800
Newburgh Conspiracy	Shays' Rebellion	U.S. Constitution ratified	War in the Northwest Territory	Whiskey Rebellion	Quasi-War

TIMELINE

Chapter 4

Challenges in the Early Republic, 1783–1815

The United States faced a host of challenges in the generation after winning its independence. These included internal revolts, hostilities with Indians, conflict on the high seas, and one large conventional war. But political differences hampered the establishment of military institutions. Many Americans remembered how redcoats had enforced repressive British policies before the War of the American Revolution and opposed creating standing forces. Others recalled the Continental Congress' difficulties maintaining a regular army and the wartime shortcomings of militia. The U.S. Constitution embodied a compromise between these views, acknowledging a role for both state-maintained militias as well as standing armies and navies.

It would fall to the U.S. Congress and the president, though, to create and maintain such forces. Early efforts suffered from political suspicions between those who favored strong national government and those who feared it. But by the early nineteenth century, American political leaders had worked out another compromise: The country would maintain a small regular army and navy to confront limited threats, and would supplement them with militia and armed merchant vessels in case of a larger war. With this system, the United States successfully addressed a variety of threats in the 20 years after the Constitution was ratified. But over time, problems generated by the French Revolutionary Wars increased tensions between the United States and Great Britain. By June 1812, they were once again at war, one that would demonstrate the weaknesses of America's military institutions.

In this chapter, students will learn about:

- How political differences shaped the development of U.S. military institutions.
- How the U.S. Constitution addresses armed forces.
- Indian wars in the Old Northwest and the Old Southwest.
- The impact of the French Revolutionary Wars on the United States.
- America's early naval wars.
- U.S. military performance in the War of 1812.

1801–05	1812–15	January 1815
Tripolitan War	War of 1812	Battle of New Orleans

Challenges at the End of the Revolutionary War

The Second Continental Congress had no authority to govern in its own right but served as a forum where representatives of individual colonies, later states, could interact and establish common policies. Following the Declaration of Independence of July 4, 1776, efforts to create America's first national government produced the Articles of Confederation. Although agreed to by the Congress in 1777, disputes delayed its ratification by the individual states until 1781. The Articles of Confederation created a government that had little more authority than the Second Continental Congress and explicitly placed political sovereignty in the individual states. This central government consisted solely of a legislature, called "the United States in Congress assembled," or simply, the Confederation Congress.

The Articles gave the Confederation Congress the right to declare war and make treaties but not to impose taxes or raise armed forces on its own authority. Standing military units in peacetime were also prohibited, except for men needed to garrison forts or crew ships for coastal defense. Yet the individual states were required to "always keep up a well-regulated and disciplined militia, sufficiently armed and accoutered." The Articles thus reflected a bias against regular forces that stemmed from such events as the Boston Massacre. Although Americans had accepted the need for the Continental Army during the war, many rejected the idea of maintaining such a force in peacetime. For them, state militias were adequate to meet the country's military needs.

Developments at the end of the War of the American Revolution heightened fears of standing forces. In spring 1783, Henry Knox, Washington's chief of artillery, helped create the Society of the Cincinnati, a fraternal organization of Continental Army officers. But membership could be passed to sons and succeeding generations, and critics saw it as an interest group that would push for a stronger national government and a peacetime army. At about the same time, some Continental troops mutinied. The end of the war had been announced, and soldiers expected to receive back pay and be discharged. But Congress did not want to disband the army before a signed copy of the Treaty of Paris arrived. Some Pennsylvania troops marched to Philadelphia to confront Congress, whose members left and reconvened in New Jersey.

The most disturbing incident, however, was an event called "the Newburgh Conspiracy." In 1780, Congress had promised Continental officers an annual pension of half their pay when the war ended. But it had taken no action by 1782 and army officers, concerned about returning to civilian life and the sacrifices endured by themselves and their families, worried that Congress would not keep its pledge. In late December, some officers from the army's camp at Newburgh, New York, arrived in Philadelphia. They proposed that the half-pay pension be "commuted" to annual payments equivalent to their full salaries but for only five years. The officers also hinted that tensions within the army were high enough that failure to act might provoke violence. Congress deferred making any decision, partly because of its poor finances. The continued delay disturbed army officers but also frustrated a group of Congressional delegates and government officials. They hoped to use the commutation issue as a means to induce Congress to adopt a more robust financial system (such as passing an amendment to the Articles

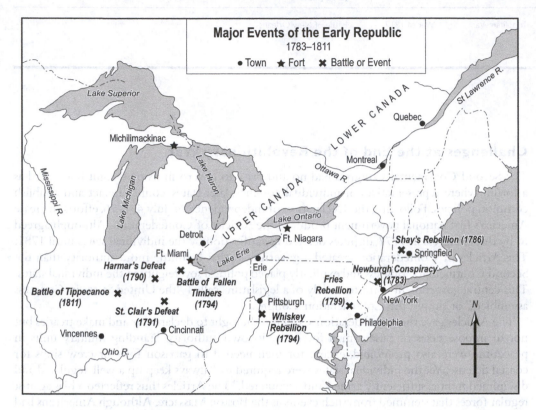

Map 4.1 Major Events of the Early Republic, 1783–1811

of Confederation that would give it the ability to impose taxes) and strengthen the national government.

In February 1783, correspondence with officers in Newburgh implied that if the Army acted in a threatening manner, it might scare Congress into accepting commutation of officers' half-pay. An outright overthrow of the government was apparently not contemplated. Whatever the specific details, in March anonymous notices circulated through the Continental Army camp, sometimes called "the Newburgh Addresses." These called for officers to meet and discuss their grievances and played upon their fears of destitution and abandonment by civilian leaders after years of hardship and sacrifice. More ominously, the Addresses suggested the army should refuse to disband after the war, or perhaps abandon the United States, if Congress did not meet officers' demands.

George Washington was aghast. He sympathized with his officers but firmly believed in civilian control of the military. Such threats as advocated by the Newburgh Addresses would weaken the authority of the Confederation Congress and its capacity to safeguard the political rights Americans had fought for in the Revolutionary War. Washington quickly convened a meeting of the army's officers. Confronting the Addresses and the gravity of what they suggested, he assured them Congress would meet its obligations and reminded the men of the army's accomplishments and their common shared sacrifices. Washington's speech worked: His men adored their commander, and some wept. The officers rejected any ideas of confronting Congress—which not long thereafter agreed to commutation.

The Nationalists

The Newburgh Conspiracy reflected prolonged frustration with the weakness of the Second Continental and Confederation Congresses. For example, failures to support the Continental Army had appalled military officers and civilian officials. By the end of the war, the national currency—the Continental dollar—was all but worthless, and the Congress could not impose taxes to shore it up (or pay its war debt or other expenses). With the return of peace in 1783, Great Britain did not open its markets to American exporters, provoking a severe economic depression. When individual states established their own tariffs, British merchants simply shipped to those with the lowest customs rates—Congress was powerless to intervene (it could not impose one national tariff). Many American officials, wary of the problems using state-organized militia units during the Revolutionary War, wanted the national government to control the organization and training of U.S. armed forces.

The men who wanted a stronger national government were known as "nationalists." The Newburgh Conspiracy was a dangerous and reckless effort by a few to manipulate the anxieties of army officers and scare the Confederation Congress into adopting reforms. But most sought change in a more reasonable and cooperative manner, such as George Washington. In the spring of 1783, Alexander Hamilton, previously an aide to Washington and now a member of Congress, asked the general for his thoughts on a peacetime military for the United States. Washington, though he wanted to maintain regular troops, recognized popular apprehension toward them and preference for militia. In a letter entitled "Sentiments on a Peace Establishment," he outlined a program that encompassed both.

Washington's plan recommended a standing force of about 2,600 men to garrison frontier outposts, confront hostile Indian groups, and guard against possible incursions from Canada and Florida (the latter returned to Spanish control in 1783). He also advocated a "well-regulated militia" to provide manpower in case of major emergencies but proposed an innovation. While all males ages 18 to 50 would be liable for militia service, younger men with "a natural fondness for Military parade" could be formed into a "Continental militia" that would receive more training, be subject to national (rather than state) standards, and be the first men called up in a crisis. Washington also called for building a series of arsenals and magazines (supply depots), as well as a military academy. "Sentiments on a Peace Establishment" balanced the need for regular troops and national control of military units against popular political suspicions of standing armies and preferred reliance on militia. Regular units would be limited and mostly relegated to the frontiers. Militia would provide the bulk of the country's manpower for a major war, but national authorities would set training and preparedness benchmarks for men who would serve as an initial reserve force.

Members of the Confederation Congress rejected the proposal, concerned they did not have the authority to raise troops in peacetime. (In the early twentieth century, the United States adopted a system that greatly resembled Washington's, with National Guard units fulfilling the role of his Continental militia.) But most Congressmen realized armed force was needed on the western frontiers, and not just because of possible invasions or Indian wars. The Confederation Congress could not impose its own taxes—but it could raise revenue by selling rights to western lands. Doing so required promoting settlement, which in turn required policing and guarding these territories. Yet Congressmen remained vexed over whether they could raise troops. On June 2, 1784, they disbanded the few Continental units left over from the Revolutionary War, excepting about 80 soldiers to garrison West Point and Fort Pitt. The next day, Congress "recommended" to four states that they provide militiamen to serve in a 700-man unit for service in the Northwestern territories.

This act created the First American Regiment, the first peacetime U.S. military unit. Individual states raised men who reported to both national and state officials to serve for one year. In 1785, Congress required replacements to serve three-year enlistments, giving it a more "regular" character. The First Regiment was nonetheless undermanned, undersupplied, and suffered from poor morale and discipline. Troops escorted diplomatic missions to Indian nations and built forts (mostly on the Ohio River). But they were too few to staunch escalating violence between settlers and native groups in the Old Northwest.

Whereas the Newburgh Conspiracy had alarmed Americans wary of strong national government, nationalists became greatly disturbed by Shays' Rebellion in western Massachusetts. For years, farmers there had suffered from heavy debt loads and high taxes, exacerbated by national depression. Whereas other states passed relief measures, Massachusetts had not. In the summer of 1786, mounting frustration exploded and mobs prevented local courts (which adjudicated debt cases) and governments from operating. Massachusetts militiamen from the eastern part of the state dispersed crowds and put down the revolt. Congress authorized creating units to address the crisis but failed to recruit men in time. What was particularly galling was that Massachusetts troops had to defend the national arsenal at Springfield, Massachusetts. Moreover, although militiamen put down the rebellion, numerous rebels were also members of the state militia. The inability of Congress to confront domestic insurrection spurred nationalists to establish a new, stronger government for the United States.

The Military Provisions of the U.S. Constitution

Delegates to the Constitutional Convention of 1787, while seeking a stronger national government, were sensitive to fears of creating a repressive regime. They thus devised a system of checks and balances that shared power between the individual states and the national—or federal—government, and among the different branches of the latter. These safeguards are evident in the Constitution's treatment of armed forces.

Under the Constitution, only Congress can declare war, though the president can use force without such a declaration. It splits authority over standing forces between branches of the federal government. The President is the Commander-in-Chief of the Army and Navy, but only Congress has the authority to "raise and support" armies and to "provide and maintain" a navy. Armies can only be funded for two years or less. Forcing the executive branch to solicit Congress for money every two years helps the legislative branch oversee the use of regular troops. The Constitution also empowers Congress to enact laws to regulate and administer military forces, and only the legislature can issue letters of marque (authorizing private ship captains to use force on behalf of the United States—making them privateers).

Regarding the militia, the Constitution splits authority between the states and national government, and between different federal branches. The President is the Commander-in-Chief of "the militia of the several states, when called into actual service of the United States." When not in such service, militias remain under the control of their states. Moreover, the Constitution grants Congress the ability to determine when state militias will enter into federal service, and only for particular reasons: "[T]o execute the laws of the Union, suppress insurrections and repel invasions." Congress is also authorized to "provide for organizing, arming, and disciplining the militia," and enact laws to "govern" them when in federal service. But under the Constitution, states appoint officers and have the responsibility for training militia forces according to federal laws.

In its treatment of both regular and militia forces, the Constitution formalized what scholars such as Allan R. Millett and Peter Maslowski call "a dual-army tradition." It specifically recognizes that both the federal government and the individual states can raise and maintain military forces. (Today—similar to ideas expressed in Washington's "Sentiments"—individual states maintain their own National Guard forces while the federal government funds and sets standards for these units). Dividing authority between the executive and legislative branches helped ensure national armies posed no threat to the states. The Constitution gave the federal government a right to employ state forces, but only within certain circumstances, and its capacity to oversee militias was balanced by state control over personnel and training.

These protections satisfied many that the national government would not acquire excessive power. But some politicians remained unconvinced. Those who favored ratifying the Constitution became known as "Federalists," and those who opposed it, "anti-Federalists." The former prevailed and agreed to 10 constitutional amendments that explicitly guaranteed personal liberties. Known collectively as the "Bill of Rights," two amendments touched on military issues. The Third Amendment forbade quartering soldiers in civilians' homes without homeowner approval in peacetime; during war, any such quartering had to be done "in a manner prescribed by law." The Amendment reflected widespread outrage over the practice before the Revolutionary War. The federal government has long since built housing for its troops, hence today the amendment is of only historical interest. But the Second Amendment still receives much attention. In contemporary debates about gun control, people defending gun ownership cite it to oppose limitations on weapons possession. Yet in its entirety, the Second Amendment states: "A well-regulated Militia, being necessary to the security of a free State, the right of the people to keep and bear Arms, shall not be infringed." Thus the Second Amendment explicitly tied the individual's right to bear arms to militia service, a civic obligation whereby able-bodied men shared responsibility for protecting their states and communities.

In 1788, enough states ratified the Constitution—nine of 13—to bring it into force. National elections were held late in the year, and in 1789 the United States installed its first government under the new regime, with George Washington serving as president. Convening in New York, the new U.S. Congress needed to create departments for the executive branch such as the War Department, and had to draft and pass the amendments that would become the Bill of Rights. The latter was ratified in 1791, by which time the Washington administration had become embroiled in an Indian war.

War in the Northwest Territory, 1790–95

Warfare between settlers and Indians had occurred since Europeans first established colonies in America. By the late eighteenth century, such hostilities engulfed the Trans-Appalachian region (west of the Appalachian Mountains). These began with native attacks against Pennsylvania and Virginia in the French and Indian War, and continued with events such as Pontiac's Rebellion, Dunmore's War, and the American Revolutionary War. George Rogers Clark led one of the most famous American campaigns in the latter, but British and native forces pursued their own operations, winning some victories such as the Battle of Blue Licks in 1782.

The 1783 Treaty of Paris ceded to American control the area north of the Ohio River to the Great Lakes, between Pennsylvania and the Mississippi River—then known as the Northwest Territory (today the Old Northwest). But the treaty was between the United States and Great Britain. The Confederation Congress sent emissaries to negotiate peace with regional Indians, but some refused. Recognizing a need for a military force on the frontier, it created and dispatched the First American Regiment to the area in 1784, but its few hundred men were not enough to maintain order. Hostilities escalated, with reprisals between Kentucky settlers (sometime called "Long Knives" by native peoples) and the Miami and Shawnee becoming particularly severe.

By 1790, the Washington administration was compelled to act. After some fumbled attempts at diplomacy, the commander of the First American Regiment (now renamed the Regiment of Infantry), Josiah Harmar, led troops to punish the region's Indians, called "Harmar's expedition." In October, his 300 regulars and 1,200 militiamen from Kentucky and Pennsylvania marched north from Fort Washington (today, Cincinnati, Ohio). Reaching the Maumee River, his men destroyed abandoned Miami towns and crops. They were returning, concerned about the onset of winter, when Harmar ordered an attack on a nearby Shawnee town. His men fell into a trap, with warriors luring militia forces away and then massing against the isolated regular troops. Afterward, Harmar's forces quickly retreated back to Fort Washington.

The expedition's poor performance fueled criticism of Washington's administration. The President and his Secretary of War, Henry Knox, blamed militia troops, which had broken when confronted with serious combat. Kentucky and Pennsylvania authorities also apparently allowed militiamen to provide substitutes. Reports described many of them as old men or boys with minimal or no military training, and their officers little better. Washington and Knox hoped to avoid using militia for the next, larger campaign. Congressmen were wary of its cost and the prospect of exacerbating conflict, but with new reports of Indian attacks in the Northwest, they agreed. Federal authorities raised a force of 3,000 men, including a new regiment of regular infantry and about 2,000 "levies" who enlisted for only six months.

Box 4.1   Lyrics to "St. Clair's Defeat," a.k.a. "Sinclair's Defeat"

Throughout American history, battles and campaigns have been memorialized in song. Below are the first two stanzas to a ballad erroneously entitled "Sinclair's Defeat," published in 1836, as it narrates St. Clair's defeat of 1791. For the full lyrics, and a link to a modern rendition of the song, see the companion website to this textbook at www. routledge. com/cw/muehlbauer.

November the fourth in the year of ninety-one
We had a sore engagement near to Fort Jefferson
Sinclair was our commander, which may remembered be,
For there we left nine hundred men in the Western Territory.

At Bunker's Hill and Quebec, where many a hero fell
Likewise at Long Island, 'tis I the truth can tell.
But such a dreadful carnage, never did I see,
As happened on the plains, near the River St. Marie.

(*United States Songster,*
Cincinnati: U. P. James, 1836, p. 123)

Though Washington wanted to avoid militia for the main 1791 campaign, he approved of it for other operations. He asked Congress to help fund raids by mounted Kentucky frontiersmen against Indian communities. In the event, the main field army included militia, for by August only a few hundred federal troops had reached Fort Washington. Led by Arthur St. Clair—governor of the Northwest Territory and a Revolutionary War veteran—this force marched into the Ohio country in October 1791 with 1,400–1,500 regular troops, levies, and militiamen (although many had already deserted or died from disease). However bad the militia may have fought on Harmar's expedition, St. Clair's levies and newly recruited regulars were not much better, having received little or no training. The commander himself was ill when the campaign began (at times carried on a litter). The supply system also broke down, reducing the army's progress to a few miles a day.

The result was a disaster worse than the previous year. Shortly before dawn on November 4, 1791, about 1,000 warriors surprised St. Clair's army encamped near the Wabash River. Chiefs, including Little Turtle of the Miami and Blue Jacket of the Shawnee, led assaults from multiple directions. Many of St. Clair's troops broke and ran; when the battle ended, over 600 soldiers were dead and 250–300 wounded. To this day, the Battle of the Wabash (or St. Clair's defeat) remains one of the worst debacles in U.S. military history and offers a powerful example of what can happen to an ill-trained and poorly led army when confronted by a well prepared foe.

The Legion of the United States

Criticism of the Washington administration now became shrill, as neither diplomacy nor two military campaigns had brought peace to the Northwest. In 1792, it dispatched envoys to treat with native leaders. But Congress also approved funds for a larger army of up to 5,000 regular troops, though it was chronically understrength. The administration offered higher pay to attract better-quality recruits and officers, and appointed Anthony Wayne, one of the highest ranking and experienced Revolutionary War veterans, commander. Washington and Knox adopted a new organization and name for this army: the Legion of the United States, which was divided into four "sub-legions," each with its own components of infantry, cavalry, and artillery that could act independently in combat situations. Moreover, the administration did not rush military preparations, for it recognized that one more defeat could destroy its credibility. Hence, Wayne had ample time to train his men. Washington and Knox also took the opportunity to revamp the administration of the War Department.

By September 1793, negotiations had failed. But historians such as Richard White note the native alliance in the Northwest was starting to fracture. Some peoples, tired of the incessant and brutal raids between them and mounted Kentucky raiders, sought peace. Others could not agree on negotiating terms, with various chiefs refusing to concede land north of the Ohio River to the United States. Though the defeats of Harmar and St. Clair had greatly boosted Indian morale, maintaining the capacity to mass enough warriors to counter U.S. military moves required supplies, and native leaders such as Little Turtle and Blue Jacket sought British assistance. These developments set the context for American victory.

Later that year Wayne marched his army into the Ohio country, but it soon stopped for the winter. His men built Fort Greenville, and then Fort Recovery on the site of St. Clair's defeat. In June 1794, over 1,000 warriors led by Little Turtle and Blue Jacket attacked 250 soldiers defending the latter post but withdrew after two days of attacks. In July, Wayne advanced with 2,000 Legion soldiers and 1,500 volunteer Kentucky militiamen, occupying native villages around the Maumee and Auglaize Rivers. After constructing Fort Defiance, they advanced down the Maumee River. (Unlike St. Clair's, his army took the time to construct fortifications around their camp each night.)

The subsequent engagement is called "the Battle of Fallen Timbers" for the numerous fallen trees around the battlefield from a recent tornado. On August 20, a few hundred warriors and some Canadian militia attacked an advance guard, after which the bulk of the American army drove them from the battlefield. The Indians fled to nearby British Fort Miami but were refused entrance and any assistance. Thereafter, native resistance in the Northwest collapsed. Chiefs no longer trusted British promises and made peace with the United States in the 1795 Treaty of Greenville. They ceded lands in what is now Ohio and Indiana to American control, and for years the region was fairly tranquil.

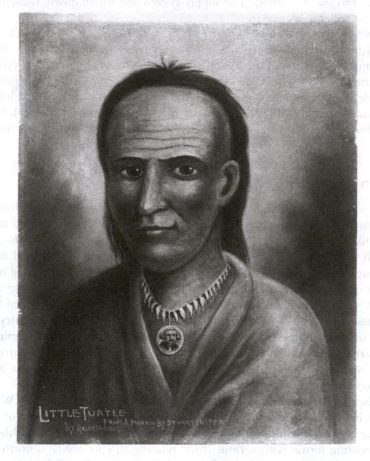

Figure 4.1 "Little Turtle"

An image of a mixed-media painting by Ralph Dille, after a portrait by Gilbert Stuart, 1797.
Chicago Historical Museum

The War in the Northwest Territory resembled earlier conflicts in that American troops sought to destroy native towns and fields to induce hostile Indians to come to terms. But the United States had hastily fielded armies in 1790 and 1791, and better organized and tactically proficient warriors exploited their weaknesses to defeat both Harmar's and St. Clair's expeditions. The Legion of the United States, though, was better trained, and Wayne's 1794 campaign achieved the victory Washington's administration sought. But as historian Richard Kohn observes, the War in the Northwest Territory had a longer-lasting impact on U.S. military policy: It established a peacetime role for the regular U.S. army that was agreeable to the nation's differing political factions. Although Congress formally abolished the Legion of the United States in 1796 and reduced army troop levels to less than 3,000, from that point forward it consistently devoted funds to maintain federal forces on the country's western frontiers. Until the late nineteenth century, the primary role of the U.S. Army was as a frontier constabulary.

The Whiskey Rebellion, 1794

In 1794, Washington's administration also confronted a major rebellion. To help retire preexisting debt and fund the national government, Congress had taxed whiskey production in 1791 as part of a larger program developed by Alexander Hamilton, the Treasury Secretary. The tax was very unpopular in the American backcountry. Protests became particularly intense in western Pennsylvania in the summer of 1794, which became known as the Whiskey Rebellion. After some farmers attacked the home of a tax collector, Washington and his cabinet acted.

Their initial problem was acquiring men to put down the rebellion and restore order. The administration's regular soldiers were then in the Ohio country with Anthony Wayne. Washington decided to use state militiamen, a contingency specified in the Constitution. But initial consultations indicated Pennsylvania officials were very cool to the idea. Realizing that many people felt likewise, Washington changed his approach, sending officials into western Pennsylvania in August to negotiate with the revolt's leaders. Doing so allowed his administration to solicit public support for any actions it might have to take later.

Washington took pains to comply with the law. In accordance with its constitutional prerogative, in 1792 Congress had passed the Calling Forth Act to stipulate how the president could muster state militias into federal service. It allowed him to do so on his own authority in the case of foreign invasions and at the request of state officials in order to suppress insurrection. The Constitution also allowed the president to call up militia to "execute the Laws of the Union," which the Calling Forth Act defined as a situation where normal law enforcement could not proceed due to "combinations too powerful to be suppressed in the ordinary course of judicial proceedings." But in that case, the Act required the president to acquire a judge's certification that the law could not otherwise be enforced. The Washington administration did so, forwarding documents and reports to Supreme Court Justice James Wilson, who granted it the authority to call up militia forces in early August.

Washington took his time. Many rebels in western Pennsylvania would accept a peaceful resolution, but a core of extremists refused. He waited until late September, after his administration had circulated public reports of federal efforts to diffuse the crisis. Washington then called upon Pennsylvania, New Jersey, Virginia, and Maryland to mobilize militia units. The states complied, and militiamen congregated at Carlisle, Pennsylvania, and Cumberland, Maryland. In early October, Washington led the army of 12,000–15,000 men into western Pennsylvania.

They met no resistance. As the army advanced, the rebellion evaporated. A few ringleaders were arrested, but only two were actually tried and convicted of treason (later pardoned). In November, militia units started returning home. As with the Legion of the United States' victory that summer, the suppression of the Whiskey Rebellion had larger implications for U.S. military institutions. It demonstrated that the national government could employ state militias to maintain law and order without threatening personal liberties. Federalists certainly saw the quelling of the revolt in this way, though others were not so sanguine.

The Early Impact of the French Revolution

By 1794, two distinct political groups had emerged in the United States: the Federalists and the Democratic Republicans, or simply Republicans (not to be confused with the current Republican Party that formed in the 1850s). The Federalists were the same group that had produced and promoted adoption of the Constitution. They favored a strong national government and drew support from large landowners, businessmen, and regions such as the American seaboard and eastern areas. Many anti-Federalists who had initially opposed the Constitution later became Democratic Republicans. Preferring a weak central government to stronger local and state ones, they generally came from areas where agriculture dominated economic activity, particularly in southern and western regions. A few people, however, switched views: James Madison, who in 1787–88 wrote essays in support of the Constitution, later became a prominent Republican.

With the adoption of the Constitution and the Bill of Rights, opposing political factions had compromised to create an enduring foundation for the new country and its representative government. But suspicions persisted. Moreover, the concept of a "legitimate opposition"—a political party that opposed government policies but sought to work within a defined constitutional system and not overthrow it—had not yet developed in the late eighteenth-century United States. American leaders, in fact, tended to fear the rise of political parties.

The Washington administration's efforts to construct a government under the Constitution and implement national policies exacerbated preexisting political anxieties. Alexander Hamilton's fiscal program and efforts to raise troops for the Northwest frontier provoked worries that the national government might become too strong and stimulated the formation of the Democratic Republicans. Conversely, strong criticism of the administration's policies intensified Federalist worries of the opposition, and some feared Republicans might seek to overturn the Constitution.

The beginning of the French Revolution in 1789 further exacerbated United States political tensions. Americans of all stripes initially regarded it favorably, as it started with the French working toward building a more equitable representative government. Although war erupted in 1792, it only affected the United States in 1793, after Great Britain joined Austria and Prussia in fighting France. By that year, the French Revolution had also entered its most radical phase. In 1793–94, the Committee of Public Safety, which had come to dominate the new French legislature—the National Convention—executed tens of thousands people in the name of defending the Revolution, a period known as the Reign of Terror. Though the Convention overthrew the Committee and was itself replaced in 1795, France remained at war (with intermittent pauses) until 1815. It would fight different countries at different times, but the one persistent enemy throughout the period was Great Britain.

Their conflict challenged American policymakers. Federalists favored Britain. As it remained the United States' largest trading partner, they felt it was best to maintain a workable Anglo-American relationship. Federalists were also repulsed by France's violent excesses under the Terror. Republicans preferred France. They were drawn to the French Revolution's ideals of "liberty, equality, and fraternity." In addition, the United States and Great Britain disagreed on many issues, and Republicans sought a more pro-French foreign policy to check British influence. For example, British troops continued to occupy forts in territory ceded via the 1783 Treaty of Paris—which had encouraged native resistance in the Northwest. Shippers and southern slave owners still sought compensation from Britain for losses during the Revolution, while the British wanted American Loyalists reimbursed for their lost and confiscated property. U.S. merchants still could not trade with the British West Indies.

In 1793, President Washington declared U.S. neutrality in the war between Great Britain and France. But American trade with the French West Indies irked British officials, and Washington asserted the right of neutrals to trade with any country. In retaliation, the British began capturing ships sailing to French islands and impressing American sailors for service on their vessels. In 1794, Congress passed laws to prepare the United States for a possible war. It authorized fortifications to protect American harbors and formed units of engineers and artillerymen to construct and garrison them. In addition to its frontier duties, building and manning harbor defenses now also became an accepted role for the peacetime U.S. Army. Congress also passed the Naval Act of 1794, addressed below.

In that same year Washington dispatched U.S. Supreme Court Chief Justice John Jay to Britain. He successfully negotiated a compromise known as Jay's Treaty. Taking effect in 1796, it averted war between the United States and Great Britain but sparked a political firestorm in America. The British evacuated illegally occupied forts, compensated American shippers for losses sustained in the current war between Britain and France, and allowed U.S. merchants access to the British West Indies and India. But Great Britain received "most-favored nation" status for its ships trading in American ports. The treaty also required the United States to retract its insistence on neutrals' rights to trade anywhere in time of war, effectively barring Americans from commerce with the French West Indies. Jay's Treaty failed to address impressment or compensation for American slave owners (or losses of American Loyalists).

Republicans hated the treaty. To them, the United States had buckled to Britain, and sacrificed the interests of landowners (particularly southern Republicans) to merchants and traders (especially those in the Federalist north and east). Washington had succeeded in maintaining peace with Great Britain. But French officials were also furious at news of Jay's Treaty—which helped precipitate an undeclared war with the United States.

The Quasi-War With France, 1798–1800

A new French regime came to power in 1795, and a committee known as "the Directory" held executive power. It saw Jay's Treaty as the start of an Anglo–American alliance. After John Adams, a Federalist, won the 1796 U.S. presidential election, France retaliated. French vessels raided American shipping, ultimately capturing hundreds of ships with cargoes worth millions of dollars. In 1797 John Adams dispatched a delegation to negotiate a solution and diffuse escalating tensions. The American envoys were rebuffed and insulted: Three subordinates to the French foreign minister demanded a personal bribe for him and a U.S. loan to France of $12 million before opening negotiations. When the Adams administration reported the incident in early 1798, it became known as the XYZ Affair (with the three French officials identified by those letters). Infuriated, Americans rallied behind the Federalists. Adams did not request a declaration of war, but in May 1798 Congress proclaimed U.S. "public vessels" could capture armed French ships off the American coast, and later anywhere on the high seas.

What became known as the Quasi-War was an undeclared, low-intensity naval war between the United States and France. American vessels mostly raided French shipping in and around the Caribbean Sea, though some ships protected merchant convoys. Most engagements pitted armed merchantmen against French privateers, though the U.S. Navy grew to about 30 warships and 5,000 sailors, and a few battles occurred between warships. By the end of the conflict, American vessels had captured dozens of French ones. In this regard, the U.S. commerce-raiding strategy (also known as *guerre de course*) succeeded, for French attacks on American shipping decreased. But France was simultaneously fighting the Royal Navy, the world's largest. While Anglo–American naval cooperation was limited, the British helped protect U.S. merchant shipping.

During the Quasi-War, Congress appropriated money to purchase ships, authorized privateering attacks on French shipping, and agreed to finish building all six frigates authorized by the 1794 Naval Act. Prior to that law, the United States did not possess any warships, having long disposed of any left from the American Revolution. Although tensions were rising with Britain in 1794, the frigates were actually meant to combat corsairs from Algeria, one of the Barbary states of Northwest Africa. These pirates were exploiting the French Revolutionary War to prey on merchantmen around the Mediterranean, as Europe's navies were too busy fighting each other to patrol sea lanes. But negotiations produced the 1796 Treaty of Tripoli, whereby the Barbary states agreed to stop attacking U.S. shipping in return for annual payments.

The Washington administration, though, had convinced Congress to continue work on three of the frigates. These—the USS *United States*, *Constellation*, and *Constitution*—were completed in 1797, and with other measures taken during the Quasi-War, became the foundation for a permanent U.S. Navy. In addition to building the remaining frigates specified in the Naval Act, in 1798 Congress created the Marine Corps and the Department of the Navy. Marines for shipboard security had been organized during the Revolutionary War but disbanded afterward. The War and Treasury Departments had handled responsibility for naval affairs before 1798, but with the increasing demands and workload generated by the Quasi-War, Congress authorized the new department and installed Benjamin Stoddert as the first Secretary of the Navy.

American success in this conflict stemmed partly from Stoddert's administrative and logistical skills, and partly from the operational and tactical skills of U.S. ship and squadron commanders. Stoddert, though, wanted ships for missions other than commerce raiding. He initially proposed a navy of more than 40 ships, including a dozen ships of the line, the battleships of the age of sail. Though the United States could not build enough to engage in large battles with either the British or French navies, his logic was that some would help deter possible invasions. He also argued that big ships took the longest to build, whereas smaller ships could be built quickly or purchased, hence the United States should maintain a few of the largest warships. Congress agreed to build six ships of the line but ceased construction at war's end, and also sold off all but 13 frigates (only maintaining six). During the war, though, Stoddert created a basic naval infrastructure for the future, constructing a number of dry docks and shipyards.

The New Army and the Federalists' Fall From Power

Though actual combat was limited to the seas, the Quasi-War also spurred army preparations. By the time of the XYZ Affair, numerous Federalists were anxious about Republicans. The latter included many who had originally opposed the Constitution, and their denunciations of government policy were becoming shriller. Moreover, Republicans were sponsoring pro-French meetings, and Federalists saw France's revolutionary regime as one that sought to subvert other countries' governments. Historian Richard Kohn asserts that with the outbreak of the Quasi-War, some Federalists feared Republicans might collude with French agents to overthrow the U.S. government. Others not as worried about a possible *coup d'etat* nonetheless saw an opportunity to stifle political opposition.

Historical treatments of the Quasi-War emphasize the Alien and Sedition Acts of 1798. These restricted personal liberties, allowing the deportation or jailing of aliens in wartime, and imposing fines or imprisonment for statements against the government that could be construed as "false, scandalous and malicious." But some Federalists, dreading possible invasion or civil strife, wanted to enlarge and guarantee the political reliability of American military forces. These consisted of Alexander Hamilton and his supporters (the "High Federalists"), who now saw the army as a means to contain Republican opposition and exert political control.

In 1798 and early 1799, the Federalist-controlled Congress did not just expand the regular Army—it created many armies. The Volunteer Army, for example, would have been composed of volunteer units the president could accept into federal service; the Provisional Army would have raised up to 10,000 men if a land war had erupted, and the Eventual Army would include an additional authorized 24 regiments of infantry. But beyond the regular U.S. Army, these others never existed except on paper, with one exception: the New Army, to consist of 12 infantry regiments and which George Washington agreed to command only if a land war began. Meanwhile Alexander Hamilton started issuing officer commissions but only to men with good Federalist credentials, explicitly excluding Republicans. As Richard Kohn notes, such recruitment made the New Army the only overtly politicized military force in U.S. history.

Not all Federalists agreed with Hamilton, including President John Adams. He thought the High Federalists' worries of insurrection and civil war overblown and was much more concerned with ending the conflict with France. Adams also realized the New Army was a political liability. To pay for new military spending, Congress passed the Direct Tax of 1798, which imposed levies on property such as buildings, land, and slaves. It was widely hated, and in early 1799 provoked Fries' Rebellion, an uprising in southern Pennsylvania. As with the Whiskey Rebellion, resistance dissolved once troops arrived—but these included not just militia but regular soldiers as well. Adams realized that new taxes, a growing military establishment, and use of regular troops to disperse protest was enflaming Republican fears of a despotic national government and eroding Federalist support among Americans in general.

In late 1798, Adams sent another delegation to France that ultimately negotiated the Convention of Mortefontaine. Signed on September 30, 1800, it ended the Quasi-War. But by then news of France's willingness to negotiate a peace removed the need for the New Army, and Congress and the Adams administration dismantled it. The president wanted to protect the Federalists' political position, but he also sensed the New Army threatened the democratic institutions of the young American republic and acted to counter the danger. Hamilton and the High Federalists, however, never forgave him. Lacking their support, Adams lost the election of 1800, making Republican Thomas Jefferson the next president.

Jefferson and the Army

For close to a decade, Republicans had fretted that the national government would become too powerful. Many expected Jefferson would shrink or possibly dissolve the U.S. Army. His administration did reduce troop levels under the Military Peace Establishment Act of 1802. But historian Theodore Crackel observes the intent was actually to depoliticize, rather than shrink, the army. The Military Peace Establishment Act reduced it to two infantry regiments and one artillery regiment, about 2,500 men. But the army was already understrength, and few enlisted men actually left. Significant changes only affected the officer corps, dominated by Federalists. The Act of 1802 reduced the number of preexisting officer positions but also created new ones (and a new rank, second lieutenant). Jefferson used the law to make the U.S. Army more politically neutral: He did not discharge all Federalist officers, just the ones with the most extreme views, while using new slots to grant commissions to men with Republican leanings.

The Military Peace Establishment Act took other steps along these lines. It created a permanent Army Corps of Engineers and the United States Military Academy at West Point, New York. Both have been viewed as ways to make the standing army more politically palatable to the general public: West Point soon emphasized a science and engineering curriculum, and its graduates, along with the Engineering Corps, helped develop the country by building roads, canals, and other infrastructure. Crackel observes, though, that these institutions offered Jefferson more tools to diversify the army's officer pool. The Act reserved appointments and promotions within the Corps of Engineers to the president, whereas in the regular Army, promotion was based rigidly on seniority. Each member of Congress was allowed to appoint one young man to each entering class at the Military Academy, offering the prospect of a college education to many families (especially in Republican constituencies) that could not otherwise afford it.

In depoliticizing the army, Jefferson sought to make it a reliable tool of executive authority, one that Republicans would be comfortable supporting. He recognized that only the army could enforce federal policies in many circumstances, especially on the frontier. A powerful example occurred in 1803, when Jefferson arranged the Louisiana Purchase. The only organization that could assume control and enforce American authority over the new territory was the U.S. Army. Immediately after the Purchase, most army units went to New Orleans, the region's most important city and the one that controlled access to the Mississippi River from the Gulf of Mexico.

The Tripolitan War, 1801–05

While it reorganized the army, the Jefferson administration pursued a naval war. But whereas the Quasi-War was mostly limited to commerce raiding and a few small battles in the nearby Caribbean, the Tripolitan War was the United States' first major projection of force overseas. Its enemy was Tripoli, which along with Algiers, Morocco, and Tunis, comprised the Barbary states (the conflict is also known as the First Barbary War). Pirates from this area had long threatened Mediterranean shipping, but up until the French Revolutionary Wars, a combination of the Royal Navy and payments to Barbary rulers had restrained them. After Britain went to war with France after 1793, piracy escalated, prompting Congress to pass the 1794 Naval Act. But following the 1796 Treaty of Tripoli, Barbary raids on U.S. shipping ended in exchange for annual payments.

By 1800, though, this settlement was breaking down. Promised payments to Tripoli had not been made, and attacks on American shipping resumed in 1801. When its ruler, the bey or pasha of Tripoli, indicated these would stop if the United States would pay more tribute, Jefferson refused, fearing it would prompt other Barbary states to make similar demands. Instead, the president dispatched four vessels, including three frigates, to blockade Tripoli's harbor. But this squadron had too few ships for the mission, and the frigates were too big to patrol close to the shoreline. Another flotilla in 1802 did little better.

The next year, the U.S. Navy's Mediterranean Squadron acquired more ships, including many smaller vessels, and a new commander—Edward Preble. In October 1803, the USS *Philadelphia* ran aground in Tripoli's harbor, and its crew was captured. But Preble soon turned the mishap into victory: In early 1804, he ordered Stephen Decatur to lead a raid that destroyed the *Philadelphia* and prevented its use by Tripolitan forces. This episode remains the best known event of the war and brought Preble and Decatur acclaim in the United States. Preble soon escalated operations, dispatching forays into Tripoli harbor to bombard the city and destroy portions of its fleet.

The war ended not long after its only land battle. Early in 1805, a U.S. official in Egypt approached the pasha's brother—Tripoli's previous ruler before being overthrown. He agreed to fund an expedition for promises that the United States would restore him to power. In March 1805 about 500 men, mostly Arab mercenaries but including eight U.S. Marines, began a westward trek of over 500 miles. By late April, they had reached the Tripolitan town of Derna, in what is now eastern Libya. Although outnumbered, attackers led by Marines and assisted by gunfire from the Mediterranean Squadron overran a harbor fortress and captured the town, and then repelled attempts to retake it in May. The Battle of Derna encouraged the pasha to conclude a peace. The United States agreed to a modest one-time payment to release the *Philadelphia*'s crew, and for the next decade, U.S. shipping was unmolested by the Barbary states. (The pasha continued to rule Tripoli for decades to come, to his brother's chagrin.)

The Tripolitan War demonstrated that the United States could project force overseas to protect its interests. It also had a unique impact on American naval policy. The utility of small gunboats for blockade duty and harbor combat had sparked Jefferson's interest. He believed these vessels, along with artillery batteries, offered a cheap alternative for guarding American ports and coastlines, compared to constructing large, expensive warships. Between 1805 and 1807, Congress allocated funds to build about 260 small boats, most of them about 50 feet long and armed with a single gun. To save costs, these boats would be beached in peacetime and manned by naval militia in times of war. But the program was not well supported: More than 80 of the craft were never built, and of those that were, only 60 were still serviceable by 1812. Moreover, such small vessels were useless on the high seas, where British actions soon provoked a crisis.

The War of 1812, 1812–15: Prelude

As with the Quasi-War and the Tripolitan War, the origins of the War of 1812 stemmed from the French Revolutionary Wars. Although the Peace of Amiens temporarily ended these in 1801, by 1803 war had resumed. But now Napoleon Bonaparte ruled France, and Europe's conflicts from then until 1815 are usually known as the Napoleonic Wars. The French emperor led his armies to some of the most spectacular victories in Western military history (particularly Austerlitz and Jena-Auerstadt). By 1807, all of mainland Europe was either allied with France or under its direct control, and for years Britain was Bonaparte's only challenger. The Royal Navy won a dramatic victory of its own, destroying most of France's and (now allied) Spain's warships at the 1805 Battle of Trafalgar. Napoleon then tried to hurt Britain economically by closing European ports to its shipping, which he called "the Continental system." The British responded with their "Orders in Council," which proclaimed that neutral vessels would have to pay for access to French-controlled ports.

Caught between the two was the United States. The neutral country with the largest commercial fleet, American shippers had resumed trade with France and the French West Indies after the Convention of Mortefontaine. Another problem was impressment, the practice of compelling sailors to serve on British warships. With the demands of war and enforcing the Orders in Council, the Royal Navy was stretched for manpower. Moreover, to avoid press gangs or flee service on warships, British seamen sometimes joined crews on American merchant ships. Frustrated Royal Navy captains began confronting U.S. vessels after 1805. The most infamous incident was the Chesapeake-Leopard Affair of 1807. Stopping the USS *Chesapeake* shortly after it put to sea, the captain of the British frigate HMS *Leopard* asked to come aboard and search for deserters. When the U.S. captain refused, the *Leopard* fired its cannons, killing three sailors, wounding 18, and forcing the *Chesapeake* to surrender. The British removed four sailors, only one of whom was later confirmed as a Royal Navy deserter.

The incident stoked a popular outcry in the United States. A furious Congress increased the regular U.S. Army to 10,000 men and allocated funds to arm state militias and build coastal forts. President Jefferson tried to redress American grievances short of war with the Embargo Act of 1807, which stopped all U.S. exports to foreign destinations. The intent was to hurt Britain and France so that they would recognize American maritime rights. Instead, the embargo exacerbated tensions within the United States, hurting people in the northeast the most, where shipping was a large part of the regional economy. When smuggling with Canada rose, Jefferson deployed army troops to enforce the Embargo Act—much of which was nullified by laws passed in 1809 and 1810.

The War of 1812, though, was not simply an Anglo-American conflict. As relations deteriorated between the United States and Britain, the peace in the Northwest following the 1795 Treaty of Greenville broke down. Since then, white settlement had advanced down the Ohio River and north along the Mississippi as well as into the Trans-Appalachian regions south of Tennessee, creating new strains with native peoples. One reaction was an Indian movement that advocated separation and isolation from whites, similar to that which preceded Pontiac's Rebellion. Its most renowned leaders were two Shawnee brothers: Tenskwatawa, called "the prophet" for his visions and proselytizing, and Tecumseh, who was more of a traditional chief.

Spreading their message, they tried to unite different Indians into a confederation to oppose American encroachment.

William Henry Harrison, governor of the Indiana territory (established by Congress in 1800), had some tense diplomatic meetings with Tecumseh. Then in 1811, when the Shawnee chief was visiting southern Indians, Harrison exploited his absence to confront warriors gathered in "Prophetstown," near the Tippecanoe and Wabash rivers. His force of about 1,000 U.S. regulars and Kentucky and Indiana militiamen (including cavalry and infantry) arrived in early November. Tenskwatawa invited Harrison's men to camp nearby. Early the next morning, hundreds of warriors attacked, similar to the assault on St. Clair's army 20 years earlier. But this time U.S. troops stood firm and repelled the assault (while suffering over 60 dead and 120 wounded): Harrison was a veteran of the 1794 Fallen Timbers campaign and trained his men in tactics and techniques employed by Anthony Wayne's Legion of the United States. The Battle of Tippecanoe eroded support for the Prophet, and also highlighted another development: The British in Canada were once again offering material assistance to native leaders, especially Tecumseh. The Shawnee chief worked to maintain anti-American sentiment among peoples of the Old Northwest, many of whom allied with Britain when the War of 1812 began.

Meanwhile, President James Madison, elected in 1808, struggled to develop a policy toward Great Britain after the failure of the Embargo Act. The British remained unresponsive, focused on fighting Napoleonic France. By 1812, a group of young Republican Congressmen known as the War Hawks had grown tired of ineffectual diplomacy and economic measures. They reflected a growing belief that ongoing violations of U.S. rights undermined the country's independence and saw war as the only means to assert autonomy from Great Britain. Coming mostly from western and southern regions, they also sought to quell native resistance on the frontiers and thwart British influence among Indian peoples. Although people in other parts of the country preferred to avoid war, the rising political influence of the War Hawks pushed the question of war or peace in their favor. At President Madison's request, on June 18, 1812, the U.S. Congress declared war on Great Britain. Shortly thereafter, news arrived that Britain had revoked the Orders in Council.

The War of 1812: U.S. Plans and Problems

Madison's objective was Canada, which produced raw materials (such as lumber) that had alleviated Britain's need for trade with the United States. The president's strategy was to invade and occupy it, expecting the British would then have to negotiate and concede to U.S. demands. Many Americans also hoped war would lead to territorial annexations. But invading Canada required offensive operations encompassing large numbers of troops that, when pressed, the United States could not easily produce, despite expectations to the contrary.

The Constitution, combined with developments of the 1790s, produced an American military system consisting of a small national regular army supplemented by state-maintained militias. This arrangement had successfully confronted challenges such as Indian wars in the Northwest and internal revolts but had not yet been tested by a major conventional war. U.S. leaders expected that state militias would provide the bulk of the manpower needed for any large conflict. With over 7.5 million people in 1812, the United States could raise hundreds of thousands of soldiers—if the states had maintained their militia systems, and if the federal government had administrative capacity needed to mobilize and support large numbers of troops.

The Constitution allowed Congress to "organize, arm and discipline" the militia. But to do so required effective federal legislation. Prior to the twentieth century, the only significant law Congress passed regarding militia readiness was the Uniform Militia Act of 1792. It mandated militia service for all "free able-bodied white male" citizens between the ages of 18 and 45 (permitting exceptions) who had to maintain their own weapons and equipment. Individual states were to organize militiamen into units and train them. But the Uniform Militia Act did not stipulate any standards in this regard and imposed no penalties for noncompliance.

In the years before 1812, militias deteriorated. Many men lacked firearms, and some hired substitutes or refused to serve. States mustered units infrequently, providing few opportunities to train. Men in some towns and cities formed volunteer militia companies, regularly mustering and training under their own chosen officers. These, however, could not compensate for the larger decay of state militias. Historian C. Edward Skeen observes that militia units in the War of 1812 did not always fight poorly. Those who served under exceptionally capable leaders like Winfield Scott or Jacob Brown, or who were already experienced and highly motivated, such as Kentucky frontiersmen, could distinguish themselves in combat. But the American militia system was supposed to provide basic military training for the country's male citizenry, and its failure meant the United States lacked a large pool of men with minimal combat proficiency needed for a conventional war. Moreover, few other sources of military expertise existed to correct the problem. By 1812, the United States Military Academy had produced few graduates whose education contained more than just a little actual military training, and most Continental Army veterans were too old to serve.

The federal government also lacked the capacity to field large armies. The War Department had been organized to administer a force of just a few thousand regulars. It only expanded during the war itself, which further exacerbated confusion and logistical difficulties. Legal and political concerns also dogged Madison's strategy. The Constitution allows the federal government to employ state militias to repel invasions, suppress rebellions, or to enforce laws; it does not address invading a foreign country. Many militiamen, when ordered to cross into Canada, refused. In New England, where Federalists were prominent and opposition to war widespread, governors did not call out their militias. The war was popular in the western parts of the country, but people there preferred to fight regional Indians and had little interest in providing manpower for campaigns elsewhere. In this sense, U.S. operations in the War of 1812 consisted of many uncoordinated campaigns.

Congress had made some preparations for war. In January 1812 it authorized expansion of the U.S. Army to 35,000 men. Later it approved enlisting up to 30,000 one-year volunteers, 15,000 18-month volunteers, and the mustering of up to 100,000 state militiamen. But by the time the United States declared war in June, only 12,000 regular and volunteer troops were available. One reason was that Congress did not allow volunteer officers—who would recruit men for these units—to obtain commissions until after the war began. It also approved no additional funding for military expenses before it declared war other than printing more paper money.

Great Britain had the world's largest navy, though its army was modest compared to those fielded by other major countries during the Napoleonic Wars. Most of its forces were not deployed in North America. Naval forces will be addressed below, but as for the army, Canada had only 7,000 regulars when the War of 1812 began, though these would be supplemented by a few thousand native allies and perhaps 10,000 Canadian militiamen. The bulk of Britain's redcoats were fighting French forces in Spain. Had the United States effectively mobilized its much larger reservoir of manpower, it could have better exploited British weakness and come closer to strategic success. Instead, while Napoleon marched east to invade Russia with the largest army Europe had seen to that point, over 600,000 men, America struggled to field forces a mere fraction of that size. But over the next two years, Napoleon's forces suffered many defeats, culminating with the French emperor abdicating his throne in 1814—which then freed British troops and ships for operations against the United States.

The War of 1812: The Northern Campaigns

To succeed, Madison's strategy of invading Canada required offensives launched from northern U.S. states and territories. These occurred in three distinct theaters: northern New York and the upper St. Lawrence River valley; the Niagara frontier, where the Niagara River separates New York State from the province of Ontario, between Lakes Ontario and Erie; and the Northwest frontier, particularly around western Lake Erie. Naval forces on the Great Lakes had a crucial role in these campaigns, and Indian allies were prominent, especially for the British in western areas. Before the war, President Madison appointed Henry Dearborn, who planned initial operations in all three theaters, overall commander of American forces in the north.

Dearborn had been Secretary of War under President Jefferson and was a Revolutionary War veteran. But as a field commander he was timid and uncertain. He also faced manpower problems, especially given opposition to the war in New England—the very states from which he needed men for his campaign against Montreal. By November he had cobbled together a few thousand men in New York, but militiamen refused to cross the border. After Canadian troops and Indians repelled his advance force, he ended operations for the winter. On the Niagara frontier, militia general Stephen van Rensselaer briefly captured Queenston on October 13. He had similar problems with militiamen, but it was lack of boats that prevented his assault force from receiving timely reinforcements. By day's end, the British had retaken the town and captured 900 of the 1,300–1,500 men who had crossed the river, while suffering 120 casualties. For the next few months, operations along the Niagara consisted of minor raids.

The greatest U.S. debacle in 1812, though, was in the Northwest. Madison had appointed William Hull, governor of the Michigan Territory, regional commander. Congregating about

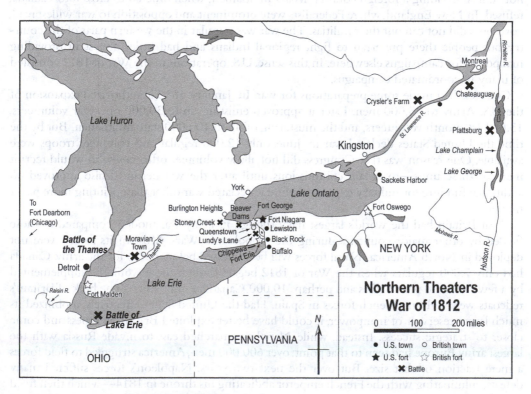

Map 4.2 Northern Theaters, War of 1812

1,800 militia and regulars at Fort Detroit, he was to advance eastward into Ontario. But after crossing the Detroit River in July 1812, Hull grew timid, only sending out patrols. In August he heard an American outpost in northern Michigan had been captured. Fearing British forces were massing at Fort Malden 20 miles away, he retreated back to Fort Detroit. British regulars, Canadian militia, and Indians promptly surrounded the fort, and when they brought up cannons to shell it, Hull surrendered—to forces half the size of his own. This loss was compounded in early 1813 by another U.S. defeat on the nearby Raisin River.

American forces won some victories that year. In April 1813, Isaac Chauncey's naval squadron ferried about 1,500 troops across Lake Ontario to attack York (later Toronto). After capturing it, an explosion killed the ground commander, and U.S. soldiers looted and ransacked the town. When the British launched a retaliatory raid against Sackets Harbor, New York—Chauncey's base—regulars and militia commanded by Jacob Brown repelled it. In May, Chauncey and Dearborn shuttled troops to the Niagara theater. They captured Fort George on the Canadian side of the river, where it empties into Lake Ontario. This victory threatened to cut off other British garrisons on the Niagara, which withdrew from forts further upstream. But when U.S. forces moved west in June, they were defeated at the Battles of Stoney Creek and Beaver Dams. Meanwhile, Chauncey's squadron had returned to Sackets Harbor, and the British Lake Ontario flotilla appeared off Fort George. Except for that post, which they held for a few more months, Dearborn's troops pulled back to the American side of the Niagara.

Farther west, U.S. forces prevailed in other battles. In September 1813, Oliver Perry took his nine warships across Lake Erie and, surprising the opposing British squadron at Fort Malden, destroyed it during the Battle of Lake Erie. The Americans now controlled shipping on the lake, and with the supply situation at Forts Detroit and Malden already severe, the British abandoned these posts. William Henry Harrison, now commanding the Northwest after Hull's humiliation, chased after them with about 3,500 regular, volunteer, and militia troops—including 1,000 mounted Kentucky riflemen. On October 5, 1813, they reached the Thames River, catching up to about 800 British soldiers and 500 native warriors led by Tecumseh. At the Battle of the Thames, American cavalry broke through the redcoats, compelled their surrender, and then engaged and defeated their Indian allies—killing Tecumseh.

The Battles of Lake Erie and the Thames were two of the most significant American victories of the war. With Tecumseh's death, the native alliance against the United States fell apart, and after 1813 the British no longer contested American control in the Old Northwest. But these battles did little to advance Madison's strategy of controlling Canada. James Wilkinson, who relieved Dearborn as top commander over the summer, launched a campaign against Montreal in the fall of 1813—and did no better than his predecessor. At the Battle of Châteauguay on October 26, a force of about 1,500—mostly Canadian militia—repelled 4,000 U.S. troops advancing north from Albany under Wade Hampton. Wilkinson transported 7,000 soldiers via Lake Ontario to the Canadian side of the St. Lawrence, bypassing British troops at Kingston. Some of the latter followed his army as it marched downstream toward Montreal, precipitating the Battle of Crysler's Farm on November 11. There, about 1,200 British troops defeated roughly 2,400 men in the American rearguard. Learning of Hampton's retreat, Wilkinson did likewise, moving his forces south over the border.

Meanwhile, transfers and expiring enlistments slowly whittled down American strength at Fort George. Fearing a British attack, the U.S. commander abandoned it in December 1813. But his men burned nearby Newark, Ontario, before returning to the American side of the Niagara. By year's end, the British not only reoccupied Fort George but had crossed the river to capture Fort Niagara and destroy the New York towns of Buffalo, Black Rock, and Lewiston. These events, along with others such as the sack of York, reveal a side of the War of 1812 that receives little attention—that military operations threatened the lives, homes, and property of thousands of American and Canadian civilians in the border regions.

The following summer, the Madison administration launched its last offensive of the war on the Niagara frontier. Following another failed campaign to capture Montreal in early 1814, Jacob J. Brown replaced Wilkinson as top commander. Brown began the war as a New York State militia general, but having demonstrated his military skills in actions such as the defense of Sackets Harbor, he was now a Major General in the regular U.S. Army. One of his key subordinates was Winfield Scott, another officer who had proven himself in engagements such as the 1812 Battle of Queenston and the capture of Fort George in 1813. Much of their success stemmed from the ability to train, discipline, and prepare men for war, whether regulars or militia. In the summer of 1814, their soldiers' prowess was displayed in the Battles of Chippewa and Lundy's Lane.

Brown's offensive began on July 3, 1814. His 3,500–4,000 men crossed the Niagara, captured Fort Erie, and then moved north to the Chippewa River, where a British force awaited. The two armies resembled each other, in that both contained regulars, militia, and Indian warriors, though the defenders only numbered 1,800–2,000. But the British commander had a low opinion of American fighting qualities and on July 5 crossed the Chippewa to attack. Scott marched his brigade out to meet them, engaging in an intense firefight with British regulars, taking and delivering volleys of musket fire. Late in the battle, his troops feigned weakness in the center of their line, luring the redcoats into U.S. artillery fire. The British retreated, having suffered about 450 casualties to the Americans' 300, with 1,000–1,500 troops engaged on either side.

At the Battle of Chippewa, U.S. soldiers tactically bested British regulars in a pitched battle. Afterward the British fell back to Fort George, which American troops could not threaten without the help from the U.S. Lake Ontario squadron (once again at Sackets Harbor). Brown's men moved west, and British forces followed. The opposing armies then fought the most intense combat of the war at the Battle of Lundy's Lane on July 25. Leading an advance force in the afternoon, Scott discovered enemy troops and cannons ready on a hill. His brigade took many casualties before the rest of Brown's forces arrived, while the British also received reinforcements. Most of the fighting occurred after dark, in a confused sequence of charges, countercharges, and close-quarters combat. Around midnight the British withdrew from the hill, giving the Americans a tactical victory—but a costly one: 861 casualties out of less than 2,500 men, with both Brown and Scott wounded; the British lost 878 out of about 3,000 men, with their commander captured. U.S. forces were too exhausted to continue the campaign and retreated to Fort Erie, which they abandoned later in the year. Lundy's Lane thus was not only an operational victory for the British but also a strategic one, for the Madison administration made no further attempts to invade Canada.

Later that year, though, American forces checked the one British attempt to invade the U.S. from the north. France's defeat in April 1814 allowed Britain to dispatch reinforcements to North America, including about 10,000 veterans of the Napoleonic Wars. They arrived too late to join the summer campaign on the Niagara frontier. But Canada's governor and military commander, George Prevost, used some for an army of 11,000 that, in September 1814, marched down the western shore of Lake Champlain. His objective was to take U.S. territory to enhance the British bargaining position at peace talks that would end the war. To oppose him, American commander Alexander Macomb gathered about 4,500 soldiers at Plattsburg, where a small naval squadron led by Thomas Macdonough was anchored in the town's harbor. Prevost's army arrived before the British Lake Champlain flotilla, and he waited so his assault could have naval support. Meanwhile, the opposing squadrons engaged each other on September 11, each with four larger vessels and 10–12 smaller gunboats.

Macdonough's forces prevailed at the Battle of Lake Champlain, and when Prevost heard the news, he returned to Canada. An American naval victory thus ended the War of 1812's last northern campaign.

Naval Conflict in the War of 1812

As demonstrated by the Battles of Lake Erie and the Battle of Lake Champlain, joint operations comprised of both land and naval forces played a key role in the northern theaters of the war. The vessels involved were smaller than large oceangoing ships, and the disparity between United States and British naval forces on the Great Lakes was not nearly as large as on the high seas. When the War of 1812 began, the Royal Navy had close to 600 warships, compared to 20 in the U.S. Navy. But as with the American Revolution, various factors mitigated this difference. British fleets, for example, had to conduct operations around the world. When the War of 1812 began, only 25 warships were based at Halifax, Nova Scotia, for operations along the American coastline; another 27 operated around the West Indies. After close to 20 years of warfare against France, manpower was a constant problem (and fueled the problem of impressment)—hence many Royal Navy crews had high proportions of untrained men.

Lacking large numbers of big warships, the U.S. Navy could not engage in big fleet actions against the British. But the country could convert much of its extensive merchant fleet into privateers to prey upon enemy shipping, pursuing a *guerre de course* strategy as it had in the War of the American Revolution and the Quasi-War. As for its few warships, U.S. Navy frigates were some of the best in the world. Those called "44s"—designed to carry 44 cannons—were bigger, with more guns and larger crews (helpful for forming or repelling boarding parties) than typical frigates. They were also fast and tough, designed by experienced shipwrights and captains from high-quality materials. Moreover, the experiences of the Quasi- and Tripolitan Wars had produced experienced officers and crews.

Box 4.2   The USS *Constitution* Versus the HMS *Guerrière*

The following is an excerpt of Captain Isaac Hull's report of the USS *Constitution*'s defeat of the HMS *Guerrière* in August 1812.

At 5 minutes past 6 PM being alongside, and within less than Pistol Shot, we commenced a very heavy fire from all of our Guns . . . which done great Execution, so much so that in less than fifteen minutes from the time, we got alongside, [Guerrière's] Mizen Mast [fell] . . . and the Hull, and Sails very much injured, which made it very difficult for them to manage her . . . the Constitution had received but little damage, and having more sail set than the Enemy she shot ahead, on seeing this I determined to put the Helm to Port [turn left], and oblige him to do the same, or suffer himself to be raked [firing cannon down the length of an enemy ship] by our getting across his Bow . . . our Helm being put to Port the Ship came [around] and gave us an opportunity of pouring in upon his Larboard [port] Bow several Broadsides, which made great havock amongst his men . . . . and did great injury to his forerigging, and sails, The Enemy put his helm to Port . . . but his Mizen Mast [having fallen], prevented her [turning], which brought us across his Bows, with his Bowsprit over our Stern. At this moment I determined to board him, but the instant the Boarders were called . . . his Foremast, and Mainmast [fell]. . . . On seeing the Enemy totally disabled

Figure 4.2 "Action Between USS *Constitution* and HMS *Guerriere*, 19 August 1812"
By Anton Otto Fischer
Artist: Anton Otto Fischer. Courtesy of Miss Katrina S. Fischer. Naval Historical Foundation.

. . . I ordered the Sails filled, to hawl off, and repair our damages and return again to renew the action . . . it being now dark, we . . . could discover that she had raised a small flag Staff . . . I ordered a Boat hoisted out . . . Lieutenant Reed returned in about twenty minutes, and brought with him, James Richard Dacres Esqr. Commander of his Britannic Majesty's Frigate the Guerri[è]re, which ship had surrendered, to the United States Frigate Constitution.

"Captain Isaac Hull to Secretary of the Navy Paul Hamilton," National Archives, Record Group 45, Captain's Letters, 1812, Vol. 2, No. 207; also available at www.history. navy. mil/docs/war1812/const5.htm

During the War of 1812, American privateers and warships raided British shipping in the Atlantic, including around the Bay of Fundy, Newfoundland, the West Indies, and the British Isles. Some saw action in more distant waters: The USS *Essex* marauded in the Pacific for over a year. Early in the war, U.S. frigates won a number of ship-on-ship encounters against British ones. In August 1812, the USS *Constitution* defeated the HMS *Guerrière* in the Gulf of St. Lawrence, earning the name "Old Ironsides" because during the battle, a broadside from the British frigate bounced off the American ship's hull. In October, the HMS *Macedonian* surrendered to the USS *United States*, another "44," in the eastern Atlantic. These victories greatly boosted morale and support for the war in the United States, making victorious captains Isaac Hull and Stephen

Decatur (both Tripolitan War veterans) famous. In December, the *Constitution*, under a different commander, sank the HMS *Java* off the Brazilian coast. Britons were baffled, having assumed the tactical and nautical skills of the Royal Navy surpassed any possible challenger.

British leaders reacted by deploying more warships against the United States, up to about 100 by early 1813—including 10 ships of the line and 38 frigates. Starting in late 1812, the Royal Navy blockaded the American coast in stages. British ships first patrolled off of Georgia and the Carolinas. By spring 1813, they barred access to Chesapeake Bay, and a year later, New England. Over time, the blockade smothered both trade and American naval operations. U.S. frigates became trapped in ports, outnumbered by squadrons of British warships waiting to intercept them. By war's end, more than half of America's warships had been captured or destroyed. American privateers also had difficulty leaving and returning to harbor, and their impact was limited. By one count, they captured over 1,000 vessels, but Great Britain's total merchant fleet numbered about 25,000. Conversely, British ships captured hundreds of American vessels, including privateers, and U.S. shipping tonnage plummeted during the war. The economies of seaboard states suffered greatly, and U.S. customs revenue fell.

Greater numbers of ships allowed the Royal Navy to conduct operations in addition to the blockade, in particular raids and campaigns against American coasts. These began in 1813 but became more extensive in 1814 after France's defeat. Before the war ended, British joint operations targeted the coasts of New England and Long Island, and included a major expedition against New Orleans. But Chesapeake Bay received the most attention.

The Chesapeake in the War of 1812

By March 1813, the Royal Navy had blockaded the Chesapeake. Then, from April to August, the British preyed on local shipping, raiding ports around the Bay and destroying depots. American reactions were mixed: Some local militia forces ran when bombarded by naval artillery, and towns often did not resist in order to minimize damage. In June, Virginia militia repelled an assault on Norfolk only for the British to then attack and pillage nearby Hampton. These operations greatly disrupted the Chesapeake's economy in 1813, but the British were also trying to draw U.S. attention and resources away from campaigns against Canada.

After August, British forces withdrew from the Chesapeake but expanded the blockade of the Atlantic coastline. When they returned the following spring, the Americans had created a squadron of about 30 small vessels and gunboats. By June 1814 the British had trapped it in the Patuxent River and proceeded to again maraud towns around Chesapeake Bay. But in August, they struck a new target: Washington, D.C., the U.S. capital since 1800. The British first sailed up the Patuxent River, and the American squadron there retreated upstream before the U.S. commander ordered the boats destroyed to prevent their capture. Then British troops landed. Advancing toward the capital in hot and humid weather on August 24, they encountered 6,000 troops, mostly militia, at Bladensburg, Maryland. Though numbering only 2,600, the British attacked and drove American forces from the field. Although the militia performed poorly, the U.S. defeat at the Battle of Bladensburg also stemmed from poor tactical decisions, such as placing lines of infantry too far away from each other for mutual support.

Despite British prior depredations in the Chesapeake, little had been done to fortify Washington. The Madison administration took hasty steps to defend Washington in July 1814, but they were too little, too late. The U.S. government and most civilians abandoned the city before enemy troops arrived on the evening of August 24. The British then burned the Capitol Building, the Library of Congress, and the White House (the Washington Navy Yard had already been torched to keep supplies, equipment, and two warships from falling into enemy hands). The next day redcoats destroyed additional government buildings and retreated after dark.

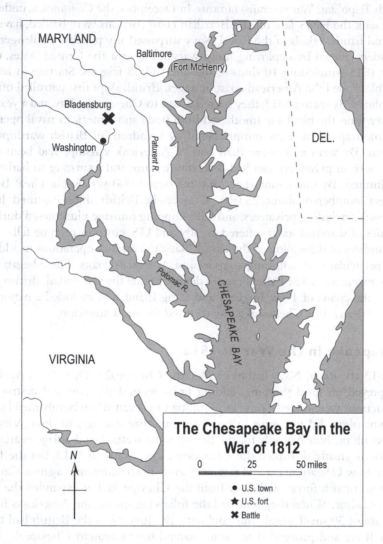

Map 4.3 The Chesapeake Bay in the War of 1812

The British next moved against Baltimore. One of America's major ports, its harbor was guarded by Fort McHenry and some shore batteries, and the entrance had been blocked by sunken vessels. On September 12, about 4,500 British troops decamped at North Point, at the tip of a peninsula some miles from Baltimore and its harbor. Marching toward the city, they drove off 3,000–3,200 American militiamen in two encounters. The following day, redcoats stopped outside Baltimore's defenses while Royal Navy vessels bombarded Fort McHenry. But the ships had to fire at very long range to avoid being hit by the fort's cannons. Beginning in the morning of September 13 and lasting into the early hours of the following day, the British maintained a prolonged bombardment that inflicted minimal damage to the fort, wounding two dozen and killing four Americans.

Then they withdrew to organize a campaign against another American port. Baltimore was saved. But the Chesapeake had again been ravaged, and the U.S. capital destroyed. These operations were partly in retaliation for devastating American raids on Ontario's Lake Erie shore earlier in 1814—which in turn were reprisals for the British destruction of Black Rock and

Buffalo the prior December. But as in 1813, the 1814 Chesapeake campaign also tried to deflect U.S. attention from the northern theaters of war, and in particular assist Prevost's invasion of New York. It dealt a great blow to American morale at the time, but ironically also led to one of the foundations of U.S. national identity. "The Star-Spangled Banner," a poem written by Francis Scott Key to describe his pride and joy at witnessing Fort McHenry survive the British bombardment, later became the U.S. national anthem.

The First Creek War, 1813–14

After the summer of 1814, British forces prepared to capture New Orleans. The most important U.S. city on the Gulf Coast, it was the gateway to the Mississippi River and interior of North America—including the "Old Southwest" south of Tennessee. The British had previously given scant attention to this area, but it had just witnessed a brutal conflict between American forces and a faction of the Creek nation. Today known as the First Creek War, its genesis lay in a combination of imperial, regional, and local tensions.

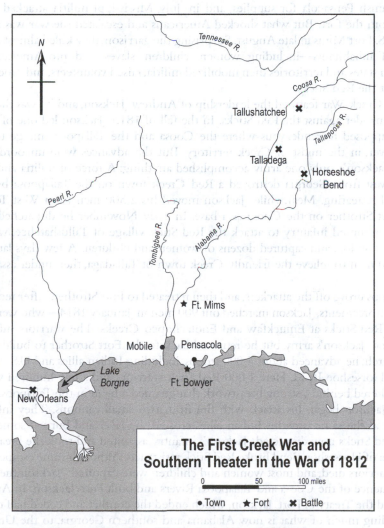

Map 4.4 The First Creek War and Southern Theater in the War of 1812

The 1783 Treaty of Paris both ended the War of the American Revolution and returned Florida to Spain. By 1812, Britain and Spain were allies against Napoleonic France. Similar to the Old Northwest and the British, many Americans feared Spain was colluding with regional Indians against the United States and that a war might provide an opportunity to annex parts of Spanish Florida. Most native peoples actually preferred to remain at peace with the United States. But a group of Creeks known as the Red Sticks were particularly upset with ongoing settler encroachment on their lands. Many had been receptive to Tecumseh's visit in 1811 seeking support for an anti-American Indian coalition, and some had returned with him to the Northwest.

When the War of 1812 began, little happened in the area. Then, in April 1813, U.S. troops captured part of Spanish West Florida: Mobile and territory west of the Perdido River (today the Perdido is Florida's western boundary with Alabama). The Creek War itself began a few months later, though by then Creeks were warring among themselves. In 1812, U.S. agents accused some Red Sticks of killing some settlers on the Duck River. When chiefs had the warriors hunted down and executed, fighting erupted between the Red Sticks and the rest of the Creek nation. By the summer of 1813, U.S. forces were also involved. Red Sticks sometimes went to Spanish Pensacola for supplies, and in July, Mississippi militia attacked one group returning from the fort. But what shocked Americans and escalated the war was a Red Stick attack on U.S. Fort Mims in late August. Surprising the garrison, they killed almost all the fort's hundreds of inhabitants—including women, children, slaves, and pro-American Indians. Southeastern states and territories then mobilized militia, raised volunteers, and procured native allies to fight the Red Sticks.

The First Creek War featured the leadership of Andrew Jackson, and he was the most successful commander against the Red Sticks. In the fall of 1813, Jackson led one of four forces that were supposed to rendezvous where the Coosa and the Tallapoosa merge to form the Alabama River, in the midst of Creek territory. But the advances were uncoordinated, and except for Jackson's, only one army accomplished anything: A force of militia and Cherokee advancing west from Georgia destroyed a Red Creek town on the Tallapoosa before being attacked and retreating. Meanwhile, Jackson moved his 2,500 men from West Tennessee to establish Fort Strother on the Coosa as a base. In early November he dispatched a force of cavalry and mounted infantry to attack the Red Stick village of Tallushatchee, which killed hundreds of warriors and captured dozens of women and children. A few days later, Jackson moved 2,000 men to relieve the friendly Creek town of Talladaga, then under assault by Red Sticks.

These troops drove off the attackers, and then retreated to Fort Strother. After receiving supplies and reinforcements, Jackson marched out 900 men in January 1814—who were promptly attacked by Red Sticks at Emuckfaw and Enotachopco Creeks. The warriors suffered more casualties than Jackson's army, but he retreated back to the Fort Strother to build up a larger force. In March, he advanced about 4,000 troops, including Indian allies and U.S. Army regulars, toward Horseshoe Bend. Here 1,000 Red Stick warriors and a few hundred women and children sheltered behind a strong breastwork that guarded a bend in the Tallapoosa River. On March 27, Jackson began his attack with fire from two small cannons. They inflicted little damage, but at the same time his Indian allies crossed the river and burned some buildings. With the Red Sticks now distracted, Jackson's infantry assaulted and took the breastwork.

The Battle of Horseshoe Bend broke Red Stick resistance. Although some escaped, 800–900 Red Stick warriors died, and most women and children were captured. Jackson then advanced to the confluence of the Coosa and Tallapoosa Rivers and built Fort Jackson. In August 1814, he concluded the Treaty of Fort Jackson, which ended the conflict and ceded half of all Creek lands, including much of what is now Alabama and southern Georgia, to the United States.

Ironically, the war with Britain would end with no change of territory, whereas the First Creek War greatly expanded the area under American control.

New Orleans, 1814–15

Based on these successes, the Madison administration appointed Jackson to defend the Gulf Coast. In September 1814, a small British force tried to capture Mobile, which could serve as a staging area for an overland advance to New Orleans. But a harbor fort repelled the assault. To deny the British another possible base, Jackson's forces marched to Pensacola. Arriving in early November, the Spanish commander surrendered. The British now had to directly transport an army to the vicinity of New Orleans rather than land elsewhere and march overland. As they concentrated forces in Jamaica for the campaign, word of their plans got to Jackson, and he moved the bulk of his forces to defend the city

When the invasion fleet arrived outside the entrance to nearby Lake Borgne on December 12, it easily brushed aside the small American squadron defending it. But the British did not have enough shallow-draft boats to move men and supplies around the bayous and waterways that surrounded New Orleans. They needed 10 days to transport troops across the lake, placing an advance force of about 1,800 a few miles from the city. When they started marching toward New Orleans, Jackson reacted. On December 23, the British stopped at a plantation on the eastern side of the Mississippi River; over 2,000 U.S. troops attacked that evening. The redcoats prevailed in confused night fighting, the first engagement in what culminated in the Battle of New Orleans early the next month.

American forces retreated about two miles to a canal. Jackson's men fortified it, building earthworks and artillery positions. He also established smaller defenses on the other side of the Mississippi in case the British crossed the river. After accumulating more men and supplies, the British ground commander, Sir Edward Pakenham, launched an assault on January 8, 1815. His infantry columns had to cross a large open area between the Mississippi River and a swamp to assault the main American line. To counter the defenders' firepower, he sent a small force

Figure 4.3 "Battle of New Orleans: Jackson's Terrific Slaughter of the British"

Andrew Jackson commanded a unique combination of units at the Battle of New Orleans. Along with U.S. regulars and militia from southern states and territories, these included free African-American men who served in companies long established by the city of New Orleans for local defense, as well as some volunteer slaves. Also assisting Jackson was Jean Lafitte and his band of pirates.

across the river to its western bank, where it would capture American cannons and use them to fire into the main fortifications on the eastern side of the Mississippi.

Unfortunately for Pakenham, these troops were swept far downstream and were still marching into position when his main assault was ready. Instead of waiting, he ordered his infantry columns forward. At that time, fog on the ground obscured the battlefield and his advancing soldiers. Pakenham also had high confidence in these forces, 5,000–6,000 men, including many veterans of the Napoleonic Wars as well as black troops recruited in the Caribbean. The roughly 4,500 men defending Jackson's line included militia from Louisiana, Tennessee, and Kentucky, as well as U.S. regulars, free African Americans from New Orleans, Choctaw warriors, and a band of pirates. Few of them had experienced conventional battle. But as the British advanced, the fog lifted, and American soldiers and artillery fired from their prepared positions and devastated the attacking columns. Only afterward did Pakenham's force on the west bank capture U.S. positions there, and it soon withdrew. British casualties totaled about 2,000 (including Pakenham), compared to less than 100 reported by Jackson. After American forts repelled a subsequent effort to sail warships up the Mississippi, the British evacuated.

The U.S. victory at the Battle of New Orleans saved the city from invasion. Ironically, it occurred after the two belligerents had technically agreed to peace. On December 24, 1814, U.S. and British negotiators in Belgium signed the Treaty of Ghent, which ended the war on the basis of the *status quo ante bellum*—the situation before the war began, thus avoiding issues of neutral shipping rights and impressment that had helped cause the war. But by late 1814, Napoleon's abdication made these issues moot: The Royal Navy no longer had to pursue operations against France or impress sailors to maintain adequate levels of manpower. (Napoleon would return briefly in 1815 only to be defeated at Waterloo.) After over 20 years of conflict, Great Britain wanted peace, while Madison wished to end an increasingly unpopular war.

Due to this timing, many observers claim Jackson's victory was irrelevant to the outcome of the war. But had the British captured New Orleans, it might have dramatically affected subsequent Anglo-American relations as well as how the war was remembered in the United States. As it happened, the battle ended the last campaign of the war, and the British were happy to focus on reestablishing peace. It also catapulted Jackson to national fame, making him the best known American commander of the war. In years to follow, this one victory would overshadow the war's other events, allowing Americans to forget U.S. military ineptness during the War of 1812. Today, many regard it as a "second War of Independence" in which the young republic confronted and established its autonomy from its former mother country.

Conclusion

The United States faced many issues after independence, the chief being the nature of its national government. The Constitution resolved this problem and set the basic framework for American military institutions, splitting authority over armed forces between the federal and state governments, and between different branches of the former. The size and role of standing military units remained a contentious point for America's first political parties, but various crises after 1788 shaped an effective compromise: a small regular army and navy, to be supplemented by militia and commissioning privateers in case of a major conflict.

This solution, despite setbacks, worked for early challenges faced by the United States. But it failed dramatically in the War of 1812. The country had failed to maintain its militia system and had not developed adequate administrative and logistical capacity to mount conventional land campaigns. Although U.S. warships won some early ship-on-ship battles, the Royal Navy's blockade subsequently smothered American naval capabilities. As the origins of the war stemmed from broader hostilities between Great Britain and France, the end of the Napoleonic

Wars resolved disputes that had fueled the Anglo-American conflict. But poor performance by U.S. armed forces highlighted the question of how the country would reform its military institutions.

Short Bibliography

Calloway, Colin G. *The Victory with No Name: The Native American Defeat of the First American Army*. New York: Oxford University Press, 2015.

Crackel, Theodore J. *Mr. Jefferson's Army: Political and Social Reform of the Military Establishment, 1801–1809*. New York: New York University Press, 1987.

Cress, Lawrence Delbert. *Citizens in Arms: The Army and the Militia in American Society to the War of 1812*. Chapel Hill: University of North Carolina Press, 1982.

Hickey, Donald R. *The War of 1812: A Forgotten Conflict*. Bicentennial ed. Urbana: University of Illinois Press, 2012.

Hogeland, William. *The Whiskey Rebellion*. New York: Scribner, 2006.

Kohn, Richard. *Eagle and Sword: The Federalists and the Creation of the Military Establishment in America, 1783–1802*. New York: The Free Press, 1975.

Lambert, Frank. *The Barbary Wars: American Independence in the Atlantic World*. New York: Hill & Wang, 2007.

Latimer, Jon. *1812: War with America*. Cambridge: Harvard University Press, 2007.

Skeen, C. Edward. *Citizen Soldiers in the War of 1812*. Lexington: University of Kentucky Press, 1999.

Stagg, J. C. A. *The War of 1812: Conflict for a Continent*. West Nyack, NY: Cambridge University Press, 2012.

Toll, Ian. *Six Frigates: The Epic History of the Founding of the U.S. Navy*. New York: W. W. Norton & Co., 2006.

Chapter 5

Expansion, 1815–1865

Though Americans celebrated the British defeat at the Battle of New Orleans, U.S. failures in the War of 1812 concerned many leaders. In later years, they took steps to improve the country's military institutions. Meanwhile, the expanding frontier continued to absorb the regular U.S. Army's attention. Although conflicts with native peoples were not new, after 1830 President Andrew Jackson's policy of Indian Removal sparked wars and forced migrations. As for the U.S. Navy, it maintained a modest fleet of smaller- to medium-sized vessels to protect American shipping and advance national interests around the world. The most prominent conflict between 1815 and the Civil War was the Mexican War of 1846–48. U.S. forces demonstrated improved leadership, organization, and planning, enough to deliver what had not been attained in the War of 1812: a clear victory that achieved the U.S. government's political goals. But that victory would produce other conflicts and complications in the years leading up to and including the American Civil War.

In this chapter, students will learn about:

- Reforms following the War of 1812.
- The experiences of antebellum soldiers and sailors.
- The Wars of Indian Removal.
- U.S. military performance in the Mexican War.
- Filibuster expeditions and Indian wars between 1848 and 1865.

Army Reforms After the War of 1812

Administrative and logistical failures plagued U.S. efforts during the War of 1812. Previously, the War Department's permanent staff had consisted of the Secretary of War and some clerks, sufficient to maintain a few thousand troops. On occasions when Congress had expanded the army's size, it had also added temporary administrative positions in the Department. Such

September 1847	1847–58	1854–56	1858–59	1861	1862	1864–1867	1864–1868	November 1864
Mexico City captured	Pacific Northwest Wars	First Sioux War	Antelope Hills and Wichita Expeditions	Apache Wars begin (end 1886)	The Dakota War	Cheyenne-Arapaho War	Snake War	Sand Creek Massacre; First Battle of Adobe Walls

happened again in the War of 1812: More personnel were hired, and a "general staff" was created. The latter was not a general staff in the contemporary sense—it did not plan campaigns—but were instead officials assigned to oversee administrative functions for the army and War Department, including positions such as the Commissary General, Inspector General, Quartermaster General, Paymaster, and so on. Hired during the war and possessing little prior experience, they actually exacerbated the logistical chaos that bedeviled American operations, which were much bigger than any since the American Revolution. But after 1815, Congress retained the staff so that the War Department could cultivate the administrative knowledge and the bureaucratic infrastructure needed to support large armies.

Congress also passed legislation to help develop military expertise. The Reduction Act of 1821 actually reduced the U.S. Army from over 12,000 authorized personnel to almost 6,000. But while losing more than half of its enlisted men, the army retained most of its officers, over 80%. The Reduction Act incorporated the idea promoted by President James Monroe's Secretary of War, John C. Calhoun, that of an "expansible army." Going forward, peacetime regular Army units would remain significantly understrength in soldiers but maintain a full complement of officers: Keeping the latter would allow them to develop and improve their military skills. In wartime, when the Army inducted recruits to bring units to full strength, officers would quickly train and prepare enlistees for military service.

The expansible army concept stemmed from disappointing military performance in the War of 1812. To that point, the United States had expected militia to provide the bulk of the manpower for any large conflict. But the war clearly demonstrated the militia system's failure to provide a reliable standard of military proficiency. Both militiamen and their officers lacked basic skills and knowledge needed for wartime service. Though men could and were trained during the war, U.S. forces were ill-prepared for its first campaigns. Moreover, there was no established system for training large numbers of new soldiers in wartime, and effective military instruction and preparation stemmed from the abilities of individual officers, Jacob Brown and Winfield Scott being the best examples.

The Reduction Act enabled the U.S. Army to better prepare officers in peacetime for training and leading greater numbers of soldiers in war. But it could only accomplish so much. Calhoun expected the regular Army could be increased to between 11,000 and 12,000 men without adding any officers, and up to 19,000 by recruiting an additional 288 officers (the Reduction Act established 540 officer billets). Any large war, though, would require larger forces, which would have to be raised from militiamen and via volunteer formations. As Congress neglected to pass any legislation to improve state militias, the quality of those units would remain uncertain.

But the Reduction Act represented a subtle shift of the place of military service in American society. In the colonial era, no distinct barriers existed between civilian and military endeavors. With some exceptions, militia service was required of all males, and in war, they were recruited for campaigns and led by men who were also leaders in their communities. After the Revolutionary War, American leaders accepted the need for a standing army, though they continued to rely upon state militias for manpower in any large war. Political bickering between

Federalists and Republicans victimized the early U.S. Army, and its small yet fluctuating size did not offer enviable long-term career prospects. By the time the War of 1812 ended, however, the Army's simple existence was no longer politically charged. Moreover, beginning with the Reduction Act, young men oriented toward service and leadership could pursue a long-term career as an army officer. As noted by William Skelton, men could now choose officership as a lifelong career, one based on military service, leadership, and expertise.

This development was an initial step toward establishing military service as a profession distinct from civilian pursuits in America. (This distinction was much more pronounced in European countries that had created standing armies in the seventeenth century.) In 1822, Calhoun implemented another policy along modern lines by establishing army recruitment offices in major American cities. Traditionally, individual officers had raised troops in their communities, utilizing personal connections and their reputations to induce enlistments. The army continued to rely on this method, but recruitment offices soon accounted for the majority of new enlistees, who were dispersed among its various units.

One other major change under Calhoun was construction of a new set of coastal forts, sometimes called "the third defense system"—the first being fortifications built during the 1790s, the second constructed between the Chesapeake-Leopard Affair of 1807 and the War of 1812. In 1816, President Monroe appointed a Board of Engineers for Fortifications, which set coastal defense priorities for the next few decades. Construction proceeded slowly at a few dozen sites, mostly in key harbors and waterways. But the program entailed a substantial financial commitment by the U.S. government, which devoted more than $35 million between 1816 and 1861 on such fortifications (today, hundreds of millions of dollars).

Military Education

Changes at the United States Military Academy (USMA) at West Point, New York, also promoted the long-term development of an American military profession. Though created in 1802, the academy had faltered before 1817, when Calhoun appointed Sylvanus Thayer as Superintendent. A few years earlier, the army had sent Thayer abroad to learn about European military practices and education. Known as the "father" of West Point, Thayer instituted many changes that today define life at the academy. For example, he organized cadets into tactical units similar to regular Army formations and introduced a demerit system to track and punish cadet infractions.

In terms of curriculum, the academy was primarily an engineering school. Cadets took numerous courses in math, science, and engineering, and only one that addressed military topics (which devoted much time to fortifications). But West Point nonetheless promoted a sense of military professionalism among its graduates, one that Samuel Huntington called "corporate-ness." Life at the academy was defined by military discipline and an emphasis on service. It shaped cadets' outlooks and established a sense of professional identity among them. Moreover, over time their attitudes spread within the army, as academy graduates received most new officer commissions (64% of officers were USMA graduates by 1830). As noted previously, in a large war, the United States would have to raise numerous volunteer and militia units, creating a great need for officers that could only be met by commissioning civilians without formal military experience (as happened during the Mexican and Civil Wars). But USMA graduates, though a minority, provided an example that new officers often emulated.

The government created other schools to promote military education. In 1824, the Monroe administration formed the Artillery School at Fortress Monroe, Virginia, and a few years later the Infantry School of Practice at Jefferson Barracks, Missouri. But troop scarcity during the Second Seminole War (see below) shut down the former in 1835, and the latter did little beyond providing new recruits rudimentary training. The 1820s and 1830s also saw the formation of some journals to promote discussion and knowledge among officers of particular branches, but these were also short-lived.

Emerging ideas of professional identity were not always shared among officers. Those assigned to the War Department were often more concerned with their particular bureaucratic division's influence. Moreover, modern concepts of military professionalism—with their emphasis on knowledge and expertise as a basis for commissioning and promotion—were not known in the early nineteenth-century United States. Instead, a distinct American military profession was just establishing itself in this period, forming the basis for more rigorous requirements based upon military proficiency in later eras. Indeed, conditions of service often retarded the cultivation of martial skills among army personnel.

Life in the Antebellum Army

Manpower was one of the biggest problems for the army, one exacerbated by other opportunities available to young men. In the antebellum period (1815–61), expanding westward settlement beckoned people who sought to farm their own property. In frontier areas, skilled workers such as blacksmiths and carpenters could also make good livings. Industrialization was beginning in the northeastern part of the country, providing factory jobs for unskilled laborers. In contrast, army pay was low. Troops received additional compensation such as housing, food, and clothing, though quality was often poor. Moreover, soldiers endured discipline stricter than in civilian life and often served in lonely, isolated garrisons.

Who enlisted in the U.S. Army? Many were immigrants. More than 20% of regular Army soldiers were foreign-born in the 1820s, rising to over 50% in the 1850s. A large proportion of them were Irish and German, the two largest migrant groups in the antebellum era. Many immigrants arrived in the United States with little or no money and, depending upon their origin, may not have known English. The army offered men a job, and opportunities to learn about America and improve their language skills. Among native-born U.S. citizens, some enlisted out of a sense of adventure or to flee uncomfortable personal circumstances. Many did so for economic reasons: Though the country was growing in general, occasional recessions and depressions affected particular regions and industries.

Recruiters often found recruits—U.S. and foreign-born—in northeastern cities, which had large numbers of single young men. Recruitment standards, or adherence to them, varied over time. For example, new enlistees were not supposed to be minors, or drunk, but were expected to know English. When violations of these standards were aggressively enforced, such as in the 1850s, they could lead to the disqualification of most new recruits.

The U.S. Army also suffered from desertion, which in a given year could reach 20% of its manpower. A soldier was most likely to desert within a few months of enlisting, after first experiencing the discipline, drudgery, and often arbitrary nature of army life. For officers, desertion was a horrid offense and severely punished, often with flogging. Though outlawed between 1812 and 1833, some officers used it illegally. Those who did not employed other forms of corporal (or simply degrading) punishment for desertion and other offenses—particularly for those who seemed to challenge their authority. Junior officers were sometimes insecure in their positions and could be quick to sense insubordination.

Attitudes toward troops varied. Many officers were prejudiced against enlisted men—or the type of men they saw as enlisting—regarding them as lazy and incompetent, and hence requiring discipline to turn them into reliable soldiers. Others demonstrated more care for their troops. Both the War Department and Congress struggled with balancing officers' requirements for discipline against positive enticements to attract new recruits and reenlistments. For example, while Congress allowed legal flogging in 1833 for cases of desertion, it

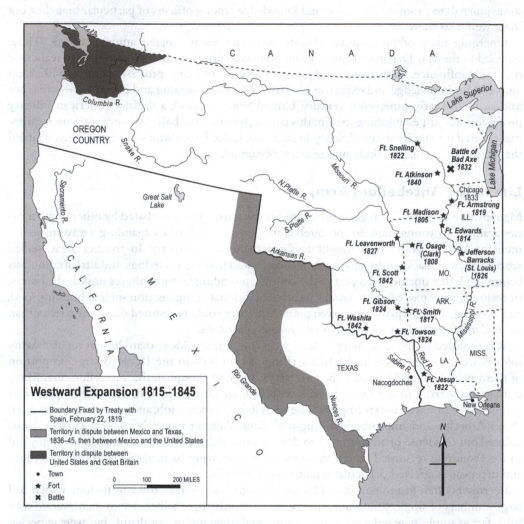

Map 5.1 Westward Expansion 1815–1845

also reduced enlistment terms to three years, increased soldier pay, and offered reenlistment bounties.

The army maintained dozens of posts in the antebellum period. Some were in large eastern cities or coastal fortifications. But most were out west, including installations in cool northern areas such as Fort Winnebago, Wisconsin, and those in arid, hotter regions such as Fort Gibson in what is now Oklahoma. A few larger facilities served as recruiting depots, such as Jefferson Barracks, Missouri. Most, though, were built just beyond expanding areas of white settlement and held small garrisons, some fewer than 100 soldiers.

Garrison routine encompassed reveille, inspections, changing of the guard, meals, drills, and maintenance of posts and troops' equipment. All soldiers periodically performed guard duty, which usually lasted 24 hours. Beyond routine responsibilities, troops also labored on projects such as constructing roads to facilitate settlement. Sometimes a commander dispatched a detachment to survey or explore an area. The various duties and small sizes of the garrisons generally prevented the concentration of enough troops for training units larger than companies.

Box 5.1   Life as a Frontier Soldier in the Antebellum Army

Dragoons were a type of cavalry unit that ranged the western frontiers. The following excerpt comes from Percival G. Lowe's *Five Years a Dragoon ([18]49 to [18]54)*, published in 1906, and provides insight into army life of the period.

And now the winter was before us, and we hoped for rest—rest that every man and every horse needed. To sum up the summer's campaign: I had ridden . . . [a] total, 3,100 miles . . .

An officer said to me when talking of this campaign, "Well, you did not have any mounted drill for some time, after that!" In a week we drilled an hour mounted in the forenoon and on foot in the afternoon, but we drilled carefully; went through the evolutions, saber exercises and pistol practice at a walk; in a few weeks a part of the time at a trot, and in a couple of months all of the gaits, never missing mounted drill every forenoon when weather and ground was suitable on week days, and, except Saturday, afternoons on foot, with inspection mounted on Sunday morning. One hour drill each time. In case of rain or snow we drilled on foot in quarters. Our horses were ridden to the river for water morning and evening before corn was fed to them which, with the hour's drill, gave them good exercise . . .

And now we were settled down in comfortable quarters for those times. A bed sack, refilled with prairie hay . . . once a month, and a pair of soldier blankets, with overcoat, or anything else one could utilize for a pillow. If the Government allowance of wood was not sufficient, we took a company team, made a detail, and hauled more from above the post. Indefatigable commissary and quartermaster Sergeant Cook managed our rations and forage so that men and horses fared well. We got vegetables and apples from Missouri. Nothing of the kind was then furnished by the commissary. Cook got some barrels and had them sawed in two for bath tubs, which we could use in the dining room. . . . The troop moved about so much that there was little company fund, and from our small pay we 'chipped in' for nearly all the extras.

Boredom was a perennial problem at isolated garrisons. Off-duty soldiers pursued a variety of outdoor distractions depending upon weather and climate, such as hunting, fishing, or gardening (which supplemented monotonous army rations). Indoor diversions included checkers and cards as well as organized activities such as dances. Chaplains were occasionally available for religious services, but alcohol was far more prevalent among army installations: Whiskey was included in daily rations. Beyond drunkenness, another long-standing hazard of army life was disease. Soldiers' afflictions depended upon season, location, and circumstances but included malaria, scurvy, and cholera.

Most men in a garrison were single. But some officers and a few enlisted soldiers had wives, and occasionally children. Officers could expect their own quarters, though junior ones had to defer to the preferences of their superiors. The crude nature of frontier installations could shock those officers' wives raised in more refined circumstances. Many women adjusted to garrison life; those who could not often resided in a larger town while their husbands served in army posts. Enlisted soldiers' wives sometimes acquired jobs as garrison laundresses or in hospitals, and acquired quarters as a perquisite of employment. Others worked as servants for officers' families and resided with them. Assignments to new posts imposed hardships upon families, though officers and their dependents often traveled in easier circumstances. Lack of schools and medical facilities posed problems for parents, though frontier postings offered children opportunities for outdoor experiences—and to meet Indians.

Troops in western and southern posts often interacted peacefully with native peoples, despite white prejudices that regarded Indians as uncivilized and barbaric. Individual soldiers traded with them, visited their homes, and shared recreational and social activities with them. Some officers and enlisted men took Indian mistresses. Conversely, disputes could arise between troops and native men over women, or regarding a purchase. While some soldiers never overcame their prejudice toward Indians, officers tasked with enforcing government policies sometimes became sympathetic to native peoples struggling to maintain traditional lifestyles and independence. For these men, President Andrew Jackson's Indian Removal policy posed a serious challenge. When tensions with native peoples erupted into violence, the army had to address the crisis—and conflict inevitably hardened troops' attitudes toward Indian foes.

Andrew Jackson and Indian Removal

One war occurred a decade before Jackson's presidency and featured him as the U.S. field commander. Tensions between Seminoles in Spanish Florida and Georgia settlers predated the War of 1812, and then escalated. After the First Creek War, many Red Stick Creeks ventured south to join the Seminoles. The latter had formed in the eighteenth century as an amalgamation of various Indian bands fleeing conflict farther north while also offering a haven for runaway slaves. In 1816, American forces destroyed the "Negro Fort" on the Apalachicola River in Spanish Florida, which warriors had been using as a base for frontier raids. In November 1817, U.S. troops also destroyed Fowltown, an Indian village that had also supported war parties. But warriors retaliated, attacking a boat on the Apalachicola carrying soldiers and civilians, killing or capturing more than 30 people.

The latter incident formally started the First Seminole War of 1817–18. The War Department appointed Andrew Jackson to command U.S. operations. By March 1818, roughly 4,500 men had congregated at Fort Scott, north of the Florida–Georgia border—including about 1,000 Georgia militia, 1,600 friendly Creeks, and 1,000 six-month volunteers Jackson had brought from Tennessee. Taking part of this force into Florida, on April 7 Jackson captured the Spanish fort of St. Marks. His men then marched on some Seminole settlements that had been abandoned. Returning to St. Marks, Jackson court-martialed three Britons his troops had captured for supplying the Seminoles, executing two of them. In May, Jackson's forces marched west and, after a three-day siege, captured the Spanish fort at Pensacola.

Here the campaign ended. Leaving a garrison, Jackson returned north to report to President Monroe and Secretary Calhoun. His campaign upset numerous people: Jackson's army had executed British subjects and captured Spanish forts to deny aid to the Seminoles. But the United States was not at war with Britain or Spain! His superiors, though, did not reprimand Jackson. Expansion-minded Americans had long coveted Spanish Florida. In 1817, the Monroe administration was trying to coax Spain into recognizing American gains in West Florida during the War of 1812 and selling the rest of Florida to the United States. Jackson's campaign demonstrated Americans could use force to resolve the issue, and may have led to the Transcontinental Treaty. Negotiated in 1819 between American Secretary of State John Quincy Adams and Spanish minister Luis de Onís, it was ratified in 1821 and ceded all of Florida to the United States.

As President of the United States, Andrew Jackson would acquire more land for white settlement. Elected in 1828, he was the first Democratic Party candidate to win the office. The party had formed in the 1820s, appealing to populist sentiments among U.S. men disenchanted with the elitism of established politicians. Jackson was their ideal candidate: Born in the Carolina backcountry, with no formal education or family wealth, he had become a successful Tennessee planter and lawyer with little more than his intelligence and perseverance. Moreover, his military successes had already made him a national figure in the United States, and he was wildly popular among white southerners. They had benefited the most from territories acquired as a result of his campaigns, and he shared with them a widespread disdain toward Indians and a desire to acquire their homelands.

By 1828, most native peoples east of the Mississippi River resided in the "Old Southwest." The largest—the Cherokees, Chickasaws, Choctaws, Creeks, and Seminoles—were sometimes referred to as the five "civilized tribes," in that many of them had adopted white American lifestyles. The Cherokee had done the most to assimilate, codifying their language into a written form, producing a newspaper and a constitution, and forming a government under the latter. But Georgia nonetheless tried to confiscate Cherokee territory in the 1820s. After first accepting a treaty of dubious legality, its government then declared the Cherokee fell under Georgia's jurisdiction, and that their land was owned by the state. Cherokee leaders resisted through the courts, asserting they were a sovereign nation that had executed treaties with the federal government and did not fall under state jurisdiction.

In 1831 and 1832, the Supreme Court ruled in their favor. But by then Andrew Jackson was president. He refused to use federal authority to stop states from expelling native peoples within their borders. He instead adopted a policy of encouraging Indian groups to migrate west beyond the Mississippi or submit to state control, the centerpiece of which was the Indian Removal Act of 1830. Congress provided money to entice native groups to sign new treaties, whereby they would abandon their traditional homelands and migrate to new lands provided by the federal government (mostly in present-day Oklahoma and Arkansas).

Jackson asserted no Indians would be forced to move, that treaties should be voluntary. But his stance toward the Supreme Court rulings indicated his administration would provide no assistance to Indians who wanted to remain on their lands. Many native peoples concluded deals with the federal government and migrated peacefully, though not happily. In some cases, treaties were negotiated in questionable circumstances, and not approved by most Indians within nations such as the Cherokee or the Seminoles (discussed below). Despite Jackson's promises, the U.S. government would use troops to enforce these questionable agreements.

Ironically, of all the wars of Indian Removal, the biggest was against the Seminoles. After the First Seminole War, most sold their land and moved to a reservation in central Florida, as per the 1823 Treaty of Fort Moultrie. Thereafter, tensions festered over slaves: Seminoles continued to welcome runaways, whereas white owners wanted them returned. After Jackson became president, U.S. and Seminole representatives concluded the 1832 Treaty of Payne's Landing, whereby the Seminoles would abandon Florida for lands out west—which led to the Second Seminole War. By then, U.S. forces had mobilized to confront another native people.

Black Hawk's War, 1832

The first conflict of Jackson's presidency was something of a tragic case. In 1832, chief Black Hawk and about 1,000 men, women, and children tried to return to their traditional homelands in northern Illinois. Previously, the federal government had forced Fox and Sauk peoples to leave for Iowa in accordance with a dubious treaty negotiated decades earlier. Black Hawk was not looking to fight and believed other native groups and the British in Canada would support him. But when his band crossed the Mississippi in April, it provoked a panic among white settlers that became Black Hawk's War.

Illinois militia quickly mobilized. In May, realizing no help would come, Black Hawk tried to return to Iowa. When militia forces approached, he dispatched emissaries to surrender. Suspicious militiamen, however, did not understand their language, and instead began a disorganized attack called "the Battle of Stillman's Run." Black Hawk's warriors repelled the assault, but now faced a larger war—one that saw the commitment of a third of the regular U.S. Army's

Figure 5.1 "Battle of Bad Axe"

In *Das illustrirte Mississippithal* (Dusseldorf: Arnz & Co., 1857)

The day prior to the actual Battle of Bad Axe, a river steamer prevented most of Black Hawk's people from crossing the Mississippi River to safety. The *Warrior* was a private vessel recently chartered by an army officer. An artillery piece had been placed aboard that fired at the shore before running out of ammunition.

Library of Congress, Prints and Photographs Division, LC-USZ62–90

strength and the mobilization of 9,000 militiamen from five states, primarily Illinois (most would not see combat, including a young Abraham Lincoln).

After Stillman's Run, Black Hawk's group fled north into Wisconsin. His warriors and some from nearby groups (Kickapoos and Potawatomies) raided settlements in the region, and efforts to track them down produced skirmishes with militiamen. Troops caught up with Black Hawk's people near the Wisconsin River in July, but at the Battle of Wisconsin Heights, warriors defended long enough for the rest of the band to escape. Language problems doomed another surrender attempt, and by August 1 Black Hawk's followers—now reduced to about 500—reached the Mississippi River near the confluence with the Bad Axe River. Perhaps 100 managed to cross it before the next day, when over 1,000 militia and U.S. regulars attacked. The vast majority of the remaining Indian men, women, and children were killed at the Battle of Bad Axe. Of those who crossed the Mississippi, most were hunted down by Sioux warriors working with U.S. forces. As for Black Hawk, he escaped and surrendered weeks later, and was returned to Iowa.

Black Hawk's War was brief—though long enough to destroy his band and prompt the mobilization of much of the country's available military manpower. Shortly thereafter, U.S. officials and Seminole chiefs began to implement the Treaty of Payne's Landing. The agreement stipulated that Seminoles would inspect reserved lands and would only move there if they approved. Moreover, migration was to occur within three years after the treaty was ratified. In 1833, government agents arranged for inspections. In the Treaty of Fort Gibson, Seminole representatives stated the land was acceptable. But upon returning to Florida, various chiefs

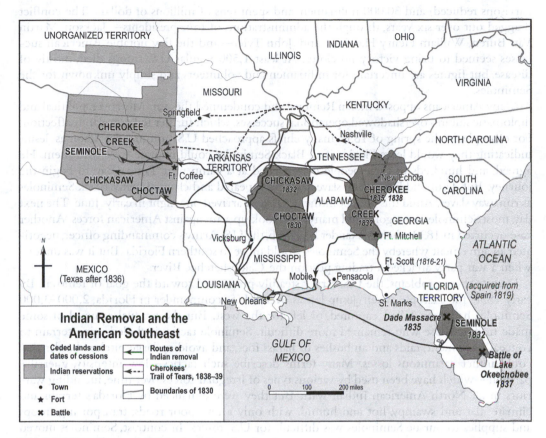

Map 5.2 Indian Removal and the American Southeast

claimed they had been forced to sign the treaty, or never had, or that they lacked the authority to make such a decision on behalf of their whole nation. Beginning in late 1834, federal agents began pressuring the Seminoles to leave. The U.S. Senate had only ratified the Treaty of Payne's Landing earlier that year, but Jackson's administration regarded the three-year window as starting when the treaty was signed in 1832.

Some chiefs agreed to go, and U.S. officials set a deadline of January 1, 1836. But when most Seminoles refused to leave, federal agents threatened them with force. In late 1835, frustrated Seminoles raided sugar plantations. Settlers fled to forts and towns. The United States increased troops in Florida to more than 500. By December 28, 1835, the Second Seminole War had begun. That day the popular warrior Osceola and a few dozen Indians killed a federal agent and settlers outside Fort King in north central Florida. Simultaneously, about 180 warriors ambushed a military convoy led by Francis Dade farther south. About half of the approximately 100 troops died in the initial volley; the rest retreated, defended themselves until ammunition ran out, and were overwhelmed. Only three men survived what became known as the Dade Massacre.

The Second Seminole War, 1835–42

The Second Seminole War, sometimes called "the Florida War," was perhaps the most unpopular U.S. war of the nineteenth century. To remove an estimated population of 5,000 Indians, the United States deployed 10,000 regular soldiers (requiring western posts be closed or garrisons reduced) and 30,000 militiamen, and spent tens of millions of dollars. The conflict dragged out over six years, through the administrations of four presidents—Jackson, Martin Van Buren, William Henry Harrison, and John Tyler—and the few notable American successes seemed to bring victory no closer. At least 1,500 regular U.S. troops died, mostly of disease, but figures are uncertain for militiamen and volunteers and simply unknown for the Seminoles.

Many Americans opposed Indian Removal and condemned the war. Moreover, political and diplomatic failures overshadowed operational successes, which further fed popular disaffection. For example, in the spring of 1837, many chiefs approached U.S. commander Thomas Jesup, indicating they would leave Florida if all Black Seminoles could migrate west with them. He agreed, and hundreds of their people congregated at a camp near Tampa Bay to begin the journey. But Jesup did little when slave catchers appeared and claimed many Black Seminoles as runaway slaves. Amid this disappointment, Osceola arrived one night in early June. The next day, most Seminoles were gone, and many soon took up arms against American forces. Another case occurred in 1839 when Alexander Macomb, the U.S. Army's commanding officer, negotiated an agreement whereby the Seminoles would move to southern Florida. But it was undone when a war party attacked a trading post on the Calooshatchee River.

Despite these problems, the U.S. Army steadily progressed toward the goal of removal. By early 1838, for example, when Jesup left as overall U.S. commander in Florida, 2,000–3,000 Seminoles had been killed, captured, or left for the west. But the gradual removal of some made finding those who remained more difficult. Seminole tactics included using terrain to conceal movement, raids and ambushes to harass foes, and avoiding large pitched battles that could inflict calamitous losses. Many terms describe such tactics—low-intensity, guerrilla, partisan—which have been used by various types of irregular forces over time, including warriors in all North American Indian wars. But they were enhanced by Florida's terrain and climate: flat and swampy, hot and humid, with only a few, poor roads; transporting troops and supplies to pursue Seminoles was difficult for U.S. forces. In contrast, Seminoles moved quickly through swamps and thickets, even when encumbered: Native casualties during the war are unknown because Seminoles usually retrieved their dead and wounded before being discovered by American troops.

Another U.S. problem was that, ironically, regular Army officers did not train to fight Indian wars. The one military course taken by West Point cadets was mostly devoted to fortifications. Moreover, most officers were biased toward conventional war against European opponents. Combat against "civilized" enemies provided the means to enhance one's martial reputation, whereas warfare against "barbarous" natives did not offer opportunities for glory—though many officers discovered fighting Indian foes was incredibly difficult. This bias shaped how some officers designed campaigns. For example Winfield Scott, U.S. commander in Florida in early 1836, organized three large columns (one each moving from the north, east, and south) to converge and trap Seminoles in their swampy refuge called "the Cove," near the Withlacoochee River north of Tampa Bay. But it took months to concentrate the requisite troops and supplies, and Seminoles easily avoided the slow-moving columns.

Thomas Jesup replaced Scott at the end of 1836. He commanded perhaps the largest concentration of American troops during the war, 8,000–9,000, about half volunteers or militia. Jesup's approach was better suited against irregular fighters. He built more outposts and sent out numerous small patrols to track down and harass Seminoles. By early 1837, cumulative U.S. operations drove many chiefs to seek peace. But Jesup suffered a political debacle in June when most of those preparing to leave Florida instead joined with Osceola. Some assert that this incident, whereby Jesup felt betrayed, led him to disregard Osceola's white flag and arrest the warrior when he came to parley the following October.

In late 1837, Jesup launched a more conventional campaign, using a few large columns to roust Seminoles from their refuges, similar to Scott's 1836 operation. One moved south down Florida's Atlantic coast, another advanced up the St. John's River, and a third commanded by Zachary Taylor moved east from Tampa Bay and then south toward Lake Okeechobee. Entering a large Seminole haven amid the swamps, Taylor's men precipitated the Battle of Lake Okeechobee, perhaps the largest engagement of the war. U.S. forces suffered 26 killed and 112 wounded out of 800 soldiers, driving off hundreds of warriors and killing 14. But with the exception of the Battle of Loxahatchee in January 1838, Taylor's force was the only one to encounter significant numbers of enemy warriors. Nonetheless, the campaign induced many Seminoles to surrender and migrate.

In May 1838, Taylor replaced Jesup as the top commander in Florida. By then, troop levels had declined by a few thousand, in part due to Congressional budget cuts following the Panic of 1837. But Congress continued war appropriations despite the conflict's unpopularity; by its end, the regular U.S. Army had increased from 7,500 to 12,500 soldiers. Taylor pursued a new approach: To provide security for settlers, he divided the northern part of central Florida into squares 20 miles on each side. In the center of each he established an outpost with an officer and a few dozen troops tasked with patrolling their square and clearing out Seminoles. His approach was similar to techniques employed in later wars to combat guerrillas and insurgents, though Taylor lacked the manpower to make it effective.

William K. Armistead replaced Taylor as commander in May 1840, and lasted a year. Unlike his predecessors, he launched summer operations, though they were limited. The following winter, the Van Buren administration gave him $1 million to induce remaining Seminole chiefs to migrate west. But Armistead undermined his diplomacy by simultaneously sending troops out to harass Seminole bands. Like Jesup and Taylor, he asked to be relieved, and was replaced as commander by William J. Worth in May 1841. Worth pursued Armistead's operational ideas further, launching a major campaign that summer. Army officers worried their men would sicken, and many did. But the Seminoles harvested food in the summer. Though none of his troops engaged in significant combat, Worth's 1841 summer campaign destroyed large numbers of crops and fields, making Seminole resistance difficult to sustain. Worth launched more operations into the Everglades that December, which also encountered minimal resistance.

In August 1842 Worth, backed by President John Tyler, unilaterally declared the war over. The hundreds of Seminoles who remained in Florida were allowed to stay on lands further south. They moved, only to see tensions arise again when planters later migrated to the area. A Third Seminole War broke out in 1855 involving a band led by Billy Bowlegs (who had fought in the prior two wars), sparked by encroachment on his people's lands. After many raids and reprisals, in 1858 his band also migrated west. About 200 Seminoles then remained in Florida, primarily around Lake Okeechobee and in the Everglades.

Evolving Military Attitudes

Worth had proposed ending hostilities earlier, echoing the opinions of senior Florida commanders going back to Jesup. Confronted with the quandaries of the war, these officers believed the time, effort, and sacrifice required to remove every last Seminole from Florida would be excessive, and advocated letting some remain in parts of the territory. The U.S. government had not been willing to accept such a concession before 1842, by which point accumulating costs and growing popular frustration made continuing the war politically unfeasible. Though commanders such as Jesup, Taylor, Armistead, and Worth disagreed with the objectives and prosecution of the Second Seminole War, they nonetheless fulfilled their missions, expressing their concerns to their superiors and, except Worth, serving until they were relieved at their own request.

Their conduct represents another aspect of military professionalism emerging in this period. This aspect is the ideal that officers should not be influenced by politics but pursue the tasks assigned to them to the best of their ability. This ethic allows for doubts about a mission to be expressed to superiors so long as an officer continues to fulfill assigned duties until reassigned. This principle has not always been observed, and when it is, other problems may arise, such as if senior officials ignore expressed concerns. But in this war, one can observe senior commanders trying to abide by this professional ideal. They also illustrated some persistent tensions within the American military establishment. Since the War of the American Revolution, regular officers had disparaged the performance of militia and short-term volunteer units, as they did again during the Second Seminole War. Toward the war's end, U.S. Army commanders relied more upon regular troops, arguing Florida militiamen in particular would better help their operations by remaining at and defending their homes.

The Second Creek War, 1836–37

Given its long duration, the Second Seminole War has overshadowed the Second Creek War, sometimes called "the Creek War of 1836." Both stemmed from Jackson's Indian Removal policies. In 1832, Creek delegates signed the Treaty of Washington, or the Cusseta Treaty. They agreed to sell most of their territory in Alabama, but a large proportion would remain in Creek hands. Individual Indians would receive land titles, which they could keep, or sell and migrate west to lands provided by the U.S. government. But this arrangement broke down amid widespread land hunger fueled by a cotton boom. White speculators defrauded Creeks of their titles, and squatters ignored them entirely. Federal efforts to protect native rights were weak.

In the spring of 1836, tensions exploded into war. As with the war of 1813–14, Creeks fought one another, some allying with and some fighting the United States. In May war parties attacked settlements near the Georgia-Alabama border, particularly around Columbus and the Chattahoochee River. The federal government dispatched 1,100 regular soldiers; about 9,000 Alabama and Georgia militiamen also participated in the conflict, as did over 1,000 Indian allies. The Jackson administration ordered Winfield Scott to leave Florida and assume command of operations against hostile Creeks. But it was Thomas Jesup who on June 16, leading militia and friendly Indians, attacked the camp of Chief Neah Emathla, capturing him and over 300 warriors. Thereafter, hundreds of other Creek men, women, and children surrendered and were held temporarily at Fort Mitchell, Alabama.

On July 1, 1836, Scott declared the war over, though that was not accurate. U.S. officials forced Neah Emathla and his followers to leave for the west, and many other bands followed. Over 14,000 Creeks left for the west in 1836—but not all. Hostilities continued throughout the summer. After a lapse, they picked up again in 1837 and spread to western Florida. Fighting then died out to the north, but sporadic violence afflicted the Florida panhandle until the 1850s. Many Creeks fled to the Seminoles or the Cherokee. Others agreed to fight the Seminoles for the United States, only to have their families forced from their lands. These Creeks migrated in 1837, after which only a handful remained in Alabama.

Forced Removal Short of War: The Trail of Tears, 1838–39

Most American students learn about the Cherokee exodus from their homelands, one of many in the age of Indian Removal. Some Indian nations such as the Choctaws and the Chickasaws moved voluntarily, as did most Creeks (ostensibly) after Neah Emaltha's expulsion. Conversely, the United States needed a prolonged war to oust Seminoles from Florida. The Cherokees refused to leave, but they did not take up arms. Instead, military units forced them out of their homes. All native peoples who moved west of the Mississippi suffered hardships, from lack of food to exposure to the elements, which sickened or killed travelers. But those of the Cherokee migration were excessive, known as "The Trail Where They Cried," or more popularly "the Trail of Tears."

The 1835 Treaty of New Echota stipulated that the Cherokee would abandon their lands for western territories and some monetary compensation within two years of ratification. Though concluded in the Cherokee capital, the signatories did not include authorized representatives of the Cherokee government. Its recognized leader, Chief John Ross, protested the treaty, but the U.S. Senate ratified it anyway in 1836. Jackson's administration made initial plans to relocate the Cherokees but actual removal fell to that of his successor, President Martin Van Buren. In April 1838, he ordered Winfield Scott to command the operation. Scott was promised 3,000 regular troops and told to have the Cherokees off their lands by May 23, 1838.

The Cherokees inhabited parts of North Carolina, Georgia, Tennessee, and Alabama. Scott divided this territory into three zones, each containing camps where Cherokees (and their slaves) would be "collected"—about three dozen in total. They would then be moved to one of three debarkation points (two in Tennessee, one in Alabama) where they would board boats to make most of the remaining journey by water, in order to minimize hardships upon the travelers.

In early May, Scott proclaimed the Cherokees had to leave. But few families reported to the camps before the deadline. He then prepared to expel them. Scott's orders stated troops should behave in a humane manner, avoiding cruelty, and that Cherokee unable to walk should ride on horses, ponies, or wagons. But the regular soldiers promised him had not arrived. Instead, Scott used a few thousand militiamen—many of whom were eager to purchase lands made available by the Cherokee's expulsion. Removal of the Georgia Cherokee began on May 26, 1838, with many families driven out of their homes at bayonet point. Often their movable property, particularly livestock, was taken and their homes burned as they were hustled away.

By mid-June, U.S. Army soldiers had arrived, and militia units were dismissed. Cherokee expulsion from other states began in July, with less chaos and mistreatment. By August, about 3,000 Cherokees had embarked on boats when, in the heat of the summer, water levels fell so low that rivers were no longer navigable. Moreover, disease had broken out among the 13,000 still in the camps. Scott allowed the Cherokees to remain until the hot weather passed. Meanwhile Chief John Ross persuaded the Van Buren administration to let the Cherokee continue their migration without armed escort.

Scott dismissed his troops. But the Cherokee continued their exodus, marching overland through the bitterly cold winter of 1838–39, with the last travelers arriving in Oklahoma that March. The exact number of Cherokee who died, either in the camps or during their journey, is not known, though estimates range from 4,000–8,000. To his credit, Scott voluntarily accompanied one band of Cherokee as an observer before being recalled to Washington. He represents another officer who, though he had doubts about his assigned mission, executed it as well as he could, comporting himself according to the ideal of officership evolving in this period.

The Trail of Tears was another case where the federal government used military units to execute its Indian Removal policy. Unlike many Seminoles and Creek, the Cherokees chose not to resist, so outright war did not erupt. But from the First Creek War to the Second Seminole War, armed force was crucial to opening up the Old Southwest to white expansion by either expelling the Indian inhabitants or inducing them to abandon their homelands.

Overview of the Antebellum U.S. Navy

Around 1810, Barbary corsairs again molested American shipping. The United States soon became embroiled in the War of 1812, but afterward President James Madison dispatched two squadrons to the Mediterranean, precipitating the short Second Barbary War or the Algerian War of 1815. Stephen Decatur's fleet of 10 vessels, including three frigates, destroyed two enemy warships and scattered others before sailing into Algiers. Its ruler agreed to release American prisoners, to end demands for tribute, and to accept trade terms that were favorable to the United States. Decatur's squadron then sailed to Tunis and Tripoli and imposed similar treaties.

The Madison administration subsequently established a permanent naval presence in the Mediterranean. This was the first of many squadrons, or "stations," that the U.S. Navy maintained in particular seas. Beyond the Mediterranean, other stations included the Caribbean (West Indies), Latin America, the eastern Pacific, and the Far East. A given squadron included a handful of ships that usually operated independently, pursuing a variety of missions. One was protecting American commerce and suppressing piracy—particularly for the West Indies Squadron. At times, ships of the African Squadron combated the illegal slave trade. U.S. Navy ships also charted and explored little-known waters and "showed the flag" in diplomatic missions to advance U.S. interests. Commodore Matthew C. Perry, for example, famously led voyages to Japan in 1853 and 1854, opening the country to American commerce for the first time.

Perry was also one of the few U.S. naval officers who embraced new technology in the antebellum period. Most were wary of developments such as steam power, screw propellers, and shell guns (cannons that could fire high velocity, explosive projectiles). Perry is sometimes known as the "Father of the Steam Navy" for his advocacy of modern technologies and for organizing the U.S. Navy's first corps of engineers. Of the four "black ships" that he took into Tokyo Bay in 1853, two were steam powered, and all had shell guns. But due to broader conservative views and limited naval budgets, most U.S. Navy warships remained wooden and reliant upon sails and wind for propulsion.

Like the army, the navy had problems with recruitment. Merchants usually offered sailors better wages and less stringent discipline: Flogging remained standard practice in the U.S. Navy until the 1850s. Foreign-born and black sailors comprised significant proportions of many naval crews. Turnover was high, as crewmen enlisted for just a few years, sometimes just for the duration of a single voyage. At sea, life was often more monotonous than at isolated army outposts. Warships had large crews to man guns: Only a small proportion was needed to sail them. Morale was low among sailors as well as officers. The U.S. Navy only had a few hundred officer billets in this period, and promotion was slow and based upon seniority. Before 1845, midshipmen (officer candidates) had practically no formal opportunities to develop skills and expertise before shipboard service. That year, President James K. Polk's Secretary of the Navy, George Bancroft, created the Naval School at Annapolis, Maryland, which a few years later became the United States Naval Academy.

Beyond fighting pirates, the U.S. Navy saw little combat in the 20 years after the Algerian War. But naval forces—and those of the Revenue-Marine service, a precursor of the U.S. Coast Guard—participated in the Second Seminole War. Vessels patrolled the Florida coast, rivers, and the Everglades in search of Seminoles and traders trying to sell them arms. Sailors and marines garrisoned forts and joined some land campaigns. For example, a joint Army-Navy force fought one of the war's larger engagements, the Battle of Loxahatchee, in January 1838. A few years later, the U.S. Navy would have more extensive duties during the Mexican War.

Manifest Destiny, Texas, and Mexico

The federal policy of Indian Removal expelled native peoples from their homelands within the bounds claimed by the United States. But white Americans had long sought additional territory, as demonstrated by the Louisiana Purchase, the First Seminole War, and the acquisition of Florida. The notion of "manifest destiny" expressed this desire in the 1840s, asserting that the United States would expand across North America to the Pacific—though it assumed that the Americans who would dominate the continent would be white Anglo-Saxon Protestants. The term itself was not coined until 1845, yet the Democratic Party effectively tapped into these sentiments during the presidential election of 1844, won by James K. Polk.

White Americans sought lands in the Pacific Northwest, a popular destination for settlers traveling the Oregon Trail in the 1840s. The boundary with Canada was disputed, and Polk's campaign bellicosely advocated a northern boundary of "54° 40' or Fight!" But in early 1846, the British and Polk's administration compromised on the 49th parallel for the common border. Polk also tried both bluster and negotiations to acquire Mexico's northern territories, but resentments over Texas doomed diplomatic efforts.

After winning independence from Spain in 1821, Mexico encouraged immigration from the United States into Texas so long as new settlers became Mexican citizens and accepted Catholicism. But as more white Americans arrived, they ignored these requirements and Mexican laws in general—such as the prohibition of slavery. Government efforts to control American settlers in the 1830s sparked tensions, which worsened after Antonio López de Santa Anna became the president and, in 1835, overthrew the Mexican constitution. Late that year, war began between Texan rebels and Santa Anna's troops.

The most renowned engagement of the Texas Revolution is the Alamo. In March 1836, a few thousand Mexican troops overwhelmed fewer than 200 defenders. Over the next few weeks, Mexican forces advanced farther east, with Santa Anna splitting his army to harass both the Texas coastline and the interior. On April 21, about 900 Texans under Sam Houston surprised Santa Anna's camp of 1,300–1,400 men at the Battle of San Jacinto. They killed over 600 Mexican soldiers and captured more than 700, while suffering few casualties.

Among the prisoners was Santa Anna, who negotiated a treaty that established the southern border of the new Texas Republic at the Rio Grande River. But the Mexican Congress rejected the agreement. It wanted the Nueces River further north—previously the provincial boundary—as the border. Amid the dispute, hostilities between Texas and Mexico resumed. These were generally skirmishes and raids between the Nueces and the Rio Grande, but at times the violence intensified. For example, Mexican forces attacked San Antonio twice in 1842, the second time occupying the city for many weeks. But the Texas Republic faced hostilities beyond Mexico, particularly ongoing raids of frontier settlements by Kiowa and Comanche warriors.

These problems prompted Texas to request annexation by the United States. Both Presidents Jackson and Van Buren demurred, suspecting it would provoke sectional animosities within the country. But President Tyler pursued the issue. Just before he left office, Congress passed a joint resolution in March 1845 "inviting" Texas to join the United States, which it accepted in July. The United States acquired both Texas and its border dispute—and Mexico broke off diplomatic relations.

The Mexican-American War, 1846–48: First Battles

Shortly after Texas accepted annexation in the summer of 1845, President Polk ordered an "Army of Occupation" commanded by Zachary Taylor to the Nueces River, which encamped on its southern bank (land claimed by Mexico). By the fall, about 4,000 soldiers had arrived, about half of the regular U.S. Army. Late that year, Polk dispatched an envoy, John L. Slidell, to offer tens of millions of dollars for Mexico's northern territories and recognition of the Rio Grande as the border with Texas. After Mexican officials refused to meet with him, Polk ordered the Army of Occupation to the Rio Grande. Arriving in March 1846, troops built Fort Texas across the river from a Mexican army in the town of Matamoros.

Tensions soon escalated. The Mexican commander demanded Taylor's force withdraw by April 15, otherwise there would be war. Taylor responded by having two navy ships attached to his command blockade the mouth of the Rio Grande, cutting off Matamoros. Later that month, a Mexican cavalry force crossed the river and overwhelmed a smaller patrol of U.S. dragoons. Taylor then took most of his troops north to fortify a base and collect supplies. A Mexican army under

Mariano Arista confronted them on their way back to Fort Texas (later called "Fort Brown"). It outnumbered the U.S. army by about 4,000 to 2,300, and was predominant in cavalry.

Although the flat terrain favored horsemen, Taylor had the advantage of more (and more modern) artillery. At the Battle of Palo Alto on May 8, 1846, American cannon repulsed Mexican cavalry charges, inflicting hundreds of casualties compared to a few dozen for the United States. Arista's men retreated and the next day took up defensive positions in a ravine. Here dense, low-lying foliage nullified the effectiveness of American artillery. At the Battle of Resaca de la Palma, Taylor ordered a cavalry charge and then an infantry advance. The fight devolved into smaller, simultaneous combats, but ultimately his troops drove off the Mexican army. Having lost hundreds of men to about 120 U.S. casualties, Arista's men fled south back across the Rio Grande.

The Mexican-American War: Initial U.S. Plans and Operations

News of the these events stirred support for war back in the United States. Polk asked Congress to enact war measures, which—with its Democratic majority—quickly agreed. After the Second Seminole War, the size of the regular U.S. army had shrunk, though along expansible lines: Congress now about doubled it to about 15,000 men by increasing numbers of enlisted men; the army already had most of the officers needed. Congress also authorized raising 50,000 volunteers to serve either one year or the duration of the war. Meanwhile, on his own authority, Zachary Taylor had requested that the governors of Texas and Louisiana organize about 5,000 volunteers to reinforce his army. Edmund P. Gaines, chief Army officer in the southwestern United States, had similarly raised about 11,000 men with three- or six-month enlistments.

Polk's objective in fighting Mexico was to acquire its northern provinces for the United States, particularly California and New Mexico. He hoped to avoid a prolonged conflict and believed that by quickly occupying these areas he could induce the Mexican government to sue for peace. In 1845, even before war began, the commander of the U.S. Pacific squadron received instructions to occupy or blockade Mexico's California ports if hostilities erupted. In May 1846, a strategy emerged to achieve the president's goals from talks and letters involving Polk, his cabinet, prominent politicians, and officers including Taylor and the U.S. Army's General-in-Chief Winfield Scott.

His administration created a small "Army of the West," commanded by Stephen Kearny, with orders to take Santa Fe and occupy New Mexico. Kearny also received authority to dispatch troops to California. John E. Wool was to lead another force from Texas to the northern Mexican city of Chihuahua, while Taylor would advance with the main U.S. field army to Monterrey. In addition, the U.S. Navy's Home Squadron would blockade ports on the Gulf of Mexico, strangling trade and preventing sea transport of men and supplies.

Prior to May 1846, Polk had done little to ready the country for war. Though public support remained strong in southern and western areas of the country, the war was unpopular elsewhere, as many Americans viewed it as an act of aggression. Yet the United States could better cope with the demands of a major conflict than Mexico. One advantage lay in potential military manpower: its population exceeded 20 million, whereas the Mexican population was about 7 million. The United States also had a larger and more robust industrializing economy. Another advantage was political: though they bickered and competed for power, U.S. political parties accepted the Constitution and worked within its framework, making the national government stable.

In contrast, Mexico's long war of independence (1810–21) had ravaged much of the country and produced political fragmentation. Mexican politicians had created constitutions, but the governments they established were often overthrown by *coup d'etats*. At the national level, liberals competed with conservatives, and centralists with federalists (the former wanted strong national government, the latter more power at the provincial level). But *caudillos*—strongmen who dominated the provinces—effectively limited the authority of the central government. In addition to

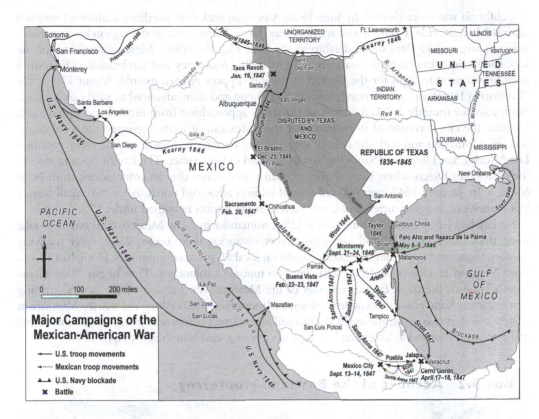

Map 5.3 Major Campaigns of the Mexican-American War

coups, Mexico also faced many rebellions, of which the Texas Revolution was the most successful. For decades after 1821, Santa Anna—a former Spanish officer of Mexican birth who fought for independence—was the most prominent figure in the country's politics. He supported numerous coups and acquired and lost power repeatedly: Santa Anna was Mexico's president 11 times.

These problems made it difficult for Mexico to raise and supply armies for operations against the United States beyond local defense forces. Similarly, generals in different regions were reluctant to part with forces under their command. During the entire war, Mexico mounted only one offensive campaign. Its political instability likely persuaded Polk that the country would offer little resistance to the occupation of its northern territories and would concede their loss after a short war. As it happened, Mexico was more resilient than he expected.

The Mexican-American War: The Far West

After a journey of about 900 miles over plains and mountains, Kearny and his 1,600 men arrived at Santa Fe in August 1846. New Mexico surrendered without resistance, and over the next few months U.S. troops occupied other parts of the territory. But in January 1847 a rebellion began. Hispanic and Indian residents in Taos killed the U.S. territorial governor, and attacks elsewhere on other "anglos" and their supporters followed. Concentrating about 350 soldiers at Santa Fe, commander Sterling Price chased the rebels back to Taos, where they took refuge in an apartment complex and a church at the Pueblo de Taos. After his forces assaulted the church, defenders fled to apartments or into the countryside. At least 150 rebels died, whereas Price's casualties totaled a few dozen. But his troops had suppressed the Taos Rebellion, ending challenges to U.S. authority in New Mexico.

California was more chaotic. In June 1846, American settlers in northern California revolted against Mexican rule. Explorer and army officer John C. Fremont, in the region leading a surveying party, quickly lent his leadership to the Bear Flag Rebellion. Meanwhile, forces of the U.S. Pacific Squadron occupied various ports, including Monterey and San Francisco. Fremont's men now agreed to fight for the United States and support American rule. About 170 of the "California Battalion" were ferried down to San Diego and then advanced toward Los Angeles. With another roughly 300 U.S. sailors and marines approaching from recently occupied Santa Barbara, the city surrendered in August. But then Mexican officials organized the local "californio" population and with the help of some cavalry overthrew American rule and recaptured Los Angeles, San Diego, and Santa Barbara by the end of September. The Pacific Squadron soon took back San Diego, where Kearny arrived with a small force after an arduous trek from New Mexico. In January 1847, over 600 sailors and soldiers advanced north. After two small battles, Los Angeles once again surrendered, and thereafter the region remained under U.S. control.

Kearny had left Alexander Doniphan as U.S. commander in New Mexico, with orders to take some troops to Chihuahua and join other forces advancing there under Wool. After receiving reinforcements and responding to Indian assaults on local Hispanic communities, Doniphan set out from Missouri in December 1846 with over 850 mounted volunteers. Thus began "Doniphan's March," one of the more famous episodes of the Mexican War because of the troops' grueling journey across hundreds of miles of brutal desert and mountain terrain. Along the way, the Missourians fought and won two engagements (El Brazito and Sacramento) before occupying Chihuahua. Wool had previously diverted to Saltillo, and Doniphan's troops joined him there by April 1847.

Box 5.2   Account of the Battle of Monterrey

Figure 5.2 Battle of Monter[r]ey—The Americans Forcing Their Way to the Main Plaza, Sept. 23th 1846

By N. Currier, 1846

Volunteers from Texas, known as "Texians," participated in the urban fighting inside Monterrey, as noted in the following account of the battle in Samuel C. Reid, Jr.'s *The Scouting Expeditions of McCulloch's Texas Rangers*, published in 1847.

Library of Congress, Prints and Photographs Division, LC-USZC4–1642

The street fight became appalling—both columns were now close engaged with the enemy, and steadily advanced inch by inch—our artillery was heard rumbling over the paved streets, galloping here and there, as the emergency required, and pouring forth a blazing fire of grape and ball—volley after volley of musketry, and the continued peals of artillery became almost deafening—the artillery of both sides raked the streets, the balls striking the houses with a terrible crash, while amid the roar of battle were heard the battering instruments used by the Texians. Doors were forced open, walls were battered down—entrances made through the longitudinal walls, and the enemy driven from room to room, and from house to house, followed by the shrieks of women, and the sharp crack of the Texian rifles. Cheer after cheer was heard in proud and exulting defiance, as the Texians or regulars gained the house-tops by means of ladders, while they poured in a rain of bullets upon the enemy on the opposite houses. It was indeed a most strange and novel scene of warfare.

Monterrey, 1846

Following the Battles of Palo Alto and Resaca de la Palma, Mexican troops pulled back from the Rio Grande. Taylor's army crossed the river and occupied Matamoras in late May 1846. In July, he advanced on Monterrey in the northern Mexican province of Nuevo León, but encountered delays. His men lacked boats and wagons, and summer rains made river navigation hazardous, while turning poor roads into muddy tracks. Moreover, at Camargo, the extreme heat, coming after intense rains, made many troops sick. In August, Taylor moved roughly 6,000 men to Cerralvo, but left thousands of troops behind who were too ill to continue. The next month his Army of Occupation—roughly half regulars and half volunteers—made its final advance to Monterrey, arriving on September 19.

The Battle of Monterrey occurred on September 20–24, 1846. Defending the city (which sat just north of a river) were a large fort to its north called "the Citadel," two smaller ones on hills to its west, and about 7,000 soldiers. Taylor divided his forces in two. One, composed primarily of regulars and Texas Rangers, attacked from the west. Its mission was to take the hills and forts overlooking the city and cut it off from the road that led west through the mountains into Mexico's interior. Another force, comprised mostly of volunteers, attacked the city from the east to distract the defenders. After reconnoitering the area on September 20, the main assaults began on September 21. By the end of next day, U.S. troops had taken the two western hills and established a position on the city's eastern end, and then made advances from both directions toward its center. Intense urban fighting comprised much of the Battle of Monterrey, with combatants fighting street to street, house-to-house, and rooftop to rooftop. On September 24, Mexican officials asked to negotiate.

The resulting armistice allowed the Mexican army to withdraw with some cannon, but it gave up the rest of its arms and ammunition, and surrendered the city and its outlying fortresses. Taylor agreed to suspend further U.S. advances for eight weeks or until either government abrogated the agreement. The terms fulfilled his objective of capturing Monterrey and provided a rest for his troops, who were exhausted and had taken hundreds of casualties. But Polk was furious that Taylor allowed a Mexican army to escape and rescinded the armistice. In November, Taylor advanced troops to the town of Saltillo and its important road junction, where forces under Wool later arrived.

U.S. Strategic Reassessment and a Mexican Offensive

More than just the enemy withdrawal from Monterrey stoked Polk's frustrations. He had hoped that U.S. occupation of Mexico's northern provinces would convince its government to sue for peace. By the fall of 1846, American troops had captured Monterrey and occupied New Mexico and much of California, while naval forces were blockading the Gulf coast. Yet Mexico's government gave no indication it was willing to stop fighting. Moreover, popular enthusiasm with the war was fading, and criticism was building. Polk and his cabinet now sought a way to compel Mexico to negotiate and end hostilities. They settled on an amphibious landing at Vera Cruz, followed by a march into the interior to the capital, Mexico City. Winfield Scott received the command.

The General-in-Chief and the president had not gotten along. Polk's urges for rapid action and Scott's attempts to implement orderly and effective war preparations produced mutual irritation. For months, Polk had denied Scott a field command. But the general had developed plans for the Vera Cruz campaign, and no one else was available who was capable of leading the expedition. The administration approved the operation in November, and by early January 1847 Scott had arrived in Mexico. Most U.S. troops mobilized for the war were serving under Taylor. Scott took more than half, over 8,000, from their camp at Camargo for the Vera Cruz campaign, including almost all the 4,000 regulars.

Taylor was then with a smaller force in Victoria, Mexico, securing communications between Saltillo and Tampico. The latter, Mexico's second-largest port, had recently been captured by the U.S. Navy. Taylor was furious when he heard most of his men had been appropriated for the Vera Cruz campaign, so much so that he ignored Scott's orders to retreat back to Monterrey. Instead, he moved most of his remaining troops a few miles south of Saltillo, ostensibly to protect U.S. gains further north. This decision helped instigate the only Mexican offensive of the war.

Santa Anna needed a victory. When the war began, he was living in exile in Cuba. But in the summer of 1846, the Polk administration allowed Santa Anna to return to Mexico, hoping he would negotiate a peace agreement if returned to power. Instead, after being reinstalled as president, he organized a force of 20,000 men, Mexico's largest wartime field army. Santa Anna knew many Mexicans were wary of him, and he could not negotiate with the United States and retain power. He needed a quick victory to improve his political standing and national morale. In January 1847, learning the United States was organizing a campaign against Vera Cruz, he decided to attack Taylor's army. That force, in an isolated position about 20 miles south of Saltillo, had less than 5,000 men, most of whom were inexperienced volunteers. To get there, Santa Anna marched his army over 200 miles of desert and mountains; thousands did not complete the journey.

Hearing of Santa Anna's approach, Taylor moved his men a few miles north, near Buena Vista. There, the main road to Saltillo passed between cliffs at the edge of a plateau on the east and broken ground before a river on the west. John Wool positioned U.S. forces to block the road and defend the plateau below a mountain ridge, with Taylor going back to Saltillo to prepare its defenses. During the Battle of Buena Vista of February 22–23, Santa Anna's soldiers attacked up the road and onto the plateau, and some advanced around the mountain ridge to get into the rear of the American positions. The Mexicans achieved some isolated successes, breaking some infantry units and briefly getting their cavalry around the U.S. left flank. But Taylor dispatched forces to repel enemy advances, and his artillery broke up many Mexican assaults. After two days, Santa Anna gave up and retreated, his force of about 14,000 men having suffered about 2,000 causalities, compared to less than 700 among Taylor's command.

Figure 5.3 "Battle of Buena Vista"
By H. R. Robinson, 1847
Library of Congress, Prints and Photographs Division, LC-DIG-pga-02525

Outnumbered and mostly inexperienced American soldiers had won an impressive tactical victory—despite about 1,500 troops deserting during the battle.

The Vera Cruz Campaign, 1847

Meanwhile, Scott was finishing plans for the war's climactic campaign. In early March, over 13,000 men put to sea to rendezvous with the U.S. Navy squadron blockading Vera Cruz. His men landed a few miles south of the city on March 9, 1847. This was the first amphibious invasion ever made by U.S. forces, with soldiers towed to shore in boats pulled by steamers. The Mexicans did not contest the landing, and within a few days Scott's army surrounded Vera Cruz. Needing to capture the port before advancing inland, U.S. artillery and naval guns began bombarding it on March 22. After a few days, the Mexican commander surrendered; scores and possibly hundreds of civilians and soldiers died from American fire.

Scott next prepared to move his forces inland to higher elevation, for yellow fever was rampant in Mexico's coastal lowlands in the spring and summer months. But transportation problems delayed his march, particularly finding enough mules to haul supplies. On April 8, U.S. forces began advancing up Mexico's National Highway toward the city of Jalapa. Meanwhile, Santa Anna organized defenses. Having lost half his army during the Buena Vista campaign, the Mexican general rushed back to Mexico City to put down political unrest and then raised thousands of men for a new army. These were mostly untrained conscripts, and many became ill. Santa Anna marched them east, beyond Jalapa and the town of Cerro Gordo, to a point where the National Highway went through a canyon. He placed most troops in positions on the southern side of the road, and only a few men and guns were located on a hill called "El Telegrafo" to the north. He assumed the terrain north of the highway was impassible to an advancing army.

Scott's men proved him wrong. Advance forces encountered Mexican positions on April 12, and the rest of the U.S. army, about 8,500 men, arrived over the next few days. Some officers (including a Captain Robert E. Lee) discovered a path that led to a hill northeast of El Telegrafo. Scott ordered the path widened and reinforced, and prepared his troops for the Battle of Cerro Gordo on April 18. Scott directed his main assault against El Telegrafo. But he also advanced some forces farther west, around the left flank of Santa Anna's army and into its rear, while some troops attacked enemy positions south of the Highway. The plan worked: U.S. troops took the hill, and the Mexican army fled. Having suffered over 400 casualties, Scott's men inflicted about 1,000 casualties and captured more than 3,000 enemy troops.

American forces reached Japala the next day. Moving on, by the end of May they had captured Mexico's second largest city, Puebla, without resistance. During this month Scott lost much of his army, with the enlistments of thousands of one-year volunteers expiring, and he waited for more reinforcements before continuing on to Mexico City. Meanwhile, guerrilla raids ravaged the National Highway, and Scott made a controversial decision for the time: He abandoned regular communications with his logistical base at Vera Cruz. Maintaining a line of communications requires invading armies to detach troops to guard roads, forts, and towns, devoting more soldiers to such duties the farther they advance. Given his depleted numbers, Scott instead concentrated his army at Puebla, retrieving men he had left to garrison towns on the highway between that city and Vera Cruz. His troops supported themselves from supplies they foraged from the countryside around Puebla.

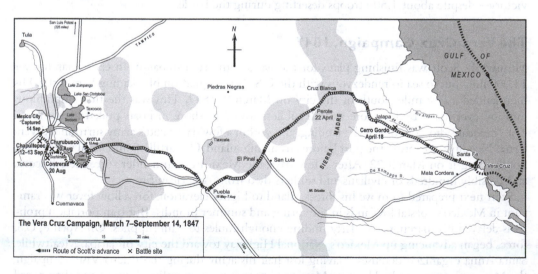

Map 5.4 The Vera Cruz Campaign, March 7–September 14, 1847

The Capture of Mexico City

By August, a few thousand reinforcements had pushed up from Vera Cruz and joined Scott's army. With the supplies he had collected and about 10,500 troops, he set out to capture Mexico City. Santa Anna had scratched together 20,000–25,000 men to guard the capital's eastern and southern approaches, ranging from experienced regulars to recently raised conscripts. He established his main defense on a rocky ridge called "El Peñón" that overlooked the National Highway as it traveled along a causeway across Lake Texcoco. U.S. advance parties discovered this position, but also found a road that branched off the Highway, one that traveled south and west around Lakes Chalco and Xochimilco to San Agustin, where it connected with another road that ran north toward the capital. Scott had this road improved and marched his army over it, reaching the town on August 18.

Santa Anna reacted by strengthening his defenses west of Lake Xochimilco to block an American move toward the capital. Along the western shore ran the road north from San Agustin. Beyond that was the Pedregal, an old, rocky and craggy lava bed. Santa Anna stationed troops around the eastern and northern edges of the Pedregal. But one commander (a political rival of Santa Anna) decided on his own initiative to move about 5,000 troops farther southwest toward Contreras. Meanwhile, U.S. officers (including Lee) found a path through the lava bed. On the morning of August 20, Scott's forces routed the isolated Mexican force at the Battle of Contreras, inflicting over 1,500 casualties. His troops then advanced around the western side of the Pedregal, while other U.S. units pushed north from San Agustin.

Scott now had two forces converging on Churubusco. The town was on the Churubusco River, north of the lava bed. Mexican soldiers were using the bridge there to escape. To defend it, Santa Anna placed troops in a convent just to the south. Scott ordered immediate assaults on the convent and the bridge. At the Battle of Churubusco, the defenders repelled some assaults, but U.S. forces ultimately captured the bridge, after which troops in the convent surrendered. This battle, combined with the one earlier near Contreras, made August 20 the bloodiest day of the war: Scott's army took about 1,000 total casualties, including 133 killed, whereas Santa Anna's lost more than 4,000 killed and wounded with over 2,500 captured—not counting thousands who fled and never returned to fight.

Box 5.3 The San Patricios

One Mexican unit at the Battle of Churubusco was the Battalion of St. Patrick, known as the Batallón de San Patricio or the San Patricios. It was composed primarily of deserters from the regular U.S. Army. Most of its soldiers were Irish, though other European nationalities were represented, including German Catholics. Their experiences illustrate how the regular U.S. Army relied upon immigrants for manpower, and the challenges these enlistees faced—including not just hard discipline and conditions of service, but also a pervasive anti-Catholic bias in nineteenth-century American society. The Mexican government offered them better pay, land grants, citizenship, and also appealed to a shared Roman Catholicism. These inducements persuaded hundreds of soldiers to desert from Zachary Taylor's Army of Occupation early in the Mexican War. Many were artillerymen, and they fought for Mexico in most of the conflict's prominent battles. They gained a reputation for fighting tenaciously and refusing to surrender, as they knew that U.S. Army regulations stipulated the execution of any man convicted of deserting to the enemy in wartime. Most of the San Patricios were captured defending the convent at the Battle of Churubusco after running out of ammunition. During the brief truce that followed, Winfield Scott ordered two courts-martial that initially sentenced 70 of 72 deserters to death. He commuted about 20 of these sentences, but 50 still hanged on September 10 and 13. Regarded in the United States as traitors, they are heroes in Mexico, with many landmarks commemorating their service.

A few days later, Scott agreed to a truce. It allowed him to resupply his army and provided an opportunity for Nicholas Trist, a diplomatic envoy dispatched by Polk, to try to negotiate a peace. But Mexican officials did not seriously consider U.S. terms, and Santa Anna improved the capital's defenses in anticipation of further fighting. Scott terminated the truce as of September 8. Between his forces and Mexico City were a number of causeways over marshy ground that led to the capital's western and southern gates. But guarding these approaches was Chapultepec. About a mile long and a perhaps a third of a mile wide, the estate contained gardens and fields, but its central feature was an old colonial mansion atop a hill that housed the Mexican military academy. Walls surrounded its southern and eastern boundaries, an old aqueduct the northern, and on its west was a large complex of stone buildings called "the Molino del Rey."

Before attacking Chapultepec, Scott ordered an assault to take Molino del Rey. Artillery fire and infantry assaults captured the complex, but U.S. troops suffered high casualties: about 880 of 3,250 killed or wounded. Scott then consulted his officers to decide if his army should first capture Chapultepec and then advance to the city gates, or bypass it and assault up the causeways; he chose the first option. Santa Anna had devoted the bulk of his army to defending Mexico City or its other approaches, and only 800 troops were guarding the estate—with some artillery, engineers, and perhaps 50 military cadets who refused to leave. On September 12, U.S. artillery pummeled Chapultepec. The bombardment started again on September 13, followed by infantry assaults on the southern perimeter and from Molino del Rey. By late morning, Scott's soldiers had won the Battle of Chapultepec and overwhelmed the defenders.

U.S. troops immediately advanced toward the capital. Forces under John Quitman rushed up one causeway to Mexico City's southwest gate. After seizing some cannons and bringing up their own artillery, his soldiers captured it but struggled to hold the gate against Mexican counterattacks. Meanwhile, William Worth led his force along another causeway to the road that led to Mexico City's northwest gate. Beating off a cavalry attack, his troops came under intense fire as they advanced toward the city. But engineers blasted into buildings on the north side of the road, creating a protected route for advancing infantry, while artillery officers (including Ulysses S. Grant) moved up guns to provide fire support. By the evening of September 13, U.S. soldiers had captured the northwest gate, and Mexican troops fled into the city.

Santa Anna had lost an estimated 3,000 men that day. Although thousands more were in the capital, local officials beseeched him not to turn Mexico City into a war zone. Lacking political support, Santa Anna withdrew that night. On September 14, 1847, U.S. forces—which had taken about 860 casualties in the previous 24 hours—occupied the capital. The Vera Cruz campaign was over. Scott's army had achieved its objective, advancing hundreds of miles into enemy territory and defeating numerically superior forces in multiple battles along the way. But the war was not over.

Occupation and Negotiation

Having lost Mexico City, Santa Anna resigned the presidency. In the confused circumstances of the war, it took some time for the Mexican government to select a new president. Even then, the new regime was hesitant to negotiate a peace that would require great territorial losses to meet U.S. demands. In the interim, Mexican society broke down, with revolts and uprisings spreading in the provinces. This violence fueled guerrilla activity against U.S. forces, including supply convoys. The motives of irregular combatants varied, from nationalism and a desire to hurt the invader, to attempts to gain advantages in local power struggles, to outright banditry.

Such hostilities were already a staple of the war. After reaching Puebla, Scott had decided against securing the road back to Vera Cruz from guerrillas due to limited manpower. When he moved on to Mexico City, the few hundred soldiers he left in Puebla were effectively besieged until October. Shortly after capturing the capital, his army suppressed an uprising among its poorer population. The city was subsequently peaceful, though tense. Scott now tried to secure the National Highway back to Vera Cruz. Though he received reinforcements, guerrilla attacks and reprisals by U.S. soldiers plagued the region for the rest of the war. Moreover, his army was not the only one bedeviled by Mexican irregulars: Guerrillas also harassed Taylor's troops in northern Mexico and U.S. forces along the Pacific coast.

But the ongoing violence took its toll. By the end of 1847, many Mexicans wished for peace—some even called for the United States to annex the whole country! Trist and Mexican negotiators recommenced talks in January 1848. On February 2, they signed the Treaty of Guadalupe Hidalgo, ratified by both governments the following May. The United States paid the Mexican government $15 million, which in turn acknowledged the Rio Grande as the border with Texas, and ceded its northernmost territories to U.S. control. Known as the Mexican Cession, it included all of what is now California, Nevada, and Utah, and parts of Wyoming, Colorado, New Mexico, and Arizona. In 1853, the United States bought additional lands from Mexico via the Gadsden Purchase, creating the current border.

Expansion and Conflict: 1848–1865

Efforts to expand U.S. borders and consolidate control over areas within them fueled more violence in the years following the Mexican-American War. In fact, hostilities in American borderlands with native peoples continued as the United States almost tore itself apart during the American Civil War (discussed in the next two chapters). But the Mexican-American War also sparked a wave of private—and illegal—military ventures designed to subjugate parts of Latin America.

These were called "filibustering" expeditions, and the men who joined them "filibusters," a term derived from the Dutch word for "freebooter" (a pirate or adventurer). Such enterprises predated the Mexican War. Private military expeditions organized in the United States had ventured into Spanish-held Florida and Texas prior to the ratification of the Transcontinental Treaty of 1821, and assisted the cause of Texan independence from Mexico after 1835. Some filibustering campaigns had even harassed Canada in the late 1830s. But these became especially prominent and destructive in the 1850s, and among their recruits were many veterans of the Mexican War. The first of these were efforts led by Narciso López to conquer Cuba in 1850 and 1851. But the most infamous of filibuster was William Walker, who led many expeditions into Central America. His forces actually subjugated Nicaragua in 1855, and he ruled parts of the country until 1857, when he was overthrown and killed. All of these filibustering ventures met defeat sooner or later. But they caused death and destruction throughout Latin America, along with great resentment of the United States—which seemed inept in its inability to prevent filibustering groups from organizing and leaving the country.

Within U.S. borders, a new wave of hostilities erupted involving native peoples. Some of these occurred in territories acquired via the Mexican Cession and the Gadsden Purchase, where the U.S. Army constructed a number of new forts. Conflict with Mescalero and Jicarilla Apaches erupted in the mid-1850s, ending following campaigns by federal troops and territorial militia. In April 1860, however, Navajo warriors attacked Fort Defiance, erected in the midst of their homelands. Then in February 1861, an attempt to arrest the previously friendly chief Cochise (known as the Bascom Incident) precipitated the Apache Wars, which featured western Apache groups such as the Chiricahua and lasted, with some lulls, until 1886.

The outbreak of the Civil War further encouraged native hostilities throughout the southwest. Not only were regular Army troops withdrawn from the territory but a small Confederate army invaded New Mexico from Texas in early 1862, which emboldened the Mescalero Apache, among other peoples. Later that year federal forces arriving from California beat off a native attack at the Battle of Apache Pass. In 1863 federal and territorial forces campaigned against the Mescalero Apache and the Navajos, and induced both peoples to move to the newly established reservation at Bosque Redondo on the Pecos River. There, conditions were so bad that after the Civil War ended both Mescaleros and Navajos abandoned it, with the latter allowed to peacefully reoccupy their traditional homelands. Meanwhile, attacks by other Apache peoples, such as the Chiricahua and the Yavapais, continued on settlements and travelers throughout New Mexico and Arizona.

Violence also erupted in the Utah Territory, including confrontations between Mormon settlers and the U.S. Army in 1857–58. By 1862 increased migration, prospecting, and traffic provoked attacks on major travel routes by Shoshonis, prompting the dispatch of a California regiment to secure communications and safe passage for gold and silver shipments. The most lethal engagement of the Shoshoni War came at the Battle of Bear Creek in January 1863, when soldiers assaulted the winter camp of Chief Bear Hunter's band in southern Idaho, killing him and 200–250 out of a village population of about 450. The carnage cowed some bands, but provoked others to raid mail and coach stations. Federal forces reacted with attacks on their camps, and by the following fall a number of treaties established peace in the region.

Hostilities also occurred in areas beyond those acquired from Mexico. Migration and prospecting, for example, inflamed tensions with indigenous peoples in the Pacific Northwest. The Cayuse War began in late 1847 and continued intermittently with raids between warriors and territorial militia for about eight years. It overlapped with the Rogue River Wars of 1853 and 1855–56 in southwest Oregon, and the beginning of the Yakima War of 1855 to 1858. All these Pacific Northwest Wars ended with defeats of native forces by army and militia units, after which Indian groups accepted relocation to reservations. The region then remained relatively peaceful until 1864, when northern Paiutes and some Shoshonis raided from southern Idaho west to the Cascades and south into northern California, Nevada, and Utah. In what is known as the Snake War (1864–68), volunteer units initially failed to prevent Indian depredations or find hostile bands, and the regular Army units that returned to the region after the Civil War fared little better until George Crook took command in late 1866 (addressed in Chapter 8).

Conflicts also erupted in various parts of the Great Plains, most of which the United States had acquired via the Louisiana Purchase. Per the 1851 Treaty of Fort Laramie, the Lakota (or western) Sioux peacefully allowed travelers along migration routes through their territory, in exchange for annual gifts. But in August 1854, the First Sioux War began when overzealous second lieutenant John Grattan confronted a Lakota band and ordered his men to fire. Enraged warriors then killed the entire command, in what is known as the Grattan Massacre, followed by raiding buildings outside Fort Laramie. A U.S. retaliatory campaign in 1855 culminated with an assault on a native village at the Battle of Ash Hollow in September, killing more than 80. By 1856 hostilities with the Lakota had ended, but incidents farther south provoked another army campaign in the summer of 1857 against the Cheyenne. This resulted in the Battle of Solomon Fork that July, wherein troopers drew sabers and engaged in a rare charge, scattering the warriors. In following months Cheyenne war parties raided along the Platte River, but thereafter remained peaceful for many years.

Similar to the Fort Laramie Treaty, the 1853 Treaty of Fort Atkinson provided presents for the Kiowa and Comanche of the southern plains as inducements to allow peaceful travel on the Santa Fe Trail, among other terms. Yet they continued to pillage the Texas and Mexican frontiers. Late in the decade both Texas Rangers and the U.S. Army embarked on campaigns to counter native raids while constructing additional forts. The Antelope Hills and Wichita expeditions defeated Comanche bands at various battles in 1858 and 1859, but native raids not only continued but began to target the Santa Fe Trail.

In Minnesota, the withdrawal of regular Army troops during the Civil War preceded the Great Sioux Uprising of 1862, also known as the Dakota War. Reacting to frustrations including rapid white settlement, loss of lands, unscrupulous traders, and delayed government payments, that August Dakota (or eastern) Sioux warriors under Little Crow assaulted farms and settlers along the Minnesota River. These hostilities culminated in attacks on New Ulm and nearby Fort Ridgely, which soldiers and civilians repelled after desperate fighting. Thereafter, militia forces advanced against hostile Dakotas, defeating and dispersing them in late September. Fearing that Sioux bands farther west might threaten settlements or travel routes, in 1863 and 1864 federal officials organized expeditions into what is now North and South Dakota, establishing new forts and defeating Sioux warriors in some engagements.

The central plains remained quiet until 1864, when incidents involving Cheyenne and soldiers commanded by regional commander John Chivington raised tensions in Colorado Territory, beginning the Cheyenne-Arapaho War (which would end in 1867). In September a delegation of chiefs met with local officials and came away believing they had established a peace. Instead, Chivington led a unit of territorial volunteers against the camp of Black Kettle, one of the foremost proponents for peace who had complied with instructions to move his people to Sand Creek. On November 29 soldiers attacked 500 unsuspecting Cheyenne and Arapahoe, killing between 130–200—mostly unarmed women and children. The Sand Creek Massacre was one of the bloodiest and cruelest attacks upon a native community in the history of the Indian wars. Public outcry led to Colorado governor John Evans' resignation, though Chivington himself was never called to account for his actions. Early in 1865, incensed Cheyenne and Arapahoe bands devastated the South Platte River valley, while that spring and summer, Lakota and other bands from Montana's Powder River region attacked the North Platte.

Meanwhile, Comanche and Kiowa depredations had continued farther south, particularly along the Santa Fe Trail. In response, famous frontiersman "Kit" Carson marched a few hundred federal troops into the Texas panhandle to defeat warriors at the First Battle of the Adobe Walls in November 1864. Carson's forces destroyed native camps and stores, but Comanche and Kiowa attacks continued.

In 1865 John Pope planned multiple campaigns to address turmoil on the plains. But horror at the Sand Creek Massacre prompted a Congressional investigation and efforts to secure peace, which stalled military operations. Although the end of the Civil War freed numerous troops for frontier service, additional soldiers strained a weakened logistical system. Moreover, volunteers wanted to go home and had poor morale. Army campaigns did advance through the Dakota Territories and into the Powder River region in the summer of 1865 but accomplished little and (in the immediate aftermath of the Civil War) were criticized as excessively expensive. That October, federal officials signed a series of treaties on the Little Arkansas River with southern nations, and at Fort Sully with northern ones. These paused the Cheyenne-Arapaho War, momentarily establishing peace, guaranteeing safety of travel routes, and resuming annual payments to native peoples. But war soon returned to the Plains.

Conclusion

The U.S. Army, assisted by militia, was crucial for implementing federal policy in the Wars of Indian Removal and the Trail of Tears, as well as on the country's western frontiers throughout this period. These experiences did not create a positive legacy for U.S. military institutions— but the Mexican War did. American armed forces fought and won a conventional war on foreign soil, erasing the stigma of the War of 1812 and greatly expanding the territorial boundaries of the United States. Regular army officers, particularly West Point graduates, demonstrated skill and capability, their wartime accomplishments thus validating previous efforts to make officership a career. The United States still needed to recruit volunteers for the Mexican War, but regulars comprised a large proportion of the forces fielded by the Polk administration. Such would not be the case, though, in the American Civil War. Those armies were so large that volunteers comprised the vast majority of combatants—which had important ramifications for military performance and the experiences of soldiers.

Short Bibliography

Ball, Durwood. *Army Regulars on the Western Frontier, 1848–1861.* Norman: University of Oklahoma Press, 2001.

Bauer, K. Jack. *The Mexican War, 1846–48.* New York: Macmillan Publishing Co., Inc., 1974.

Clary, David A. *Eagles and Empire: The United States, Mexico, and the Struggle for a Continent.* New York: Bantam Books, 2009.

Coffman, Edward M. *The Old Army: A Portrait of the American Army in Peacetime, 1784–1898.* New York: Oxford University Press, 1986.

Ellisor, John. *The Second Creek War: Interethnic Conflict and Collusion on a Collapsing Frontier.* Lincoln: University of Nebraska Press, 2010.

Jung, Patrick J. *The Black Hawk War of 1832.* Norman: University of Oklahoma Press, 2007.

Leeman, William P. *The Long Road to Annapolis: The Founding of the Naval Academy and the Emerging American Republic.* Chapel Hill: University of North Carolina Press, 2010.

May, Robert E. *Manifest Destiny's Underworld: Filibustering in Antebellum America.* Chapel Hill: University of North Carolina Press, 2002.

Missall, John, and Mary Lou Missall. *The Seminole Wars: America's Longest Indian Conflict.* Gainesville: University Press of Florida, 2004.

Prucha, Francis Paul. *The Sword of the Republic: The United States Army on the Frontier: 1783–1846.* New York: Macmillan Publishing Co., Inc., 1969.

Schroeder, John H. *Matthew Calbraith Perry: Antebellum Sailor and Diplomat.* Annapolis: Naval Institute Press, 2001.

Valle, James E. *Rocks and Shoals: Naval Discipline in the Age of Fighting Sail.* Annapolis: United States Naval Institute Press, 1980.

Watson, Samuel J. *Jackson's Sword: The Army Officer Corps on the American Frontier, 1810–1821*. Lawrence: University Press of Kansas, 2012.

———. *Peacekeepers and Conquerors: The Army Officer Corps on the American Frontier, 1821–1846*. Lawrence: University Press of Kansas, 2013.

Winders, Richard Bruce. *Mr. Polk's Army: The American Military Experience in the Mexican War*. College Station: Texas A&M University Press, 1997.

TIMELINE

1861–65	April 12–13, 1861	July 21, 1861	February 6, 1862	February 16, 1862	April 6–7, 1862	April 25, 1862
The American Civil War	Fort Sumter bombarded	First Battle of Bull Run (Manassas)	Fort Henry captured	Fort Donelson captured	Battle of Shiloh	New Orleans captured

Chapter 6

The American Civil War: Confederate Defiance, 1861–1863

By the middle of the nineteenth century, U.S. military institutions had proven their worth in the Mexican War. Yet their greatest test would not involve a conflict with a foreign power. Far more Americans fought and died in the American Civil War of 1861–65 than in all other previous conflicts put together. Its numerous engagements ranged from huge pitched battles with tens of thousands of soldiers on a side, to small skirmishes and raids involving just a few dozen. Irregular operations occurred, particularly in western areas, but campaigns by large conventional armies predominated.

The Union and the Confederacy each raised huge numbers of troops during the conflict, but effectively using them was problematic. The vast majority were volunteers with no military background. On both sides, officers with prior experience were few relative to the number needed, and no commander had previously handled armies as large as those created between 1861 and 1865, which sometimes exceeded 100,000 men. Similarly, no civilian administration had ever faced the problems of supporting such vast forces and developing effective strategies for them.

In this chapter, students will learn about:

- The causes of the American Civil War.
- The tactics and technology used to fight Civil War battles.
- The relative strengths and weaknesses of the Union and the Confederacy.
- How each side mobilized manpower.
- The initial strategies and the diplomacy pursued by both sides.
- The major campaigns and battles in 1861 and 1862.
- The military significance of the Emancipation Proclamation.

June 25–July 1, 1862	August 29–30, 1862	Sept. 17, 1862	Sept. 22, 1862	October 8, 1862	Dec. 13, 1862
The Seven Days Battles	Second Battle of Bull Run (Manassas)	Battle of Antietam	Preliminary Emancipation Proclamation issued	Battle of Perryville	Battle of Fredericksburg

Causes

Slavery was the fundamental issue that fueled the clash between Northern and Southern parts of the United States in 1861. Ever since, apologists for the Confederate cause have glossed over this point by claiming the war was over "states rights." Southern states, however, only came to fear that the federal government might threaten their "rights" after the 1860 election of the Republican candidate Abraham Lincoln to the presidency. Lincoln had campaigned on a platform stating he would outlaw slavery in federal territories, though not in states where it already existed. Yet his victory came solely from his popularity in the north, for he received no electoral votes from states south of the Mason-Dixon Line. Many Southerners thus concluded that they would eventually lack the political power to block attempts to ban slavery anywhere in the United States.

Disagreement over slavery, however, was not the sole cause of the war. American slavery predated the founding of the United States, and the institution had been tolerated since the country's founding—for more than 80 years by 1860. Instead, it was slavery, combined with the spread of sectional interests and perspectives over the previous generation, which ripped the country apart after Lincoln's election. In 1820, for example, national leaders had agreed to exclude slavery from the vast majority of federal territory at that time: All land above the line of latitude 36' 30° excepting what became the state of Missouri. But following the "Missouri Compromise," the debate over American slavery became more heated. Although abolitionist ideas were not then new, to that point they advocated the slow and gradual end of slavery. But the 1830s saw the birth of a "militant" abolitionist movement, whose leaders included William Lloyd Garrison and Frederick Douglass, that demanded its immediate end. Their speeches and writings, along with abolitionist literature mailed by the American Anti-Slavery Society, produced sometimes violent backlashes in both the North and the South, including riots and attacks on post offices.

These initial clashes were relatively few and did not yet represent a national crisis over slavery. More alarming tensions began after the Mexican War, for the huge area acquired via the Mexican Cession reopened the question of slavery in the territories. During the war itself, Pennsylvania Congressman David Wilmot proposed banning slavery from any territories acquired from Mexico (the "Wilmot Proviso"), which was rejected. But California's efforts to gain statehood soon brought the issue to a head. The resulting Compromise of 1850 owed its passage in Congress more to the procedural engineering of Illinois Senator Stephen A. Douglas than to any genuine spirit of cooperation.

California's admission to the Union meant that free states now outnumbered slave states in the Senate. (Congressmen from slave states had long been a minority in the House of Representatives due to Northern population growth.) But Southerners gained a new strong Fugitive Slave Act whose provisions threatened the liberty of Northern blacks and also worried Northern whites. The latter groups soon acquired a greater appreciation for the horrors of slavery via Harriet Beecher Stowe's *Uncle Tom's Cabin*.

The 1850s witnessed a succession of crises that continued to enflame sectional tensions. Stephen Douglas soon destroyed the 1850 Compromise by championing the Kansas–Nebraska Act of 1854. This law revoked the older ban on slavery in federal territories established by the Missouri Compromise, allowing residents of these regions to decide the question themselves— an idea known as "popular sovereignty" that had been championed in the election of 1848. When settlers in the Kansas Territory tried to vote on the issue in 1854–55, both abolitionist and pro-slavery groups sought to sway the outcome, generating a political crisis and widespread violence in "Bleeding Kansas." In the 1857 *Dred Scott* case, the U.S. Supreme Court ruled slavery could not be banned in federal territories, claiming that such would violate the Fifth Amendment's protection of property. But Chief Justice Roger Taney went further, claiming blacks were not and could never be U.S. citizens. Northerners, already alarmed over previous developments and crises—including an attack on Massachusetts Senator and abolitionist Charles Sumner on the Senate floor in 1856—were shocked by the decision. Growing Northern sympathy for abolitionism in turn upset Southerners, particularly the support John Brown received after his failed raid on Harper's Ferry, Virginia, and subsequent execution in 1859—a raid whose purpose was to acquire arms to facilitate a slave revolt against Southern slaveholders.

Ironically, most white Southerners did not own slaves. Of those who did, most had one or perhaps a few. But about half of Southern slaves lived on large plantations owned by rich landholders who comprised a tiny proportion of the entire white population. Nonetheless, slavery was a form of racial domination that shaped all of Southern society. Even the poorest white family was free. Moreover, many regarded slaveowning as a means to improve their economic and social status. A different dynamic operated in the north, where land prices were high and industrialization had dramatically increased the number of free urban laborers. Many poor Northerners dreamed of moving west to start their own farms—hopes threatened by the

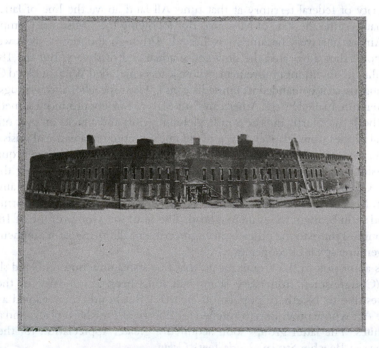

Figure 6.1 Photographs of the Exterior of Fort Sumter the Day After Its Surrender

Library of Congress, Prints and Photographs Division, LC-DIG-ppmsca-35206, LC-DIG-ppmsca-35219, and LC-DIG-ppmsca-35221

prospect of wealthy Southerners moving into new territories and buying large tracts of land to farm with slaves. Just as many in the South came to believe that all Northerners were abolitionists (most were not, and in many areas prejudices against blacks were strong), many in the north came to believe in a "slave power" or "slavocracy" that was trying to manipulate the federal government for the benefit of Southern interests. These were the underlying anxieties that successive political crises exacerbated in the late 1840s and 1850s, leading to the final one that almost destroyed the United States.

Secession and War

As the country became more polarized, it lacked the leaders and institutions that had previously been able to forge a national consensus. The Whig political party disintegrated in the 1850s, and by the 1860 election the Democrats had split, with Southern and Northern wings each running different candidates (Stephen A. Douglas and John C. Breckinridge, respectively). Many of the men who in earlier years possessed the standing to craft a possible compromise, such as Daniel Webster, Henry Clay, and John C. Calhoun, had died by the early 1850s. Among younger politicians, perhaps Stephen A. Douglas had the ability to do so. But any possibility of his championing a national reconciliation was squandered with the Kansas-Nebraska Act, and his subsequent efforts to preserve the Union were too little, too late. Instead, four presidential candidates ran in the election of 1860.

Northern states provided all the electoral votes Abraham Lincoln needed to win the presidency. For many Southerners, the North's ability to win the executive branch outright posed a mortal danger to slavery within the United States, though Lincoln and the Republicans only sought to ban it from federal territories, and abolitionists were a minority among the region's population. South Carolina was the first to act on these fears, declaring its secession from the Union on December 20, 1860. By February 1, 1861, it had been joined by Mississippi, Florida, Alabama, Georgia, Louisiana, and Texas, and soon thereafter representatives from each met in Montgomery, Alabama, to declare the birth of a new nation, the Confederate States of America—or simply the Confederacy.

These states comprised the majority of the Lower South, where large plantations with numerous slaves producing cotton and other staples for export flourished. In contrast, those in the Upper South—Virginia, Kentucky, North Carolina, and Tennessee—chose not to secede from the Union at this time, along with Arkansas. These states had more diversified, though still primarily agricultural, economies and lacked the large numbers of big plantations prevalent in the Lower South. But slavery was still legal in the Upper South, and while many there were sympathetic to the Confederate cause, they were not yet prepared to abandon the Union. Even in the original Confederate states, support for secession was not universal but strong enough to command support from the majority of the population.

What ultimately pushed the Upper South—except Kentucky—into the Confederacy was the Lincoln administration's reaction to the fall of Fort Sumter (after which Richmond, Virginia, would become the Southern capital). Lincoln would not assume the presidency until early March, and the outgoing administration of President James Buchanan did little to address the crisis. In the interim some politicians tried to craft a last-minute compromise that would maintain the Union and peace, but all efforts failed. Meanwhile, seceding states seized federal installations in their midst, leaving only three controlled by U.S. forces by the time Lincoln took office on March 4, 1861. These included Fort Sumter, located on an island in the middle of the harbor of Charleston, South Carolina—and its supplies would last only a few more weeks.

In early April, Lincoln dispatched a ship to resupply Fort Sumter, but with no arms or troops, and publicly announced its mission. Though aware this effort could provoke an armed response,

Lincoln had other alternatives if he wanted to begin a war. It appeared instead the best option for avoiding conflict while keeping the promises in his inaugural speech to retain federal posts. Confederate authorities sought to induce the fort's surrender before the ship arrived, thereby avoiding the dilemma of either allowing it through or using armed force. But the post commander, Major Robert Anderson (who was unaware of the supply mission) saw no reason to hasten his submission given that his men would soon run out of stores anyway. With the ship's approach forcing the issue, Confederate forces began firing upon Fort Sumter at 4:30 a.m. on April 12, 1861, thus beginning the American Civil War; Anderson surrendered the next day.

Changing Weapons Technology

Up through the Mexican-American War, the primary firearm used by U.S. infantry had been the flintlock, muzzle-loading, smoothbore musket that was equipped with a bayonet that could lock on the end of the barrel. Used since the seventeenth century, this weapon could only be fired two or three times per minute and required a complex series of steps to load. These included:

- Ripping open a paper cartridge containing gunpowder and bullet (usually with one's teeth).
- Placing a small amount of gunpowder in a pan and hole in the barrel that led to the firing chamber (when a soldier pulled the trigger, a flint in the hammer would strike another piece of metal—the "frizzen"—sending sparks into the pan, lighting the powder, which would burn and produce ignition in the firing chamber, propelling the bullet).
- Closing the frizzen so powder would not fall out of the pan.
- Pouring the rest of the gunpowder down the muzzle.
- Placing bullet and paper in the muzzle and then pushing them all the way down with a ramrod.

The effective range of this musket was only about 50–100 yards. To compensate, infantry formed in close order, one man right next to another in long formations a few ranks deep. Troops usually formed by company, with one adjacent to another in a battle line. Often, a second battle line formed a few hundred yards behind to support the first, with additional units in reserve further back.

These formations delivered concentrated, coordinated volleys of fire to wreak havoc on opposing troops. But the short range of smoothbore muskets, combined with the time needed to reload them, meant that a charging infantry formation might endure only one or two volleys before closing with the enemy's ranks and fighting with bayonets. Cavalry moved even faster. As artillery had much greater ranges than smoothbore muskets, they could be fired to break up enemy formations, thereby assisting infantry and cavalry charges. Such tactics did not guarantee success for the attacker, who could be thwarted by the defender's use of terrain, fire, and movement. The success of U.S. forces in the Mexican War, however, indicated that these tactics remained effective options for offensive battlefield movement.

But weapon technology was changing. One development was the percussion cap, which replaced the complicated flintlock mechanism. Made of metal, the inside contained mercury fulminate, which explodes when struck. Placed on a "nipple" that protruded from the barrel, when a soldier pulled the trigger, the hammer came down upon the cap, sending flames through a hole into the combustion chamber and lighting the main charge. The United States actually began adopting this technology just prior to the Mexican War. It continued in the 1850s under then-Secretary of War Jefferson Davis, when the U.S. Army began considering rifled muskets.

Rifled arms have grooves on the inside of the barrel that impart a spin to projectiles, giving them greater range and accuracy. Though a very old technology, they had only been used in

Western armies as specialist weapons. Early rifles took a long time to load: the bullet needed to fit tightly in the barrel, and had to be hammered down. In contrast, soldiers could load smoothbore muskets quickly, for the bullets were smaller than the diameter of the barrel—which also reduced accuracy. But the mid-nineteenth century saw the advent of rifled arms that could be loaded as fast as smoothbores. The most successful of these used the Minié bullet. Named after French officer Claude Minié, this projectile was made of lead in a conical shape and had a hollow center. When the gun fired, the force of the combustion expanded the base of the bullet into the grooving inside the barrel. In the United States, the weapon developed to use this technology was the Springfield rifle. Like all rifled muskets, its range and accuracy was hundreds of yards better than a smoothbore.

Breech-loading firearms also became available just prior to the Civil War. These were much easier to load than muskets, which had to be stood upright. But U.S. government officials were wary of breechloaders. Though some had been used in the Mexican War and on the frontier, administrators feared their ease of loading would induce soldiers to rapidly waste ammunition. Rifled muskets instead became the primary infantry weapon for both Union and Confederate soldiers. But breechloaders were ideal for cavalry, especially breech-loading carbines (a carbine has a shorter barrel than a musket or rifle, regardless of firing mechanism). Over the course of the war, officers—particularly in federal units—took pains to acquire them for their troopers. Confederate cavalry had more varied arms, including sawed-off shotguns and shortened muskets. Troopers on both sides carried pistols.

As with infantry firearms, rifled artillery was available to both sides and used with increasing frequency over the course of the war. But smoothbores were common, and generally effective at battlefield ranges. Artillery could employ various types of ammunition depending upon circumstances (though these were not new in 1861). For longer distances, cannons could fire simple roundshot balls to break up massed infantry formations or weaken fortifications, or shells that exploded above enemy positions and rained down metal to wound or kill. For close ranges, gun crews employed canister ammunition, containing hundreds of small metal fragments that essentially turned artillery into giant shotguns.

Box 6.1   The Rifled Musket

On the following page are images of the Springfield rifled musket, the typical infantry weapon of the war, with a Minié ball. The following account, written by Alexander G. Downing, a Union infantryman, describes some experiences peculiar to fighting with these weapons:

> My musket became so dirty with the cartridge powder, that in loading it the ramrod stuck fast and I could neither get it up nor down, so I put a cap on, elevated the gun and fired it off. But now I had no ramrod, and throwing down my musket, I picked up a Belgian rifle *[an imported European gun, common early in the war]* lying at the side of a dead rebel, unstrapped the cartridge box from his body, and advanced to our company, taking my place with the boys. While in this position I witnessed a wonderful sight—thickly-flying musket balls. I have never seen hail falling thicker than the minié balls were flying in the air above us, though too high to do any harm. Our ammunition soon ran out and the entire regiment was ordered to the rear to replenish our cartridge boxes.
>
> (*Downing's Civil War Diary*, Des Moines: Iowa State
> Dept. of History and Archives, 1916, p. 41)

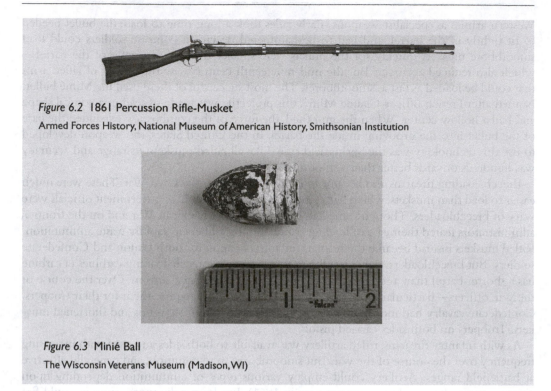

Figure 6.2 1861 Percussion Rifle-Musket

Armed Forces History, National Museum of American History, Smithsonian Institution

Figure 6.3 Minié Ball

The Wisconsin Veterans Museum (Madison, WI)

Tactics

Scholars claim U.S. authorities did not consider the tactical implications of new weapon capabilities prior to 1861. Soldiers in early Civil War combat used previously developed tactics, with troops packed into formations of two or three ranks. When these advanced upon enemy positions, they came under fire sooner and remained so for a longer period compared to earlier wars, producing more casualties. Some historians, though, question if this combination of older tactics and newer firearms was much more lethal. They note, for example, that many Civil War engagements occurred well within the maximum range of rifled muskets, close to that of smoothbores—weather and terrain could obscure an enemy's position until advancing forces were relatively close—and that firing a rifled musket accurately at longer ranges might be difficult under combat conditions.

The battles that produced the greatest casualties had the largest number of combatants. They also featured numerous assaults, with attackers often receiving fire well within the range of rifled muskets as they advanced toward defensive positions. But rifled muskets certainly had greater lethality than smoothbores and did contribute to tactical changes during the war. For example, charges by troops in close, massed formations decreased over time. Conversely, use of skirmishers increased. These soldiers deployed in open order, with a distance of many feet or yards between them, and chose their own targets and fired without direct supervision of officers, usually taking cover behind available terrain. Skirmishers had been used for centuries, with conventional armies deploying small numbers ahead of a main force to harass enemy troops as they formed for battle (though European generals made greater use of them during the French Revolutionary and Napoleonic Wars). Late in the American Civil War, soldiers also constructed field fortifications on a regular basis whenever they stopped and faced the prospect of combat—a natural progression from making use of available terrain for defensive cover in earlier battles.

For infantrymen, the most significant units were the company and the regiment. Men were recruited by regiment (sometimes a battalion) of usually a few hundred to a thousand men. Raised in particular regions, they often contained a man's relatives, friends, and neighbors, and a soldier's primary military identity was usually with the regiment. A regiment was usually divided into eight to 10 companies of a few dozen to 100 men each. This was the smallest tactical infantry unit, and drill, camp, and combat experiences were most intensely shared among men within a given company. In the field, regiments were "brigaded" together—two and up to six were joined together in one brigade, with two and up to six brigades similarly combined into a single division. Multiple divisions formed an army corps or small field army, with a large army comprised of many corps (Ambrose Burnside briefly tried grouping the Army of the Potomac's corps into "Grand Divisions").

In the American Civil War, cavalry was arguably more valuable for its operational versus tactical capabilities, whether screening the movements of a field army, performing reconnaissance, or raiding enemy rear areas. On the battlefield, cavalry generally did not engage infantry while mounted. Troopers on horses presented large targets, while rough terrain on many battlefields often precluded the possibility of a mounted charge. Instead, they usually dismounted to engage infantry forces, and in this sense served as mounted infantry rather than true cavalry from a tactical standpoint. At times, opposing cavalry forces did fight each other while on horseback, such as the Battle of Brandy Station. The cavalry equivalent of the infantry company, a troop or a company, usually had an equivalent number of men with their horses. These were also grouped into battalions and regiments. The Union army initially attached these units to larger infantry formations (such as a division). Later, it followed the Confederate practice of grouping troopers into larger pure cavalry units such as brigades and divisions.

The longer range of rifled muskets also made the aggressive employment of artillery more problematic. Gun crews could come under infantry fire (as well as counterbattery fire) if they advanced too close. For this reason, the defender's cannon often had a greater impact in Civil War battles than the attacker's. Armies on both sides followed the practice, prominent since the Napoleonic Wars, of massing artillery. In the Civil War, the basic tactical unit was the battery, usually containing six guns and crews for each, along with additional command and support personnel. Three or four batteries usually comprised a battalion or brigade. An infantry division usually had its own artillery battalion, whereas many such units usually formed a reserve for use by corps and army commanders.

Officers and Expertise

These tactical developments did not in themselves determine the outcome of battles, and their effects are debated. Some writers claim the rifled musket enhanced defensive advantages in the Civil War. They note some generals sought to fight on the tactical defensive, pursuing operations to find and hold an advantageous position and force the opposing commander to attack and suffer greater casualties. Other scholars contest this view, asserting the issue was not that new weapons technology favored the defender but due to lack of training and poor communication, attackers often bungled their assignments.

As noted earlier, given the large size of Civil War armies relative to limited personnel in the regular U.S. Army, most company officers came directly from civilian life with no or little military expertise. They had to learn their responsibilities and duties after appointed to command, often consulting available manuals, if any. Moreover, Civil War armies lacked a capacity that today is taken for granted: skilled staffs to draft and communicate orders.

Competent staff officers enable the component units of an army to understand their missions and goals in an impending action, and are required to coordinate their efforts and defeat the enemy. Civil War staff officers also learned their duties on the job—and they had few precedents to guide them. In the Mexican War, the only prior conventional conflict since 1815, the largest force fielded by the United States was Winfield Scott's army for the Vera Cruz campaign, between 10,000 and 14,000 men—the equivalent of a corps within a major Civil War army. Both Union and Confederate forces suffered from poor staff work, and many army commanders could not competently execute the operational and strategic responsibilities thrust upon them.

The Civil War does not lack examples where defenders bloodily repelled attacks. But at times, the tactical offensive succeeded, such as Stonewall Jackson's flank attack at Chancellorsville in 1863. Various circumstances explain the attackers' success in these cases: superior planning, coordination among top officers, successful exploitation of movement or numbers, a grave mistake made by defenders, and likely a combination of these. But the paucity of cases where tactical attackers prevailed demonstrates how difficult it was to combine such factors to achieve offensive success.

Yet tactical victories were not always needed to achieve operational or even strategic objectives. For example, only once during the Seven Days Battles of 1862 did Confederate attackers successfully overwhelm Union defenders. But repeated assaults induced Union general George McClellan to retreat and abandon efforts to take Richmond. Conversely, there were campaigns where operational and strategic goals required tactical success—in particular, Robert E. Lee's 1862 and 1863 invasions of the North, and early federal campaigns to capture Richmond. In fact, by the end of the war, the Union had developed a strategy that did not require large tactical offensive victories to defeat the Confederacy.

Union Versus Confederacy: Resource Comparison

Understanding strategic issues requires contrasting Union and Confederate capabilities. For example, numerous writers have noted the North's advantage in resources. The discrepancy in manufacturing was particularly acute: Many Northern areas were thoroughly industrialized by 1861, whereas the South remained primarily agricultural. Over a million Northerners worked in industrial jobs, more than 10 times the number of similarly employed Southerners; whereas the north had roughly 100,000 factories or plants, the South had less than 20,000 factories. The Union also had twice as much railroad track as the Confederacy, including more long-distance lines. Beyond industrial capacity, the Northern states had a greater population, about 22–23 million people, compared to 9 million in the South. More specifically, the Union had more than 3.5 million men who could potentially serve in its armies, compared to 1 to 1.5 million in the Confederacy. Moreover, of the 9 million people in the South, 3.5 million were slaves who would not serve in Confederate armies—though many later wore the Union blue to fight for their freedom. About 180,000 African Americans served in federal forces during the war.

Yet it would take time to convert factories to war production, and to raise and train larger numbers of troops. Moreover, both sides needed sufficient administrative and fiscal resources to mobilize men and manufacture war material. Here again, the Union had the upper hand. After 1861, its well-established government expanded to oversee more activities in the private sector and meet wartime needs. Perhaps the best example is the Lincoln administration's coordination of Northern railroads and direct management of those captured in Southern areas. In contrast, the Confederacy was creating a national government from scratch when the war began.

The North also had a robust financial system. Although the Lincoln administration printed some money, it also increased taxes and received an unprecedented amount of loans to finance the Union military machine: $2.6 billion, enough to pay for most war expenses. In contrast, the Confederacy printed money to pay most of its expenses, which fueled inflation to devastating levels: By war's end, Southerners could get less than two cents for each Confederate dollar.

These advantages made the Union well disposed to fight a long, resource-intensive war—so long as it could maintain the political will to prosecute hostilities. More recent history has provided examples of belligerents who, even with significant material, technological, and manpower advantages, still lost wars. The American Revolution was also such a conflict, with Great Britain failing to employ its empire's resources to crush Patriot resistance. In the Civil War, the Union also sought to suppress a rebellion—only the Confederacy encompassed a much greater area than the original 13 colonies. To reassert its authority, the federal government had to form and maintain large conventional forces to invade the South. Conversely, to establish their own independent country, Confederates had to create armies to defend their territory and repel invasions long enough for Northerners to tire of the war.

The question was which side was better able to endure the war's sacrifices while simultaneously punishing the enemy enough to achieve its goals. The answer would only be determined over the course of hostilities. As Gary Gallagher has noted, the outcomes of campaigns and battles shaped popular expectations for ultimate victory or defeat during the war. At its beginning, though, people on both sides had high hopes for success.

Union Versus Confederacy: Military Capabilities

Many Southerners believed their men were better fighters, as did some Northerners. By 1861 many articles, essays, and stories had depicted the image of a Southern "cavalier," the young gentleman of manners who, with advantages of a comfortable background and rural environment, was skilled in athletic and outdoor pursuits and a natural leader of men. The cavalier myth was a response to socioeconomic developments over the previous generation, providing a means for Southerners to take pride in their society as the North industrialized. Conversely, many Northerners were insecure about changes such as the pace of urbanization and the long hours workers spent inside factories.

But the actual readiness of men in both regions for war was more complex. Mandatory state militia service was generally defunct in mid-nineteenth-century America. Many communities, though, had men who banded together to form their own voluntary militia companies—and these were usually found in the North. In another sense, urban Northerners had an advantage over rural Southerners: a reduced susceptibility to disease. Prior to the twentieth century, far more soldiers died of disease than from combat. Men who lived and worked in close proximity to large numbers of people, as they did in Northern factories and urban areas, had been exposed to many more potential illnesses than those dwelling in low-population-density areas, and had a potentially greater chance of resisting illness during military service.

In both the Union and Confederate armies, the few men with some military expertise had been officers in the regular U.S. Army. At war's outbreak, about 280 of 1,080 active-duty officers resigned to fight for the South, and both sides had veterans return from civilian life to take commissions. Many had served in the Mexican War, and because experienced officers were so few relative to the size of Union and Confederate armies, the Civil War presented them with unprecedented opportunities for promotion. But not all could effectively handle larger commands. Commanding a company of a few dozen men was not as complex or demanding as leading a brigade or division of a few thousand, much less a corps of over 10,000, or a field army of many corps. In 1861, the only American alive who had ever commanded a field army was the aging Winfield Scott. Most men who had served in the Mexican War were junior or company-grade officers at the time.

A common belief is that in the Civil War, the South had more and better officers. Relative to their population within the United States, more Southerners may have served in the U.S. Army prior to 1861, but this point does not support claims of better wartime performance. The idea stems primarily from dramatic Confederate victories by the Army of Northern Virginia under Robert E. Lee. But these successes merely indicate the Confederacy found one very good field commander early in the war, as Lee assumed command in June 1862. Beyond Lee, the number of distinguished higher-ranking Southern officers is limited. Thomas J. "Stonewall" Jackson won victories in the Shenandoah Valley during the spring of 1862 before becoming one of Lee's corps commanders but died of wounds sustained at Chancellorsville in May 1863. James Longstreet was another officer known mostly for his service as a corps commander under Lee.

The Army of Northern Virginia also fought in the Eastern theater which, given the close proximity of both capitals (Washington, D.C. and Richmond, Virginia) received more media attention than other Confederate armies—all of which had poorer military records. While Lee won prominent victories early in the war, Lincoln struggled to find an effective commander to check him. After a succession of disappointing officers, he finally rectified the problem in 1864, placing Ulysses S. Grant in command of all Union armies. By then, Grant and his chief subordinate, William T. Sherman, had proven their abilities by consistently defeating Confederate armies in the west.

One must also consider the missions of opposing commanders when considering claims of superior performance. Union armies were usually on the operational and tactical offensive. The philosopher of war Carl von Clausewitz asserted that overall, a successful attack is more difficult to achieve than a successful defense. Such difficulties are arguably greater for large armies of inexperienced soldiers and officers, as was the case early in the war. Moreover, when Confederate armies took the operational offensive or initiated tactical assaults, they often did not perform any better than Union armies had.

Students should be wary of simplistic statements of combat proficiency in a conflict as large and complex as the Civil War. Given that the few experienced officers on both sides shared a common military heritage and background prior to 1861, neither belligerent had a dramatic advantage in fighting capacity, at least early in the war. Over time, the Union exploited its superior resources to enhance its military effectiveness. But one reason it did so was an advantage in political leadership, and its capacity to sustain the popular will to fight.

Union Versus Confederacy: Political Leadership

In early 1861, Southern state representatives met in Montgomery, Alabama, to create a constitution for the Confederacy. It was quite similar to that of the United States, chief differences being an explicit protection of slavery and a greater emphasis on state sovereignty—even though it created a national government with considerable authority. This inherent tension in the Confederate constitution did not make future political strains inevitable, if Southerners could find effective and cooperative leaders. In this regard, their choice of Jefferson Davis as president proved disappointing.

Davis had strong credentials. A West Point graduate who had commanded troops in the Mexican War, he was prominent among Mississippi's planter class, and was elected to the U.S. Congress as both a representative and a senator. Davis had also served as President Franklin Pierce's Secretary of War. But he did not listen or take criticism well, and was ill-suited to a position where persuasion and compromise was required to build political consensus. Davis had hoped for a field command but accepted the presidency out of sense of duty. Over time, he would come to alienate state governors and officials and much of the Confederate Congress, as well as members of his own administration and cabinet.

The Union was not immune to personality clashes among its leadership or problems developing effective policies. But its great advantage was President Abraham Lincoln. In contrast to Davis, his qualifications for high office were not impressive. Lincoln's sole military experience stemmed from the Black Hawk War, when his militia unit was mobilized but never saw combat. A successful lawyer, the Illinois state legislature accounted for the bulk of his prior political experience, though he had served a term as a U.S. Representative and in 1858 had lost his bid for a Senate seat to Stephen Douglas. But Lincoln was a man of great patience, able to listen to different perspectives and cogently express his own concerns. Capable of forging consensus among politicians and officials of disparate opinions and temperaments, he was modest enough to modify his own views to account for previous mistakes and changing circumstances.

One of Lincoln's first challenges as president was to ensure that the border states—those with legal slavery but which had remained in the Union—did not leave. Maryland, for example, was a small state, but lay between Washington, D.C., and the rest of the Union. When pro-Southern riots erupted in Baltimore in April 1861, Lincoln responded quickly, suspending the writ of habeas corpus, imprisoning Confederate sympathizers and suspected agents, and positioning troops to protect rail and telegraph lines. He took the opposite tack with Kentucky. A large state with significant resources, its border on the Ohio River would greatly enhance Southern defensive capabilities if it joined the Confederacy. When its governor declared "neutrality," Lincoln simply waited. His patience was rewarded in September 1861, when Confederate forces occupied Columbus, Kentucky, on the Mississippi River, driving the state into the arms of the Union.

To secure Missouri, Lincoln had to rely more upon military action by local commanders. In May 1861, army captain Nathaniel Lyon arrested a group of suspected secessionists outside St. Louis, fearing they would try to seize the city's federal arsenal. Street riots erupted, and pro-Union and pro-Confederate forces formed. In subsequent months, Union troops lost the Battle of Wilson's Creek in August (where Lyon died commanding) but won the Battle of Pea Ridge (Arkansas) in March 1862. Afterward, Confederate supporters could not muster the strength to challenge Missouri's pro-Union government. Fighting did not cease, though, but instead morphed into local guerilla operations that plagued the state for the rest of the war. Both sides produced groups that became infamous for atrocities, including Union "jayhawkers" from Kansas and William C. Quantrill's band, perhaps the most notorious of the pro-Confederate fighters.

Strategy

Davis and Lincoln each needed to work with military commanders to determine how the use of armed forces would achieve their war goals—the province of strategy. Both sides faced difficult choices, complicated by issues of resources and politics. Both tried different strategic approaches over the course of the war. Though victorious in the end, it took years for the Union to develop a winning strategy and find the commander to implement it.

Terrain and geography shaped strategic perspectives and created distinct theaters of war for military operations. One was the Eastern theater, between the Appalachian Mountains and the Atlantic Ocean, where campaigns generally ranged between Virginia and southern Pennsylvania. Events here received the most attention during the war, for it contained both belligerents' capitals, which were only 100 miles apart after Virginia joined the Confederacy. Moreover, the largest field armies opposed each other in this theater—the Union Army of the Potomac and Confederate Army of Northern Virginia—though other, smaller armies also fought there.

This area was actually fairly constrained compared to the Western theater, between the Mississippi River and the Appalachians. Although individual armies there were generally not as large as the Army of the Potomac and the Army of Northern Virginia, they still numbered into the tens of thousands, and pursued operations that at times traversed Tennessee, Kentucky, Mississippi, Alabama, and Georgia. West of the Mississippi River was the Trans-Mississippi theater where, though it was important in resources (particularly for the Confederacy), fighting involved relatively small forces. Beyond armies, the Union Navy was active along the lengthy Confederate coastline, blockading as well as invading and occupying ports.

Strategically, the Confederacy was on the defensive. For its leaders, the challenge was to determine the best way to resist Union invasions to the point where it would quit and recognize Confederate independence. One alternative was to fight on the operational defensive, simply countering and fighting off Northern advances into Southern territory, which occurred for much of the war. But given its size, Confederate military forces could not prevent all Union incursions, and if local units faced a large invading army they might have to retreat before commanders could concentrate enough troops to confront it. Such operations could produce political backlash, given Southern expectations that the government's function was to protect their territory and property.

An alternative strategic defense for the Confederacy was the operational offensive. That is, invade Northern territory and by winning battles or inflicting damage, induce the Union to sue for peace on Southern terms. The chief advocate for this approach was Robert E. Lee, who worried that the Confederacy could not prevail in a long conflict. He pursued such offensives twice during the war, and both times failed to win the battle needed for success (although there was no guarantee such a victory would induce the Union to negotiate an end to the war). After the Gettysburg campaign, Lee never again had the men or supplies needed for such an offensive campaign.

Conversely, the Union was on the strategic offensive. It would have to conquer or hurt the Confederacy enough to induce Southerners to relinquish their aspirations of independence and rejoin the United States, which in turn required operational offensives. As with the South, the Union had various options for pursuing this goal. The aging Winfield Scott, General-in-Chief of the U.S. Army when the Civil War began, developed the first one. His plan envisioned an advance down the Mississippi River to the Gulf of Mexico of about 80,000 men, both marching overland and conveyed by steamers. Supported by gunboats, he expected these forces to isolate and conquer rebel strongholds on the river. While this movement divided the Confederacy and prevented supplies from moving across the Mississippi, the Union Navy would blockade the Confederate coastline. If these measures were not sufficient to induce surrender, Scott proposed armies totaling 300,000 men invade and conquer Southern territory.

With its emphasis on denying the Confederacy resources to support its war effort, Scott's plan reflected hopes that the rebellion had limited support among Southerners, and that relatively mild pressure might be enough to induce them to abandon secession. But the General-in-Chief acknowledged it would take time to implement this strategy—many months for the blockade and Mississippi River campaign, and two to three years if large armies had to assault the Confederacy. As in the South, Northerners were anxious for military action at the start of the war. Many thought that simply capturing the Southern capital at Richmond would end the rebellion.

Northern newspapers, with banner headlines proclaiming "On to Richmond," derisively called Scott's strategy "the Anaconda Plan." Many historians have observed that, in the end, the Union adopted the key elements of Scott's strategy. But in the war's first years, the North gave

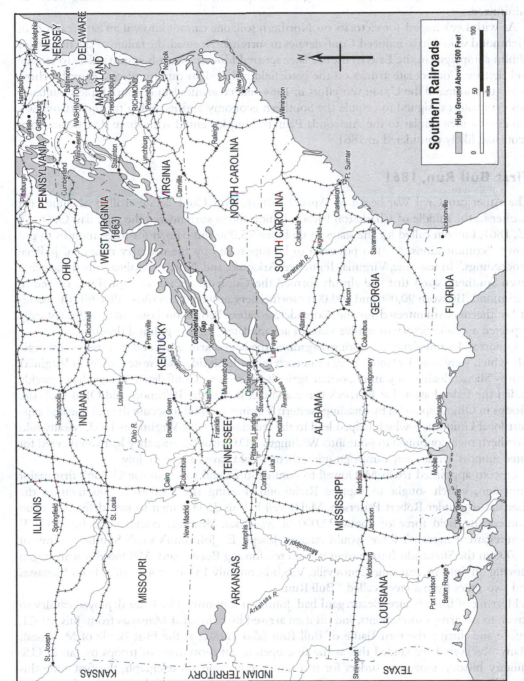

Map 6.1 Southern Railroads

more attention to operations that sought to win the war with a single offensive campaign to capture Richmond, expecting that Southerners would sue for peace after losing their capital. Northerners also argued that, by winning the war quickly, destruction and suffering would be minimized.

As with Lee's hoped-for victories on Northern soil, one cannot know if an early capture of Richmond would have induced Confederates to surrender. Instead, the failure of the first major Union campaigns in the Eastern theater later spurred Lincoln to push commanders to engage and destroy Confederate armies on the battlefield rather than capture places. After he chose Grant to command the Union war effort in 1864, federal armies launched multiple simultaneous campaigns designed to cripple the Southern economy and its ability to support military forces—an idea similar to the Anaconda Plan, but implemented with more destruction than Scott had likely considered in 1861.

First Bull Run, 1861

The American Civil War began on April 12, 1861, with Confederate artillery shelling Fort Sumter in the middle of Charleston harbor. Union forces surrendered the next day. On April 15, 1861, Lincoln called for the states to mobilize 75,000 militiamen for three months to put down "combinations . . . too powerful to be suppressed by the ordinary course of judicial proceedings." In response, Virginia, Tennessee, Arkansas, and North Carolina joined the other seven Southern states that had already formed the Confederacy, whose capital was moved to Richmond. Between 90,000 and 100,000 Northerners answered Lincoln's call, while thousands of Southerners volunteered for the Confederate cause. People on both sides enthusiastically expected a quick victory to resolve years of accumulated, intense political dissention.

Union and Confederate authorities organized the largest armies around their respective capitals, which were only 100 miles away from each other. Each side also created forces in Virginia's nearby Shenandoah Valley, an important agricultural region. Confederate troops there quickly raided the federal arsenal at Harper's Ferry and threatened the Baltimore and Ohio Railroad. Troops in Ohio responded by invading western Virginia in June to secure the rail line and support local Unionists—which helped lead to the creation of West Virginia in 1863. Meanwhile, Northern men continued to pour into Washington, D.C. But because they had volunteered for three months' service, any campaign using them would have to start in July.

Lincoln appointed Irwin McDowell to command federal forces in the Union's first major campaign, which sought to capture Richmond. Placing the 14,000–18,000 men in the Shenandoah under Robert Patterson, McDowell led his 35,000 men to first defeat the main Confederate field force of about 22,000 at Manassas, Virginia, commanded by P. G. T. Beauregard. Patterson's force would engage Joseph E. Johnston's small Southern army of 11,000 in the Shenandoah to prevent it from reinforcing Beauregard. McDowell's army began moving on July 16, reaching Centreville, Virginia, on July 18, about 4–5 miles from Manassas and two miles from a creek called "Bull Run."

Hearing of this advance, Beauregard had Johnston join him. The latter deployed cavalry to screen to his army's movements, and his men arrived by railroad at Manassas from July 19–21, before and during the First Battle of Bull Run (also known as the First Battle of Manassas). Many observers have lauded this as the first operational movement of troops by rail in U.S. military history; moreover, orders for this movement came via telegraph, the first time this technology was employed during military operations. In terms of the campaign's ultimate outcome, though, Patterson's failure to prevent Johnston's withdrawal was more significant.

Meanwhile, McDowell prepared his attack. As a distraction, he had a division assault a stone bridge across Bull Run, on the Confederate left flank. McDowell sent his main force to cross farther north and then advance against the enemy flank and rear. The attack began early on July 21, 1861, but difficulties delayed the primary assault. By late morning, Union troops had pushed back defenders and occupied Mathews Hill. Throughout the course of the day, Beauregard shifted forces from the Confederate right to the left, while Johnston moved reinforcements up from the railhead. Both organized a new defensive position on the Confederate left at Henry Hill. Following a lull in the early afternoon, McDowell renewed the Union attack, trying to capture the hill. Fierce combat raged over two hours, but the Confederates prevailed after a final counterattack drove off Union forces.

McDowell's plan was fine in conception but flawed in the execution. Poor reconnaissance missed crossing points on Bull Run that would have saved the main assault force miles' worth of marching. Confusing orders added unnecessary marches to units already tired after advancing from Washington. Units often failed to coordinate, attacking individually without support. Officers were new to their responsibilities, and McDowell had to perform much of his own staff work—by the time of battle, he may have exhausted himself. Even so, his army might have been successful if Johnston's men had not arrived to support Beauregard, for Confederate leaders also made mistakes. Beauregard's reconnaissance before the battle was also poor, and his initial troop dispositions flawed. But the relative complexity of McDowell's tactical offensive plan amplified Union errors, and the discrepancy between it and his troops' abilities was likely the biggest reason for defeat.

Figure 6.4 "Battle of Bull Run—July 21st, 1861"
By Kurz & Allison, 1889–90

Many volunteer units wore their own uniforms at the First Battle of Bull Run, for soldiers' clothing was not yet standardized. A popular fashion of the era stemmed from the Zouaves, originally North African fighters who wore loose pants and open jackets. Their garb became popular after the French Army adopted similar units during its conquest of Algeria. In the above image, the soldier in the bottom center, fleeing to the left, is part of a Northern "Zouave" unit.

Library of Congress, Prints and Photographs Division, LC-DIG-pga-01843

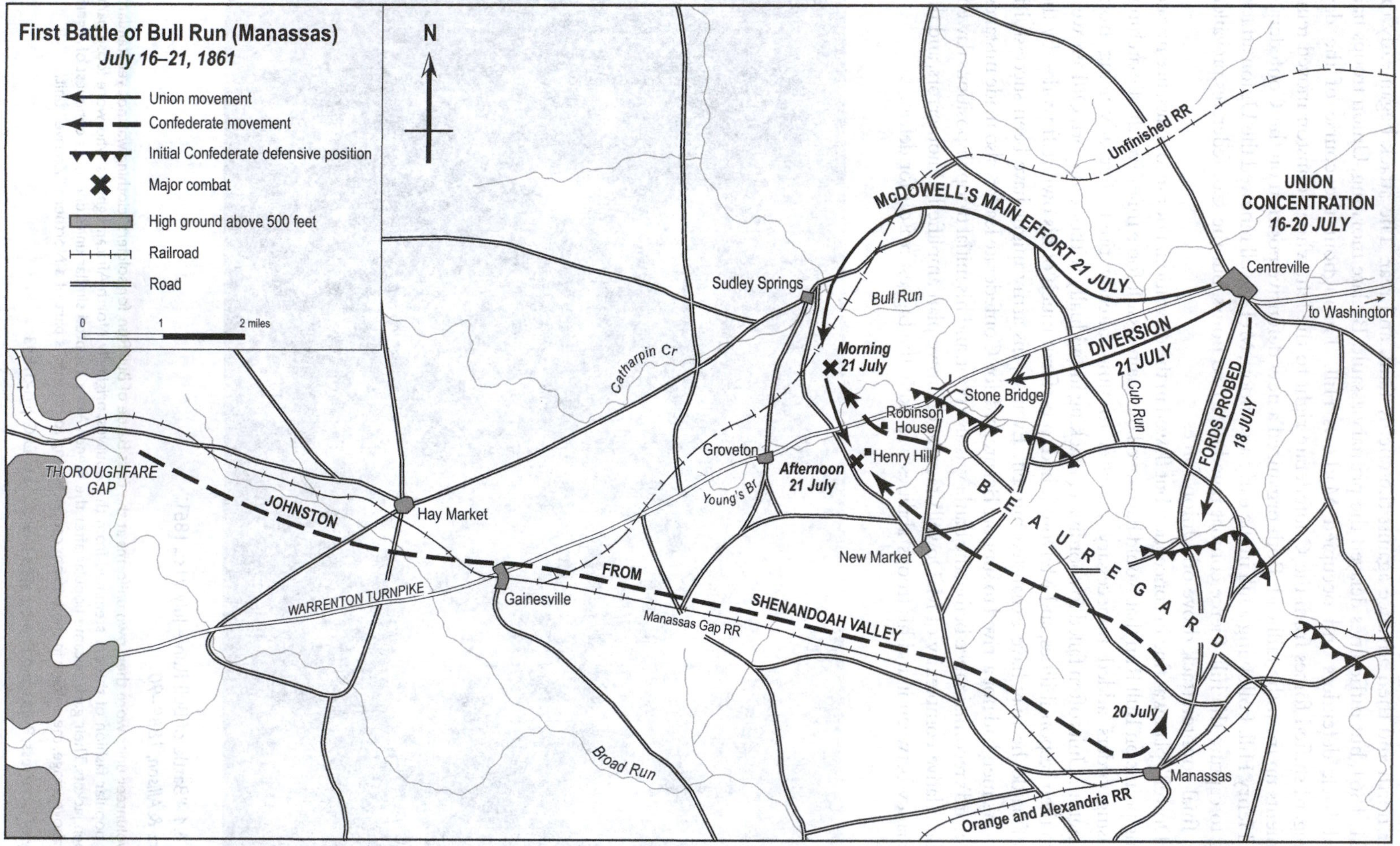

Map 6.2 First Battle of Bull Run (Manassas) July 16–21, 1861

First Bull Run is also infamous for the rout that immediately followed. Many civilians had come out from Washington, D.C., to observe what they thought would be a great Union victory and the end of the war. As McDowell began to retreat, some troops panicked, and many fled north; civilians and soldiers raced for the safety of the Union capital. But the danger of attack was minimal. Confederate forces were also exhausted and disorganized after fighting what was then the largest battle in American history: about 65,000 total combatants, of whom 3,000 Northerners and 2,000 Southerners became casualties. Larger and more grisly battles would soon follow. For the moment though, the Confederacy rejoiced in having defeated Union's initial attempt to squash the rebellion. Conversely, Northerners began to realize greater efforts were required to preserve the United States.

Raising Armies

By First Bull Run, the Lincoln administration had recognized the need for more men with longer terms of service. On July 4, the president had asked a special session of Congress to raise 400,000 volunteers for three years' service. Instead, it authorized 500,000 to serve in military units designated "United States Volunteers," as distinct from the regular U.S. Army (which had been increased to 22,000 men). By summer's end, the Union had 700,000 men under arms, most of them three-year volunteers. In March 1861, before the attack on Fort Sumter, the Confederate Congress had authorized an army of up to 100,000 volunteers for 6–12 months' service. Two months later, it called for up to 400,000 men who would serve either for three years or the duration of the war. By the time fighting stopped, many more men had donned a uniform. Over the course of the war more than two million men fought for the Union, though no more than one million served at any one time. The Confederacy raised 750,000–900,000 soldiers during the conflict, with perhaps up to 450,000 serving at any one time.

Early in the war, ideals motivated men to volunteer. Southerners wanted to defend their homes and establish a new country. Many thought the Confederacy was the true heir to the values of the American Revolution, regarding the Union as corrupt and tyrannical. Conversely, Northern men fought to save the Union and suppress the rebellion. As Gary Gallagher has observed, nineteenth-century Americans regarded the United States as possessing a special place in history. Relatively few democracies or republics had existed over the course of human civilization, of which the United States was the biggest. If successful, the secession of the Southern states could lead to the Union's dissolution, implying a large republic could not survive. Many Northerners fought to ensure that did not occur.

Local ties also spurred enlistment. As in previous wars, states organized units for national service, issuing commissions to men who would raise volunteers from their communities. When some heeded the call to serve, they were often joined by brothers, cousins, neighbors, and friends. As a result men from specific towns, cities, or regions often comprised the majority or all of an individual regiment's strength. A desire for adventure was also a factor for many young recruits. Another was social pressure stemming from popular conceptions of honor and manliness. Many Southern men of privileged background subscribed to the cavalier myth mentioned previously, seeing themselves as natural leaders. But common cultural values throughout nineteenth-century America expected that men would bear sacrifices for the larger communal good. Women in local communities, at least at the beginning of the war, often held young men to these standards, providing sometimes not-so-subtle hints to enlist.

The great need for manpower provided special opportunities for regular Army officers. In peacetime, promotion was slow and based upon seniority. But states needed leaders to raise and command large numbers of volunteer regiments. Hence, a young regular Army lieutenant or captain could become a colonel of his own regiment in the United States Volunteers or the

Confederate Army. Even so, such officers were few compared to the need, and states issued numerous commissions to local leaders, notables, and politically connected men to raise and command military units.

Whatever the motivations, popular volunteerism soon ebbed, and both sides pursued other means to find men for their armies. The Confederacy established a national draft law before the Union, the first in American history. The idea of a draft was not new, but before the Civil War only individual states (or colonies) had imposed them. In early 1862, Confederate leaders realized that about half of their soldiers had only enlisted for one-year terms that would soon expire. In response, they passed the Confederate Conscription Act in April 1862, which made all able-bodied men 18–35 years old (including current one-year volunteers) eligible for a draft, with inductees providing three years' service—though it allowed draftees to hire substitutes.

Almost immediately and throughout the remainder of the war, the Confederate Congress enacted additional laws to modify the Conscription Act. One of the first allowed exemptions to the draft and excluded men such as government officials, militia officers, workers in important industries, clergymen, and teachers. In 1863, the Congress forbade hiring substitutes, and the following year required all Confederate soldiers to serve for the duration of the war. By war's end, age limits for eligible draftees had expanded to between 17 and 50 years of age. In comparison, the Union enacted its Enrollment Act in March 1863, making all able-bodied men aged 20 to 45 eligible for the draft, and allowing draftees to either hire substitutes or avoid service by paying a $300 "commutation" fee. This law gave the federal government a role in military recruitment for the first time, particularly in setting manpower quotas and creating an administration to oversee local draft boards.

As with prior drafts, Civil War conscription laws were actually designed to spur more volunteer enlistments, rather than induct draftees directly. In 1862, for example, the Lincoln administration prompted states to raise over 400,000 additional troops by simply threatening a draft. The following year, the Enrollment Act stipulated that conscription would only be imposed upon a local district if too few men volunteered to meet stipulated goals. In the nineteenth century, much of American society looked down upon individuals forced into military service, and upon communities that had to rely upon them to meet manpower quotas. In this regard, the conscription laws worked: Fewer than 200,000 Confederate soldiers served as draftees or substitutes, most joining as volunteers. After the passage of the Enrollment Act, more than one million men enlisted (or reenlisted) in Union armies, which took in only about 160,000 draftees or substitutes.

Though successful, conscription laws both reflected and aggravated social tensions. The Confederate Congress, for example, prevented draftees from hiring substitutes when prices for the latter reached up to $6,000 Confederate dollars (or $600 in gold), prompting complaints that only the rich could afford them. Conscription exemptions sparked similar anger. One provision allowed plantation owners to exclude a white man from the draft for every 20 slaves they owned, which was not appreciated by soldiers who owned no or few slaves. This aspect of the law led to cries of "a rich man's war but a poor man's fight." Many Southerners opposed the simple existence of the Conscription Act, which imposed national requirements and obligations upon a people who had supposedly left the Union so that their states would have more political autonomy. In this regard, some Southern states reduced the burden of conscription by either creating additional categories of men excluded from the draft or placing more men than necessary in preexisting ones.

The Union avoided the furor over substitutes by creating a commutation fee. But it suffered problems stemming from bounties: cash bonuses offered to men upon enlistment to stimulate volunteering. Federal bounties were capped at $300, but states, cities, districts, and even private and civic organizations also offered bounties to encourage recruitment for their own local regiments. Nearby areas often competed for the same pool of volunteers, driving up prices. In 1864, a new Union recruit could potentially receive $800 in total bounty money, sparking complaints from poorer areas. Draft riots were another problem in the North, the most infamous of which occurred in New York City. There, large populations of free African Americans and Irish immigrants competed for employment, particularly in factories. In the summer of 1863, by which time President Lincoln had issued the Emancipation Proclamation and Congress had passed the Enrollment Act, many Irish were upset at the prospect having to serve in the ranks of the Union armies while African Americans acquired jobs. In July their frustration exploded, with mobs attacking and killing dozens of black residents. After a few days troops from the Battle of Gettysburg arrived to restore order.

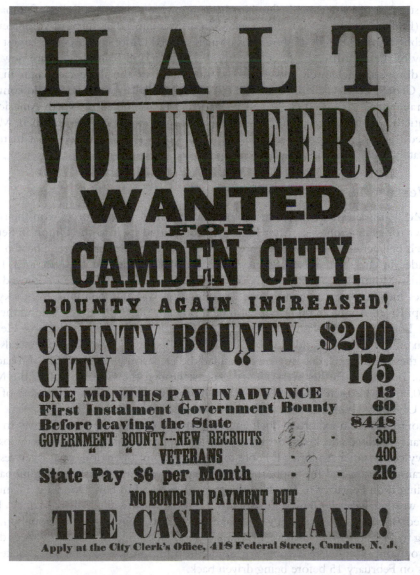

Figure 6.5 Civil War Recruiting Poster

Courtesy of the New-York Historical Society

The New York City Draft Riot was the largest and most lethal of many that occurred in Northern towns and cities late in the war. But numerous immigrants and African Americans served in Union armies. The German and Irish communities provided many regiments, including both men recently arrived in America and those from families who had already established themselves. Early in the war Northern, free African Americans enlisted in a few units, of which the 54th Massachusetts is the most famous. But after President Lincoln issued the Emancipation Proclamation, large numbers of slaves fled bondage in the South and enlisted. The federal government organized these men into regiments that were part of a separate military entity, the "United States Colored Troops." Unlike units formed by state authorities, these were raised by federal officials. A total of about 180,000 African Americans served in Union armed forces over the course of the Civil War.

In the summer of 1861, though, few Northerners envisioned the possibility of so many black soldiers. (Ending slavery was not then even a Union war aim.) The spirit of volunteerism had not yet ebbed, and hundreds of thousands of men swelled Union armies. The largest one was the Army of the Potomac, the force recently defeated at Bull Run. To prepare new recruits, Lincoln dismissed McDowell and turned to the victor of the June campaign in western Virginia, George B. McClellan. As will be discussed, McClellan was a poor field commander. But he trained and organized the largest field force ever assembled in North America before the twentieth century, for the Army of the Potomac soon exceeded 100,000 men. McClellan performed this task with great skill, creating such a high sense of morale that many troops affectionately called him "Little Mac."

The Western Theater in Early 1862

Before McClellan led the Army of the Potomac in the field, federal forces won their first significant victories in Tennessee. After Kentucky committed itself to the Union in September, 1861, each belligerent concentrated troops near its border with Tennessee. The Confederate commander in the west, Albert Sydney Johnston, had to defend the vast area, from the Appalachian Mountains to Arkansas. In early 1862 he had only 43,000 men, deployed to block key routes into Southern territory. One concentration was at Columbus, Kentucky, on the Mississippi River. About 25,000 troops also held Bowling Green, Kentucky, along the railroad between Louisville and Nashville. Other Confederate troops manned Forts Henry and Donelson on the Tennessee and Cumberland Rivers, respectively. Two Union generals oversaw forces in the area. Don Carlos Buell commanded the Department of the Ohio and had 40,000 soldiers at Louisville. Farther west, Henry Halleck headed the Department of the Missouri. About 20,000 of his men were based at Cairo, Illinois, under the direct command of his subordinate Ulysses S. Grant.

For months, Lincoln exhorted Buell and Halleck to cooperate in an offensive. In January 1862, Grant proposed attacking Fort Henry. Halleck approved, and Grant worked closely with U.S. Navy commander Andrew H. Foote to develop a joint operation, with river vessels providing transportation and fire support. Fort Henry surrendered shortly after gunboats began bombarding it on February 6. Much of the garrison escaped to Fort Donelson 11 miles away, and bad weather delayed Grant's attempts to attack it. Meanwhile, Albert Sydney Johnston abandoned Bowling Green, sending thousands of men to reinforce Fort Donelson, the rest retreating to Nashville. By February 14, Grant's 25,000 men outnumbered the fort's defenders about two to one. Confederate troops withstood the initial gunboat assault and attacked Union positions on February 15 before being driven back.

By then their commanders had had enough. When asked for terms, Grant responded that he would only accept "unconditional and immediate surrender." Most high-ranking Confederate

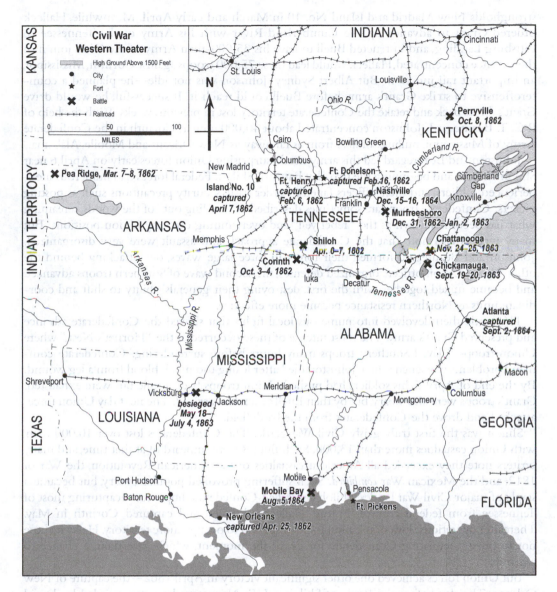

Map 6.3 Civil War, Western Theater

officers fled, and the vast majority of the defenders, 12,000–13,000 men, surrendered on February 16. Albert Sydney Johnston thus lost much of his total strength in the Western theater. Operationally, these victories also gave Union forces the capacity to penetrate further into Confederate territory along the Tennessee and Cumberland Rivers. Johnston had to abandon Nashville, especially when Buell began advancing there from Louisville. As a result, all of Kentucky and most of Tennessee—an important granary for the Confederacy—came under Union control in the weeks after Fort Donelson's capture.

Lincoln then appointed Henry Halleck overall Union commander in the Western theater. Halleck dispatched troops under John Pope who, working with Foote's naval flotilla, moved south down the Mississippi River. This Union Army of the Mississippi captured Confederate strongholds New Madrid and Island No. 10 in March and early April. Meanwhile, Halleck ordered Grant to advance up the Cumberland River with his Army of the Tennessee to Pittsburg Landing, and instructed Buell to have his 35,000-man Army of the Ohio join him there. Once concentrated, Halleck would lead these 75,000 troops against Corinth, Mississippi, an important rail junction. But Albert Sydney Johnson was not idle—he planned a counteroffensive to strike Grant's army before Buell could reach it. If successful, he would drive Grant's forces back and retake the Confederate territory lost in previous weeks. With the help of P. G. T. Beauregard, Johnston concentrated about 40,000 men at Corinth in the Confederate Army of Mississippi, pulling soldiers from as far away as New Orleans and Mobile, Alabama.

Johnston and Beauregard led this army north, surprising Union forces early on April 6 near Shiloh church, and beginning the two-day Battle of Shiloh. Federal forces had numerous inexperienced soldiers, and their officers failed to order basic security precautions such as posting pickets. Confederate troops are sometimes described as "boiling out" of the woods, screaming what has become known as the "rebel yell" and overrunning outlying Union positions. But many writers also note that the Confederate approach and assault were very disorganized. Johnson and Beauregard formed their forces in three large waves, one attacking behind the other. But as Union officers organized defenses, the second wave of Southern troops advanced and became mixed together with the first, destroying their generals' ability to shift and coordinate units as Northern resistance became more effective.

The battle then devolved into numerous local fights that slowed the Confederate advance and preserved Grant's army. The most intense of these occurred at the "Hornet's Nest," where Union troops delayed Southern troops many hours before surrendering. Confederate command problems worsened when Johnston died after losing too much blood from a leg wound. By the end of April 6, his soldiers had pushed Union troops back a mile but were exhausted. Grant's troops were also weary, but by then Buell's men had arrived. The next day Union forces attacked and drove the Confederates from the battlefield.

Shiloh was the first truly grisly Civil War battle. The Confederates lost over 10,000 men, with Union casualties more than 13,000. Such figures were unheard of at that time, and many writers note they exceeded all American casualties of the American Revolution, the War of 1812, and the Mexican War *combined*. Such suffering provoked popular outcry, but became a staple of major Civil War battles. Shiloh also killed Confederate hopes for recapturing most of Tennessee from federal control. Instead, Halleck advanced and captured Corinth in May. Thereafter operations slowed, as Union forces dispersed to occupy more territory. Halleck chose not to pursue retreating Confederate forces for the moment, which gave them a chance to regroup.

But Union forces achieved one other significant victory in April 1862—the capture of New Orleans. The day before the Battle of Shiloh, a U.S. Navy squadron commanded by David Farragut appeared before Forts Jackson and St. Philip, which guarded the Mississippi River about 75 miles below the city. After many days of shelling, most of his 17 vessels pushed past the forts on April 24, 1862. Defeating a Confederate flotilla of smaller vessels and a few incomplete ironclads, they arrived at New Orleans the next day. Weeks earlier, soldiers protecting the city had left to join Johnston's army at Corinth (just before the Battle of Shiloh), and Union troops easily occupied New Orleans.

The loss of the Confederacy's largest port prevented the use of the Mississippi as a shipping route. Moreover, New Orleans was one of few centers of Southern industry and finance, and its capture was a huge blow to the Southern war effort. Combined with other gains since the beginning of 1862, the Union was well on its way toward splitting the Confederacy in half and occupying large portions of its territory, as initially envisioned in Scott's Anaconda Plan. But many Northerners still thought the Union would win the war with one climactic campaign and looked to George McClellan's Army of the Potomac to deliver victory.

The Peninsula Campaign, 1862

McClellan had been training and organizing what would become the largest army of the Civil War. When Winfield Scott retired as General-in-Chief in the fall of 1861, Lincoln elevated the 35-year old general to that position as well, giving him more duties. But Northerners were becoming impatient. Having prepared the Army of the Potomac to fight, McClellan gave no indication of when it would. In January 1862, Lincoln issued presidential "War Order No. 1," stipulating Union forces should advance by February 22. The Army of the Potomac did not, but the order at least prompted McClellan to state his operational plans.

The general proposed using Union naval capacity to ship his forces down Chesapeake Bay to a point close to Richmond, bypassing the main Confederate army in northern Virginia, then commanded by Joseph E. Johnston. The Army of the Potomac would then advance inland to Richmond or another place it could fortify before Johnston's army arrived; McClellan envisioned Confederates then having to attack his men in prepared defensive positions. Lincoln preferred that Union troops advance overland to Richmond, so they could move back to protect Washington if enemy forces threatened. But McClellan promised to leave enough men behind to defend the capital, and Lincoln agreed. The Army of the Potomac began the Peninsula campaign in March, sailing down the Chesapeake and debarking at Fort Monroe. Located at the tip of the peninsula formed by the James and York Rivers, 75 miles east of Richmond, it had remained under Union control when Virginia seceded.

McClellan's forces advanced west. About 15 miles beyond Fort Monroe, they encountered a line of trenches and fortified positions stretching across the peninsula, the northern end terminating at Yorktown. A trained engineer, McClellan paused until large siege guns could be brought up to bombard the defenses. He failed to realize, though, that enemy forces initially numbered 10,000–15,000 men, many fewer than his available manpower. The local Confederate commander, John Magruder, deceived McClellan with ploys such as marching troops behind his works and producing noise and dust that implied the presence of more men—ruses that exploited the Union general's overly cautious nature. Throughout the campaign, McClellan claimed his forces were outnumbered, sometimes by a two to one ratio, when in fact the Army of the Potomac always had more men than the Confederates before it. Stopped in front of the Yorktown line, he did not heed reports of weaknesses in the enemy's positions, or explore alternatives to a siege.

As McClellan delayed, Johnston moved his army onto the peninsula. But realizing the Union Navy controlled both rivers and could land troops behind him, the Confederate commander then fell back toward Richmond. Johnston began retreating on the night of May 3, just before federal artillery bombarded the Yorktown line. Union troops caught up with the rearguard on May 5, precipitating the Battle of Williamsburg, but Johnston's troops successfully held up McClellan's forces. The Confederate army escaped and took up positions in front of Richmond.

The Army of the Potomac, now composed of five army corps, advanced cautiously to within a few miles of the city. Doing so required two corps to cross the Chickahominy River, which separated them from the rest of the McClellan's army to the north. Late in the month, rains flooded the river, and Johnston massed most of his army to attack the two isolated Union corps. But his staff had problems disseminating clear orders for an assault involving about 30,000 men. For example, Johnston intended his units to advance on multiple roads. Instead, all attacking forces used one road, bogging them down and preventing many troops from entering the fight. On May 31, Union troops repelled Confederates at the Battle of Fair Oaks (also called "the

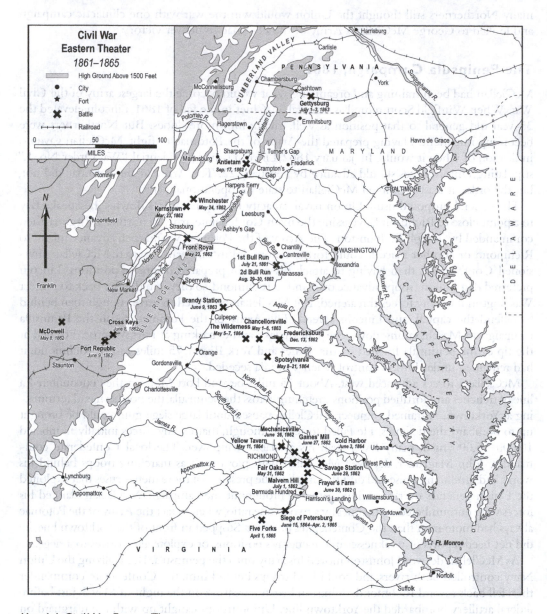

Map 6.4 Civil War, Eastern Theater

Battle of Seven Pines"). After Johnston fell wounded, President Jefferson Davis turned to a friend then serving as his key military advisor to become the new army commander: Robert E. Lee.

About that same time, Lincoln removed McClellan from the post of General-in-Chief, leaving him as simply the Army of the Potomac's commander. The decision reflected mounting frustration. For months before the Peninsula campaign, McClellan had arrogantly boasted about his abilities, and his delays and caution since had destroyed the general's popularity in Washington. His case was not helped when Lincoln and his Secretary of War, Edwin Stanton, realized the troops left to defend the capital were fewer than they had been led to believe.

Lincoln then prevented Irwin McDowell's army corps from debarking for Fort Monroe, instead sending it to Fredericksburg, Virginia, to protect approaches to Washington. McClellan subsequently railed about this decision, claiming political interference had sabotaged his ability to win the campaign. But at the time, the Army of the Potomac was stalled before Yorktown, and McDowell's corps could make no immediate difference. Moreover, from Fredericksburg it could march about 50 miles to join Union forces on the peninsula—a fact not lost on Lee.

Jackson in the Valley, Lee and the Seven Days

Lee had noticed another development. In late March, forces under Thomas "Stonewall" Jackson had attacked Union troops commanded by Nathaniel Banks at Kernstown, in Virginia's Shenandoah Valley. Though Jackson lost, Banks had stopped transferring troops east to help with the Peninsula campaign. After McDowell's corps advanced to Fredericksburg, Lee kept it there with operations that seemed to threaten Washington. He contacted Jackson and had him attack Union forces around the Shenandoah, producing the Valley campaign of May–June 1862. Having previously earned the sobriquet "Stonewall" for his brigade's steadfast defense of Henry Hill during the First Battle of Bull Run, the Valley campaign catapulted Jackson to broader fame.

On May 8 he defeated federal forces under John C. Fremont at McDowell, Virginia. He then raced northeast, combined with troops led by Richard Ewell, and using a small valley to screen his movements, surprised Union troops at Front Royal on May 23. Jackson then threatened to cut off Banks' army a few miles east at Strasburg. The Union commander retreated north toward the Potomac, but Jackson's Army of the Valley caught up and won another battle at Winchester the next day. The Confederates had now captured large stores of supplies, arms, and ammunition, and about 2,000 prisoners. Lincoln and Stanton ordered Fremont and McDowell to send troops to the Valley, hoping to trap Jackson's army of 16,000–17,000 men before it could escape south. But Union forces moved too slowly, and it slipped past. When federal troops later caught up with Jackson, his Confederates prevailed in two separate battles at Cross Keys and New Republic on June 8 and 9, respectively.

Jackson's Valley operations used speed, deception, and terrain to prevail over an enemy with overall numerical superiority. Union forces in and near the Valley totaled more than 60,000—but except for Cross Keys, Jackson's troops outnumbered their enemies in all the battles of the campaign. Union troops were organized into three distinct formations with different commanders (Banks, Fremont, and McDowell), which themselves were deployed in multiple positions. Put another way, federal forces lacked a unified command: The position of General-in-Chief remained vacant, and Lincoln and Stanton tried to coordinate military movements on their own. Many claim that responsibility should have been delegated to a senior officer, though doing so would not have guaranteed a different outcome. Most important was not Jackson's victories in themselves but that they achieved Lee's goal of distracting Union attention and preventing more troops from joining operations on the Peninsula.

That success helped prompt Johnston to launch the Battle of Fair Oaks. Though a Southern defeat, Lee also decided to attack when he assumed command of the main Confederate field army, called the Army of Northern Virginia. But first, he wanted to bring Jackson's forces down from the Valley to join him. Even then, the Army of the Potomac's 105,000–110,000 men would still outnumber Lee's more than 90,000 troops. But he took steps to check this numerical disparity. Lee ordered more entrenchments dug before Richmond, positions that could be held with fewer men. He then concentrated troops to attack the Union Fifth Corps on the right flank of the Army of the Potomac—by then McClellan's only corps north of the Chickahominy—so that the Army of Northern Virginia had a numerical advantage at that location. After defeating it, Lee planned to strike the Union rear, cutting McClellan's troops off from their supply base at White House on the York River—and possibly destroying the federal army.

To prepare, Lee sent cavalry commander J. E. B. Stuart to reconnoiter the area. Lee gave Stuart discretion in executing his orders. Stuart turned the mission into an event in itself, known as "Stuart's Ride" or the "Ride around McClellan." Over the course of four days in mid-June, Stuart's 1,200 troopers rode around the entire Army of the Potomac, evading pursuers, raiding rear areas, and capturing scores of prisoners. As with Jackson in the Valley, this ride propelled Stuart to fame. Both episodes brought elation to Southerners desperate for good news following months of Union successes in the Western theater. But both paled in comparison to what Lee accomplished against McClellan.

The Seven Days Battles actually began with a Union attack. After Fair Oaks, McClellan moved two more corps across the Chickahominy and prepared to besiege Richmond. His troops improved roads, brought up guns and equipment, and fortified their positions. McClellan envisioned a series of battles in which he would bring up guns and pulverize the defenses before the Confederate capital. On June 25, his troops advanced into Oak Grove, from where he would launch a subsequent assault to take high ground for his artillery. But then Confederate forces attacked on June 26, with A. P. Hill initiating the Battle of Mechanicsville. Lee planned to have 60,000 troops, including Jackson's force, attack the 30,000-man Fifth Corps. But Jackson's men, traveling all the way from the Shenandoah Valley, got lost, and Union soldiers repulsed A. P. Hill's assault. McClellan, however, then pulled Fifth Corps back onto a low plateau with more defensible terrain. Lee's troops (now including Jackson's men) converged there, and the resulting Battle of Gaines Mill on June 27 involved about 95,000 Northern and Southern troops combined; close to 15,000 became casualties. After hours of intense combat that lasted well after dark, Confederate troops won, pushing through the defenders' positions.

McClellan, realizing the threat to the White House, moved his base. Exploiting Union control of the rivers, he established a new one at Harrison's Landing on the James River, and ordered the Army of the Potomac to retreat there (protected in part by U.S. Navy warships). Lee's troops, exhausted after the Battle of Gaines Mill, paused a day before chasing federal units south and attempting to cut them off. These operations produced battles at Savage's Station on June 29, Glendale on June 30, and the climactic Battle of Malvern Hill on July 1. At the latter, terrain protected the flanks of defending Union forces positioned on the heights, and artillery devastated Confederate infantry attacks. After prevailing at Malvern Hill, McClellan's army continued on to Harrison's Landing with little interference.

Box 6.2   Account of the Battle of Malvern Hill

Combat lasted well after dark at the Battle of Malvern Hill. In the following account, Confederate officer McHenry Howard described how this and other factors adversely affected soldiers' morale:

> Once, if not oftener, the General [Windner] and his staff . . . went back in the swamp thicket, just behind us, to bring or drive out some of the men who were scattered through it. Force is quicker, if not more effective than persuasion in such cases and without taking time to parley, we used the flats of our swords freely, not infrequently, may be, on commissioned officers. Sometimes there would be half a dozen or more men in a long single line behind one tree, and it was comical, even in that awful time to see a shiver pass up the file when the hindmost was struck with the flat of a sword,

> or how the line would swing to the right or left when a shell passed by. But I wish not to do any injustice to men who were availing themselves of shelter at hand in such a trying time, and perhaps the picture I have drawn may give an exaggerated impression. Most of these men whom we got up with such scant ceremony were not cowardly skulkers, but in the rapid marching up in the dark and on such ground they had become separated from their commands and did not know which way to turn to find them. And all this while the advance was being held by men stubbornly standing under as terrific a fire as can well be imagined, and, mixed up as they were, each one sustained by his own individual courage.
>
> (McHenry Howard, *Recollections of a Maryland Confederate Soldier and Staff Officer Under Johnston, Jackson and Lee*, Baltimore: Williams & Williams, 1914, p. 154)

Tactically, Union defenders had actually prevailed over Confederate attackers during the Seven Days Battles, the one exception being Gaines Mill. But operationally, the threat these attacks posed to McClellan's base prompted the Union commander to retreat after each engagement and abandon attempts to capture Richmond. As result, the Seven Days was a strategic victory for the Confederacy, whose capital was saved. Moreover, Lee's troops captured great stocks of supplies and arms.

The cost of Lee's success was high—over 20,000 casualties from the Seven Days as a whole, compared to 15,000 for the Army of the Potomac. Such losses have spurred critics to bemoan Lee's offensive tendencies, complaints that usually stem from arguments that the ultimate Confederate defeat in the Civil War stemmed from Union advantages in manpower. But that was not Lee's concern in June 1862. His pressing objective then was to save Richmond, whose loss could have immediately destroyed the Confederacy. He achieved that goal, though he did not accomplish his other objective of annihilating the Army of the Potomac. Here, McClellan deserves credit for saving his army, and his devotion to his men was commendable. But he also undermined the Army of the Potomac's chances of victory, and its entire purpose for venturing to the Peninsula. McClellan's caution provided his opponents ample time to counter his moves and develop plans to thwart him.

Second Bull Run, 1862

To revive Union fortunes in the war, Lincoln made significant command changes in July. He appointed John Pope to command the Union Army of Virginia, created from the disparate forces that had failed to trap Jackson in the Shenandoah. Pope had acquired his reputation capturing Confederate strongholds on the Mississippi River in the spring. Lincoln also made Western theater commander Henry Halleck General-in-Chief. After coming east, Halleck first visited the Army of the Potomac at Harrison's Landing. McClellan requested large reinforcements to continue his campaign, claiming he was outnumbered. Lincoln instead decided to withdraw the army via water to the Potomac River, where it could then move to join Pope's army.

Meanwhile, Pope moved his force into Virginia, toward Gordonsville, threatening an important rail link to Richmond. Lee initially dispatched about 12,000 men under Jackson to watch the Union Army of Virginia, which grew to about 24,000 by early August. Advanced units fended off a Union attack by Nathaniel Banks' troops at Cedar Mountain on August 9. By then, Lee realized McClellan's men at Harrison Landing were no longer a threat, whereas Pope's army was mounting a serious campaign. Leaving some troops to defend Richmond, Lee moved to drive it from Virginia. Apparently he hoped to outmaneuver Pope, threatening his rear to induce retreats—but the result was a dramatic victory.

The Confederate Army of Northern Virginia now totaled 55,000 men divided into two corps, one commanded by Jackson and the other by James Longstreet. Lee concentrated his army on the southern bank of Rappahannock River, opposite Pope's Army of Virginia. Then, while Longstreet's corps distracted the federals, Jackson's advanced northwest, using some low mountains to screen its movements. Reaching the Manassas Gap Railroad, Jackson's force turned east. His cavalry raced to Manassas Junction, where it raided and destroyed Pope's key supply center. The Union army retreated, but Pope now looked to engage Jackson's corps while it was separated from the rest of Lee's army.

Jackson positioned his men near the old Bull Run battlefield, on a wooded hill behind an unfinished railroad line. Pope's Army of Virginia began uncoordinated frontal assaults on August 29, precipitating the Second Battle of Bull Run (or Second Battle of Manassas). Jackson's men fended off the Union attacks, and Pope renewed them the next day. But Pope had not detected the arrival of Longstreet's corps, which took up positions on his army's left flank. On August 30, assaults on Jackson's corps did not begin until mid-afternoon, but Longstreet waited until Union forces were heavily engaged. Massed Confederate artillery then blasted into the flank of Pope's army, followed by infantry attacks. Union troops fled the field, having suffered 16,000 total casualties to Lee's 9,000–10,000.

At Second Bull Run, the Union Army of Virginia outnumbered the Confederate Army of Northern Virginia by 65,000 men to 55,000. Moreover, Lee had split his army while facing Pope's larger force. That choice defied conventional military thinking, which stipulated that forces should be massed together. But Lee realized that speed and surprise could create conditions to drive back the federal army. They did because Pope—fixated upon Jackson after the raid on the Manassas Junction depot—failed to keep track of Longstreet's corps. Had he done so, or simply deployed some forces to contest access routes to the battlefield, Union forces may have come closer to defeating Jackson's corps.

Second Bull Run, following so closely on the Seven Days, brought Lee fame and adulation in the Confederacy. But he did not destroy Pope's army. Union troops had held a key bridge that allowed most federal units to escape. Moreover, the bulk of McClellan's soldiers had then arrived on the Potomac River. Faced with these enemy forces, and concerned about the devastation recent campaigns had inflicted on Virginia, Lee pursued a bold course: an invasion of Maryland. He did so at a time when Southern armies in the west were also advancing into Union territory. The result was one of only two Confederate strategic offensives of the war, and the only one that involved multiple campaigns.

Antietam, 1862

Lee clearly saw his strategic objectives. He sought to move onto Union soil, defeat federal forces, and threaten a major city such as Washington, Baltimore, or Philadelphia. With Congressional elections scheduled for the fall, Lee hoped such developments would prompt Lincoln to negotiate and recognize Southern independence. If not, they might persuade Britain or France to either recognize the Confederacy or lend significant aid, similar to what had happened after the Battle of Saratoga in 1777. Many Southerners also believed numerous Confederate sympathizers lived in Maryland. Operationally, Lee wanted to cut rail lines between the Eastern Seaboard and interior states. Shifting the fighting onto Union territory would also enable his forces to consume and destroy enemy resources while preserving his own. Lee was particularly concerned about allowing Virginia farmers the opportunity to reap the eminent harvest unmolested.

Second Bull Run created favorable circumstances for Lee's campaign. Stunned and confused Union troops had retreated to the defenses of Washington. In early September, the Army of Northern Virginia crossed the Potomac River into Maryland. Lee then dispersed his forces. Some went west to hold passes over South Mountain and into the Cumberland Valley beyond to collect supplies. Jackson led the largest detachment to Harper's Ferry, Virginia, to capture the 10,000-man Union garrison that would otherwise threaten Lee's communications back to the Shenandoah Valley. Dividing his army created the danger that separated parts could be crushed. But Lee did not expect Union forces to react quickly to these moves and assumed he would have ample time to reconcentrate his army before any large battle.

Amid the shock suffered by Second Bull Run, Lincoln felt compelled to reinstate McClellan as his top commander in the east. No other available officer had a better field record, and despite recent defeats, McClellan remained popular with the troops. The Union Army of Virginia was disbanded and its troops incorporated into the Army of the Potomac, which set out to pursue Lee. On September 13, a soldier at a campsite previously used by Confederate troops picked up some cigars on the ground. They were wrapped in Lee's orders—and detailed the dispositions of the Army of Northern Virginia! McClellan moved his army the next day, pushing through passes over South Mountain.

Lee could have abandoned Maryland immediately to protect his army—which would have ended his campaign. On September 15, he learned Jackson's troops had captured Harper's Ferry. He ordered his scattered forces to Sharpsburg, Maryland, and prepared to confront the Army of the Potomac. Operationally, this location was in the middle of the Army of Northern Virginia's dispersed units, facilitating its concentration. Tactically, Lee's troops would defend behind Antietam Creek—but the Potomac River circled around the rear of the position, which threatened to destroy Lee's forces if they were driven from the battlefield.

On September 17, 1862, the Army of the Potomac began the Battle of Antietam. Ostensibly, it had about 85,000 men to face the Army of Northern Virginia's 55,000. But McClellan did not commit all of his available troops, whereas not all Lee's men had reached Sharpsburg when combat began. The battle consisted of a series of Union attacks on different positions. In the early morning, McClellan sent the corps on his right flank against the Confederate left. After that was driven back, other units advanced toward Lee's center, which also held. The battle's climax occurred in the afternoon. After hours of struggle, the corps on the Union left was finally pushing beyond Antietam Creek when late-arriving Confederate reinforcements hit it in the flank, prompting a Northern retreat. At day's end, Lee's army remained on the battlefield. McClellan did not renew the battle, but neither could the Army of Northern Virginia advance. The following evening, Lee retreated back across the Potomac River.

The Confederate army left the battlefield first, making the Union army the tactical victor—though many did not feel that way. Lee left when he chose to, rather than having his army forced from their positions. Launching attacks sequentially, McClellan had allowed Lee to shift forces from quiet sections of his line to threatened areas. Simultaneous, coordinated attacks would have better exploited the Army of the Potomac's advantage in numbers (admittedly, an ordered diversionary attack that morning never occurred). McClellan also had thousands of troops who never fought in the battle. Yet despite these tactical failings, the Battle of Antietam was a definitive operational and strategic success for the Union: It repulsed Lee's invasion, dashing Confederate hopes of a quick victory that could lead to independence. The cost, though, was exceedingly high. The Battle of Antietam was the bloodiest single day in American history (other battles generated more casualties, but lasted many days). Of 70,000 Northern soldiers who fought, 12,000–13,000 became casualties; Southern forces lost over 10,000 of the 40,000 who saw combat.

Figure 6.6 The "Sunken Road" at Antietam

By Alexander Gardner

Photography was just establishing itself as a medium when the Civil War began. Immediately after the Battle of Antietam, Alexander Gardner took the first pictures of slain soldiers on the battlefield (before they had been removed for burial), which produced powerful responses when viewed by the public. This double image was designed for a stereograph, a nineteenth-century device that gave a viewer a three-dimensional perspective.

Courtesy of the New-York Historical Society

Confederate Western Campaigns of Late 1862

Western Confederate offensives were mostly opportunistic reactions to Union weaknesses. In June 1862, Northern troops had captured Corinth, Mississippi. Union forces then occupied most of Tennessee and much of the Mississippi River Valley. But Halleck, Union western commander until July, faced competing priorities. He needed troops for operations against other important targets such as Vicksburg on the Mississippi and the important rail junction of Chattanooga. But he also needed soldiers to hold captured rebel regions and protect supply lines. After Halleck went to Washington to become General-in-Chief, it became apparent that Union forces lacked the manpower or the leadership to address all these demands.

In the summer of 1862 Confederate cavalry commanded by Nathan Bedford Forrest and John Hunt Morgan raided parts of Tennessee and Kentucky, attacking railroads and federal supply depots. Union cavalry were then too inexperienced to counter or track down the marauders. Local guerrillas also cut rail lines. These operations all but paralyzed the main Union campaign following the capture of Corinth, an advance east to take Chattanooga. The federal commander, Don Carlos Buell, stopped his troops repeatedly to fix damaged bridges and railroads, to the consternation of the Lincoln administration. Moreover, the new overall Confederate commander in the west, Braxton Bragg, exploited Buell's lethargic pace. In August, he sent more than 30,000 troops by rail over a long, circuitous route that nonetheless got them to Chattanooga before Buell.

After advancing into Tennessee, Bragg continued on into Kentucky, hoping it would compel Buell to retreat and free central Tennessee from Union occupation. In addition, Southerners believed many Kentuckians supported the Confederacy and might help or join Bragg's Army of Tennessee. As his force was outnumbered by Buell's 50,000-man Army of the Ohio, he hoped to combine with a smaller army led by Edmund Kirby Smith. Other Confederate forces would attack into western Tennessee from Mississippi to keep Union troops there from joining Buell and possibly recapturing the area.

All these operations failed. Those in western Tennessee culminated in the two-day battle in Corinth on October 3–4. It was similar to Shiloh, in that Southern troops made impressive gains the first day but, exhausted from both combat and high heat, were driven back when defenders led by William Rosecrans counterattacked (and some Union divisions left to join Buell's army). Meanwhile, the Confederate Army of Tennessee moved north, with the Union Army of the Ohio following. Bragg could not remain in Kentucky without driving off Buell, but first he wanted to combine with Kirby Smith's army to even the odds. Advancing on a separate route to the east, Kirby Smith instead marched to Frankfort, Kentucky's capital. Then Buell dashed forces into Louisville.

By that time, Confederate forces in northern Kentucky were scattered, and Union efforts to discover the enemy precipitated the Battle of Perryville. On October 8, portions of Buell and Bragg's armies bumped into each other (sometimes called "a meeting engagement"). Other units responded, culminating in a confused battle in which the right flank of each army attacked and drove back the left flank of the other. Facing superior numbers of Union troops, Bragg pulled back. He retreated all the way to Chattanooga while Kirby Smith's men returned to Knoxville, ending the Confederacy's one major offensive in the west.

Emancipation

By September 1862, Lincoln realized he needed to change the Union's war aims. The failure of the Peninsula campaign meant the war would continue for some time, and also indicated most Southerners supported the rebellion and Confederate independence, contrary to what many Northerners had supposed in 1861. These realizations induced the Lincoln administration to change its policies toward noncombatants, a process examined by historian Mark Grimsley.

At the beginning of the conflict, federal officials directed military officers to respect civilian property in rebellious areas, believing that limiting damage would induce Southerners to return to the Union. Instead, Lee's victories in 1862 bolstered hopes that the Confederacy could win the war. Some officials and officers such as McClellan and Buell continued to believe that harm to civilians must be minimized. But others came to see that doing so helped the Confederacy's war effort, in that civilian property helped support and maintain Southern armies. Accompanying this strategic concern were operational and logistical ones. Union field armies that did not confiscate property were more dependent on supplies from the North—and Confederate raids during the summer of 1862 demonstrated the vulnerability of railroads that carried them.

Lincoln, though, came to focus on a particular form of property, one unique to the South: slaves. Their labor produced most Southern crops, and also freed white males to fight with Confederate armies. Yet slaves were not simply property but people who could accept their servitude or, through escape or violent confrontation, contest it. Before the war, white Southerners feared slave revolts, though the few that occurred had been easily suppressed. More common had been flight, though that was difficult given the distances most runaways had to travel to reach free states.

When the Civil War began, many slaves tried fleeing to nearby federal troops or forts—which posed a dilemma for Union commanders. Some, obeying regulations to preserve civilian property, returned slaves to their owners. Others protected runaways. For example, in the spring of 1861 Benjamin Butler, then commanding Fort Monroe, refused to return the slaves of a Southern colonel, calling them "contraband of war," or property seized because it would otherwise benefit the enemy. Thereafter, runaway slaves were often called "contrabands." John C. Fremont and David Hunter went further. The former, commanding in Missouri in 1861, declared the slaves of owners helping the Confederate cause freed; the latter, in charge of Union forces occupying South Carolina and Georgia islands in early 1862, similarly announced emancipation for all slaves in those states and Florida.

Neither Fremont nor Hunter possessed the authority to free slaves. Lincoln quickly revoked these orders, both for that reason and because early in the war, there would have been staunch political opposition to emancipation. For decades, abolitionists had championed freeing slaves, and politically their views were represented by the radical wing of the Republican Party, or the Radical Republicans (both Freemont and Hunter supported the Radicals). But most Northerners were not abolitionists, and racial prejudice was widespread. In 1861, the idea of fighting the South to free slaves would have offended broad segments of the Northern public whose primary aim was to save the Union—views represented by Democrats and conservative Republicans in Congress.

But by the summer of 1862, Lincoln detected signs that the Union electorate would accept emancipation, if presented as a means to weaken the Confederacy and destroy the Southern rebellion. In July, Congress passed the Second Confiscation Act, which freed the slaves of "traitors." That month John Pope, when assuming command of the Union's short-lived Army of Virginia, ordered his troops to confiscate the property of Southern civilians. When Lincoln consulted his cabinet about emancipation, they concurred but advised him to wait for a Union victory before taking such a step, for otherwise it might seem an act of desperation.

Lincoln bided his time, and was rewarded with the Union victory at Antietam. Five days later, on September 22, 1862, he announced the Preliminary Emancipation Proclamation. This stated that as of January 1, 1863, slaves "within any state or designated part of a state, the people whereof shall then be in rebellion against the United States, shall be then, thenceforward and forever, free; and the executive government of the United States, including the military and naval authority thereof, will recognize and maintain the freedom of such persons." Lincoln issued the Final Emancipation Proclamation on January 1, 1863, which stipulated the specific areas in which slaves were now free. In this regard, Antietam was one of the Union's most important strategic victories of the war, for it enabled Lincoln to pursue emancipation.

Figure 6.7 "Bombardment of Port Hudson by Admiral Farragut's Fleet, Assault of the Second Louisiana (Colored) Regiment on the Rebel Works at Port Hudson, May 27 [1863]"

Frank Leslie's Illustrated Newspaper 27 June 1863, pp. 216–217

About 180,000 African Americans fought for the Union during the war. Roughly 90,000 were former Southern slaves, 40,000 came from Union border states (where slavery remained legal until the war's end), and 50,000 were free, Northern blacks. Though fighting for the Union, black troops nonetheless faced widespread racism. Most units, for example, were led by white officers, as blacks were not regarded as capable of command. African-American soldiers were also often assigned labor and construction duties loathed by white troops. Although often held back from combat, "colored" troops did fight: for example, black Louisiana infantry regiments (which did have black officers) were prominent in actions at Port Hudson—depicted in the 1863 illustration above—and Milliken's Bend, whereas the famous 54th Massachusetts participated in assaults on Fort Wagner, South Carolina.

Library of Congress, Prints and Photographs Division, LC-USZ62–133081

Ostensibly, the preliminary Proclamation provided rebellious states an opportunity to rejoin the Union before it was enforced, which helped make it more politically palatable to Northerners still hesitant about emancipation. It actually only freed slaves in areas not under Union control at the time, though it set the precedent that ultimately ended slavery throughout the United States. In this regard, the Proclamation's effectiveness relied upon future Union campaigns into yet unconquered Confederate territory. But it also depended upon the actions of slaves themselves. In essence, advancing federal troops would provide a catalyst to encourage slaves to flee, depriving their Southern masters of the labor needed to support the Confederacy and its armies.

It worked. Thousands and thousands of slaves ran away to Union lines, helping to cripple the Southern economy. Moreover, many men who fled bondage then fought for the Union—as did many free blacks already in the North when the war began. About 180,000 African Americans served in the Union armed forces over the course of the war. Some served in the U.S. Navy, others enlisted with state regiments early in the war such as the famous 54th Massachusetts. But most served in special units created and maintained by the federal government following the Emancipation Proclamation: the regiments of the United States Colored Troops.

Diplomacy

The Emancipation Proclamation also had international ramifications and helped settle the biggest diplomatic question of the Civil War—would any foreign powers intervene? The Confederacy hoped for either overt military assistance or for international pressure to force the Union to end the war and recognize Southern independence. Great Britain was most important in this regard—it had the greatest trade with the Americas, and no other country would intercede if it did not. But first the Confederacy had to convince the international community it was a viable nation. Hence diplomatic recognition, specifically by Britain, became Southern officials' most important foreign policy goal.

The Lincoln administration claimed the Southern states were in rebellion and did not constitute a separate country. But the imposition of the blockade in April 1861 complicated the issue, particularly when the British government responded by declaring itself neutral. That decision—soon adopted by other countries—implied the Confederacy was a belligerent power, which under international law could make purchases in neutral countries and dispatch cruisers onto the high seas.

Other developments further complicated the Union's relations with Britain. In late 1861, a Union warship stopped a British merchant vessel, the *Trent*, and seized Confederate envoys on board. While supported by the Union public, the incident raised numerous legal issues and insulted Britain. The Lincoln administration defused the crisis by apologizing and releasing the Confederate officials. Another problem stemmed from commerce raiders. British law forbade the construction of warships for belligerents, but Confederate agents exploited ambiguities in the statutes to build and launch two raiders from British shipyards before Union protests prompted Crown officials to seize other such vessels.

The Confederacy also made some missteps with Britain. Early in the war, Southern exporters imposed a trade embargo, believing if they stopped cotton sales to Britain and France, these countries would suffer so much they would have to intervene on the Confederacy's behalf. Known as "cotton diplomacy" or "King Cotton diplomacy," it was not official policy of the Davis administration—but neither did the Confederate government condemn it, and it was widely adopted in the South. The cotton embargo did cause unemployment among British textile workers in 1862–63. But the impact was limited by accumulated cotton stocks at the beginning of the war followed by a switch to alternative sources of supply, such as Egypt. Ironically, by the time Southerners abandoned the embargo, the Union blockade was becoming effective (see the next chapter).

Both the Confederacy and the Union had supporters in Britain. In general, the upper classes tended to favor the former with its aristocratic Southern planter society, whereas the working and middle classes tended to favor the more industrial North. There were exceptions: Some British nobles respected the democratic values in the Union's political system, and some textile workers saw their jobs as tied to Southern cotton. Whereas the cotton embargo alienated much of British society from the Confederate cause, Lincoln greatly enhanced the Union's standing with Britons with the Emancipation Proclamation. Britain had ended its participation in the slave trade in 1807 and abolished slavery throughout its empire in 1834. Royal Navy efforts to combat the slave trade were popular among facets of the British public. Once Britons realized that the Union was committed to emancipation, their support for it increased, while that for the Confederacy ebbed.

After initially declaring neutrality, Queen Victoria's government took no further steps toward recognizing the Confederacy. British Prime Minister Lord Palmerston and his cabinet were not prepared to risk a serious confrontation with the Union. They would instead act only if military developments demonstrated the Confederacy had a good chance of successfully seceding. The closest the British ever came to interceding in the American Civil War was in the late summer of 1862. Following Lee's victories at the Seven Days and Second Bull Run, the British cabinet contemplated extending on offer of mediation to the belligerents—but abandoned the idea after the Battle of Antietam.

Union Operations to 1863

After the collapse of Confederate campaigns in September and October 1862, Lincoln urged his generals to seize the initiative and advance before Southern forces could recover. Instead, McClellan delayed crossing the Potomac for over a month. Exasperated, Lincoln relieved him of command in November and appointed Ambrose Burnside to command the Army of the Potomac. The President had less patience for Don Carlos Buell, who after the Battle of Perryville hesitantly pursued Bragg's army. At the end of October, Lincoln replaced him with William Rosecrans, the victor of Corinth, whose forces were thereafter known as the Army of the Cumberland.

Burnside had gained renown for successful operations on the North Carolina coast early in the war. He had previously turned down command of the Army of the Potomac, claiming he was not qualified, and tried to do so again—but Lincoln was so frustrated with McClellan that he appointed Burnside anyway. The new commander made a promising start, quickly marching the Army of the Potomac to the Rappahannock River, across from Fredericksburg, Virginia. When it arrived, few Confederate forces were in the area. Burnside intended to cross the river and advance to Richmond, but the War Department had not delivered the pontoon bridges the army needed. While he waited, Lee moved the Army of Northern Virginia onto the heights behind Fredericksburg. The Army of the Potomac still outnumbered its adversary (over 110,000 troops compared to about 75,000), but Burnside had lost the element of surprise, and Lee's men now occupied formidable defenses. Instead of leaving and trying to outmaneuver Lee, the Union commander chose to attack.

The resulting Battle of Fredericksburg has become infamous for the futility of the federal assaults. Prior to the battle, Union troops crossed the river, pushing Confederate units out of Fredericksburg itself and establishing lodgments on the Rappahannock's southern bank further downstream. Burnside had divided his army into three "Grand Divisions," and the one on the left advanced after fog lifted on the morning of December 13, 1862. A unit commanded by George G. Meade reached a wooded ridge before being driven back by Confederate counterattacks. Its advance was the best progress made by the Army of the Potomac that day.

In the afternoon, on the Union right, officers launched a sequence of assaults on Marye's Heights, the ridge behind Fredericksburg held by Longstreet's corps. Confederates at the base of the hill defended a sunken road protected by a stone wall, while Union troops advanced across an open area between Fredericksburg and the Heights, moving gradually uphill and at one point having to cross a stream or ditch. None of the dozen attacks reached the enemy. Each one consisted of a single division (two to three regiments) or brigade (two to three divisions), and in later ones, assaulting federal units were impeded by having to bypass clumps of soldiers sheltering from Confederate fire in slight depressions.

By day's end, Burnside's army had suffered 12,000–13,000 casualties for no appreciable gain, compared to about 5,000 for Lee's forces. Having decided to attack the Army of Northern Virginia in strong defensive positions, he compounded his error with successive assaults on Marye's Heights, regardless of the fact that the first advances were clearly too small and unsupported to succeed. After taking a day to collect the wounded, the Army of the Potomac retreated back across the Rappahannock.

In the west, Grant began a series of efforts to capture Vicksburg at the end of 1862. Though ultimately successful, initial efforts failed, producing more Northern frustration; these operations will be addressed in the next chapter. Meanwhile, the other major Union commander in the Western theater achieved some success. After replacing Buell, Rosecrans reprovisioned his supply base at Nashville before moving his Army of the Cumberland toward Braxton Bragg's Army of Tennessee in late December. By then Bragg had advanced his men to Murfreesboro in hopes of ultimately capturing Nashville.

Learning of the federal approach, Bragg placed his men in positions around a small river outside the town. From December 31, 1862, until January 2, 1863, the two armies clashed at the Battle of Stones River (or the Battle of Murfreesboro). On the first day, an attack from the Confederate left bent but did not break the Union right. Rosecrans held his ground on the second day, which saw only minor skirmishing, and his troops foiled a Confederate attack on the Union left on the third day. By that time, about a third of the Army of Tennessee had become casualties (compared to the about 30% of Union forces), and Bragg retreated. A relieved Lincoln telegraphed his thanks to Rosecrans. But relief soon turned to exasperation, for Rosecrans did not move his army again for another six months.

Conclusion

Between 1861 and 1863, both the Union and the Confederacy mobilized resources and manpower to prosecute a large conventional war. But the unprecedented size of their armies and limited numbers of men with prior military experience made using them difficult. Operational offensives or tactical attacks were especially problematic, with the few successful ones including Jackson's Valley campaign, Grant's operations in early 1862, and some of Lee's victories with the Army of Northern Virginia. But even Lee faltered when he first tried to invade the North, being checked at the Battle of Antietam. Believing a long war might exhaust the Confederacy's ability to fight before the Union's, he sought a victory that would so demoralize Northerners that they would seek a quick peace and would do so again in 1863. But in most Civil War campaigns, the Union pursued the strategic offensive. Though its forces obtained successes in the Western theater in 1862, the Army of the Potomac's numerous defeats produced mounting frustration. These failures prompted federal leaders to adopt a different, tougher approach to the war, one that Lincoln began with the Emancipation Proclamation but which continued to evolve until 1865.

A Short Bibliography of Civil War readings appears at the end of Chapter 7.

TIMELINE	1861–65	January 1, 1863	May 1–6, 1863	May 18–July 4, 1863	July 1–3, 1863	Sept. 19–20, 1863	November 24–25, 1863	May 5–7, 1864
	The American Civil War	Emancipation Proclamation issued	Battle of Chancellorsville	Siege of Vicksburg	Battle of Gettysburg	Battle of Chickamauga	Battle of Chattanooga	Battle of the Wilderness

Chapter 7

The American Civil War: Union Triumph, 1863–1865

As 1863 began, Union and Confederate armies continued to face each other across America. Hundreds of thousands had already died from sickness and combat, as would hundreds of thousands more before the Civil War ended. A combination of tactics, technology, and the size of the armies produced particularly lethal combat; wounded veterans numbered hundreds of thousands more. In both the Union and the Confederacy, such horrific carnage fueled frustration and efforts to pursue military operations that would bring final victory.

Noncombatants also suffered in the war's first years, but the extent paled compared to the misery at its end. Much of this stemmed from Union strategy, though Confederate weaknesses also contributed. Even before 1863, the Lincoln administration targeted Southern economic and logistical capacity with a naval blockade and by emancipating slaves. But these measures had their greatest impact in the war's final two years. Moreover, starting in 1864, Ulysses S. Grant directed federal armies in a strategy that neutralized the operational effectiveness of Confederate forces and wreaked greater destruction in Southern territories. By April 1865, all these factors had so eroded Southern morale as to induce Southern capitulation.

In this chapter, students will learn about:

- Naval operations.
- How men and women experienced the Civil War.
- How Union strategy evolved from 1863 to 1865.
- The major campaigns and battles from 1863 to 1865.

The Naval War

The Union naval blockade helped paralyze the Confederate economy, though it took some time to organize it. At the start of the Civil War, the U.S. Navy had only a few dozen vessels. By war's end, thanks to Navy Secretary Gideon Wells and his assistant Gustavus Fox, it had

May 8–20, 1864	June 15, 1864–April 2, 1865	Sept. 2, 1864	Nov. 15–Dec. 21, 1864	December 15–16, 1864	Feb. 1–April 13, 1865	April 9, 1865
Battle of Spotsylvania Courthouse	Siege of Petersburg	Atlanta captured	March to the Sea	Battle of Nashville	March through the Carolinas	Robert Lee surrenders at Appomattox Court House

about 670, maintaining about 150–200 on blockade duty at any given time. Naval personnel increased from fewer than 10,000 officers and sailors to about 60,000. Even at its height, the blockade did not stop all Confederate shipping. But it dramatically curtailed Southern overseas trade to perhaps less than a third of prewar levels. For example, at war's end, about 50% of ships that tried to evade the blockade succeeded. But that number was very low relative to shipping before 1861. Moreover, blockade running put a premium on speed, hence successful ships were smaller vessels with limited cargo space. In addition, though the chances of evading the blockade on any one voyage were decent, most blockade runners ultimately ran afoul of Union patrols.

Patrolling about 3,500 miles of Southern coastline was a daunting task. The hundreds of ships required included traditional wooden-hulled sailing warships, naval vessels with modern steam engines, and converted civilian ferries and merchantmen. Moreover, they needed to be maintained and supplied. Throughout the war, the Union Navy pursued operations to capture ports and harbors to use as bases for the blockade—and deny them to Confederate shipping. These campaigns often included both army troops and naval forces, or were "joint operations" in modern parlance.

Such operations began in 1861, with assaults around Cape Hatteras and the seizure of Port Royal, South Carolina. In 1862, the Union Navy captured a number of coastal enclaves on the southern Atlantic and Gulf Coasts, as well as New Orleans. By 1863, just a few Southern ports remained in Confederate hands: Mobile, Wilmington, Charleston, and Galveston. The Union Navy captured Mobile Bay in August 1864, and cut off Wilmington by taking Fort Fisher in January 1865. Federal forces captured Charleston the following month but never took Galveston.

The blockade was the Union Navy's biggest effort during the Civil War. It supported the broader strategic goal of undermining the Southern economy and hampering Confederate ability to maintain its war effort. But the Union Navy also participated in river operations to assist the advance of federal armies, including the capture of Forts Henry and Donelson and campaigns on the Mississippi, as addressed previously.

Whereas the Union Navy was small and dispersed at the war's beginning, the Confederacy had no naval vessels and—except for Norfolk and Pensacola (both captured in 1862)—no shipyards. Relying more heavily on purchasing and leasing than his Union counterpart, Confederate Navy Secretary Stephen Mallory acquired about 130 vessels over the course of the war, mostly small and of limited seaworthiness. To compensate, Confederate officials turned to technology, using what was then called a "torpedo" but would today be recognized as an underwater mine. These devices helped keep Union blockaders at bay and approaches to ports such as Mobile and Charleston open. The Confederate Navy also built a submarine, the CSS *Hunley*. After the loss of some prototypes (and their crews), it succeeded in sinking a Union ship near Charleston in 1864 and then sank itself.

The most famous new naval weapon in the Civil War was the ironclad. This was a steam-powered vessel with either a wooden hull overlaid with iron plates, or a vessel whose hull was

Figure 7.1 "Battle of Mobile Bay, 1886"

Although the USS *Monitor* versus the CSS *Virginia* remains the most famous confrontation between Civil War ironclads, such vessels participated in other battles as well. The above painting depicts the 1864 Battle of Mobile Bay. Note the Union ironclads steaming in a line closest to the Confederate fort and ships, protecting the wooden vessels behind (the sinking ironclad is the USS *Tecumseh*, which hit a mine).

Library of Congress, Prints and Photographs Division, LC-DIG-pga-04035

constructed completely of metal to provide protection from enemy cannons. Confederate officials built their first ironclad, the CSS *Virginia*, in the hope that it would pose a lethal threat to the Union Navy. On March 8, 1862, the *Virginia* steamed out of Norfolk toward wooden warships patrolling off Hampton Roads in Chesapeake Bay. By day's end, it had sunk two vessels and ran a third aground while only suffering minor damage from cannon fire. But federal officials had been constructing their own ironclad, the USS *Monitor*, which met the *Virginia* the next day.

On March 9, the two odd-looking vessels slowly maneuvered and fired at each other for hours, both withdrawing at day's end. Thereafter, the *Virginia* posed no danger to the blockading fleet. The two ironclads never fought again, and just before the Army of the Potomac captured Norfolk during the Peninsula campaign, the *Virginia* was scuttled to prevent its capture. Both sides built more ironclads over the course of the war, but the Union launched dozens more than the Confederacy, nullifying the technological advantage Southerners had sought.

Confederate officials also pursued a naval strategy to reduce Northern overseas trade, dispatching commerce raiders to attack Union merchant shipping. The most successful ones, such as the CSS *Alabama* and the CSS *Florida*, each destroyed dozens of vessels over the course of the war. Such raiding—and the resulting surge in insurance costs—effectively drove much

Union maritime commerce from the seas. But while Northern shippers suffered, the damage to the overall Union economy was limited, as British and other foreign vessels that Confederate raiders would not attack carried cargoes instead.

The Soldiers' Experience: Camp Life

Tens of thousands of men served at sea, whereas millions served in Civil War armies. Combat only comprised a portion of their military experience. Most of the time, soldiers were marching or in camp. Marches occurred at all times of the year, in all types of weather. Most roads were dirt, and in dry weather clouds of dust created by men, horses, and wagons at the head of columns would choke troops marching further back. Conversely, wet weather turned these roads into mud, making movement slow and difficult. Occasionally, armies could travel along routes covered with wooden planks, or "corduroyed" roads. At other times, trains might be available to move troops to particular destinations. Miles and miles of marching destroyed soldiers' boots, requiring some to wrap their feet in rags or go barefoot. The latter problem was more common for Confederate troops, for the Union's extensive industry, along with its robust rail network and shipping capacity, kept federal soldiers well supplied with clothing, equipment, arms, and ammunition.

Northern soldiers generally received enough food, though they had challenges eating it. Their bread ration was a biscuit made of water and flour called "hardtack" because, though it would last a long time, it was incredibly difficult to break up and chew. It also had a tendency to host weevils or other insects if it got wet and moldy. Union troops also received a ration of pork or beef so heavily salted as to be nearly inedible, and "desiccated" or dehydrated vegetables. Confederate soldiers usually received corn meal, frying it in bacon grease and meat (if available) to produce "Johnny cakes." Soldiers on both sides prepared their own meals and foraged for fresh vegetables, fruits, and meat from the countryside. All Civil War soldiers loved coffee, brewing their own from bean rations. When coffee beans became increasingly scarce in the Confederacy late in the war, Southern troops substituted chicory and other plants or seeds for them. Shortages, federal raids, and a poor rail network reduced food supplies for Confederate armies as the war continued. Although Southern troops usually did not starve outright, their rations were often reduced and at times hunger drove them to consume items such as roots, grasses, and meat from animals other than livestock.

Camp life was a mixture of routines and efforts to fight boredom. The former included morning reveille and roll call, scheduled meals, picket and sentry duty, drill and training periods, constructing roads and fortifications, and collecting firewood and fresh water. (Slaves performed manual labor for Confederate armies, and escaped slaves often did the same for Union forces.) In their free time, soldiers engaged in a variety of activities. Some were more licentious, such as gambling, drinking, and sex. Other men sought spiritual solace, attending formal religious services with army chaplains or forming informal worship and study groups among themselves. Soldiers read whatever books, magazines, or journals they could acquire, and were avid letter writers. Other activities included amateur theatrical productions, competitions, and sports; the modern version of baseball became quite popular among Union camps, for example. Campfires provided a social focus in the evenings, and for much of the war troops slept in small tents, or blankets and rolls in the open air (the latter more common for Confederate soldiers).

One danger was disease. As with all warfare before the twentieth century, illness claimed the majority of men who died in the American Civil War, with perhaps just a third succumbing to combat wounds. Knowledge such as germ theory was not available to doctors and medics of the period, nor were modern vaccines or antibiotics. Northern organizations such as the U.S. Sanitary Commission dispatched volunteers to try to improve hygiene in federal army camps. But exhaustion and exposure to the elements, a daily diet lacking in vitamins, camps located near swamps and marshes, and poorly placed latrines all helped spread disease. Recent recruits also faced exposure to new illnesses upon joining a field army. The war's more lethal ailments included smallpox, diarrhea/dysentery, typhoid, pneumonia, and malaria, not to mention nonfatal illnesses such as tonsillitis.

Combat and Its Consequences

Combat was the soldier's chief concern. Officers were responsible for preparing their men and leading them in combat. Training occurred within individual regiments and focused on weapons instruction and company drill and maneuver. But it might be minimal if recruits joined an army shortly before a major battle. Early in the war, volunteer units on both sides tended to elect many of their officers. Over time, ability played a greater role in officer commissioning and promotion.

Combat varied in the Civil War from short skirmishes to large battles that could last for days. A major Civil War battle was unlike anything people of the time had experienced. Artillery fire, musket volleys, the whir of speeding projectiles, officers' shouts, and the screams of wounded and dying men all created a cacophony on the battlefield. Moreover, attacking troops often yelled to both raise their own morale and undermine that of the enemy (Confederates were known for the "rebel yell"). Smoke created by cannons and small arms fire shrouded the battlefield, and loss of daylight was a problem if fighting lasted past sunset. Smells also contributed to the unique experience of heavy combat, including the odors of spent gunpowder, tilled earth, horse manure, as well as urine and feces from wounded or nervous soldiers.

Amid these overwhelming sensory stimuli, soldiers struggled to obey commands and maintain good order while not succumbing to the fear of death or maiming. In this regard, company officers did not just issue orders but were supposed to provide examples of how to act bravely in combat, leading advances and directing their troops' fire. Soldiers had to advance, charge, retreat, shoot, reload, and repeat firing in response to commands while simultaneously enduring enemy fire themselves. Fright, uncertainty, and confusion placed a great burden on them.

At times, the stress was too much. When soldiers sensed that unstoppable danger was imminent, they "broke," fleeing to save their lives. Officers then had to chase their men and induce them to reform and listen to commands. Conversely, desperate circumstances could provoke individual soldiers to perform acts of tremendous bravery and sacrifice. Battlefield success might inspire troops to feats of great boldness. To an extent, experience mitigated the possible reactions to combat. Seasoned soldiers were not as likely to flee as green troops but were also not as prone to acts of rashness.

After combat ended, battlefields were strewn with wounded and dead bodies—both men and horses—and destroyed and discarded equipment and arms. Fighting also razed or damaged structures and buildings. But some carnage continued in the hospitals just beyond the combat zone. Rifled muskets fired large bullets, bigger than a half-inch in diameter. When it struck a soldier, any bone it hit would likely shatter, and bullet and bone fragments could then cause more internal damage. Not all battle-inflicted wounds were dreadful: Projectiles sometimes only struck the skin and muscle, and if bandaged and kept clean, full recovery was expected. But wounds to the torso were generally mortal because of damage to internal organs or the likelihood of infection. Soldiers were much more likely to survive wounds to limbs. But if bullets struck bones, they were usually destroyed, and surgeons needed to amputate limbs before infection set in and spread to the rest of the body.

As a result, hospitals often looked like "charnel houses," with doctors working feverishly near piles of amputated limbs amid the cries of wounded soldiers. But surgeons were not cruel: they used chloroform and other medicines to anesthetize patients, who then received morphine, laudanum, and other painkillers afterward. Unfortunately, supplies sometimes ran out, in which cases alcohol or "biting the bullet" might be the only means to assist wounded soldiers through surgery. The speed with which doctors worked did not reflect callousness but the effort to treat as many soldiers as possible before infection set in. An estimated 14–18 percent of wounded soldiers died of subsequent infections. However crude, such medical care was only available to soldiers transported off the battlefield. Many were not, particularly in large battles early in the war, a problem later mitigated by the creation of ambulance services.

One large battle produced thousands of corpses. Scholars such as Drew Gilpin Faust observed that more men died in the Civil War than in all other wars fought by the United States from the American Revolution to the Korean War *combined*, perhaps two percent of the entire U.S. population in 1861. Long-standing estimates of 620,000 troops killed on both sides are being challenged by new research by J. David Hacker that indicates the figure might be closer to 750,000.

Faust has examined how soldiers and civilians struggled to cope with the Civil War's unprecedented scale of death. To intern large numbers of corpses, soldiers often created mass graves and sometimes did not adequately finish the task. Local residents also helped intern bodies, such as after Gettysburg. Because record-keeping was often a low priority for armies on the move, civilian organizations such as the U.S. Sanitary Commission sent agents to help identify the slain, inform their families, and either bury their remains or ship them home. After the war, government officials and private organizations gave more attention to the dead. Internments and identifications continued, and numerous cemeteries were created just for Union and Confederate soldiers. In the years that followed, public commemorations remembered the fallen and their sacrifices but also provided former enemies a means to join together and dispel bitter feelings left over from the war.

Given the arduous nature of camp life, horrors of combat, and the risk of wounds, disease, and death, many soldiers deserted. More than 100,000 Confederates left their units during the war, with the pace of desertion increasing toward the end. For example, from mid-February to mid-March, 1865, about eight percent of the Army of Northern Virginia vanished in this manner. In the war's final months, Confederate troops faced worsening supply shortages—and so did their families at home. Simultaneously, Union armies were then advancing unchallenged through areas previously untouched by war, and many Southern soldiers went home to protect homes and provide for loved ones. Federal forces suffered perhaps 200,000 desertions over the course of the war. They accounted for approximately the same proportion of total troops compared to Confederate armies, but the Union had a larger pool of potential manpower to replace them. Ostensibly punishable by death, few deserters were executed. Appeals were made for them to return, and if they did so they were usually welcomed back.

Most men stayed with their units. Some remained motivated by patriotism and a sense of duty that had spurred many to volunteer. Others drew upon faith to sustain them. But many soldiers remained to support each other. For these men, leaving was tantamount to abandoning friends in crisis, and their sense of pride and self-respect came from fighting with their comrades. Such feelings compelled many federal soldiers to reenlist. Southern troops had no such option, for the Confederate Congress ultimately compelled them to serve for the war's duration. In the North, enlistments lasted three years. Starting in 1864, Union officials offered enticements to persuade men to remain in the service, including bounties and furloughs. They also promised soldiers would continue to fight with their comrades if 75 percent of their unit reenlisted and that they would receive special badges for their uniforms to mark their veteran status. More than 135,000 federal soldiers chose to return. But about 100,000 did not, a quiet testament to the war's hardships and brutality.

Chancellorsville, 1863

Lincoln's strategic ideas evolved over the war. After the failure of the Peninsula campaign, he struck at Southern capacity to maintain Confederate field armies with the Emancipation Proclamation. By 1863, Lincoln realized the Army of the Potomac's priority should not be to capture Richmond but to destroy the Army of Northern Virginia. Lee's victories had greatly boosted Southern morale. Defeating his army would not only undermine Confederate support for the war but facilitate taking other objectives. Early that year, Lincoln appointed "Fighting Joe" Hooker to command the Army of the Potomac. Hooker was another general who had achieved success at lower levels of command, and he developed an operational plan that reflected Lincoln's strategic views. He also reinstated corps as the largest unit within the Army of the Potomac, creating distinct patches for each one to foster troops' pride in their units.

Hooker had about 130,000 men to Lee's 60,000, and developed a plan to exploit this numerical advantage. In late April, he left John Sedgwick with 40,000 troops across the Rappahannock River from Fredericksburg to hold the Confederates' attention. He then sent other corps northwest before crossing over the Rappahannock and Rapidan Rivers. By May 1, they had arrived in the rear of the Army of Northern Virginia. Hooker concentrated about 70,000 soldiers at a crossroads called "Chancellorsville," in the midst of a large wooded area roughly 10 miles west of Fredericksburg. But then he hesitated. Hooker moved troops a few miles east on May 1 before pulling back to Chancellorsville to await a Confederate attack. Lee obliged, but not in the manner Hooker expected. According to conventional military thought, the

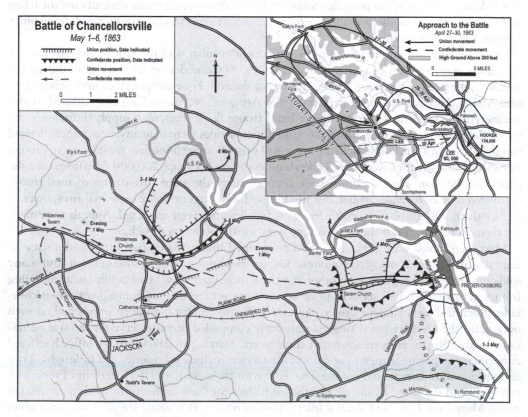

Map 7.1 Battle of Chancellorsville, May 1–6, 1863

Army of Northern Virginia—outnumbered more than two to one—should have withdrawn and remained concentrated. Instead, Lee seized the initiative and attacked (which Hooker anticipated), splitting his army into three parts (which Hooker did not). His boldness bordered on recklessness, but once again Lee successfully bet on the timidity of the opposing commander.

Leaving about 10,000 men near Fredericksburg to check any movement by Sedgwick's forces, he moved the rest of his army west. Consulting with "Stonewall" Jackson, Lee decided to hit the Union right flank. J. E. B. Stuart's cavalry had skirmished with federal troops as they approached Chancellorsville and knew that the Union Eleventh Corps was strung out on the Orange Turnpike that led west from the crossroads. But the end of the army was not situated on any terrain feature, such as a hill or river that would help protect it. The Union right flank was "in the air," whereas the Union left flank rested on the Rappahannock River, and the center at Chancellorsville was on higher ground whose approaches were protected by dense undergrowth. Lee gave Jackson about 26,000 soldiers, the bulk of his army. On May 2, Jackson led them along a circuitous route to a position just west of the Eleventh Corps. The movement took many hours, and if detected, Hooker could have assaulted the Army of Northern Virginia while it was split into different parts, destroying each one separately.

Some Union soldiers observed the Confederate march, reported it, and fired at the enemy. But Hooker did not understand the significance of the information, apparently believing Lee's army was retreating. In the late afternoon Jackson's men arrived a few miles west of Chancellorsville. Forming for battle, they attacked east along the Orange Turnpike. The Union Eleventh Corps was completely surprised and routed. Luckily for Hooker, the flank attack began late in the day. By the time Jackson's exhausted soldiers approached Chancellorsville, night was falling, and Union officers scraped together a defense that stopped the Confederate assault. In the darkness, Jackson moved ahead of his lines to reconnoiter and was mistakenly shot by his own men. He was removed from the field and died later that month.

The battle did not end, though. Stuart took over Jackson's corps, and on May 3 the Confederates squeezed federal forces at Chancellorsville from the east, south, and west. By late morning Hooker had extracted his men from this pocket, and they retreated toward the Rappahannock. The next day, May 4, Sedgwick crossed the river at Fredericksburg and pushed back defending Confederate troops under Jubal Early. Hooker had actually ordered Sedgwick to attack on May 3, but Union communications broke down and he received the order late. To address this new threat to his rear, Lee left 25,000 troops with Stuart and took the remainder to join Early. About 20,000 Confederates then attacked an equivalent number of Sedgwick's men near Salem Church, about three miles west of Fredericksburg. Union troops repelled the assault, but when Sedgwick learned of Hooker's retreat, he also moved his forces back to the river. By May 6, the entire Army of the Potomac had returned to the northern bank of the Rappahannock.

The Battle of Chancellorsville and Second Bull Run rank as Lee's greatest victories. From May 1–6, 1863, he wrenched the initiative from an enemy army twice the size of his own, one whose tactical position threatened to destroy the Army of Northern Virginia. Instead, he exploited Hooker's sudden timidity to surprise and drive back federal forces. These suffered 17,000 casualties, compared to 12,000–13,000 Southerners. Yet the Army of the Potomac was not destroyed and would resume operations after it had recovered from the battle. Meanwhile, Lee's triumph spread gloom among Northerners already disappointed over Grant's failure to capture Vicksburg and the stalemate between federal and Confederate forces in Tennessee. Sensing this despair, Lee again decided to invade the Union, gambling that a victory would so devastate the Lincoln administration that it would sue for peace.

Gettysburg, 1863

Jefferson Davis and other Confederate officials were hesitant. In May, federal forces commanded by Grant advanced to besiege Vicksburg, and some argued it should be reinforced. But Lee, his reputation soaring after Chancellorsville, argued the city could hold out long enough for the Army of Northern Virginia to a win a battle on Union soil. As with his short-lived 1862 invasion, Lee argued such a campaign would also transfer the fighting north, relieving Virginia of the devastation generated by military operations and enabling Southern soldiers to live at the enemy's expense.

Davis endorsed the plan. As Lee prepared, he had to confront the loss of Jackson, perhaps his most trusted subordinate. The Army of Northern Virginia had been structured into only two corps, led by Jackson and Longstreet, making them much larger than the more numerous corps in the Army of the Potomac. After Jackson fell, Lee did not think any other officer could handle such a large unit and reorganized his army into three corps, now led by Longstreet and two former division commanders, Richard Ewell and A. P. Hill.

In early June, Lee began moving his army west from Fredericksburg. Once it reached the Shenandoah Valley, his troops advanced north, crossing the Potomac River into the Cumberland Valley. Hooker hesitated, and unlike the previous September when Union forces quickly checked its advance, the Army of Northern Virginia moved through Maryland unimpeded. As the Army of the Potomac began following, Confederate forces continued on into southern Pennsylvania, with Lee once again dispersing his troops to collect supplies. Hooker appeared to be developing the same anxieties that had plagued McClellan, and Lincoln lost patience. On June 28, George G. Meade became commander of the Army of the Potomac—just days before the Battle of Gettysburg began.

By that time, Lee was concentrating his dispersed units. But he did not know exactly where the Army of the Potomac was, as J. E. B. Stuart's cavalry force was out of contact with the Army of Northern Virginia. In early June, Union cavalry had surprised Stuart's troopers at the Battle of Brandy Station. Although the Confederate horsemen prevailed, Stuart's reputation was sullied. Two weeks later, when Lee gave Stuart discretionary orders for the advance north, Stuart took the liberty to ride completely around the Army of the Potomac, apparently recreating the "Ride around McClellan" that had gained him fame the previous year. But it kept him out of touch with the Army of Northern Virginia during the crucial last days of June, as the two armies approached each other.

Lee instructed his unit commanders to avoid triggering a large battle until the army had regrouped—which happened anyway. Numerous roads intersected at Gettysburg. Confederate troops had passed through the town earlier in June, and reported large stocks of shoes. On the last day of the month, men sent to collect them were repulsed by some recently arrived Union cavalry. The troopers' commander, John Buford, understood the importance not only of the road junction, but of the high ground just south of the town, called "Cemetery Hill." It dominated the surrounding countryside. Buford placed his men northwest of town and prepared to block the road until help arrived.

On July 1 the Confederate division commanded by Henry Heth became embroiled in fierce combat with these Union horsemen, who fought dismounted, as infantry. More divisions from A. P. Hill's corps came up and deployed, and Buford's men held off the attack long enough for infantry from the Union First Corps to enter the fray. By midday, more Confederates from Ewell's corps were arriving from the north, along another road, and federals from O. O. Howard's Eleventh Corps came up and advanced beyond Gettysburg to engage them.

In the afternoon, Ewell's soldiers pushed through Eleventh Corps—which had been victimized at Chancellorsville—and the right of the Union line. Federal troops fled back into and beyond Gettysburg. But Howard had held some men back to dig entrenchments on Cemetery Hill. When the Union line broke, soldiers retreated to these positions. Lee, again issuing discretionary orders, instructed Ewell to attack Cemetery Hill "if practicable." With little daylight left, and considering the Union defenses, Ewell feared an immediate assault would fail, and he rested his exhausted corps for the night.

The Union line at Gettysburg is sometimes described as a "fishhook," which was taking shape by July 2. Just to the southeast of Cemetery Hill is another, Culp's Hill, which anchored the right flank. After swinging northwest around Cemetery Hill, federal positions continued along Cemetery Ridge, a low rise to the south. Ultimately, the Union line extended to two more hills, Little and Big Round Top, but they were not yet occupied on the morning of July 2. By then, Lee had most of the Army of Northern Virginia in the vicinity, while Meade was still bringing up much of the Army of the Potomac. Recognizing the strong defenses on Cemetery Hill, Lee decided to hit the flanks. Longstreet would lead the main assault against the Union left to the south, while Ewell's men would launch a diversionary assault on Culp's Hill.

Both efforts misfired. Longstreet had problems getting his two divisions in position, at one point backtracking to avoid detection. Their attack began about 4:00 p.m., hours late. In the interim, a Union officer reported the hills south of Cemetery Ridge unoccupied, and commanders rushed troops to Little Round Top in the afternoon. When Longstreet's divisions advanced, they pushed Union forces out of rough terrain known as the Devil's Den but were repulsed when they tried to take Little Round Top. Confederate soldiers also took a peach orchard west of the main Union line but became embroiled in an intense battle for a nearby wheat field that lasted well into the night. The Union left held. On the right, Ewell launched his attack on Culp's Hill after Longstreet's had begun and made little headway beyond taking some unoccupied positions.

By July 3, most of the Army of the Potomac had arrived, totaling 85,000 men. Much of the Army of Northern Virginia's 75,000 men were exhausted. But Lee had some fresh men in A. P. Hill's corps and Longstreet's third division. With these troops he made one last gamble. Assuming that Meade had strengthened his flanks to meet the previous days' assaults, he instructed Longstreet to attack the Union center on Cemetery Ridge. Attacking troops would have to cross about three-quarters of a mile of open ground, so Lee ordered his batteries to bombard Union artillery positions prior to the infantry advance, which began in the early afternoon. Federal cannons soon stopped counterbattery fire, and when informed that Confederate gun ammunition was running low, Longstreet began the assault.

Box 7.1   Account of the Battle of Gettysburg

The following account of the Battle of Gettysburg comes from William Wheeler, a Union artillery officer whose battery moved to Cemetery Ridge in the midst of the climactic Confederate assault on July 3.

> [A]t about 1 P.M. Lee's one hundred pieces (I believe that he had more in position [closer to 150]), opened all at once, and, as far as noise went, it was the most terrible cannonade that I ever witnessed, and the air was literally alive with flying projectiles, from the six-pound solid shot, which looks like a cricket ball, to the long Whitworth

rifled shot, which has probably given rise to the story of the rebs firing railroad iron. My pieces stood in a peculiarly bad place, as they were at the foot of *[Cemetery]* hill, and got the fire from all three sides; but the enemy's artillery practice was not as good as it used to be, and the situation was not as deadly and dangerous as on Friday afternoon *[August 29]* at *[Second]* Bull Run, or on Sunday morning *[May 3]* at Chancellorsville. In this place I lost some horses but no men. The fire was still at its height, when a request came from General Hunt, Chief of Artillery, to Major Osborne to send him a battery for General Webb of the Second Corps *[on Cemetery Ridge]*, who feared an infantry attack . . . . As I came up and unlimbered on this crest, the rebels were within four hundred yards and were making a charge across our front upon a battery which stood at my right. Luckily for us, they did not see us until we had got into position, and had poured a couple of rounds of canister over the heads of our own infantry, who were lying behind a stone fence in front of us. Then they turned their attention somewhat to us and a battery of theirs opened very fiercely upon us, and made things very hot; but we paid no attention to their battery, and just kept the canister going into them. Once a double round of canister struck close to their flag, and I saw a dozen of them drop, and the whole column wavered and halted; but the standard-bearer waved his flag and they moved on again, but in a weary and spiritless manner. Just at this moment what should the infantry in front of us do but get up and leave! The Battery seemed lost, but I got hold of some of them, told them not to let the Eleventh Corps' boys laugh at them, and in this way, first a squad, and then the whole regiment, was rallied and got back to the fence again, and about every reb who came up on to that hill was either killed, wounded, or captured. We then went back to our Corps and soon the fighting for the night was over.

(Letters of William Wheeler of the class of 1855, Y.C. [Yale College], Cambridge: H. O. Houghton, 1875, pp. 413–14)

What followed is known as "Pickett's Charge." George Pickett led Longstreet's third division, one of three Confederate divisions attacking that day. Pickett's men were on the right of the assault column, which totaled 14,000–15,000 men. They began their march in a slight depression, and as they marched forward farm buildings screened some of their movement from federal guns on the Round Tops. As a result, they did not endure as much enemy fire as other assaulting units. Many of Pickett's men managed to reach the Union line, but their numbers were too few. Federal troops repulsed them, and Pickett's division broke. In contrast, Union artillery and infantry had broken up the other advancing Confederate units long before they reached Cemetery Ridge.

The three-day Battle of Gettysburg was the bloodiest of the Civil War, producing 23,000–24,000 Union casualties to 27,000–28,000 Confederate. Among the latter were about half of all the men who attacked Cemetery Ridge on July 3. Gettysburg did not end the Civil War, but it finished Lee's campaign, dashing hopes for a Southern victory on Northern soil that would end the war on Confederate terms. The Army of the Potomac had thus won a strategic victory, as well as an operational and a tactical one. After Gettysburg, the Army of Northern Virginia retreated back across the Potomac and never again invaded the Union. For these reasons, many people regard the battle as the Confederacy's best chance to win the war, and have intensely analyzed it to explain the Southern defeat.

One factor was Lee's decision to continue the battle. He was not looking for a fight at Gettysburg on July 1, but after it started, he chose to attack on each of the following two

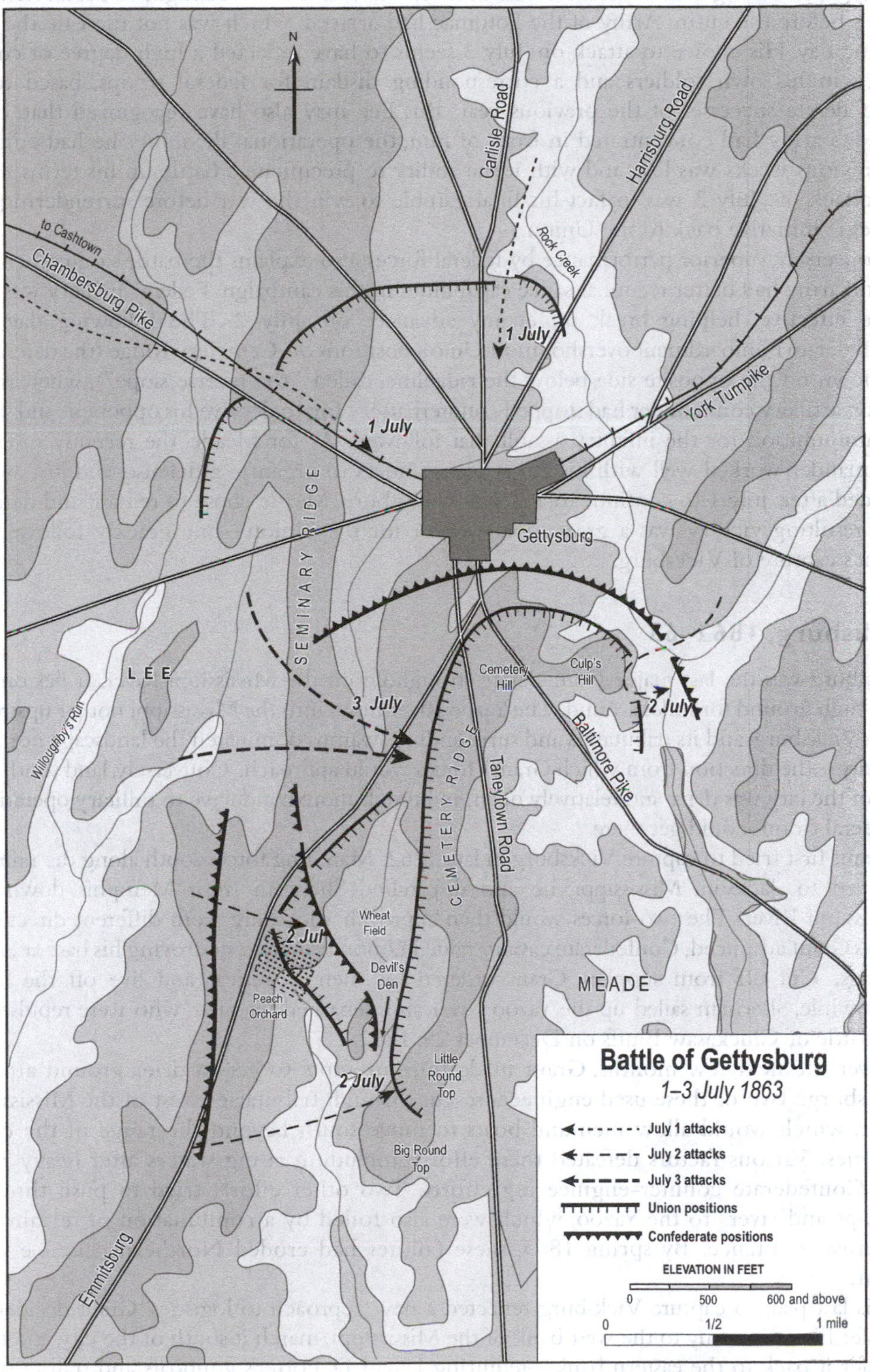

N

Carlisle Road

Harrisburg Road

Rock Creek

to Cashtown

Chambersburg Pike

1 July

1 July

York Turnpike

S E M I N A R Y   R I D G E

Willoughby's Run

Gettysburg

3 July

L E E

Cemetery Hill

Culp's Hill

2 July

Baltimore Pike

C E M E T E R Y   R I D G E

Taneytown Road

M E A D E

2 July

Wheat Field

Devil's Den

Peach Orchard

Little Round Top

2 July

Big Round Top

Emmitsburg

Battle of Gettysburg
1–3 July 1863

◄------ July 1 attacks
◄— — July 2 attacks
◄ — — July 3 attacks
⊤⊤⊤⊤⊤ Union positions
▼▼▼▼▼ Confederate positions

ELEVATION IN FEET

0   500   600 and above

0   1/2   1 mile

Map 7.2 Battle of Gettysburg, July 1–3, 1863

days, despite strong Union defenses. His decision on July 2 at least sought to defeat Meade's forces before the entire Army of the Potomac had arrived, which was not the case the following day. His choice to attack on July 3 seems to have reflected a high degree of confidence in his own soldiers and a corresponding disdain for federal troops, based upon Confederate successes of the previous year. But Lee may also have recognized that, once Meade's army had concentrated in front of him, the operational flexibility he had enjoyed in previous weeks was lost, and with it the ability to precipitate a battle on his terms. If so, the attack on July 3 was in fact his final gamble to win the war before surrendering the strategic initiative back to the Union.

Conversely, superior performance by federal forces also explains the battle's outcome. The Union army had better reconnaissance capabilities in this campaign. Federal artillery was also more effective, helping break up enemy advances on July 2. The following day, the Confederate bombardment overshot most Union positions on Cemetery Ridge (the defenders lay down on the opposite side below the ridgeline, called "the reverse slope"), whereas the Union artillery commander had stopped counterbattery fire to deceive his opponent and saved his ammunition for the infantry assault that followed. As for Meade, the recently installed commander worked well with his corps commanders to organize a defense, and just as Lee decided after July 1 to continue to attack at Gettysburg, Meade chose to remain and defend. The resulting victory was a great morale boost for the Union—one quickly followed by Grant's capture of Vicksburg.

Vicksburg, 1862–63

Vicksburg was the last major Confederate stronghold on the Mississippi River. It lies on the only high ground for miles around. The Yazoo River flows into the Mississippi not far upstream from Vicksburg, and its tributaries and surrounding swamps dominated the landscape north of the city—the direction from which Grant's forces would approach. Conversely, land south and east of the city was drier and relatively open, and much more conducive to military operations, if federal troops could get there.

Grant first tried to capture Vicksburg in late 1862. Marching forces south along the railroad that led to Jackson, Mississippi, he also dispatched Sherman from Memphis down the Mississippi River. The two forces would then approach Vicksburg from different directions. But as Grant advanced, Confederate cavalry raided Union rear areas, destroying his base at Holly Springs. Cut off from supplies, Grant ordered his men to retreat and live off the land. Meanwhile, Sherman sailed up the Yazoo River and debarked his men, who were repulsed at the Battle of Chickasaw Bluffs on December 29, 1862.

Over the next few months, Grant made four attempts to get to drier ground around Vicksburg. Two of these used engineers to cut through tributaries west of the Mississippi River, which would allow men and boats to move south beyond the range of the city's batteries. Various factors defeated these efforts, including rising waters after heavy rains and Confederate counter-engineering efforts. Two other efforts tried to push through swamps and rivers to the Yazoo, which were also foiled by a combination of terrain and defensive resistance. By spring 1863, these failures had eroded Northern patience with Grant.

His last plan to capture Vicksburg reflected a new approach to logistics. Grant decided to transfer his main army to the west bank of the Mississippi, march it south of the city, and then transfer it back to the eastern bank—requiring David D. Porter's gunboats and transports to sail past Vicksburg and endure artillery fire to rendezvous with the infantry downstream. Once placed on the eastern bank, Union troops would be out of supply after they moved inland: They would have to live off the land, which Grant noticed they could do months earlier after cavalry raids destroyed his supply base. In addition to these operations, Grant sent federal cavalry raiding though the state of Mississippi to distract and confuse the Confederates, similar to what Tennessee and Kentucky had experienced at the hands of Southern marauders such as Nathan Bedford Forrest.

On April 16, Union horsemen began their ride. That night, Porter sent some of his boats past Vicksburg, the remainder a few days later; only three were lost. On the last day of the month, these vessels ferried Grant's Army of the Tennessee to the eastern bank of the Mississippi at Bruinsburg. To further distract Confederate commanders, Grant had Sherman land troops just north of Vicksburg to launch a diversionary attack simultaneously with the river crossing. From May 1 until May 18, Grant's more than 40,000 men advanced rapidly, moving about 180 miles and winning five battles along the way. Knocking aside Confederate resistance at Port Gibson on May 1 and at Raymond on May 12, the Army of the Tennessee took Mississippi's state capital, Jackson, on May 14. Turning west, it fought the biggest of the five battles on May 16 at Champion Hill, and then secured a crossing over the Big Black River the following day. On May 18, Grant's army surrounded and besieged Vicksburg.

These movements befuddled Confederate commanders, who could not agree on a common plan to oppose Grant. John C. Pemberton commanded forces at Vicksburg, and his nominal superior was Joseph E. Johnston (now Western theater commander after recovering from wounds suffered at the Battle of Seven Pines). But Jefferson Davis had sent Pemberton direct orders to hold the city. When Grant's army moved inland, Johnston urged Pemberton to leave Vicksburg and join him. Johnston only had a few thousand men under his direct command, who were repulsed at the Battle of Jackson. After hesitating, Pemberton finally moved about 20,000 soldiers to Champion's Hill only to retreat back to the city after Grant's troops defeated them. When the Union Army of the Tennessee besieged Vicksburg, it trapped the majority of available Confederate troops there.

Grant immediately ordered his army to assault Vicksburg's defenses, thinking he could quickly capture the city. Southern troops repelled assaults on May 19 and 22; thereafter, Grant settled for starving out the defenders. His army was now back in contact with the Mississippi River and well supplied, whereas provisions within Vicksburg started running out. Before the city's surrender, soldiers and civilians cooked meat from mules, rats, and pets for food. They also endured shelling from Union artillery, with some fleeing to caves for shelter. As the situation deteriorated, people in Vicksburg hoped Johnston would attack their besiegers. But Johnston was scrambling to find more soldiers and did not think he had enough to challenge Grant's grip on the city. He urged Pemberton to break out and join him, but Vicksburg's commander did not believe his men could do it. On July 4, 1863, Pemberton surrendered Vicksburg and about 30,000 Confederate troops to Grant.

Military historians hail Grant's final campaign against Vicksburg as a model of operational movement. Using speed to confuse and divide enemy forces, he isolated the city and forced its capitulation. At the time, Vicksburg's capture enthralled Northerners and shocked Southerners who had just learned of Lee's defeat at Gettysburg. Only one Southern outpost remained on the Mississippi River, which soon surrendered. The Union thus achieved one of its top strategic goals: splitting the Confederacy in two and denying it access to western resources. Moreover, the South could ill afford the loss of tens of thousands of soldiers. Grant's victory propelled him to national acclaim. By 1864, he would be overseeing the Union's entire conduct of the war. But first he had to save another western campaign.

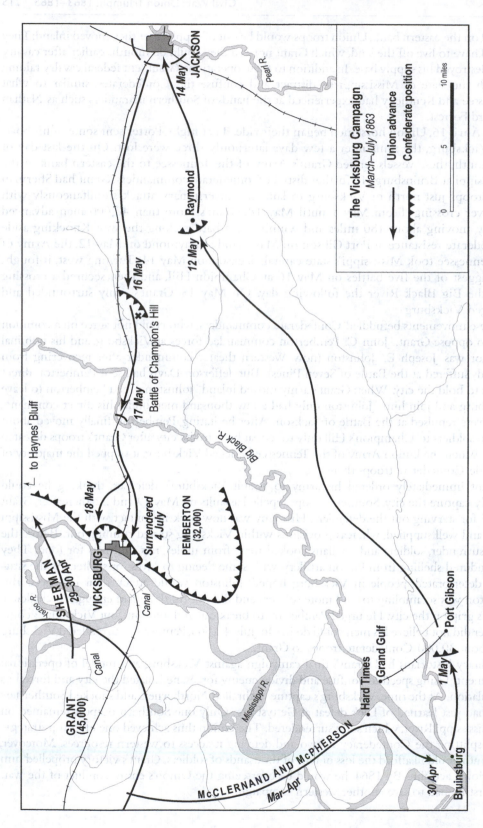

The Vicksburg Campaign
March–July 1863

Union advance
Confederate position

0 5 10 miles

JACKSON

Pearl R.

14 May

16 May

Raymond

12 May

17 May
Battle of Champion's Hill

Big Black R.

to Haynes' Bluff

18 May

SHERMAN
29–30 Apr

VICKSBURG

Surrendered
4 July

PEMBERTON
(32,000)

Yazoo R.

Canal

Canal

GRANT
(45,000)

McCLERNAND AND McPHERSON

Mar–Apr

30 Apr

Bruinsburg

Mississippi R.

Hard Times

Grand Gulf

Port Gibson

1 May

Map 7.3 The Vicksburg Campaign, March–July, 1863

Chickamauga and Chattanooga, 1863

As the Vicksburg campaign reached its climax, William Rosecrans began another offensive in Tennessee. On June 24, his Army of the Cumberland moved out from Murfreesboro. Employing superior numbers, Rosecrans feinted in different directions to conceal the movement of his main body, which advanced around the right flank of Bragg's Army of Tennessee. With the Confederate rear threatened, Bragg retreated back to Tullahoma. But when he realized that Rosecrans was again moving to outflank him, Bragg's army fell all the way back to Chattanooga.

By the beginning of July, Rosecrans had induced his opponent to abandon central Tennessee, suffering fewer than 600 casualties in the process. After delaying a few weeks to organize the Army of the Cumberland's logistics, he then captured Chattanooga with a similar lack of bloodshed. In mid-August, feinting toward the Tennessee River upstream of the city, most of his troops actually crossed downstream. Federal forces then began advancing southeast through the mountains to cut off Chattanooga. In early September, Bragg's army abandoned the city and moved south into Georgia. Simultaneously, a smaller Union army captured Knoxville.

Chattanooga was the major railroad junction that linked the Confederacy's eastern regions with those farther west. The Army of the Cumberland had captured it and pushed Bragg's forces out of Tennessee without a major battle or large casualties. In this regard, Rosecrans' operations from late June to early September have been widely admired. But they have been overshadowed by the large dramatic Union victories at Gettysburg and Vicksburg, and the fact that shortly after capturing Chattanooga, Rosecrans fell into grave trouble.

After retreating into Georgia, Bragg stopped and looked to surprise Rosecrans. The Union commander had dispersed his army to move them quicker through the mountains, assuming that he was chasing a fleeing foe. Bragg tried attacking isolated elements of the Army of the Cumberland between September 10 and 13. But his relations with his officers had greatly deteriorated over the prior year, and they found reasons to delay or avoid action. Rosecrans then concentrated his army west of Chickamauga Creek. Bragg planned another assault to place his Confederate Army of Tennessee between the Union Army of the Cumberland and Chattanooga, and then drive federal forces into a valley where they would have to surrender or be destroyed.

Joining Bragg for the Battle of Chickamauga were reinforcements from the Army of Northern Virginia. After Gettysburg, Lee's army had retreated back into Virginia, and the Army of the Potomac cautiously followed. Then the two armies sat across from each other on the Rappahannock River, with Meade initiating no major operations. Davis ordered Lee to send troops west, over the general's objections. Only part of two divisions commanded by James Longstreet arrived in time to participate in the battle, but they played a crucial role.

On September 19, Bragg's other forces, having advanced to the western side of Chickamauga Creek, attacked. George Thomas' XIV Corps on the left (northern) flank of the Army of the Cumberland received the brunt of these assaults. By the end of the day, brutal fighting among the heavily wooded and hilly terrain had failed to dislodge Union forces. That evening, Longstreet's men arrived. Bragg reorganized his army into two halves, assigning the northern part to Leonidas Polk, the southern to Longstreet.

Polk assaulted the Union left on the morning of September 20. Soon after, Longstreet attacked as well, and his men penetrated enemy positions through a gap created when Union officers moved troops to cope with attacks on the left. As a result, the Union right flank collapsed, with troops fleeing toward Chattanooga. Had the rest of the Army of the Cumberland done likewise, Bragg's forces might have destroyed it. But George Thomas saved the situation, earning the sobriquet "The Rock of Chickamauga." His corps fell back to a new defensive position on high ground, and held off Confederate attacks until the rest of Rosecrans' army was out of danger. That night his men cautiously retreated to Chattanooga.

Casualties at the Battle of Chickamauga were among the worst in the Civil War. Bragg lost about a quarter of the 66,000 troops then in the Army of the Tennessee, compared to about 16,000 of Rosecrans' roughly 55,000 men. Given the carnage, Bragg chose not to chase the Army of the Cumberland—which upset his officers, who believed they missed a rare opportunity to destroy an entire Union field army. The Army of the Cumberland, however, was in a precarious situation. Confederate forces soon occupied the mountain ridges around Chattanooga, particularly Lookout Mountain and Missionary Ridge, and thereby prevented all access to the city except for one small trail. By October, Union forces were besieged in the city and Rosecrans seemed paralyzed, or as Lincoln put it, "stunned like a duck hit upon the head." With supplies running out, the Army of the Cumberland faced the prospect of starving or abandoning Chattanooga.

Taking a cue from Jefferson Davis, Lincoln and Secretary of War Stanton transferred more than 20,000 men from the Army of the Potomac west. They also promoted Grant to command all Union forces west of the Appalachians (except for the federal army in Louisiana). Rosecrans was relieved and replaced with Thomas. Grant arrived in Chattanooga in late October, and consulting with the Army of the Cumberland's officers, ordered operations to improve logistics. Federal forces cleared the area south of the Tennessee River and west of Chattanooga, opening up a railroad (dubbed the "cracker line") and pushing enemy troops away from ground that dominated the river. Meanwhile, recriminations between Bragg and his subordinates became so acrimonious that Jefferson Davis left Richmond to personally address the crisis. Davis kept Bragg (like Lee, a friend of his) in charge of the Army of Tennessee, transferring or giving commands to many of his chief officers.

In November, Bragg let Longstreet leave with 15,000 men in a failed attempt to capture Knoxville. About that time, Sherman arrived at Chattanooga with a force that had marched from Mississippi. With a numerical advantage of about 60,000 to 40,000, Grant attacked. The Confederate left flank occupied Lookout Mountain, which overlooked Chattanooga from the southwest. Bragg's troops also held Missionary Ridge to the east, which ran north to the Tennessee River. On November 24, troops led by Joe Hooker— who helped open the "cracker line"—captured Lookout Mountain in an action sometimes called "the Battle of the Clouds" because much of the combat occurred in fog. Simultaneously, Sherman's men crossed the Tennessee River to assault the northern end of Missionary Ridge. But they found themselves in front of a separate hill to the north, which was stubbornly defended.

On November 25, the second day of the Battle of Chattanooga, Grant ordered Thomas to advance his troops against the Confederate center along Missionary Ridge. This was supposed to be a limited, diversionary attack to help Sherman's force, for defenses on the ridge looked formidable, and Union troops had to cross open ground to reach them. Instead, Thomas' men captured the forward defenses quickly, and then—without any apparent orders—swarmed up the hill. Yelling "Chickamauga! Chickamauga!" federal soldiers routed the Confederates and took Missionary Ridge. Bragg's army fled south, leaving Grant and his troops the victors and in secure possession of Chattanooga.

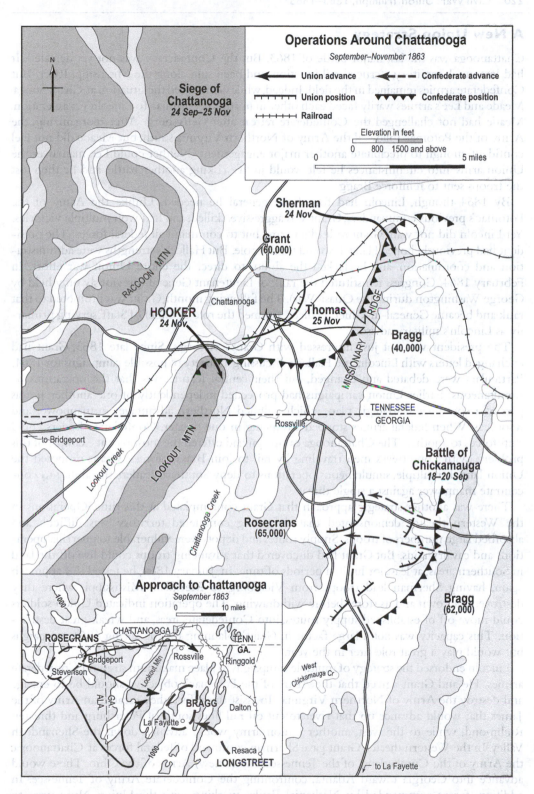

Map 7.4 Operations Around Chattanooga, September–November, 1863

A New Union Strategy

Chattanooga was the last major battle of 1863. But the Confederacy was not yet defeated. It had lost much territory, a crucial rail junction, and been split along the Mississippi River. But Confederate armies remained in the field. Indeed, while Grant saved the situation at Chattanooga, Meade and Lee's armies warily faced each other in northern Virginia. To Lincoln's exasperation, Meade had not challenged the Confederate retreat after Gettysburg. After reorganizing, the Army of the Potomac followed the Army of Northern Virginia south, but Meade did not feel confident enough to precipitate another major engagement. Neither could Lee maneuver the Union army into circumstances he felt would justify risking another battle, and he then lost the troops sent to reinforce Bragg.

By 1864 though, Lincoln had found the general he needed. Unlike the Army of the Potomac's previous commanders, Grant was aggressive, skilled, and had won multiple victories. Yet Lincoln did not want Grant to lead an army but to command all federal forces. The president had previously hoped Halleck would fill that role. But Halleck's strengths were administration and coordination, and he lacked the ability to direct the entire Union war effort. In February 1864, Congress reinstituted the rank of Lieutenant General (previously only held by George Washington during the Quasi-War). The following month, Grant was promoted to that rank and became General-in-Chief. Halleck assumed the role of Chief of Staff, serving primarily as Lincoln's military advisor.

The president was not just impressed with Grant's victories. Since late 1863, Grant had exchanged letters with Lincoln and Halleck discussing a variety of possible campaigns for 1864. Particulars were debated and changed, but their central feature was that the operations be simultaneous. Earlier Union campaigns had proceeded independently of one another, not as part of a coordinated strategic plan, which nullified Northern advantages in manpower and resources: When federal armies stopped advancing in one theater, Confederate leaders could shift forces to another. The Chattanooga campaign had offered the most recent example of this problem, with Longstreet's men traveling by rail to join Bragg's forces. Grant proposed the Union launch multiple, simultaneous operations to deny Southern leaders the ability to concentrate manpower against a single threat.

There was another strategic approach that Grant contemplated at this time. Operations in the Western theater demonstrated that defending conquered territory was difficult and absorbed large numbers of troops. Supply routes and depots were vulnerable to guerrilla operations and cavalry raids. But Grant had discovered that advancing troops could live off the land in Southern areas, at least for limited periods of time. In January 1864, he tested this approach again, having Sherman lead troops from Vicksburg to Meridian, Mississippi, where they destroyed the town and its stores before withdrawing. The operation indicated Union soldiers could move off of established supply routes, into Confederate areas, and wreak great destruction. This capacity was not a large factor in Grant's planning for the spring 1864 campaigns but would play a great role later in the year.

Lincoln endorsed the strategy of multiple campaigns to place maximum stress on Confederate armies. He and Grant agreed that the Army of the Potomac's objective should be to engage and destroy the Army of Northern Virginia. To assist this effort, they created an Army of the James that would advance up that river to cut off rail lines south of Petersburg and threaten Richmond, while to the west, another Union army would advance down the Shenandoah Valley. In the Western theater, Grant gave Sherman command of federal forces at Chattanooga: the Army of the Cumberland, of the Tennessee, and (a new) Army of the Ohio. These would advance into Georgia toward Atlanta, confronting the Confederate Army of Tennessee. In addition, forces commanded by Nathaniel Banks, working with the Union Navy, were to

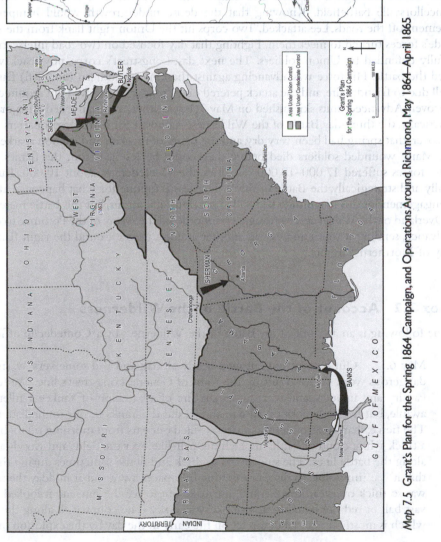

Map 7.5 Grant's Plan for the Spring 1864 Campaign, and Operations Around Richmond, May 1864–April 1865

assault Mobile, Alabama—but only after completing a campaign up the Red River into north-western Louisiana and eastern Texas that Lincoln wanted to support local Unionists.

The Overland Campaign, 1864

Excepting the Mobile expedition, the Union campaigns began in early May 1864. In the east, the most vital effort lay with the Army of the Potomac. Grant attached his headquarters to Meade's, accompanying his army and using telegraph messages to communicate with Washington and other federal forces. His presence produced a different type of Civil War campaign. Previously, after a major battle, the loser withdrew and both armies avoided another big fight while they recuperated and reorganized. Grant changed this dynamic.

On May 4, the Army of the Potomac, about 120,000 men, left its camp. Grant wanted to get around the Army of Northern Virginia (roughly 65,000 men) before initiating a major battle, and he directed Meade's army to cross the Rapidan River and move eastward. On May 5, federal forces moved through a wooded area called "the Wilderness," a few miles west of the Chancellorsville battlefield. Knowing that the dense undergrowth would hamper tactical movement off the roads, Lee attacked. Two corps hit the Union right flank from the west, and Meade's forces turned to meet them. Fighting that day focused on two road intersections suc-cessfully defended by Union soldiers. The next day, Longstreet's corps, now back with Lee, joined the battle. His force was advancing against the Union southern (now left) flank when he fell due to friendly fire, and the attack petered out. Longstreet survived but required months to recover. Advanced units skirmished on May 7, but neither army launched a major assault.

Tactically, the three-day Battle of the Wilderness is known for hard, close-quarters fighting. Moreover, that spring had been very dry, and the firing of muskets and cannon sparked brush-fires. Many wounded soldiers died before they could be rescued from the flames. Overall, Union forces suffered 17,000–18,000 casualties, the Confederates about 10,000. But opera-tionally and strategically, the Battle of the Wilderness is unique for what happened afterward. An engagement of this magnitude had ended previous operations, but this battle merely began the Overland or the Wilderness campaign. Grant ordered the Army of the Potomac to continue its advance, sending it south and east in another attempt to get around the right flank of the Army of Northern Virginia.

Box 7.2   Account of the Battle of the Wilderness

The following is an account of the Battle of the Wilderness by a Confederate officer:

> May 6. . . . Our battery was engaged nearly all day, and had some very warm and dangerous work on hand just on the right of General Longstreet's line. We fought cavalry and infantry, and were under the fire of a battalion of Yankee artillery for awhile, but held our position all day, and so did the Yanks in our immediate front. The fierce, sharp roar of deadly musketry filled our ears from morning till night, and a thick white cloud of battle smoke hung pall-like over the fields and woods all day along the battle lines. The smoke was so thick and dense sometimes during the day that it was impossible to discern anything fifty paces away, and at midday the smoke was so thick overhead that I could just make out to see the sun, and it looked like a vast ball of red fire hanging in a smoke-veiled sky. The country all along the lines, which is mostly timber land, was set on fire early in the day by the explosion of shell

and heavy musketry; a thousand fires blazed and crackled on the bloody arena, which added new horrors and terrors to the ghastly scene spread out over the battle plain. A thousand new volumes of smoke rolled up toward the sky that was already draped with clouds of battle smoke. The hissing flames, the sharp, rattling, crashing roar of musketry, the deep bellowing of the artillery mingled with the yelling of charging, struggling, fighting war machines, the wailing moans of the wounded and the fainter groans of the dying, all loudly acclaimed the savagery of our boasted civilization and the enlightened barbarism of the nineteenth century.

(Michael Neese George, *Three Years in the Confederate Horse Artillery*, New York: Neale Publishing, 1911, pp. 261–62)

In this sense, the Battle of the Wilderness was a Confederate defeat, for it failed to stop the Union campaign. But Grant had yet to get his forces around Lee's. He was trying to place the Army of the Potomac between the Army of Northern Virginia and Richmond, which would have forced Lee to attack at a disadvantage. Grant tried again, moving out his forces on the night of May 7–8. But Confederates detected the move, and cavalry harassed and delayed the federal advance long enough for Lee to place infantry around Spotsylvania Courthouse ahead of Union troops, where they dug trenches and built extensive fieldworks.

The Battle of Spotsylvania Courthouse began late on May 8, but the first concentrated effort to break through Confederate lines came on May 10. Troops commanded by Emery Upton attacked a salient, or bulge, that extended out and away from adjacent trenches, known as the "Mule Shoe." The initial assault succeeded, but reinforcements were repulsed before reaching the position, and Upton's exhausted men were driven off by a Confederate counterattack. Grant ordered another attempt on May 12.

Amid a heavy rain, the federal assault drove through the Mule Shoe and beyond, threatening to split the Confederate army and capturing a division before counterattacks drove Union forces back. Combat raged for hours and into the night along a section of entrenchments called "the Bloody Angle," and was among the most intense of the war. In the early morning of May 13, Southern troops retreated to a new trench line constructed at the base of the Mule Shoe. Efforts to push through Confederate positions in the following days failed, and Grant again decided to move around Lee's army. By the time the Battle of Spotsylvania Courthouse ended on May 20, Union forces had suffered 17,000–18,000 casualties (about 6,000–7,000 on May 12 alone), whereas Confederate losses are estimated at about 10,000–12,000.

The Army of the Potomac marched south, and Lee moved the Army of Northern Virginia to block it at Hanover Junction. As the Confederates had a strong defensive position, with the North Anna River protecting their center, the Battle of the North Anna (May 23–26) did not involve any major assaults. Combat stemmed from federal probing actions to test Confederate defenses, though Grant took the opportunity to destroy railroads leading to Richmond. Again the Army of the Potomac disengaged, and again Lee's army raced to man defenses north and east of Richmond. Fighting resumed on June 1 as both armies finished occupying and fortifying their positions, and would continue until June 12. But the main action occurred on June 3, when Union troops assaulted Confederate defenses at Cold Harbor, near the old Gaines Mill battlefield. Grant thought he detected a weakness, and after four weeks of the most intense and bloody operations seen in the war, believed a breakthrough could cripple Lee's army or capture Richmond, possibly ending the war. But the attack failed dismally, producing 7,000 Union casualties for no tactical gain.

Grant made one more attempt to outflank Lee. His forces began withdrawing from the Cold Harbor area on the night of June 12–13, using feints and a cavalry screen to conceal its movement. Crossing the James River to the south, their destination was Petersburg and its rail hub. If captured, Richmond and Lee's army would be cut off from the rest of the Confederacy. Advanced federal units took some thinly held defenses on June 15. But P. G. T. Beauregard, the local Confederate commander, rushed troops to the area who constructed additional field works and repelled Union attempts to reach the city. On June 18, Grant initiated siege operations at Petersburg, thereby ending the Overland campaign.

The amount of combat over the prior six weeks distinguished this operation from others in the Civil War. The casualties were staggering: From the beginning of the Overland campaign until the Cold Harbor assault, the Army of the Potomac lost roughly 55,000 men, up to about 65,000 by the time it reached Petersburg. The Army of the Northern Virginia suffered about 35,000 casualties over the entire campaign. Such losses bewildered people on both sides, but were especially demoralizing in the Union. After the dramatic successes of 1863, Northerners had high hopes that federal armies would quickly crush the Confederacy. Instead, the Overland campaign ended with Lee's army undefeated in Petersburg. The resulting disappointment helped create the view that Grant was a "butcher" who would win by using the Union's advantage in manpower to offset high casualties.

That perspective is unfair. Grant had constantly attempted to get his force around Lee's to place the Confederate general in a position of having to attack the Army of the Potomac and sustain higher casualties. Grant had maneuvered effectively in the Western theater, but Lee was the Confederacy's best general, and he successfully blocked these moves. At times, particularly at the Mule Shoe and Cold Harbor, Grant had ordered large assaults on Confederate positions. But in these cases, he believed such attacks could succeed and potentially yield great gains (as Lee had thought at Gettysburg). At other times, such at the North Anna River, he saw that defensive works were too formidable to attack. By the time federal forces reached Petersburg, he recognized his operations had failed to lure Lee into a disadvantageous position, and so chose another approach: to pin down the Army of Northern Virginia. The concept behind his 1864 strategy had been to use superior Union manpower and resources to place maximum stress upon Southern forces. By besieging Lee's army, Grant prevented it from pursuing operations elsewhere.

Additional 1864 Operations in the Eastern Theater

The Union's other eastern operations were just as disappointing. On May 5, the 30,000 men of Butler's Army of the James landed between Richmond and Petersburg. With few Confederate troops nearby, its chances of cutting the railroad between the two cities and isolating Lee were excellent, had it moved quickly. But Butler dawdled, allowing P. G. T. Beauregard to arrive and concentrate Southern troops in the area. When the Army of the James finally advanced in mid-May, the Confederates attacked, and Butler retreated to a line of entrenchments between the James and Appomattox Rivers. Beauregard's men also constructed fortifications, effectively stuffing Butler's troops on the peninsula like a "cork in a bottle," as Grant described it. There the Army of the James remained, doing little until the Army of the Potomac crossed the James River in mid-June and Beauregard retreated toward Petersburg. The Shenandoah campaign did no better. Franz Sigel's 6,500 men advanced down the valley in early May. On May 15, a scratch force of 5,000 Confederates—including some Virginia Military Institute cadets—attacked them at New Market, and drove the federals back up the valley.

Grant made some command changes. He replaced Sigel with David Hunter, and after the Battle of the Wilderness gave most of the Army of the Potomac's cavalry to Philip Sheridan, who had previously made his name in the Western theater. Sheridan took his troopers on a two-week raid around Richmond, generating panic in the city and clashing many times with Confederate horsemen (in one, J. E. B. Stewart fell mortally wounded). In early June, when the Army of the Potomac was at Cold Harbor, Grant sent Sheridan's force westward to link up with Hunter's 15,000 at Lynchburg, hoping to distract Lee. Hunter and Sheridan were also to wreck railroads and confiscate or destroy provisions that could supply Confederate armies.

Lee reacted by dispatching his own cavalry. It caught up to the federal troopers at the Battle of Trevilian Station, which compelled Sheridan to abandon his junction with Hunter. Lee also sent Jubal Early and a corps to the Shenandoah, which arrived at Lynchburg before Union forces. Hunter discovered Confederates there on June 17–18, and fell back. But he retreated west, leaving the route up the valley exposed. Early pounced on the mistake. In late June and early July, as the Armies of the Potomac and Northern Virginia entrenched around Petersburg, his troops moved up the Shenandoah and into Maryland. On July 11, his forces skirmished with federal defenders in the suburbs of Washington (which Lincoln observed). But Grant had dispatched reinforcements, and with their arrival, Jubal withdrew to the valley.

Frustrated, Grant consolidated administrative departments and Union forces, and appointed Sheridan to lead a newly minted Army of the Shenandoah, with instructions to pursue Early "to the death." After organizing his men, Sheridan advanced and defeated Confederates at Winchester on September 19. The Army of the Shenandoah pursued and bested them again at Fisher's Hill on September 22. After Early's men retreated to the southern end of the valley, Sheridan's soldiers focused on their other mission: turning the Shenandoah into "a barren waste." The Shenadoah was an important agricultural area, and stripping the region of supplies would prevent Confederate armies from moving up the valley until the following year. Hunter's

Figure 7.2 Confederate Fortifications Around Petersburg, Virginia, April 1865

Library of Congress, Prints and Photographs Division, LC-DIG-cwpb-02790 troops had begun such confiscations, but under Sheridan, federal forces were more efficient, removing or killing thousands of livestock and destroying 2,000 crop-filled barns by October 7. Early made one last attempt to drive off the federal army, with Confederate troops surprising and routing Union forces near Cedar Creek on October 19. But when Sheridan arrived on the scene, he rallied his troops and led them in a counterattack that scattered Early's army, leaving the Shenandoah firmly under Union control.

Meanwhile, the siege of Petersburg continued, and would last until April 1865. Both sides constructed elaborate fortifications, including deep trenches, redoubts, breastworks, and forts, as well as roads and bridges. Photographs of the battlefield bear a striking resemblance to entrenchments used in World War I. Such works were first constructed east of Petersburg and then expanded north toward Richmond, as well as south and west. Numerous combat actions occurred during the siege, stemming from efforts to extend fortified positions and test those of the enemy. One notable event occurred on July 30, when federal engineers exploded a huge mine dug underneath Confederate positions. The shock of the blast was wasted, however, when Union troops advanced into the resulting hole, not around it, and defenders who rushed to the area easily trapped the attackers at the Battle of the Crater.

In the short term, Lee successfully countered Grant's attempts to outflank his positions by similarly lengthening his own defensive lines. But these efforts played to the Union advantage in manpower, and the Confederate commander realized at some point he would run short of men. Moreover, as positions expanded westward, federal troops cut off roads and rail lines leading to Petersburg from the south, requiring supplies to arrive via a circuitous route from the west.

The siege of Petersburg was unique in that the opposing armies were in continual contact, with ongoing combat occurring for more than nine months. The Overland campaign had also seen continual fighting, but of a much higher intensity over a shorter period of time. For the entire siege, federal forces suffered about 42,000 casualties, Confederate ones 28,000. The Civil War had other sieges, but none of the duration or with troop numbers as large as Petersburg. Long and bloody, it achieved Grant's strategic goal of fixing Lee in place. But he needed another Union commander to exploit the situation and win a victory.

The Atlanta Campaign, 1864

William T. Sherman commanded three armies around Chattanooga. These included the 60,000-man Army of the Cumberland, 25,000 troops in the Army of the Tennessee, and 13,000 troops in the new Army of the Ohio. Like the Army of the Potomac, they began their spring campaign in early May, marching through northern Georgia toward Atlanta, with Sherman seeking chances to destroy or break up enemy forces. Opposing them was the 50,000-man Confederate Army of Tennessee, now commanded by Joseph E. Johnston (Davis dismissed Bragg after the Battle of Chattanooga), though early in the campaign, reinforcements from the Army of Mississippi brought its strength up to about 65,000.

Operational movements in the Atlanta and Overland campaigns resembled each other, for in both, Union armies kept moving around the flanks of opposing Confederate armies. But unlike eastern Virginia, northern Georgia is very mountainous. With some quick field fortification, Johnston's men could easily create formidable defensive positions. Hence Sherman did not commit his troops to heavy combat before entering the vicinity of Atlanta, with one exception.

When federal forces began advancing, the Confederate Army of Tennessee held a position on Rocky Face Ridge, about 25 miles south of Chattanooga and above the main railroad to the city. While the Armies of the Cumberland and the Ohio "demonstrated" or drew the attention of Johnston's men, Sherman sent the Union Army of the Tennessee south to get around their flank. But the Confederates detected this movement, and Johnston fell back 15 miles to Resaca. Again, the Cumberland and Ohio armies tested the enemy position while the Army of the Tennessee moved around the Confederate left. Once more Johnston disengaged, retreating 10 miles to Cassville. After another federal flanking maneuver, he fell back again, to Allatoona Pass. Sherman now sent all three armies south to try and get around the Confederates, but Johnston's men blocked them around Dallas and New Hope Church.

For three weeks federal forces had progressed rapidly, marching roughly 60 miles through mountainous terrain while outmaneuvering a large enemy force. But operations bogged down over the next month, as rains turned roads to mud. Both forces slowly inched to the east. By late June, both sides faced each other northwest of Marietta, on the main north–south rail line. Frustrated by the campaign's slow pace, Sherman thought he needed to reinvigorate his soldiers' combat capabilities after weeks of marching and constructing fieldworks. Reasoning his prior movements had led the Confederates to strengthen their flanks, he ordered an attack for June 27 on their center, resting on Kennesaw Mountain. The result was a smaller version of Cold Harbor, with 2,000–3,000 federal troops lost for no tactical gain.

This battle was the only major Union assault in the entire Atlanta campaign. Within a week, Sherman returned to maneuvering around Johnston's army. On July 9, federal soldiers crossed the Chattahoochee River, and Southern troops fell back to defenses outside Atlanta. Excepting Kennesaw Mountain, Sherman had used numbers and movement to maintain his operational offensive without resorting to tactical attacks. But he had not found an opportunity to cripple Confederate forces. Johnston had given up ground to preserve his army. Military historians have praised him for this decision, but at the time, his operations produced great frustration in the Confederacy. Union troops were now outside the Confederacy's most important city besides Richmond, and Johnston had not initiated a battle to bloody his foe and raise Southern morale.

If Johnston had Lee's record of prior victories, perhaps Southerners would have had more patience with him. Instead, Jefferson Davis replaced Johnston with John Bell Hood in mid-July. Despite having lost an arm and a leg in prior battles, Hood retained his penchant aggressive action, and between July 20 and July 28 his troops attacked Union forces three times, at the Battles of Peachtree Creek, Atlanta, and Ezra Crossing. These were all repulsed, producing 15,000 Southern casualties to 6,000 Northern. But the assaults stopped Sherman's immediate attempts to surround Atlanta. The city remained in contact with the rest of the Confederacy through one rail line to the south. While Union armies remained entrenched in an arc around the city's northern defenses, Sherman used cavalry to try to isolate the city, which Hood countered with his horsemen.

Farther west, federal cavalry were searching for Nathan Bedford Forrest's troopers and threatening raids in Mississippi. These operations successfully distracted Confederate cavalry and helped keep rail lines between Sherman's forces and Chattanooga safe during the Atlanta campaign. The summer also brought a significant strategic gain for the Union with the capture of Mobile Bay. This operation had been delayed by the fruitless Red River campaign, which cost Nathaniel Banks his command. On August 5, David Farragut led 18 ironclads and wooden warships with one army division into Mobile Bay. When the lead vessel struck a mine and sank, Farragut personally directed his squadron through the minefield, yelling "Damn the Torpedoes! Full speed ahead!" After reaching the bay and pummeling the ironclad CSS *Tennessee*, the small Confederate flotilla surrendered, ending the Battle of Mobile Bay. Farragut lacked the troops to take Mobile itself but had enough to capture the forts guarding entrance to the bay, thereby cutting off one of the Confederacy's few remaining ports to shipping.

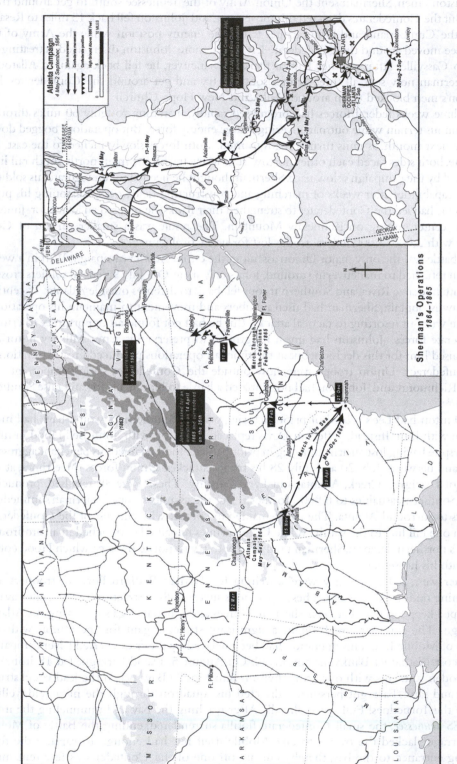

Map 7.6 Sherman's Operations, May 1864–April 1865, and the Atlanta Campaign, May 4–September 2, 1864

Figure 7.3 "Columbia Demands Her Children!"

By James Baker, 1864

This illustration captures Northern frustration and disillusionment in the summer of 1864. In the nineteenth century, the female character of Columbia appeared in popular media as a symbol of America. Here she is castigating Lincoln, demanding the return of her "500,000 sons," men serving in the Union armies. The president responds by offering a story, while a bill to raise another 500,000 men lies on the floor.

Library of Congress, Prints and Photographs Division, LC-DIG-ppmsca-15768

But this strategic victory did not dispel deepening gloom among Northerners. Already dejected over the results of the Overland campaign, they fell into even greater despair when Sherman's armies stalled outside Atlanta. Once again Confederates seemed to have thwarted federal generals, and a successful end to the fighting seemed beyond reach. Sensing this mood, the Democratic Party endorsed a platform for the 1864 presidential election that called for an immediate armistice followed by negotiations with the Confederacy. They also nominated former general George B. McClellan as their candidate. By late August, Lincoln came to believe he would lose the November election.

Southerners hoped for that result. By the summer of 1864, Lee, Davis, and other Confederate leaders grasped that by countering Union advances and inflicting casualties, they could facilitate the replacement of the Lincoln administration with one that would cease hostilities. But Southern morale still had to be bolstered during the campaigns. In this regard, Lee's battles with Grant, while bloody for both sides, demonstrated that Confederate troops were hurting federal forces. Conversely, Johnston's constant retreats had exasperated Southerners to the point where Davis replaced him.

These attitudes explain the importance of Sherman's capture of Atlanta on September 2. Leaving just a few troops behind in their trenches, at the end of August he moved all three federal armies out and around the western outskirts of the city to sever its rail and road communications to the south. Belatedly realizing what was happening, Hood dispatched a corps to protect the railroad at Jonesboro. But Union troops were already there and repulsed Confederate attempts to drive them away at the Battle of Jonesboro. Facing possible encirclement, and not wanting to repeat Pemberton's mistake at Vicksburg of losing an army, Hood abandoned Atlanta on September 1. Federal forces occupied it the next day, producing elation throughout the Union. Support for Lincoln and his handling of the war surged. Lincoln's reelection in November—by an overwhelming margin, especially among soldiers—reaffirmed the Union's commitment to fight until the Confederacy was defeated militarily. That came about after one more evolution in federal strategy.

The March to the Sea, 1864

Although Atlanta's capture stoked Northern spirits, Southerners were still willing to fight. Shortly thereafter, Davis visited Hood's army to bolster morale. The challenge for Grant and Sherman was how to crush Southern ability and willingness to continue the war. Part of the answer was continued operations against Confederate military forces, particularly the siege of the Army of Northern Virginia at Petersburg. But in the war's final months, the Union increasingly sought to exhaust Southerners by confiscating and destroying resources that could sustain resistance. Moreover, the scale of destruction was much more than foreseen at the beginning of the conflict, for federal officers no longer sought to shield civilians from the war's effects. Instead, Sherman came to believe that noncombatants had to feel pain from hostilities if they were to stop supporting the rebellion. Although this strategic approach did not end the war in itself, it created circumstances whereby the final Union military victories would induce Confederate surrender in the spring of 1865.

Sheridan demonstrated the effectiveness of exhausting Southern resources with his Shenandoah campaign in late September and October 1864. But even before then, Sherman began taking a tougher approach to the war. On September 7, he ordered Atlanta's population to evacuate the city; one reason was that, with no civilians, supplies coming in on the rail line would all be for military use. The order provoked bitter protests. When Hood complained it "transcends, in studied and ingenious cruelty, all acts ever before brought to my attention in the dark history of war," Sherman calmly observed that Confederate commanders—including Hood himself—had previously destroyed property or forced noncombatant evacuations from combat zones. As it happened, most of Atlanta's population had already fled by the time Sherman's soldiers arrived, and scholars such as Mark Grimsley observe that not all those who remained were forced to leave while federals occupied the city.

As Sherman contemplated his next move, Hood began a new campaign. In early October, 40,000 Confederate soldiers moved north to harass the federal supply link back to Tennessee. Sherman and most of his forces followed, driving Hood's troops away from the railroad. But the Union commander soon realized he would not need to protect it if his men advanced to the Atlantic and foraged along the way. Although federal forces had lived off the land previously, the distance to be traveled and numbers of troops in Sherman's' proposed operation gave Lincoln and Grant pause. They acceded to it, but Hood's army (which had retreated to northern Alabama) still threatened Tennessee. Sherman dispatched John Schofield with two corps to check Hood and join forces concentrating around Nashville under George Thomas.

On November 12, 1864, Sherman and more than 60,000 soldiers began the March to the Sea. Traveling close to 300 miles, they reached the Atlantic by December 10 and captured

Savannah within the next two weeks. Before leaving, Union troops destroyed everything of military value in Atlanta, including railroads and buildings. En route they faced minimal opposition, brushing aside the small numbers of militia and cavalry in the area. Advancing through the middle of Georgia while avoiding major towns, Sherman's four corps spread out over a path that at times measured 60 miles wide. Foraging along the way, they also destroyed anything that could be used to supply Confederate military forces. They burned caches of grain, warehouses, rolling stock, and mills; ripped up and bent rails; and drove off livestock.

While similar to Sheridan's campaign in the Valley, the March to the Sea inflicted destruction on a much greater scale. Various authors note it was essentially a giant raid. Sherman's troops did not occupy any territory between Atlanta and the coast, but simply foraged and destroyed supplies and infrastructure in the areas they crossed. But beyond logistical goals, Sherman knew the March would horrify Southerners (he claimed he would "make Georgia howl"), and wanted to demonstrate one point in particular: that the Confederacy lacked the power to protect its civilians. The Davis administration could muster no effective resistance to the 60,000 enemy troops advancing through the heart of its territory. Sherman was perhaps more successful than he could have imagined. The outrage the March provoked has been recounted and retold in popular culture and Southern memory ever since, the most famous example being *Gone With the Wind* (novel and film).

Such recollections of the March to the Sea depict wanton federal destruction, but overlook its limits and broader context. For much of the war, Union forces tried to respect civilian property, attitudes that changed when it became clear most Southerners supported the Confederacy. Numerous Southern families truly suffered, but they were not left destitute as a matter of policy. Sherman's orders entailed the destruction of supply caches that could be used to feed enemy troops, and facilities and equipment that could produce and transport provisions and equipment. But private dwellings were to be spared, and families left with enough subsistence for their own

Figure 7.4 Print of Engraving of "Sherman's March to the Sea" by Alexander Hay Ritchie, 1868

Library of Congress, Prints and Photographs Division, LC-DIG-ppmsca-09326

Figure 7.5 "'The Halt'—a Scene in the Georgia Campaign" by Thomas Nast, in *Harper's Weekly*, June 30, 1866

Different images of Sherman's March to the Sea: The first is typical of the long-standing view that emphasizes the destruction of federal armies, whereas the second comes from a Northern publication of the period, depicting compassion of Union soldiers toward Southern civilians. The actual experiences of Southern families generally fell between these two extremes, though loss and privation were common. (Note the African-American family in the foreground of the first image.)

Library of Congress, Prints and Photographs Division, LC-USZ62–98261

needs. Some Union troops—called "bummers"—ignored or exceeded such orders and plundered residences, as did some Confederate deserters and runaway slaves. Yet available evidence indicates such incidents, while too frequent, were not predetermined or calculated acts of deprivation.

As for violence against noncombatants, scholarly research has discovered an absence of documented crimes such as rapes and murders during the March, indicating they may be overblown in popular memory. Whatever the actual incidence of such violence, what has become clear is that blacks also suffered. From the time Lincoln issued the Emancipation Proclamation until the end of the war, slaves had to flee their masters to realize the dream of freedom. Those who did so faced numerous dangers, including starvation, abuse, and illness. While research is ongoing, possibly hundreds of thousands of them died during the Civil War.

When Sherman's troops marched through Georgia, thousands of slaves flocked to them. But his forces, on the move and foraging for their own needs, were not prepared to help so many. While some runaways found employment with federal units or received help, others were denied assistance. Some incidents of abuse occurred, and in one case an officer abandoned hundreds of runaway slaves after crossing a river. The March produced a major refugee crisis, and one way Sherman addressed it was with Field Order No. 15: This settled thousands of black runaways on lands confiscated by Union forces in coastal Georgia and South Carolina. For the moment, these former slaves had acquired land as well as freedom—but the order would be revoked after the war ended.

As Sherman marched, Hood began his last campaign. In November, the Army of Tennessee advanced into its namesake state, trying to surprise and defeat Schofield's corps. Union troops fell back and entrenched at Franklin, and on November 30 Hood attacked. In assaults that continued past dark, 6,000–7,000 Confederate soldiers became casualties, compared to 2,000–2,500 Northerners. Schofield retreated during the night, joining Thomas' troops in prepared positions around Nashville. Hood followed, and realizing his army was outnumbered (less than 40,000 men compared to 55,000 federals), had his men entrench to await a Union assault. Thomas carefully planned his attack, and on December 15 began the Battle of Nashville. After two days, flank assaults captured over 4,000 Confederate troops and drove off the rest, who were chased by Union cavalry. By the time Hood's army reached Mississippi in January 1865, it had lost about half of the 40,000 troops it possessed in November, the rest being exhausted and demoralized. Hood lost his command, and the Army of Tennessee—the only remaining major Confederate force after Lee's Army of Northern Virginia—was broken up.

Women and the War

Women fought in the Civil War. But their numbers totaled perhaps a few hundred. Women were not allowed in the ranks, so female soldiers had to hide their gender, and if discovered were sent home. Many served as musicians—positions often filled by boys, who were easier to impersonate than adult men. Hundreds of other women, instead of serving with armies, acted as spies, collecting information on enemy positions in their vicinity. But the most prominent contributions women made in the combat zone were medical. Many thousands served as army nurses, including numerous volunteers. Women also accompanied armies in other capacities, such as laundresses, servants, and cooks.

With so many men away at war, women at home took over farms and businesses. Those in cities acquired jobs in factories and offices. For those who did not have to work, the war provided numerous volunteering opportunities. Union and Confederate women formed thousands of relief organizations to assist soldiers, most with a local or regional membership. They raised funds and sent clothing, blankets, food, and other items to troops in the field. A few agencies had a broader, national scope, particularly in the North. The Women's Central Relief Association coordinated the efforts of regional and neighborhood groups. Both the U.S. Sanitary Commission and the U.S. Christian Commission sent representatives to armies on campaigns; though run by men, both had extensive female memberships. The former strove to improve hygiene and medical conditions at army camps, while the latter tended to both the spiritual and material needs of soldiers, providing Bibles, writing materials, and fresh food. Whether at home or as nurses in the field, upper- and middle-class women were more prominent as volunteers, whereas those from more modest backgrounds had to devote time to jobs, businesses, and families.

Wartime developments posed special challenges to Southerners. Scarcity of crucial staples such as food, salt, and clothing became more common as the war progressed. Shortages reflected many factors, such as the Union blockade, fighting in agricultural regions or their occupation by federal troops, and poor Southern rails. Depending upon the item, prices for goods increased by many dozens in Confederate dollars or more: A barrel of flour cost better than $1,000 in Richmond by the war's end. The approach of Union armies also posed the difficult choice for families of whether to remain or leave.

The brunt of these problems fell upon women, who sometimes dramatically expressed their frustration. Protests erupted in a number of Southern cities during the war, the most infamous being the Richmond Bread Riot of April 1863. Women comprised the majority of the crowd and were protesting the high price of bread. More common than such public, collective denunciations were individual reproofs expressed in letters to local newspapers and journals, government officials, friends, and family—including spouses and other male relatives serving in

Confederate armies. Such correspondence did not simply lament rising prices and the lack of crucial provisions such as meat, bread, and cloth; some also described flight, as many families abandoned homes before advancing Union forces. They became refugees and placed an added burden on relatives and communities already facing problems of scarcity.

Families who remained and tolerated federal occupation generally did not endure the scarcity afflicting other areas of the South. Although some Union officers could be heavy-handed, most did not impose occupation harshly, seeing residents as Americans who would soon come under local civilian rule under reestablished federal authority. However onerous occupation may have been, it provided stability that greatly contrasted with the growing chaos in many Southern areas during the war's last months. In places law and order broke down, with families worrying not just about raiding armies such as Sherman's, but Confederate deserters and bandits as well. White families also feared the actions of runaway slaves. But black families faced the difficult choice of flight. As noted above, running away entailed numerous dangers, and some black women chose to remain with their masters' households, believing it would better preserve their families.

Box 7.3   The Collapse of the Confederate Homefront

The following letter between Elvira Worth Jackson and Mrs. Jonathan Worth demonstrates many problems Southern women faced late in the war:

Asheboro, March 16 1865

We have had more peaceable times with the deserters since you left. I hear of no robbing being committed since these troops came in, and a large number of cavalry and wagons, etc. have passed here on their way to Raleigh. You ought to have seen us hiding meat, corn, etc. the other day. We heard that 4000 Cavalry were to pass here and we knew if they did we would be eaten out and so we went to hiding hay and provisions. Fortunately for us the Cavalry turned off and went by Thomasville. We expected a train of 150 wagons a day or two ago and they turned off at Page's toll house and went to Franklinsville, and yesterday 100 Cavalry and 100 wagons passed here and they went to the same place. I guess they are about eat out at the Factory now. I hope you will write to me as long as there is any communication for I shall continually be uneasy. William Stanton arrived here from Fayetteville yesterday—says Uncle B. G. Worth's house, barn, provisions, etc. were all destroyed—Is it not horrible—said brother was at Roxana's. I hope he may escape. Don't you suppose Sis Julia is in the greatest trouble about him? Not knowing where he is, etc. Roxana had not been pressed for provisions up to that time. Uncle Addison said he intended to stay and tough it out. Pittsboro is full to overflowing with refugees from Fayetteville. I think it is getting time now for this war to cease. It will never be settled by the sword. Peace now would be more acceptable to the people than all the wealth of the world even a peace on Lincoln's terms. I fully concur with the great Dr. Franklin that "there never was a good war or a bad peace.

(Letter from Elvira Worth Jackson to Mrs. Jonathan Worth, March 16, 1865, in *The Correspondence of Jonathan Worth*, vol. 1, Raleigh: Edwards & Broughton, 1909, pp. 368–69)

White Southern women powerfully expressed their fears, anxiety, and frustration over these developments in letters. Ironically, when the war began, many had championed cultural ideals that held men as protectors of the community who should volunteer for the Confederacy. But most people, Southerners and Northerners, then believed the war would be short. As the war continued, the Confederate government failed to protect and adequately provide for its soldiers' families. Toward the end, with wives and mothers confronting mounting challenges and dangers, more and more soldiers abandoned their units to return home. In early 1865, Robert E. Lee noted that hundreds were leaving his army every week.

The Final Campaigns, 1865

Time was running out for the Confederacy. In March 1865, the Confederate Congress became so desperate that it passed a bill to recruit black soldiers, though few were raised and none served before the war's end. As the year began, though, Southerners were still prepared to fight. Lee and the Army of Northern Virginia continued to defy the Union, defending Petersburg and Richmond, and Gary Gallagher has argued that so long as they remained in the field, Confederates could cling to the hope of victory and endure the war's travails. The Army of the Potomac crushed that hope in the spring of 1865, though other forces also pushed Southerners to surrender.

In January 1865, federal forces captured Fort Fisher, blocking access to Wilmington, North Carolina, the Confederacy's sole remaining port east of the Mississippi except Charleston. Sherman's armies advanced again in February. In fact, the March through the Carolinas was longer, more challenging, and more destructive than the March to the Sea. Again, one objective was logistical, with Sherman's men destroying supplies and resources that would otherwise support the Army of Northern Virginia. But Lee's army was a target itself, for Sherman's troops were supposed to join forces with the Army of the Potomac to crush it. As they marched, other Union operations targeted Alabama, most of which (like the interior of the Carolinas) had not yet been troubled by federal armies.

Sherman's forces did not reach Virginia before the war's end, and after 10 weeks arrived at Raleigh, North Carolina. The destruction they had wrought in Georgia paled in comparison to that inflicted upon South Carolina (the first state to declare secession in December 1860). Whereas in Georgia senior Union officers had exercised a fair amount of discretion over what buildings and structures were razed, in South Carolina some entire towns burned. The most dramatic example was Columbia, the state capital, although Sherman had ordered the city spared. Both sides blamed the other for the fire that erupted shortly after federal soldiers arrived on February 17, and there were many possible causes. Sherman's troops had avoided Charleston, but they prompted Confederates to abandon the city on February 18 by severing its rail connection to the interior; Union blockaders then occupied it.

Unlike during the March to the Sea, the Confederate government concentrated some regular soldiers to stop Sherman's advance, though it made little difference. Joseph E. Johnston, commanding Southern forces in the region, cobbled together about 20,000 men to confront Sherman in North Carolina. At the Battle of Bentonville from March 19–21, Johnston's men attacked an isolated component of Sherman's force but were driven off when federal reinforcements arrived. Johnston's army, suffering desertions every day, never fought again. After Bentonville, Sherman paused at Goldsborough to rest his men and collect supplies before continuing to the coast. At about that time, more than 13,000 Union cavalrymen left Tennessee to devastate Alabama—including both Selma, one of the Confederacy's sole remaining industrial centers, and the state capital, Montgomery.

But it was the surrender of Robert E. Lee and the Army of Northern Virginia that effectively ended the war. Besieged at Petersburg since the summer of 1864, federal troops had steadily extended their lines westward, compelling outnumbered Confederate soldiers to do likewise. In late March, Sheridan's forces returned from the Shenandoah Valley, raiding areas north and west of Richmond along the way. With about 120,000 troops to Lee's 55,000, Grant began operations to force Lee's army out of Petersburg.

On March 29, a federal infantry corps moved to envelop the Confederate right flank, while Sheridan's cavalry swung out farther west to cut the city's last rail link and attack the enemy rear. Lee countered by sending more than 10,000 troops under George Pickett to stop Sheridan. Union forces prevailed at the Battle of Five Forks on April 1, with Sheridan leading an assault that captured half of Pickett's force and scattered the rest. On April 2, federal pressure drove in the Confederate right flank and penetrated positions elsewhere. Lee evacuated Petersburg that night, prompting the Davis administration to abandon Richmond.

The next few days became a race. Lee hoped to join Johnston's army in North Carolina. But federal forces advanced faster and kept blocking routes to the south. Exhausted and lacking rations, Confederate soldiers could not march rapidly enough. Union troops harassed Lee's rearguards and, at Sayler's Creek on April 6, captured 6,000 men. About that time Sheridan's cavalry reached Appomattox Courthouse, blocking the Army of Northern Virginia's retreat.

On April 7, Grant initiated surrender talks. Lee was reluctant, but after one last attack failed to puncture the growing cordon around his outnumbered and near-starving troops, he agreed. On April 9, the two opposing commanders met at the McLean House in Appomattox Courthouse. Grant offered generous terms: Southern soldiers would be "paroled," allowed to go home upon a promise not to take up arms again. Grant also offered to feed Lee's men. Confederate troops had to surrender weapons, but soldiers could keep horses and officers their sidearms. Lee agreed, and when his more than 28,000 men marched to relinquish their arms and battle flags a few days later, Union troops stood at attention and saluted.

In the following weeks, other Confederate forces surrendered. Johnston's men capitulated later in April. On May 10 federal troops captured Jefferson Davis, and all hostilities had ceased by the end of the month. After fleeing Richmond, Davis had tried to rally support for continuing the war. One member of Lee's staff suggested ongoing guerilla operations. But Lee, Johnston, and other senior officers refused, noting Southerners were simply too tired. By April 1865, Union forces had so pummeled the Confederacy that, after the surrender of Lee, its people could no longer bear the sacrifices the war demanded. After four years of struggle, the Lincoln administration had saved the Union.

Conclusion

In the American Civil War, a system of preexisting institutions, customs, and procedures created armies larger than any previously seen in the Western Hemisphere. Designed to raise manpower for war with a major external enemy, Northerners and Southerners instead used them against each other in the most destructive conflict ever fought in North America. The vast majority of combatants produced by this system were volunteers, though professional officers served as top commanders and advisors. Soldiers endured a form of combat more brutal than they could have imagined, and the scale of killing scarred the American public consciousness for years thereafter. Civilians organized and mobilized to help troops in the field and, especially in the South, faced dangers from invading armies. Both sides struggled to find and execute a strategy that would bring final victory. In the end, the Union pursued various means to exhaust the Confederacy and destroy the Southern will to fight. The war preserved the United States, but its end brought other challenges, some of which would also only be resolved through additional conflict.

Short Bibliography

Note: an extended bibliography appears at www.routledge.com/cw/muehlbauer

Ash, Stephen V. *When the Yankees Came: Conflict and Chaos in the Occupied South, 1861–1865.* Chapel Hill: University of North Carolina Press, 1995.

Attie, Jeanie. *Patriotic Toil: Northern Women and the American Civil War.* Ithaca, NY: Cornell University Press, 1998.

Blair, William Alan. *Virginia's Private War: Feeding Body and Soul in the Confederacy, 1861–1865*. New York: Oxford University Press, 1998.

Caudill, Edward, and Paul Ashdown. *Sherman's March in Myth and Memory*. Lanham, MD: Rowman & Littlefield Publishers, 2008.

Faust, Drew Gilpin. *Mothers of Invention: Women of the Slaveholding South in the American Civil War*. Chapel Hill: University of North Carolina Press, 1996.

———. *The Republic of Suffering: Death and the American Civil War*. New York: Knopf, 2008.

Gallagher, Gary W. *The Confederate War*. Cambridge: Harvard University Press, 1997.

———. *The Union War*. Cambridge: Harvard University Press, 2011.

Geary, James W. *We Need Men: The Union Draft in the Civil War*. Dekalb: Northern Illinois University Press, 1991.

Glatthaar, Joseph T. *The March to the Sea and Beyond: Sherman's Troops in the Savannah and Carolinas Campaigns*. New York: New York University Press, 1985.

———. *Forged in Battle: The Civil War Alliance of Black Soldiers and White Officers*. Baton Rouge: Louisiana State University Press, 2000.

Grimsley, Mark. *The Hard Hand of War: Union Military Policy toward Southern Civilians, 1861–65*. New York: Cambridge University Press, 1995.

Guelzo, Allen C. *Fateful Lightning: A New History of the Civil War & Reconstruction*. New York: Oxford University Press, 2012.

Hacker, J. David. "A Census-Based Count of the Civil War Dead." *Civil War History* 57, 4 (December 2011): 306–47.

Hall, Robert H. *Women on the Civil War Battlefront*. Lawrence: University Press of Kansas, 2006.

Jenkins, Wilbert L. *Climbing up to Glory: A Short History of African Americans during the Civil War and Reconstruction*. Wilmington, DE: Scholarly Resources, 2002.

Kennett, Lee B. *Marching through Georgia: The Story of Soldiers and Civilians during Sherman's Campaign*. New York: HarperCollins, 1995.

Linderman, Gerald F. *Embattled Courage: The Experience of Combat in the American Civil War*. New York: Free Press, 1987.

McPherson, James. *Battle Cry of Freedom: The Civil War Era*. New York: Oxford University Press, 1988.

———. *Tried By War: Abraham Lincoln as Commander in Chief*. New York: Penguin, 2008.

Mitchell, Reid. *The Vacant Chair: The Northern Soldier Leaves Home*. Oxford: Oxford University Press, 1993.

Nolan, Alan T. *Lee Considered: General Robert E. Lee and Civil War History*. Chapel Hill: University of North Carolina Press, 1991.

Rable, George. *Fredericksburg! Fredericksburg!* Chapel Hill: University of North Carolina Press, 2002.

Rafuse, Ethan S. *A Single Grand Victory: The First Campaign and Battle of Manassas*. Wilmington, DE: Scholarly Resources, 2002.

Reardon, Carol. *Pickett's Charge in History and Memory*. Chapel Hill: University of North Carolina Press, 1997.

Reid, Brian Holden. *America's Civil War: The Operational Battlefield 1861–63*. Amherst, NY: Prometheus Books, 2008.

Roberts, William H. *Now for the Contest: Coastal and Oceanic Naval Operations in the Civil War*. Lincoln: University of Nebraska Press, 2004.

Royster, Charles. *The Destructive War: William Tecumseh Sherman, Stonewall Jackson, and the Americans*. New York: Alfred A. Knopf, 1991.

Sears, Stephen W. *To the Gates of Richmond: The Peninsula Campaign*. New York: Houghton Mifflin, 1992.

Shea, William L., and Terence J. Winshell. *Vicksburg Is the Key: The Struggle for the Mississippi River*. Lincoln: University of Nebraska Press, 2003.

Stoker, Donald J. *The Grand Design: Strategy and the U.S. Civil War*. New York: Oxford University Press, 2010.

Symonds, Craig L. *The Civil War at Sea*. New York: Oxford University Press, 2009.

Weigley, Russell F. *A Great Civil War: A Political and Military History, 1861–65*. Indiana: University of Bloomington Press, 2000.

Woodworth, Steven E. *Six Armies in Tennessee: The Chickamauga and Chattanooga Campaigns*. Lincoln: University of Nebraska Press, 1998.

———. *Beneath a Northern Sky: A Short History of the Gettysburg Campaign*. Wilmington, DE: Scholarly Resources, 2003.

1866		1866–68	1867	1867–1870	1868	November 1868	1870–71	1872–73	1873	1874
TIMELINE	Memphis and New Orleans Race Riots	Red Cloud's War	Medicine Lodge Treaty	Congressional Reconstruction	Treaty of Fort Laramie	Battle of Washita	Enforcement Acts Passed	Modoc War	Colfax Massacre	Battle of New Orleans

Chapter 8

Transitions: Force in Domestic, Frontier, and Imperial Contexts, 1865–1902

The deadliest conflict in American history ended in the spring of 1865. But even as hundreds of thousands of soldiers returned home, U.S. Army units began coping with postwar problems in the South and a new round of Indian wars in the west. By the late 1870s, regular troops were no longer present in the Southern states, and frontier conflicts with native peoples were ending. The latter development raised the question of the army's future peacetime role. Army officers strove to prepare for a conventional war against a major Western power and improved professional standards and training to that end. Volunteer militias also adopted new roles and a new name, the National Guard, during this period. But the U.S. Navy saw the greatest changes in its composition and mission. The emergence of America as a great industrial power, combined with the growing popularity of imperialist ideas that called for a greater American role in global affairs, bolstered arguments for a larger, more modern, and more powerful fleet.

The Spanish-American War of 1898 tested both services. The navy won some dramatic victories that bolstered national pride and reaffirmed its new role. In contrast, the army had problems deploying a force to Cuba, though it prevailed once there. The end of the war against Spain led to a rebellion against U.S. control in the Philippines. Here too, the U.S. Army successfully defeated resistance in 1902. But its difficulties in these conflicts later led to a reevaluation of U.S. military policies in the early twentieth century.

In this chapter, students will learn about:

- The use of armed forces during Reconstruction and the Southern insurrections (1865–77).
- The last wars against native peoples in the American West.
- The changing roles of the U.S. Army, U.S. Navy, and volunteer militia.
- American military performance during the Spanish-American War (1898–99) and the Philippine-American War (1899–1902).

Overview of Reconstruction

With the defeat of the Southern states' attempted secession, the fundamental political issue became under what terms they would be admitted back into the Union. Closely related to this question, however, was which branch of the federal government should set and enforce these requirements. The problem first arose during the war, particularly where much of a rebellious state was occupied by Union troops, such as Tennessee and Louisiana. President Lincoln tried to work with loyalists in these areas to produce new state governments and rejoin the Union. But with the main exception of West Virginia, which seceded from Virginia to become a new state in 1863, Congress did not recognize any governments formed in Southern states during the war.

Before the spring of 1865, the main focus of the president and the Congress was winning the war. Historians can only speculate on how Lincoln would have handled Reconstruction thereafter, for on April 14, 1865, John Wilkes Booth assassinated him during a theatrical performance at the Ford Theater in Washington. Vice President Andrew Johnson—a War Democrat from Tennessee chosen by the Republicans in 1864 to broaden their political appeal—became the new president. His efforts to direct Reconstruction soon infuriated the Republican-dominated Congress so much that it not only took control of it but initiated the first impeachment proceeding against a sitting president in U.S. history.

From May 1865 until the spring of 1867—the period known as Presidential Reconstruction—Johnson tried to implement and defend his program, which he initially called "restoration." Johnson allowed white Southerners to reclaim their rights and property (except slaves) if they took oaths to the Union, with some exceptions. Men who had held high civilian or military rank in the Confederacy, who had been federal officers before joining the rebellion, and who had held property exceeding $20,000, for example, would have to apply directly to the president for a pardon. While appointing provisional governors, Johnson allowed the Southern states to create new governments so long as they ratified the Thirteenth Amendment to the U.S. Constitution (which abolished slavery), nullified their ordinances of secession, and repudiated Confederate debt issued during the war.

To many in the North—though not Radical Republicans—these terms seemed reasonable. But Johnson pardoned the vast majority of men who applied. Moreover, some states formed governments and elected representatives to Congress without abiding by the president's criteria: Texas and Mississippi refused to accept the 13th Amendment, and South Carolina did not revoke its secession ordinance. To the dismay of many Republicans, Johnson did not require Southerners to guarantee black suffrage. Instead, in 1865–66 most Southern states instituted Black Codes: sets of laws that, while acknowledging some basic rights (such as marriage), restricted the mobility and freedoms of black people so as to create a new system of white racial dominance short of outright slavery.

Johnson had implemented his plan while Congress was in recess. Angry Republican legislators returned to Washington at the end of 1865 and became more irate when committees began investigating conditions in the South and the status of freedmen and women. Congress refused to seat representatives elected from the Southern states and soon confronted the president. In early 1866, for example, it overrode Johnson's veto power to both reauthorize the Freedman's Bureau (discussed below) and pass the Civil Rights Act. The latter sought to protect the rights of freedmen and women, but because of the Supreme Court's 1857 *Dred Scott* decision—which ruled that black people could never be citizens—Congress passed the Fourteenth Amendment, which made all people born in the United States citizens with equal protection under the law. The effort to have the individual states ratify this amendment became the dominant political question in the Congressional elections of 1866. Johnson campaigned vigorously against it, infuriating Republicans and alienating much of the Northern electorate. When Congress reconvened afterward—with large Republican majorities in both houses—it proceeded to legislate its own terms for Reconstruction.

The spring of 1867 marks the transition from Presidential Reconstruction to Congressional Reconstruction. This was also known as "Radical Reconstruction," because the program of racial equality and protection for black rights was pushed by Radical Republicans and sought sweeping changes in Southern society; it was also known as "Military Reconstruction." Between March and July, Congress passed three Military Reconstruction Acts, and a fourth the following year. Declaring their current governments "provisional," these laws stipulated Congressional requirements Southern states had to meet in order to reenter the Union. First, eligible voters had to elect delegates to a convention that would draft a new state constitution. That constitution had to include guarantees of suffrage to all male citizens, including blacks. Once voters passed the new constitution, and the new government passed the Fourteenth Amendment, that state would be readmitted to the Union. Congress also made the U.S. Army responsible for enforcing these laws, placing the 10 unreconstructed states (not Tennessee, which had been readmitted to the Union in 1866 after it ratified the Fourteenth Amendment) into five military districts. Each one was commanded by an army general with troops at his disposal. Congress gave these commanders authority over state governments in their districts, with responsibility for registering eligible voters, appointing and removing civilian officials, and overseeing elections and judicial proceedings.

Tasking the U.S. Army with ensuring Southern states met Congressional Reconstruction requirements created another problem for Republicans. Constitutionally, the president commanded the army—and not surprisingly, Johnson bitterly opposed the Military Reconstruction Acts; Congress enacted them only by again overriding his veto. In early 1867 Republican legislators passed two laws to limit Johnson's authority over the army and capacity to interfere with Congressional Reconstruction. The Tenure of Office Act stipulated that, if a federal official had been appointed with the advice and consent of the Senate (such as a member of the Cabinet), the president could not remove that appointee without the Senate's consent. The particular concern here was to protect Secretary of War Edwin Stanton, a Republican who supported Congressional Reconstruction. Congress also passed the Command of the Army Act, which required the president to issue all army orders through the General of the Army— Ulysses S. Grant—and not directly to any other officers. This act also prevented the president from removing the General of the Army from his post without the Senate's consent, and required army headquarters to remain in Washington.

Johnson viewed the Tenure of Office Act as unconstitutional, and in early 1868 fired Stanton—precipitating his impeachment by Congress. That spring he was tried in the Senate, and came within one vote of being removed from office. In the end, some moderate Republicans worried about the precedent set if Congress removed a sitting president for what they saw as a disagreement over policy. Johnson remained president, though he no longer interfered with Congressional Reconstruction. Congress soon admitted six Southern states back into the

Union, and the Fourteenth Amendment was ratified in July 1868. The remaining states of
Georgia, Mississippi, Texas, and Virginia rejoined in 1870, passing both the Fourteenth and
Fifteenth Amendments to do so. Republicans thus successfully imposed their political criteria
upon Reconstruction—but at the cost of alienating conservative Southern whites who despised
the Republican state governments created in the process. Events soon demonstrated that they
did not regard these governments as legitimate or regard Congressional Reconstruction as the
final word on the political and racial complexion of the postwar South.

Army Duties During Reconstruction

In a sense, the army's duties during Reconstruction constituted its largest occupation mission
before the twentieth century. The American South was not a foreign country, though, but a
region of the United States whose inhabitants had failed to overthrow the federal government.
Initially, the army's task was to ensure stability, order, and relief. Chaos prevailed throughout
the South in the immediate aftermath of the war. Military operations had destroyed transportation networks and infrastructure, making basic goods scarce in many areas. Much of the
population was unsettled: Many searched for better economic conditions, while others returned
home or tried to locate relatives. These movements further paralyzed already anemic economic
production while exacerbating resource problems for communities hosting numerous refugees.
Many Southern municipal officials had stopped performing their duties, unsure if the federal
government would consider them rebels or criminals.

In many areas, the army took on the functions of government. Soldiers enforced the law and
kept the peace, while officers administered local courts, ensured the provision of services such
as sanitation, and selected civilians to fill municipal positions. The army also directly helped
needy Southerners, white and black, in particular, distributing tens of millions of rations.
Military engineers rebuilt destroyed roads, rail lines, bridges, and buildings. Officers also managed railroads.

Military provision of these services diminished as state governments formed during
Presidential Reconstruction. Army personnel then gave more attention to assisting freedmen
and women in late 1865 and 1866. To this end, Congress had created the Bureau of Refugees,
Freedmen, and Abandoned Lands, known as the Freedmen's Bureau, in March 1865.
Organizationally, it was a separate agency within the War Department, distinct from the army.
But its top official was a general, O. O. Howard, while current and former army officers com-
prised much of its personnel.

In the chaos that followed the war's end, Bureau agents gave priority to stabilizing Southern
society. The quickest method (and stipulated by Johnson) was to return abandoned lands to white
owners, and black laborers to the fields. Though the latter were hired as free laborers, the policy
quashed dreams of landownership for thousands of African-American families. Over time though,
Bureau agents gave more consideration to the needs of former slaves, in particular, overseeing the
construction of hundreds of schools and providing legal services to ensure labor contracts were
not abusive. Moreover, army officers had the authority to suspend judicial proceedings and conduct their own if they believed civilian courts were biased against black people.

Army officers in the postwar South were often frustrated implementing political policies for
which they received little guidance. These men held a wide range of views, from conservatives
with doubts about black suffrage, to committed Radical Republicans, to men who strove to
avoid any appearance of any political influence. But whatever their sympathies, all officers at
times upset Southern whites with exertions of federal authority, such as replacing obstructionist
and recalcitrant local officials. Southerners sometimes retaliated by trying to pursue legal action
in local courts against officers and Freedmen's Bureau agents.

Box 8.1   A General's View of Reconstruction

After serving in the Civil War, Philip Sheridan held high rank in the late nineteenth-century army, ultimately succeeding William Tecumseh Sherman as the Commanding General of the United States Army. In 1867 Sheridan became commander of the Fifth Military District, created as part of the Military Reconstruction Acts to encompass Louisiana and Texas, and aggressively enforced these laws. The following excerpt is taken from Sheridan's memoirs, and addresses his use of military courts ("commissions"):

Although Military Commissions were fully authorized by the Reconstruction acts, yet I did not favor their use in governing the district, and probably would never have convened one had these acts been observed in good faith. I much preferred that the civil courts, and the State and municipal authorities already in existence, should perform their functions without military control or interference, but occasionally, because the civil authorities neglected their duty, I was obliged to resort to this means to ensure the punishment Of offenders . . .

In the State of Texas there were in 1865 about 200,000 of the colored race—roughly, a third of the entire population—while in Louisiana there were not less than 350,000, or more than one-half of all the people in the State. Until the enactment of the Reconstruction laws these negroes were without rights, and though they had been liberated by the war, Mr. Johnson's policy now proposed that they should have no political status at all, and consequently be at the mercy of a people who, recently their masters, now seemed to look upon them as the authors of all the misfortunes that had come upon the land. . . . [W]hen outrages and murders grew frequent, and the aid of the military power was an absolute necessity for the protection of life, I employed it unhesitatingly—the guilty parties being brought to trial before military commissions—and for a time, at least, there occurred a halt in the march of terrorism inaugurated by [Southern white conservatives].

(*Memoirs of P. H. Sheridan*, 2 vols., part 5, chap. XI, New York: C.L. Webster, 1888, e-book available via Project Gutenberg)

During both Presidential and Congressional Reconstruction, one of the army's most important duties was maintaining peace and order. When competently led, soldiers fulfilled this task well, as Southerners did not confront federal units. But the army lacked the manpower to station troops in every community. Federal forces totaled over a million men in May 1865, but six months later most had been discharged, with somewhat more than 200,000 soldiers remaining. In the Southern states, federal troop numbers fell from about 39,000 in April 1866 to less than 18,000 the following October. These declines reflected the desire of volunteers to return home, Congressional efforts to reduce military expenditures, and deployment of troops to the West.

The Politicization of Violence

Violence was endemic in the American South following the Civil War, partly because law and order had broken down at war's end. But questions of race also fueled the problem. Slavery was over, but most Southern whites would not countenance the idea that former slaves should be their social equals. Many used violence to express their frustrations and to try to keep African Americans in a subservient status. The number of robberies, beatings, murders, and other crimes against blacks will never be known with any certainty. Many were spontaneous rather than premeditated acts, and the majority occurred in the countryside. Two very large urban disturbances, however, erupted in 1866: the Memphis and New Orleans Race Riots.

On May 1, white mobs that included policemen and firemen began a multiple-day rampage of robbery and destruction through Memphis' black neighborhoods. When it ended, 46 people were dead, 75 injured, and over 100 buildings burned. On July 30, violence erupted in New Orleans over a political convention. White mobs attacked African-American men marching in support of the conference; the mobs also attacked the meeting hall itself. By the time soldiers arrived, 48 people were dead and well over 100 wounded, with black men comprising the vast majority of the casualties. For Republicans, the Memphis and New Orleans riots clearly demonstrated how Presidential Reconstruction had abandoned the needs of freedmen and women, and pushed Congress toward passing the Fourteenth Amendment and pursuing its own plan for Reconstruction.

But race riots did not occur in the vast majority of communities where troops were stationed. Moreover, scholars such as George Rable note an important difference between the Memphis and New Orleans riots. Memphis' black population grew markedly after the war, with former slaves arriving in search of new opportunities. The riot was thus a spontaneous release of social tensions building since the end of the war, similar to violence throughout the South early in Reconstruction. The violence in New Orleans, however, had an overtly political purpose—disrupting a convention whose members sought a new Louisiana state constitution that would guarantee black rights. In this regard, the New Orleans riot presaged an important change in the South: harnessing violence and terror to achieve political goals.

The activities of the Ku Klux Klan (KKK) provided another indication of this trend. The KKK was the most infamous of many groups Southern whites formed to intimidate those who supported black rights and federal policies. Louisiana, for example, had the Knights of the White Camellia. The Klan itself originally formed in 1866 as a social club for Confederate veterans. But the advent of Congressional Reconstruction in 1867 spurred many members to become terrorists. Whether part of the Klan or another group, these men generally operated at night, traveled on horseback, and wore hoods or masks to hide their identities. Their targets included Republican leaders of both races, schoolteachers, and blacks deemed not sufficiently deferential to whites. Intimidation ranged from issuing threats, burning down churches and schools, to beatings, whippings, and murder. These acts, sometimes called "night riding," were all designed to scare the black population into submission and frighten away their white allies.

In 1868, many Southern states were ratifying new constitutions and anticipating that year's presidential election. Political tensions were high. The U.S. Army, however, successfully supervised political processes required by Congressional Reconstruction. Soldiers determined who was eligible to vote and hold office. They oversaw conventions to write new state constitutions, and managed elections to ratify those constitutions, the Fourteenth Amendment, and to create new state governments. In June and July, Congress admitted Alabama, Arkansas, Florida, Louisiana, North Carolina, and South Carolina back into the Union. That fall, Republicans gave Ulysses S. Grant the electoral votes for six of the eight Southern states that participated in the national election—which he won.

But in some areas, political violence was pervasive. Hundreds of murders occurred in Arkansas and Louisiana. In the latter, state Republican voters—who in the spring of 1868 had ratified a new constitution and installed a Republican government—were so cowed by the fall that Democratic presidential candidate Horatio Seymour won its electoral votes. In Georgia, conservatives attacked white and black Republicans at Camilla that September, killing at least nine. The Georgia legislature had also recently expelled its black members, and an infuriated Congress revoked the state's reconstructed status.

Even in areas where voters elected Republican candidates fairly peacefully, there was an ominous development: Most white Southerners boycotted the political process. Much of their outrage with Congressional Reconstruction was not just black males receiving voting rights but that army officers—in accordance with a clause of the Fourteenth Amendment—disenfranchised white men who had held federal or state office and then "engaged in insurrection or rebellion" against the United States. As a result, blacks and a white Republican minority created new state constitutions and Republican governments in 1868 and also 1870, when Georgia, Mississippi, Texas, and Virginia rejoined the Union. Southern white Republicans consisted of Northerners who had migrated south (who Southern conservatives derisively called "carpetbaggers") and Southern white Unionists ("scalawags").

Once Congress recognized a state's reconstruction, it returned to civilian rule. The army no longer had any special authority or responsibilities, and troops stationed there could only act at the request of state officials. But political and racial violence continued. Within a few years, it helped install conservative governments committed to white racial dominance throughout the South.

Southern Insurgencies and Redemption

An insurgency is an attempt by a group within a political community to take over its government using force, one that relies more upon intimidation and terror than conventional military operations. Unlike regular forces, insurgents are usually people who live and work in the areas where they perpetrate violence. The Southern insurgencies of the Reconstruction period were unique, though, in their political and racial objectives. Southern white conservatives did not seek to overthrow the *federal government*—in that regard, they accepted the outcome of the Civil War. Their objective instead was to remove the *Republican state governments* that formed during Congressional Reconstruction and replace them with Democratic ones. Doing so would not only destroy the regimes Southern conservatives regarded as illegitimate and imposed upon them by Congress but would enable them to undermine black rights and reestablish a system of white racial dominance short of slavery.

Installing conservative Democratic state governments and reinstituting white supremacy became known as "redemption." For generations thereafter, popular memory—created and reaffirmed by media written for whites—regarded redemption as having "saved" the South from the horrors of "Black" Republican rule. But it varied by state. Unlike the Civil War, there was no single leadership overseeing or directing these efforts throughout the entire South. Instead, local conservatives concentrated on "redeeming" their own states. Klansmen in local dens, for example, generally acted on their own initiative, regardless of the organization's nominal hierarchy.

In all areas, white conservatives employed both legitimate political activities as well as intimidation and terror to bolster Democrats and undermine support for Republicans. But the degree of violence varied, as did the time redemption required. For example, by 1871, Republican governments had fallen in North Carolina, Tennessee, and Virginia, whereas they lasted longest in Florida, Louisiana, and South Carolina. After January 1877, Democrats governed in all Southern states and repressed African-American rights without federal interference. That outcome reflected the actions of white conservatives, waning federal willingness to intervene on Southern affairs, and confusion and hesitancy among Southern Republicans.

Insurgent efforts had begun by 1868, when groups such as the KKK first used political terror to prevent black and white Republicans from participating in Congressional Reconstruction. Except for the presidential races in Louisiana and Georgia, this intimidation failed, though hundreds of Republicans died and many more were victimized. But such violence did not stop

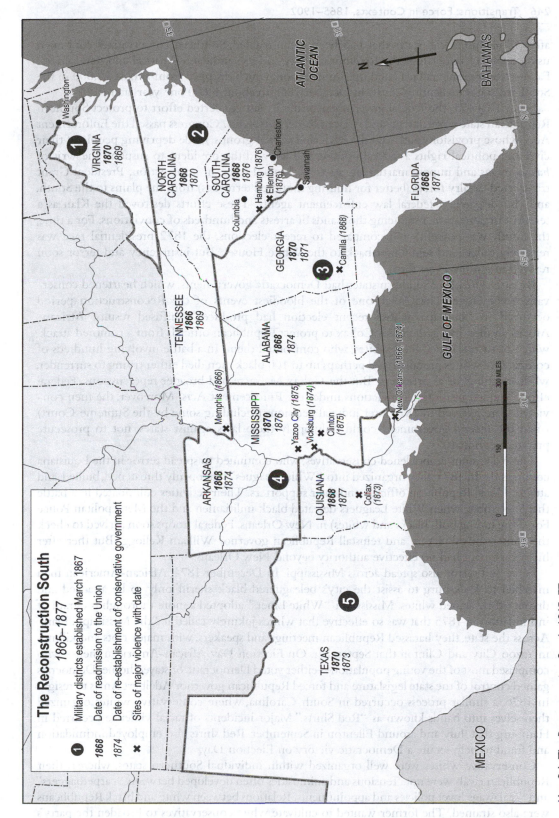

The Reconstruction South
1865–1877

1	Military districts established March 1867
1868	Date of readmission to the Union
1874	Date of re-establishment of conservative government
✕	Sites of major violence with date

Washington

VIRGINIA
1870
1869

NORTH CAROLINA
1868
1870

SOUTH CAROLINA
1868
1876

Columbia

✕ Hamburg (1876)
✕ Ellenton (1876)
Charleston

Savannah

FLORIDA
1868
1877

GEORGIA
1870
1871

✕ Camilla (1868)

TENNESSEE
1866
1869

ALABAMA
1868
1874

✕ Memphis (1866)

MISSISSIPPI
1870
1876

✕ Yazoo City (1875)
✕ Vicksburg (1874)
✕ Clinton (1875)

ARKANSAS
1868
1874

LOUISIANA
1868
1877

✕ Colfax (1873)

✕ New Orleans (1866, 1874)

TEXAS
1870
1873

MEXICO

ATLANTIC OCEAN

BAHAMAS

GULF OF MEXICO

N

0   150   300 MILES

Map 8.1 The Reconstruction South, 1865–77

after 1868. Instead, in states that had been reconstructed, Southern conservatives continued using terror to undermine the Republican Party and its candidates for local and state offices. Falling troop numbers facilitated this intimidation, which dropped from almost 12,000 in the Southern states (excepting Texas) in October 1868 to about 6,600 one year later.

From 1870–71, the federal government made its last concerted effort to protect Southern Republican state governments and African-American rights. Congress passed the Enforcement Acts, whose provisions outlawed the KKK and similar groups, made depriving people of their civil and political rights a federal offense, and allowed the president to suspend the writ of *habeas corpus* and impose martial law in areas deemed to be in insurrection. President Grant transferred cavalry forces (better for hunting mounted terrorists) from the plains to the South, and also dispatched federal law enforcement agents. These efforts destroyed the Klan as a terrorist organization, producing thousands of arrests and hundreds of convictions. For a time, the South was peaceful, and compared to recent elections, the 1872 presidential race was relatively quiet (and sent Grant back to the White House). But insurgency and terror soon revived in a more overt form.

By early 1873, five Southern states had Democratic governments, which heartened conservatives elsewhere. That April, one of the bloodiest events of the Reconstruction period occurred in Louisiana, whose recent election had produced confused results. African-American men had gathered in Colfax to protect Republican officials from a rumored attack, which in turn alarmed local whites, who confronted them. In a battle involving hundreds of combatants, whites prevailed, and perhaps up to 100 black men died either trying to surrender, while escaping, or as prisoners. But the Colfax Massacre had broader repercussions. Federal efforts yielded just a few convictions under the Enforcement Acts. Moreover, the men convicted were released in 1874 after judicial decisions (including some by the Supreme Court) ruled the federal government could only apply these laws against states, not to prosecute private individuals.

These decisions emboldened conservatives, who continued to spread terror in the Louisiana countryside. In 1874, they organized into "White Leagues" that openly threatened, bullied, and attacked local Republican officials and their supporters. Their activities culminated in a battle that September, when White Leaguers defeated black militiamen and the Metropolitan Police Force (including both blacks and whites) in New Orleans. Federal troops soon arrived to check the conservatives' victory and reinstall Republican governor William Kellogg. But thereafter his government had no effective authority beyond New Orleans.

Force and terror also spread across Mississippi. In December 1874, African-American men marched to Vicksburg to assist the city's beleaguered black sheriff only to be attacked and driven off by armed whites. Mississippi "White Liners" adopted a more thorough program of intimidation in 1875 that was so effective that whites jokingly called it "the Mississippi Plan." Across the state, they harassed Republican meetings and speakers, with major riots and killings in Yazoo City and Clinton that September. On Election Day, African-American men—who comprised most of the voting population—either voted Democratic or stayed home. Democrats gained control of the state legislature and forced Republican governor Adelbert Ames to resign. In 1876, a similar process occurred in South Carolina, where conservative whites organized themselves into bands known as "Red Shirts." Major incidents of racial violence occurred in Hamburg that July and around Ellenton in September. Red shirts also employed intimidation and fraud to help secure a Democratic victory on Election Day.

Conservative whites were well organized within individual Southern states, whereas their Republican rivals were not. Tensions and animosities often developed between "carpetbaggers" and "scalawags" over policies and appointments. Relations between white and black Republicans were also strained. The former wanted to cultivate white conservatives to broaden the party's base and quell racial tensions, but such efforts alienated blacks. Given prejudices of the time, the only way white Republicans could fully satisfy conservatives would be by abandoning commitments to protect African-American rights. Fumblings among Southern Republicans only encouraged white conservatives' use of threats and confrontation to secure political office.

Militia and paramilitary groups were crucial to the conservatives' ultimate success, whereas Republicans were hesitant to use armed units. In the summer of 1865, Southern states began to reorganize their antebellum militia forces. Comprised of Southern white men including ex-Confederate soldiers, these could be used to repress freed men and women. Congress responded in 1867 by disbanding militias in all unreconstructed states as part of the Military Reconstruction Acts. After these states reentered the Union, the militias established by Republican governors had many black units to create a politically reliable force—one that could counter conservative militancy.

But these forces exacerbated the fears and hatred of many whites. Antebellum white Southerners had lived in fear of slave revolts, and the creation of black militia units sparked accusations that Republicans were fostering a potential race war. Such cries helped Democrats and made Republican governors tentative about employing black militiamen. Moreover, sometimes conservative paramilitary organizations such as the White Leagues and the White Liners were better armed than official militia units.

State leaders could request federal assistance to cope with conservative violence. But such help was limited and not assured. Federal troops propped up Kellogg's government after White Leaguers captured New Orleans in 1874. But the following year, President Grant denied Mississippi governor Adelbert Ames' similar request to cope with the White Liners, asserting that state governments needed to exhaust their own resources before calling for federal help. His response was indicative of changing Northern attitudes toward Reconstruction in the mid-1870s. Radical Republicans who had previously championed black rights now had another issue—fighting government corruption. Northerners in general cared much more about the West, with its apparent opportunities for wealth and success, than the South. The United States was also suffering through an economic depression in the 1870s.

These trends culminated with the presidential election of 1876. Returns from Florida, Louisiana, and South Carolina were disputed. Without them, neither Democratic candidate Samuel J. Tilden nor Republican candidate Rutherford B. Hayes could win the presidency. After weeks of negotiation, the two parties reached an agreement in January, called "the Compromise of 1877." Democrats gave the disputed electoral votes to Hayes, and Republicans agreed to withdraw federal troops from Louisiana, Florida, and South Carolina—the only Southern states where Republican governments and army garrisons remained. Republicans also pledged to refrain from any future interference in Southern affairs. The Compromise of 1877 thus ended Reconstruction. Thereafter, Democrats came to power in all the Southern states and proceeded to repress African-American rights.

The West

During Reconstruction, the West absorbed most of the U.S. Army's attention. Earlier in the century, before and during the period of Indian Removal, many writers asserted that once the last major native nations in the East moved West, indigenous peoples would no longer have to cope with white settlers. Much of western North America was dubbed the "Great American Desert," too barren and arid for conventional agriculture, and some commentators envisioned a "Permanent Indian Frontier" to separate native peoples from whites. But developments soon destroyed such a notion. Reports of fertile lands sparked large-scale overland migration to the Pacific Northwest in the 1840s, the most famous route being the "Oregon

Trail." By the end of the decade, another huge stream of migrants was journeying to California as part of the Gold Rush.

By the late nineteenth century, the U.S. government sought to concentrate native peoples on reservations and have them adopt Western lifestyles. But before the Civil War, federal policies toward Indians in the West were milder. For example, neither the 1851 Treaty of Fort Laramie nor the 1853 Treaty of Fort Atkinson removed Indians from their lands but instead sought safe passage for immigrants traveling west. Native signatories agreed to peace among themselves and with the United States, allowed the federal government to build roads and facilities on their lands, and received annual gifts of goods and equipment. But local tensions nonetheless produced a number of conflicts from the late 1840s to the end of the Civil War. After violence erupted again in 1866, Congress formed a Peace Commission to treat with western peoples. (For a review of Indian wars from 1848–1865, see Chapter 5.)

The result was the 1867 Medicine Lodge Treaty and the 1868 Treaty of Fort Laramie, both of which sought to confine Indians to reservations. In the Medicine Lodge Treaty, Kiowa, Comanche, Kiowa Apache, Cheyenne, and Arapahoe peoples agreed to move to designated areas in Indian Territory north of the Red River, relinquished claims to other lands except some hunting privileges, and agreed not to harm white settlers and their property or oppose construction of forts and railroads. The federal government promised to keep unauthorized whites off reservations, to distribute goods and equipment, and provide teachers to help Indians become farmers. The 1868 Fort Laramie Treaty repeated these provisions. It also created the Great Sioux Reservation (all of present-day South Dakota west of the Missouri River) and designated lands north, west, and south of it as "unceded Indian territory"—available to the Sioux and other signatory peoples for hunting but forbidden to whites. Like many treaties with native peoples, both of these ultimately failed, though the Fort Laramie Treaty established peace on the northern plains for a few years.

White expansion posed difficult decisions for Indian leaders, as it had for centuries. Resistance created the threat of military reprisals. Negotiated accommodation could maintain peace but required surrendering lands needed to support traditional ways of life. Chiefs within a nation often could not agree; some federal negotiators signed agreements with just a few chiefs and then argued that the terms applied to an entire people. Leaders who signed treaties trusted U.S. government officials to abide by stipulated terms, and were often disappointed. For example, conditions on some reservations were so bad that many Indians fled, as with Bosque Redondo in New Mexico in the 1860s. White civilians posed other problems, for numerous settlers and prospectors did not respect reservation boundaries. Such transgressions heightened tensions with native peoples, but the army had limited abilities to cope with them. If encroachments provoked a violent Indian reaction, though, white civilians would frequently demand a military response.

Reservations, also called "agencies," were the responsibility of the Bureau of Indian Affairs (BIA), particularly the agents who resided on them. Once part of the War Department, the Interior Department acquired the BIA in 1849, and its officials often bickered with army officers over native policy. Chronically underfunded, many officials were accused of corruption. Promised goods and equipment often failed to arrive on reservations in a timely manner, in sufficient quantity, or with adequate quality. Moreover, though Indians were supposed to learn farming, they were often settled on lands poorly suited for agriculture.

BIA agents also pursued policies that enflamed native animosities. In the mid-1870s, for example, officials concentrated Arizona's Apache peoples onto the San Carlos Reservation, off of lands previously promised to them. Many of these Apache groups detested each other. After a few years, some Apache chiefs led their followers off the reservation to pursue raiding, the most famous of whom was Geronimo. Such developments frustrated army officers who, lacking administrative authority over Indian agencies, could not address native grievances before they exploded into violence.

San Carlos was established in the early 1870s, not long after the 1869 announcement of President Grant's Peace Policy, which embodied the ideas of assimilation and concentration. The U.S. government would place Indian groups on reservations, where they would be protected, introduced to Christianity, and educated—particularly in how to become self-sufficient farmers. Responding to criticism of the BIA, the Peace Policy allowed humanitarian and religious groups to select or supply civilian Indian agents. But the policy also encompassed coercion: Native groups that refused to go to, or who subsequently left, reservations would be forced onto them by the army. As such, Grant's Peace Policy did not live up to its name, for hostilities with Indian peoples plagued the West for years thereafter. Nor did assimilation efforts usually succeed, for efforts to impose white Christian American culture generally reduced native groups to poverty and dependence on government assistance. But the U.S. Army did concentrate Indian nations on reservations.

The Army on the Frontier

Policing the frontier was the U.S. Army's primary peacetime mission in the nineteenth century. But the annexation of Texas, the acquisition of the Oregon Territory, and the Mexican Cession greatly expanded the area in which troops had to maintain order. The army had about 16,000 men in 1861, but the federal government then withdrew regulars from western garrisons to fight the Confederacy. Those troops were replaced by volunteers that also comprised the bulk of the Union Army. But in the West, these recruits were settlers who often had wary attitudes toward Indians, and hence a capacity to exacerbate rather than quell violence with native peoples. The worst such incident was the Sand Creek Massacre of 1864, when a Colorado unit attacked a peaceful Indian village, killing about 150–200 men, women, and children.

After the Civil War, regular Army units replaced volunteers manning western posts. In 1866, Congress initially authorized a relatively large peacetime force of 54,000. Over the next decade it slashed this figure, to slightly more than 27,000 soldiers in the 1870s. The army continued to protect settlements and travel routes, punish hostile Indians, and enforce treaties on the western frontier—which encompassed hundreds of thousands of square miles, and extremes in terrain and climate, including the high plains, deserts, and mountains. Given this vast area, cavalry units were prominent, although infantry units were also used and sometimes mounted if enough animals were available.

The army also built scores of forts, which served various functions depending upon their location. Some offered protection to white settlements, roads, and railroads. Other posts sought to defend Indians peacefully dwelling on reservations, and ostensibly to detect movement of any native groups leaving or returning to those areas. Forts also provided bases from which army units could mount campaigns to find and engage hostile bands. Many also stimulated the growth of towns.

Western native peoples, especially on the plains, were traditionally nomadic. Warriors were skilled horsemen, and a determined group could easily evade a fixed post to assault areas beyond. Hence forts were usually more effective as bases for offensive operations rather than preventing Indian attacks. Locating a mobile band of hostile Indians, however, was difficult. Troopers often took wagons to carry provisions, limiting their ability to travel away from roads or flat ground, whereas native horsemen could usually travel faster and through rougher terrain. Cavalrymen who did catch up with a hostile band sometimes fell into ambushes. Warriors used guerrilla or hit-and-run tactics, generally avoiding pitched battles and attacking only when they held a significant advantage, such as surprise, numbers, or terrain (such as holding high ground).

Army officers adopted various means to address these difficulties. As in previous native wars, troop commanders often targeted native villages and communities in reprisal campaigns, which were easier to locate than speedy bands of warriors. Phil Sheridan, for example, organized winter operations, when lack of forage greatly diminished the mobility of native horsemen and army logistics would be an advantage rather than a disadvantage. Successful officers also used Indian allies to track and help fight indigenous foes. In addition to these techniques, George Crook also became known for using mules that could travel over difficult terrain to carry provisions. These solutions, however, depended upon the intelligence and ability of individual commanders. Despite its long-standing mission on the country's frontiers, the army lacked a doctrine for fighting native peoples, and the topic was barely mentioned in the curriculum at the United States Military Academy.

Soldiers had a technological advantage over warriors, though not an overwhelming one. Artillery could have a decisive impact in battle if present, for it had to be light and durable enough to travel long distances and over rough ground. After the Civil War, all army soldiers carried breech-loading weapons (both long arms and pistols) that fired metallic cartridges, providing great improvement in handling and rate of fire over muskets. Some cavalry units used the multiple-shot Spencer carbine. In the mid-1870s, however, the army issued single-shot 1873 Springfield "trapdoor" muskets and carbines (so called because of the design of the breech). By that time, Indians could sometimes acquire (through trade or capture) modern multiple-shot rifles, including the Winchester, often regarded as the best such weapon of the era. Such armament was not universal for warriors, though. Many used older or outdated firearms such as smoothbore muskets, or even bow and arrows when firearms or ammunition were not available.

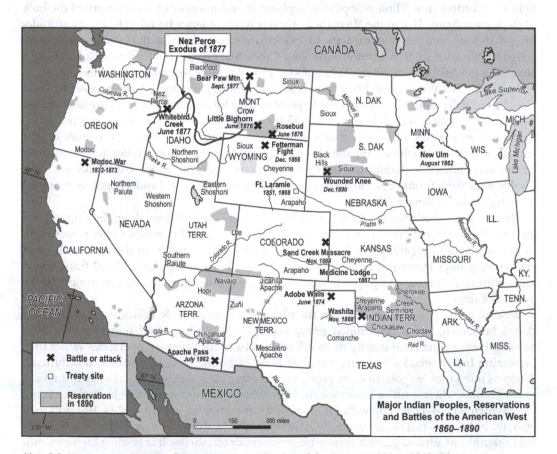

Map 8.2 Major Indian Peoples, Reservations, and Battles of the American West, 1860–90

Federal cavalrymen also carried sabers, but they usually fought as infantry that dismounted to use firearms, with every fourth trooper back behind the firing line to hold the horses.

Garrison life after the Civil War was similar to the antebellum period. Soldiers served in isolated outposts, though they frequently campaigned for weeks or months at a time. Such operations took them across rough terrain, and men and beasts might endure climactic extremes from desert heat to mountain blizzards. Life on posts was often boring and monotonous, and with garrisons regularly understaffed, training was infrequent. Until the end of the century, promotion was based solely on seniority, frustrating officers; one might have to wait over 10 years before advancing in rank. Finding and retaining enlisted men was difficult, given low pay and other opportunities beckoning in the West. Immigrants comprised a large proportion of the rank-and-file, while those who were American-born included the poor, those with difficult personal circumstances, and young men seeking adventure. Scholars such as Kevin Adams argue officers from middle- and upper-class backgrounds often looked down on enlisted men, whatever their origin. Desertion was a persistent problem: By some calculations, of more than a quarter million men who enlisted in the army between 1867 and 1891, a third deserted.

One group of soldiers generally did not desert. In 1866 Congress established the 9th and 10th Cavalry Regiments and the 24th and 25th Infantry Regiments as black units. They were similar to the regiments of the United States Colored Troops formed during the Civil War, in that white officers commanded African-American men. Within a few years, they became known as "buffalo soldiers." They were crucial during the western Indian wars, particularly in operations on the southern plains and southwest. Buffalo soldiers fought scores of battles and skirmishes, and over a dozen won the Congressional Medal of Honor for bravery in combat. Despite their successes and service, black troops suffered racism. Civilians often derided and abused them in places like the Texas frontier, while some senior officers assigned them old and inferior equipment, horses, and housing. For black men, a key reason for joining and remaining with the army was the relative lack of opportunities for them in American society, given the prejudices of the era.

Figure 8.1 **Buffalo Soldiers of the 25th Infantry**

"Buffalo Soldiers" at Fort Keogh, Montana, 1890. Note some are wearing buffalo robes.

Library of Congress, Prints and Photographs Division, LC-DIG-ppmsca-11406

The Last Indian Wars: The Pacific Northwest

A number of conflicts had ravaged the Oregon and Washington Territories from the late 1840s into the 1850s as white immigration increased. The region was then at peace until northern Paiutes and Shoshonis began raiding white settlements in 1864, beginning the Snake War. When he arrived with regular Army units in late 1866, George Crook used techniques that also proved effective in later conflicts: pack mules to carry provisions over difficult terrain, Indian allies to track his foes and fight them with regulars, and relentlessly driving his forces after hostile bands to deny enemies time to rest and recuperate. Crook personally led over a dozen operations that, by late 1868, induced the Paiutes to sue for peace.

The best known conflicts in the Pacific Northwest were the Modoc War and the Nez Perce War. In late 1872, a band of Modoc Indians, unhappy with their reservation, left to return to their homelands on the California-Oregon border. When army troops confronted them in November, they escaped and killed some settlers before fleeing to the lava beds south of Tule Lake. In January 1873, army troops failed to force out the estimated 60 warriors and their families, after which federal officials tried negotiations. This led to disaster in April when Modoc leaders assassinated the commanding general leading the peace talks, Edward Canby. The Modocs then escaped following a second attempt to capture them. Thereafter, one group abandoned the rest, was captured, and agreed to hunt down the others. The Modoc War ended in June 1873 after six months, long enough to fuel criticism of Grant's Peace Policy.

Relative to the Modoc, the American media expressed great sympathy for the plight of the Nez Perce. Most had moved onto reservations, but some refused, and government officials applied great pressure on them to sell their lands. In 1877, these last Nez Perce reluctantly complied, but as they were traveling to a reservation, a group of angry warriors attacked some settlers. Then in June an expedition of federal cavalry and local volunteers precipitated (and lost) the Battle of White Bird Canyon, beginning the Nez Perce War.

Over the next three-and-a-half months, the Nez Perce fled Oregon east over the Rocky Mountains to the Montana plains, trying to reach Canada—about 1,700 miles. The general of the main pursuit forces, O. O. Howard, struggled to catch them. When U.S. troops did so, Nez Perce warriors either repelled attacks or escaped with their families. Finally in September, forces commanded by Nelson A. Miles advanced from southern Montana and found the Nez Perce about 40 miles from the Canadian border. After warriors won a defensive victory at the Battle of the Bear Paw Mountains, Miles besieged the native camp. A few days later about 400 Nez Perce led by Chief Joseph surrendered, while another 300 escaped to Canada. More than 100 likely died during the war, including women and children.

Compared to the Modoc and Nez Perce conflicts, the Bannock War received relatively little media attention. In 1878 Howard more successfully coordinated his troops, who displayed greater tactical prowess against Bannock and Pauite marauders. The main hostile band was broken up in July, though some warriors did not surrender until the fall. But no Indian groups took up arms again. By 1880 the army, with aid from territorial militia, had subjugated the native peoples of the Pacific Northwest.

The Last Indian Wars: The Southwest

Before 1861, conflicts had erupted with Mescalero Apache and the Navajo peoples in western Texas and New Mexico. By the time the Civil War ended, these hostilities were over, but a new set had begun called "the Apache Wars," which featured the Chiricahua Apaches in the

Arizona Territory (created in 1863 from the western half of New Mexico Territory). After 1869, army officers implementing Grant's Peace Policy created many stations where Indians seeking peace could relocate and obtain food. But in April 1871, Tucson residents furious at ongoing native raids assaulted one, slaughtering between 80 and 150 peaceful Apaches at the Camp Grant Massacre. In 1871–72 the Grant administration dispatched federal officials to Arizona. They negotiated settlements with recalcitrant native groups who agreed to peace and to move onto reservations.

But Apache depredations continued, with some perpetrated by warriors living on reservations. George Crook, Arizona's regional commander since 1871, began operations against remaining hostile bands in 1872–73. Launched during the winter, when lack of provisions would hinder enemy movement, he dispatched multiple forces to scour the Tonto Basin and its surrounding mountains. He employed the proven techniques from the Snake War, using Indian allies to track and help fight enemy warriors, and mules instead of horses and wagons to carry supplies. The resulting engagements killed scores of warriors. In the spring, native bands surrendered, with thousands of Apache and Yavapais moving to camps and reservations by year's end.

Peace in Arizona only lasted a few years, and in the interim, Apache warriors raided settlements and roads in Mexico's northern provinces. In the late 1870s, relocation of disparate native peoples onto the San Carlos Reservation drove the Mimbres Apache chief Victorio to take up arms. From September 1879 to October 1880, his warriors marauded in New Mexico, Texas, and Chihuahua. They often fought U.S. cavalry (particularly buffalo soldiers of the Ninth and Tenth Cavalry), but Mexican militiamen with Indian allies killed Victorio and defeated his band in Chihuahua.

The last stage of the Apache Wars began in late 1881. Many Chiricahua and Warm Springs Apache left San Carlos following a botched army attempt to arrest a native mystic. Fleeing across the border, Geronimo and his warriors raided settlements and fought off troops in northern Mexico, New Mexico, and Arizona in early 1883. George Crook, recently returned from an assignment on the northern plains, dispatched forces against marauding Apache bands, which defeated one group in Mexico. Negotiations followed, and hostile chiefs surrendered at San Carlos Reservation until early 1884. In May 1885, however, Geronimo fled again. Eluding army forces for months, he agreed to surrender in early 1886—and immediately escaped from an escort with a few dozen followers. Crook was soon relieved of command, and his replacement, Nelson Miles, dispatched an expedition to locate Geronimo. But Miles also banished the Chiricahua and Warm Springs peoples to Florida. Once informed of this development, Geronimo surrendered in September 1886 on the condition he could join his family in Florida. With his submission, the Apache Wars—and native resistance to U.S. authority in the southwest—ended.

The Last Indian Wars: The Plains to 1875

The Great Plains encompasses a vast area and numerous native groups. In the mid-nineteenth century, Sioux peoples predominated north of the Platte River, and the Lakota (or western Sioux) were often the U.S. Army's most prominent foe. South of the Arkansas River, the most feared peoples were the Comanche and the Kiowa. The Cheyenne and Arapahoe were prevalent on the central plains, though their northern bands tended to ally with the Lakota, the southern ones with the Comanche and Kiowa. Some native groups were friendly to the United States and assisted army campaigns as scouts, such as the Crow and the Pawnees.

As with the northwest and the southwest, plains Indian wars began before 1861. The army had to pursue various campaigns to reestablish a tense peace after the Grattan Massacre of

1854. Violence exploded again during the Civil War, beginning with the Great Sioux Uprising of 1862 in Minnesota, followed by the 1864 Sand Creek Massacre in Colorado. Federal negotiators established a fragile truce on the plains in the fall 1865, but soon violence exploded again.

The opening of Montana goldmines and the Bozeman Trail through the Powder River country, along with construction of new army forts to protect travelers, had upset many Lakota bands. In the summer of 1866 raids along the Trail began Red Cloud's War, also known as the Powder River War (Red Cloud was the most prominent of the hostile Lakota chiefs). Attacks culminated on December 21 in the Fetterman Massacre. Over 1,500 warriors lured Captain William Fetterman and a force of 80 men out of Fort Phil Kearny into a trap, killing everyone in his command. Civilian traffic all but stopped along the Bozeman Trail in 1867, and military units traveled in large convoys for security. The army suspended a planned campaign for that summer due to the dispatch of Congress' Peace Commission, but Lakota and Cheyenne warriors attacked again in early August, surprising isolated groups outside Fort C. F. Smith (the Hayfield Fight) and Fort Phil Kearny (the Wagon Box Fight). In these battles, outnumbered soldiers defended improvised positions for hours using newly issued breech-loading rifles until rescued.

In the spring of 1867, an army campaign farther south provoked a new conflict called "Hancock's War." Winfield Scott Hancock's column was supposed to "awe" native bands on the southern plains and induce them to remain peaceful. When his troops approached a village at Pawnee Ford, Indians fled. Hancock interpreted their reaction as preparation for war, and burned the village. For the next few months Sioux and Cheyenne warriors retaliated by ravaging travel routes and harassing forts between the Platte and Arkansas Rivers. Hancock's War helped prompt Congress to form the Peace Commission, which then negotiated the 1867 Medicine Lodge Treaty and the 1868 Treaty of Fort Laramie. The latter ended Red Cloud's War, created the Great Sioux Reservation, and conceded to all major Lakota demands: The United States abandoned the Bozeman Trail, removed forts from the Powder River country, and placed the region in "unceded Indian territory" from which whites were banned.

The Fort Laramie Treaty calmed the northern plains for a few years. Not so the Medicine Lodge Treaty. In the summer of 1868, violence involving Cheyennes erupted in western Kansas. Moreover, Kiowa and Comanche raids into Texas and Mexico continued: Their warriors had done so for generations but were supposed to stop. To chastise belligerent bands, Philip Sheridan organized a multipronged campaign against their winter camps in Indian Territory. One column advanced eastward from New Mexico, and another southeast from Colorado, but it was George Custer's force moving south out of Kansas that fought the major engagement of the campaign: the Battle of the Washita. Ironically, he attacked the camp belonging to Black Kettle, who had continued to work for peace since escaping from the Sand Creek Massacre.

At dawn on November 27, 1868, Custer divided his forces to assault the village from multiple directions. Troopers surprised the inhabitants, killing perhaps a hundred—including Black Kettle—and capturing about 50 women and children. When warriors from camps further downriver responded, Custer withdrew, destroying Indian supplies and hundreds of ponies. After Washita, operations continued into 1869, which were particularly difficult on draft animals who died in large numbers. But the Army's willingness to campaign in winter, and its ability to destroy necessary provisions and vital livestock, convinced thousands of Indians to submit and report to the agencies.

Violence nonetheless continued. Kiowa and Comanche warriors raiding into Texas exploited Grant's Peace Policy, which barred army troops not on reservations from entering Indian

Territory. After some hostile chiefs were arrested, federal officials promised to release them if depredations ceased. The winter of 1872–73 was fairly peaceful, and the chiefs were freed the following autumn. But by that time, white hunters moving west had decimated the buffalo herds that were crucial for southern plains Indians, while supplies arriving at the agencies had been poor and inadequate. In the spring of 1874, Kiowa, Comanche, and Cheyenne warriors flooded out of Indian Territory to ravage settlements and travelers in Texas and Kansas, beginning the Red River War. In response, the Grant administration allowed army troops onto, and to control, reservations.

That summer, Sheridan directed five army columns toward tributaries of the Red River in the Texas panhandle and nearby Indian Territory, particularly the Staked Plains, where hostile bands remained. The troop movements were not well coordinated, and some bogged down due to lack of supplies. Moreover, whereas Sheridan's campaign of 1868–69 required that soldiers and beasts endure brutal cold and snow, now they suffered blazing heat and drought until the weather turned stormy, cold, and wet in the early fall. The war encompassed numerous battles from August to November. In some, troops defended wagon trains from Indian assaults, and in others soldiers attacked native forces and destroyed camps, provisions, and pony herds. The onset of winter weather and supply issues prompted the columns' return to their bases in November, having chased belligerent Indians for months and destroyed crucial supplies and livestock. Hostile bands subsequently drifted back to reservations and surrendered, the last ones submitting in mid-1875. Native peoples on the southern plains remained peaceful thereafter, and consigned themselves to life on the reservations.

The Great Sioux War and the Battle of the Little Bighorn, 1876–77

Within a year another war began. Not all peoples on the northern plains had signed the 1868 Fort Laramie Treaty, including the prominent Lakota chief Sitting Bull. Using "unceded" Indian Territory as a sanctuary, hostile bands had instead raided settlements and harassed friendly and reservation-dwelling Indians. But the catalyst for the Great Sioux War of 1876–77, also known as "Sitting Bull's War," was the discovery of gold in the Black Hills within the Great Sioux Reservation. Army troops tried to keep out prospectors, but thousands invaded the region. The federal government offered to buy the Black Hills, but talks with the Sioux, who regarded the area as sacred, broke down. With frustrations rising, in December 1875 the Bureau of Indian Affairs ordered all Indians abandon the unceded territory and report to reservations by January 31, 1876. Given short notice and poor seasonal weather, few complied.

In February, the army prepared to scour the region between the Yellowstone River and the Bighorn Mountains, west of the Powder River. Once again, Phil Sheridan planned multiple columns for a winter campaign, but transportation and supply difficulties delayed coordinated operations until the spring. In April, John Gibbon's column began advancing east along the Yellowstone, while in May troops under George Crook moved north along the Bighorn Mountains as another force commanded by Alfred Terry proceeded west from Fort Abraham Lincoln on the Missouri River; George Custer's Seventh Cavalry Regiment comprised the bulk of the latter.

Meanwhile, numerous Indians abandoned reservations to join Sitting Bull and other Lakota and Cheyenne bands in the unceded territory. But contrary to typical practice, these bands all joined together. A native camp usually consisted of perhaps a few hundred men, women, and children, and was located a good distance from others to ensure livestock herds would have adequate grazing and hunters could find game. But given the threat posed by the U.S. Army, these peoples concentrated closer for mutual defense in a set of neighboring camps that totaled between 10,000–15,000 people; at least 1,500 but perhaps as many as 4,000 were warriors.

Figure 8.2 Custer's 1874 Expedition on the Plains

In 1874, George Custer led an expedition into the Black Hills. Reports soon spread that gold had been discovered, prompting the subsequent rush of prospectors into the region. This photograph of the 1874 expedition indicates the wagons, horses, and other equipment used by U.S. Army troops used on large campaigns in the West.

The Denver Public Library, Western History Collection, [X-31704]

Because so many Indians quickly taxed local resources, these camps moved every few days. But they exploited their numbers to launch an attack. On June 17, warriors surprised Crook's command at the Battle of the Rosebud. After more than six hours the attackers withdrew, technically leaving U.S. forces with a tactical victory. But operationally, the Lakota and Cheyenne prevailed, for Crook was so shaken by the battle that he withdrew south, and his command played no role in the subsequent battle later that month.

A few days later, Terry and Gibbon's forces met on the Yellowstone River. They had no knowledge of the Rosebud battle, but had received reports of an Indian camp on the Little Bighorn. To create a trap, Gibbon sent his infantry up the Bighorn River toward the Little Bighorn, while Custer's faster cavalry would advance all the way up the Rosebud valley, move west, and then descend down the Little Bighorn valley from the opposite direction. But Custer cut west a day early, and precipitated the Battle of the Little Bighorn without waiting for Gibbon's troops. The result was one of the worst disasters in U.S. military history.

Custer had planned to rest his men, but believing his movements had been detected, spurred his troopers to attack on June 25. After first dispatching 125 men under Frederick Benteen south to look for Indians, he sent Marcus Reno with 112 soldiers across the Little Bighorn to advance north and attack. Custer kept 210 troopers and continued moving north over the bluffs on the east side of the river. Apparently he saw Reno's detachment charge the southern edge of the Indian encampments (which extended three miles downstream) before dispatching a message for Benteen to return with ammunition and moving his own force out of sight to attack farther north.

What Custer did not witness were swarms of warriors who checked Reno's advance and drove him back across the river, a retreat that cost him a quarter of his men. Lakota and Cheyenne farther downstream then crossed the river and surrounded Custer's force on the heights. Neither he nor any of his men survived their "last stand." Meanwhile, Benteen's command returned and reinforced Reno's troopers on high ground. That force repelled additional attacks until the next day, when Gibbon's infantry drove the warriors away.

Box 8.2   An Indian Account of Custer's Last Stand

Lakota Chief Red Horse was one of the combatants at the Battle of Little Bighorn. His account of the battle was recorded in 1881, and the following section describes the conduct of soldiers commanded by Custer at their "Last Stand."

> The soldiers charged the Sioux camp about noon. The soldiers were divided, one party charging right into the camp. After driving these soldiers across the river, the Sioux charged the different soldiers [i.e., Custer's] below, and drive them in confusion; these soldiers became foolish, many throwing away their guns and raising their hands, saying, "Sioux, pity us; take us prisoners." The Sioux did not take a single soldier prisoner, but killed all of them; none were left alive for even a few minutes. These different soldiers discharged their guns but little. I took a gun and two belts off two dead soldiers; out of one belt two cartridges were gone, out of the other five.
>
> The Sioux took the guns and cartridges off the dead soldiers and went to the hill on which the soldiers were, surrounded and fought them with the guns and cartridges of the dead soldiers. Had the soldiers not divided I think they would have killed many Sioux. The different soldiers [i.e., Custer's battalion] that the Sioux killed made five brave stands. Once the Sioux charged right in the midst of the different soldiers and scattered them all, fighting among the soldiers hand to hand.
>
> (Garrick Mallery, "Picture Writing of the American Indians,"
> *Tenth Annual Report of the Bureau of American Ethnology, 1888–89,*
> Washington: Government Printing Office, 1893, pp. 563–66)

Reports of Custer's defeat shocked the American public. Ever since, commentators have speculated on his decisions and the performance of Reno and Benteen. But Custer's decisions accorded with prior experiences during the Indian wars. Dividing one's force and attacking a much larger enemy without adequate reconnaissance was foolish against a foe prepared to stand and fight. But against a smaller target that would flee at the sign of danger, and to prevent its escape, such tactics were appropriate—as demonstrated by Custer's own performance at the Battle of Washita. At the Little Bighorn, his biggest failing was an inability to perceive a tactical situation different from what he had assumed.

After Custer's demise, the army rushed reinforcements to the region. Little happened for the remainder of the summer, as U.S. commanders displayed a newfound caution. But Lakota and Cheyenne bands could no longer sustain themselves together in one location. They had dispersed when new army operations began in the fall. Troops under Nelson Miles built a camp on the Tongue River near the Yellowstone and then chased Lakota peoples in the region. On November 25, cavalry led by Ranald Mackenzie attacked and destroyed the camp of Cheyenne chief Dull Knife. At the Battle of Wolf Mountains on January 8, 1877, Miles' forces repelled a Lakota and Cheyenne attack led by Crazy Horse, who had been a prominent leader at the battles of the Rosebud and Little Bighorn. Thereafter, most native bands surrendered. The main exception was Sitting Bull and his people, who first fled into Canada. But lack of game and other resources prompted them to return and submit to U.S. authorities in 1881.

Following the war, the federal government pushed Indian groups out of the Black Hills to other areas. But the conflict had an epilogue. By 1890, poor conditions had aroused resentment on the reservations, and a religious movement known as the Ghost Dance had become popular. Some Lakota favored a more militant variant that alarmed federal authorities. Sitting Bull died during a botched arrest attempt, and soldiers' attempts to disarm a group of Lakota warriors instead produced a battle on December 29, 1890. About 150 Lakota men, women, and children died in the Battle of Wounded Knee or the Wounded Knee Massacre, as well as 25 soldiers. Thousands of other Lakota then fled to a camp on White Clay Creek. Surrounding them with thousands of troops, Nelson Miles used a combination of threats and diplomacy to induce surrender. Wounded Knee is generally regarded as the last engagement of the Indian wars.

Evolving U.S. Military Institutions

Since its founding, the United States had relied upon a small regular Army and militia system for its military needs. Maintained by the individual states, the latter was supposed to impart military skills to male citizens who could then be mobilized in the case of a major war. The system raised hundreds of regiments to fight the Civil War, though mandatory peacetime militia training was essentially defunct by the mid-nineteenth century. Volunteer militia units, though, had remained active in some American cities. Interest in them plunged just after the Civil War but revived in the 1870s. Volunteer militia units then began adopting the name "National Guard," the term by which they are now known.

In the late 1800s, the federal government neither financed nor controlled them. But many state governments devoted more funding to their National Guard organizations and made efforts to better organize, administer, and train them. One reason was to cope with labor unrest. For example, over a dozen states called out Guard units to cope with the Great Railroad Strike of 1877, and governors in the Northeast and Midwest were more prone to use Guardsmen for this purpose. In the South, state officials often called out the Guard to prevent race-related violence such as mob lynchings.

In the early twentieth century, after the Spanish-American War had revealed mobilization problems, the federal government adopted reforms that funded and imposed common standards upon National Guard organizations, making these units true first-line reserves that could operate with the regular U.S. Army. Decades before then, though, officers were considering how to make the regular Army more professional. Many felt high Civil War casualties stemmed in part from the inexperience of civilians who had been awarded commissions to lead volunteer units. But part of this effort reflected the ending of the Indian wars—which had been the regular Army's prominent traditional peacetime function—spurring officers to find a new institutional purpose.

After the Civil War, William Tecumseh Sherman took the first steps toward promoting greater professionalization of the U.S. Army. He helped revive the Artillery School in 1868, and as Commanding General from 1869–83, he created the School of Application for Infantry and Cavalry at Fort Leavenworth in 1881. He also helped form a voluntary association of officers known as the Military Service Institute. The Institute published a well-regarded journal that inspired the creation of other military professional periodicals such as the *Infantry Journal* and the *Journal of the U.S. Artillery*. After Sherman retired, professionalization efforts continued. In 1890, the army required all officers seeking promotion up to the rank of major to pass examinations that tested their military knowledge. Shortly thereafter, the army imposed regular character and efficiency reports for all officers.

For the late nineteenth-century U.S. Army, professionalization meant improving its capacity to employ conventional military forces. In both America and Europe, the model to emulate was Prussia. Its powerful and well-trained army had quickly defeated enemy forces in the Austro-Prussian (1866) and Franco-Prussian (1870–1) Wars. Compared to the United States, the Prussian Army had a more rigorous system of training and greater control over military policy. While attractive to American officers, these circumstances reflected important differences between the two countries. Prussia had a much more autocratic and conservative society than the United States, and shared borders with neighbors that possessed large standing armies.

Of the two services, the U.S. Navy underwent more dramatic changes in the late nineteenth century. During the Civil War, it expanded to about 700 vessels and had adopted modern technology such as steam power, rifled cannons, and ironclads. Afterward the navy returned to the stations system, and by 1870 a money-conscious Congress had reduced it to about 50 older wooden ships that relied upon sails and carried smoothbore guns. These vessels were cheaper to maintain and adequate for the navy's traditional peacetime mission.

But attitudes about the navy soon changed. In the late 1800s, imperialist ideas became very popular in the United States and in Europe. Some argued that an industrialized country needed reliable access to overseas foreign markets. One variant, Social Darwinism, saw global affairs as a competition wherein peoples had to dominate others to avoid being subjugated themselves, and often embodied racist views. A more benevolent but still ethnocentric view espoused bringing the benefits of Christianity and Western culture to the peoples of Africa and Asia. Whatever their specific beliefs, American imperialists called for a larger and modern navy to project power worldwide and safeguard U.S. interests.

They soon found a champion in naval officer Alfred Thayer Mahan, author of numerous works, including the 1890 book *The Influence of Sea Power Upon History*. Known as the "prophet of American navalism," he linked successful commerce with a large navy. Mahan advocated building large fleets of big warships that could dominate international sea lanes, and overseas bases to support them. His works took a skewed view of history, tending to take the experiences of the British as normative and ignoring technological developments, but they were popular among the general public and naval officers, both in the United States and abroad.

With such support, the U.S. Navy underwent significant changes in the late nineteenth century. Rear Admiral Stephen B. Luce championed professional development, helping to establish the U.S. Naval Institute in 1873 and the Naval War College in 1884. In the 1880s, Congress authorized funds to build modern warships. The first vessels were cruisers designed to support the traditional peacetime missions of commerce protection and diplomatic support. But from 1889 to 1893, Secretary of the Navy Benjamin F. Tracy pushed to construct fleets of big ships and acquire overseas bases. Congress agreed to build nine battleships by 1898, the year the Spanish-American War began.

The Spanish-American War, 1898–99

By 1898, the only colonies remaining in Spain's once-expansive Latin American empire were Cuba and Puerto Rico. The rest had won their independence in the Wars of Liberation that ended in 1825, though Spain still controlled the Philippines in the western Pacific. In 1895, a guerrilla war began in Cuba, with rebels under the leadership of Máximo Gomez fighting for independence. To undermine support for them, Spanish governor Valeriano Weyler isolated much of the rural population in camps (one of the first modern uses of concentration camps), and disease killed thousands.

United States concern steadily mounted. For decades, economic and business interests had sought a greater American presence in Cuba. But the guerrilla war aroused humanitarian fears for its people, whereas imperialists saw the opportunity to exploit Spain's troubles and establish an overseas U.S. empire. "Yellow journalism" also played a role, with many newspapers brazenly calling for American intervention in Cuba. The chance came after the visiting battleship USS *Maine* exploded on February 15, 1898, while in Havana harbor. The reasons for the blast remain uncertain to this day, but the press immediately blamed Spain, and demands for confrontation reached a fever pitch. After the Spanish rejected President William McKinley's call for Cuban independence, Congress authorized intervention. Spain formally declared war on April 23, and Congress reciprocated two days later.

The McKinley administration sought Spanish withdrawal from, and independence for, Cuba. It saw the war as mostly a naval conflict, with the Caribbean as the primary theater of operations. But U.S. officials envisioned attacks elsewhere, both to divert enemy forces from Cuba, and to capture other Spanish possessions that would enhance the American position at peace talks to end the war. The U.S. Navy was well prepared, for in previous years, students at the Naval War College had simulated possible war with Spain. After the *Maine* sank, naval officers

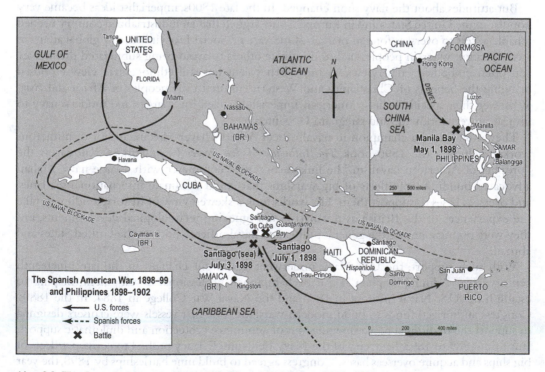

Map 8.3 The Spanish-American War, 1898–99, and Philippines, 1898–1902

quickly readied the fleet. They established five squadrons, assigning the North American Squadron under William Sampson the responsibility for Caribbean operations. But it was George Dewey's Asiatic Squadron that won the war's first battle.

The Navy Department ordered Dewey to take his ships from Hong Kong to the Philippines. Arriving on the morning of May 1, 1898, his sailors fought the Battle of Manila Bay and destroyed the Spanish fleet. The six U.S. warships were cruisers or smaller, but bigger than the seven Spanish vessels commanded by Patricio Montojo. The American ships were of metal construction, had more and bigger guns than their adversaries, and had crews with better training and morale. Dewey found the Spanish ships anchored off the Cavite peninsula. By noon, Montojo had lost three warships, and shortly thereafter he surrendered. Dewey's sailors then destroyed the remaining enemy vessels and captured the naval base at Cavite. His squadron had won an impressive victory that destroyed Spanish naval power in the Pacific and made Dewey a hero in the United States. But any extension of American power into the Philippines would have to wait until the arrival of troops.

In the Caribbean, Sampson's North Atlantic Squadron began the war by blockading the northern coast of Cuba. When news came that a fleet commanded by Pascual de Cervera was crossing the Atlantic, Sampson took his ships to Puerto Rico to deny Spanish warships access to their base at San Juan; other U.S. vessels continued to blockade Havana. In May, Cervera, searching for a port, put in at Santiago on Cuba's southern coast. By June, Sampson's squadron arrived outside the harbor, trapping Cervera's warships. But defenses including fortresses and mines made any American attempt to enter the harbor dangerous. Nor could Sampson leave, for the Spanish squadron was what is sometimes called "a fleet-in-being": a threat if left unchecked. For help, the navy looked to the army.

The U.S. Army's war had not gone well. Top commanders initially assumed its role would be restricted to manning coastal defenses against possible Spanish raids and perhaps landing a few troops in Cuba to assist the rebels. Weeks before the war began, they sought to increase the army's size along expansible lines so that regular officers would command new recruits, many of whom they expected to come from National Guard units. Congress rejected this idea, though it enlarged the regular Army from almost 40,000 men to 67,000.

Instead, it authorized the president to call up National Guardsmen as volunteers who would serve in their own state-organized units. Army leaders thought McKinley would mobilize only modest numbers of Guardsmen but he instead called up 115,000 in April 1898 and another 75,000 in May. About 200,000 men served as volunteers during the war, most in state units, but a few in federally organized ones. The Spanish-American War was the last time in U.S. history that the majority of mobilized men served in units organized by the individual states— and most of them never left the country.

These decisions caused problems. The existing army bureaucracy had maintained a prewar establishment of 28,000, and was not prepared to support forces that ultimately exceeded 250,000. Men arriving at army training camps found confusion and supply and housing shortages. States often failed to completely outfit their Guard units, exacerbating the army's logistical problems. Numerous Guardsmen also proved medically unfit for duty or refused to volunteer, prompting units to recruit untrained men—many of whom were later disqualified for medical reasons.

Santiago de Cuba, 1898

As the army coped with mobilization and supply problems, the McKinley administration changed its operational role in the war. Initial ideas focused on dispatching just a few thousand troops to support Cuban guerrillas, a mission assigned to the 5th Corps concentrating in Tampa under the command of William Shafter. Shortly after the war began, officials contemplated a larger landing and assault upon Havana. After Cervera's fleet was discovered at Santiago, the administration ordered Shafter's force to land near the city. But its mission was unclear. Navy commanders assumed these troops would help reduce defenses guarding the harbor entrance, while Shafter and army officers believed they should capture the city first, then the harbor.

Logistical problems, such as congestion on the rail line into Tampa and difficulties finding shipping, delayed the 5th Corps' departure. Shafter's 17,000 men sailed in mid-June. Most were regular Army soldiers, but there was one volunteer unit raised under federal (not state) auspices: the 1st U.S. Volunteer Cavalry Regiment, also known as the "Rough Riders." Its officers included Theodore Roosevelt, who had recently resigned as Assistant Secretary of the Navy to fight. By the end of the month Shafter's force had landed on Cuba's southern shore and was advancing west toward Santiago.

On July 1, the Battle of Santiago began. The Spanish had established defenses on heights just east of the city, particularly San Juan and Kettle hills, as well as at El Caney farther north. Shafter sent some forces to capture the latter position, which would then join soldiers assigned to assault the former. El Caney's defenders put up a stiff resistance. Meanwhile, exposed American troops waiting to advance up San Juan and Kettle hills took casualties from Spanish fire. Their officers decided to attack without reinforcements, and advancing up the heights drove off the Spanish, who retreated into the city. Accounts of the battle gave much credit for the U.S. victory to Roosevelt and the Rough Riders. But they were only one of the assaulting units that day, which also included buffalo soldiers of the Ninth and Tenth Cavalry regiments.

Despite this tactical success, Shafter was worried. The Spanish still held Santiago, and he doubted his ability to take it. Much of the victory stemmed from greater numbers—U.S. troops outnumbered the Spanish by more than 10 to 1 at both El Caney and San Juan and Kettle hills— although American artillery and machine-gun fire had proved effective. But Shafter's troops had taken over 1,300 casualties, mostly from enemy infantry using modern Mauser rifles, and the Spanish still had thousands of troops nearby; Shafter was also concerned about his supplies. But the Battle of Santiago yielded one immediate strategic result: the destruction of the Spanish fleet.

Fearing the city would soon fall, Cuba's governor-general ordered Cervera to flee. The result was the sea Battle of Santiago of July 3. The Spanish had six warships to the American seven, but the latter included four battleships, whereas Cervera's largest vessels were cruisers. Moreover, the Spanish ships had to exit the harbor one at a time. Two of Cervera's cruisers briefly escaped to the west, but in the end, Sampson's warships sank the entire Spanish fleet. Over 450 Spanish sailors were killed or wounded, and around 1,700 captured. In contrast, only one American sailor died, and only a few U.S. vessels sustained minor damage. Moreover, the victory saved the U.S. Navy from a strategic dilemma. Reports indicated the Spanish were preparing another fleet to challenge Dewey in the Philippines. With Cervera's fleet destroyed, the navy could now dispatch reinforcements to the Pacific.

Box 8.3   An Account of the Sea Battle of Santiago

The *Vizcaya* was one of the Spanish cruisers destroyed by Sampson's North Atlantic Squadron at the sea Battle of Santiago on July 3, 1898. Joseph Mason Reeves, who served as an engineer on the USS *Oregon* during the battle (and later became an admiral) described the *Vizcaya*'s end in the following letter:

> I never dreamed of such a terrific cannonade as the first few minutes of that scrap. . . .
> The rapid fire guns of the Spanish fleet were going fast enough but, great guns they
> were going screatch [sic], shriek over head. The result of ours we have since learned

Figure 8.3 Wreck of the *Vizcaya* After the Battle of Santiago, 1898
Library of Congress, Prints and Photographs Division, LC-D4–21538

was too terrible to relate. The ALMIRANTE and the VIZCAYA are simply torn and ripped to pieces: the VIZCAYA the OREGON destroyed almost alone and she did it most mercilessly. A 13" shell tore through her bows, she turned and ran for the beach and then 13", 8", 6", and 6pdr tore her from stem to stern. She was afire in a dozen places a guns crew could not stand up at her guns, three of her magazines blew up, a torpedo exploded in the tube, she was afire forward and aft: her loss of life must have been frightful, and the OREGON never once stopped nor turned she kept straight on for there was another ahead and there were others of our fleet behind.

(Letter from Joseph Mason Reeves to his mother, July 7, 1898, currently available at www. spanamwar.com courtesy of Thomas Wildenberg)

Meanwhile, despite his anxieties, Shafter demanded the Spanish surrender Santiago and began a siege. His initial demand was rebuffed, but it led to a truce and negotiations. On July 17, to Shafter's surprise, the acting Spanish commander surrendered not just the city but all of eastern Cuba! Whatever Shafter's concerns about supplies, the Spanish were in worse straits. They only had about 8,000 troops to face both U.S. conventional troops as well as Cuban guerrillas (because of the latter, few Spanish soldiers were available to defend El Caney and San Juan and Kettle hills). Shafter's bold demands exploited a dire situation for the Spanish, producing dramatic gains. Combat operations now ceased for the 5th Corps. But until peace was established, it had to care for both Cubans and Spanish in the region, and in the interim, disease felled large numbers of American soldiers.

At the end of July, U.S. forces invaded Puerto Rico, and throughout the summer, American troops also arrived in the Philippines to besiege Manila (addressed below). But the surrender of eastern Cuba crushed the Spanish war effort. On August 12, both sides signed a protocol ending fighting until a formal peace treaty was signed, which occurred on December 10, 1898. The Treaty of Paris granted Cuba independence and ceded Puerto Rico, Guam, and the Philippines to American control. Spain received $20 million in compensation. Despite protests from anti-imperialist groups, the Senate ratified the treaty in early 1899, formally ending the war. Much of the American public reveled in the victory, one that stemmed from superior U.S. naval capabilities. The army, too, had made a notable contribution, though its performance was marred by problems with logistics and disease.

Though Cuba was nominally independent, the United States exerted great influence over the country for decades to come. The other former Spanish colonies acquired from the treaty now provided the foundation for an overseas American empire, which was not universally welcomed. In fact, as war with Spain ended, another began with an enemy who preferred political independence rather than switching rule from one imperialist power to another.

The Philippine-American War, 1899–1902

The Philippines consist of thousands of islands spread across hundreds of miles in the western Pacific. The capital of Manila is on Luzon, the largest island in the north of the archipelago. Like Cuba, the Philippines had its own independence movement in the 1890s, and the Spanish had banished its primary leader, Emilio Aguinaldo. But he returned once the Spanish-American War began. In the spring and summer of 1898, Aguinaldo helped form a government that declared independence and extended control over much of the Philippines. The Filipinos also organized an army of about 13,000 men that besieged Spanish forces in Manila. Meanwhile, the McKinley administration, reacting to Dewey's destruction of the Spanish Pacific fleet, sent U.S. troops to the Philippines: 15,000 by August.

The rebels initially welcomed the Americans, allowing them into positions along their siege lines. But they became wary when the United States did not acknowledge Filipino independence. Suspicions grew after the Battle of Manila (not to be confused with the Battle of Manila Bay, won by Dewey's Asiatic Squadron the prior May). On August 13 (word had not yet reached the Philippines of the August 12 peace protocol), Filipino and American forces assaulted the city. By secret arrangement, however, Spanish troops only offered token resistance against U.S. attackers. At day's end, American troops controlled Manila—but did not allow in their Filipino allies. Later the Treaty of Paris exacerbated tensions further, as it denied Filipinos independence. The final break came in early 1899. On February 4, with the U.S. Senate on the verge of ratifying the treaty, fighting erupted between United States and Filipino forces around Manila.

Over the next few months, U.S. forces commanded by Elwell S. Otis drove the Filipino army away from the city and captured much of Luzon. Although outnumbered 40,000 to 20,000, American troops were better led than the Filipinos, who had no traditions or experience with conventional units. But in May, Otis' campaign stalled, partly due to the onset of the wet season and the spread of fatigue and disease among his soldiers. Moreover, volunteers comprised most of his army, and their enlistments were expiring. By then Congress had voted to maintain the regular Army at 65,000 men, and authorized President McKinley to raise 35,000 more volunteers. Unlike most volunteer units (but like the Rough Riders), these would be organized by the federal government, not the states. But reinforcements did not start arriving in the Philippines until the fall. In October, Otis resumed offensive operations, and by November U.S. forces had broken the Filipino army, whose remnants scattered into the mountains at the northern end of Luzon. American troops then controlled the rest of the island and numerous others as well.

The nature of the war now changed. Aguinaldo and other rebel leaders abandoned conventional forces and instead contested U.S. rule with an insurgency and guerrilla operations. They sought to maintain resistance in the hopes that a Democrat sympathetic to Filipino independence would defeat McKinley in the 1900 U.S. presidential election, or that another foreign power would intervene to assist them against the Americans. Militarily, rebels employed ambushes and hit-and-run tactics, pursued sniping and sabotage, laid traps, and fled when confronted with superior forces. Politically, they used terror to induce compliance from communities and local officials. Filipinos known to be helping U.S. forces might become victims of theft, torture, or murder. In many cases, insurgents formed "shadow governments" in towns and villages, and people who seemingly cooperated with Americans by day often worked with rebels by night.

These tactics and techniques were similar to those seen in other, later guerrilla conflicts and insurgencies. But the Philippines had regions of rough terrain such as mountains, jungles, and rice paddies. Coordinating resistance among its numerous islands was difficult, especially given U.S. Navy patrols. Hence local conditions often shaped conflict in particular regions, and in some places "guerrilla" actions were little different from criminal activity.

In response, the U.S. war effort followed a trajectory similar to changing Union attitudes during the Civil War, going from lenient to harsh. U.S. officers thought resistance was all but over after dispersing the Filipino army in late 1899. They focused on establishing civic programs to cultivate goodwill and assist the population. In the countryside, U.S. soldiers built roads, bridges, schools, and telephone and telegraph lines. The army also pursued a public health campaign to reduce smallpox and infant mortality. Many Filipinos appreciated these programs, though not the cultural arrogance and ignorance of local customs many Americans demonstrated. By mid-1900, Filipino insurgents in many areas had checked political gains made by army civic action programs. As a result, Arthur MacArthur, who replaced Otis as army commander in the Philippines in May, adopted a harsher stance toward the guerrillas, while maintaining civic programs.

To guide his policies, MacArthur invoked General Orders 100, originally issued to Union armies during the Civil War. This directive utilized prior laws and conventions of war to dictate how officers should treat civilians in occupied areas. For example, uniformed soldiers captured by U.S. troops would be treated as prisoners of war. But fighters caught in civilian clothes, or who spent much time among noncombatants, would be treated as criminals. General Orders 100 stated that at times, military necessity might inflict harm on civilians, but noncombatants and their property were to be protected if possible, and at no times should soldiers engage in cruelty.

Under MacArthur, U.S. forces pursued numerous operations to hunt down guerrilla bands. Rebel leaders were targeted for "neutralization," which could mean imprisonment, deportation, or execution. The frequency of such operations increased after McKinley won reelection in November 1900, itself a great disappointment for the insurgents. But working with the new U.S. colonial administration headed by William Taft, MacArthur also supported the Filipino Federal Party. This organization offered a political alternative to independence, with its members advocating acceptance of American rule, peace, and the goal of U.S. statehood.

By early 1901, these policies had produced results. Between the carrot of the Federal Party working with local communities, and the stick of U.S. forces hounding insurgents and their leaders, rebels in many areas laid down their arms. Moreover, the resistance suffered a great blow that March when American soldiers and Filipino scouts captured Aguinaldo himself. But the war was not over. Guerrillas remained strong and defiant in a few regions, and the army once again faced a manpower crisis: Though 70,000 soldiers were in the Philippines when 1901 began, that summer the enlistments of volunteers recruited in 1899 would expire. Moreover, the U.S. and other imperialist powers had dispatched thousands of troops to suppress China's Boxer Rebellion. Congress responded by raising the size of the regular Army to 100,000, while American military officers and civilian officials recruited thousands of Filipinos to serve as scouts or police.

In July 1901 Adna Chaffee became the top U.S. army commander in the Philippines, replacing MacArthur. By that time, fierce resistance to American rule remained on the eastern island of Samar and the Batangas province on Luzon. On September 28, rebels and villagers launched a surprise attack on a company of U.S. soldiers stationed at Balangiga, on Samar. Of 78 men, 48 died and 21 were wounded, with the survivors fleeing. The American response was harsh. Forces led by Jacob H. Smith launched retaliatory operations on Samar, while others under J. Franklin Bell pacified Batangas. U.S. soldiers chased rebels and destroyed crops, livestock, and homes. Similar to the Spanish in Cuba, they moved civilian populations into camps to isolate them from guerrillas. At one point, Smith instructed a subordinate to "kill and burn," slaying anyone who could carry a weapon. When asked to clarify, Smith indicated his criteria included males over 10 years old. U.S. forces did not actually target children in these campaigns. But at times they engaged in indiscriminate killings, and there were cases of torture and executions.

Samar and Batangas were not the first campaigns where American troops employed brutal measures. Previous cases of destroying property and relocating populations, however, had been more limited, and were employed simultaneously with both civic action programs to help communities, and political activity to persuade them to accept American rule. By the middle of 1901, these efforts had defused resistance to U.S. authority in most areas. On Samar and Batangas they had not, and coercive measures employed late that year led to rebel leaders surrendering in early 1902. Theodore Roosevelt (president since McKinley's September 1901 assassination), declared the Filipino resistance over in July.

Even as the Philippine-American War ended, a guerrilla conflict was just starting on the southern island of Mindanao with the Moros, one that would last intermittently until 1913. More immediately, the cruelty inflicted by U.S. forces had not gone unnoticed, with American media attention and the resulting the public outcry prompting Congressional investigations and court martials in 1902. These produced only mild penalties: Some junior officers received suspensions and fines for use of torture, while Littleton "Tony" Waller, Smith's subordinate who led operations on Samar, was acquitted of charges. Smith himself was convicted of a minor charge, and Roosevelt retired him. Otherwise, the violence that accompanied the genesis of the American overseas empire was soon forgotten. Over 125,000 U.S. regular or volunteer soldiers served in the Philippine-American War of 1899–1902, with 4,000 dying (mostly from illness) and another 3,000 wounded. In contrast, up to 20,000 Filipino combatants died during the conflict, and estimates of civilian deaths range into the hundreds of thousands, reflecting the impact of relocation, crop destruction, and disease.

Conclusion

In the period from 1865–1902, the United States faced a variety of challenges. The U.S. Army played a crucial role in the political process by which southern states rejoined the Union after the Civil War. But when confronted with political opposition and insurgencies thereafter, the federal government ultimately allowed white conservatives to impose a system of racial domination throughout the South. Instead, it employed army units to confine Indian peoples of the west onto reservations, thereby freeing land for white expansion. As these hostilities ended, growing imperialist ideas drove support for projecting American power abroad, particularly via the U.S. Navy. This service performed well in the Spanish-American War that acquired significant overseas territories. Conversely, the army's problems in that conflict and the resulting Philippine-American War indicated that the country's land forces needed reform if the U.S. was going to pursue a greater role in world affairs.

Short Bibliography

Adams, Kevin. *Class and Race in the Frontier Army: Military Life in the West, 1870–1890*. Norman: University of Oklahoma Press, 2009.

Coffman, Edward M. *The Old Army: A Portrait of the American Army in Peacetime, 1784–1898*. New York: Oxford University Press, 1986.

Cooper, Jerry M. *The Rise of the National Guard: The Evolution of the American Militia, 1865–1920*. Lincoln: University of Nebraska Press, 1997.

Cosmas, Graham A. *An Army for Empire: The U.S. Army in the Spanish-American War*. College Station: Texas A&M University Press, 1998.

Dawson, Joseph G. *Army Generals and Reconstruction: Louisiana, 1862–77*. Baton Rouge: Louisiana State University Press, 1982.

Grimsley, Mark. "Wars for the American South: The First and Second Reconstructions Considered as Insurgencies." *Civil War History* 58, 1 (March 2012): 6–36.

Linn, Brian M. *The Philippine War, 1899–1902*. Lawrence: University Press of Kansas, 2000.

May, Glenn Anthony. *Battle for Batangas: A Philippine Province at War*. New Haven: Yale University Press, 1991.

McBride, William M. *Technological Change and the United States Navy, 1865–1945*. Baltimore: John Hopkins University Press, 2000.

Ostler, Jeffrey. *The Plains Sioux and U.S. Colonialism from Lewis and Clark to Wounded Knee*. Cambridge: Cambridge University Press, 2004.

Rable, George C. *But There Was No Peace: The Role of Violence in the Politics of Reconstruction*. Athens: University of Georgia Press, 1984.

Seager, Robert. *Alfred Thayer Mahan: The Man and His Letters*. Annapolis: Naval Institute Press, 1977.

Sefton, James E. *The United States Army and Reconstruction, 1865–1877*. Baton Rouge: Louisiana State University Press, 1967.

Sweeney, Edwin R. *From Cochise to Geronimo: The Chiricahua Apaches, 1874–1886*. Norman: University of Oklahoma Press, 2012.

Trask, David F. *The War with Spain*. New York: Macmillan, 1981.

Utley, Robert M. *Frontier Regulars: The United States Army and the Indian, 1866–1891*. Lincoln: University of Nebraska Press, 1973.

West, Elliot. *The Last Indian War: The Nez Perce Story*. New York: Oxford University Press, 2009.

Zuczek, Richard. *State of Rebellion: Reconstruction in South Carolina*. Columbia: University of South Carolina Press, 1996.

1903	1908	1914–18	1916–17	1917–18	April 6, 1917
The Militia Act	U.S. Navy's first dreadnoughts	First World War	Mexican Punitive Expedition	U.S. in the First World War	U.S. Declaration of War

Chapter 9

Early Twentieth-Century Reforms and the Great War, 1902–1918

The triumphant United States emerged from the Spanish-American War and the Philippine-American War as a member of the great-power fraternity. With this elevated status came new territories in the Caribbean and the Pacific Ocean and requirements of administering those possessions. The United States was poised on the threshold of what would become "the American Century." These strategic and political realities meant that the U.S. military would need to adjust its plans, missions, and forces to protect the nation's interests.

Just as had happened after the Civil War in 1865, however, the federal government cut military expenditures following the end of hostilities with Spain. The U.S. Army slipped from 125,000 soldiers in 1898 to 75,000 in 1903. The war with Spain also exposed weaknesses in organization and mobilization that hampered the creation of a modern army that could maintain readiness in peace and expand during war. Unlike the army, the U.S. Navy did not suffer such serious downsizing after the end of the Spanish-American War. Quite the contrary, it continued to modernize into a world-class naval force because of support from successive presidents, secretaries of the navy, and legislators in Congress. America's other seaborne service, the Marine Corps, began its shift from shipboard security to constabulary and amphibious operations.

Then a long, bloody war broke out in Europe in 1914. After watching for three years, the United States entered the First World War in April 1917 and fought until November 1918. Mobilizing for war and fighting in this conflict put severe strains on the U.S. military as it expanded from 200,000 men to nearly five million over the next 20 months.

In this chapter, students will learn about:

- Reforms in the U.S. Army to solve problems experienced during the Spanish-American War.
- Expansion of roles of the Navy and Marine Corps to project American force and protect American interests.
- The causes and conduct of American entrance into the First World War.
- Applications of new tactics and technologies in combat in Europe.

May 18, 1917	May 29, 1918	June 1–26, 1918	September 12–16, 1918	September 26–November 1918	November 11, 1918
Selective Service Act	Battle of Cantigny	Battle of Belleau Wood	Battle of St. Mihiel	Meuse-Argonne Campaign	Armistice

Elihu Root's Reforms and the Creation of a Modern Army

The unacceptably high number of American noncombat deaths in the Spanish–American War gave Army leaders much to consider in the postwar period. The logistical and medical efforts broke down even before the conflict because America's frontier Army and militia units were not prepared for the fight. To help solve these wartime problems, President William McKinley appointed Elihu Root as Secretary of War in August 1899. He never served in the military, but he did bring experience as a successful Wall Street attorney to the War Department. Root spent the next four-and-a-half years in office, serving first McKinley and then President Theodore Roosevelt. Root's efforts are collectively known as the "Root Reforms."

Root applied progressive principles as he recast the Army and the War Department as flexible and adaptable institutions in a new century. Surfacing as a movement in the United States during the late nineteenth century, progressivism called for order and efficiency in business, education, politics, and other areas of modern life. Root was not alone in making such improvements. Others included Frederick Winslow Taylor, who applied his scientific management to industry, and John Dewey, who developed his experiential approach in education.

Root faced many problems at the War Department. He focused on three key improvements: the creation of a General Staff, the establishment of new education programs, and formation of a relationship between the regular Army and the National Guard. Root drew on ideas outlined by the late Emory Upton in his essay "The Military Policy of the United States from 1775" and by Spenser Wilkinson in his book, *The Brain of the Army*. Writing in the late nineteenth century, Upton called for an end of American faith in volunteer militias. While ostensibly offering a massive pool of manpower, the questionable levels of training, skill, and discipline of these citizen-soldiers reduced efficiency and increased battlefield losses. Upton believed the Army should instead be a large standing force of well-trained professionals supplemented by conscripts and volunteers in wartime.

Root also took inspiration from Spenser Wilkinson, a prominent British military commentator and theorist. Published in 1890, Wilkinson's *The Brain of the Army* examined the German Army's organization and particularly its General Staff. Based on what Wilkinson wrote, Root wanted the U.S. Army to have a General Staff like the Prussian Army had, which was so successful in the Wars of German Unification between 1864 and 1871.

In what was likely Root's most sweeping reform effort, he attempted to convince Congress to create a strong General Staff of the Army in 1902. However, anti-military factions in Congress and jealous traditionalists like the Army's commanding general, Nelson A. Miles, stymied Root's efforts. Some in Congress equated Root's proposed General Staff to the militaristic specter of the German General Staff, which in turn aroused American fears of tyranny or territorial expansionism. For his part, Miles had a personal stake in opposing Root's move because his own position as commanding general would be eliminated.

Root tried again in 1903 and succeeded in convincing Congress to pass the General Staff Act. This watered-down version called for a small General Staff of 45 officers that would be assigned to the War Department. The Chief of Staff replaced the position of commanding general. The new chief thus became the titular head of the Army, directing the General Staff, and serving as principal military advisor in the War Department.

Apart from creating the General Staff, Secretary Root knew that he needed a pool of professional Army officers who were skilled experts in the art and science of warfare. To this end, Root established the Army War College in 1901. It became the pinnacle of the Army's education system for officers of major's rank or above. Students studied the strategic level of warfare, learned about policy-making processes, and assisted the Army's new General Staff in formulating war plans. The first class entered the War College in 1904.

Secretary Root initiated other changes throughout the Army's education system. He expanded the School of Application for Infantry and Cavalry at Fort Leavenworth, Kansas. The new School of the Line was open to captains from all branches and focused on studying military art and science. Graduates subsequently entered the Army Staff College, where they received training in staff work. After several name changes, the School of the Line and the Army Staff College would eventually evolve into the Command and General Staff College in the 1920s.

Not content with reforms in the Army's structure and educational system, Secretary of War Root also worked to redress the serious problems in state militia units in the Spanish-American War with the Militia Act of 1903. He received help from Representative Charles W. Dick (Republican-Ohio), who was himself a major general in his state's National Guard. What became known as the "Dick Act" differentiated between two American militias: the unorganized reserve militia, including all able-bodied American men, and the organized state militia known as "the National Guard." Under this act, the federal government paid for equipping, arming, and training the guardsmen. When on maneuvers, in training, or in federal service, the guardsmen received pay equal to their regular Army counterparts.

Other legislation followed over the next decade that helped create a more expandable American force structure. Congress established the Naval Reserve in 1914. Thus, by the start of the First World War in 1914, the U.S. military possessed three manpower components—regular, guard, and reserve—on paper, if not in reality—at full readiness. The guard and reserve components were citizen-soldiers who lived civilian lives and worked civilian jobs, except for periodic drills and exercises with local units of men like themselves or except for periods of emergency when they were called to active duty.

Despite Root's best efforts, the actual staff of the General Staff numbered only 22 officers, not its original 45, on the eve of the First World War. In the enlisted ranks, the Army faced disciplinary problems such as absenteeism, desertion, and dereliction, as well as the perennial challenges of recruitment, retention, and funding. These combined to undermine the soldiers' morale and the Root Reforms so that, when the United States did enter the First World War in 1917, the Army was only marginally better prepared than it was in 1898.

Expansion of the U.S. Navy and Transformation of the Marine Corps

Unlike the Army and its much-needed reforms after the Spanish-American War, the U.S. Navy accelerated along a trajectory of expansion and modernization already set in motion in the late nineteenth century because it benefited from two catalysts in the new century. First, the American victory over Spain gave the United States territories in the Caribbean and across the Pacific Ocean. The new possessions, particularly the Philippines in the western Pacific, shifted the Navy's strategic mission from defending the continental United States and the Caribbean to projecting American force across the Pacific. American commercial interests in East Asia suddenly became significant and needed to be protected. The U.S. fleet needed a force structure with deepwater capability to fight set-piece ship-to-ship battles. In these ways, the Navy's existence became intertwined with the new globalism in American foreign policy.

The second catalyst, Theodore Roosevelt's ascension to the presidency in 1901, also flowed from victory in the Spanish-American War. He had served as Assistant Secretary of the Navy from 1897 to 1898 before fighting in that conflict. A proponent of American greatness, progressive in his outlook, and a disciple of naval theorist Alfred Thayer Mahan, the new president made the modernization of the Navy one of his major projects. Roosevelt inherited a good foundation for achieving these goals from Secretary of the Navy John D. Long, who had served from 1897 until 1902. Long helped make the U.S. Navy into the fourth most powerful naval force in the world—behind only Great Britain, France, and Russia—and superior to the navies of Germany, Italy, and Japan. Among his reforms, Long worked to centralize administrative power in the Navy. He created the General Board of the Navy in 1900 and named Admiral George Dewey as its first president. Dewey advised the secretary and the president on strategic planning, ship construction, and force structure. Over the next four years, Long's efforts paralleled those of Elihu Root in the War Department.

After John Long left the Navy Department in 1902, President Roosevelt and Admiral Dewey dominated the U.S. Navy during the first decade of the twentieth century. They continued the ambitious shipbuilding program. The impetus for new warship construction took on new urgency in 1906 when the British Royal Navy launched the HMS *Dreadnought*. This first all-big-gun warship became the world's premier capital ship, making all existing warships obsolete because it boasted a potent combination of larger guns, more armor, and greater speed than any other warship afloat. The term "dreadnought" became synonymous with the term "battleship" for several decades to follow. The HMS *Dreadnought* revolutionized design and accelerated a naval arms race among the great powers. Under Roosevelt and Dewey, the U.S. Navy launched its dreadnoughts in form of two *South Carolina*-class battleships in 1908.

A powerful fleet of these warships gave President Roosevelt the "big stick" he wanted to reinforce his foreign policy decisions and guarantee expanding American commerce around the world. By 1909, the U.S. Navy became the second most powerful force behind the British Royal Navy.

Apart from attempts to increase American naval power and international prestige, President Roosevelt established the Joint Army and Navy Board in 1903. He tapped his ally and supporter Admiral Dewey to be its first chairman. The board started formulating colored war plans—for example, "Orange" for Japan, "Red" for Great Britain, and "Black" for Germany. Each plan laid out strategic scenarios to defeat those potential adversaries at sea or on land. Of these, the ORANGE War Plan would emerge over the next decades as the most important for the U.S. Navy and the Marine Corps.

Box 9.1   Lessons Learned and Ignored in the Russo–Japanese War

The Russo-Japanese War of 1904–1905 was an ideal conflict for American observation and analysis of combat, strategy, and technology. During the ground war, Russian machine guns firing 10 rounds per second, for example, delivered withering fire that made massed Japanese infantry assaults into deadly and pointless exercises. American and European observers and analysts learned that Japanese soldiers were fierce fighters with high morale. However, both Europeans and Americans ignored Japan's enormous casualties and the reasons behind them, and their oversight would contribute to gross overestimations of offensive capabilities during the First World War in Europe a decade later.

As outgrowths of lessons from the Russo-Japanese War together with Secretary of War Elihu Root's reforms, the U.S. Army codified new doctrines in the *Field Service Regulations* (1905), the *Infantry Drill Regulations* (1911), and *Cavalry Service Regulations* (1915). The term doctrine can be understood as those principles and techniques that guide actions. These documents and others like them ingrained American soldiers with beliefs that aggressive offense, good morale, and daring leadership could win battles. However, Root's reforms were organizational reforms, not operational or tactical. The increasing killing power stemming from higher cyclic rates of fire, rifled barrels, longer-range artillery, more potent explosives, and other technological advances did not play significant roles in these manuals.

The naval component of the Russo-Japanese War also held some lessons learned and not learned. The decisive Japanese naval victory at the Battle of Tsushima demonstrated the primacy of the battleship, the continued relevance of classic fleet tactics, and the acceptance of principles laid down by naval theorist Alfred Thayer Mahan. American naval planners and strategists meticulously studied this battle, and future American naval commanders yearned to duplicate its results. Yet America paid no attention to Japan's willingness to launch a surprise attack before a declaration of war had been made when their warships damaged the Russian fleet at anchor in Port Arthur in Manchuria in 1904. Japan emerged victorious from this conflict as the rising power in East Asia and as a legitimate threat to America's interests in that region.

When Woodrow Wilson became president in 1913, the future of the Navy did not necessarily look brighter. He appointed a southern political supporter named Josephus Daniels as his Secretary of the Navy. Daniels had experience in government service and as a newspaper publisher, but no military service. In fact, because he tended toward pacifism, he would be the last member of Wilson's cabinet to support a declaration of war against Germany in April 1917.

Despite his anti-military beliefs, Daniels did direct the continued expansion of certain elements of the American fleet. He de-emphasized new battleship construction in favor of increasing the number of destroyers and antisubmarine vessels to combat Germany's submarine attacks after 1914. In other areas, Daniels brought a reformer's spirit to the Navy Department by actively instituting progressive changes to improve the morality and morale of the American sailor. Daniels mandated vocational training for sailors, increased the number of Navy chaplains, and banned alcoholic beverages on board warships. He believed that outstanding sailors should have the opportunity for advancement as commissioned officers, so he started a program that admitted 100 of them into the U.S. Naval Academy each year. Daniels' many programs, however, did not extend to African-American sailors. Like so many other Caucasians at the time, the navy secretary held racist views about blacks, whom he saw as inferior. Consequently, blacks remained relegated to duties in ships' galleys and dining rooms.

Beyond the benefits enjoyed by the Navy in the early twentieth century, the U.S. Marine Corps also found a new mission after the Spanish-American War. No more would Marines serve primarily as shipboard security. Instead, the Corps developed its capabilities of conducting amphibious assaults against enemy beaches and of maintaining American influence as a constabulary force (addressed in the next section).

Amphibious operations were hardly new to the Marines, who had conducted minor ship-to-shore operations in every American conflict to date. But the prominence of amphibious capability took on new significance after 1898 because of the increased American presence in the Pacific Ocean. Suddenly, the scope and size of naval operations grew exponentially because of the need to defend and attack islands. Although U.S. Army units defended the Philippines, the Marine Corps assumed responsibility for holding Midway, Wake Island, Guam, and other islands dotting the Pacific. These advanced bases could be used as coaling stations and anchorages for American warships, and later as refueling points for military aircraft. In addition to advanced base defense, the Marines also prepared to assault enemy-held shores across the Pacific and establish defensible bases for future operations of the U.S. Fleet.

The Corps' defensive and offensive components constituted a dual amphibious mission that fit into the 1906 ORANGE War Plan to defeat Japan as formulated by the Joint Army and Navy Board. Should hostilities with Japan occur, for instance, the U.S. Fleet would sortie from the West Coast or from Hawai'i, and then steam westward across the Pacific. The U.S. Fleet would use the Marine-held island bases as stepping stones, and the Marines would in turn assault Japanese bases. After hopping from island to island in the western Pacific, the Americans would defeat the Japanese in a decisive battle. This strategic mind-set also echoed aggressive naval theories espoused since the late nineteenth century by Alfred Thayer Mahan, who influenced the Navy's war plans well into the new century.

Interventions in Latin America

The sudden increase in American territory after victory in the Spanish-American War required the deployment of thousands of Marines and soldiers as agents for American corporate influence, if not outright American imperialism. In Latin America, they went into the Dominican Republic from 1904 to 1907 and from 1916 to 1924; Cuba from 1906 to 1909 and again in 1912; Nicaragua from 1909 to 1910 and 1912 to 1925, and again from 1926 to 1933; Mexico in 1914 and in 1916; and Haiti from 1914 to 1934. Bringing order to these nations entailed establishing democratic institutions, building government infrastructures, constructing new military bases, protecting American investments, deterring foreign intrusions, and quelling indigenous revolutions. These sorts of activities have since been called stability, counterinsurgency, or national security missions.

Presidents Theodore Roosevelt and later Woodrow Wilson believed that the American dreams of prosperity and democracy could be projected to other regions. For these two presidents, there could be no better goal to pursue. Their attitudes also revealed the influence of progressivism so prevalent in American society and politics during the early twentieth century. The term "paternalism" can be used to describe attempts to remake other less-developed nations in the United States' own image, whether indigenous peoples wanted to do so or not. The fatherly Americans could raise up the child-like others. Paternalism thus can be considered a form of imperialism. Not all Americans, however, possessed such seemingly benign motivations for sending Marines and soldiers to Latin America. Some supported military intervention for reasons of strategic planning for territorial expansion, racial superiority, commercial interest, or Protestant religious zealotry. The resulting problems slowly soured world opinion and American public opinion against the military efforts in the region.

Several of these motivations can be seen when President Roosevelt deployed American forces to stop Colombian attempts to repress a revolution in Panama. He succeeded in ensuring that a new, friendly government took power in Panama. This in turn set the stage for the United States to start construction efforts in 1904 on a canal across the Panamanian isthmus connecting the Atlantic and Pacific Oceans. The Panama Canal constituted a prime example of American commercial and strategic interests converging in Latin America. Building the canal paid huge commercial dividends by reducing the voyage from the Pacific to the Atlantic by several weeks and thousands of miles. The canal likewise fit into Roosevelt's Mahanian vision for a powerful oceangoing U.S. Navy that could move quickly through the canal between the two oceans.

After becoming president in 1913, Woodrow Wilson was even more active in Latin America and the Caribbean than either Roosevelt or Taft. Wilson possessed a moralistic vision—first in Latin America and later during the First World War—that favored diplomacy where possible yet employed force where necessary. According to Wilson's messianic vision, the United States would spread stability, democracy, and prosperity across the globe. He raised expectations for results beyond any reasonable hope for success. Indeed, presidents' overestimations of the ability of American military force to solve crises would reverberate throughout the twentieth century and into the twenty-first.

Between 1914 and 1916, for example, President Wilson used military force several times, notably in Mexico, then in Haiti, and again in Mexico. Aside from wanting to establish order in the often-chaotic nations, Wilson worried that Germany might take advantage of the region's weaknesses to project its power into the Caribbean. He also believed that ongoing political upheaval endangered American commercial interests.

Wilson first sent troops to Mexico in 1914. Plagued by political upheaval and bloody revolution since 1910, American citizens and commercial interests were not safe in Mexico. Such instability in a neighbor so close to the United States worried Wilson. Incidents in the coastal city of Vera Cruz in April 1914 provided a pretext for armed intervention. Mexican soldiers threatened and insulted several American sailors going ashore to find fuel for their warship anchored in the harbor. After unsuccessful attempts at conciliation, poor relations between the United States and Mexico deteriorated still further. Meanwhile, Mexico's President Victoriano Huerta purchased weapons and equipment from Germany to help suppress revolutionary forces in his country.

When a German ship carrying arms arrived off the coast of Vera Cruz, Wilson directed American forces to land at Vera Cruz and occupy the city. In what can be legitimately considered an invasion, nearly 1,000 American sailors and Marines landed in the port city in late April and fought a short battle. The two nations nearly went to war, but the Mexican government could not oppose American occupation forces because an ongoing revolution in Mexico undermined that nation's ability to project its military force. Some 3,000 American troops remained in Vera Cruz until November 1914, when the revolutionaries overthrew President Huerta and established a constitutional, albeit weak, government.

A year later in 1915, President Wilson decided to use military force to restore order in Haiti on the western side of Hispaniola. The Haitian dictator had been recently killed in an uprising, a revolution endangered American investments, and a German military intervention loomed as a real possibility. Wilson reacted by directing American Marines to land in Haiti to stop the revolution and restore order. They established and served as officers of a national police force. The Marines spent much of their time chasing, fighting, and subduing the *cacos*, who were Haitian bandits, revolutionaries, and mercenaries. Their insurgent activities declined by 1920 after their leaders were killed or captured. American occupation forces then turned to improving Haitian infrastructure by initiating public works, reforming the nation's corrupt judicial system, and laying foundations for democratic elections. These positive effects lasted only as long as the Marines remained in Haiti. Their deployments to Latin American came to be known euphemistically as "banana wars" and officially as "small wars." In the twenty-first century, these conflicts are referred to as "counterinsurgencies."

Reality never matched the goals of the Marines, nor of the progressive intentions of Presidents Roosevelt and Wilson. Cycles of revolution and counterrevolution erupted because Latin American peoples resisted the United States' occupation forces, and they resented being exploited by American commercial interests. Even so, hard fighting under difficult conditions gave practical experiences to young Marine officers like Holland M. Smith and Alexander A. Vandegrift that would pay dividends later in the Second World War when these officers assumed senior leadership roles.

Not all interventions in Latin American were made by the U.S. Marine Corps or Navy. In the most significant exception, Army units massed in the spring of 1916 on the United States' southern border for what would be known as the Mexican Punitive Expedition. The soldiers tried to capture Francisco "Pancho" Villa, who was a revolutionary leader in Mexico. Villa had grown angry at the United States and felt betrayed by President Wilson when he supported another successor to Huerta's recently overthrown regime rather than siding with Villa. In response, Villa and his men lashed out by attacking American citizens and destroying American property in northern Mexico in 1915 and 1916. The newly established Mexican national government could provide no protection. Then, on March 9, 1916, some 500 of Villa's followers crossed into the United States and raided a town in New Mexico, killing American civilians and U.S. soldiers stationed there. The *Villistas*, as they were called, took machine guns, ammunition, and mules and horses back across the border into Mexico.

An enraged President Woodrow Wilson dispatched Spanish-speaking Brigadier General John J. Pershing with 4,800 soldiers on March 15 to cross the border, track down Pancho Villa, and capture him. The first American soldiers entered Mexico four days later. Over the next few months, more than 11,000 soldiers fought several indecisive battles with the *Villistas*. American forces also clashed with Mexican Federal troops and antagonized their new government. Failing to capture Villa himself and fearing war with Mexico, President Wilson ordered the withdrawal of American soldiers in February 1917. He subsequently called more than 100,000 National Guardsmen to federal service to secure the border against future incursion by Villa's revolutionaries.

The U.S. Army culled many benefits from the Mexican Punitive Expedition, however. The expedition represented a test case for the General Staff and Militia Acts of the Root Reforms, from which many organizational, operational, and logistical lessons were learned. Moreover, a new generation of American soldiers and officers gained experience in what was the largest concentration of troops since the Spanish-American War. Among them was a young Lieutenant named George S. Patton, Jr., who personally killed one of Villa's key subordinates in combat. The American forces also experimented with such new technologies as motorized vehicles for logistics, airplanes for reconnaissance, and wireless telegraphs for communications.

The Great War in Europe, 1914–17

While the U.S. military went through reforms and deployed to the Caribbean, the European nations slipped slowly toward the bloodiest conflict in history to date. For several decades, a delicate balance of power divided Europeans into two armed alliances. Territorial expansion, geographical location, and national fervor contributed to this division. By 1914, the German Empire, the Austro-Hungarian Empire, and Italy formed the Triple Alliance (or more widely called the "Central Powers"); and in opposition stood the United Kingdom, France, and Russia comprising the Triple Entente (or more widely called the "Allies"). The nations in each bloc were tied to one another with treaties that guaranteed mutual support if any nation were attacked.

In anticipation of a conflict, each European nation drew up intricate mobilization schedules and strategic plans for war. The most famous of these, Germany's Schlieffen Plan, outlined how the German Army could win a two-front war by defeating France to the west in a few weeks and then wheeling around eastward to attack Russia in the east thereafter. Other factors pointed to future conflict. Arms races occurred between European nations vying for the largest land and sea forces. Another powerful ideological force—nationalism—spiraled out of control among the populations hoping for battlefield glories, territorial expansion, or political independence. Nationalism could bring together people with very different political, social, economic, or religious beliefs in service of flag and country.

Perhaps most ominous was the ignorance of so many European military leaders about the incredible destructiveness of machines guns, poisonous gas, submarines, and other new weapons. Too many Europeans believed that patriotic zeal, aggressive leadership, and elaborate plans could overcome the new weapons systems to win battles. All these factors could be considered a powder keg waiting for the right spark to cause an explosion and plunge the continent into war.

That spark occurred in Bosnia on June 28, 1914, when a terrorist assassinated Austro-Hungary's Crown Prince Franz Ferdinand. The assassination started a chain reaction: European nations mobilized their massive armed forces, initiated their long-standing war plans, activated their alliance systems, and issued declarations of war. None of Europe's leaders could halt the chain reaction once the blood lust started, and the Great War began in early August.

The conflict's opening moves did not meet the belligerents' prewar hopes and plans. The German Army initiated the Schlieffen Plan but failed to defeat France. September 1914 proved to be a pivotal month as French and British forces stopped the German offensive at the Marne River, just 30 miles from Paris. With their manpower and resources depleted, each side settled in and dug defensive trenches thereafter. The battle lines on what would become known as the Western Front solidified along earthen fortifications so massive and complex that they stretched from neutral Switzerland to the English Channel.

What had been expected to be a short, glorious war turned into an endless stalemate. Meanwhile on the Eastern Front, German forces fought a war of maneuver on a grand scale against Russia. At the Battle of Tannenberg in September 1914, the Germans surrounded the Russians and won a decisive victory, killing or capturing one-third and routing the other two-thirds of the 350,000-man Russian Army.

The second year of the Great War saw the introduction of chemical weapons at the battles of Ypres and of Loos in northern France. The Germans first employed these fearsome weapons, and later the French and British tried them, too. Delivered by artillery shells, murky clouds of chlorine, phosgene, or mustard gas settled in enemy trenches and caused death or blindness to thousands of troops unable to put on their protective gas masks quickly enough. The gas attacks caused physical pain and death as well as psychological distress. The soldiers experiencing a gas attack could only hope that the seal of the mask around their faces was airtight, and that the filter in the mask worked properly. Today, in the twenty-first century, chemical weapons are regarded as weapons of mass destruction.

Despite this devastating new application of technology by the Germans and British, the attacking forces at Ypres and Loos could not penetrate enemy defensive positions. The defenders enjoyed advantages in artillery and machine-gun fire that killed assaulting soldiers as they climbed "over the top" of their own trenches and crossed into "no man's land" to attack the enemy trenches. No man's land was the hellish landscape marked by huge craters and rotting flesh. Once at the enemy trenches, the assault forces had to cut their way through barbed wire, endure small arms fire, and engage in bloody hand-to-hand combat to capture and secure the enemy position. Then they pushed still further through more trench systems, while suffering casualties so debilitating that a sustained breakout beyond those trenches into the enemy's interior was impossible. Instead, the assaulting troops licked their wounds and awaited the inevitable counterattack, which frequently pushed them back across no man's land to their original starting points.

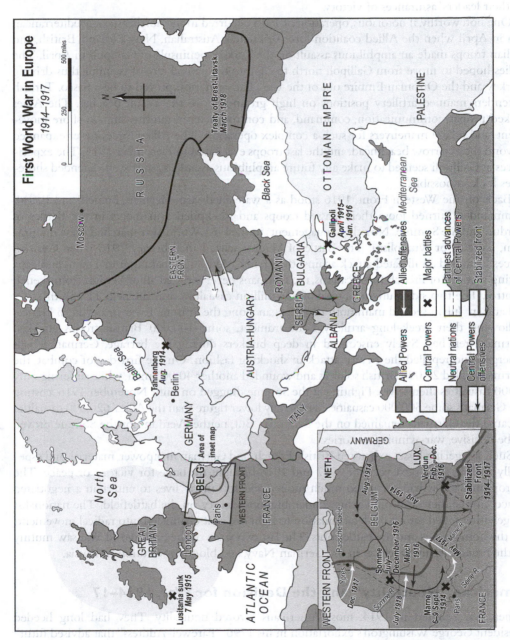

Map 9.1 The First World War in Europe, 1914–1917

Throughout 1915, patriotic fervor nonetheless continued to spur enlistments and conscriptions on the home fronts across Europe. Factories continued to churn out billions of rounds of ammunition, millions of rifles, and thousands of artillery pieces to be used in future campaigns. The Europeans blindly believed in the righteousness of their national causes and clung to their leaders' assurances of victory.

One noteworthy, if notorious, operation of 1915 occurred in the northeastern Mediterranean Sea in April when the Allied coalition force of French, Australian, New Zealand, British, and Indian troops made an amphibious assault on the Turkish peninsula of Gallipoli in April. The Allies hoped to move from Gallipoli north to capture the capital city of Istanbul, thus driving Turkey and the Ottoman Empire out of the war. The operation proved to be a fiasco. Turkish defenders manned artillery positions on high ground above the assault beaches. The Allies lacked proper communication, command, and control of naval gunfire, ship-to-shore movement, and inland maneuvers for such a complex operation. The Allied forces never expanded beyond their narrow beachhead, and the last troops evacuated in December 1915. The experiences at Gallipoli seemed to make any future amphibious assaults against well-defended shorelines look impossible.

Back on the Western Front, 1916 stood as a watershed year. German, French, and British commanders turned loose their massed troops and stockpiled armaments in the Battles of Verdun and the Somme. No other engagements in the First World War matched these in duration, ferocity, or symbolism. The Battle of Verdun started in February 1916 when German forces launched an ill-fated attack against the French. Although making initial gains and capturing sections of French fortifications, the Germans never wrested all of Verdun from French control. The two sides suffered a total of one million casualties over the next 11 months.

Later in July, a second mammoth battle began along the Somme River in northern France. Following their week-long artillery bombardment, some 100,000 British troops attacked German trenches. Safely ensconced in deep bunkers during the barrage, German troops emerged and repelled the British attack in shocking fashion. On the first day of combat, the Germans killed 20,000 British soldiers and wounded another 40,000 men, while suffering only 8,000 casualties themselves. Fighting at the Somme dragged on until November 1916, costing the Germans some 500,000 casualties, a relatively lower figure than the Allies' 620,000 casualties because the Germans remained on the defensive. But, neither Verdun nor the Somme proved to be decisive, war-winning victories.

Such staggering losses exhausted British, French, and German manpower, material, and especially morale. The next years of 1917 and 1918 brought no hope for victory or peace. The European nations had spent too much money and too many lives to entertain a negotiated peace, and neither side could achieve unambiguous victory on the battlefield. The nationalist surge either faded into stoic determination to fight on, or it channeled into radical movements on the home fronts and the battlefronts. The last two years of the First World War saw mutiny in the French Army, rebellion in the German Navy, and bloody revolution in Russia.

American "Neutrality" and the Decision for War, 1914–17

When war erupted in 1914, most Americans favored neutrality. They had long heeded President George Washington's exhortation in his 1796 "Farewell Address" that advised future American generations to avoid entangling foreign alliances. Americans followed Washington's advice throughout the 1800s and stayed out of formal involvement in Europe's wars. Even so, as conflict in Europe dragged on into 1917, the American people increasingly spurned the Central Powers and supported the Allies. Just as important were commercial and economic ties among the United States, Great Britain, and France. American products sold to the British and France brought in 10 times more revenue than sales to Germany or Austria-Hungary. The United States also changed from a debtor nation to creditor nation that financed the Allied governments. Thus, it grew more and more important for France and Britain to defeat Germany and repay those loans to United States.

Unconvinced by American moralist claims of neutrality, Germany's leaders knew all too well that the United States served as the breadbasket, armory, and bank for the Allies. Merchant ships transported clothing, food, and eventually munitions from the United States to Britain and France. To destroy this supply system, the Germans utilized a new weapon—the submarine, translated as *Unterseeboot* in German and abbreviated at "U-boats"—to blockade the British Isles and the French coastline. But doing so was problematic. According to international maritime law, submarines should surface and offer the crews on targeted vessels the chance to abandon ship or surrender before being sunk. In fact, the German U-boat crews followed these rules but fell victim in turn to cannon fire from armed British merchant ships. Thus, the U-boats needed to remain safely submerged and launch torpedoes against unsuspecting targets. Their surprise attacks sank hundreds of British, French, and American vessels. It was one thing to attack enemy shipping, but the Germans also sank other vessels from neutral nations like the United States.

The most infamous attack occurred on May 7, 1915, when a German U-boat torpedoed and sank the British luxury ship RMS *Lusitania*. Of the 1,959 passengers and crew on board, 1,198 perished; 128 of them were American citizens. The Germans justified this attack by accusing the British of using civilian vessels to transport military cargo. Outrage in the United States over the loss of life reached a fever pitch. Americans increasingly began to see Germany as an aggressor and a threat. In the short term, President Wilson issued an ultimatum in July 1915 that pressured the Germans to restrict their submarine warfare. Yet, he did not ask for a declaration of war. He still wished to maintain the façade of American neutrality. Indeed, Wilson would adopt the slogan, "He kept us out of war," for his successful reelection campaign in 1916.

Despite the threats and realities, the U.S. War Department failed to consider how to mobilize, train, and transport troops to Europe in the event of American entry into the conflict. Instead, the planners focused on the military side of war planning while paying little attention to the logistical necessities of their plans. With the possibility of conflict becoming more real in 1915, a few farsighted Americans decided to increase the level of preparedness through unofficial means. Private citizens created a camp in Plattsburgh, New York, where thousands of middle-class American men went through training in military procedures and leadership. Dubbed the "Plattsburgh Movement," more camps popped up in other areas of the United States, and more than 20,000 Americans received their officer training by 1917.

While the British, French, and German soldiers fought the bloody battles of the Somme and Verdun in 1916, the United States edged closer to war through two significant pieces of legislation. President Wilson may have tried to maintain American neutrality during the European conflict, but he also worked with hawks in Congress who wanted the United States to be better prepared in a dangerous world. In 1916, Congress passed and Wilson signed two acts into law: the National Defense Act and the Naval Act. Each gave the federal government's civilian and military leadership greater flexibility to meet the requirements of fighting a war. They also expanded Elihu Root's Militia Act and the General Staff Act from a decade earlier.

The National Defense Act of 1916 set the Army and the War Department on the road to preparedness. The title itself connoted a nonbelligerent yet watchful stance that drew support from across the American political spectrum. The act garnered support from all but the most pacifist and isolationist Americans. It called for the U.S. Army to double its peacetime manpower to 175,000 and expand still further in wartime to 285,000 regulars. Congress also decided to utilize the National Guard as the trained reserve for the regular Army, appropriated additional funding for its fourfold expansion to 450,000 men, and gave Wilson the power to call them to federal service.

Increasing the number of soldiers and guardsmen among the enlisted ranks, however, was not enough. The National Defense Act of 1916 established the Reserve Officer Training Corps for students at universities and colleges, and it authorized funds for facilities, equipment, and other operating expenses for officer training camps like those in the Plattsburgh Movement. Lastly, in what was likely its most significant feature, the 1916 Act also stipulated that in wartime, the National Guard, the Army Reserve, and the Regular Army would combine to form the Army of the United States. This provided a platform for wartime expansion and a foundation for an evolving relationship between the three components ever since.

Several events outside the United States precipitated the passage in 1916 of the Naval Act. Russia and Japan signed an alliance that could control the Far East. Tensions with Mexico could mean war with this southern neighbor. Lastly, the Battle of Jutland between German and British fleets revealed how the powerful new dreadnoughts made all older warships obsolete and vulnerable.

The Naval Act of 1916 enlarged and modernized the U.S. Navy. Most admirals believed that building more battleships and battlecruisers should be the main goal of this new legislation. Adhering to Mahanian principles, they saw these massive vessels as benchmarks for naval supremacy: The more battleships and battlecruisers, the more power and influence that the United States could wield. The Naval Act of 1916 thus provided the foundation to build the world's most powerful fleet, including four battleships and four battlecruisers to be constructed in the next three years. This constituted the largest naval expansion program to date in American history.

Despite the groundswell of support for new construction and the supposed primacy of the capital ship in naval warfare, the main threat to American shipping remained the German U-boats lurking beneath the Atlantic Ocean's waves. Their captains mostly acted as commerce raiders who targeted merchant ships. Secretary of the Navy Josephus Daniels recognized this danger and disagreed with the battleship proponents in the admiralty and Congress. Aside from completing the new battleships already being built, he only approved the construction of new destroyers that would bring the U.S. Navy's total to 273 in 1917. These light, fast warships could detect and sink the submerged U-boats. Destroyers and similar sub-chasing vessels acted as screens for merchant ships making the transatlantic voyage through submarine-infested waters of the Atlantic Ocean.

In late 1916, this reduced effectiveness of their U-boats persuaded Germany's leaders to make the fateful decision to reinstitute unrestricted submarine warfare in February 1917. The Germans gambled that a U-boat blockade could starve the French and British home fronts into submission before the United States could enter the conflict. Regardless, lifting restrictions meant that German submarines would target vessels flying the flags of neutral nations such as the United States. The actions angered Wilson and most Americans, tipping the scales and finally pushing the United States into the conflict.

On April 2, 1917, the American president addressed a joint session of Congress, enumerated Germany's transgressions and asked for a declaration of war. Wilson wished to enter the war to "make the world safe for democracy." Couched in these terms, he planned to apply progressive principles to the international arena, just as he had done in his Latin American interventions. He hoped to enter the fight in part to gain a seat for the United States in the treaty process. The idealistic American president believed he could broker that postwar peace based on national self-determination, maritime rights, free trade, and open diplomacy. Congress overwhelmingly voted in favor of the declaration of war.

The Great War Over Here: American Mobilization

After entering the First World War, the U.S. military needed to mobilize, train, transport, and supply a force capable of fighting Germany on the land, in the air, and at sea. The U.S. Army stood at 133,000 men, the National Guard at 185,000 men, and the new Reserve at 17,000 men in April 1917. Wilson promised to send several American divisions to Europe to help the French and British in April. But when he asked his senior American leaders, he discovered that not even one Army division existed on paper, let alone in reality. No blueprint existed for the herculean expansion from 200,000 men in all America's armed services in April 1917 to a 4.7 million-man strength in the next 19 months. The state of readiness was equally poor in the Marine Corps, and only marginally better in the Navy.

Stray regiments, brigades, and battalions were scattered across the United States and overseas. The Army quickly cobbled together enough units to constitute the 1st Expeditionary Division in May 1917. After being redesignated as the 1st Division, elements of this unit sailed for France in August. According to the Army's newly established tables of organization and equipment, a division should have 28,000 soldiers. It contained two infantry brigades, each of which had two regiments. Some 18,000 soldiers served as infantrymen in these units, which became known as a square division because of its four infantry regiments. Additional units included one field artillery brigade, one engineer regiment, one signal battalion, one machine-gun battalion, and a full supply train. The Army eventually fielded 43 divisions with more than one million American soldiers seeing combat by the war's end in 1918.

The understrength 1st Division's 18,000 men arrived in France piecemeal during the summer and fall of 1917. Next, the U.S. 2nd Division was activated and steamed to Europe in October. This inauspicious start pointed to severe shortages in men and materials that hampered planning and training in the new American Expeditionary Force (AEF) in 1917 and 1918. President Wilson originally chose to give command of the AEF to General Frederick Funston, a Medal of Honor recipient who fought in the Spanish-American War and the Philippine Insurrection. After Funston's unexpected death, however, Wilson reached down the list of senior officers to select Major General John J. Pershing to command the AEF in May 1917. He received a promotion to general five months later in October. While relatively junior, Pershing possessed decades of Army service on the western frontier, in the Spanish-American War, and most recently as commander of American forces in the Mexican Punitive Expedition.

No Army officer had worn four stars since Phil Sheridan in the 1880s. Making Pershing a general raised his status to where he could interact as an equal with other Allied senior officers, such as French General-in-Chief Henri Phillippe Pétain, French Marshal Ferdinand Foch, and British Field Marshal Douglas Haig. President Wilson gave Pershing great latitude to direct the AEF, negotiate with the Allies, and act independently in theater. Pershing did not abuse his sweeping prerogatives, because maintaining the coalition was paramount.

Filling the military's ranks took priority beginning in the spring of 1917. Many Americans heeded the nation's call and voluntarily entered military service. Some two million men eventually volunteered. They came from all parts of American society, including rural farming, working class, and wealthy backgrounds. The volunteers also represented many racial and ethnic groups in the United States. They felt compelled to join because of love of country, anger over Germany's actions, thirst for adventure, desire to prove their manhood, or pressures from peers, families, or communities.

Box 9.2   Robert R. McCormick as Citizen-Soldier

Some three million Americans heeded the call and volunteered for military service during the First World War. Many left family farms, factory floors, or business offices to go to war. A few volunteers like Robert R. McCormick came from the wealthiest families in America. The 37-year-old McCormick was the owner, editor, and publisher of the *Chicago Tribune*. He joined the Illinois National Guard in 1916, which had just been called to federal service. McCormick then spent time patrolling the border with Mexico in support of the Punitive Expedition. Once the United States entered the Great War and his Illinois Guard unit was federalized in 1917, McCormick went with his unit to France.

When offered a safe post on General John J. Pershing's headquarters staff, McCormick refused. He wanted to see action and sought transfer to a combat unit. Major and later Colonel McCormick commanded the 1st Battalion, 5th Field Artillery Regiment in the U.S. 1st Division. His unit fought at Cantigny, where his guns laid down effective barrages to support infantry attacks against German defenses. He earned the Purple Heart and the Distinguished Service Cross in combat.

Looking back in 1937 on service in the First World War, the retired Colonel McCormick could say, "May my first words express an undying affection for the comrades who fought beside us in many a famous victory. Let us never forget the men who laid down their lives with ours in brotherly heroism." Only exceeded by his work for the *Tribune*, serving in the 1st Division represented the greatest activity in McCormick's full life. He therefore can be considered a citizen-soldier of the First World War's generation. (Robert R. McCormick, speech, "The First Division," 9 August 1937, File 1989.22, Box 342, Robert R. McCormick Papers, McCormick Research Center, Cantigny Park, Illinois.)

Similar motivations could also be found among American women. Several million went to work in war-related industries. Some 21,000 women also joined the U.S. military to serve in the Army and Navy Nurse Corps, a role that was perfectly accepted in the gender norms of the early twentieth century. An additional 13,000 volunteered for clerical jobs in the U.S. Navy and Marine Corps, but these women never received military rank and served only for the duration of the war. To be sure, American women made their greatest advances after the conflict ended when they gained voting rights. But a precedent was set during the First World War nonetheless for women serving in the military.

President Wilson and his advisors realized that volunteers alone could not project American force across the Atlantic Ocean to France. Thus, they decided to conscript or draft additional manpower. Conscription, otherwise known as "the draft," had been utilized during the American Civil War to swell the ranks of Union and Confederate militaries. Such a compulsory policy generated resistance—sometimes violent—because economic inequalities meant many draftees came from the poorer segments of society.

To reduce such inequities, Congress passed the Selective Service Act on May 18, 1917. This program of universal conscription registered some 24 million men for the service as part of a national lottery. Initially, the eligible ages ranged from 21 to 31 years old but later expanded to include the men from 18 to 45 years old. After the first number in a lottery was drawn in July 1917, some 4,600 local draft boards followed suit across the United States. Once their numbers were called in the lottery, the men endured several examinations to determine their physical fitness, moral uprightness, and mental acuity. They also could claim exemptions for family dependents, alien status, critical vocations, or pacific religious beliefs. The draft boards drew lottery numbers for about twice the required manpower because around half of those were unfit or unwilling to serve in the military or were given exemptions from duty. By war's end in 1918, the conscription process inducted nearly three million men into the U.S. military of the total 24 million registrants.

In theory at least, the draft included a cross section of American society with 368,000 African-American inductees and 2,443,000 Caucasian inductees. However, in practice, these figures revealed how some local draft boards chose poorer Caucasians and African Americans because these men were deemed expendable. Blacks made up about 10 percent of the population of the United States, but 15 percent of the men drafted. Racism and social elitism thus tainted the draft process.

Of the draftees, immigrants made up as many as 20 percent or 600,000 men. Although many immigrants' loyalty was not scrutinized, suspicions of German-Americans abounded and a vicious propaganda campaign portrayed their homeland as evil, but very few German immigrants undermined the American war effort. Instead, they willingly proved their allegiance to the United States and thus became fully assimilated into their adopted nation. Military service had long been a means of legitimizing citizenship in the United States.

Not all draftees or registrants served in uniform. Some received exemptions for having dependent families or skilled occupations essential to the war effort. Conscientious objectors with their pacifist religious beliefs could opt out of military service, and they could instead serve in noncombat roles in medical units. Other Americans, such as socialists and some Mennonites, were unwilling to support the American war effort and fell victim to harsh penalties like incarceration under the auspices of the separate Espionage, Alien, and Sedition Acts in 1917 and 1918. Among these was the socialist labor leader Eugene V. Debs, who received a prison sentence for speaking out against the war.

Conscription brought tens of thousands of African Americans into service in the U.S. Army. Very few blacks served in the Navy, and no blacks entered the Marine Corps at all because of long-standing prejudices against them. Victims of racial discrimination at every stage, from induction through training, black draftees or volunteers served in segregated Army units led by Caucasian American officers. No black officers outranked white officers in units. Moreover, African-American soldiers were issued inferior equipment and lived in substandard housing, when compared to their white counterparts.

An incident in Houston, Texas, hurt the already negative public perceptions about African Americans in uniform. In August 1917, a fight broke out between white police and African-American soldiers over rumors and misunderstandings about one of their fellow black soldiers being killed by the police. Several people died in the ensuing riot. In the largest court-martial in Army history, 19 African-American soldiers received death sentences, and another 41 received life sentences in prison. Sadly, this incident fanned fears among many bigoted Caucasians from Southern states that arming blacks would cause more problems. It also lent false credence to the racist assumption that African Americans lacked the self-discipline, intelligence, and skill to be full-fledged combat soldiers. Thereafter, Secretary of War Newton Baker mandated that African Americans should serve only in labor units, where they could be more easily controlled by their white officers.

Although facing racial discrimination, the African-American community in the United States overwhelmingly supported the American war effort. For many blacks, military service, despite institutionalized racism, represented the best means of validating their claim to full and equal American citizenship. Even the ardent civil rights activist, W. E. B. Dubois, urged his fellow blacks to set aside their anger and frustration with racism in the United States and rally to flag and country. In all, 380,000 black draftees and volunteers served in the military in the

Figure 9.1 African-American Soldiers in a Labor Unit

Very few African-American soldiers saw combat in the First World War. Most blacks in the U.S. Army dug trenches like these soldiers, or they helped move supplies in labor units.

© Robert R. McCormick Research Center

First World War. Of these, nearly 90 percent would be assigned to labor units supporting logistics efforts on the home front or behind the front lines. The other 10 percent saw combat in units like the U.S. 92nd and 93rd Divisions after Secretary Baker relented under pressure from the African-American community to allow some blacks to serve on the front lines.

When the volunteers and draftees started basic training in 1917, none of the necessary facilities or equipment existed in the U.S. military. Making matters worse, experienced drill sergeants were too few to inculcate raw recruits with military discipline or help transform them into soldiers. Their training was also flawed or outdated. The existing U.S. Army *Field Service Regulations* (1917) and *Infantry Drill Regulations* (1911) emphasized the importance of rifle marksmanship in infantry tactics.

Part of this emphasis on the rifleman and marksmanship can be traced to Pershing's own career. As a junior officer in the early 1890s, he qualified as one of the Army's top five marksmen with both rifle and pistol. Pershing also served as an instructor of military tactics and commanded a drill company at the University of Nebraska. These factors doubtlessly predisposed him toward maintaining discipline and marksmanship among soldiers.

As he looked forward to fighting in Europe, General Pershing favored what he called "open warfare." He wanted masses of fast-moving American troops to make aggressive attacks against German positions over open ground, overwhelm them, and drive them from those positions.

After breaking through these defenses, American units could move swiftly into the interior behind enemy lines and achieve victory. The Army, however, neglected to account for deadly machine-gun and artillery fire in its training or doctrine. Pershing did not heed the hard lessons of the European armies who tried to fight their versions of open warfare over the last three years.

Mobilizing American manpower, revising doctrine, and adopting new tactics were not the only challenges facing the United States as it plunged into the First World War. The country also possessed insufficient equipment, weapons, ammunition, clothing, and vehicles for the large amount of men entering its armed forces. American industry produced huge amounts of war materials between 1914 and 1917, but most went to France and Britain. Hence American soldiers arrived in France in 1918 using French and British equipment and weapons manufactured back in the United States. Other problems emerged in mobilizing the nation's industrial resources to support the new American war effort.

Shortly after declaring war in April 1917, President Wilson established the War Industries Board and made Wall Street investor Bernard Baruch its chairman. This board and dozens of similar government agencies extended the federal government's influence over all parts of American social and economic life during wartime. The War Industries Board centralized control of wartime American manufacturing in the hands of a committee of experts in business and technology. The First World War ended in November 1918 before the War Industries Board could harness the full production capabilities of the United States. As experiments, however, these types of agencies provided precedents for centralization of government control later in the New Deal and the Second World War.

Once American soldiers were trained, new weapons manufactured, and food harvested, the last great challenge occurred in making a safe voyage across the Atlantic. German U-boats posed a serious threat to this transit. During the entire conflict, they sank more than 12 million tons of Allied shipping. This nearly brought Great Britain and France to their knees, but three factors mitigated these losses. First, the American shipbuilding industry helped compensate for the sinkings by constructing more than seven million tons of ships during the war, of which less than 400,000 tons were lost. This meant that American shipyards produced more vessels and faster than German U-boats could sink them.

Second, Secretary of the Navy Josephus Daniels differed from the battleship proponents among the American admirals and in Congress. Instead of finishing the huge building program with its new battleships, Daniels redirected resources toward constructing destroyers. The Navy's total force reached 273 destroyers in 1917 and then grew to more than 400 antisubmarine vessels in the next year. Destroyers were small, fast warships that could detect U-boats with sonar and destroy them with depth charges. An acronym for Sound Navigation and Ranging device, "sonar" allowed vessels on the surface to locate submerged U-boats by measuring sound pulses echoing off submarine hulls or by listening for noises made by U-boat engines. Once located, the surface vessels could drop depth charges into waters near the submerged U-boat. The large metal containers filled with explosives would detonate at predetermined depths. The resulting explosions would send shock waves through the water powerful enough to crack or crush the U-boats' thin hulls.

Third, at the urging of Vice Admiral William S. Sims, who commanded U.S. Navy forces in Europe during the First World War, American and Allied merchant ships began sailing from ports in large convoys in 1917. This represented a marked change from individual ships or small groups making transatlantic voyages, as was common earlier in the conflict. Sims recognized that hundreds of solitary vessels transiting the Atlantic made easy targets for the German U-boats. However, in the convoy system, destroyers and other antisubmarine vessels served as escorts that located and destroyed U-boats lurking beneath the surface. The convoy presented the U-boat captains with the challenge of finding one large group of merchant ships with escorts in an ocean area some 3,000 miles long and 1,500 miles wide. Admiral Sims' success in converting American and Allied shipping to the convoy system likely stood as the greatest contribution by any U.S. Navy officer in the First World War.

The Great War Over There: Combat in France, 1918

By 1918, the Germans realized their U-boat campaign would not by itself drive Great Britain from the war. But American mobilization difficulties meant they would not have to face large numbers of U.S. troops until sometime over the summer. In the interim, two revolutions had rocked Russia and enabled the communist Bolsheviks to overthrow the government and take power. In early March 1918, the Bolsheviks negotiated a peace with Germany that placed harsh penalties on Russia but ended the fighting between the two countries on the Eastern Front. This freed up German units to move to the Western Front where they came under control of Generals Paul von Hindenburg and Eric Ludendorff, both heroes of the German victory at the Battle of Tannenburg in 1914. They planned to launch several massive offensives against the Allied trenches in France, hoping to score decisive war-ending victories before the fresh American soldiers entered the Allied lines. The first offensive, code-named Operation MICHAEL, began in late March. Four more assaults occurred later in the spring and summer, with the last one stalling out in July 1918.

When soldiers in the U.S. 1st Expeditionary Division arrived in France back in 1917, they encountered countless obstacles before they could be sent to the front. Among the most vexing were the nonexistent American logistical system, inadequate combat training, and problematic Allied command relations. Solving these problems meant working with the French and British in a coalition in which these Allies dictated strategy and, as newcomers, American forces executed that strategy at the operational and tactical levels. The AEF commander, General John Pershing, could not always sway major decisions about the overall Allied plan to halt the German spring offensive and then roll back those enemy forces, but he did have input on particular sectors and operations where his "doughboys" would fight.

The term "doughboy" has several possible origins dating back to the Mexican War in the 1840s, but none are based on concrete documentation. One possible explanation could be that the soldiers cooked their flour-based food by wrapping it around their bayonets like a doughnut. Another theory speculates that the dust covering American soldiers marching through Mexico made them look like the adobe buildings. Thus, phonetically, "adobe" was an easy jump to "doughboy." Regardless of its origins, the nickname became very popular in the First World War, but it would not be used in American conflicts thereafter.

That the United States needed 13 months until May 1918 to place substantial numbers of Americans in Europe occurred in large part because the military had no logistical system to support the millions of soldiers. Some of the worst shortcomings occurred in such mundane areas as finding good boots for the doughboys and replacing the AEF's horses killed in combat.

In reality, French or British trucks carried American soldiers and equipment across France and to the front. In their first battles, the doughboys utilized the British Lee-Enfield MkIII rifle, the British Vickers machine gun, the French Chauchat assault rifle, and the French 75mm gun. In some cases, as in the Vickers and the 75mm, these Allied weapons proved equal to or superior to AEF weapons. But, in other instances, the Americans developed their own more effective weapons, such as the M1918 Browning Automatic Rifle that replaced the poorly performing and unpopular Chauchat in September 1918. As American manufacturing slowly geared up for the war effort, doughboys were gradually issued the U.S. Army's standard issue M1903

Springfield rifle. This five-shot, bolt-action rifle gained a solid reputation for its accuracy and reliability.

Once in Europe, Americans discovered that their training back in the United States did not prepare them for combat in the trenches. The Americans would suffer casualty rates proportionate to the European losses. In the seven months of most severe fighting from May 1918 to November 1918, the AEF saw approximately 30 percent (a total of 300,000 men) killed, wounded, or missing in action out of the approximately one million Americans who saw combat. Of this figure, 100,000 died in combat or succumbed to wounds or the effects of German gas attacks.

Nevertheless, General Pershing remained adamant that open warfare could succeed in the face of withering German machine gun and artillery firepower as well as bloody impediments of barbed wire and land mines. He consistently stressed the rifle as the infantryman's basic weapon and marksmanship as his fundamental skill. Writing more than a decade later, the still-stubborn Pershing stated, "The armies of the Western Front in recent battles that I had witnessed had all but given up the use of the rifle. Machines, grenades, Stokes mortars, and one-pounders had become the main reliance of the average Allied soldier. These were all valuable weapons for specific purposes but they could not replace the combination of an efficient soldier and his rifle."[1] At any rate, the soldiers themselves became weapons systems.

Pershing approached combat in 1918 with a mind-set like that of the Europeans dating back to 1914. He had faith that the marksmanship of soldiers and the aggressiveness of their officers would yield victory. Moreover, it is not a stretch to say that American tactical doctrine in 1917 had barely moved beyond the use of massed infantry formations during the American Civil War. Such doctrinal conservatism would have tragic results for the doughboys in coming battles.

Figure 9.2 American "Doughboys" Being Trained in Trench Warfare
Hundreds of thousands of American Doughboys like these in the 6th Engineer Regiment received additional training in trench warfare after their arrived in France in late 1917 and 1918.
Source: U.S. Army Signal Corps Photograph, U.S. Army Engineer School History Office Archives

Despite Pershing's preference for open warfare, his doughboys did receive current training from the French and British to help them adapt to the tactical realities of trench combat. The British, having become proficient in laying down preparatory artillery barrages before their infantry assaults started, taught these techniques to the Americans. The doughboys likewise learned to use entrenching tools in hand-to-hand fighting, and they developed skills in combat engineering that helped increase their mobility in the barbed wire-infested and mine-strewn battlefields. Whereas expert marksmanship could help achieve tactical success, accurate rifle fire could not guarantee victory. Only proper coordination with artillery and armor—known as "combined arms operations"—could minimize casualties and maximize chances of reaching the point where rifle fire mattered. Methodical preparatory bombardments helped destroy enemy defenses and rolling artillery barrages kept the enemy's heads down during the American advance. Although hardly perfect, these gave the doughboys their best means of getting troops across no man's land in sufficient numbers to seize enemy trenches and break through enemy lines.

Aside from tactics and doctrine, the command relationships between the AEF and the French and British Allies were fraught with problems from the start of coalition efforts. The two Allies wanted to place the newly arrived American brigades and regiments into British and French units under their respective commands. This rankled General Pershing, because he did not want AEF units to be fed into the Franco–British line and placed into their formations piecemeal. The arguments between Pershing and French Marshal Ferdinand Foch and British Field Marshal Douglas Haig grew into the "amalgamation controversy," which lasted until September 1918 when the recently formed U.S. First Army went into action as an independent force.

If the AEF was going to fight, Pershing wanted them to fight as independent divisions, allowing their American commanders to make decisions in the heat of battle and guaranteeing that their units played conspicuous roles in the conflict. Whereas Pershing jealously guarded AEF autonomy, the general benefited from ironclad support from Secretary of War Newton Baker and President Woodrow Wilson back in Washington. Wilson wanted independent American participation because he saw this as the path to giving him a prime seat at the postwar negotiations table. While resisting pressure to amalgamate AEF units into the Allied Armies, Pershing did remain under Allied strategic control, and his commanders followed plans drawn up by the Allied staff.

One exception to an independent AEF occurred when Pershing relegated African Americans in the 92nd and 93rd Divisions to direct French command. This move represented a departure from Pershing's treatment of black soldiers earlier in his career. As a young officer in the 1890s, he commanded a troop of "Buffalo Soldiers," as they were known, in the 10th Cavalry Regiment in Montana. Pershing then went to the U.S. Military Academy at West Point as an instructor, where his heavy-handed leadership style caused his cadets to nickname him "Nigger Jack" or the less vicious "Black Jack" Pershing. Although derogatory, the latter nickname "Black Jack" stuck with him for the rest of his career. Pershing later led African-American soldiers in combat during the Spanish-American War in 1898 and the Mexican Punitive Expedition in 1916. While a strict disciplinarian, he cared for his black soldiers' well-being and worked to get them assigned to combat duty when possible.

In placing African-American divisions under French control, Pershing apparently bowed to political pressure among Southerners in Congress and President Wilson's administration. The French split up the 93rd Division and sprinkled its units, including the 369th Infantry Regiment "Harlem Hell Fighters," into several French Army divisions. The black soldiers in the 93rd fought effectively under the French command. They garnered high praise and received individual and unit citations from the French leadership.

The other African-American division—the 92nd—did not always fare as well in combat. After much training early in 1918, the division fought effectively in its first engagement in

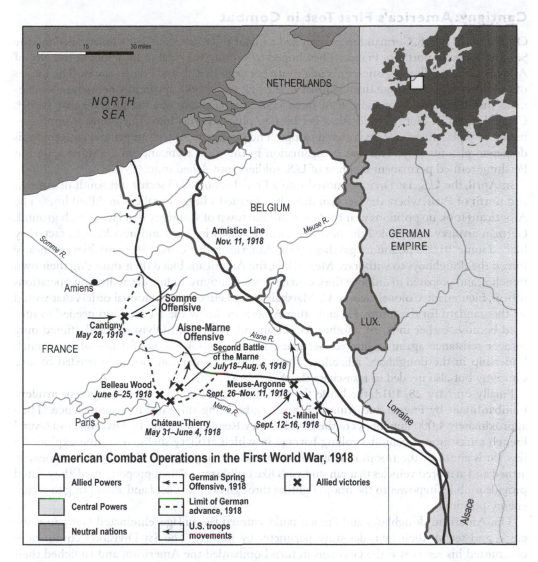

Map 9.2 American Combat Operations in the First World War, 1918

August 1918, but then it failed to capture some heavily fortified German trenches and suffered high casualties in the Meuse-Argonne Offensive later that fall. Racist critics used this setback to disparage the fighting ability of all black soldiers. In truth, that attack was not planned well, led effectively by white officers, or supported adequately by artillery. None of these factors can be blamed on the African-American soldiers.

Problems on the American home front, the frictions with coalition forces, and the slow transit to Europe caused interminable delays. But by the end of 1917, General Pershing's fledgling AEF included 120,000 soldiers and only four combat divisions deployed to Europe. They conducted limited combat operations in relatively quiet sectors on the Western Front until spring 1918. These figures amounted to a very small portion of the more than two million Americans and 43 U.S. Army divisions destined for France.

Cantigny: America's First Test in Combat

On March 21, 1918, German forces launched a major offensive along a 40-mile line along the Somme River in northern France. They hoped to capture the vital railway link at the city of Amiens, disrupt Allied logistics, and cut a swath between British and French forces. The masses of Germans advanced more than 35 miles in the first two weeks, apparently breaking the stalemate that had existed for more than three years. So relentless was the pressure that French General-in-Chief Henri Pétain asked Pershing to plug his units into Allied lines as reinforcements or replacements for his battered troops. The pragmatic American general answered this desperate plea for help. This was amalgamation in the short term and on a limited scale, but Pershing refused permanent melding of U.S. soldiers into Allied units.

In April, the U.S. 1st Division moved into a French-controlled sector just south of Amiens and north of Paris, where the German drive had formed a bulge or salient in Allied lines. The Americans took up positions near the German-held town of Cantigny that lay on high ground. German artillery bombarded the new American position in April and into May. In fact, they lobbed some 10,000 poisonous gas shells at the Americans that caused 800 casualties and nearly forced the doughboys to withdraw. Meanwhile, the Americans bided their time, dug their own trenches, and prepared to dislodge the Germans from Cantigny. In his role as division operations officer, Lieutenant Colonel George C. Marshall crafted effective operational orders that would set the standard for the future. He and other Americans knew the 1st Division needed to succeed because, earlier in April, another American unit—the 26th Division—had offered only meager resistance against a limited German raid. This shook the confidence of the French leadership in the doughboys' reliability. The 1st Division therefore not only needed to take Cantigny but also needed to resuscitate the AEF's reputation.

Finally on May 28, 1918, the battle for Cantigny started with a short but potent artillery bombardment by French and American artillery, breaking the early morning silence. Then approximately 4,000 doughboys of the 28th Infantry Regiment (of the 1st Division) and several French tanks moved behind a rolling barrage in which artillery shells were time-exploded a few yards ahead of the troops moving toward the German positions. The tanks were heavily armed and armored vehicles that ran on treads like bulldozers. When properly used, they could provide mobile firepower to the troops fighting through no man's land and attempting to secure enemy positions.

The American doughboys and French tanks entered the village, eliminated German resistance, and set up their own defensive perimeter by midday. The 1st Division's commander committed his reserves as the Germans in turn bombarded the Americans and launched their own counterattacks against the village. The doughboys survived the barrages and repelled the assaults, securing the village by May 30. The Battle of Cantigny stood as the first American victory, albeit on a small scale, for the 1st Division and for the AEF's reputation. It did, however, come at a high price. The 4,000-man-strong 28th Regiment suffered a 25 percent casualty rate that amounted to 1,067 men killed, wounded, gassed, or missing in action.

The Battles of Chateau-Thierry and Belleau Wood

On May 27, one day before the fighting at Cantigny started, the Germans launched another offensive near Craonne, France. Over the next week, the Germans threw French forces back on their heels and drove southwest deep into the French line across the Aisne River and to the Marne River. The Germans advanced to within 50 miles of Paris. They had not achieved such significant gains since 1914. To help stop the onslaught, General Pershing again sent AEF units into the breach in what is known as the Aisne-Marne campaign.

The U.S. 2nd Division and elements of the 3rd Division went into action on June 3, 1918, at the village of Chateau-Thierry, which was the most southwestern edge of the German advance. The Americans succeeded in pushing the German forces out of Chateau-Thierry and back from the Marne River, providing some relief for the hard-pressed French forces. Then the 2nd Division shifted westward about two miles, where 9,500 Marines of the division's 4th Brigade were ordered to dislodge the Germans from Belleau Wood and an adjacent village of Bouresches. This brigade included the only Marines to see action in the First World War. The American attack would also be a test of open warfare: Could the Marines, courageous fighters and great marksmen that they were, traverse the wheat field before losing too many men to enemy fire and losing forward momentum?

In the morning of June 6, the Marines formed on line to make their frontal assault. They moved through the wheat and into Belleau Wood and Bouresches village, suffering 1,000 casualties on that first bloody day of their attack. The Marines did wrest control of the wood and village. But then the Germans counterattacked. While the enemy never recaptured Bouresches, Belleau Wood proper changed hands several times over the next three weeks. Eventually, however, the sheer American numbers overwhelmed the Germans and expelled them from Belleau Wood on June 26, 1918.

The American victories first at Chateau-Thierry and Belleau Wood stopped German offensives and set up the Allied forces for a counteroffensive in the Aisne-Marne campaign later in the fall of 1918. Even these battles, particularly Belleau Wood, exacted a heavy toll on the American units. The 4th Marine Brigade lost more than 5,000 killed, wounded, or missing out of its original 9,500 men in only three weeks of combat. This casualty rate, though nowhere near the massive scale of losses suffered by French, British, or Germans, matched proportionate losses at Verdun and the Somme. Thus, if the battle is evaluated as a test case for the American concept of open warfare, then it did not achieve success. This 55 percent casualty rate could not be indefinitely sustained in practice.

The Second Battle of the Marne

The German Army began its fifth (and last) effort to break through the Allied lines on July 15, 1918. In the Second Battle of the Marne, 40 German divisions moved southwest from the Aisne River toward French city of Reims and then on to the Marne River. Generals Ludendorff and Hindenburg conceived this operation as a feint to draw Allied forces away from their proposed main strike against the British in Belgium to the north. The German units attacking to the east of Reims made no progress because, on the first day of the offensive, the National Guardsmen of the U.S. 42nd Division helped to stop the Germans in its sector. A colonel named Douglas MacArthur distinguished himself as the division Chief of Staff, having been wounded twice and earned decorations for heroism. He later rose to command his own unit. The 42nd ranked among the top American divisions in combat time—objectives achieved and casualties incurred, the latter being a dubious distinction.

Those German divisions driving toward the Marne on the western side of Reims, however, made impressive initial gains. They penetrated the French front lines, captured the city of Soissons, reached Belleau Wood, and established a bridgehead on the southern side of the Marne River. Soon, however, the Germans lost momentum when Franco-American forces stopped the advance on July 18. The U.S. 3rd Division helped prevent the German expansion south of the Marne. While so many nearby French units retreated, the 3rd doggedly stood its ground and earned its nickname "Rock of the Marne."

Marshal Foch quickly ordered a counterattack to crush this new German salient that bulged far into the Allied lines. In this Aisne-Marne Offensive, he wanted to push the Germans back across the Marne and beyond Reims. The combined 24 French divisions and eight American divisions made immediate inroads into the enemy positions beginning on July 18.

Once again placed under overall French control, the U.S. 1st and 2nd Divisions played key roles in the French XX Corps. Composed of Moroccan, Senegalese, French, and American troops, this multinational force moved eastward and captured the German logistics hub at Soissons. In the case of the battered U.S. 2nd Division, rest and recuperation from the Battle of Belleau Wood was cut short when the unit was ordered back into the fight. The division's soldiers and Marines bravely attacked German positions over open ground under deadly German machine gunfire. Several units in the 2nd Division suffered a staggering 50 percent casualty rate in the two days of combat. Cumulative casualties outpaced the AEF's ability to train replacements to fill those individual slots. Too often, the replacement soldiers and whole units went directly from the troopship on the French coast to the battlefield.

At the strategic level, losing the supply and communication hub at Soissons sounded the death knell for German hopes for victory. Thereafter, the exhausted Germans began their slow retreat. Two weeks later on August 3, the Franco–American forces pushed them back to their original starting point. The Second Battle of the Marne did prove costly for Allied forces. The French suffered 95,000 casualties, and the Americans 12,000 killed, wounded, or missing. They inflicted nearly 170,000 casualties on the Germans. The battle's outcome finally marked a decisive shift in 1918. No more could the demoralized and devastated German Army mount attacks.

The St. Mihiel Salient, the Meuse-Argonne Offensive, and the Armistice, September–November 1918

In late July 1918, General John J. Pershing finally secured permission from Marshal Foch to form an operationally independent American force called "the U.S. First Army." Indeed, so large was the new force structure that Pershing set up several corps, each with divisions attached to them. He took personal command of the First Army, while maintaining his position leading the entire AEF. Pershing also negotiated for an American sector in the Allied lines.

In the meantime, the Allies planned to take the initiative and launch a decisive war-ending campaign across the Meuse River and northeastward into the German lines. First, however, the

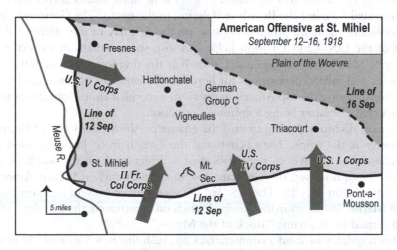

Map 9.3 American Offensive Operations at St. Mihiel, September 12–16, 1918

German salient at St. Mihiel extended several miles into Allied lines on the southern flank of proposed Allied path of attack. The Allies needed to collapse the salient. This attack presented Pershing and the AEF a golden opportunity to embark on an independent American campaign using his new U.S. First Army. He had amassed some 550,000 American soldiers in three corps with 14 divisions. One of Pershing's headquarters staff, recently promoted Colonel George Marshall, played an important role in planning this operation as well as the Meuse-Argonne Offensive that followed later in September. He possessed an innate ability to assimilate details and complexities into clear objectives and orders. Thus, it was no mistake that Pershing relied on Marshall to formulate the First Army's operational plans.

On September 12, the Battle of St. Mihiel commenced when the American doughboys flung themselves into the German line. This attack represented another first for the AEF—a combined arms operation using artillery, aircraft, tanks, and infantry. Pershing maneuvered his corps and their divisions in a double envelopment of enemy forces with pincers from the northwest and southeast corners of their salient. The two American pincers would drive toward one another surrounding Germans unable to escape.

On its face, Pershing's plan worked brilliantly. The Americans captured 16,000 Germans at St. Mihiel, and their own casualties remained relatively light compared to previous battles. However, unbeknownst to Pershing, the German forces had already begun their withdrawal from the salient. Thus, as the Americans pressed hard, the Germans gave ground more easily than if they had mounted a spirited defense. The First Army can only be given marginal praise for successfully collapsing the salient by September 16, after just four days of battle.

With the southeastern flank secure after St. Mihiel, the Franco-American forces launched the massive Meuse-Argonne Offensive on September 26. Some 1.2 million American doughboys saw action in the 47 days of the Meuse-Argonne Campaign. This constituted the largest concentration of manpower in a single operation to date in American military history.

Figure 9.3 German Pillbox Destroyed by American Attacks

AEF units destroyed German defensive positions like this pillbox at Avancourt.

Source: U.S. Army Engineer School History Office Archives.

The U.S. First Army pushed eastward and northward into the Argonne Forest, but their advance slowed because of the Germans' heavy resistance and effective artillery fire. The Americans broke through the German line of defense and seized some high ground. The cost in casualties, however, drained the AEF's manpower. Poor logistical support added to the problems. Consequently, the Americans stood on the defensive for several days. Then in early October, General Pershing ordered another advance against the German positions. Veteran reinforcements and experienced unit leaders helped the Americans drive the enemy from the Argonne Forest. Casualties rose to some 100,000 men, including many noncombat cases of influenza.

Box 9.3   The "Lost Battalion" in the Argonne Forest

Many American units performed well despite horrific conditions of the First World War. Among the most noteworthy was the "Lost Battalion" that saw action during the AEF's Meuse-Argonne Offensive in the fall of 1918. This unit was not a battalion proper but instead several companies in the U.S. 77th Division totaling 554 American officers and men under command of Major Charles White Whittlesey. The 77th, nicknamed the "Metropolitan Division" or the "Statue of Liberty" Division, drew most of its 28,000 soldiers from New York City's Lower East side. They spoke more than 40 different dialects or languages.

On October 2, 1918, Major Whittlesey and his men took part in a rapid advance into the Argonne Forest that outdistanced friendly units on their flanks. German forces easily surrounded these troops in a ravine, isolating them from resupply and reinforcement for six days. The beleaguered Americans dug in to defensive positions. They desperately fought off numerous enemy attacks despite running low on food and ammunition. The Americans could only replenish their water by crawling to a nearby stream in the face of enemy gunfire. The Americans suffered from artillery barrages, ground assaults, sniper fire, and even a flame thrower attack. Communication with other American units was only possible by using carrier pigeons. Despite his seemingly untenable situation, however Major Whittlesey held his position and ignored German requests to surrender.

The Americans lost 360 men killed, wounded, missing, or captured before being relieved on October 8. That the "Lost Battalion" could mount this defense, costly though it was, represented a real accomplishment for the Americans. It proved their mettle in combat. Nevertheless, that the communications breakdown placed these doughboys in such a predicament raised serious doubts about American command and control. For his intrepid leadership and courage under fire, Major Whittlesey received the Medal of Honor, as did four fellow officers, one sergeant, and one private. Twenty-eight other American soldiers also received the Distinguished Service Cross, the second-highest award for valor in combat.

After a brief respite in a defensive posture and some restructuring of its force structure in mid-October, the AEF again took the offensive in the Meuse-Argonne Campaign. The Germans desperately tried to slow that advance, but to no avail. The Americans sent the enemy retreating to a new line north of the Meuse River. In all, the campaign saw the U.S. First Army lose 117,000 men killed, wounded, or missing in action. The AEF did, however, inflict 100,000 casualties on the enemy.

By late October 1918, the reality of their dismal situation became clear to Germany's military and political leadership. No victory against the Allies or Americans was now possible. The irresistible surge of doughboys combined with attacks of renewed vigor by French and British forces spelled ultimate defeat for Germany. It was now a matter of crafting a negotiated peace that could forestall invasions of the homeland proper. The Central Powers contacted Allied leaders requesting an Armistice, and the German Navy ceased its unrestricted submarine warfare at the same time. The fighting ended as the last artillery shells exploded on the 11th hour of the 11th day of the 11th month—11:00 a.m. on November 11, 1918.

Conclusion

The First World War, or the "Great War" to contemporaries, can be understood as a truly modern conflict in its scope of destruction and participation. At least 60 million people from dozens of nations served in uniform, and as many as 10 million combatants died and another 20 million lived with physical and psychological scars. Yet the war can likewise be seen as transitional in its pointing to future doctrines, policies, tactics, and strategies. New applications of technology appeared in all areas of the conflict, and several key individuals in the U.S. military embraced those modern technologies during the war and laid foundations for their use in the coming decades.

In ground warfare, the use of railroads, motorized vehicles, machine guns, and poisonous gas changed military operations in many ways. Railroads had been in existence for many decades, but the iron horse had never been harnessed for military use to such a great degree as in the First World War. The railroad likewise made modern war at least as much about meticulous planning, complex management, and fixed time schedules as about men fighting in combat. Motorized vehicles like the truck also made their first appearance in large numbers in the First World War. Trucks helped to bring the transportation gap between the railhead and the battlefield proper.

Machine guns proved to be devastating weapons when arranged in trenches so that their fields of fire could overlap with nearby machine-gun emplacements. Each weapon could spew 10 to 12 bullets each second and continue to fire indefinitely if barrels were switched or cooled by water before melting down from the heat of firing and friction. It was suicide for infantry advancing on line to assault fortified machine-gun emplacements. Casualty rates for battles in the First World War reached 50 percent of the assaulting force's manpower.

Beginning in 1915, the use of chemical weapons made these high casualties even higher. Chlorine or phosgene gas delivered in artillery shells caused either a quick death or a long painful one. Less lethal mustard gas produced severe irritation to the lungs or blisters on uncovered skin. During the entire conflict, gas attacks killed more than 100,000 soldiers and incapacitated another 1.3 million as nonfatal casualties for all combatant nations. Of these totals for gas attacks, the AEF lost at least 2,000 killed and another 70,000 nonfatal casualties. The first figure of 2,000 represented a tiny percentage of the total of 53,000 American combat-related deaths. But, the latter figure of 70,000 Americans incapacitated by gas was one-third of the total of 216,000 American soldiers wounded in the conflict. Some of those 70,000 nonfatal gas victims also died from complications and long-term illnesses after the war's end.

Two other new weapons systems emerged during the First World War. First, the tank made appearances on several battlefields, most notably at the Somme, Cambrai, and Soissons. They achieved only marginal success because their slow speeds often stalled advances beyond enemy trenches, frequent malfunctions caused delays, and huge silhouettes made easy targets. By 1918, the German soldiers learned their weaknesses and began destroying tanks in great numbers with artillery fire or land mines. Some officers in the U.S. Army did recognize the tank's potential and helped start the Tank Corps. Among them was the Corps' first commander, George S. Patton, Jr. While in France, he trained soldiers in the AEF's fledgling tank units that saw action in the Battle of St. Mihiel and later engagements. The Americans used the light and relatively fast French-built Renault FT-17 tanks and the heavier British-built Mark VI tanks. Patton would go on to play a prominent yet controversial role in armor doctrinal development in the postwar years.

Second, aircraft made many appearances in the skies over the battlefields. But like the tank, none of the combatants realized the fullest potential of airpower at the tactical or the strategic levels. Early in the conflict, aircraft played mostly reconnaissance roles, spying out troop movements or spotting for artillery fire. Soon opposing sides started flying pursuit missions to shoot down enemy reconnaissance aircraft, and conversely to start flying escort missions to protect their own observer planes. These latter roles required small, maneuverable, fast airplanes like the French-built SPAD S.XIII, the British-built Sopwith Camel, and the German-built Fokker D VII armed with machine guns. Skilled pilots such as America's "Ace of Aces" Eddie Rickenbacker and Germany's "Red Baron" Manfred von Richthofen became heroes who harkened back to a chivalric age of medieval warfare when knights fought one another as individuals. They may have captured the imagination of the public on the home fronts, but they never decisively affected the outcomes of any ground battles.

Another application of aircraft in warfare—strategic bombing—slowly attracted attention during the First World War. All nations recognized that, given a large airplane with great range and heavy carrying capacity, it would be possible to strike at enemy home fronts far behind the front lines. Potential targets could include factories, railroads, shipyards, and other logistics or war production facilities, all of which were of strategic value. Targets could also be the enemy civilian populations. After all, whole societies became part of national war machines. Targeting civilians represented a departure from what were considered the legal limitations of war, but killing them or terrorizing them could hurt those war efforts. A U.S. Army officer and pilot named William "Billy" Mitchell emerged as an outspoken supporter of military aviation to include strategic bombing. He would become a controversial figure in both Army and Navy circles in the postwar years because he saw applications for airpower in bombing targets on land and ships at sea.

During the First World War, strategic bombing never achieved the mass or scope to affect industrial production or the outcome of the conflict. The aircraft used as strategic bombers carried too few bombs to cause significant damage to targets, and they flew at speeds much too slow to evade the nimble single-engine pursuit planes. Even arming the bombers with their own machine guns offered no real protection.

Despite some bravado during the First World War, however, tanks and aircraft remained in their infancy in terms of tactical applications and combined armed operations. Looking ahead, however, combined arms doctrine slowly evolved during the 1920s and 1930s and achieved operational maturity during the Second World War. That conflict demonstrated how coordinated infantry, armor, artillery, and aviation forces could overcome even the strongest defensive fortifications. The Second World War would likewise reveal the horrific impact of strategic bombing as a mature weapons system used on a massive scale.

Note

1. John J. Pershing, *My Experiences in the World War*, Vol. 1 (New York: Stokes, 1931), pp. 153–54.

Short Bibliography

Abrahamson, James. *American Arms for a New Century: The Making of a Great Military Power.* New York: Free Press, 1981.

Beaver, Daniel R. *Modernizing the American War Department: Continuity and Change in a Turbulent Ear, 1880–1920.* Kent, OH: Kent State University Press, 2006.

Chambers, John Whiteclay, II. *To Raise an Army: The Draft Comes to America.* New York: Free Press, 1987.

Coffman, Edward M. *The War to End All Wars: The American Military Experience in World War I.* New York: Oxford University Press, 1968.

Davenport, Matthew J. *First Over There: The Attack on Cantigny, America's First Battle of World War II.* New York: Thomas Dunne Books, 2015.

Feuer, A. B. *The U.S. Navy in World War I: Combat at Sea and in the Air.* Westport, CT: Praeger, 1999.

Grotelueschen, Mark E. *The AEF Way of War: The American Army and Combat in World War I.* New York: Cambridge University Press, 2007.

Hendrix, Henry J. *Theodore Roosevelt's Naval Diplomacy: The U.S. Navy and the Birth of the American Century.* Annapolis: Naval Institute Press, 2009.

Keene, Jennifer D. *World War I: The American Soldier Experience.* Lincoln, NE: Bison Books, 2011.

Kennedy, David M. *Over Here: The First World War and American Society.* New York: Oxford University Press, 1980.

Kuehn, John T. *America's First General Staff: A Short History of the Rise and Fall of General Board of the Navy, 1900-1950.* Annapolis, MD: Naval Institute Press, 2017.

Langley, Lester D. *The Banana Wars: United States Intervention in the Caribbean, 1898–1934.* Lexington: University of Kentucky Press, 1985.

Lengel, Edward G. *Thunder and Flames: Americans in the Crucible of Combat 1917–1918.* Lawrence: University Press of Kansas, 2015.

Owen, Peter F. *The Limit of Endurance: A Battalion of Marines in the Great War.* Texas A&M University Press, 2007.

Rossano, Geoffrey L., and Thomas Wildenberg. *Striking the Hornet's Nest: Naval Aviation and the Origins of Strategic Bombing in World War I.* Annapolis: Naval Institute Press, 2015.

Sammons, Jeffrey T., and John H. Morrow, Jr. *Harlem's Rattlers and the Great War: The Undaunted 369th Regiment and the African American Quest for Equality.* Lawrence: University Press of Kansas, 2014.

Smyth, Donald. *Pershing: General of the Armies.* Bloomington: Indiana University Press, 1986.

Williams, Chad L. *Torchbearers of Democracy: African American Soldiers and World War I.* Chapel Hill: University of North Carolina Press, 2010.

TIMELINE

1920	1920	1922	1929	1931
Treaty of Versailles	National Defense Act	Washington Naval Arms Treaty	Stock Market Crash	Japan invaded Manchuria

Chapter 10

Transformations in the Interwar Years, 1918–1941

After the First World War ended in November 1918, two intertwined trends affected the U.S. military for the next two decades. One can be seen in the international arena where victorious French, British, and American leaders hammered out the Treaty of Versailles and established the League of Nations in 1920. The treaty determined the fate of Germany. The belligerent nation was required to accept responsibility for the war, pay reparations to the Entente Powers, and disarm its military forces. Thereafter, most leaders and people in France, Great Britain, and the United States saw little need for maintaining expensive armed forces. Into the late 1920s and the early 1930s, these nations made several additional attempts to ensure peace by controlling production of weapons and arbitrating disputes among nations. Their efforts yielded temporary solutions that could not, however, prevent the slide toward another global conflict by the end of the 1930s.

The second trend occurred as the American military demobilized from 4.7 million personnel in 1918 to 250,000 in 1920. The subsequent stagnation of the Army, Navy, and Marine Corps was closely tied to public and Congressional support, entities which both grew isolationist in the postwar years. The onset of the Great Depression in 1929 caused further reductions in military budgets and exacerbated anti-military sentiments. New weapons systems developed at a slow pace in this austere environment. Strategic planning matched neither the nation's military capabilities nor its foreign policy priorities. Meanwhile, the Depression's effects expanded to Europe and Asia, triggering the rise of a resurgent Germany and expansionist Italy and Japan in the 1930s. These nations, with their growing military power, increasingly threatened a tenuous global peace.

In this chapter, student will learn about:

- Political and fiscal restraints on the U.S. military during the 1920s and in the Great Depression.
- Evolution of armor, strategic bombing, naval aviation, and amphibious capabilities and doctrine.

- Matching strategic plans to increasing threats on the land, in the air, and at sea.
- The gradual American slide into the Second World War.

Allied Occupation of Germany and the Treaty of Versailles, 1918–20

By the time the last shell exploded on the morning of November 11, 1918, the United States emerged as the world's most powerful nation relative to the permanently weakened United Kingdom, France, and Germany. The outcome gave President Woodrow Wilson the opportunity to restructure the postwar order in a way that fit his progressive worldview. American efforts took two forms in the years immediately following the Armistice. The first entailed American forces occupying part of Germany, and the second involved Wilson's attempt to influence the peace negotiation process.

Fighting on the Western Front may have stopped, but the need for American and Allied troops in Europe did not end. German ground forces still numbered in the millions and could have continued to resist even after the Armistice. Four years of conflict had wrecked Germany's economy, and its civilian populace suffered horrible deprivations on the home front. After Kaiser Wilhelm's abdication in 1918, a new liberal democratic government, nicknamed the Weimar Republic after the city where it was formed, took power. Germany's new democratic government struggled to achieve the best possible results in the postwar treaty negotiations.

Western Europeans and Americans also feared a communist revolution across war-torn Europe. In war-weary Russia, Tsar Nicolas II's abdication in the previous spring of 1917 had created a political vacuum that fostered the vicious Russian Civil War between a communist group called "the Bolsheviks" and a loose coalition of socialists, liberal democrats, and monarchists referred to as the "White Russians." Watching from the wings, the Allied nations were prompted to intervene to help stop the communists for two reasons. First, they feared that the large cache of weapons and supplies sent to the Tsar's government and military during the First World War would now fall into unfriendly Bolshevik hands. Second, the Bolsheviks blocked 40,000 Czechoslovak troops who wanted to ride the Trans-Siberian Railroad to the Russian port of Vladivostok on the Pacific coastline. They then hoped to travel by boat and return home to Eastern Europe or possibly fight the Germans on the Western Front. At the same time, the Allies did not want a declared war against the Bolsheviks.

To stop either fear from materializing, two American regiments landed at Vladivostok in eastern Russia on the Pacific Ocean in 1ate 1918. They joined French and Japanese units in Siberia but did not see action while guarding supplies and railroads. In a separate operation, however, some 5,000 additional American troops landed in northern Russia at Arkhangelsk to assist British units in combat operations against the Bolsheviks. By 1920, all the Allied forces departed from Russia after the communist leader Vladimir Lenin won the Russian Civil War. There was no more reason to continue because Lenin and the Bolsheviks established the new

Soviet Union. Even so, the American deployments to Russia started animosities that would fester for decades until the start of the Cold War in the 1940s.

Back in Europe, elements of the French, British, and American armies quickly moved into Germany to establish security and maintain stability. These Allied units transitioned to become occupation forces. Following the Armistice in 1918, some 230,000 United States servicemen began marching into Germany toward the Rhineland. The Americans busied themselves with setting up defensive positions and training for possible German resistance should the Weimer Republic refuse to sign the peace treaty. Those fears, however, were not realized because the Americans faced no serious resistance or problems in dealing with German soldiers or civilians. Despite French requests to stay longer, American units began returning to the United States in 1919, with the last ones departing for home four years later.

During this occupation, President Woodrow Wilson tried to shape the postwar peace in accordance with his lofty goals outlined in the Declaration of War speech of April 1917 and the Fourteen Points of January 1918. He hoped that the world would never again endure horrific suffering on the scale of the First World War. Wilson traveled to France in 1919 to participate in the Paris Peace Conference, where he joined France's Prime Minister Georges Clemenceau and Great Britain's Prime Minister David Lloyd George. The conference lasted from January 1919 to January 1920.

The idealistic Wilson arrived in Paris with several goals in mind. He favored lenient treatment of Germany, believing that nation should be stripped of offensive military capabilities but not completely ruined. First, he reasoned that a productive Germany would be a healthy member of the international community and a bulwark against communism. The American president also desired that the victorious powers write elements of his Fourteen Points into the postwar treaty. Key among these were Wilson's two other goals: self-determination, which was the right of peoples to determine their own governmental systems without external compulsion, and collective security, which was the right of protection of territory and sovereignty of nations against external threats.

Wilson's desire for lenient treatment of Germany garnered no support from Lloyd George and Clemenceau. They wanted to defang their mutual enemy. They did, however, agree to apply Wilson's principle of self-determination to some people living in the now-defunct German, Austro-Hungarian, and Ottoman Empires. However, in other cases, Lloyd George and Clemenceau ignored self-determination altogether. For example, despite large numbers of ethnic Germans in these regions, Germany had to return Alsace-Lorraine to France and relinquish large tracts of East Prussia to a newly independent Poland. Elsewhere, Germans in the Sudetenland on the southeast border of Germany were given no choice when they became part of the new nation of Czechoslovakia.

Lloyd George and Clemenceau did find common ground with Wilson's principle of collective security as a function of the proposed League of Nations. Each legitimate nation-state would have a vote in this organization that they hoped would keep the peace. If arbitration or economic sanctions failed to resolve differences and if the League voted to do so, then military force could be directed against any rogue nations. The League's members would then provide the manpower and weapons for punitive operations to reestablish peace. However, the reality of pacifism in Great Britain and France and growing isolationism in the United States would preclude them from committing armed forces to any such punitive actions.

Negotiations in Paris dragged on for several months until the Treaty of Versailles was unveiled in June 1919. The end product represented a victory for Georges Clemenceau and David Lloyd George and a repudiation of Wilson regarding postwar treatment of Germany and self-determination of all nations. Germany endured a harsh peace settlement: accepting full blame for the First World War, paying heavy reparations to Britain and France, losing most of its army and all its navy, and relinquishing millions of people and huge swaths of land to its neighbors. Most German civilians and veterans saw the Treaty of Versailles as humiliating and debilitating to their national pride and economy. Just as galling, representatives of the Weimar Republic arrived in Paris only to see the completed agreement, and then they were coerced into signing the Treaty or risk resuming hostilities.

Back in the United States, President Woodrow Wilson faced strong resistance against the Treaty of Versailles, because it entailed his nation's full and active membership in the League of Nations. Many Americans did not share Wilson's vision of the League as a vehicle for maintaining world peace. Specifically, the League's prerogative to use military force against a rogue nation meant that member nations were mandated to provide men and weapons in coalition forces. Those nations' military forces would thus be subordinated to the League's control. Put in constitutional terms, this meant a possible loss of American sovereignty to the League, because the United States government would not have complete control of when, where, and against whom a war might be fought. This fear helped drive the U.S. Senate to reject the Treaty of Versailles. The United States therefore never joined the League of Nations. Without this key member, the League possessed no teeth and thus no legitimacy.

Personal antagonisms between the president and senators also helped stop ratification, as did the increasingly isolationist American people who wanted no global military actions. Later, Wilson turned the elections of 1920 into referenda on the Treaty and the League, but his last-ditch effort met final defeat when the Democratic Party lost the presidency and control of Congress to the Republican Party.

The American Military in the Postwar Era of Normalcy

While the political fight raged over the Treaty of Versailles, proponents of American military reductions and stable international relations initiated two other important measures: the National Defense Act of 1920 and the Washington Naval Arms Limitation Treaty of 1922. Both fit into the nation's historical pattern of the flow of postwar demobilization following the ebb of wartime expansion. In late 1918, the Army boasted 3.7 million men, the Navy stood at 430,000, and the Marine Corps' strength peaked at more than 75,000. Amid calls for returns to prewar tranquility, more than 90 percent of these men left military service. Demobilization also included major budget reductions. The Army's expenditures reached more than $9 billion in 1918, then fell to $1 billion in 1920, and finally dropped still lower to $250 million in 1925.

Secretary of War Newton D. Baker and Army Chief of Staff General Peyton C. March tried to slow this steep drawdown in 1919 and 1920. Because the United States needed to be better prepared for future conflicts, they wanted to maintain the system established by the National Defense Act of 1916. Harkening back to Emory Upton's theories in the late nineteenth century, the Army would utilize reservists to fill out understrength Regular Army units. Centripetal pressures for demobilization, however, were too strong. Congress rejected Baker and March's plan and instead passed the National Defense Act of 1920. The Regular Army, the National Guard, and the Organized Reserves remained intact, along with the possibility that the Army could expand during emergencies. The new act likewise acknowledged the need for a cadre of commissioned officers in the reserves and continued to support the Reserve Officer Training Corps (ROTC) in colleges and universities.

Nevertheless, the National Defense Act of 1920 departed from Emory Upton's expansible Army of the late nineteenth century with its skeletonized units. It amended the preceding 1916 Act in significant ways. In making these changes, Congress took its cues from Colonel John M. Palmer, a highly intelligent Army officer and veteran. Per his recommendations, the 1920

Act called for a peacetime standing Army of 280,000 regulars who filled a few operationally ready divisions tasked with expeditionary duties and border defense. The Regular Army would also train some 435,000 National Guardsmen and several hundred thousand federal reservists in the Enlisted Reserve Corps and the Officer Reserve Corps. According to Palmer's thinking, these citizen-soldiers and citizen-officers could then fill their own units reinforcing the Regular Army as needed in times of emergency. War Department General Staff Planners believed that, under the new National Defense Act's system, the wartime Army could field more than two million regular soldiers and citizen-soldiers after 60 days of training.

Although the 1920 Act may have authorized a Regular Army of 280,000 men, the reality of Congressional funding levels supported a paltry 135,000 men in the Regular Army. Few units could be considered operationally ready because the Army was stretched so thin. On a practical level, the existing units were little better than skeletons. Thus, Palmer's vision was not fully realized in the years after 1920.

Apart from manpower issues, the National Defense Act of 1920 transformed many other structures and functions of the War Department and the Army. It created administrative head-quarters in the War Department for the Infantry, Cavalry, Artillery, and Field Artillery Branches. Learning hard lessons from the First World War, the Act added new elements to the Army when it made the Chemical Warfare Service and the Air Service permanent organizations. The Tank Corps, however, did not achieve permanent autonomy. It was absorbed into the Infantry Branch, where it languished in doctrinal uncertainty and budgetary poverty.

Under the auspices of the National Defense Act, the Army's new Chief of Staff, John J. Pershing, began to consolidate and organize the Army's structures and functions in 1921. He modeled the War Department's General Staff on his General Headquarters staff of the AEF in the First World War. Pershing divided the General Staff into five divisions with designated functions: G-1, Personnel; G-2, Intelligence; G-3, Operations and Training; G-4, Supply; and WPD, the War Plans Division. The last division articulated the Army's missions in strategic plans formulated to fight potential conflicts in Europe and the Pacific.

Like the Army, the Navy suffered budget cuts in the postwar years, but the cuts' fullest effects were delayed for several years. In 1918, the United States boasted the world's largest navy with 29 capital ships. These powerful vessels, including battleships and battlecruisers, were the most powerful warships afloat. President Wilson's ambitious plan to maintain American naval supremacy continued in 1919 when the battleships USS *Tennessee* and her sister ship, the *California*, were launched. These formidable vessels displaced 32,000 tons and carried twelve 14-inch guns. Additional construction also began on eight even more powerful capital ships.

Once Warren G. Harding became president and his Republican Party took control of Congress in 1921, however, the U.S. Navy also felt the full effects of demobilization. Harding decided to reduce spending on the seaborne service. Construction of the new capital ships slowly ground to a halt. Only three new *Colorado*-class battleships armed with 16-inch guns were completed, and two other American battlecruisers were converted into aircraft carriers. Thereafter, the United States did not build any new battleships until 1937.

Harding also made other diplomatic moves to reduce the need for a large American fleet when he convened the Washington Naval Conference in 1921. Worries that a naval arms race might cause another conflict motivated many nations to attend. Representatives from eight nations, including Great Britain, France, Italy, and Japan met with their American counterparts to discuss reduction in the size, number, and armament of capital ships. Of these, the American, British, and Japanese delegations exerted by far the most influence. Each nation came to the negotiating table with goals in mind and strategic realities to consider. The key debates centered on the ratios of each nation's capital ship tonnage.

Box 10.1   Realities of Military Life in the Interwar Years

In the 1920s and 1930s, recruiting advertisements lured young American males into the military with promises of travel, adventure, employment, education, or rites of passage into manhood. But their service was seldom glamorous or exciting. The realities of low pay, antiquated equipment, and sluggish promotions would seem to make enlistment unappealing. For example, after completing four months of service in the Army, privates received $30 per month, and this figure did not increase between 1922 and 1940. True,

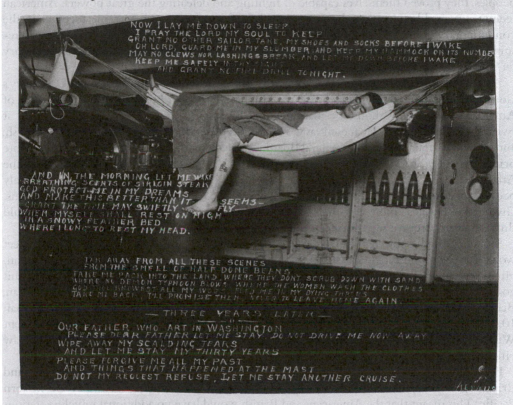

Figure 10.1 A Sailor's Prayer

A photograph of an American sailor sleeping on a hammock near five-inch shells on USS *Nevada* in the 1920s. This sailor learned to be thankful for employment during the Great Depression. The handwritten prayer on the photo appeared as the following poem:

Now I lay me down to sleep/I pray the Lord my soul to keep/Grant no other sailor take, my shoes and socks before I wake/May no clews nor lashing break, and let me down before I wake/Keep me safely in thy sight/And grant me no fire drill tonight.

And in the morning let me wake/Breathing scents of sirloin steak/And make this better than it seems/Grant the time may swiftly fly/When myself shall rest on high/in a snowy feather bed/where I long to rest my head.

Far away from all these scenes/From the smell of half done beans/Take me back into the land, where they don't scrub down with sand/Where no demon typhoon blows, where the women wash the clothes/God thou knowest all my woes, feed me in my dying throes/Take me back, I'll promise then, never to leave home again.

Three Years later: Our father who art in Washington/Please dear father let me stay, do not drive me now away/Wipe away my scalding tears/And let me stay my thirty years/Please forgive all my past/And things that happened at the mast/Do not my request refuse, let me stay another cruise.

Source: U.S. Naval History and Heritage Command.

those privates did receive housing and food, but their yearly income of $360 was approximately 50 percent of the national average income. This pay rate notwithstanding, serving in the U.S. military meant employment, which was especially important during the Great Depression when one out of four Americans was jobless.

Secretary of State Charles Evans Hughes led the American delegation. Dealing with the Japanese proved to be the biggest sticking point. Japan's Navy stood as a potential obstacle to American interests in East Asia and the western Pacific. Beginning in the 1890s, Japan's rise to power in Asia had worried American naval strategists. Alone among the non-Caucasian peoples, they proved themselves capable of fighting and defeating the great powers. American feelings wavered between racial contempt and fearful suspicion. These came together in the contemporary epithet "Yellow Peril," which denoted how the Japanese combined the presumed Asian traits of deviousness and cruelty with the skills in using Western military technologies.

Against these strategic and cultural backdrops, the high-ranking admirals on the U.S. Navy's General Board offered advice to Secretary Hughes. The Board argued that the number of American capital ships should be maintained at parity with the British Royal Navy and at twice the strength of the Japanese Navy. This would mean of ratio of 10:10:5 for U.S., British, and Japanese capital ships. The General Board reasoned that the Japanese Navy would operate primarily in the western Pacific Ocean, while the U.S. Navy needed to operate in both the Atlantic and Pacific. For its part, the British Royal Navy was stretched even more thinly because of interests in the Mediterranean Sea and the Atlantic, Pacific, and Indian Oceans. Giving the Japanese more than half the sea power of the Americans and the British would thus bequeath decisive superiority in the Pacific to Tokyo.

Secretary Hughes rejected the General Board's argument because he knew that the U.S. Fleet would have to build more capital ships to reach the point of doubling the number of Japan. Hughes recognized that Congress would never accede to spending more money to reach this goal. Instead of a 10:10:5 ratio, he proposed the ratio of 5:5:3 for tonnage of the American, British, and Japanese capital ships. Such vessels were defined as those displacing more than 10,000 tons and carrying several 8-inch guns or greater. In these strokes, he ended President Wilson's plans to build a U.S. Navy second to none. Many admirals and naval strategists saw Hughes' proposals as invitations to Japan to assert naval supremacy in the Pacific.

For their part, the Japanese achieved a significant concession when the Americans and British agreed they would not build any new fortifications or add naval bases in the western Pacific. This meant that the Americans and British would have no additional refueling stations and repair facilities. As with the 5:5:3 ratio, American naval strategists saw this concession to Japan as another step toward impeding American interests in that region. The conference concluded in 1922 and delegations signed the Washington Naval Arms Limitation Treaty, setting the tone for American naval policy and strategy for the next 15 years. In years since, the U.S. Navy of the 1920s and 1930s garnered the derogatory nickname the "Treaty Navy." Apart from issues of warship construction, the Washington Treaty also prohibited American fortifications of new bases in the western Pacific during those decades. This added yet another aspect to Japan's military superiority in that region.

Groping for Strategies: Planning for Future Wars

At face value, the settlements in Paris and Washington looked like steps toward a peaceful future. None of the great powers were ready to fight another war, nor were their populaces willing to contemplate entering another bloody conflict. For the near future, the impetus for creating strategic plans was reduced. However, threats to American security still loomed just over the horizon. Most probable among these was Japan. That nation gladly expanded its presence in the western Pacific Ocean by assuming control of "Micronesia" from the defeated Germans. Micronesia included the Marshall, Caroline, and Marianas island chains. Possession of the Philippines, Guam, Wake, and Midway gave the United States vested strategic interests in the Pacific ever since victory in the Spanish–American War in 1898. American and Japanese islands were intermingled in the central and western Pacific.

Beginning in the 1920s, American planners continually updated the ORANGE War Plan, the color designation referring to Japan. Although the plan to defeat Japanese forces did evolve from 1906 to 1939, all its variations shared several tenets. American strategists expected the Japanese to launch a preemptive strike, probably without a declaration of war. That attack would be directed against U.S. Army bases in the Philippines and Marine bases on Guam or Wake. The U.S. Fleet would sortie from Hawai'i or the North American West Coast and sail across the Pacific. Meanwhile, U.S. Marine Corps units would seize Japanese bases, which in turn would become refueling stations, safe anchorages, repair facilities, and supply depots for future American offensive operations. After crossing the Pacific, the fleet would relieve U.S. Army forces in the Philippines. American planners then expected the Japanese Navy to contest the American offensive. This ensuing naval battle, as was unquestioningly assumed in all versions of the ORANGE War Plan, would result in a decisive American victory. But if Japan chose not to fight, the U.S. Fleet would blockade their home islands. In any case, an American victory would reduce Japanese power in the region.

The American military formulated plans in several locations and organizations, and each service possessed its own war plans division. Promising officers such as the Army's George C. Marshall and Dwight D. Eisenhower, the Navy's Richmond Kelly Turner, and the Marine Corps' Thomas Holcomb and Holland M. Smith did tours in their services' war plans divisions and later put their experiences to use as senior leaders during the Second World War. The Army War College and the Naval War College devoted significant portions of curricula to planning and simulating conflicts. Students played out scenarios in war games that pitted the United States against individual adversaries such as Japan (Orange), German (Black), and even Britain (Red). They analyzed American capabilities, anticipated possible enemy movements, and recommended options to defeat those forces. This process, however, proved problematic in the interwar years because the United States possessed no coherent national policies that identified potential foes other than worries about a vague Japanese threat. Meager budgets, personnel shortages, and antiquated equipment also hampered planners from crafting realistic courses of action.

Returning to the context of the early 1920s, changes to the ORANGE War Plan occurred because the Japanese controlled bases in Micronesia in the western Pacific following the Treaty of Versailles. These lay in the path of any American advance westward across the Pacific. Two American officers played instrumental roles in revising the ORANGE War Plan to account for the Japanese control of these island bases.

The relatively unknown Rear Admiral Clarence Stewart Williams worked from the top down as head of Navy's War Plans Division in 1921 and 1922. He did not think a quick dash across the Pacific toward the Philippines and Japan was feasible, given the long distances and the localized Japanese advantages. Instead, he favored a broad and deliberate offensive campaign through Micronesia that would keep the U.S. Fleet from being overextended or cut off from logistical support. Williams recognized that the Marine Corps could make significant contributions to this westward drive.

Another gifted planner, the more well-known Marine Corps Lieutenant Colonel "Pete" Ellis developed part of the operational level of the ORANGE War Plan. He predicted with uncanny accuracy how the American amphibious operations eventually occurred in the Pacific

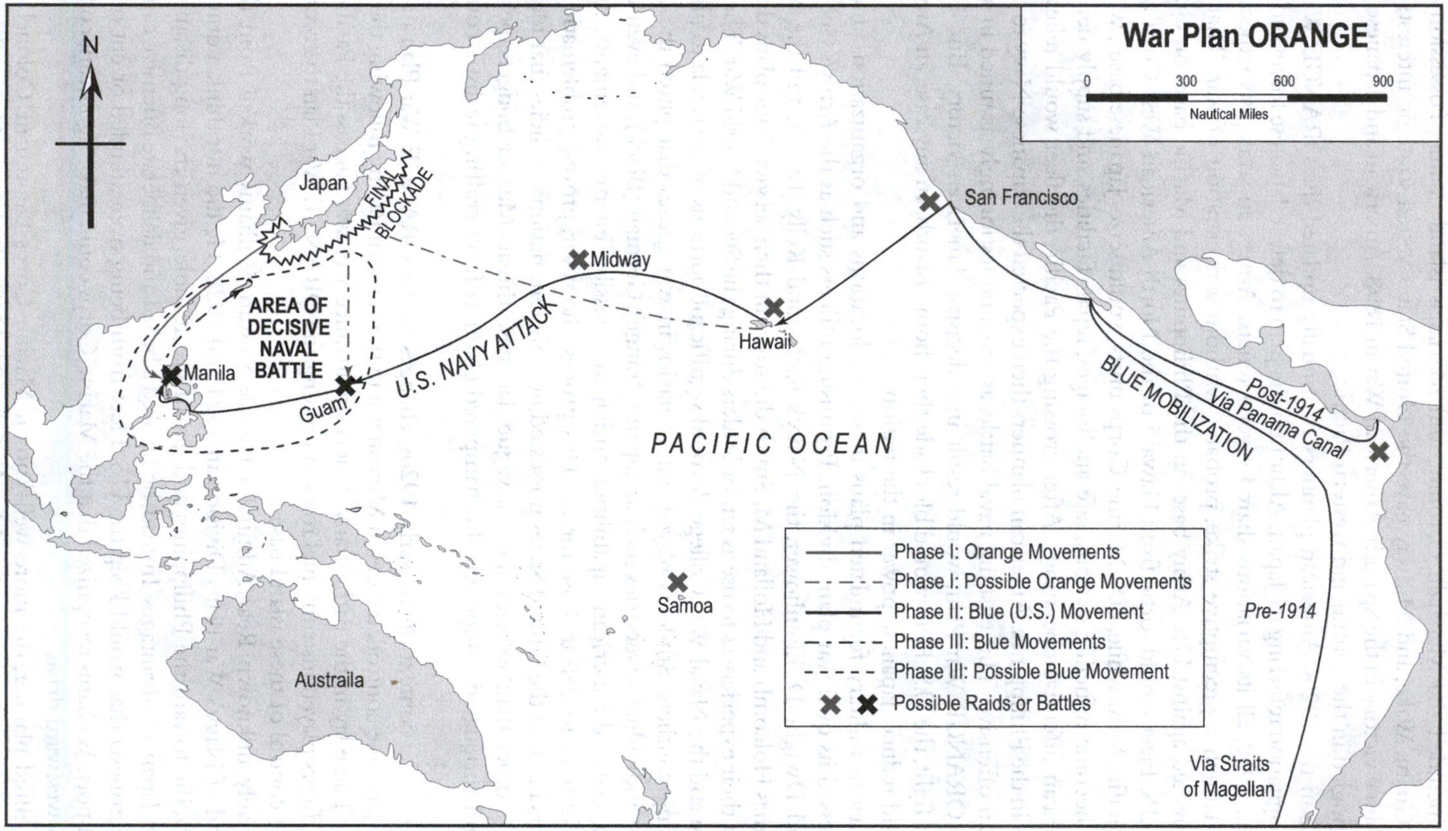

War Plan ORANGE

Nautical Miles
0   300   600   900

Post-1914
Via Panama Canal

Pre-1914
Via Straits
of Magellan

BLUE MOBILIZATION

San Francisco

PACIFIC OCEAN

Hawaii

Midway

Samoa

Guam

Manila

Japan

Australia

U.S. NAVY ATTACK

FINAL BLOCKADE

AREA OF DECISIVE NAVAL BATTLE

N

Phase I: Orange Movements
Phase I: Possible Orange Movements
Phase II: Blue (U.S.) Movement
Phase III: Blue Movements
Phase III: Possible Blue Movement
Possible Raids or Battles

Map 10.1 ORANGE War Plan

War two decades later. Apart from this contribution to strategic planning, Ellis laid the foundation for the Marine Corps' firm establishment as an operational partner, albeit very junior, to the Navy. With support from Admiral Williams, Ellis argued that the Marine Corps represented the only logical choice to assault enemy-held island bases like Eniwetok or Truk and subsequently hold them against counterattack. For the Corps, these integral missions in the naval contingencies represented institutional survival. Not only was it practical for the Marines, as soldiers of sea, to support the Navy's fleet operations, it was also shrewd because the Navy could utilize Marines and thus exclude the Army from many aspects in the ORANGE War Plan. Such competition between Army and Navy for strategic prerogatives persisted through the prewar planning and preparations as well as into wartime operations.

Grasping for New Technologies: Proponents and Detractors

Although fought mostly in the trenches, the First World War also heralded the rise of the tank and the airplane as weapons systems. Popular images of armored tanks bearing down on enemy trenches and agile airplanes diving and veering in dogfights belied their limited contributions to outcomes of battles. Tanks and airplanes nonetheless did show great potential to change war-making at tactical, operational, and strategic levels. In the case of the airplane, similar potential also existed to launch aerial attacks on enemy warships and shift naval warfare away from ship-to-ship engagements.

Throughout the interwar years, American officers debated the viability of armor and aviation in warfare. On one side were innovative, often younger, and sometimes controversial officers who supported the exploitation of their new weapons systems. They believed airplanes or tanks offered decisive advantages if properly employed. Some may also have seen proponency as a means of personal advancement. On the opposing side stood detractors and skeptics. These parochial and occasionally reactionary officers viewed the new technologies with uncertainty because they doubted whether tanks or airplanes could change warfare. To them, committing scant resources to these new weapons systems in already lean budgets was not a viable option. Some officers also worried that their personal power would be displaced by innovators who promoted new missions for the tank or the airplane. Thus, a tug-of-war over armor and aviation occurred in not only practical but also political terms. Three case studies involving the tank, aerial bombardment, and naval aviation revealed how and why the Army and the Navy grasped for new technologies in the 1920s and 1930s.

The tank barely survived the end of the First World War. After 1918, the Army had ordered the construction of more than 23,000 tanks, but only 1,100 outlived the Army's postwar budget cuts and loss of interest among senior leaders. Never an enthusiastic supporter of the tank, the new Army Chief of Staff General Pershing willingly allowed the Infantry Branch to subsume the Tank Corps, as mandated by the National Defense Act of 1920. This move pointed to a belief that the tank could best be used as an infantry-support weapon to provide fire support or protection for foot soldiers. As a result, no new American tanks were brought online until the next decade.

Despite this lack of interest among high-ranking leaders, the tank survived because of support from British military theorists and young U.S. Army officers. Two of the most influential foreign advocates were B. H. Liddell Hart and J. F. C. Fuller, both of whom served in the British Army during the First World War. In fact, as a founding officer of the Royal Tank Corps, Fuller planned the armor operations in the Battle of Cambrai in 1917. In the postwar years, Liddell Hart and Fuller criticized the Allied commanders for failing to end the bloody stalemate in the trenches and overcome the defenders' advantages in this type of warfare. They believed the tank represented the best possibility to do so in the future because, as part of increasingly mechanized and motorized ground forces, they could provide the speed and firepower necessary to return initiative to the offense. Concentrated attacks at key points in enemy lines, exploitation of those ruptures behind enemy lines, or sweeping envelopments around enemy positions would be possible in this new maneuver warfare. Liddell Hart and Fuller asserted that these armored units constituted one of several combat arms, including infantry, artillery, and eventually aircraft, that could be coordinated on battlefields.

Back in the United States, a few junior Army officers took up the fight to preserve tanks in the early 1920s. Captains George S. Patton, Jr., and Dwight D. Eisenhower had served in the Tank Corps during the First World War. They saw armored vehicles as potentially decisive battlefield weapons and published articles that argued for their viability in maneuver warfare. However, the accepted wisdom in Army doctrine relegated tanks to infantry-support roles. Challenging this dominant view could stall career advancement, and neither Patton nor Eisenhower was willing to sacrifice promotions for the sake of preserving armor. When they could not change the views of their superiors, both left the Tank Corps.

Patton transferred to the Cavalry Branch, where he continued to call for the formulation of armor doctrine. Yet, he also maintained allegiance to horse cavalry. This may have been his pragmatic realization that advancement in rank required loyalty to his new branch. Later as a colonel, Patton eventually found his way back into tank units in 1940, when he took command of the newly formed 2nd Armored Brigade, 2nd Armored Division. For his part, Eisenhower moved to the Infantry Branch and later rotated through several staff tours, including aide to Army Chief of Staff General Douglas MacArthur in the mid-1930s. Although Eisenhower never again served in armored units and spent the interwar years becoming a mobilization expert and skilled war planner, he never forgot the tank's potential. Patton and Eisenhower were not the only advocates for armor doctrine and development. Another Army officer, Major Adna R. Chaffee, Jr., gradually brought the tank out of obscurity in late 1920 and into the 1930s (see the section on Ongoing Developments).

While tank development faded into obscurity, the airplane was also being scrutinized, but in a more conspicuous way. Like armor, American aviation never reached its fullest potential in the First World War. Daring pilots fought aerial battles with opposing pilots for control of air space over battlefields, thus enabling the winning side's aircraft to conduct reconnaissance and artillery spotting missions against enemy ground forces. American pilots would also bomb or strafe enemy positions in support of infantry movements. These roles constituted uses of air power at the tactical level or in the close air support role. The American use of aircraft in the First World War did not, however, include strategic bombing—hitting targets on the enemy's home front with the goal of destroying the enemy's moral will and material capacity to make war.

After the conflict ended, the Army Air Service shrank during demobilization, just like the rest of the U.S. military. The Air Service slipped from its maximum wartime strength of 195,000 men to 10,000 men during the 1920s. Of these, only a few hundred were pilots. Air Service budgets also precipitously fell from $800 million in 1918 to $12 million in 1924. This left very little money for developing new aircraft and for maintaining the Air Service's inventory of several hundred planes.

Most Army officers, steeped as they were in ground warfare, believed that aircraft should remain as an auxiliary arm that supported ground forces and remained under the ground commander's control. From their perspective, this represented air power's practical application. U.S. Army pilots, however, saw much greater potential for aviation. They were inspired by the independent air forces in France and Great Britain and enamored of air power theories espoused in Italian General Giulio Douhet's book *Command of the Air* in 1920. The American pilots hoped that the Army Air Service could be expanded, and that new aircraft and doctrines would be developed. These would help turn airplanes into offensive weapons with significant strategic missions.

Chief among the Army's air power proponents was Brigadier General William "Billy" Mitchell. Following the end of the First World War, Mitchell began making appeals that a department of aviation be created. He joined the Army in the Spanish–American War and advanced quickly through the ranks from private to general by 1918. He commanded all American aviation forces in the First World War, flew combat missions, and planned air campaigns. Although Mitchell impressed his subordinates and superiors alike with his skills as a pilot and a planner, he also possessed flamboyant, if not insubordinate, attitudes. He wanted this new organization placed on equal footing with the War and Navy Departments.

Mitchell drummed up support in the U.S. military, in Congress, and among the American people by staging demonstrations of the airplane's destructive potential. The most dramatic of these occurred in July 1920. Several Marine Corps, Navy, and Army airplanes took turns dropping bombs on the battleship *Ostfriesland*, an unmanned target vessel that had been part of the German Navy during the First World War. Although the bombs eventually sank the battleship, this test's conclusions proved to be dubious because of its staged conditions. The vessel had no crew on board to man antiaircraft batteries, and it made no evasive maneuvers. Nevertheless, Mitchell and other air power supporters claimed success. He later undertook other demonstrations in which aircraft sank obsolete American battleships.

Mitchell also embraced doctrines regarding strategic bombing outlined by Douhet. Both officers believed that bombers could fly long distances behind enemy lines to destroy factories, railroads, shipyards, and other logistical targets, all of which had strategic value. Bombing enemy home fronts also opened possibilities of targeting the enemy civilian populations, who supported their national war efforts. However, this also represented a departure from what were considered legal limitations of warfare at that time.

Mitchell ran into stiff opposition in the Army and Navy establishments. Blocking his goals were powerful senior leaders, including Army Chiefs of Staff General John J. Pershing and later General Charles P. Summerall and Chief of Naval Operations Admiral William S. Benson. They chafed at the idea of an independent "air force." Such an organization would not only detract from their influence in Washington but also potentially reduce the primacy of infantry and artillery on land and the battleship at sea.

The outspoken Mitchell made his worst mistake when he criticized his superiors for ignoring the airplane's potential. In 1925, he publicly accused the Army and Navy's senior leadership of "incompetency," "criminal negligence," and "almost treasonable administration of the national defense." His strident words were a reaction to two deadly accidents that, for Mitchell, revealed the poor condition of aviation equipment, rather than the weakness of air power. Because such outburst could not be tolerated, Mitchell was charged with insubordination later that year and court-martialed. The military judges, none of whom were aviators, stripped him of rank, suspended him from active duty and command, and ordered his pay be withheld for five years.

Ultimately, it was not merely Mitchell's ideas that challenged the conventional Army wisdom about air power; his attitudes and bearing also angered senior officers. Herein lay an interesting case study in personality. Mitchell's presumptuous style helped to bring down the wrath of the military establishment on himself. Despite his weaknesses and failings, Mitchell attracted several disciples like Carl Spaatz and Henry Arnold. Both Army officers served as aviators in the First World War, testified on Mitchell's behalf at his court-martial, maintained their interest in Army aviation in the interwar years, and later assumed powerful positions in the U.S. Army Air Force during the Second World War.

Although destructive to Mitchell's own career, the publicity from his court-martial did pay long-term dividends for Army aviation. Congress passed the Air Corps Act in 1926. This made important changes by renaming Army Air Service as the Army Air Corps, creating a new position of Assistant Secretary of War for Air, and increasing aviation's presence on the War Department's General Staff. The act called for expansion of the Air Corps' manpower and aviation units. Sadly, budget restrictions slowed this growth process during the rest of the decade and into the next. Nevertheless, officers in the Air Corps began to formulate doctrines for strategic air power in the interwar years, austere though they were.

Billy Mitchell's decision to destroy battleships and validate aerial bombing provides a convenient segue into naval aviation during the interwar years. The idea of arming airplanes with bombs or torpedoes to sink warships resonated with Vice Admiral William S. Sims and Rear Admiral William A. Moffett, both of whom were senior naval officers. Sims had commanded the U.S. forces based in England during the First World War. Once the conflict ended, Sims criticized Secretary of the Navy Josephus Daniels because he believed the Navy was unprepared to fight the war. Sims also returned to the Naval War College for a second term as its president from 1919 to 1922. In this post, he helped to mold the next generation of officers to understand the potential of aviation in naval operations. This sowed seeds for aviation to become a premier combat function in the Navy.

During the interwar years, the most noteworthy proponent of naval aviation was William A. Moffett. Commissioned in 1890, he served during the Spanish-American War and later received the Medal of Honor for leading a daring night raid into Vera Cruz harbor, where he landed Marines and sailors who occupied the Mexican city. Captain Moffett remained in the continental United States during the First World War, where as commander of the Great Lakes Training Center in Chicago, Illinois, he started a pilot training program. He continued to take interest in naval aviation after the conflict ended. Moffett rose to the rank of rear admiral when he became the first chief of the Navy's new Bureau of Aeronautics in 1921. Serving three terms in this capacity until his accidental death in 1933, he shepherded naval aviation from relative obscurity to an ascendant element of the Navy. Moffett supported the development of the new aircraft carrier as a major component in the U.S. Fleet. Lastly, he helped formulate doctrine for the use of air power during naval operations.

Despite Moffett's successes, he did face strong resistance inside the Navy. He fought running administrative battles with senior admirals. These provincialists and conservatives saw fleets of battleships fighting decisive Mahanian engagements as the ideal. The airplane, if at all useful, could support this fleet in reconnaissance and gunfire spotting missions, not unlike the use of airplanes supporting artillery and infantry in ground operations. That Moffett overcame the centripetal inertia of the battleship-centric Navy can be credited to a combination of his character traits and interservice circumstances.

In temperament and approach, Moffett stood on the opposite pole from Billy Mitchell. Moffett carefully maneuvered through the Navy Department's bureaucracy to avoid making serious enemies to his cause. He even turned Mitchell's aggressiveness to his own advantage. Mitchell wanted to bring all aviation under a single cabinet-level organization, thus potentially combining Army with Navy and Marine Corps aerial assets into a single entity. Moffett countered this threat by appealing to the loyalties of his fellow Navy officers, albeit most of whom were battleship and surface warfare proponents. Moffett reasoned that, even if some admirals failed to comprehend the full potential of airplanes, they would prefer that the Navy control its own aviation arm.

Proof of Moffett's legacy can be seen during his lifetime and after his untimely death. The Navy added three aircraft carriers to the fleet on his watch. The USS *Langley* became the Navy's first aircraft carrier in 1922. The two others, sister ships USS *Saratoga* and *Lexington*, were commissioned in 1927. These displaced more than 35,000 tons, boasted complements of 90 airplanes, and made top speeds of 33 knots. Just as important as these new vessels were Moffett's efforts to carve niches for the aircraft carrier and naval aviation in fleet exercises and war plans.

Economic Depression and Emerging Global Threats, 1929–39

The world of the 1920s seemed to be relatively stable and peaceful. The people in France, Great Britain, and the United States tried to forget the horrors of the trenches of the First World War. These nations, as well as Japan, abided by principles and policies established in the Treaty of Versailles and the Naval Arms Limitation Treaty. The U.S. military, beleaguered as it was by meager budgets, seemed to have no immediate threats.

Serious problems, however, festered under the surface of the postwar normalcy. The Soviet Union remained politically and economically isolated, but the specter of communism cast a dark shadow over the rest of Europe. Rumblings could be heard in Italy, where dictator Benito Mussolini established his fascist regime, began enlarging his military forces, and greedily eyed territories in the Mediterranean basin and on the African continent. The League of Nations criticized Mussolini's imperialistic foreign policies, but given the League's weakness these words rang hollow. Elsewhere in Europe, the German economy collapsed under the weight of reparations and hyperinflation, and worries of revolution and upheaval prompted the United States to provide financial support to the Weimar Republic. These efforts stabilized the German economy only in the short term.

Existing international and financial problems exploded after the stock market crash in the United States in October of 1929. In a matter of days, American investments lost 30 percent of their value. This set off a chain reaction that caused bankruptcies, foreclosures, and bank failures across the United States, plunging the country into the Great Depression. American consumers purchased fewer and fewer items, which in turn lowered production of those items, reduced income for businesses, and forced the businesses to lower wages or lay off employees. Unemployment rose sharply from two percent in 1929 to 24 percent in 1932.

The economic catastrophe reverberated across the globe, causing the collapse of international trade, and triggering financial crises in other nations. Between 1929 and 1932, unemployment rates doubled in Great Britain and Japan and tripled in Germany. The suffering and anxiety of millions of people prompted changes in governments in almost every industrialized nation in the early 1930s. The citizens blamed parties in power for the economic downturns and voted them out of office. Some governments like the United States moved slightly to the left, while others moved far to the right toward authoritarianism. A new Nazi government in Germany and a militarist government in Japan sought to solve the economic problems by increasing expenditures on military forces and annexing or invading nearby territories. These actions portended grave threats to American security.

As the President of the United States from 1929 to 1933, Herbert Hoover could not stop the problems caused by the stock market crash, nor could he mitigate the effects of the Depression. Hoover exhibited uneven leadership in military, international, and domestic arenas. On the proactive side in 1930, he sent an American delegation to an international conference in London that sought to limit the size, firepower, and number of warships in the world's navies. The Senate ratified the resulting treaty. Hoover also began withdrawing American occupation forces from Latin America in the "Good Neighbor" Policy. He started the process of turning control of those nations over to indigenous governments.

On the negative side, Hoover's poor leadership was evident in dealing with crises in Asia and inside the United States. When Japan invaded Manchuria in 1931, Hoover condemned this aggressive act and refused to recognize the Japanese conquest of Manchuria. His words meant nothing to the Japanese, who likewise ignored the condemnations leveled at them by the League of Nations. Hoover never supported a strong U.S. military, and as such was in no position to stop expansion. Budget cuts during the Great Depression and fears that the United States might get sucked into another global war combined to make the early 1930s years of famine for all the armed services.

In domestic military affairs, Hoover made his greatest blunder during the Bonus Army March in 1932. This sad event occurred when American veterans of the First World War gathered in Washington to demand early payment of their monetary "bonuses" for service in that conflict that many unemployed veterans desperately needed during the Depression. Hoover reacted first by denying their request. The president could not, however, control his overzealous Army Chief of Staff General Douglas MacArthur, whose soldiers wounded many veterans and even killed one man in the violence that followed.

Box 10.2 Bonus Army March, 1932

In 1924, Congress authorized the federal government to make payments of $1,000 to 3.6 million veterans. The payments were not scheduled to be made until 1945, but many veterans needed that money sooner. Like so many Americans, they lost jobs in the Great Depression. In summer of 1932, nearly 20,000 veterans and their families gathered in Washington, D.C. The well-organized and peaceful veterans decided to set up camps, occupy abandoned government buildings, and stay until they received their bonuses. Hoover refused to give in to their demands, and he eventually decided to use the U.S. Army to eject the veterans from the capital. Using tear gas, bayonets, and gunfire, the soldiers drove them away.

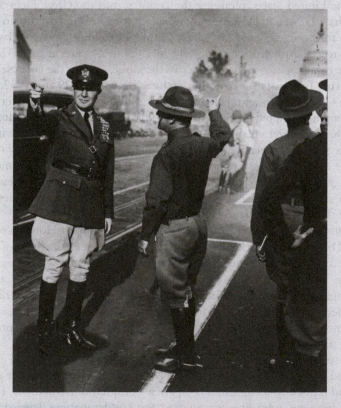

Figure 10.2 MacArthur and the Bonus Army

General Douglas MacArthur gives order to soldiers to eject the Bonus Army veterans from Washington, D.C. (Library of Congress)

MPI/Archive Photos/Getty Images

Although Hoover ordered the attacks to stop, the Army Chief of Staff General Douglas MacArthur ignored this order and sent his troops into the veterans' main camp. He believed that communists had infiltrated the ranks of the Bonus Army. No proof of this was ever found. The soldiers burned the camp, and the remaining veterans fled the area.

In the aftermath of the Bonus Army March, President Herbert Hoover never held MacArthur accountable for disobeying his orders and using force against the veterans. Hoover could have relieved MacArthur or called for court-martial proceedings against him. Instead, the president accepted responsibility for the decisions and actions of his general. But the political damage was done. The images of soldiers attacking veterans shocked the American people. This added to public opinion that Hoover was incompetent at best and cruel at worst. The bonus was eventually paid in 1936 during Franklin D. Roosevelt's presidency.

The Bonus Army fiasco stood as only one of Hoover's many perceived lapses in leadership. By November 1932, most Americans looked to the Democratic Party and its candidate—Franklin Delano Roosevelt—to restore confidence in the American system. He attained a landslide victory, winning not only the presidency but also bringing overwhelming Democratic majorities in Congress on his coattails.

Most of these new members of Congress tended toward isolationism, pacifism, and anti-militarism. Their constituents worried very little about faraway dangers in Asia or Europe when they could not feed their own families, find employment, or pay debts. Congress focused on pushing domestic legislation to support Roosevelt's series of policies and programs collectively called the "New Deal" in 1933 and thereafter. This constituted a major break with the federal government's limited efforts to resuscitate the American economy during Hoover's presidency.

Not all focus remained on America's domestic economic woes, however. A few members of Congress, such as Representative Carl Vinson of Georgia and Senator Park Trammell of Florida, used their positions on key committees to strengthen the American military preparedness. In his role as the new chairman of the House Naval Affairs Committee, Vinson worked with Trammell in the Senate to pass the 1934 Naval Appropriations Bill. Nicknamed the Vinson-Trammell Act, this legislation authorized the U.S. Navy to start building more than 100 new warships in the next eight years. Although Vinson came under fire from isolationists worried that this construction could cause another naval arms race, the Vinson-Trammell Act actually fulfilled the requirements of American warships as fixed by the 1922 Naval Arms Limitation Treaty. President Roosevelt also believed that the United States needed stronger armed forces. In 1933, he issued an executive order that directed $238 million to be spent constructing 32 new warships.

Not incidentally, Roosevelt's executive order and the Vinson-Trammell Act of 1934 created jobs in steel mills and shipyards. Throughout the rest of 1930s, Roosevelt worked with Vinson, Trammell, and a few others in Congress to reverse more than a decade of stagnation in military appropriations. Even so, they could not spend too much money on armed services as long as isolationist, pacifist, and anti-militarist feelings remained so dominant in Washington and across the United States. The politicians opposing military buildups wielded enough power to pass Neutrality Acts in 1935, 1936, and 1937. If war broke out, these acts prohibited the supply of American weapons and loans to combatant nations, and American travel on board combatant ships. Thus, from an isolationist perspective, the United States could never be placed in a position like that of 1917. Most Americans remained oblivious to international events in the 1930s, but the realities did not bode well for the future. Roosevelt's first years as president saw the situations in Europe and Asia grow more alarming as Germany, Italy, and Japan began their expansionist programs.

Ongoing Development of Tanks and Strategic Bombers

While growing anxieties drove American war planning in the 1930s, the worries also highlighted the need for technological development in the American military. Two factors, however, muddled the process of acquiring new weapons systems like the tank and the strategic bomber: first, the austere budgetary environment made building prototypes difficult; and second, unending debates over doctrines hampered the progress toward bringing tanks and bombers from drafting boards to functional models.

The tank languished within the Army's Infantry Branch for most of the 1920s. The existing tanks were too few and too antiquated to demonstrate any great battlefield potential. In 1927, however, then-Secretary of War Dwight F. Davis witnessed exercises using tanks from the British Experimental Mechanised Force. This demonstration impressed him so much that, on his return to the United States, he directed a mechanized force be created in the U.S. Army. This decision provided an opening for an American officer named Major Adna R. Chaffee, Jr., to formulate armor doctrine and bring the tank out of purgatorial irrelevance.

During the First World War, Chaffee experienced firsthand how trench warfare favored defensive forces and made offensives too costly. He later took a post in the Army's General Staff from 1927 to 1931, where he grew increasingly interested in armor warfare and asserted that the mobile tank could dominate future ground operations. Later in the 1930s, Adna Chaffee helped design new tanks and commanded "mechanized" Army units where he could test his ideas.

Chaffee's efforts did receive some support from Douglas MacArthur and Leon Kromer. While serving Army Chief of Staff from 1930 to 1935, General MacArthur encouraged motorization of the Army and mechanization of the Cavalry Branch in particular. In terms of logistics, MacArthur recognized that the limited speed and range of horse-drawn wagons paled in comparison to the speed, range, and endurance of trucks.

As Chief of Cavalry from 1934 to 1938, Major General Kromer remained loyal to horse cavalry, but he also wanted to transform his branch into a fighting arm capable of decisive battlefield contributions rather than a force merely providing reconnaissance for infantry units. Kromer envisioned using armored combat cars alongside horses to form fast-moving, mobile units capable of flanking maneuvers. This mind-set restricted the development of larger, more powerful tanks until the very late 1930s. Chaffee, for example, favored a more expanded role for medium tanks. They would provide firepower and speed for spearhead attacks against enemy lines as well as envelopments around enemy flanks. This notwithstanding, the key factor was Kromer's support for mechanization of cavalry units.

Like aviation proponents in the Army and Navy, Chaffee faced ever-present budgetary constraints. Aside from fiscal problems, Chaffee encountered resistance from the next Chief of Cavalry, Major General John K. Herr. Between 1938 and 1942, Herr stubbornly objected to the full mechanization of his branch, favoring instead the continued use of horse cavalry.

Under these circumstances, Chaffee made the most of his opportunities. He put armor doctrine down on paper and worked to design tanks that could realize those doctrines. This latter effort saw less progress, since the Army took so long to adopt a viable tank. The Army missed an excellent opportunity by rejecting a superb tank design by a brilliant civilian named J. Walter Christie.

An inventor of automobiles, fire trucks, and naval gun turrets, Christie turned his attention to developing a viable medium tank—the M1928—in the late 1920s. He solved several existing problems for all tanks by devising a suspension capable of operating at high speeds and in off-road environments. Christie also added sloped armor that deflected the kinetic energy of incoming shells upwards, rather than absorbing their full force. When the Army's Tank Board observed the prototype in action, members decided they did not want to make a mass purchase. They instead preferred a more heavily armored and armed, albeit slower, tank that could support infantry. The Board's decision stood as yet another example of narrow thinking about a weapons system.

Christie next took his M1928 to the Cavalry Evaluation Board for similar testing. One member, Major George Patton, liked Christie's design and supported its adoption, but he was in the minority. The Cavalry Branch favored armored cars, not tanks, so the board only wanted Christie's off-road capable suspension but not the whole tank. Ultimately, the Army decided not to purchase the M1928. The angered Christie turned to the other nations to sell his tank. The Soviet Union purchased it and eventually adapted the M1928 into the T-34, the most effective medium tank in the Second World War.

The tank was not the only American weapons system to experience progress in the 1930s. The Army's strategic bomber made still greater strides in terms of doctrines and designs. The air power principles of Billy Mitchell and Giulio Douhet in the previous decade continued to attract attention. Operating under the rationale of defending American coasts from enemy naval forces, the U.S. Army achieved significant advancement in the development of a strategic bomber. Touting the coastal defense application of the aircraft appealed to isolationist Americans who would not support offensive weapons.

The enduring doctrinal basis for American strategic air power had been irrevocably established inside the Army Air Corps by 1930. Aerial bombardment targeting enemy centers of industrial production and transportation stood as the primary missions for America's aviation forces. Publications emanating from the Air Corps Tactical School stated and restated this goal. They explained that bombing the enemy's strategic targets could best be achieved through accurate strikes by masses of American heavy bombers flying long distances and precisely delivering their bomb loads during level flight from high altitudes in daylight. Many officers in the Army Air Corps assumed that the United States could produce so many bombers and drop so many bombs on vital targets behind the front lines that no enemy could maintain moral will and material means to fight a long war. This last point represented a major selling point: End wars quickly with air power and avoid bloody ground combat. The rising officers of this mind-set, which included Henry Arnold, Carl Spaatz, James Doolittle, and Curtis LeMay, comprised a group nicknamed the "Bomber Mafia."

Not all Army aviators agreed that bombers represented a strategic panacea. Captain Claire Chennault, for instance, countered that bombers would be vulnerable to attack by enemy fighter aircraft. The Army used the term "Pursuit" for its fighter aircraft that engaged in air-to-air combat against enemy aircraft. Chennault taught at the Air Corps Tactical School from 1931 to 1936, where he argued that air-to-air combat missions also deserved serious consideration. Swarms of fast, nimble fighter aircraft could direct their deadly gunfire against the slower, less-maneuverable bombers. Despite his protests, Chennault remained in the minority. The Bomber Mafia ignored his warnings because they believed that large, four-engine bombers bristling with defensive machines in turrets would be impervious to gunfire from enemy aircraft or by ground fire from antiaircraft artillery.

Apart from solidifying a strategic bombing doctrine in the Air Corps, the most striking advances in air power occurred in the aircraft designs. At the end of the First World War, biplanes with their double-stacked wings could be found in all the world's air forces. In the next two decades, aircraft had made truly impressive gains in speed, armament, horsepower, and endurance. New American airplanes like the Curtis P-40 Warhawk were monoplanes, meaning they had one wing. Propelled by a 1,150-horsepower engine, the P-40 could reach a maximum speed of 350 miles per hour. It also boasted impressive armament of six heavy machine guns. A metal frame made the P-40 sturdy and safe as well as capable of handling stresses of higher speeds and more radical maneuvers. Larger fuel capacities meant lengthier patrol or loiter times over targets and longer combat engagements.

It is worth noting that the P-40 did not rank as the most lethal fighter in the world by the late 1930s. The U.S. Navy was developing its own fighter, the Grumman F4F Wildcat. Meanwhile, the Japanese, German, and British designed prototypes of the formidable Mitsubishi A6M Zero, Messerschmitt Bf 109, and Supermarine Spitfire, all of which were single-seat monoplanes superior in speed or maneuverability to the U.S. Army's P-40 Warhawk.

Nowhere were advances in American aircraft design more marked than in strategic bombers. The best example can be seen in the Model 299 aircraft, which was built by the Boeing Airplane Company for the U.S. Army Air Corps. Years of research and experimentation culminated in 1935 when the prototype flew from Boeing's facilities in Seattle, Washington, to the Air Corps' Wright Field in Dayton, Ohio. The one-winged Model 299 averaged a speed of 250 miles per hour in the flight that took just over nine hours. This performance surpassed everything else in the Air Corps' inventory.

Redesignated as the Y1B-17 in 1936, the aircraft upgraded existing Army Air Corps bombers in many ways. The Y1B-17's extended wingspan allowed another engine on each wing, to make a total of four engines. The aircraft carried more than two tons of bombs on flights exceeding 2,000 miles. Initially the new bomber was equipped with five heavy machine guns, but this number more than doubled in the Second World War. These guns, it was assumed, would give the bomber the ability to defend itself against attacking enemy aircraft. The Y1B-17 also possessed a sleek profile that captivated people who saw it sitting on runways or flying overhead. It thus served as a publicity vehicle to raise the Air Corps' visibility with the American public. The Y1B-17 was quickly dubbed the "Flying Fortress." Four years later in 1939, another American heavy bomber, the XB-24, made its test flights. When war erupted in Europe that same year, the Y1B-17 and XB-24 gave the Army Air Corps what the bomber mafia believed were unstoppable weapons that could destroy strategic objectives.

Amphibious Doctrine, Landing Craft, and the U.S. Marine Corps

While the U.S. Army and Navy developed new weapons systems and formulated new armor and aviation doctrines, the Marine Corps achieved its own notable successes in marrying amphibious doctrine to equipment in the 1930s. This process played out in different ways from the airplane or the tank, both of which were existing weapons systems that required new doctrines and missions. Instead, the Marine Corps needed to develop specialized equipment to execute its particular mission. All versions of the ORANGE War Plan gave the Marines a strategic mandate to seize islands in support of U.S. Fleet operations in the Pacific. To accomplish these daunting tasks, Marines spent the 1930s establishing a force structure that could conduct amphibious assaults by using the principles that revolutionized amphibious warfare and by identifying two civilian designs that became viable amphibious landing craft.

The end of deployments to Latin America in the early 1930s gave the Marines an opening to shift their service's limited resources away from constabulary security. No more would Marines be involved in the so-called "small wars" or "banana wars" they had undertaken since the Spanish-American War. Instead, amphibious warfare represented the new Marine mission for which some Marines touted their Corps as ideal and uniquely qualified.

An ascendant group of Marine officers, including Holland M. Smith and Thomas Holcomb, saw this type of warfare as the key to the Corps' survival, if not expansion. They firmly believed a future conflict with Japan (Orange) required better amphibious capabilities. The Marine Corps, however, needed a new force structure that could perform amphibious operations. It had to be a combined arms force with infantry, artillery, and aviation elements under command of a single officer. At the same time, this overarching purpose could not appear to be too offensive or aggressive in the eyes of isolationists in Congress or the American public. The force could not be called a "Marine Expeditionary Force" because the word "expeditionary" harkened back to the American Expeditionary Force in the First World War. Such a connotation would have meant certain failure in acquiring funding and resources from Congress.

Finally in 1933, the Navy's leadership filled the void with the "Fleet Marine Force." This name set off fewer warning signals than others might have done. However, because Americans saw the U.S. Fleet as the nation's first line of defense against foreign aggression, Marine units serving on warships did not sound overly belligerent. Early on, the Fleet Marine Force included

Figure 10.3 Grounds Crewman Unloading Bombs on a Trolley
Three Army Air Corps grounds crewmen placing bombs under the fuselage of a YIB-17 bomber in August 1939.
Mondadori/Getty Images

a few thousand marines in two brigades stationed at San Diego, California, and at Quantico, Virginia. Because the Marine Corps numbered fewer than 18,000 men, the brigade was the largest unit that could be organized.

Beginning that next year, 1934, the Fleet Marine Force conducted exercises in the Caribbean, on the East Coast, and on the West Coast with the U.S. Fleet. These simulated amphibious assaults were far from ideal due to small numbers of Marine and Navy participants. Fiscal restraints continued to plague the entire U.S. military. Nevertheless, they provided opportunities for the Marine Corps and Navy to solve nagging problems of communications, naval gunfire, command relations, logistics, close air support, and landing craft.

While the Fleet Marine Force conducted these exercises, faculty and students at the Marine Corps Schools in Quantico worked to formulate viable doctrines for amphibious operations. The normal classes for junior officers were suspended in 1933 and 1934 so their efforts could be focused on researching and writing. The Marines challenged the conventional wisdom that the advances in artillery and machine-gun firepower made amphibious assaults suicidal. This was seemingly affirmed in 1915 at Gallipoli, where British forces barely succeeded in landing on hostile shores and failed to expand inland from their tenuous beachhead. The Marines in Quantico nonetheless gleaned lessons from Gallipoli that they codified into doctrinal concepts. They asserted that effective plans, training, equipment, and coordination could overcome the advantages of firepower, cover, and concealment enjoyed by an enemy defender on shore. The Marines completed their work on the *Tentative Manual for Landing Operations* in June 1934. This document's long-term significance cannot be overstated. It either solved or accounted for all the difficulties facing the British at Gallipoli. The manual thus provided the blueprint for all American amphibious operations in both the Pacific and Europe during the Second World War. As such, it formed the basis for similar documents later adopted by the U.S. Navy and the Army.

Therefore, by the mid-1930s, the Marine Corps possessed the doctrine and the force structure to fulfill its mission in the ORANGE War Plan. However, the Marines still needed landing craft for the dangerous ship-to-shore transit. An amphibious assault could be made or broken during this stage. The Navy's existing assault boats were not well suited for the transit. They lacked not only speed to get the Marines to the shore but also ease of extraction from sandy beaches once they disembarked.

The Marines did not create their own newer, faster, better protected, or more agile amphibious assault vehicles. Instead, they identified and adapted civilian designs already in use. The first, called the "Eureka" boat, could maneuver in the swampy bayous of southern Louisiana. This craft had a shallow draft that allowed it to extricate itself from sand bars or beaches quickly and easily. When it was later modified with a bow ramp, 36 men could run straight out the boat's bow onto the beach without making themselves vulnerable by climbing over the sides. Following several tests in the late 1930s, the Marine Corps designated the Eureka boat as the Landing Craft, Vehicle, Personnel (LCVP).

The other landing craft was the Alligator amphibian tractor. Thanks to a suggestion by an observant Navy admiral, the Marines discovered this vehicle in *Life* Magazine in 1937. Designed to rescue hurricane victims in Florida's Everglades, the Alligator possessed dozens of paddles that propelled it through the water. They in turn functioned as tank treads on land, allowing it to traverse sand bars, beaches, and coral reefs. Like the Eureka boat, the Alligator needed modifications for military use. It was eventually designated the Landing Vehicle Tracked (LVT). It could land 20 men on a beach. Together, the LCVP and the LVT stand as examples of how amphibious doctrines and missions drove choices of equipment, as opposed to the tank and the airplane that seemingly drove the development of doctrines and choice of missions.

Apart from the ground-breaking efforts in amphibious doctrine, force structure, and landing craft, the 1930s saw the Marines compile two other important doctrinal publications: the *Tentative Manual for Defense of Advanced Bases* in 1935 and the *Small Wars Manual* in 1940. The former document explored how best to defend American island bases against enemy amphibious and aerial assaults. It also satisfied the Marine Corps' collateral mission to hold advanced island bases against Japanese assaults. The *Small Wars Manual* enumerated the lessons learned over several decades of Marine deployments in Latin America. Among other topics, this document analyzed the methods of fighting insurgent forces, building infrastructure, and supervising elections in occupied nations. Latin America would not be the only place these activities would play critical roles in instituting stability, order, and peace.

Box 10.3   The Marine Corps Schools' *Small Wars Manual* and Lessons Learned in the Interwar Years

During the first three decades of the twentieth century, thousands of U.S. Marines did tours of duty in Latin American. They performed a variety of roles, such as training indigenous forces, conducting counterinsurgency operations, supervising elections, providing disaster relief, and creating infrastructure. The Marines were agents of empire, tools of capitalists, or mentors to underdeveloped peoples, depending upon political slant. Just as the Marines were leaving Latin America in the mid-1930s, a major transition occurred as the Marine Corps shifted its focus to amphibious warfare. Nevertheless, the Corps' leadership wanted to retain lessons about Marine operations, roles, and activities in small wars. To this end, Colonel E. B. Miller, then-Assistant Commandant of the Marine Corps Schools, requested that Marine officers serving in Nicaragua fill out a 40-part Questionnaire in 1933.

One of these officers was a First Lieutenant named Vernon E. Megee, who served in Nicaragua from 1929 to 1932 as an aviation supply officer. (Later in his long career, he saw action in the Second World War and went on to become Assistant Commandant of the Marine Corps from 1956 through 1957.) The Marine Corps Schools' Questionnaire concentrated on tactical, operational, and logistical aspects of small wars. For the most part, the survey did not deal with matters of politics, strategy, or diplomacy. Megee provided several intriguing answers. Three of his answers follow. These showed that he had a flair for descriptive writing as well as a candid air in that writing.

Megee did not directly answer Question 8-a, which asked, "What do you think of the suitability of the Browning Machine Gun, 30 calibre, for use on combat patrols? Of the 3 [inch] Trench Mortar? The Rifle Grenade? The Hand Grenade?" However, Megee made these observations about automatic weapons that square with common sense and practicality:

> Serious study might be given to the question of replacing the [Browning Automatic Rifle] with the [Thompson Submachine Gun] for bush warfare. At the close ranges prevailing, the Thompson is the more deadly weapon, its blunt nose .45 caliber bullet has a deadly knockdown effect—sometimes lacking in the spitzer type .30 caliber bullet. The advantages of portability, both of gun and ammunition, are obvious, and the general handiness and speed of fire of the [Thompson] make it a murderous weapon in a surprise attack.

The Nicaraguan insurgents often ambushed Marine units on patrol; and much of the fighting occurred in jungle areas.

Megee also offered some criticisms regarding the Marines' training in Question 38-a. which asked, "Do you think that a training center, and an Infantry-weapons School should have been established in Managua?" Megee responded:

> It is my opinion that a Brigade training center at Managua, or possibly Ocotal, where newly arrived [Marine] officers and men could have received two months of intensive training in scouting and patrolling work, would have been of inestimable value. The training center at Pont Beudet, Haiti, through which I once passed with my company, taught me more about minor tactics, musketry, and kindred subjects in two months than I had previously assimilated in several years.

Several other questions also dealt with the issues of if and how the Marines were adequately trained.

Lastly, Megee commented on the Marines' use of animals in operations. One of his answers merits mention because of its somewhat whimsical nature. Question 21 asked, "Do you prefer horses or mules, and why?" Megee makes an intriguing reply:

> Personally, I would choose mules in mountain country, both for saddle and pack. They are more sure-footed than horses, and more philosophical about the inevitable abuse they receive on the trail. They are also possessed of an easier gait than the average tropical horse. On the other hand, they mire easily in deep mud, and are stubborn about being pushed when tired, and do not have the responsive intelligence of the horse. For real tough going on long trails where forage is scarce and of poor quality, the mule is generally conceded to be superior.

Answers to the 40 questions provided raw data to help faculty and students at Marine Corps Schools develop small wars doctrine. This process of systematic self-examination and self-criticism regarding practical lessons and experiences of Marines contributed to the great value of the *Small Wars Manual* of 1935 and the more well-known version in 1940. This process also demonstrates the institutional adaptability that has been the hallmark of the U.S. Marine Corps.

The *Small Wars Manual*'s 15 chapters explored such operational topics as organization, training, logistics, infantry patrols, convoy escorts, and aviation, all of which the 1933 Questionnaire covered to one degree or another in its sections. Megee's own answers to questions did factor into the *Small Wars Manual*, if not verbatim, then in spirit and tone. The justifications for why he favored the Thompson Submachine Gun over the Browning Automatic Rifle resembled the descriptions in sections on "Weapons" and "Infantry Weapons." Interestingly, his opinions about the Browning Automatic Rifle's shortcomings were consistent with the *Small War Manual*, but not the Thompson, which the *Small Wars Manual* found to have many shortcomings of its own.

Several sections dealing with "Training in the Theater of Operations" echoed the need, just as Megee so strongly suggested, for a training center in Managua. Language like his comparisons of horses and mules can be found in the sections titled "Pack Horses" and "Pack Mules." Beyond these, the *Small Wars Manual* also laid out more politically oriented principles by which cultural differences may be understood, military governments established, democratic elections administered, and withdrawals of military forces performed.

Moreover, the topics and issues addressed in Colonel E. B. Miller's 1933 Questionnaire are relevant to the counterinsurgency operations and nation-building activities in Afghanistan and Iraq between 2001 and 2016. In fact, many principles in the 1940 manual helped lay the foundation for the U.S. Army Field Manual 3–24/Marine Corps Warfighting Publication 3–33.5 *Counterinsurgency*, which was completed in 2006. (All quotes cited in Vernon Megee, letter to E. B. Miller, 24 April 1933, Box 1, Vernon Megee Papers, Dwight D. Eisenhower Library, Abilene, Kansas; see also David J. Ulbrich, "Revisiting Small Wars: A 1933 Questionnaire, Vernon E. Megee, and the *Small Wars Manual*." *Marine Corps Gazette* 90 [November 2006]: 74–75.)

Wars in East Asia and Europe, 1937–40

Many ominous events occurred across the globe in the 1930s that presaged the start of another World War. In Asia, Japan invaded Manchuria in 1931, withdrew from the League of Nations in 1933, and started a war with China in 1937. No amount of condemnation could stop Japanese expansion further onto the mainland. The Imperial Japanese Navy shrugged off the naval treaties of 1922 and 1930, and began a massive construction program that resulted in the creation of a powerful fleet of warships. They also drew up their own war plans to fight the United States. Finally, as the 1930s ended, the Japanese turned their gaze toward the resource-rich region of Southeast Asia.

Meanwhile, in Europe during the 1930s, Adolf Hitler's Nazi Party took power in Germany after unseating the Weimar Republic in elections. Hitler established an authoritarian regime, promised to alleviate economic woes, and pledged to reinvigorate Germany's former military might. He used government spending on military construction projects and armed services to stimulate the German economy and put its people back to work. By 1938, Germany menaced neighboring nations in Europe. Benito Mussolini's Fascist Italy represented another threat in the Mediterranean Sea and North Africa. Indeed, Germany and Italy eventually aligned with each other in May 1939 in the Pact of Steel.

The antiwar moods in France, Great Britain, and the United States restricted their leaders' abilities to halt ongoing conquests by Japan, Germany, and Italy. The most conspicuous example of this occurred in Munich, Germany, in September 1938. The great powers of Europe met in this city to negotiate an agreement that allowed Germany to annex the Sudetenland, a region along the border in neighboring Czechoslovakia. Hitler wanted to liberate several million ethnic Germans living in the Sudetenland, thus reversing the perceived injustices to Germany under the Treaty of Versailles. British Prime Minister Neville Chamberlain and the leaders of France and Italy decided to appease Hitler and signed the Munich Pact. They naively hoped they could satisfy his hunger for more territory. For their part, the Czechoslovakians felt betrayed because the Munich Pact ignored their existing military alliance with Britain and France. Chamberlain's fateful decision of "appeasement" has since taken on a very negative connotation of weak leaders making diplomatic concessions to avoid war.

With no fear of British or French recrimination, Adolf Hitler freely grabbed not only the Sudetenland but also the rest of Czechoslovakia. By the summer of 1939, Germany was poised

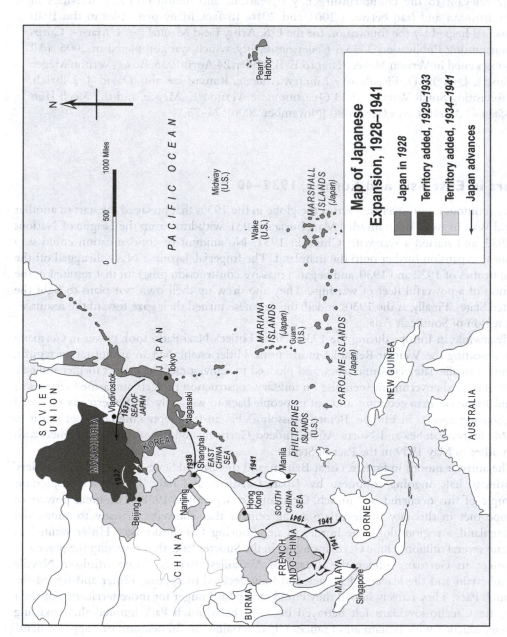

Map 10.2 Japan's Expansion in Asia and the Pacific Ocean, 1928–1941

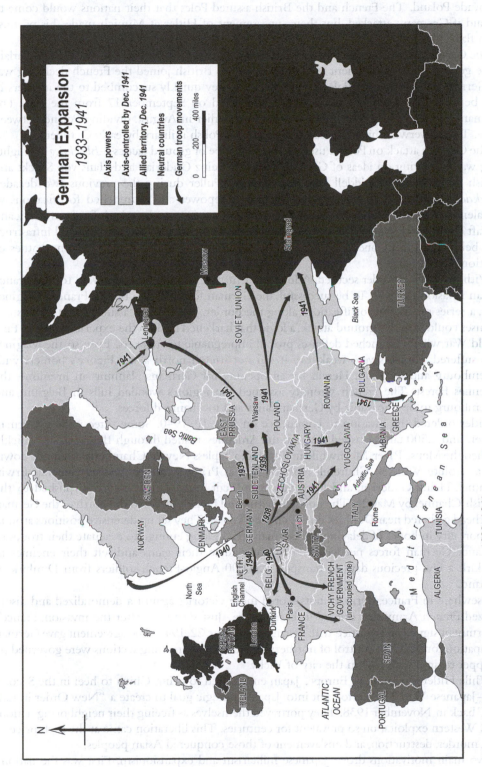

Map 10.3 Germany's Expansion in Europe, 1933–1941

to invade Poland. The French and the British assured Poles that their nations would come to her aid if Germany attacked, but their appeasement of Hitler at Munich made this promise seem flat.

The German Army invaded Poland on September 1, 1939. Just two days later, Chamberlain made good on his commitment to Poland when the British joined the French declaring war on Germany. Although the Poles fought valiantly, they quickly succumbed to the invaders in part because the Soviet Union also attacked Poland on September 17 from the east. The Germans and the Soviets had signed a secret pact earlier in August, dividing Poland between them. These overwhelming foes easily defeated the Polish military by early October.

The German attack on Poland ushered in a new type of ground tactics—*Blitzkrieg* or "lightning war." Drawing on ideas of German Generals Heinz Guderian and Hans von Seeckt and British theorists B. H. Liddell Hart and J. F. C. Fuller during the previous two decades, *Blitzkrieg* overcame the advantages of defensive firepower and entrenched fortifications so prevalent in the First World War. Combined arms operations with tanks, infantry, artillery, and aircraft could quickly penetrate or flank enemy positions, menace enemy logistical infrastructure behind the front lines, and achieve decisive victories rather than fight long battles of attrition.

With his eastern border secured, Adolf Hitler turned his attention westward toward France and an invasion in 1940. To be successful, the German forces had to breach France's Maginot Line, a series of massive fortifications along the border. The French assumed that these static defenses could stop any ground attack, a logic that harkened back to the experience in the First World War when entrenched defenses proved impregnable to attackers. Even so, the Maginot Line suffered from a severe weakness. It did not stretch north along France's borders with Luxembourg and Belgium. Herein lay an opening for Germans planning an invasion—the Ardennes Forest. The French wrongly assumed the region's wooded hills in Belgium and Luxembourg to be impassible by German tanks and mechanized forces.

Hitler ordered the invasion to commence on May 10, 1940. Some three million German soldiers and 2,500 tanks crashed through the Ardennes, rushed through Belgium, and quickly reached the Meuse River. Meanwhile in England, a hapless Neville Chamberlain stepped down, and a resolute Winston Churchill replaced him as Prime Minister. Led by Generals Erwin Rommel, Heinz Guderian, and Gerd von Rundstedt, the German *Blitzkrieg* pushed to the English Channel by May 21. The isolated British and French forces to the north of the German spearhead gathered near Dunkirk on the channel's coast. They set up defensive positions around this port city in hopes of delaying the German attacks long enough to evacuate their troops to England. German forces needed time to consolidate their gains and left their enemies in Dunkirk a few precious days to transport 338,000 Anglo-French soldiers from Dunkirk to England.

Elsewhere in France, German units scored more victories against a demoralized and disorganized French Army that offered little resistance. Just six weeks after the invasion, France's government signed an armistice with Germany on June 22, 1940. The agreement gave German occupation forces direct control of northern France. The remaining sections were governed by a puppet regime with base in the city of Vichy.

While Hitler ran amok in Europe, Japan endeavored to bring China to heel in the Second Sino-Japanese War. These efforts fit into Japan's strategic goal to create a "New Order in East Asia" back in November 1938. They portrayed themselves as freeing their neighboring nations from Western exploitation so prevalent for centuries. This liberation came at the high price of rape, murder, destruction, and enslavement of those conquered Asian peoples.

Two main motivations drove Japanese militarism and expansionism. First was the nation's pressing need for raw materials. Japan's home islands possessed little arable land and negligible raw materials. Anything other than subsistence living for the overpopulated nation and minimal production for its war machine required looking to the Asian mainland or to Southeast Asia. Second was virulent racism. The Japanese believed themselves to be superior to all other peoples. The term *Yamato minzoku* (Japanese race) legitimized the nation's destiny because of its biological purity and cultural homogeneity. Reinforcing these notions were hyper-nationalism and blind obedience to their deified emperor.

Despite committing two million soldiers in China, Japan made little progress in reaching the goal of regional hegemony between 1937 and 1941. The Japanese gained control of major cities and ports along the coastal areas of China, but their efforts bogged down in endless fighting against Chinese nationalist forces led by Chiang Kai-Shek and the communist forces of Mao Zedong since 1937. The Japanese could never lure their opponents into a decisive battle. Chiang retreated farther into the Chinese mainland, and Mao directed his guerrilla war against the Japanese occupation forces.

With its quagmire in China not improving, Japan turned to Southeast Asia as another area ripe for conquest. The region held incredible natural resources of oil and rubber in French Indochina, the Dutch East Indies, and British Malaya. By late 1940, only the British and American forces could stop the Japanese. Although fighting for survival against Germany in Europe, the British maintained a major naval base in Singapore. It stood in the way of Japanese expansion into the "Southern Resource Area." In addition, American forces under General Douglas MacArthur's command in the Philippines, Marine Corps units on Pacific islands, and movement of the Pacific Fleet from the West Coast to Pearl Harbor posed serious threats to Japanese territorial ambitions. For their part, the Japanese, most notably Admiral Isoroku Yamamoto, began planning to launch several preemptive strikes against Anglo-American forces that would buy Japan time to finish mobilizing for war against those nations.

In September 1940, another alarming event occurred when representatives of Germany, Italy, and Japan signed the Tripartite Pact. Although not binding like a treaty, this pact unified the three nations in a common cause to continue consolidating their gains, expanding further beyond their borders, and assisting one another if attacked. It was an indication that the regional conflicts in East Asia and Western Europe were evolving into a truly global war.

These events in Asia and Europe were not lost on President Franklin Roosevelt. He reacted by slowly increasing diplomatic and economic pressures against these potential adversaries. He initiated an embargo on exporting American aircraft and aircraft parts to Japan in January 1939. Later in November, the president convinced Congress to modify the strict Neutrality Act of 1937 to allow American sale of arms to France and Great Britain.

After the defeat of France in 1940, Roosevelt adopted a short-of-war strategy that gave him more flexibility in supplying weapons, equipment, and financial support to the British. This support tipped the American hand to Adolf Hitler and the Germans. Repeating their efforts during the First World War to blockade the British home islands, the German Navy's U-boats once again searched the Atlantic Ocean for merchant ships to attack. In the closing months of 1939, the U-boats German teamed with surface vessels and aircraft to sink 700,000 tons of shipping and inflicted another four million tons of losses in both 1940 and 1941. Few of the victimized ships, however, flew American flags until late 1941.

Even so, Roosevelt agreed in late 1940 to trade 50 obsolete U.S. Navy destroyers to the British for several of their bases in the Caribbean and South America. More symbolic than substantive, this "Destroyers-for-Bases Agreement" sent an unequivocal signal to Prime Minister Churchill and the British that Roosevelt wanted to help them, despite the ongoing isolationist tendencies of many Americans and the American status as a neutral nation. On a practical level, the destroyers did serve as escorts protecting the convoys of transport ships carrying vital supplies from the United States through the U-boat-infested waters of the Atlantic Ocean to the British islands.

Meanwhile, the U.S. Navy, Army, and Marine Corps planners increasingly turned their attention to determining where and when the Japanese blow might fall, and what forces the United States might muster to react to such attacks. In addition, the increasing German and Italian threats required the American planners to add more contingencies for fighting two or more enemies in multiple fronts. The ORANGE War Plan thus became obsolete by 1939 because it envisioned only an American-Japanese conflict.

No more could Americans expect to fight a one-on-one war against the Japanese in the Pacific Ocean. This realization culminated in the five RAINBOW Plans, ranging from a unilateral American defense of the Western Hemisphere against enemy incursions to a wider conflict with allies fighting against enemy forces in the Pacific and Europe. Each time Germany or Japan made another aggressive move and achieved another victory, the United States adopted a different RAINBOW Plan.

Roosevelt recognized that he needed senior military leaders to manage the mobilization of the American military, direct the planning for a possible conflict, and advise him on strategic matters. In addition to Commandant Thomas Holcomb, who led the Marine Corps, the president chose Admiral Harold R. Stark to be the new Chief of Naval Operations in August 1939, and the next month selected General George C. Marshall to be Army Chief of the Staff. All three capable officers played instrumental roles in preparing the United States to fight in another global war.

By late 1940, only RAINBOW Plan 5 could be applied to the United States' situation, but it needed clarification. Admiral Stark reacted by articulating the "Germany First" strategy: if the United States entered the war, the main American offensive focus would be on Germany in Europe; and the secondary defensive focus would be on Japan in the Pacific. Stark reasoned that Britain needed the immediate support in the face of the German (and Italian) threats to the British home islands and supply lines. The United States would have to stand on the strategic defensive in the Pacific, waiting to concentrate its forces against Japan until Germany was defeated. With this strategy in mind, Stark, Marshall, and other senior American leaders met with their British and Canadian counterparts in early 1941 to discuss how best to fight the Axis powers and especially Germany.

Apart from strategic and defense-related efforts to prepare for war, Roosevelt began girding the United States to generate a heretofore unimaginable war effort. In September 1940, after Congress passed the Selective Training and Service Act (Burke-Wadsworth Act), President Roosevelt signed this act into law. It required all American men aged 21 to 35 to register with local draft boards. This stood as America's first peacetime draft. Once registered, up to 900,000 men were chosen by lottery. They could then expect to serve in uniform up to 12 months, but only in the Western Hemisphere. The years 1939 and 1940 also saw dramatic increases from $2 billion to $10 billion in government spending on military mobilization, but Roosevelt remained careful to couch these measures as protecting the United States proper.

In March 1941, Congress took another momentous step with the passage of the Lend-Lease Act. This act sent $50 billion worth of supplies to the British, Chinese, and later the Soviets to help them fight the Axis powers. For all practical purposes, Lend-Lease constituted outright grants to these allied nations. Both symbolically and substantively, this act marked a break with isolationist foreign policies, even if most Americans still opposed entrance in the Second World War. No more could the United States claim neutrality.

The Last Six Months Before the Attack on Pearl Harbor, 1941

Beginning in June 1941, the rush of events exerted more pressure on the United States, pulling and pushing the nation into the Second World War. On June 22, 1941, Nazi Germany violated the standing agreement with the Soviet Union and surprisingly launched Operation BARBAROSSA, in which some three million soldiers from Germany and its allies invaded the Soviet Union. Hitler decided on this course of action for several reasons, including the Nazis' ingrained ideological and racial hatred for Russians as Slavic communists. The first few months of the campaign once again proved the operational effectiveness of the combined arms of *Blitzkrieg*. The ill-prepared Soviet Army fell back in full retreat, giving up thousands of square miles of territory. In the first month of the invasion alone, the Soviets suffered more than three million soldiers killed, wounded, or captured. It looked like Germany might defeat the Soviet Union.

During mid-1941, the United States began sending Lend-Lease support to the Soviets as well as the British, Chinese, and other nations. Later that fall, British Prime Minister Winston Churchill and President Franklin Roosevelt met in Newfoundland, Canada, where they agreed on the "Atlantic Charter." Although having no legal standing, this document laid out future Anglo-American goals if the United States entered the conflict as an ally of Britain.

These conspicuous efforts helped escalate confrontations between American warships and German U-boats in the Atlantic, where the U-boats tried to stop of the flow of supplies from the United States to Britain and the Soviet Union. Given sanction by President Roosevelt to defend against attacks, American warships escorting convoys of merchant ships fired on the U-boats and dropped depth charges on them. The U-boats, in turn, launched torpedoes at several American warships. These incidents constituted acts of war, though neither side was ready to declare war. There remained too strong an isolationist mood in the United States, and Adolf Hitler preferred to focus on the Soviet Union and North Africa rather than risk war with the United States.

In the Mediterranean region south of Europe, Italian forces occupied parts of northern Africa. Fighting in the region began in June 1940, just weeks before the fall of France to Germany. Italian and British units launched attacks on the other's outposts. The Italians hoped to push the British out of Egypt so they could extend their control from northern Africa through Egypt to eastern Africa. This would give Italy and then Germany by extension access to the Suez Canal and Arabian oil, and deny the British this invaluable supply route from the Indian Ocean.

The British could never let this happen. It would mean that raw materials and oil from the Middle East and India would have to be transported southwest around the Cape of Good Hope in South Africa. This would add weeks and thousands of miles of sailing time. In December 1940, the British Commonwealth forces soundly defeated the Italian Army and drove it out of Egypt, westward back into Libya. Adolf Hitler immediately sent a major German force led by Lieutenant General Erwin Rommel to Libya to stop the impending Axis defeat. The year 1941 saw several campaigns in which Germany slowly pushed the British eastward well into Egypt and menaced the Suez Canal. The German momentum in North Africa and in the Soviet Union by December did not bode well for the forlorn British and Soviet forces fighting desperately for survival.

On the other side of the world, in Asia and the Pacific Ocean, the strategic situation looked just as dismal in the last six months of 1941. Try as he might, Roosevelt could not deter Japan from expanding its influence further into Southeast Asia, China, or the western Pacific. Moving the U.S. Pacific Fleet from California to Pearl Harbor in Hawai'i had not stopped Japanese ambitions in 1940. When Japan sent forces to occupy French Indochina (modern-day

Vietnam, Laos, and Cambodia), Roosevelt reacted first by freezing Japanese assets in the United States and later by initiating an embargo on sales of American oil to that nation.

Instead of deterring the Japanese, these acts speeded their expansion into resource-rich Southeast Asia. It also spurred Japanese plans to make a surprise attack against the United States. This preemptive strike, the brainchild of the brilliant Admiral Isoroku Yamamoto, would hope-fully damage the American war-making capabilities in the Pacific and give the Japanese time to consolidate and fortify their gains. Yamamoto's plan had multiple phases, including destroy-ing the U.S. Pacific Fleet at Pearl Harbor and U.S. Army forces in the Philippines, capturing American island bases on Guam and Wake, and eliminating the British threat in Singapore in Malaysia in Southeast Asia. Yamamoto reasoned that, at best, Japan had six months of freedom of movement before the United States would launch a counterattack. He wanted to cripple the American material and moral will to fight before the full power of the United States could be directed at Japan.

While Yamamoto and his staff worked out all details of his ambitious gamble, the diplomatic relations between the United States and Japan deteriorated in the closing months of 1941. The two governments were at loggerheads. Each side would propose agreements that the other could never accept. One major point of contention centered on whether the Japanese would relinquish control of their newly absorbed territory in Southeast Asia. With no compromise possible, the Japanese decided in September to attack the United States. That next month, the belligerent Imperial Japanese Army general Hideki Tojo became Prime Minister. The new leader quickly set to work pushing his nation closer to war.

In November, the opposing governments exchanged one last set of counterproposals that yet again neither side could tolerate. In the last week of that month, a powerful Japanese fleet of aircraft carriers set sail in secret, made its way through the storm-swept northern Pacific, and approached Hawai'i from the north. Simultaneously, other Japanese air and naval forces pre-pared to attack American bases in the Philippines and on the islands of Guam and Wake in the Pacific Ocean.

Such senior American military leaders as Chief of Staff General George C. Marshall, Chief of Naval Operations Admiral Harold R. Stark, and Commander-in-Chief of the Pacific Fleet Admiral Husband E. Kimmel fully expected some incident to precipitate American entrance into the Second World War. Yet they remained unsure where or when that might occur as late as December 6, 1941. Among the anticipated Japanese targets were the Philippines, Guam, and Wake. None of them, however, took seriously the possibility of a massive attack on Pearl Harbor. Small strikes by submarines in the port and saboteurs on the airfields seemed more plausible. American military cryptologists tried without success to decipher the encoded Japanese Navy's message that directed the attack on Pearl Harbor. This left the U.S. military without intelligence on the specifics of the Japanese intentions.

Conclusion

Although great strides had been made in aviation, armor, and amphibious doctrines, the U.S. military's meager budgets did not allow these ideas to be translated into new weapons and vehicles. Even as late as December 1941, the U.S. military remained unprepared to fight either Japan or Germany, let alone both nations. For example, too few American tanks could be used in maneuvers and exercises designed to train soldiers in armor doctrine. Soldiers solved this problem by painting the word "tank" on trucks to allow simulated armor movements. Broom sticks were also mounted on the trucks as fake machine guns. In terms of force structure, the Army adopted a smaller, more mobile "triangular division" with three regiments and 16,000 men rather than the larger, more unwieldy "square division" of the First World War with its four regiments and 28,000 men. This triangular division represented a practical effort to make the Army units more effective on battlefields, but the Army lacked the manpower to fill more than a few divisions on paper. Many other examples also punctuated the entire U.S. military's poor level of preparedness. In contrast, the Axis powers boasted militaries numbering in the many millions of men, thousands of aircraft, and hundreds of warships. On paper, it looked like the German, Japanese, and to some degree the Italians enjoyed critical advantages in manpower, experience, and momentum in December 1941.

Short Bibliography

Bickel, Keith. *Mar Learning: The Marine Corps' Development of Small Wars Doctrine, 1915–1940.* Boulder, CO: Westview Press, 2000.

Budreau, Lisa M, *Bodies of War: World War I and the Politics of Commemoration in America, 1919–1933.* New York: New York University Press, 2011.

Coffman, Edward M. *The Regulars: The American Army, 1898–1941.* New York: Oxford University Press, 2004.

Johnson, David E. *Fast Tanks and Heavy Bombers: Innovation in the U.S. Army, 1917–1945.* Ithaca: Cornell University Press, 1998.

Kuehn, John T. *Agents of Innovation: The General Board and the Design of the Fleet That Defeated the Japanese Navy.* Annapolis: Naval Institute Press, 2008.

Linn, Brian. *Guardians of Empire: The U.S. Army in the Pacific, 1902–1940.* Lawrence: University Press of Kansas, 1997.

Matheny, Michael. *Carrying the War to the Enemy: American Operational Art to 1945.* Norman: University of Oklahoma Press, 2011.

Miller, Edward S. *War Plan Orange: The Strategy to Defeat the Japanese, 1897–1945.* Annapolis: Naval Institute Press, 1991.

Moy, Timothy. *War Machines: Transforming Technologies in the U.S. Military 1920–1940.* College Station: Texas A&M University Press, 2002.

Muth, Jörg. *Command Culture: Officer Education in the U.S. Army and the German Armed Forces, 1901–1940, and the Consequences for World War II.* Denton: University of North Texas Press, 2011.

Prange, Gordon W., Daniel M. Goldstein, and Katherine V. Dillon. *At Dawn We Slept: The Untold Story of Pearl Harbor.* New York: Penguin, 1981.

Renda, Mary. *Taking Haiti: Military Occupation and the Culture of U.S. Imperialism, 1915–1940.* Chapel Hill: University of North Carolina Press, 2001.

Trimble, William F. *Admiral William A. Moffett: Architect of Naval Aviation.* Washington: Smithsonian Institution Press, 1994.

Ulbrich, David J. *Preparing for Victory: Thomas Holcomb and the Making of the Modern Marine Corps 1936–1943.* Annapolis: Naval Institute Press, 2011.

Wildenberg, Thomas. *Billy Mitchell's War with the Navy: The Interwar Rivalry over Air Power.* Annapolis: Naval Institute Press, 2014.

TIMELINE

1941–45	December 7, 1941	May 8, 1942	June 4, 1942	August 7, 1942–February 7, 1943
Second World War	Japan attacked Pearl Harbor	America surrendered in the Philippines	Battle of Midway	Campaign of Guadalcanal

Chapter 11

Mobilizing for the Second World War, 1941–1943

By the end of 1941, bloody conflicts had engulfed Europe for more than two years and East Asia for a decade. The Axis powers—Nazi Germany, Fascist Italy, and Militarist Japan—expanded to dominate vast swaths of territory on three continents. It looked like they would continue to achieve victory after victory. Against them stood a hobbled British Empire, a devastated Soviet Union, and a divided China. Since the outbreak of war in 1939, the United States of America gradually provided food, vehicles, weapons, and financial support to these nations fighting the Axis powers, but most Americans remained unwilling to enter the conflict. Isolationist tendencies still held sway over public opinion even in late 1941.

That the United States eventually entered the Second World War should not have surprised any Americans. Tensions between Japan and the United States over commercial trade, immigration policy, natural resources, and strategic influence had simmered since 1898. In Europe, fears of Germany's seeming insatiable thirst for power and territory increasingly threatened American and Allied interests in the Atlantic. Nevertheless, the specific target of Pearl Harbor caught the U.S. military off guard on December 7, 1941.

The story of the United States in the Second World War is one of a suddenly awakened giant that halted the Axis expansion by 1943 before throwing the enemy back on its heels. After an inauspicious start, decisive American victories in the Pacific came at Midway in June 1942 and on Guadalcanal by February 1943. Americans made slow progress in North Africa in 1942, however, and then on Sicily and Italy in 1943 and 1944. Although each of these campaigns almost resulted in disaster, the United States helped shift momentum toward the Allies.

In this chapter, students will learn about:

- How and why the "Day of Infamy" happened.
- Midway and Guadalcanal as twin turning points in the Pacific War in 1942.

- Maintaining the American logistical lifeline to Europe by winning the Battle of the Atlantic.
- Successes and shortcomings of harnessing resources on the American home front to support a global war effort.
- The American operational learning curve that led to victories in North Africa in 1942 and in Sicily and Italy in 1943–1944.

The "Day of Infamy"

The Sunday morning of December 7, 1941, dawned to find the U.S. Pacific Fleet at peace in Pearl Harbor on the island of Oahu in Hawai'i. Among the fleet were seven battleships, including the USS *Arizona*, moored in "battleship row" near Ford Island in the middle of the harbor. An eighth battleship rested in dry dock. These vessels constituted the pride of the U.S. Fleet and the main surface force in the Pacific Ocean. The unsuspecting crews on board began their day by raising flags to the sounds of "Morning Colors."

The respective U.S. Navy and Army commanders, Admiral Husband E. Kimmel and Lieutenant General Walter C. Short, planned to spend the pleasant Sunday morning playing golf. While both worried about the Japanese threat in the western Pacific, neither could have predicted what would happen in the next few hours. The beliefs of Kimmel, Short, and many other Americans pointed to a systemic pattern of underestimating Japanese ingenuity and audacity.

Despite the apparent serenity, several ominous signs pointed to something being amiss early that Sunday. An American destroyer sank a small Japanese submarine off the coast of Hawai'i near the entrance to Pearl Harbor. Two more of these two–man submarines were damaged and abandoned off the coast of Hawai'i. However, these possible sightings and sinkings caused no alarm among American commanders because destroyers had chased other suspected submarines that turned out to be hoaxes.

Another incident portended disaster on that morning. At about 7:00 a.m., one of the U.S. Army radar centers sighted a large number of aircraft flying from the north toward Oahu. The unsuspecting Army lieutenant in charge decided that the unidentified planes were American aircraft arriving from the continental United States. Consequently, he did not alert higher headquarters. This mistaken assumption was plausible enough given the circumstances, but it would contribute to the tragedy of errors that morning.

Those radar blips were actually 183 Japanese planes bearing down on Pearl Harbor after a two–hour flight from six aircraft carriers 230 miles to the north of Oahu. At 7:40 a.m., the first wave's commander achieved complete surprise and ordered the message "Tora, Tora, Tora"[1] to be radioed back to the Japanese carriers under command of Vice Admiral Chuichi Nagumo. Shortly after 8:00 a.m., the Japanese began making their torpedo, bomb, and strafing runs. The next two hours of carnage and destruction started with the first wave followed by a second

Figure 11.1 An Aerial Photograph of Pearl Harbor in Late October 1941

Looking toward the southwest in an aerial view of the U.S. Naval Operating Base, Pearl Harbor. Ford Island Naval Air Station lies in the center, with several American vessels moored in "battleship row" along the left shoreline of Ford Island. The airfield in the upper left-center is the U.S. Army's Hickam Field, and the narrow channel leading from Pearl Harbor to the Pacific Ocean is visible in the center top of the photograph.

Source: U.S. Navy History and History Command

attack of another 163 Japanese planes at 9:00 a.m. All the while, American servicemen desperately fought back, manning antiaircraft batteries and even shooting small arms at the planes passing overhead.

Explosions erupted at every Army, Navy, and Marine air field on Oahu. The Japanese destroyed dozens of aircraft sitting neatly in rows on the open ground, a measure General Short had decided was the best way to protect his planes from enemy saboteurs infiltrating the air fields. Out in the harbor, geysers of water and towers of flame rose into the air as the Japanese armor-piercing bombs and torpedoes hit American warships. General quarters sounded, and air raid sirens wailed. A desperate message went out over American radios: "Air raid, Pearl Harbor. This is no drill."

All eight American battleships and many smaller warships sustained damage. The most tragic loss occurred at about 8:05 a.m. when 10 Japanese planes flying at 10,000 feet targeted the USS *Arizona*. Four of the Japanese 1,760-pound bombs scored direct hits on the American battleship. Three caused relatively minor damage, but the fatal blow came from the last bomb that penetrated the deck armor near one the *Arizona*'s main gun turrets. It detonated near the ship's forward ammunition magazine. The resulting explosion sent shock waves and flames throughout the 30,000-ton vessel, wrecking its interior and killing 1,177 of the 1,400 crewmen on board. This figure amounted to half of all American deaths during the attack. The ship settled quickly to the bottom of the harbor, and fires burned out of control for days.

Several time zones away in Washington, D.C., most Americans were finishing their lunches on the cold Sunday. At about 1:30 p.m., Secretary of the Navy Franklin Knox called President Franklin D. Roosevelt to deliver the terrible news that Japanese aircraft attacked Pearl Harbor. Reports began rolling in that detailed staggering losses. A shaken yet still resolute Roosevelt spent the rest of the day in emergency meetings with his cabinet and senior military advisors. Alerts went out to commanders across the Pacific to be ready for more Japanese attacks.

Back in Hawai'i, Admiral Kimmel arrived at Pearl Harbor to find his ships burning out of control and sinking. All eight of his battleships and 10 other warships were disabled or sunk, 188 aircraft were destroyed, and 2,402 American service personnel were killed or missing. An errant bullet from the battle hit Kimmel standing where he was on shore, but he was uninjured. In anguish, he lamented, "It would have been merciful had it killed me." The attack on the seventh, however, effectively ended his career. General Short suffered similar judgments. Both men were relieved of command a few days later. Then they were accused of, if not scapegoated for, dereliction of duty for failing to be as ready as possible for an attack.

Box 11.1   Pearl Harbor in History and Memory

Hindsight allows for better understanding of what happened at Pearl Harbor on December 7, 1941. Although there could have been routine patrol flights around Hawai'i, improved communication with radar operators or destroyer captains, and more intelligence sharing between Pearl Harbor and headquarters in Washington, it is unlikely that such a great disaster could have been averted on the morning of December 7, 1941. The U.S. Pacific Fleet would still have suffered serious losses because of the sheer numbers of Japanese aircraft.

In its broadest context, the attack revealed that American military commanders and planners alike underestimated Japanese capabilities, audacity, and resolve, while they overestimated American capacities to react and defeat the Japanese. Part of this dismissive attitude about the Japanese can be seen in racially motivated beliefs about the Japanese as brutal, yet inferior and incompetent. How could Japanese be expected to plan and execute such a grand attack that involved sailing undetected across the North Pacific and launching 346 planes in two attack waves against the Americans? This was inconceivable to most American minds. Furthermore, when the antiwar and isolationist moods of the American public are factored into the equation, it becomes clear that Admiral Kimmel and General Short were part of a collective inertia infecting the American military establishment.

Such inertia can be seen in many of the initial engagements between the U.S. military and foes in the nation's wars. Whether at the Battle of Bull Run in 1861 in the case of a set-piece battle or in the terrorist attack on September 11, 2001, there seems to be a pattern of American planners and commanders underestimating enemy capabilities. In both cases, as in the attack on Pearl Harbor, the results of such assumptions cost thousands of lives.

Neither Admiral Kimmel nor General Short deserved the serious charges of dereliction of duty, but they can be held accountable for passivity and acts of omission. Military commanders have ultimate responsibility for those forces they lead to defeat or victory. After being defrocked of their commands later in December 1941, Admiral Kimmel and General Short spent the rest of the war and the rest of their lives defending themselves against accusations and trying to exonerate themselves.

From the Japanese perspective, the attack on December 7, 1941, represented decisive tactical and strategic victories. The severe losses of American battleships, aircraft, and lives notwithstanding, the attack on Pearl Harbor did not permanently cripple the U.S. Navy for two important reasons. First, all three American aircraft carriers were out of port on maneuvers, so the Japanese did not destroy what would become the new decisive arm in naval warfare—carrier-based aircraft fighting over the horizon. Second, Nagumo and the Japanese gave little or no thought to destroying the repair facilities and fuel reserves at Pearl Harbor. These targets represented greater potential disadvantages for future American naval operations in the Pacific than sinking a few battleships. With no dry docks in Hawai'i, for example, the American warships would have had to return to the western coast of the United States. Instead Nagumo decided to withdraw from the area because he worried that American aircraft carriers might be lurking nearby and could attack his fleet. His superior, Admiral Isoroku Yamamoto, did not see his subordinate's efforts as completed victories. He recognized that aircraft carriers represented the main target, and he realized that the surprise attack would spark American resolve to mobilize almost limitless resources to fight his nation.

The arousal of such resolve could be heard in President Roosevelt's declaration of war speech given to Congress and broadcast to the American people on Monday. In his assertive but calm voice, he began, "Yesterday, December 7, 1941—a date that will live in infamy—the United States was suddenly and deliberately attacked by naval and air forces of the Empire of Japan." In the next few minutes, Roosevelt cataloged the deceitfulness of the Japanese government in a cleverly worded speech that made the enemy appear completely evil and the United States completely innocent. He then rallied the nation, portrayed the coming conflict as a crusade for God and country, and urged the American people to unite and fight a war that had to achieve unconditional victory. Except for only one Representative, both houses of Congress cast votes to declare war on Japan. The isolationist sentiments pervading so much of public opinion also melted away when the American people heeded Roosevelt's call to gird themselves for war.

On December 11, Italy and Germany joined Japan's cause when they declared war on the United States of America. This set the three Axis powers against what became known as the "Grand Alliance" and included the United States led by Franklin Roosevelt, the United Kingdom led by Winston Churchill, and the Soviet Union led by Joseph Stalin. These three boasted overwhelming superiority in manpower and material. When China was added as an ally against Japan, the Grand Alliance (the United States, the United Kingdom, the Soviet Union) fielded a military force exceeding 60 million men and women, as opposed to the Axis that barely passed 20 million men in uniform. The Grand Alliance could also outproduce the Axis powers several times over in every category of weapon or vehicle.

Japan's Tide of Victories Until May 1942

The Japanese strike against Pearl Harbor began a string of victories lasting for the next five months. On December 7, 1941, Japanese aircraft also attacked American bases in the Philippines, and Japanese forces later landed on the Philippines to begin their five-month campaign to wrest the archipelago from American control. Japanese aircraft bombed Wake Island on the same day as Pearl Harbor and destroyed most of the American aircraft stationed there. Three days later, Guam fell into Japanese hands without serious resistance by the handful of Americans stationed on the island.

In the Philippines in December 1941, one high-ranking American military officer escaped condemnation for his serious oversight that cost many lives and much equipment: General Douglas MacArthur. All U.S. Army Forces in the Far East fell under his command, including 31,000 American and Filipino soldiers and 120 American aircraft based in the Philippine capital of Manila. News of the Japanese attack on Pearl Harbor began trickling into American bases in the Philippines at about 3:00 a.m. local time. Over the next several hours, confusion reigned as conflicting reports and indecisive orders kept the American aircraft from preparing for an attack by hostile air strike. Neither MacArthur nor his subordinate commanders could decide upon a course of action. Just before 1:00 p.m., Japanese aerial attacks on American air fields destroyed about half of the American planes, most of which sat in rows on the ground just as at Pearl Harbor.

No Congressional investigations like those of Admiral Kimmel and General Short were called to determine MacArthur's culpability in the Philippine debacle after he received warning at least 10 hours before the attack. Indeed, ordinarily he should have been relieved, if not court-martialed for such mistakes. Various reasons curbed the accusations made against MacArthur. His prestige made him all but invulnerable to criticism because of his stature in government, military, and public eyes. The severity of the attack on Pearl Harbor also occupied most of the headlines, radio broadcasts, and newsreels back in the United States.

During December 1941, the American strategic situation looked very grim. Only one piece of good news lifted American spirits. Several hundred U.S. Marines and civilian contractors held out against repeated Japanese attacks on Wake Island. Although isolated from help 2,000 miles west of Hawai'i, the Leathernecks succeeded in stopping an amphibious assault against their island on December 11. The courageous Marines boosted morale back in the United States, where headlines, radio broadcasts, and newsreels praised their tenacity. The Japanese successfully landed on Wake in a second, more determined amphibious assault on December 23. The defenders surrendered and spent the rest of the conflict in captivity as prisoners of war. The Japanese may have scored a victory on Wake, but the island and its Marines gave Americans hope for the future.

The spirited defense of Wake notwithstanding, the first four months of 1942 looked no more positive than had December 1941. The Japanese quickly secured most of the Philippines in early 1942 and drove MacArthur's outnumbered and outgunned forces to his last defensive positions on the Bataan Peninsula and on Corregidor Island in Manila Bay. The sieges of Bataan lasted until April and of Corregidor until May. The American and Filipino soldiers endured daily air, naval, and artillery bombardments and infantry attacks. They also suffered from mal-nutrition and disease. So desperate did the defenders' plight become by March that President Franklin Roosevelt ordered General Douglas MacArthur to evacuate to Australia. Although Roosevelt disliked MacArthur, the president believed the general was too valuable a leader and public figure to fall into Japanese hands. MacArthur reluctantly left the Philippines, but he uttered his famous words, "I shall return," as a promise to liberate the Japanese-held islands. More than 75,000 American and Filipino on Bataan surrendered to the Japanese on April 9, 1942. The remaining troops on Corregidor Island laid down their arms on May 8, judging further resistance to be pointless. In total, the American and Filipino forces lost 25,000 killed and 21,000 wounded in action during the first four months of the conflict.

The Japanese were neither prepared to feed nor house so many prisoners, nor did their cultural mind-set believe that surrendering soldiers were worthy of humane treatment. The already malnourished and diseased captives were forced to walk 70 miles for six days through the tropical heat to a prisoner of war camp. Along the way, men who fell out of line by the roadside were brutally killed where they lay by Japanese guards. This infamous "Bataan Death March" lasted from April 12 to April 18, and cost another 18,000 lives.

Such atrocities left indelible impressions on American civilians and service personnel alike. Already steeped in racist beliefs about the Japanese, the American public embraced government-sponsored and media-driven propaganda that painted the Japanese as vicious animals that needed to be exterminated. Such racial epithets as "slant eye," "monkey," "vermin," "ape,"

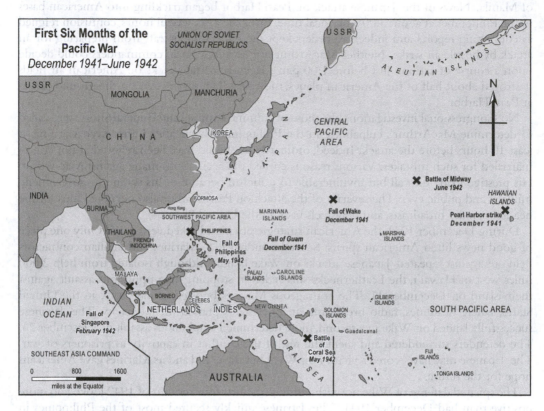

Map 11.1 First Six Months of the Pacific War, December 1941–June 1942

"beast," and "rat" helped dehumanize the Japanese, making it easier for American combatants to kill them and for Americans at home to applaud enemy deaths. These attitudes had permeated the United States dating back well into the nineteenth century. The Japanese attack on Pearl Harbor and the Bataan Death March validated these racially charged beliefs.

Initial American Reactions in Washington and in the Pacific

Changes in the U.S. Navy's highest levels of command occurred later in December 1941. Roosevelt chose Admiral Chester W. Nimitz shortly after Pearl Harbor to be commander-in-chief of the Pacific Fleet. Although quiet and unassuming, Nimitz nonetheless possessed the daring and wisdom to manage a theater of operations encompassing most of the world's largest ocean. Back in Washington at the end of December, Roosevelt made Admiral Ernest J. King the commander-in-chief of the U.S. Fleet and then in the spring of 1942 made him the chief of naval operations. King possessed the strategic prescience that allowed him, even in that year, to predict with uncanny accuracy what the next three years of the Pacific War would look like. He proved himself to be instrumental in securing resources for the Navy in the face of competing needs for manpower and material in the Southwest Pacific and Europe.

The U.S. Navy was not alone in restructuring to fight a global conflict. The Army's Chief of Staff, General George C. Marshall, also made some sweeping changes in March 1942. Prior to this date, for example, the War Department and the Army possessed a bewilderingly confusing structure. More than 100 commands and agencies had direct access to Marshall. Yet the Chief of Staff could not wrangle control of this bureaucracy, especially the oversight of logistics shared by two offices in the War Department, the six technical services (including the Quartermaster Corps, Signal Corps, Ordnance Department, Chemical Corps, Medical Corps, and Corps of Engineers), and eight other administrative departments. No decisions could be made without multiple concurrences, confusing flow charts, and meandering implementations. Such decentralization of authority had plagued the Army for decades. Its unwieldy structure proved completely unequal to the task of mobilizing a huge Army of eight million men and women, let alone maintaining units deployed thousands of miles across the globe. Marshall solved these problems in part by expanding the War Plan Division and renaming it the Operations Division. As the War Department General Staff's central command post responsible for formulating strategic plans and issuing orders in the Army, the Operations Division influenced every decision and policy flowing downward through the War Department.

Using progressive management principles like those used by Secretary Elihu Root four decades earlier, General Marshall also created new administrative commands in the Army proper, such as the Army Air Forces, led by Lieutenant General Henry H. "Hap" Arnold. Apart from directing aviation-related activities, Arnold served as a member of the Joint Chiefs of Staff. He joined General Marshall and Admirals King and William D Leahy in this group that advised President Roosevelt on strategy. The fact that Arnold was elevated to this post on the Joint Chiefs of Staff bore witness to growing importance of air power as a tool of war. Arnold, Marshall, King, and Leahy also served with their senior British counterparts on the Combined Chiefs of Staff where they formulated Anglo-American strategy.

Reeling from the Japanese victories, the United States remained on the strategic defensive throughout the first six months of 1942. This did not mean, however, that the American forces remained completely passive, as evinced by the "Doolittle Raid" in April. Named for the raid's commander, Lieutenant Colonel James H. "Jimmy" Doolittle of the U.S. Army Air Corps, this daring mission called for 16 twin-engine B-25 medium bombers to be transported onboard an aircraft carrier to within 600 miles of the Japanese home islands. All the B-25s got airborne after precarious takeoffs from a few hundred feet of carrier deck. They then dropped their bombs on targets in Japan and flew toward friendly Chinese forces on the Asian mainland. This risky venture endangered not only the bomber crews but also the American carrier tasked with their transport. A wrong move or accidental sighting could have brought the overwhelmingly powerful Japanese fleet down on the meager American naval forces.

Because they achieved complete surprise, the American flyers met no antiaircraft fire or enemy fighters. Apart from raising American morale, the Doolittle Raid shook Japanese confidence because it exposed how vulnerable their home islands were. It had been more than six centuries since the Japanese endured an attack on their homeland. After their raid ended, all but eight of the 80 American crewmen landed safely in China. The Japanese captured those eight and executed three of them.

Stopping Japan's Advance in the Southwest Pacific: Battle of the Coral Sea, May 1942

The Doolittle Raid motivated Admiral Yamamoto to accelerate his plans to sink the remaining American aircraft carriers. The first of two major Japanese efforts to achieve this goal occurred in the Southwest Pacific in May 1942. Yamamoto decided to deploy his warships to the Coral Sea and capture Port Moresby on the southern coast of New Guinea. These moves would allow Japanese forces to strike Australia and cut it off from the logistical supply route stretching 7,000 miles back to the United States. Just as important, Yamamoto believed that the U.S. Pacific

Fleet would try to block his advance. If this happened, he could destroy the American aircraft carriers.

Yamamoto sent a fleet with three Japanese aircraft carriers, troop transports, and several other warships to the Coral Sea to engage American and Australian forces there. Nimitz anticipated this move and reacted to halt Japanese expansion. He dispatched two American aircraft carriers, the USS *Lexington* and *Yorktown* under the command of Rear Admiral Frank Jack Fletcher to sail to the Coral Sea in the southwest Pacific. Although Fletcher was a "black shoe" or surface warfare admiral, he grasped the new dimension of air power. He intuitively understood how to utilize the airplane as an offensive weapon in naval operations.

In what would be the first naval battle fought completely over the horizon by opposing aircraft, American and Japanese carrier-based planes attacked enemy fleets on May 7–8, 1942. The Americans sank a Japanese light carrier and crippled two heavy carriers. For their part, Japanese torpedo and dive bombers inflicted serious losses on the Americans by sinking the *Lexington* and crippling the *Yorktown*. The latter carrier was towed back to Pearl Harbor. Instead of the anticipated month of repairs, workers at Pearl Harbor worked around the clock to send the *Yorktown* back to sea in only three days, in time to see action at the Battle of Midway.

The Battle of the Coral Sea was a tactical victory for the Japanese because they sank one American aircraft carrier in exchange for the loss of one light carrier and damage to two more. According to the estimations by Yamamoto and his staff, the U.S. Pacific Fleet was now down to two carriers. However, at the strategic level, the Battle of the Coral Sea constituted an American victory for two reasons. First, deprived of their offensive aerial capabilities, the Japanese withdrew their invasion fleet and ended their attempt to capture Port Moresby. Second, the damage to the two Japanese carriers required several months of repairs in dry docks. These two carriers, therefore, were not available for operations at Midway in June.

Apart from strategic and tactical considerations, the Battle of the Coral Sea further solidified aviation as the prime offensive combat arm in naval warfare. Carrier-born aircraft dropping bombs and torpedoes proved beyond all doubt the capability of sinking enemy warships from the air. The dreams of American General Billy Mitchell and Admiral William Moffett dating back to the 1920s were realized.

Stopping Japan's Advance in the Central Pacific: The Battle of Midway, June 1942

An important event occurred behind the scenes in the spring of 1942 when U.S. Navy cryptographers successfully deciphered the Japanese Navy's encoded messages. This intelligence allowed them to project future enemy operations near Midway and gave Nimitz sufficient evidence to commit his three remaining aircraft carriers to lay a trap for the Japanese.

Midway lay 1,100 miles west of Hawai'i in the central Pacific, almost exactly midway between the continental United States and Japan's home islands. This atoll included several small islands surrounding a shallow lagoon. Americans constructed a runway on one of them. By June 1942, more than 3,000 Marines with antiaircraft and coast artillery batteries defended Midway. Approximately 100 American aircraft were also stationed there. As such, the atoll became a *de facto* aircraft carrier.

In the first days of June, Admiral Nimitz sent three aircraft carriers to defend Midway. He wanted to make the aggressive Vice Admiral William "Bull" Halsey the commander of these warships. But because Halsey was hospitalized in early June, Nimitz gave overall command to Rear Admiral Frank Jack Fletcher and sent Rear Admiral Raymond A. Spruance to Midway as his second-in-command. Like Fletcher, Spruance had little direct experience with naval aviation. He did, however, possess a unique combination of good judgment and audacity. Nimitz gave the following guidance to the two admirals regarding the coming battle: "You will be governed by the principle of calculated risk, which you should interpret to mean the avoidance of exposure of your force to attack by the superior enemy without good prospect of inflicting, because of such exposure, greater damage on the enemy."[2] Spruance sailed with the aircraft carriers USS *Enterprise* and *Hornet* to a spot about 150 miles northeast of Midway. Joining Spruance about 20 miles away was Fletcher on the now fully operational *Yorktown* on June 3. Their trap laid, the Americans then waited to see if they could ensnare the Japanese.

Meanwhile, Admiral Yamamoto sent four aircraft carriers with 350 airplanes under Vice Admiral Chuichi Nagumo. These would close to within 200 miles of Midway, soften up the island defenses with bombing raids, and destroy any nearby American aerial or naval forces in anticipation of an amphibious assault against Midway. Once secure, the island could be used as a base for long-range Japanese aircraft to threaten Hawai'i. Yamamoto knew that Nimitz could not let this happen. He wanted to lure the Americans out to fight his supposedly superior force. The outcome of the Battle of Midway hinged on one question: Who would surprise whom? Unbeknownst to Yamamoto, the Americans waited for him. What happened next became one of the decisive naval battles in history, let alone in the Second World War.

Before dawn on June 4, 1942, the Japanese sent several dozen airplanes to destroy Midway's defenses. Nagumo kept his remaining aircraft armed with torpedoes and armor-piercing bombs in reserve in case American carriers were discovered. Both sides launched reconnaissance aircraft to search for opposing ships in 180-degree arcs. However, the one Japanese scout plane that would have detected the nearby American carriers experienced mechanical problems. Repairs delayed its takeoff. Conversely, at 5:20 a.m., American reconnaissance aircraft located the Japanese carriers some 250 miles northwest of Midway steaming toward the island.

American aircraft from Midway took off to defend the island against the coming Japanese or to attack the Japanese carriers. At 6:30 a.m., the Japanese hit Midway but failed to destroy all its defenses. For their part, the American planes from Midway did no damage to the Japanese fleet. Yet this seemingly futile raid by the Midway-based aircraft convinced Nagumo that he

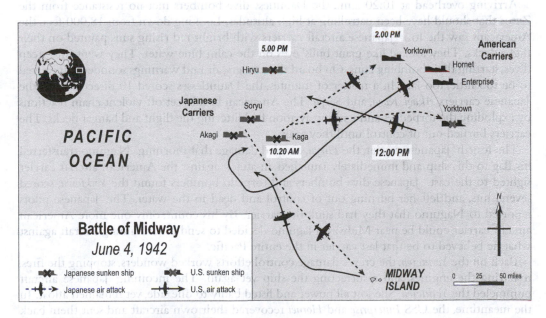

Map 11.2 Battle of Midway, June 4, 1942

should switch the armaments on his remaining aircraft for a second strike at Midway. He remained oblivious to the existence of the American carriers barely 200 miles to his east.

As planes made their return flights to the Japanese carriers and Midway respectively, Admirals Fletcher and Spruance ordered approximately 150 torpedo bombers, dive bombers, and fighters to converge on the Japanese carriers in a coordinated strike. However, delays and confusion en route caused the American squadrons to lose contact with each other, and they eventually attacked the Japanese carriers piecemeal.

Finally at 8:30 a.m., the one Japanese scout plane, having been delayed by repairs for 40 minutes, located a single American aircraft carrier (the *Yorktown*) to the east of the Japanese fleet. Bewildered by this revelation, Nagumo found himself unsure what to do. He decided to switch out his aircraft armaments once again. The bombs intended to finish off Midway's defenses needed to be replaced with torpedoes and armor-piercing bombs. Rearming 150 Japanese airplanes took time. This process left explosives strewn on his carrier's flight and hangar decks, and it was 9:30 a.m. before they were ready to launch.

Two other events further frustrated Nagumo's plan. First, Japanese aircraft began returning from Midway and landing on his carriers. This cluttered their decks. Second, beginning at 9:00 a.m., several dozen American TBD "Devastator" bombers commenced their unsuccessful torpedo runs. This aircraft's nickname belied its ineffectiveness. Slow, vulnerable, and without American fighter aircraft to defend them, all the Devastators fell victim to the deadly Japanese "Zero" fighters that had been flying at high altitudes screening the Japanese carriers against possible dive bombing attacks. Once they sighted the Devastators, the Zeros spent the next hour chasing the doomed Americans at sea level. This left no Japanese planes flying high cover.

There should have been dozens of American SBD "Dauntless" dive bombers from USS *Yorktown* and *Enterprise* rendezvousing with the Devastators in a coordinated strike. However, the dive bombers did not arrive at 9:00 a.m. as planned, because they got lost. Fortuitously, the Dauntless pilots sighted a solitary Japanese destroyer running at full speed. They decided to plot a course toward the main Japanese fleet based on that destroyer's path.

Arriving overhead at 10:20 a.m., the Dauntless dive bombers met no resistance from the Zeros that should have been patrolling at high altitudes. Looking down from 18,000 feet, the Americans saw the four Japanese aircraft carriers with bright red rising suns painted on their flight decks. They looked like giant bulls' eyes on the calm blue water. They went into steep dives, starting their bombing runs. On board the carriers, air raid warnings sounded but proved to be too little, too late. In a matter of minutes, the Dauntlesses scored 10 direct hits on the Japanese carriers *Akagi*, *Kaga*, and *Soryu*. The American bombs set off violent chain reactions by exploding the torpedoes and igniting aviation fuel littering the flight and hangar decks. The carriers burned out of control until they sank.

The fourth Japanese carrier, the *Hiryu*, escaped damage that morning. Nagumo transferred his flag to this ship and immediately launched an attack against the American aircraft carrier sighted to the east. Japanese dive bombers and torpedo bombers found the *Yorktown*, scored several hits, and left her burning out of control and dead in the water. The Japanese pilots reported to Nagumo that they had sunk the carrier. By his count, only one more American aircraft carrier could be near Midway. Nagumo decided to send his remaining aircraft against what he believed to be that last carrier in the entire Pacific.

Back on the *Yorktown*, the crew's damage control efforts worked wonders, stopping the fires, restarting the engines, and resurrecting the ship yet again. The incoming Japanese aircraft pummeled the *Yorktown*. She lost all power and listed badly to one side, yet remained afloat. In the meantime, the USS *Enterprise* and *Hornet* recovered their own aircraft and sent them back aloft to hunt down the *Hiryu*. Later on June 4, the Americans sank this last enemy carrier. That same day, an American destroyer began slowly towing the gallant *Yorktown* back to Pearl Harbor, but a Japanese submarine sunk both ships with torpedoes.

Many factors contributed to the outcome of the Battle of Midway. The American analysis of deciphered enemy messages set the conditions for the Americans to surprise the Japanese. Nagumo's wavering in decision making and ignorance of air power completely contrasted the audacity and understanding of Admirals Spruance and Fletcher and their subordinates. Ultimately, the Battle of Midway cost the Japanese their advantages in seaborne air power, both in aircraft carriers and in well-trained naval aviators. The Imperial Japanese Navy never recovered fully from Midway.

Going on the Offensive: America's Campaign for Guadalcanal, 1942–43

Whereas the Battles of the Coral Sea and Midway halted Japanese expansion, the United States launched its first major counteroffensive against the island of Guadalcanal in the fall of 1942. The fighting in the air, on land, and at sea would last six long months before American forces could secure Guadalcanal. The eventual victory proved not only that Americans could best the Japanese in combat but also that American logistical support could outlast the enemy's supply system.

In the spring of 1942, the Japanese worked their way from their massive base at Rabaul on New Britain southeastward through the Solomon Islands, a chain of several dozen islands lying to the east of New Guinea. The Japanese started construction on an airfield on Guadalcanal near the southeasternmost tip of the Solomons. Because aircraft on this island could interdict American supply routes to Australia or strike American naval forces operating in the Southwest Pacific, the Americans could not tolerate this presence. Chief of Naval Operations Ernest King in Washington and Admiral Chester Nimitz at Pearl Harbor decided to make Guadalcanal the starting point for an American counteroffensive. They hoped to use this island as a base to isolate and capture Rabaul. However, attacking the Japanese on Guadalcanal just eight months after Pearl Harbor would stretch the meager American naval, aviation, logistical, and manpower resources.

During early summer of 1942, Navy planners decided that the 1st Marine Division under Major General Alexander A. Vandegrift would make the initial assault on Guadalcanal. This would be no easy task. The Americans lacked supplies for more than one month of combat, and they also possessed insufficient intelligence about the island's defense and terrain. Tensions rose between Vandegrift and the more senior naval commanders, Vice Admiral Robert Ghormley and Rear Admiral Frank Jack Fletcher, both of whom believed this assault should not be attempted with so few resources at hand. Fletcher especially did not wish to make his precious aircraft carriers vulnerable to Japanese aerial attack. Nevertheless, orders came down that the assault on Guadalcanal would take place eight months to the day after Pearl Harbor.

Admiral Fletcher's warships and transports carrying Vandegrift's 18,000 Marines arrived offshore Guadalcanal late on the night of August 6, 1942. The American attack the next morning, August 7, achieved complete tactical surprise. The Japanese on the island fled into the jungle while Marines made their way on landing craft to the shore. When they faced no significant opposition on Guadalcanal, they easily established a beachhead, expanded inland to the airfield, and started to construct a defensive perimeter. After the landing's success, Fletcher decided to withdraw his carriers one day later. His decision met with loud protests from Vandegrift and other subordinates. Already, Japanese aircraft began bombing raids against the Marines on Guadalcanal that would continue almost every day for the next several months. Fletcher's departure left the transports with only six American or Australian cruisers forming a protective screen against counterattacks.

The enemy's retaliation occurred more quickly and in a deadlier manner than any American could have predicted. Overnight on August 8, seven Japanese cruisers sailed undetected past Savo Island toward Guadalcanal. They caught the patrolling American and Australian cruisers completely off guard. In a few minutes, the Japanese sank one Australian and three American cruisers but suffered no ships lost and just a few casualties. The Japanese could have struck a death blow against the Americans at Guadalcanal by steaming 20 miles to destroy the transports, which would have left the Marines without desperately needed extra food and ammunition. However, the Japanese admiral hesitated and withdrew before dawn because he worried that his ships would be hit by American carrier-based aircraft. He was unaware that the carriers left the area the day before. After this devastating defeat, the American transports offloaded supplies and sailed away. The Marines, as one officer recalled, felt like they were the "1st Maroon Division."[3]

The next two weeks saw the Marines strengthen their nine-mile perimeter around their beachhead and the all-important airfield—now named "Henderson Field" to honor a Marine pilot killed in action in the Battle of Midway. On August 20, several dozen Marine aircraft landed at Henderson Field, giving Vandegrift the resources to fight off the daily Japanese bombing raids. In all, American pilots shot down five enemy planes for every one American plane lost.

Incessant Japanese aerial bombing raids sent the Marines running for cover daily, and enemy artillery barrages harassed them nightly. Pitched ground battles occurred intermittently over the next five months. The most determined ground offensive against the Marines came on September 13. Some 3,000 Japanese soldiers trekked through the jungle and attacked north-ward from the inland side of the Marines' perimeter, intending to overrun those defenses and capture Henderson Field. For three days beginning on September 12, the Japanese advanced along the spine of a low ridge just south of the airfield. Facing them were 1,250 Marines led by Lieutenant Colonel Merritt A. Edson. His men gave ground each day, but they inflicted such heavy losses that the Japanese withdrew after three days. While the Marines suffered

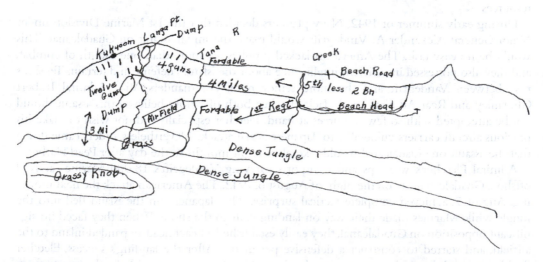

Figure 11.2 American Hand-Drawn Map of Guadalcanal, Dated August 12, 1942

This map of the northern coast of Guadalcanal was drawn just days after the 1st Marine Division's amphibious assault on August 7, 1942. This map was sent with a report back to Headquarters Marine Corps in Washington. The key features include the "grassy knob" south of the "airfield" that will be the scene of the Battle of Edson's Ridge in September 1942.

© Courtesy U.S. Marine Corps University

250 casualties, the Japanese lost 600 killed and 600 more wounded, most of whom later died in the jungle. The Battle of Edson's Ridge earned its namesake the Medal of Honor.

As bloody fighting on Guadalcanal continued, Americans and Japanese sent thousands of reinforcements to help their comrades. At their peak strengths, some 40,000 American and 25,000 Japanese were on the island. The hot, humid, rainy conditions on the tropical island reduced these numbers significantly due to disease and, for Japanese troops, starvation. The Japanese Navy tried to resupply them at night, but interference by American naval and air forces meant that the Japanese on the island remained chronically short of food, medicine, and ammunition.

At sea, American and Japanese naval forces traded blows in several battles near Guadalcanal. Vice Admiral Ghormley reluctantly committed American warships piecemeal. The opposing forces tried to protect their own convoys of supply ships steaming toward Guadalcanal while hoping to destroy enemy convoys. Suffering exhaustion from non-stop command pressures since Pearl Harbor, Ghormley was relieved by Nimitz on October 18 and replaced by Vice Admiral William "Bull" Halsey. The new commander brought his aggressive mindset to the American naval forces in the South Pacific. Halsey fully committed his resources to supplying the American troops on Guadalcanal and defeating the Japanese Navy in the region.

The opposing fleets fought several battles in which their warships traded blows in point-blank melees at night. Both sides suffered heavy losses in lives and ships. Meanwhile, the Japanese tried in vain to reinforce and resupply the starving troops on Guadalcanal through December. Finally, they evacuated the remaining Japanese forces from the island a few hundred at a time until February 7, 1943, and thereafter the Americans declared the island secure.

Thus ended the first major American offensive in the Pacific War. The six months of fighting in the Guadalcanal Campaign cost the Americans 29 warships sunk, 1,600 Marines and soldiers killed, and another 5,000 wounded. But the Japanese suffered worse losses of 38 warships sunk and 25,000 Japanese ground troops killed. A closer examination revealed how striking the American strategic and logistical victories really were. The United States forces exposed the critical weakness in Japan's logistical system that grew worse over the next three years.

As victory in Guadalcanal looked more certain, American planners turned their attention to completing the conquest of the Solomon island chain and to isolating the Japanese base at Rabaul. The next step was New Georgia, an island 150 miles to the northwest of Guadalcanal where the Japanese built an airfield. After American amphibious landings in June 1942, weeks of combat followed as the Japanese lost their airfield by August. This in turn gave the Americans their own base for further aerial operations in the northern Solomons and the surrounding waters. Then came the invasion of Bougainville in early November. Allied American, Australian, and New Zealand troops landed by the tens of thousands and advanced eastward across that island. Bitter fighting on Bougainville lasted until 1944 before the Allied forces could secure Bougainville and eventually isolate Rabaul.

American Home Front: Building the "Arsenal of Democracy"

Japan's attack on Pearl Harbor in December 1941 sparked increases in United States government expenditures to unprecedented heights to fund the "Arsenal of Democracy." Americans needed to feed, clothe, and arm not only the Allies, but also the U.S. military. This in turn simulated the American economy and ended the Great Depression once and for all. Unemployment rates dropped from 14.5 percent in 1941 to 4.7 percent in 1942, to 1.9 percent in 1943, and then to the wartime low of 1.2 percent in 1944. The average work week rose from 32 hours in the 1930s to 48 hours in the war years.

The American war effort caused sweeping changes that affected society, government, business, and politics. Carefully orchestrated propaganda aroused patriotism and volunteerism as well as played on American fears and prejudices by portraying their enemies as evil, inferior, inhuman, or worse. When such appeals or depictions were not sufficient to engender support, the federal government turned to means that bordered on authoritarianism, including censorship of the press and suspension of civil rights. Thus, the arsenal of democracy was sometimes not very democratic.

The U.S. military needed to expand dramatically to meet anticipated challenges of fighting wars on opposite sides of the globe. Hundreds of thousands of Americans flooded military recruitment centers, but these four million volunteers could not swell the ranks to the 16 million personnel that eventually served in uniform. To make up the difference, Congress amended the Selective Service of 1940 to mandate the term of service to be the conflict's duration plus six months. The amendment also lowered the minimum age for draft registration from 21 years in the original act of 1940 to 18 years. In all, some 50 million American men were registered, of whom 25 percent were inducted through conscription.

Many of the remaining 38 million men received "4-F" classifications during medical and psychological examinations. This disqualified them from service because they did not meet minimum physical, emotional, intellectual, or moral standards. Fully one-third of all would-be service personnel were rejected because they exhibited such physical problems as flat feet, poor vision, bad teeth, or low weight. Other registrants were rejected due to emotional deficiencies like depression, or to certain behaviors judged to be sexually or morally deviant. For example, homosexuality and lesbianism were believed to be either diseases or crimes during the Second World War. Neither openly gay men nor suspiciously feminine men would be tolerated in the American military.

Once judged fit for duty and sworn into military service, new recruits entered several weeks of basic training or officer training facilities. They learned discipline, military customs, and combat tactics, and they acquired rudimentary skills with weapons, vehicles, and other equipment. Many young men received regular medical care for the first time in their lives. Many also put on 20 or 30 pounds of muscle and grew at least one inch in height. They lost their civilian individuality after drill instructors molded them into soldiers, sailors, airmen, or Marines. Volunteers or draftees with one or more years of college could be singled out to become officers. Their training lasted for only three months, giving them the derisive nickname of "90-day wonders." Such abbreviated periods were hardly long enough to prepare them for the responsibilities and pressures of command, whether in combat units or behind the lines in support units.

Women and Minorities in Uniform

Despite the need for able-bodied service personnel, not all American volunteers or draftees served as freely as Caucasian Americans. Neither women nor African Americans could enter service without scoring sufficiently high on entrance examinations and demonstrating relatively high intelligence. Even then, they could not expect to rise to the flag ranks or to command white men in combat units. Such assumptions and limitations look sexist and racist from a twenty-first-century perspective, but sadly, those stereotypes were commonplace in American society and its military in the 1940s.

In 1942, Congress passed legislation establishing the Women's Auxiliary Army Corps (WAAC), the Navy's Women Accepted for Voluntary Emergency Service (WAVES), and the

Marine Corps Women's Reserves. Shortly thereafter, the Coast Guard's *Semper Paratus*—Always Ready (SPAR) and the civilian Women Airforce Service Pilots (WASP) added still more opportunities for women to contribute directly to the war effort. In all, more than 350,000 women joined the U.S. military. Although they initially performed 200 tasks in clerical and similar fields, they later added 200 more tasks in logistical and technical fields that had previously been exclusively male, though not combat-related.

During the Second World War, women flocked to recruiting stations for many reasons. Many responded to the nation's powerful appeals to patriotism exemplified by the famous advertising quote "Free a Man to Fight." Other women sought adventure or escape from their civilian domestic roles. The clear majority were rejected because of health issues, educational deficiencies, or moral questions. Those few accepted into military service always possessed more education and experience than did men of equal rank. To serve in the enlisted ranks, women needed to have at least some college-level education, if not a granted degree. Entering the officer ranks often required graduate-level education and significant expertise in government or business. Oveta Culp Hobby, for instance, left her prewar position as vice president of the *Houston Post* newspaper to become a colonel and director of the WAAC.

Once in the military, women needed to prove their competence at standards higher than men while enduring suspicion, discrimination, harassment, or assault. The U.S. military was, after all, a male-dominated and masculine institution. Women in uniform tried to balance the inherent contradictions of civilian society's expectations of them as females with the military's expectation of them as soldiers. Ultimately, they were seen as women first and as soldiers second. Nowhere was this contradiction more poignant than in accusations of rape and allegations of lesbianism. Justice in sexual assault investigations was rare, because rapes were often dismissed as the victim's fault or as normal, albeit rough, sexual intercourse. Defending against allegations of deviant sexual behaviors proved to be equally difficult for women in uniform. Smear campaigns painted women as lesbians when they entered military service or as becoming lesbians thereafter in the masculine culture of the military.

Despite entering environments of strict moral codes and unflinching performance standards, the overwhelming majority of servicewomen made significant contributions to the American war effort that far surpassed their small numbers. Women not only freed men to fight but they also brought better qualifications to those noncombatant positions they held. Servicewomen possessed the skill and knowledge to direct complex organizations, manage inventories, repair machines, and fly airplanes, all of which were tasks previously designated for men.

In ways similar to women, African Americans faced ongoing restrictions on their civil rights imposed by Jim Crow laws and other racist practices. Blacks were treated as second-class citizens throughout American society. They attended segregated but hardly equal schools, used separate restrooms, and sat in the back seats of buses. Some also became targets of harassment, assault, or even murder. Nevertheless, just as African Americans had done in the First World War, they rallied to the flag after Pearl Harbor. In the Second World War, they wanted to achieve the "Double V"—victory over racism abroad and racism at home in the United States. Black leaders recognized that fulfilling the ultimate obligations of citizenship—fighting, killing, and dying for the United States—gave them the most convincing arguments to claim the full legal and political benefits of American citizenship.

In all, more than one million black volunteers or draftees entered the U.S. military. After passing entrance examinations more stringent than those for whites, they entered segregated basic training camps, lived in segregated barracks, ate in segregated mess halls, and then fell under the control of Caucasian officers in segregated units. Considered incapable of independent action, quick decision making, or leadership roles, most African Americans served in what were euphemistically called "labor" units. They never experienced combat. Instead, they spent the war years driving trucks, unloading supplies, or performing other menial tasks, often far from the front lines. This should not, however, be construed to mean that those were not significant contributions to the nation's war effort. Quite the contrary, African Americans helped to make the massive American logistical system function smoothly. Without timely deliveries of supplies, the combat units could not effectively fight.

It should also be noted that, regardless of race, the overwhelming majority of Americans in uniform never experienced extended combat. Only 15 percent of them (2.5 million men) spent significant time on the front lines. Combat was thus not the norm in the U.S. military. It was instead the exception for the 16 million Americans in uniform.

Approximately 10 percent of the blacks in the U.S. military, or 100,000 men, eventually served in combat units on the front lines. Among the most famous of these were the Tuskegee Airmen of the 332nd Fighter Group. They entered the Army Air Force and learned to fly at the Tuskegee Institute in Alabama. Despite institutionalized racism and inferior equipment, nearly 1,000 pilots persevered to become the first blacks to earn their wings. Some of these pilots deployed with the 332nd to North Africa and Sicily in 1942 and 1943. Moving to southern Italy in 1944, the Tuskegee Airmen achieved their greatest notoriety escorting the U.S. 15th Air Force's strategic bombers on long missions against German targets. The 332nd's fighter aircraft had distinctive "red tails" that identified them to the American bomber crews. Once they started flying the new North American P-51 Mustang fighter aircraft, the Red Tails could remain with the American bombers during their entire missions.

In all, the 332nd Fighter Group boasted an impressive combat record: three Distinguished Unit Citations and 400 enemy aircraft damaged or destroyed on 15,500 sorties (flights by individual planes) during 311 missions. The Red Tails reputedly never lost an American bomber to enemy fighters. Subsequent research, however, has shown that perhaps two dozen bombers did fall victim to German fighters. This does not degrade the Tuskegee Airmen's heroic efforts, because they successfully protected more than 7,500 bombers. Contrasted to this huge total, two dozen lost bombers represents a negligible percentage. There were other effective African-American units in the Army, including the "Black Panthers" of the 761st Tank Battalion and the "Buffalo Soldiers" of the 92nd Infantry Division (Colored).

Whereas the Army allowed some blacks to see combat, neither the U.S. Navy nor the Marine Corps opened combat units to African Americans. They served as stewards in ship wardrooms or stevedores on harbor docks. The Navy did not commission black officers until February 1944, and even then, they only received reserve commissions. The Marine Corps never permitted blacks to become commissioned officers at all during the Second World War. The history and culture of the Corps made its prejudice against African Americans the most extreme in the American military. Prior to 1942, no black individual had ever entered the Corps, and so there was no tradition or lore associated with African-American Marines.

During the Second World War, other racial and ethnic groups in the United States experienced varying degrees of discrimination. But none was treated with such a double-standard as Japanese Americans. Of the 115,000 people of Japanese descent residing in the western United States in 1941, approximately two-thirds emigrated from Japan. The remaining one-third—the "Nisei," or second generation—was born in the United States and thus possessed American citizenship. The attack on Pearl Harbor aroused suspicion and fueled racial hatred toward

Japanese Americans. President Franklin D. Roosevelt reacted to these fears by issuing Executive Order 9066 on February 19, 1942. This mandate called for all Japanese Americans in the western states to be removed from their residences and relocated to camps far away from any potential American military or civilian targets. There was no due process of law, not even for the majority who claimed American citizenship by birth or naturalization. While there may be legitimate worries about the loyalty or safety of those people of Japanese descent, the process clearly violated their constitutional rights.

Japanese American families received notices that they had to vacate their homes and assemble at local train stations with what they could carry. After being herded into train cars, they found themselves living in shacks behind barbed wire fences under military guard in "internment camps" in the Rocky Mountains and other isolated areas. They carved out an existence with few resources, little food, and substandard living conditions. Appeals to the U.S. Supreme Court to redress this violation of their rights met with rejection. Despite government investigations into their backgrounds, no substantive charge of espionage or sabotage could be proven against the Japanese Americans living in the continental United States.

The Japanese Americans doubtlessly felt scared, betrayed, or angry during the Second World War. Even so, 20,000 Japanese American left the camps to serve in the U.S. military during the Second World War. They believed that they could demonstrate their loyalty to the nation on the battlefield and thus make their demands for return of their rights more legitimate. The most well-known unit of Japanese Americans was the U.S. Army's 442nd Regimental Combat Team. Rated at a full strength of 4,000 men, this unit's soldiers saw action in Italy, where it became the most highly decorated unit of its size. In all, 14,000 men served in the 442nd and earned 9,500 Purple Hearts, 21 Congressional Medals of Honor, and eight Presidential Unit Citations.

Box 11.2   Daniel Inouye—Japanese American Veteran and Recipient of the Congressional Medal of Honor

One of those Japanese Americans serving in the 442nd Regimental Combat Team was a young man named Daniel Inouye. Born to Japanese parents in Hawai'i in 1924 and living there when Pearl Harbor was attacked, he did not get interned like those Japanese Americans in the continental United States. However, like the 140,000 people of Japanese descent in Hawai'i during the conflict, Inouye did endure martial law, with nightly curfews and random identification checks.

He eventually enlisted in the U.S. Army in 1943 and saw combat in Italy. In one engagement near the German Gothic Line in 1945, then-Lieutenant Inouye suffered severe wounds in combat. His bravery merited the award of the Distinguished Service Cross, the nation's second-highest combat decoration. Decades later in 2000, Inouye's DSC was upgraded to the Medal of Honor. Excerpts of his citation follow:

With complete disregard for his personal safety, Second Lieutenant Inouye crawled up the treacherous slope to within five yards of the nearest [German] machine gun and hurled two grenades, destroying the emplacement. Before the enemy could retaliate, he stood up and *neutralized a second machine-gun nest. Although wounded by a sniper's bullet, he continued to*

Figure 11.3 Photograph of Sen. Daniel Inouye From World War II

Inouye as a young officer in the 442nd Regimental Combat Team.

Courtesy, U.S. Army Museum of Hawaii (USAMH2986)

engage other hostile positions at close range until an exploding grenade shattered his right arm. Despite the intense pain, he refused evacuation and continued to direct his platoon until enemy resistance was broken and his men were again deployed in defensive positions. In the attack, 25 enemy soldiers were killed and eight others captured . . .

Inouye received an honorable discharge, finished his college education, and began a law practice after the conflict ended. When Hawai'i received statehood in 1959, Inouye devoted himself to more than five decades of public service, most notably as a nine-term U.S. Senator. He passed away in 2012.

Building the American War Machine and Controlling Wartime Beliefs

While 16 million Americans entered the military's ranks, an equally dramatic expansion occurred in industrial production between the years 1940 and 1945. The massive output of the nation's factories boggles the mind:

- 1,200 warships (from submarines to battleships).
- 300,000 aircraft of all types.
- 4,900 merchant ships (with freight capacity of 51 million tons).
- 25 billion rounds of .30-caliber ammunition.
- 88,000 tanks of all types.
- 675,000 "deuce and a half" trucks.
- 128 million pairs of shoes and boots.
- 14.4 million first-aid packets.
- 900 billion cigarettes.

The raw materials for these items came from the continental United States, its territories like Alaska, and the Allied nations in South America and Africa.

The agricultural production levels of the United States were no less impressive as evinced in the following figures:

- 460,000 tons of beef.
- 1.3 billion eggs.
- 1 million tons of sugar.
- 428,000 tons of butter.

To reduce consumption by American civilians, the government issued ration cards that limited sales of gasoline, coffee, flour, sugar, milk, and meat. "Victory gardens" sprang up across the nation as Americans grew their own fruits and vegetables to supplement their rationed diets.

Producing so much required rapid increases in the American workforce. Men and women unemployed or underemployed in the Great Depression found jobs aplenty in the civilian sector and in the U.S. military. Between 1941 and 1943 alone, for example, some five million American women entered the workforce for the first time, popularized by the iconic "Rosie the Riveter" in posters and other media. Yet women also broke into skilled labor positions like welding, plumbing, and operating stamp presses or cranes. Other women contributed to the war effort by working as scientists and in other white collar professions.

African Americans also benefited from the growth of American industry during the Second World War. Many blacks migrated from the South to industrial centers in the North, East, and West of the United States. The South's discriminatory employment policies favored whites over blacks for jobs in newly built factories springing up all over the region. African Americans could not hope to rise above subsistence-level sharecropping on old cotton plantations or low-paying unskilled work in factories as long as they lived in the South.

There may have been greater economic mobility for blacks outside the South, yet discrimination also occurred in northern cities. Tensions occasionally erupted in race riots, as in Detroit,

Michigan, in 1943. Relations between blacks and whites in that city deteriorated after a minor racial incident spiraled out of control into three days of fighting, looting, and burning. By the time American soldiers restored order, more than 1,800 people were arrested, 400 wounded, 30 dead, and $2 million of damage was done to property. Detroit's African-American community bore the brunt of these effects.

Looking at the American war effort at the macro-level, the total cost in 1940s dollars of every item manufactured, mined, processed, or grown in the United States exceeded $300 billion. This amount equates to approximately $4 trillion in 2017 dollars. Producing and distributing so many materials across the globe required heretofore unparalleled levels of managerial efficiency as well as government power. The activism of the New Deal agencies during the Great Depression paled in comparison to the activism of the so-called superagencies during the Second World War. Yet it can also be argued that the New Deal in the 1930s gave government administrators and military officers invaluable experience in managing complex projects that blurred public-private lines. During the conflict, the United States government exerted control over every sector of the economy and society by creating superagencies like the War Production Board and the Office of War Information.

In January 1942, President Franklin Roosevelt issued an executive order that established the War Production Board. It exercised control over war materials to be manufactured, contracts to be awarded for those materials, products to be purchased by American civilians, and resources to be allocated to best support the nation's building programs. The War Production Board thus stood as a prime example of the United States government utilizing private-sector expertise to supervise public-sector projects. Elsewhere, in a different segment of life, the United States government regulated the flow of images, ideas, and words that Americans absorbed during the Second World War. Later in June 1942, President Roosevelt issued another executive order that created the Office of War Information. It acted as the central conduit for the collection, evaluation, and selection of posters, radio broadcasts, articles, newsreels, motion pictures, and even matchbooks that portrayed the war effort in positive ways. Implicit and explicit messages found in these sources played up patriotism and propaganda.

Box 11.3 Wartime Propaganda in the United States

American propaganda took many forms during the Second World War. Some attempts to portray the Axis enemy were blatant in their biased portrayals that fed on America racial or ethnic prejudices. Other types of propaganda sought to present the Americans as crusaders for freedom and democracy. The Office of War Information and other governmental and military agencies monitored the creation and dissemination of all types of print, audio, or cinematic presentations to Americans at home or abroad. The American media cooperated with the government in this process of demonizing the Axis enemy and celebrating the American and Allied efforts. This popular magazine cover is just one example available on the internet, at museums, and in libraries and archives.

Figure 11.4 Cover of *Collier's* Magazine, December 12, 1942

The popular *Collier's* magazine (December 12, 1942) looked back to the attack on Pearl Harbor one year earlier. The cover clearly depicted the Japanese enemy as a flying demon with squinty eyes, fangs, and pointy ears. In his hands is a bomb and below is Pearl Harbor on Oahu. This image combined the racially charged American beliefs about Japanese and the popular image of the Wicked Witch's flying monkeys in the film *The Wizard of Oz* released in 1939. Every American in 1942 grasped the implicit and explicit meanings in this cover.

Galerie Bilderwelt/Hulton Archive/Getty Images

Winning the Battle of the Atlantic

All the hard work on the American home front would be pointless if the resulting products could not be safely transported across the Atlantic to the Allies. The German Navy attempted to do to the British in the Second World War what they had failed to do during the Great War: starve them into submission by creating a blockade of U-boats. Anglo-American sailors and merchant mariners made dangerous voyages across thousands of miles of ocean to the United Kingdom and the Soviet Union. British Prime Minister Winston Churchill coined this term "Battle of the Atlantic" to describe this four-year struggle. The resulting battles rarely reached the magnitude of the massive fleet actions in the Pacific, but the engagements in the lonely, cold North Atlantic were no less significant.

German U-boats represented the main threat because the German Navy was outnumbered by the combined U.S. and British Royal Navies. While Germany boasted the largest submarine fleet in the world, it possessed relatively few surface vessels. In 1941 before the attack on Pearl Harbor, German U-boats targeted shipping in the northeastern Atlantic. Then, after the American entrance into the conflict, the U-boats started operating off the coast of North America, where they lay in wait to prey on ships leaving American ports. Once sighting a target silhouetted by lights along the shoreline, they fired their torpedoes at those vessels. The merchant mariners onboard those ships felt helpless because they could only sail 12 knots in zigzagging paths and pray for safety. These seamen were nicknamed "shark bait" by sailors on American warships.

In just a few weeks in early 1942, the U-boats sank 160,000 tons of shipping flying the American flag. During that entire year, the United States lost 400 ships, two million tons of shipping, and 8,400 merchant mariners dead. These figures constituted about 25 percent of the total Allied losses of 1,600 merchant ships at 8.25 million tons in 1942. This year represented the high point for German U-boats' effectiveness.

The next year, 1943, stood out as the watershed year in the Battle of the Atlantic because the momentum shifted dramatically to favor the Allies. American losses dropped to 200 merchant ships in 1943, then to 65 in 1944, and only 30 in 1945. It is worth noting that American construction of merchant ships eventually outpaced the German ability to sink them. The new construction of American shipping skyrocketed from 700 vessels in 1942 to 1,900 new vessels in 1943, then 1,800 in 1944, and to 1,200 in eight months of 1945. This totaled a wartime production of 5,500 merchant ships. Most of these were prefabricated "Liberty Ships" that American shipyards built in a matter of days. Meanwhile, Allied escort vessels and aircraft sank progressively more U-boats at sea, and others were demolished in their submarine pens along the European coast by Allied aerial bombing raids. The Germans lost 780 U-boats destroyed and 30,000 submariners killed, or more than 75 percent of their U-boat force.

The Battle of the Atlantic could be best described as a series of cat and mouse games. In one such game, the German U-boats hunted for the Allied merchant ships and tried to sink them. Those merchant ships tried to evade the Germans. In the second cat and mouse game, Allied escort vessels tried to locate the U-boats and then dropped depth charges to destroy them underwater or force them to the surface, where they were vulnerable to Allied gunfire.

The Allies developed their tactical and technological countermeasures that offset the German advantages. The U.S. Navy adopted the convoy system in early 1942, which meant that the U-boats had to be massed in "wolfpacks" at the right place at the right time to do any serious damage. A convoy could fill 20 square miles of ocean. But the possible routes from the United States to Europe stretched 3,000 miles east to west in a corridor 1,000 miles wide. If the

German captains failed to locate the convoy, then the merchant ships would make the Atlantic crossing without incident.

The year 1943 marked the decisive shift in the Battle of the Atlantic toward the Allies because technological advances gave the American and British more tools to destroy the U-boats. More accurate SONAR (Sound Navigation and Ranging Device) enabled Allied warships to track submerged U-boats by identifying sound pulses echoing off their hulls or by listening for sounds of their running engines. Once located, the surface vessels dropped depth charges into the water near the U-boats. The large metal containers filled with explosives detonated at predetermined depths, sending powerful shock waves that cracked the U-boats' thin skins. Anglo-American cryptographers also successfully broke the German Navy's codes sent on their Enigma machines after capturing the code books and machines on damaged U-boats. Intelligence gleaned from intercepting messages proved to be an effective countermeasure to German attacks.

Faltering Steps and Stumbling Victories in North Africa, 1942

By December 1941, fighting in North Africa had seesawed for 18 months. Italian forces crossing from Libya eastward into Egypt were thrown into retreat by British forces in 1940 and early 1941. Then the Germans entered the fray to reinforce, and later replace, the Italians. The opposing forces traded territory in repeated attacks and counterattacks. In early 1942, recently promoted Field Marshal Erwin Rommel's units in his *Afrika Korps* gained the upper hand by driving the British far back into Egypt to El Alamein, where in June the British finally halted the German advance less than 250 miles from the invaluable Suez Canal. This canal, connecting the Mediterranean Sea with the Red Sea, was a critical link in the British supply line to the Middle East and India. Losing the Suez Canal would have reduced the British fighting power and further hurt production and living standards on the British home front.

In August 1942, Lieutenant General Bernard Law Montgomery assumed command of the British ground forces in North Africa. Two months later, he launched a major assault against Rommel at El Alamein. The British defeated the Germans, destroying many tanks and pushing the *Afrika Korps* into retreat westward through Libya toward Tunisia.

Other than stationing a few aircraft in the region, the U.S. military played limited roles in North Africa during 1942 because the United States lacked the transportation resources to place troops on the ground and the logistical system to support them in ground operations thereafter. This all changed on November 8, 1942, which marked D-Day for Operation TORCH. The amphibious landings by American forces in North Africa stood as the first major American military efforts against German and Italian forces. The decision to invade resulted from diplomatic and practical considerations. Because the Soviet Union barely survived the German invasion in 1941 and remained hard-pressed in 1942, Stalin wanted the United States and Great Britain to open a second front in Northern Europe to draw German ground forces away from fighting his Soviet forces in Eastern Europe. The Anglo-American members of the Grand Alliance, however, could not make that cross-channel attack due to insufficient personnel and resources. So concentrating on the Mediterranean represented the only viable option. British Prime Minister Winston Churchill especially favored this choice because it protected his nation's supply lines and offered possibilities for further invasions on Sicily and Italy.

Many challenges faced the untested U.S. Army units. Most of these 63,000 soldiers had never undertaken an amphibious assault or experienced combat of any sort. Many other problems

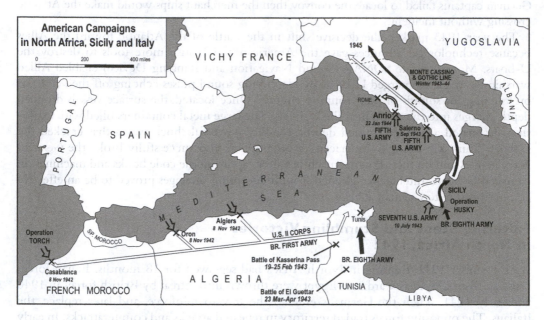

Map 11.3 American Campaigns in North Africa, Sicily, and Italy, 1942–1944

demanded attention: ensuring naval and air superiority along a coastline stretching 600 miles from the Atlantic side of northwest Africa into the Mediterranean, and confronting possible resistance from French forces in Morocco and Algeria supposedly loyal to the Vichy puppet government and thus aligned with Nazi Germany.

Anglo-American forces succeeded in this initial landing at several points in Morocco and Algeria. Scattered resistance by French units erupted in each area, but none lasted longer than a few days. The Anglo-Americans consolidated their positions before moving up 1,500 miles eastward into Tunisia, toward which the Germans retreated from the east in early 1943. The Anglo-American forces intended to capture the port city of Tunis, which would prevent Rommel from being resupplied from southern Europe and escaping from Tunisia.

Defeat at Kasserine Pass and Victory at El Guettar

Although debilitated by attrition and running short on supplies, Rommel's *Afrika Korps* could still sting the opposing forces. One such defeat occurred at the Battle of Kasserine Pass near Tunisia's western border with Algeria. Having just crossed this border, the Americans established positions to hold this pass. For his part, Rommel wanted to move through the pass to reach American supply depots across the border in Algeria.

When fighting in the Kasserine Pass began on February 19, 1942, the initial German and Italian attack against American defenses made only slow progress. Elements of the 1st Infantry Division and the 19th Combat Engineer Regiment held their ground for the first day of the German onslaught. The next day saw reinforced German forces smashing through the lines. After routing the American units, the Germans raced through the pass and prepared to go still further on the next day. By February 21, however, American and

British reinforcements arrived and halted the enemy advance. Running low on supplies, the overextended Germans were forced to withdraw three days later. Rommel needed to send his units south to block the British advance. The Kasserine Pass stood as the last high point for Rommel in North Africa. Even so, he failed to turn that tactical victory into a strategic one. His momentary gains only delayed the inevitable Anglo–American pincer movement from the west and the east.

The American units lost the Battle of the Kasserine Pass not only because of superior German numbers but also because of several systemic problems. The green troops did not properly prepare their defenses to stop German armor. American units were scattered throughout the area and mixed with other units, so that principles of unity of command and economy of force were violated. No effort was made to coordinate a combined arms approach integrating air, armor, infantry, and artillery assets into the fight.

Exercising overall control of all American forces in North Africa, General Dwight D. Eisenhower started to remedy these problems by placing Major General George S. Patton, Jr., in command of the American forces in March of 1942. Patton set about increasing discipline, morale, and combat effectiveness among the American soldiers. Patton likewise understood combined arms operations as well as any officer in the Army. During the month after the debacle at the Kasserine Pass, his units regrouped and prepared for the next test against the Germans.

In southern Tunisia, British forces under Montgomery broke through the German defenses and sent the enemy into retreat northward toward Tunis. Meanwhile, American units moved eastward toward the coast and threatened to cut off the Germans. Realizing his predicament, Rommel shifted westward to stop the American advance. The two forces clashed on March 23 at the Battle of El Guettar. Early in the morning, 50 German tanks quickly pushed through the first defensive line into what they assumed was the American rear. However, a well-placed minefield stalled the German progress long enough to allow American artillery to direct a devastating barrage against them. The Germans lost 30 tanks and withdrew an hour later. They tried another assault late in the afternoon with similarly poor results against a resurgent U.S. 1st Infantry Division.

The Americans gleaned several lessons from El Guettar. When coupled with combat engineers performing countermobility functions, American artillery and antitank fire could stop German armor attacks. Nevertheless, the Americans still needed to develop better offensive tactics to overcome German defenses. Combined arms practices needed more time to mature. Regardless, Patton did infuse the soldiers with new fighting spirit.

The final withdrawal of the Germans toward Tunis in early April sealed their fate in North Africa. Six weeks after the American victory at El Guettar, more than 200,000 German and Italian troops found themselves stranded near Tunis and low on supplies and ammunition. They finally surrendered on May 13, 1943. Rommel was not present for the ignominious end of his *Afrika Korps* because he became ill and was evacuated to Europe.

The Anglo-American Invasion and Capture of Sicily, 1943

While fighting continued in North Africa in early 1943, the Allies looked toward the next phase of the Mediterranean campaign—Operation HUSKY—the invasion of the island of Sicily. Once senior Anglo-American leaders agreed on the time and place for the invasion, they made General Eisenhower the Commander-in-Chief of the Allied Expeditionary Force. His immediate subordinates, Lieutenant Generals George Patton and Bernard Montgomery, jockeyed for resources and for top billing in news headlines on the home fronts.

The American airborne and amphibious assault portions of Operation HUSKY began early on July 10, 1943. Mistakes plagued both efforts from the start. The paratroopers intended to drop inland behind the beaches at Gela and protect this division from counterattacks. But when American aircraft carrying the paratroopers flew over Allied warships near the coast of Sicily, panicky antiaircraft gunners mistook those American planes for Germans and opened fire on them. They shot down 23 of 144 planes, causing 320 casualties. The remaining aircraft evaded the friendly fire but dropped the paratroopers far away from the intended landing zones. Although widely scattered, they did cause confusion among the Axis units trying to counterattack against Allies that landed later in the morning.

The American amphibious assaults fared little better. Some units landed in the wrong places, while others took hours longer to reach their objectives. Landing craft ran aground on an unseen sandbar. The coastal defense forces could not react in the first few hours of the attack. But later that day Italian and German units tried to push the Americans back into the sea. They failed to do so, and by the end of July 10, all seven Allied divisions established stable beachheads on shore.

In the days that followed, the British and Canadian forces drove northward along the eastern Sicilian coast. Montgomery's offensive eventually stagnated because German resistance stiffened near Mount Etna. In the American sector, Patton moved slowly inland from

Figure 11.5 American Soldiers Firing 105mm Howitzer, in Sicily

Soldiers of the 1st Infantry Division loading and firing a 105mm howitzer at a German position on Sicily in August 1943. The hilly terrain was visible in the distance.

© Robert R. McCormick Research Center

his beachhead. According to the plan, American units would drive straight north across Sicily to cut the island in half while protecting Montgomery's left flank. Patton did not like this supporting role because he believed it left his American forces to fight a determined enemy in sweltering heat in mountainous terrain, while Montgomery gained greater glory for his progress on the coast.

Three weeks after the Allied landings, the German and Italian forces had pulled back to a defensive line running from the foot of Mount Etna on the eastern coast through the town of Troina and on toward the northern Sicilian coast. The ensuing Battle of Troina raged for seven days until August 6, 1943, as Italian and German forces stubbornly held the town against repeated Americans attacking uphill in open terrain. They inflicted heavy casualties on the Americans and took severe losses themselves. Finally, the Americans captured the high ground overlooking Troina, which enabled the emplacement of their artillery that swept the town. With their position untenable, the Axis units withdrew to their next defensive positions.

At the end of July, the Axis commander, Field Marshal Albert Kesselring, realized that Sicily was lost, so he decided to evacuate his forces across the narrow channel to Italy. Masked by a few units delaying the Allied forces, more than 40,000 German soldiers escaped to Italy along with 90 artillery pieces and 45 tanks by August 18, 1943. The six weeks of combat cost American forces some 2,900 killed, 6,400 wounded, and 600 captured. The British suffered 12,600 casualties. The Axis Powers lost many more men, including 28,000 German and 145,000 Italian soldiers killed, wounded, or captured. Operation HUSKY yielded several other benefits. It helped topple Italian dictator Benito Mussolini from power, and the new Italian government ended hostilities with the Allies.

Invading Italy and the Slow Advance Toward Rome, 1943–44

With North Africa and Sicily secure, the Anglo-American leaders faced a decision: either continue the Mediterranean campaign into Italy, or consolidate forces in England in preparation for a cross-channel attack into France. The Soviet Union's Joseph Stalin clamored for the latter option. However, the massive amount of resources necessary for such an invasion still did not exist in 1943. The fall of Mussolini from power and subsequent armistice with the new Italian government by early September 1943 also made an Allied invasion of Italy more feasible. Nevertheless, Kesselring's German forces occupied and would prove to be stubborn foes. Aiding the Germans was a mountainous terrain cut by river valleys that heavily favored defenders against any incursion driving northwest toward Rome and beyond.

The initial invasion of Italy occurred in three places. The primary landing started near the city of Salerno on the "shin" of the Italian boot on September 9, 1943. Lieutenant General Mark W. Clark commanded joint Anglo-American units in the U.S. 5th Army making an assault on a broad 35-mile front. Further south, two smaller British landings occurred several days earlier, on September 3, when Montgomery's British force landed farther south in Italy, but faced less serious opposition.

Despite attempts at achieving surprise by skipping the pre-assault naval bombardment at Salerno, the German defenders knew that Clark's forces were coming on September 9. The Anglo-Americans landed and established beachheads, but the slow offloading of troops and supplies from transports meant that Clark's three divisions formed a tenuously thin line that could barely be expected to fend off enemy counterattack, let alone drive inland on the offensive. Four days later and after the arrival of German reinforcements, the enemy launched several determined assaults against the American positions that almost drove their adversaries back into the sea. German gains were reversed the next day when more Anglo-American units entered the fight, aircraft provided effective close air support, and the ground artillery and British Royal Navy's guns contributed effective fire support. After September 16, Clark's 5th Army began the drive inland from Salerno, and Montgomery's forces advanced northwestward up the Italian boot. Together they pushed the Germans into retreat.

By the end of September, the Anglo-Americans entered the port city of Naples and secured airfields near Foggia. The former gave them a key point for logistical support, and the latter gave them the bases for strategic bombing strikes against German targets in southern Europe. Rome appeared to be well within reach less than 120 miles up the coast from Naples. The Allies advanced to the Volturno River in early October. However, just beyond that river lay the Volturno Line, the first of several strongly fortified German positions stretching across the spine of the Italian peninsula. What lasted for the next eight months was bitter fighting against the German-held Volturno, Barbara, Bernhardt, and finally the Gustav Lines.

In the meantime, the close of 1943 brought changes in the Allied highest levels of command. Mark Clark remained commander of the 5th Army, but Montgomery and Eisenhower departed to England to start preparations for the cross-channel attack into northwestern France. Patton had departed for England earlier that year. It was left to Montgomery and Eisenhower's replacement, British General Sir Harold Alexander, to complete the Allied drive toward Rome and beyond. However, the rough terrain cut by river valleys made excellent natural barriers that the Germans exploited with devastating effectiveness. The shrewd Field Marshal Albert Kesselring held his defensive lines until the last possible moments and evacuated his troops before the Allies could kill or capture his men. The Germans thus made the Allied forces pay dearly for every mile of Italy gained.

Bloody Battles of the Italian Campaign

Nowhere was the fighting costlier than during the four Battles of Monte Cassino lasting from January 17 until May 18, 1944. The initial engagement in mid-January formed part of a larger offensive against the German forces manning the Gustav Line that stretched from the western coast of Italy along the Rapido River through the town of Cassino to the feet of the Apennine Mountains in central Italy. Germans enjoyed decisive advantages in defending the Gustav Line. The Benedictine monastery on the mountain crest of Monte Cassino overlooked the town of Cassino and the lowlands of Rapido River valley. Despite this monastery's strategic location along the line, the Germans decided not to station troops there because the historic structure had stood since the sixth century.

The Allies made their first attack against the Gustav Line along a 30-mile front on January 17. Five days later, an American amphibious force hit the beach of Anzio, behind enemy lines and about 60 miles up the coast toward Rome. This ground attack on the Gustav Line would, it was hoped, draw German resources away from the coastline near Anzio and thus enable the Americans landing there to establish a beachhead before cutting off the German retreat from the Gustav Line. This was a daring Allied plan that assumed operational timetables could be met.

The initial attempts to break through the German's Gustav Line did not go well because, although American, British, New Zealand, Punjabi, French, and Moroccan soldiers penetrated the German defenses in places, they could not exploit those breaches before German reinforcements arrived. In some cases, such as the U.S. 36th Infantry Division and the U.S. 19th Engineer Regiment at the Rapido River just north of Cassino, the attacking units met with complete defeat. They hoped to cross the river, drive the Germans from the high ground on the opposite shore, and wrest the town of Cassino from their control. However, from the start, the Rapido crossing ran into problems due to the inexperienced infantrymen and to ill-equipped combat engineers. There were not enough boats, nor the right kind of boats to ferry the American troops across the deep, swift Rapido. The infantry then ran into minefields that the engineers did not have time to clear. Worse still, when the Americans lost the element of surprise, they came under intense enemy fire that, in one case, killed 30 soldiers out of a company of 130 men with one exploding artillery shell. Only a few hundred Americans made it to the far side of the Rapido. They got pinned down by German fire, or they retreated back across the river. The next two days saw more American attempts to force a crossing, but these failed. By nightfall on January 22, the engagement ended. Of the approximately 7,000 men from the U.S. 36th Division, some 2,100 were killed, wounded, missing, or captured. Dug in as they were on the high ground, the Germans suffered almost no casualties.

Two days later, on January 24, far up the Italian coast, approximately 40,000 American and British soldiers of the U.S. VI Corps made an unopposed amphibious landing at Anzio. This looked like a turn of events that promised quick movement to Rome. The German attention and resources had been drawn southward to the Gustav Line. However, this ideal outcome did not occur. Instead of immediately moving inland, the Americans decided to fortify their beachhead against German counterattacks. This wasted valuable time and invited what it was designed to prevent. This lapse gave Kesselring the chance to rush reinforcements to Anzio that eventually totaled 100,000 soldiers. Although the VI Corps also grew to more than 100,000 strong by early February, the Germans kept them bottled up in a beachhead that was 20 miles wide and 15 miles deep. A stalemate developed as fighting dragged on interminably until May when the Americans at Anzio were ultimately relieved by Allied forces that broke through the Gustav Line.

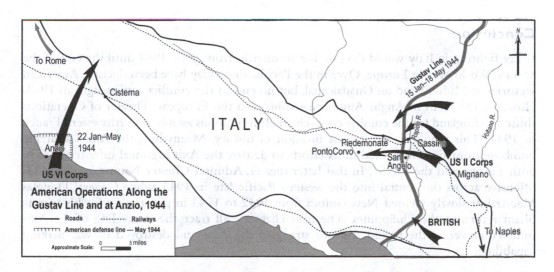

Map 11.4 Operations Along the Gustav Line and at Anzio, January–May 1944

Meanwhile three more battles occurred around Monte Cassino between February and May. Allied troops tried in vain to dislodge the German defenders from this key point in the Gustav Line. In mid-February, the Allies observed what they thought were German soldiers in the Monte Cassino monastery, so they decided to direct heavy aerial and artillery bombardments against the ancient structure. The upper floors were demolished, but the lower levels and tunnel network remained intact. With the monastery reduced to rubble, the Germans moved into the remains and utilized the position to its fullest potential as a vantage point and an artillery fire base. The Allies immediately launched a ground assault against the monastery, but Indian, Gurkha, and New Zealand soldiers could not wrest it from German control. Ensuing counterattacks drove the Allies away from the monastery. Yet another attempt to capture the monastery occurred in mid-March, but this again failed. These defeats resulted as much from poor Allied coordination as from stubborn German defenses. The fourth and final assault on the monastery occurred two months later, in May. This time, Allied forces totaling 20 divisions advanced against German positions all along the Gustav Line and crossed the Rapido at several points with infantry and armor units. Then, after a week of hard combat, elements of a Polish unit raised their nation's flag over Monte Cassino monastery early on May 18, 1944. Just as they did time and time again, the remaining Germans evacuated the night before, rather than risk being captured.

With the Gustav Line breached, the Allied forces pursued the retreating Germans to the northwest up the coast toward Anzio. In the meantime, the U.S. VI Corps broke out of the Anzio beachhead and drove north in hopes of cutting off several German divisions retreating from the Gustav Line. However, in a controversial decision, Mark Clark ordered VI Corps to turn westward toward Rome. Although he had legitimate motives like giving his troops some rest, the ambitious Clark seemingly wanted the honor of entering the famous city to go to American units. Kesselring did not attempt to stop American units capturing Rome on June 4, 1944. Regardless, Clark's decision to seize Rome deprived the Allies an opportunity to cripple German fighting power in Italy. With no Americans blocking their escape route, Kesselring's forces moved well beyond Rome and took up strong positions in the Gothic Line that bisected Italy north of Florence.

Conclusion

Bitter fighting in Italy would drag on for 20 months from June 1944 until the end of the Second World War in Europe. Over in the Pacific, there may have been decisive American victories at Midway and on Guadalcanal, but no end to the conflict was in sight in 1943. However, the focus of Anglo-American resources in the European Theater of Operations shifted to England for the coming cross-channel amphibious assault in northwestern France in 1944. This would be the largest invasion in history. Meanwhile, the Allied strategic bombing campaign intensified in its efforts to destroy the Axis logistical infrastructure in both Europe and the Pacific. In that latter theater, Admiral Chester Nimitz launched his offensive across the central into the western Pacific late in 1943, while General Douglas MacArthur slowly secured New Guinea from 1942 to 1944 in preparation for his triumphant return to the Philippines. The next chapter will trace the unraveling of the Axis military power as the Grand Alliance strangled the Axis and destroyed its war-making capabilities.

A Short Bibliography of Second World War readings appears at the end of Chapter 12.

Notes

1 The word "Tora" translates as "tiger" in English.
2 Commander-in-Chief Pacific Operation Plan No 29–42, cited in Samuel Eliot Morison, *Coral Sea, Midway, and Submarine Actions, May 1942–August 1942* (Boston: Little, Brown, 1949), p. 84.
3 Merrill B. Twining, *No Bended Knee: The Battle for Guadalcanal, the Memoir of Gen. Merrill B. Twining, USMC* (Novato, CA: Presidio Press, 1996), p. 73.

1941–45	November 20–24, 1943	June 6, 1944	October 23–25, 1944	December 16, 1944–January 1945	February 19–March 26, 1945
Second World War	Battle of Tarawa	D-Day	Battle of Leyte Gulf	Battle of the Bulge	Battle of Iwo Jima

TIMELINE

Chapter 12

Winning the Second World War, 1943–1945

The Allied landings on North Africa, Sicily, and Italy in 1942 and 1943 served as preludes to D-Day on June 6, 1944. This invasion of Normandy was the largest amphibious assault in history as well as one of the greatest gambles. Subsequent operations to defeat German ground forces took another 11 months, including the massive Battle of the Bulge in December 1944. On the other side of world, two irresistible American offensive campaigns continued in the Central Pacific under Admiral Chester W. Nimitz and in the Southwest Pacific under General Douglas MacArthur. These would eventually bring American forces to the shores of the Japanese home islands by the summer of 1945. Combined arms operations using air, ground, or naval assets characterized American fighting in the Pacific and Europe.

Throughout the Second World War, the new doctrines and technologies so hotly debated in the 1920s and 1930s were validated or altered to help achieve victory. Armor tactics, amphibious operations, and strategic bombing stand as representative case studies. The last of these included the most striking application of air power doctrine—the atomic bomb.

In this chapter, students will learn about:

- Tracing the two-pronged American strategy in the Pacific, 1943–44.
- Putting interwar doctrines and weapons systems to the test in wartime operations.
- Winning the logistics war against the Axis Powers.
- Planning and executing Operation OVERLORD.
- Fighting the bloody battles on Iwo Jima and Okinawa.
- Practical, strategic, and ethical factors in using the atomic bombs.

American Offensives Against Japan, 1943–44

The hard-fought American victory on Guadalcanal in February 1943 shifted the momentum irrevocably against the Japanese. Then the next month, control of American operations in the Solomon Island chain switched from Admiral Nimitz to General Douglas MacArthur, enabling

April 1–June 21, 1945	May 7, 1945	August 6, 1945	August 9, 1945	August 15, 1945
Battle of Okinawa	Germany surrendered on V-E Day	Atomic bombing of Hiroshima	Atomic bombing of Nagasaki	Japanese surrendered on V-J Day

the latter commander to start his own offensive on New Guinea. This was one prong of a two-pronged American strategy in the Pacific Ocean. In the Southwest Pacific Theater, MacArthur's campaign against the Japanese in New Guinea in 1943 set the stage for his promised return to the Philippines in 1944. The other prong can be seen in the Central Pacific Theater, where Admiral Nimitz started planning his own offensive campaign that would seize the Gilberts in 1943, then move to the Marshalls, and finally into the western Pacific in 1944 and 1945.

Pragmatic military and political considerations drove American decision makers to adopt a two-pronged strategy. Given his popularity and ego, the Army's General MacArthur pushed hard for command of all American and Allied naval, ground, amphibious, and air forces in the entire Pacific Ocean. But he had to settle for control of the Southwest Pacific Theater. Back in Washington, both the Navy's members on the Joint Chiefs of Staff, Ernest King and William Leahy, argued that Central Pacific would primarily be a naval campaign supported by amphibious and ground forces. It thus made sense for the Navy's Nimitz to exercise theater command. His campaign harkened back to concepts outlined in the ORANGE War Plan during the prewar decades. The Southwest Pacific, on the other hand, would include amphibious operations followed by lengthy ground operations by Army units. Naval assets would play supporting roles. Consequently, giving MacArthur control of Allied forces in the Southwest Pacific made good sense.

Apart from the Central and Southwest Pacific, Japan faced enemies in two other major theaters that put severe stress on the nation's severely stretched forces. First was mainland China, where millions of Japanese troops had tried to subdue the Chinese nationalist and communist forces since 1937. As many as 500,000 Japanese perished during this eight-year conflict, referred to as the Second Sino-Japanese War. In August 1945, approximately one million Japanese could not return to defend their home islands because there were stranded in China. This commitment of manpower and resources made the Sino-Japanese War into a quagmire.

Second was the China–Burma–India Theater (CBI) where the Japanese tried to maintain control of Burma and Southeast Asia after conquering these areas by 1942. The Japanese wanted to cut the Anglo-American overland supply lines from India to China that supported Chinese forces there. American forces came under command of General Joseph Stillwell until 1944, but actual units fell under control of British or Chinese leadership. After that, several American generals shared command of American forces in the CBI. Inclement weather, rampant disease, and rough terrain made movement and supply difficult for Americans, British, Indians, and Japanese forces. From 1942 to 1944, repeated Allied (Anglo-American-Indian) offensives into Burma did not expel the Japanese from the region. In 1944, the Japanese attempted to invade India but failed. Later in November of that year, the Allies launched offensives that eventually drove nearly all the weakening Japanese forces from Burma by July 1945. These eight months of fighting cost the Japanese more than 30,000 casualties. Operations in the CBI drained the limited Japanese resources that might have been better deployed elsewhere. Ultimately, fighting on these four fronts—the Southwest Pacific, Central Pacific, the CBI, and China proper—slowly overwhelmed Japan's war-making capacity.

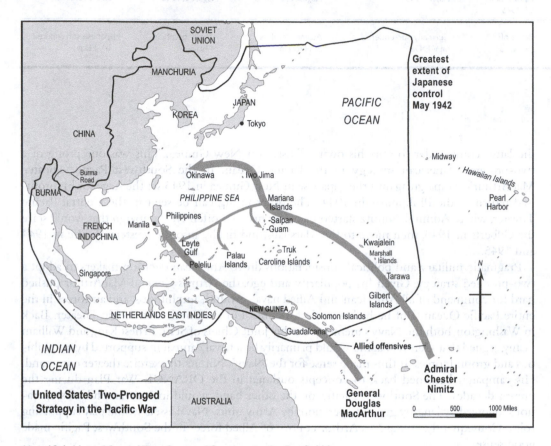

Map 12.1 United States' Two-Pronged Strategy in the Pacific War

Testing Amphibious Capabilities in the Central Pacific, 1943–44

In the Central Pacific, large-scale operations did not occur until late 1943 because the U.S. Navy did not possess enough aircraft carriers to gain, let alone maintain, tactical air superiority. Finally in the fall of 1943, the production of the new *Essex*-class aircraft carriers tipped the scales of naval aviation against the Japanese. This lead vessel and her 23 sister ships carried 90 air planes each, made top speeds of 33 knots, and boasted heavier armor plating and more antiaircraft guns than the older American carriers. For their part, the Japanese could only react to American attacks across the Pacific while losing their assets to attrition.

With several *Essex*-class carriers coming on line, Admiral Nimitz started his Central Pacific campaign with assaults in the Gilberts island chain that lay 1,200 miles northwest of the Solomon Islands. In this chain, the Tarawa atoll stood as the key prize. The Japanese chose the largest islet of Betio for an airfield. This long and narrow island reached three miles in length east to west but no more than 900 yards at its widest point. Although landing on the northern shoreline would mean crossing a shallow lagoon to the north of Betio, the American planners decided that this area had fewer gun emplacements than the southern shoreline facing the open sea. The intelligence analysts and planners, however, failed to predict tide levels because existing hydrographic charts did not provide accurate soundings or tidal time tables.

On November 20, the Battle of Tarawa began with an amphibious assault phase by the U.S. 2nd Marine Division. The Marines encountered an unexpectedly low tide in the lagoon. The anticipated five feet of water was reduced to inches in some places, much too shallow for the Marines' Landing Craft, Vehicle, Personnel (LCVP). These assault boats ran aground on the coral, leaving Marines to disembark the useless boats, make the dangerous trek on foot across more than 500 yards of coral, and brave withering enemy fire. Conversely, the other craft—the LVT—successfully climbed up and over the coral because the paddles for propulsion in water doubled as treads for movement on solid surfaces. However, these lightly armored amphibious vehicles presented easy targets for the Japanese because their silhouettes rose several feet above water level. Only half of the 125 LVTs were still operational at the end of that first day.

Of the 5,000 Marines making this treacherous assault on November 20, more than 1,500 were killed or wounded. The remaining Marines found themselves clinging desperately to a tiny beachhead barely 600 yards wide and 400 yards deep. They set up a defensive perimeter for the night and prepared for a major counterattack that never came. Although the naval and aerial bombardment had not inflicted large numbers of casualties on the defenders, one shell from an American warship killed the Japanese commander and his staff. Thereafter, the Japanese never launched synchronized counterattacks to drive the Marines back into the sea.

On November 21, thousands more Marines with artillery and tanks landed on Betio. Bitter fighting raged that second day as the Marines drove southward, cutting the islet into two parts and securing the western half of the islet. As the third day dawned, more Marine reinforcements moved eastward along Betio's long axis, where they overwhelmed the remaining enemy positions. By November 23, only a few hundred Japanese continued their resistance until the afternoon when combat ceased. The Marines suffered another 1,500 casualties after the first day on November 20. The four days of brutal combat exacted a heavy toll on the Marines: 1,000 killed and 2,250 wounded. The Japanese, however, lost 4,800 of their 5,000 men on Betio. Of the remaining 200 survivors, very few Japanese surrendered of their own free will. Others were too badly wounded to continue resistance.

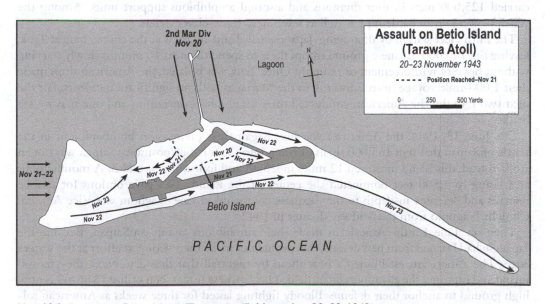

Map 12.2 Assault on Betio Island (Tarawa Atoll), November 20–23, 1943

The amphibious assault on Betio in the Tarawa Atoll validated the principles laid out by the U.S. Marine Corps in the *Tentative Manual for Landing Operations* in 1934. Nevertheless, many hard lessons needed to be learned for future operations. The first day's initial assault could have ended in disaster because planners failed to account for the low tide. The Marines' experiences during inland fighting revealed that artillery and tanks needed to be offloaded as quickly as possible. The learning curve in future operations would be steep, for the Japanese and Americans alike.

Barely two months after Tarawa, Admiral Nimitz set his sights on capturing the Marshall island chain, the next stepping stone some 600 miles northwest of the Gilberts. Of interest were the Kwajalein and Eniwetok atolls in the Marshalls. Both atolls could be used as aircraft bases, and Eniwetok formed a natural harbor capable of holding even deep-draft American aircraft carriers and battleships.

American forces conducted amphibious assaults against Kwajalein and Eniwetok in February 1944. Although the fighting was fierce, the small Japanese defense forces soon succumbed to the overwhelming American forces. Consistent with the island-hopping strategy, U.S. Navy seabees and Army engineers set about making Kwajalein into a major naval, aircraft, and logistics base to support future operations. This put American land-based bombers within 1,000 miles of the Marianas island chain to the northwest. American aircraft also flew sorties against the massive Japanese base on Truk in the Caroline island chain to the west.

In the early spring of 1944, Admiral Nimitz faced a strategic decision point. American forces could continue the island-hopping campaign by jumping from the Marshalls west to the Carolines and then north to the Mariana island chain; or they could neutralize the offensive capabilities in the Carolines, then leapfrog that chain, and finally strike the Marianas. Weighing savings in time, resources, and lives in bypassing the entire Caroline chain against the value of attacking Truk directly, Nimitz chose the bold leapfrogging movement code-named Operation FORAGER. He appointed Admiral Raymond Spruance to command this effort. Just as he demonstrated at Midway two years earlier, Spruance remained calm and calculating in his decision making. Unlike Midway, however, he enjoyed decisive advantages in quality and quantity of forces. His U.S. Fifth Fleet was an armada of 530 major warships and transport vessels that carried 125,000 men in four divisions and assorted amphibious support units. Among the warships were seven battleships as well as seven new *Essex*-class carriers

The Fifth Fleet started by destroying Japanese naval and air assets at the enemy base at Truk, leaving the 100,000 Japanese ground troops there to spend the next 16 months slowly starving without hope of reinforcement or resupply. Once Truk was isolated, the American ships made their 1,000-mile voyage from Eniwetok to the Marianas with no significant incidents. For the next two months, the American conducted three amphibious operations and one massive sea battle.

On June 13, 1944, the American warships began their preinvasion bombardment in the Battle of Saipan that sent 165,000 shells hurtling into the fortified positions. Saipan was not an atoll; instead, this island measured 12 miles in length and four miles in width. A mountainous area rising to 1,500 feet dominated the center of the island. This gave options for mobile reserves and defenses-in-depth to the Japanese commanders, one of whom was Vice Admiral Chuichi Nagumo from the Midway disaster in 1942.

Then on June 15, the Americans made their amphibious assault on Saipan. Because the Japanese had learned from past defeats, they would not make their strongest effort at the water's edge. The Americans established a beachhead by nightfall that first day. Next, they moved inland and captured the all-important airfield. The Japanese forces then utilized Saipan's central high ground to anchor their defense. Bloody fighting lasted for three weeks as American soldiers and Marines used artillery, demolitions, and flamethrowers to kill the Japanese in Saipan's many caves. On July 7, more than 4,000 Japanese soldiers, including the wounded, made one last, desperate *banzai* charge that nearly overwhelmed two U.S. Army battalions. Their charge failed. The Japanese commanders, including Nagumo, committed suicide. Saipan was declared secure on July 9, 1944.

The combat on Saipan cost the Americans 13,500 casualties out of 71,000 men, and the Japanese defenders lost almost their entire garrison of 30,000 men. Also new in this battle were civilian casualties. Of the 25,000 Japanese civilians inhabiting Saipan, an estimated 22,000 perished. Some perished in the crossfire during combat, while others committed suicide by jumping off cliffs. Japan's Emperor Hirohito had offered equality with soldiers in the afterlife to those civilians committing suicide on Saipan.

While fighting raged in Saipan, the U.S. and Japanese fleets faced off in the Battle of the Philippine Sea to the west of the Marianas. Admiral Nimitz and his staff knew that the Japanese Navy would never sit idly by and let the Marianas fall into American hands without conducting a major interdiction against Admiral Spruance's Fifth Fleet. Just 1,300 miles from the Japanese homeland, this chain allowed long-range American aircraft based on Saipan, Guam, or Tinian to strike at the heart of Japan.

As expected, the Imperial Japanese Navy's five remaining heavy aircraft carriers sailed on June 13, 1944, toward the U.S. Fifth Fleet with its seven aircraft carriers. The adversaries made strikes against each other beginning on June 19. The American side enjoyed advantages in improved radar as well as the introduction of the superior F6F "Hellcat" fighter. The fast, rugged, heavily armed new plane gave air superiority against the Japanese Zero. Over the next two days of aerial combat, the Japanese lost more than 300 planes and three aircraft carriers but failed to sink a single American vessel. The Battle of the Philippine Sea—nicknamed the "Great Marianas Turkey Shoot"—resulted in the final destruction of Japan's carrier-based air power. With the surface and aerial threats eliminated, American forces seized Tinian and Guam in July. These islands, together with Saipan, gave the United States the ability to bomb strategic targets on the Japanese home islands. (See the section on Strategic Bombing later in this chapter.)

The Southwest Pacific Campaign: From New Guinea to the Philippines, 1943–44

While the Navy and Marine Corps' primary focus shifted to the Central Pacific Theater in 1943, General Douglas MacArthur's joint American and Australian forces continued their long campaign to secure New Guinea in the Southwest Pacific Theater. The concept of island-hopping proved to be particularly useful to MacArthur because his forces hopped from base to base, eliminating the Japanese presence along 1,000 miles of New Guinea's northern coastline.

Using the airfield and harbor at Milne Bay at the southeastern tip of New Guinea as a staging point, Australian and American soldiers found themselves slogging overland to Japanese Buna and Gona. They trudged through tropical jungles where malaria, dysentery, and bush typhus reduced some units to less than half-strength. Their initial assaults failed to penetrate the well-constructed Japanese fortifications. It took three months of fighting until January 1943 to seize these bases.

The next hops against the towns of Lae and Salamaua were made later that spring. Lae became an Allied supply base for future aerial and ground operations on New Guinea just as island-hopping (or base-hopping) dictated. While the fighting for Salamaua dragged on in August 1943, MacArthur decided to attack the next major Japanese base at Wewak, some 400 miles northwest up the New Guinea coast. After establishing air superiority over the Japanese,

MacArthur's forces were to leapfrog that base and make an attack farther up the coast against Hollandia. This largest Japanese base on New Guinea quickly fell to the American amphibious assault forces with minimal losses.

The victories on New Guinea seemed to open the way for the next major jump to the Philippines about 1,000 miles to the northwest. Before this could happen, the Japanese base on Peleliu Island needed to be neutralized. Its airfield could interdict American shipping en route to the Philippines, which seemed to make the Peleliu's capture necessary. However, as Admiral William Halsey believed, the island could also have been leapfrogged, leading him to question whether an amphibious assault against Peleliu was necessary. Ultimately, Admiral Nimitz overruled Halsey and ordered the attack on the island.

American planners wrongly predicted that the Battle of Peleliu could be won in less than four days of combat. The 1st Marine Division conducted its amphibious assault against Peleliu on September 15, 1944. Once on the beach, the Marines faced unexpected heavy enemy fire from extensive fortifications on high ground. They slowly moved inland into a series of ridges and valleys that funneled them into killing zones.

Writing one of the most vivid combat memoirs ever published, Marine veteran Eugene B. Sledge recalled how "the crazy-contoured coral ridges and rubble-filled canyons" resembled "an alien, unearthly, surrealistic nightmare like the surface of another planet." On another occasion, he revealed how combat had cheapened life. He watched a fellow Marine toss pebbles "into the open skull of the Japanese machine gunner. Each time his pitch was true I heard a splash of rainwater in the ghastly spectacle. My buddy tossed the coral chunks as casually as a boy casting pebbles into a puddle . . . . The war had so brutalized us that it was beyond belief."[1] Sledge and other Marines endured stifling humidity and daytime temperatures reaching 115 degrees. Swarms of insects feasted on bodies of the dead, and the smell of rotting flesh permeated everything on the island. After four weeks of hard fighting, the debilitated 1st Marine Division was replaced by the U.S. Army 81st Infantry Division. Combat on Peleliu ended on November 27, 1944, but not before 1,800 Americans were killed and 8,000 wounded, out of a total of 28,500 going ashore. Nearly the entire Japanese garrison fought to the death. For veterans and historians alike, this island was the costliest American battle of the Pacific War.

Fighting on Peleliu lasted 10 weeks, but American forces took control of the island's airfield in the first few days. This gave General Douglas MacArthur the confidence to launch his massive invasion of the Philippines in October. He chose Leyte Island in the east central part of the archipelago. American aircraft based on Leyte could also strike any target in the Philippines, including the powerful Japanese forces near Manila on Luzon. Some 200,000 American soldiers landed in Leyte Gulf on October 20, 1944. The self-satisfied MacArthur had made good on his promise back in 1942 to "return" to the Philippines. Facing little resistance, the Americans quickly established a beachhead before capturing an airfield and moving inland.

The biggest threat came not from enemy ground forces on Leyte but from remnants of the Imperial Japanese Navy. Although bereft of naval aviators, the Japanese still possessed a formidable surface component, including the twin superbattleships *Yamato* and *Musashi* with their 18-inch guns and seven other smaller battleships. Looking at Japan's predicament from a strategic perspective, MacArthur's invasion of the Philippines presented a serious dilemma: The fall of this archipelago meant that the Japanese Navy would be cut off from Southeast Asian fuel supplies. Without that fuel, the fleet was useless to defend the home islands. Consequently, the Japanese decided to execute their SHO-Plan and commit all remaining warships in a do-or-die operation to destroy MacArthur's transport ships at Leyte.

As with so many schemes, the SHO-Plan rested on assumptions about American leaders and Japanese capabilities. In this case, the Japanese decided to exploit the aggressive nature of the

U.S. Third Fleet's commander, Admiral William "Bull" Halsey. Because he did not see action in the Midway or the Philippine Sea battles, Halsey was spoiling for a fight with the Japanese Navy. He hoped to sink the remaining aircraft carriers and perhaps even fight the enemy battleships in a surface engagement. Halsey believed his Third Fleet, with its eight large aircraft carriers and six battleships, would be more than a match for the Japanese fleet.

The SHO-Plan called for a northern force of four Japanese aircraft carriers to lure Halsey's Third Fleet away from its station near Leyte Gulf out to the open sea. This in turn would permit the two other Japanese center and southern forces of several superbattleships and battleships to converge from the north and south on MacArthur's transport ships anchored off Leyte proper. They would then defeat any escort vessels and sink the transports in a grand pincer movement. The ensuing Battle of Leyte Gulf would be the largest naval battle in history with 70 Japanese and 200 American warships.

The Japanese SHO-Plan got off to an inauspicious start when, on October 24, American dive bombers and torpedo bombers struck the center force, sinking the mighty *Musashi* with at least 15 torpedo and 15 bomb hits. Once the American aircraft departed, Vice Admiral Takeo Kurita, commanding the *Yamato* and three other battleships, sailed on undetected for the next 24 hours toward Leyte Gulf.

Meanwhile, Admiral Halsey took the bait that was the northern force of four aircraft carriers. He chased those decoy carriers 300 miles, effectively taking his Third Fleet out of the Battle of Leyte Gulf. Far to the south, the Japanese southern force lured six additional American battleships hundreds of miles away from Leyte Gulf. On October 25 in the Surigao Strait south of Leyte, lethal gunfire from these American battleships and torpedoes from American destroyers sank two more Japanese battleships and crippled several other warships.

Early that same morning of October 25, Admiral Kurita's center force of four battleships and smaller warships suddenly appeared in Leyte Gulf. Opposing this powerful fleet were four American destroyers, four destroyer escorts, and 15 escort aircraft carriers with planes armed to support MacArthur's ground forces. The Americans did not have the types of bombs or torpedoes necessary to damage the enemy's powerful warships. All the guns on those American ships did not equal the firepower of the *Yamato*, let alone the entire center force. However, the destroyers and destroyer escorts did carry several torpedoes.

Despite overwhelming odds, the American naval commander decided to fight the Japanese in hopes of delaying them. The destroyers and destroyer escorts—known as "tin cans" because they were not heavily armored—sailed out to meet the Japanese, firing their 5-inch guns and launching their torpedoes at targets of opportunity. Then the American tin cans retreated to lay smoke screens to obscure American ship movements. The light carriers launched their planes, which then bombed and strafed the Japanese ships. They planted seeds of fear in Admiral Kurita's mind that maybe Admiral Halsey's as-yet unseen Third Fleet would ambush his ships. As it turned out, Kurita had no idea that the northern forces had indeed succeeded in luring the Third Fleet out of range, because he could not communicate with that northern force. The Japanese admiral also assumed that he faced cruisers and heavy carriers, not tin cans and light carriers.

In less than three hours, the Americans sank or crippled three Japanese heavy cruisers. On balance, the Japanese sank one escort carrier, two destroyers, and one destroyer escort. So audacious were the American actions that Kurita withdrew his battered center force from the area, rather than risk more damage. Herein lay a tactical error that had rippling effects at the strategic level of war. Had Kurita been willing to commit his ships with the zeal of a *banzai* charge, the Japanese could have pushed through to destroy MacArthur's supply ships and bombard the Americans on shore on Leyte. However, by October 26, 1944, the battered Japanese fleet limped back to their home ports.

The removal of the Japanese naval threat opened the way for General MacArthur to continue his expansion on Leyte with no worries about his seaborne logistical support. After securing this island on December 31, 1944, American and Filipino forces made two amphibious landings on the island of Luzon just days later in the new year. They then advanced toward Manila, the capital of the Philippines and site of an excellent harbor. The city fell at the end of February, but fighting lasted in the rural areas of Luzon until August 1945.

American Logistics: Key to Victory in the Second World War

Although amphibious assaults and sea battles dominate most histories of the Pacific War and with good reason, another contest occurred beneath the waves of that vast ocean where submarines vied for control of the sea lanes. American submarine operations slowly strangled the Japanese seaborne logistical system. They thus succeeded in doing to Japan what German U-boats failed to do against Great Britain in two world wars. Conversely, Japanese submarine operations never stopped American seaborne logistics.

For the U.S. military, logistics entailed the administration, procurement, maintenance, transportation, and storage of supplies and equipment; the housing and transportation of personnel; and the evacuation and hospitalization of casualties. This inclusive list spanned nearly every activity, civilian or military, other than combat. No other nation could match the American ability to move and supply its armed forces.

The Japanese military possessed a similar understanding of logistics—those military activities other than strategy, operations, and tactics. Dating back to the late nineteenth century, the Japanese needed to establish and protect sea lanes back to their home islands to feed their people and provide fuel and material for their war machine. By late 1941, their flimsy lines of transportation stretched across an empire measuring 5,000 miles east to west, and 4,000 miles north to south.

At the time of the attack on Pearl Harbor in December 1941, Japan possessed approximately six million tons of merchant shipping. During the next 44 months, the Japanese captured, salvaged, or built an additional four million tons of merchant shipping for a grand total of 10 million tons during the Second World War. However, this figure dwindled to 1.5 million tons of operational transport ships because American submarines, warships, aircraft, and mines sank 8.5 million tons and 2,500 vessels.

By contrast, the United States added more than 50 million tons of merchant shipping—or some 5,000 ships—during the Second World War. These vessels carried staggering 85 billion tons of cargo tens of thousands of miles across the globe. It should be noted that the United States fought a two-ocean war, while supplying British, Soviet, Chinese, and other Allies with 25 percent of that total weight. Such an extraordinarily high industrial output made it possible for the United States not only to make the U.S. Pacific Fleet self-sustaining during ongoing combat operations but also to help win the Battle of the Atlantic.

Apart from the marked disparities in tonnage totals, the Japanese and American logistical systems exhibited two other striking differences: the prioritization of enemy transport ships as targets, and the appreciation of logistics in combat effectiveness. Throughout the Second World War, Japanese and American submarine captains targeted different types of enemy vessels. The Japanese concentrated on sinking American warships. They let many American transports slip by unmolested, sinking only 170 vessels totaling less than two million tons. This fixation on targeting warships came in part from the influential nineteenth-century American naval thinker Alfred Thayer Mahan, who was so deeply ingrained in the Japanese naval psyche. He advocated massive fleets of warships fighting decisive battles against enemy fleets. Conversely, the American submarine captains readily sank Japanese warships and transport vessels. Thus, the Americans recognized that winning the Pacific War required the destruction of Japanese military and material capabilities.

Leaders in the U.S. Navy and Army also realized that well-fed, well-supplied troops could maintain their combat effectiveness over time. For every soldier or Marine hitting the beaches in the Pacific, there were at least 15 other servicemen and servicewomen working in the logistical system stretching back to the continental United States. Ensuring that letters from home or extra pairs of clean socks reached the front lines raised morale and increased physical comfort. Thus, mastery of logistics became a force multiplier for the U.S. military: Well-supplied troops were better fighters, and better fighters meant quicker victories. In 1944, Operation FORAGER in the Pacific and Operation OVERLORD in Europe stand as prime examples of American logistical success. Conversely, the Japanese never prioritized health or nutrition for their service personnel in this way and thus lost combat effectiveness over time.

Strategic Bombing: From Theory to Reality to Victory, 1942–45

Logistics also provided a major impetus for American air power. Since the 1920s and 1930s, the maverick Billy Mitchell and others believed that long-range, high-speed aircraft could make decisive strikes deep into enemy territory to hit targets of strategic value such as railroads, bridges, factories, or oil refineries. If destroyed, these logistical targets would have strategic, operational, and tactical ramifications. Eliminating them would deprive the enemy of the material ability to fight. Civilian (noncombatant) populations in urban areas could also be considered targets with the goal of degrading the enemy's will to fight.

Strategic bombardment needs to be differentiated from tactical airpower and close air support. The term "tactical" reveals the purpose of this specific application of airpower: the use of aircraft to establish and maintain control of the airspace over a finite area above a battlefield, city, region, or area of water. To achieve air superiority, fighter aircraft need to patrol that airspace and shoot down enemy aircraft. In both the Pacific and Europe, tactical air superiority yielded such advantages as freedom of ground maneuver and the ability to disrupt enemy maneuver and supply. The words comprising "close air support" also point to a purpose: the use of aircraft to strike enemy targets or units on the ground in "combined arms operations."

At the beginning of the Second World War, the U.S. Army Air Force focused almost entirely on strategic bombardment. The B-17 "Flying Fortress" and the B-24 "Liberator" were designed during the prewar years to fulfill this mission. During the conflict, American manufacturers built more than 12,500 Flying Fortresses and 18,000 Liberators. These four-engine bombers could carry up to 8,000 pounds of bombs at cruising speeds of 180 miles per hour and hit targets at combat ranges of 800 miles for the B-17 and 1,200 miles for the B-24. Although they bristled with .50-caliber machine guns that supposedly provided protection against enemy fighters, reality proved to be much different. Even when flying in tight box formations that gave their gunners overlapping fields of fire, the American bombers remained vulnerable to enemy fighter attacks.

The first American strategic bombing missions were limited in scope, such as in June 1942, when a small squadron of 13 newly arrived B-24 Liberators flew 1,200 miles from Egypt to strike the German oil refineries in Ploesti, Romania. This raid did little damage to the massive facility, and only eight B-24s safely made it back to base. The Germans realized their vulnerability, so they increased the antiaircraft defenses around Ploesti. Thus began a deadly competition to determine whether the American bombers could destroy enough targets before the Germans could shoot down too many of them. In subsequent raids, the Germans shot down or damaged 20 percent of the American bombers flying on most missions.

Most of the USAAF missions were flown at high altitudes during daytime. But other experiments were undertaken to try to break the German aircraft and artillery defenses. One such mission occurred in Operation TIDAL WAVE, a massive daytime raid on Ploesti in August 1943 flown by American B-24 "Liberator" bombers. These aircraft and their crews came from the 98th and 376th Bombardment Groups from the U.S. Ninth Air Force and the 44th, 93rd, and 389th Bombardment Groups from the U.S. Eighth Air Force.

American airpower planners speculated that if a force of 175 Liberators could fly undetected at low tree-top level, they could achieve the element of surprise and do irreversible damage to the German war effort. In this case, the target would be the oil refineries at Ploesti in Romania. If the American bombers could destroy these facilities, then the German tanks, aircraft, and submarines would slowly run out of vital fuel reserves.

However, navigation problems plagued the Americans making the long flight from Egypt to Ploesti. German radar tracked the approaching American bombers, so their arrival over Ploesti was no surprise. Instead, the Germans set a trap from them. Once over the target, the Americans faced one of the most formidable antiaircraft defense networks in Europe, which included hundreds of 88-millimeter guns. During the mission, 53 Liberators were shot down by German fighters or ground fire, while only 33 returned to their bases in southern Italy undamaged. Of the 1,700 crewmen participating in the raid, the Americans suffered 660 crewmen killed, wounded, missing, or captured. Although oil production slowed because of the damage caused in this very costly raid, the Germans quickly repaired their facilities and resumed fuel production. Operation TIDAL WAVE failed in a spectacular fashion. Never again would the American attempt this type of low-level bombing raid.

Such devastatingly high attrition rates plagued the U.S. Army Air Force throughout 1943. German fighters attacked incoming American bombers until they neared their target area. Next, enemy antiaircraft artillery threw up barrages of "flak"—exploding shells that spread clouds of deadly shrapnel—into the airspace over the targets. Finally, after the Americans finished their bombing runs, the German fighters preyed on damaged bombers as they returned to their bases. For example, American B-17s of the U.S. 8th Air Force faced these tactics when they took off from England and raided ball-bearing factories in Schweinfurt, Germany, on October 14, 1943. Destroying these facilities would, it was hoped, create a production bottleneck, thereby crippling German tank and aircraft engines needing ball bearings to operate. On this single day, "Black Thursday," the Army Air Force experienced the highest loss rate of any mission in the war: 650 American crewmen were killed, wounded, or captured; and 60 B-17s were shot down out of the 251 aircraft and 2,500 crewmen starting this mission.

Such losses limited the American long-range bombing effort until early 1944 when the new P-51 "Mustang" came on line. These high-performance, long-range fighters immediately made their presence felt in the skies over Europe by successfully escorting bombers from England to targets in Germany and back. Eventually, more than 15,000 of the P-51s model were built. The sleek Mustang boasted a top speed of 435 miles per hour, a combat range of 800 miles with external fuel tanks, and the impressive firepower of six .50-caliber machine guns. No German aircraft could outperform the Mustang until the arrival of enemy's jet-propelled aircraft in late 1944, but their advent was too little too late to stop the mass bombing missions.

The arrival of the Mustang made it possible for the Army Air Force to fly missions in what became known as "Big Week." Some 3,000 bombers of the 8th Air Force and 500 from the 15th Air Force hit German aircraft factories and other strategic targets for five days beginning on February 20, 1944. These concerted efforts cost 250 American bombers shot down or disabled, but their defensive gunfire and the Mustangs eliminated at least more than 350 German fighters. Meanwhile, American industrial output built more aircraft than the German fighters or ground fire could shoot down.

By 1944, the American and British bombers ignited massive firestorms by dropping so many bombs on enemy targets with combustible materials. Firestorms occur when structures start burning uncontrollably and then spread over large areas. The flames require more and more oxygen, which gets sucked toward the inferno by tornado-force winds. As temperatures increase to more than 1,000 degrees, the flames rise hundreds of feet in the updraft of heated air. This in turn draws more oxygen and movable objects that fuel the fire, and so on. In one such raid on February 13, 1945, more than 1,300 British and American bombers dropped 4,000 tons of incendiary bombs on the city of Dresden, Germany. At least 25,000 civilian noncombatants died in the firestorm. Sadly, the city lacked any significant military or industrial facilities that merited such an effort. Dresden was, however, one of the few undamaged urban areas left in Germany by February 1945, so it made a likely target.

The increasing aerial bombardment of civilian populations paralleled the escalation of the Second World War toward "total war"—the complete mobilization of a nation's resources and population in wartime. To put it another way, if the family members or industrial workers contributed to the enemy's military success on the battlefield, then they could be targets. This practice of striking civilian populations has been labeled terror bombing and criticized as immoral. In the Pacific War, no ethical ambiguity existed regarding strategic bombardment in part because of the complete dehumanization of the Japanese foe in the eyes of most Americans. Racist attitudes also permeated the American military and home front alike. Lastly, memories of the attack on Pearl Harbor in 1941 and the horrors of the Bataan Death March in 1942 were etched on the American psyche.

Once the Marianas came under American control in the summer of 1944, the new B-29 "Superfortress" could make long-range raids on Japan's home islands. As the new generation of strategic bomber, the Superfortress boasted the combat range of 1,800 miles, a maximum speed of 350 miles per hour, and a capacity of 20,000 pounds of bombs. In all, 4,000 Superfortresses entered service during the Second World War. By late 1944, large squadrons of B-29s dropped incendiary bombs designed to start firestorms in Japanese cities with their tightly packed wooden structures. In his role commanding the American strategic bombing campaign in the Pacific, Major General Curtis LeMay was the architect of the firebombing of Japanese cities. He exhibited no regrets about such incredible destruction. By war's end, his bombers hit nearly all that nation's cities with more than 100,000 residents. On March 10 of the next year, the most destructive firestorm started, when 330 Superfortresses dropped 3,000 tons of incendiary bombs on Tokyo. The resulting maelstrom destroyed 25 percent of the city and killed an estimated 100,000 Japanese people.

D-Day: The Planning and Execution of Operation OVERLORD, June 6, 1944

In 1943, two important meetings occurred between U.S. President Franklin Roosevelt and British Prime Minister Winston Churchill. In January at the Casablanca Conference in Morocco, they authorized the feasibility study for a cross-channel amphibious operation. Then in August at the Quadrant Conference in Canada, they approved the study's recommendations for a landing on a sheltered coastline where millions of Anglo-American-Canadian troops could be disembarked and supplied thereafter as they moved inland. The province of Normandy appeared to be the best choice for an assault in 1944. The Soviet leader Joseph Stalin would finally get his wish—an attack in northern Europe.

The Casablanca and Quebec Conferences were noteworthy for two other diplomatic decisions. At the first conference, Roosevelt and Churchill concurred on the Allied policy of "unconditional surrender" as their grand strategic objective for the Second World War. This entailed defeating the Axis military forces on the battlefield and avoiding a postwar settlement like that of the Treaty of Versailles in 1918. Subsequently at Quebec, the two leaders forged a secret agreement regarding research and development of a new super-weapon—the atomic bomb—with incredible destructive power. They also decided that neither of their militaries would use this weapon without mutual consent.

Against these strategic and diplomatic backdrops, the planning for the invasion of Normandy began in earnest during the fall of 1943. The Allies would face formidable German defenses called "the Atlantic Wall." The Germans hoped that this series of coastal fortifications would either stop the Allies from landing or allow time for their reserves to drive them back into the sea. By mid-1944, the German Army in northwestern France totaled 50 divisions with more than 600,000 men. However, the Allies established overwhelming tactical air superiority over Normandy, thereby restricting some of the enemy's mobility.

Box 12.1 The Allies Deceive the Germans About the D-Day Invasion

Because the Germans certainly expected an Allied amphibious assault somewhere on the French coastline, the Allies also needed to find ways to decoy or confuse the Germans about the exact place and time of that invasion. The Allies deceived the Germans with a ruse that was code-named Operation FORTITUDE during the Spring of 1944. One part of this operation entailed double agents feeding false intelligence about the location of the amphibious assault to the Germans. Another part of it had the Allies create a fictitious "First U.S. Army Group" under Lieutenant General George S. Patton's command. He and his small staff exchanged fake radio messages as if there really were major troop concentrations arrayed in southern England. The Americans also placed inflatable tanks and other dummy vehicles in fields to add to the realism, should the Germans analyze aerial reconnaissance photographs.

Figure 12.1 Inflatable Decoy Tank Sitting Next to a Real M-4 Sherman Tank, May 1944

Source: U.S. Army Signal Corps Photograph, U.S. Army Engineer School History Office Archive

The elaborate Allied deceptions led the German leaders, particularly Adolf Hitler and Field Marshal Erwin Rommel, to assume that the main Allied invasion would occur at the Pas-de-Calais. This area lay in north Normandy just across the narrowest part of English Channel, and it was also the best starting point for the future Allied advance into Germany proper. The German's 15th Army remained tied down in Calais during the actual D-Day invasion in Normandy on June 6, 1944.

Adding to all these operational complexities were worries among the Allies about weather and tides along the Normandy coastline. The timing needed to be perfect on both accounts, so that neither rough seas nor wrong sea levels would halt the invasion before it even started. The first week in June stood as one of the only viable windows for the ideal tide levels, if weather permitted.

The ultimate responsibility for Operation OVERLORD rested on the shoulders of General Dwight D. Eisenhower. Fresh from his successes in North Africa in 1942 and Sicily in 1943, he assumed the role of Commander of Supreme Headquarters, Allied Expeditionary Forces (SHAEF). Just beneath Eisenhower was General Sir Bernard Montgomery, who exercised operational control over the entire Allied invasion force making the actual assault. The operational commander of American invasion forces was Lieutenant General Omar N. Bradley. After many months of preparations and planning, some 1.5 million American soldiers waited in England to make the assault in early June 1944. Joining those American soldiers were hundreds of thousands of British and Canadians. On June 4, General Eisenhower hoped to initiate the attack on the next day. However, the forecast called for high winds, rough seas, and overcast skies that made the amphibious and airborne components of Operation OVERLORD impossible. He waited one more day when the forecasts called for marginally better weather with clearer skies and calmer seas. At a meeting with his senior subordinate air, naval, and ground commander late on the evening of June 5, Eisenhower made the fateful decision to order the launch of history's greatest amphibious operation.

Finally "D-Day" arrived on the sixth of June.[2] In early morning, the 130,000 soldiers and 24,000 paratroopers made their assaults on the beach and their jumps behind the lines. The amphibious components did not go as planned for the U.S. 1st Infantry Division landing on the code-named "Omaha Beach," nor for the U.S. 4th Infantry Division on "Utah Beach."

The initial attempts by 34,000 soldiers in the 1st Infantry Division (to which the 29th Infantry Division was also attached for the assault phase) to reach the six-mile wide Omaha Beach went awry from the start at "H-Hour." U.S. Navy landing craft got swamped in the rolling waves, veered off course in the strong eastward current, ran aground on shoals, or hit German obstacles that disabled them. Once on Omaha Beach, the American soldiers endured withering artillery, mortar, and machine-gun fire as they ran toward the base of steep hills rising to a height of 170 feet. Running parallel to the shoreline, this high ground was divided by several small draws (valleys) that allowed inland access from the low-lying beaches. These heights gave the German defenders overlapping fields of fire that killed or wounded hundreds of Americans.

This tenuous situation gradually changed through the remainder of D-Day. The 16th Infantry Regiment's commander, Colonel George Taylor, saw that too many American soldiers were pinned down on Omaha Beach, unable or unwilling to move. Urging them into action, he said, "There are two kinds of people who are staying on this beach: those who are dead and those who are going to die. Now let's get the hell out of here." His soldiers slowly gained control of the draws. The men pushed through the draws and moved behind the German positions along the nearby heights.

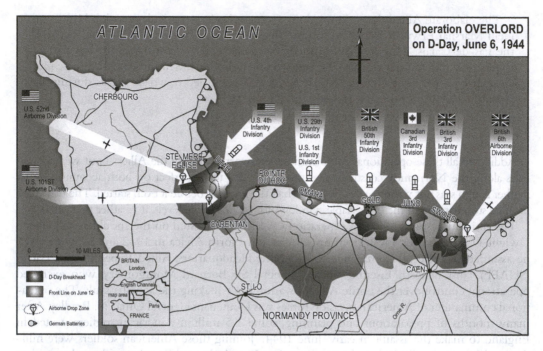

Map 12.3 Operation OVERLORD on D-Day, June 6, 1944

Meanwhile on Utah Beach to the west, the 4th Infantry Division's landing craft also ran off course during their ship-to-shore transit. Confusion reigned as American units attempted to reach their objectives. Once ashore, the assistant division commander Brigadier General Theodore Roosevelt Jr. rallied his troops with the famous words, "We'll start the war from here!" The son of the former American President took charge, redirected the units, and coordinated their movement. For his cool leadership under fire, the younger Roosevelt joined his father as a Congressional Medal of Honor recipient. By the end of D-Day, some 23,000 soldiers and 1,700 vehicles disembarked on Utah Beach. Unlike Omaha Beach, the 4th Infantry Division faced less German resistance on Utah Beach because the preinvasion aerial bombardment destroyed many enemy fortifications, and because the strong tidal current pushed the American landing away from planned landing areas which were better defended by the Germans.

The casualty rates provided the most compelling contrast: The 1st lost 3,000 men killed and wounded on Omaha, but the 4th lost only 200 men. There was another significant reason for the low casualties on Utah. In the predawn darkness, the 13,000 paratroops and glider troops of the 82nd and 101st Airborne Divisions landed and provided protection for Utah Beach against German counterattacks. Nevertheless, those two units paid dearly with 2,500 casualties.

As the American forces made their own assaults on D-Day, some 75,000 British and Canadian soldiers landed to the east on beaches code-named Gold, Juno, and Sword. Suffering little more than 2,000 casualties, the British and Canadians did not encounter the stubborn opposition that the Americans did on Omaha Beach. Although British and Canadians easily broke through the beach defenses, they soon bogged down when moving inland due to German counterattacks and to congestion of vehicles and men.

By the end of June 6, 1944, the Allied forces consolidated their positions, and even the situation on Omaha, while still tenuous, had stabilized. Looking at D-Day from the German perspective reveals that they lost the initiative in the first hours. Several failures to assess the enormity of the invasion or make decisive counterattacks cost the Germans their best opportunity to drive the Allies back into the sea.

First, the Germans possessed a confusing command structure that hampered the decision-making process. As the commander of German forces in the Normandy Area, Field Marshal Erwin Rommel believed the best means of defense was to stop the Allied invasion at the water's edge before a beachhead could be established. However, Rommel's superior officer, Field Marshal Gerd von Rundstedt, disagreed because he wanted to employ a mobile armor reserve to counterattack against any Allied invasion. Adolf Hitler resolved their dispute by ordering a hybrid defense with some German units being detailed to Rommel along the coast and other units to von Rundstedt as a mobile reserve. Hitler also made the decision to require that all use of German armor units required his personal order. This command structure severely handicapped the defenders' ability to react decisively when the Allies hit the beaches.

Second, the Allied deception efforts convinced Adolf Hitler and his senior officers that the invasion would come at Pas-de-Calais to the north, up the French coast. Making matters still worse, Hitler slept late on the morning of June 6 as he often did, and none of his generals were willing to wake him and get his authority to utilize the German tanks of the 15th Army massed in the Pas-de-Calais. Even when the significance of the Normandy landings became more obvious, Hitler refused to shift the 15th toward Normandy. He was unsure whether this was a diversionary landing. Thus, these armor units did not start moving soon enough to stop the Allies.

Hell in the Hedgerows and Breakout of the Bocage

Within the week following June 6, 1944, enough Allied infantry and armor units had disembarked to repel any German counterattack. The Allied forces in Normandy swelled to 850,000 men and 150,000 vehicles by month's end. Consequently, the Germans could only hope to stall the Allied breakout of Normandy.

The adversaries spent the next several weeks fighting countless bloody engagements in a region known to Allies as the "hedgerows" and to the French as the "bocage." The key terrain feature were hedges—earthen embankments measuring several feet tall and several feet wide at their bases that were covered with thickly tangled bushes rising several more feet. The hedgerows divided small plots of land that local farmers used to raise crops or graze livestock. These fields were laid out in irregular grids with small openings onto one-lane dirt roads. The hedges allowed the Germans direct and indirect artillery and machine-gun fire as well as concealment from Allied aircraft.

Endless fighting in the hedgerows stretched from days into weeks. Allied success was measured in yards, and casualties in the tens of thousands. But by the end of July, the German resistance in Normandy collapsed when the Omar Bradley's U.S. 1st Army launched Operation COBRA in the southern part of Normandy. Massive pre-attack aerial and artillery bombardment stunned the Germans in an area 6,000 yards long and 2,000 yards deep. They were unprepared for the American ground onslaught that followed. Bradley's units cut deep in the German lines to the southeast, leaving enemy units to retreat or be surrounded. American bombers devastated the enemy positions and limited their mobility.

Then, on August 1, a new American unit—the U.S. 3rd Army—was activated and placed under command of the recently arrived Lieutenant General George S. Patton. At the same time, Lieutenant General Courtney Hodges assumed command of the U.S. 1st Army. Omar Bradley took overall command of both armies and their generals that comprised the new U.S. 12th Army Group. He was wholly independent of Field Marshal Montgomery because they became equals as army group commanders. For his part, Montgomery retained control of the British 21st Army Group with its British and Canadian forces. General Dwight D. Eisenhower commanded the entire Anglo–American–Canadian coalition as Supreme Commander of the Allied Expeditionary Force (SHAEF).

Patton's arrival gave Operation COBRA even more momentum. The aggressive American general had been spoiling for a fight for months while acting as a decoy back in England to confuse the Germans about the main invasion on D-Day. He immediately ordered his 3rd Army to press still further into German-held territory. In the next fortnight in what has been called "the Breakout," some of Patton's units moved 100 miles south and then swept eastward 100 miles.

The dizzying speed of Patton's giant flanking maneuver left the bewildered Germans trapped near the city of Falaise, which lay about 40 miles south of the Normandy beaches. The Battle of the Falaise Pocket lasted another week until August 20. The Canadian forces attacked southward, and the American forces drove east and north. They hoped to tighten the noose and encircle two entire German Panzer armies still fighting in three directions near Falaise. Although 100,000 Germans did escape the trap, the Allies killed 10,000 Germans and captured more than 40,000 more. The Allies reached the Seine River and liberated Paris from Axis occupation by the end of August 1944. With the fall of the capital, the Germans essentially lost France. The open country east of the city offered the enemy few viable defensive positions, forcing the Germans to withdraw eastward toward the borders of Belgium and Germany.

Broad Fronts, Spearheads, and a Bridge Too Far

So successful was the Allied drive through France that General Eisenhower decided not to stop in Paris. Instead, he ordered his forces to chase the fleeing Germans farther into eastern France. In mid-September, Montgomery's 21st Army Group crossed the border into Belgium and captured the major ports of Le Havre in France and Antwerp in Belgium. To the south, Bradley's 12th Army Group fared just as well: The 1st U.S. Army reached the Marne River, while Patton's 3rd U.S. Army reached the Moselle River. In some places like the Ardennes Forest in southern Belgium, Allied units stood just 15 miles from the German border.

Nevertheless, the situation in mid-September 1944 required a pause in the broad advance because the Allied logistical efforts, as impressive as they were, could not keep pace with the fuel, water, food, and ammunition required by three million Allied soldiers and their vehicles. Together, the U.S. 1st and 3rd Army Groups, for instance, required 800,000 gallons of fuel each day. Pausing would thus allow the supply lines to catch up to the front-line units. This respite also provided Field Marshal Montgomery an opportunity to appeal for a shift from the broad front offensive favored by General Eisenhower to a narrow spearhead offensive that he preferred. Despite the objections by Bradley and Patton, Montgomery eventually convinced Eisenhower that a narrow spearhead would be the best use of the limited supplies.

In September after the capture of the key port city of Antwerp in Belgium, the usually cautious Montgomery broke with his pattern of slowly developing maneuver operations. Having witnessed firsthand the horrific casualties in the First World War when commanders brashly committed units to massive offensives, he seemed hardwired to favor the safer, more moderate approach of a grinding offensive campaign. Thus, it was surprising that Montgomery came up with a daring plan, Operation MARKET, to send more than 30,000 Allied airborne paratroops up to 60 miles behind enemy lines to seize three key bridges over rivers in the Netherlands. While these paratroops held the bridges, In Operation GARDEN, Montgomery's British XXX

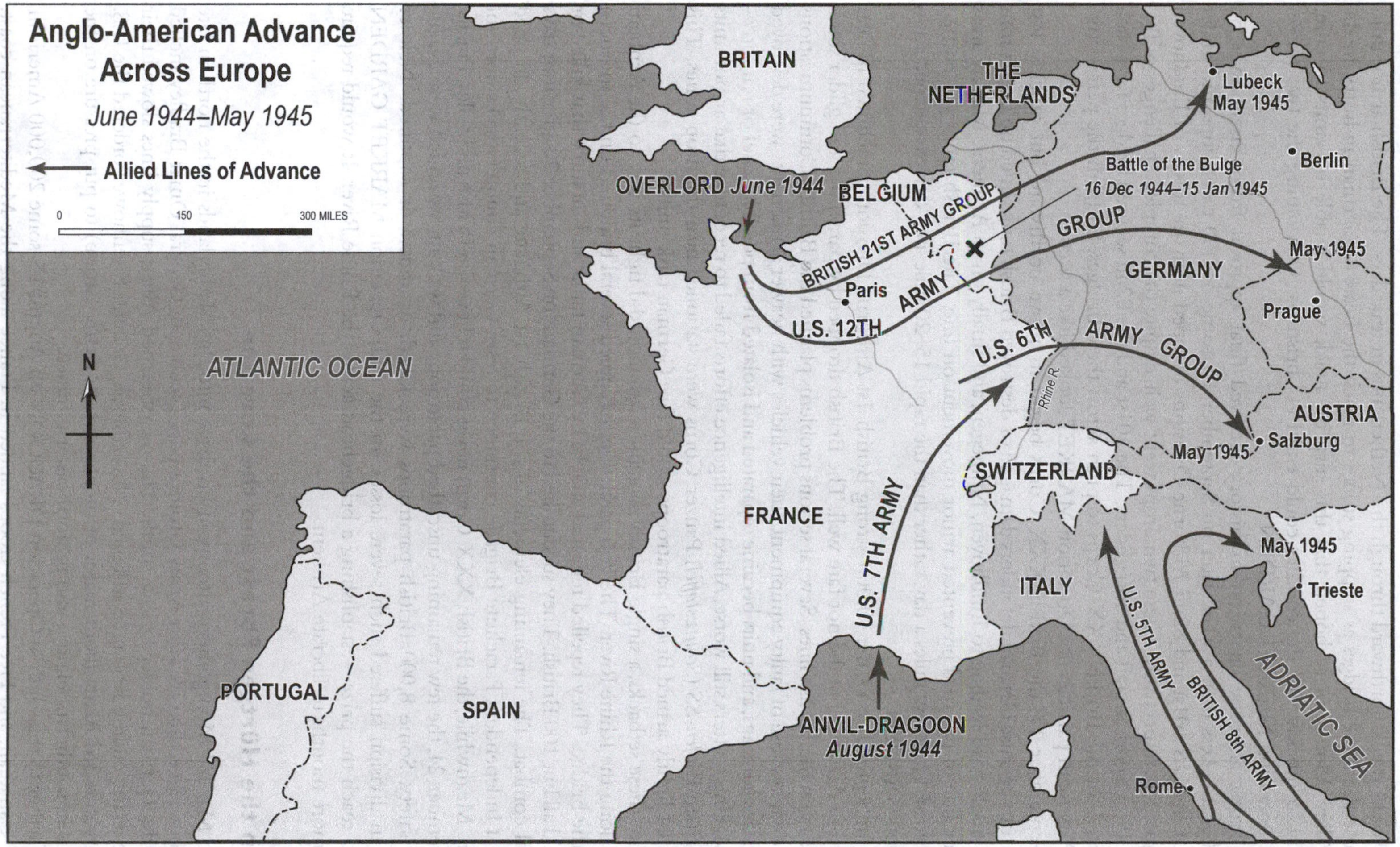

Map 12.4 Anglo-American Advance Across Europe, June 1944–May 1945

Corps would attack northward through the Netherlands in four days. The British armor units would use the three bridges as stepping stones to reach the heart of German industry in the Ruhr Valley. Montgomery hoped that this surprise attack would enable his units to enter Germany so quickly that the conflict could end by Christmas. Combining the two phases created Operation MARKET GARDEN.

The largest airborne operation in history received final approval from Eisenhower on September 11. Less than a week later on September 17, some 34,000 paratroops and glider troops of the U.S 101st and 82nd Airborne Divisions dropped near the towns of Eindhoven and Nijmegen, respectively. These two drops went well, despite the complex challenges of flying 1,500 transport aircraft and 500 gliders. The 101st and the 82nd secured bridges near each and waited for the British XXX Corps to push across these bridges. So from the perspective of the American participants, Operation MARKET looked like a success.

On September 17, the British XXX Corps began its move northward but quickly lost momentum because German defenders damaged or destroyed British tanks lined up in columns along a single road leading to Eindhoven, Njimegen, and finally on to Arnhem. Marshy areas on either side of the road prevented armor movement on line. The British tanks got bottled up and slowed to a few miles a day, rather than the rapid 15–20 mile-per-day pace expected in Operation GARDEN.

Also on September 17, the 10,000-strong British 1st Airborne Division parachuted in near the town of Arnhem but did not fare well. The British dropped by parachute and glider some 60 miles from the British lines. Several serious problems plagued the British: Communications broke down because of faulty equipment, their vehicles with heavier armaments were destroyed in the glider landings, and units became separated and isolated from possible relief or reinforcement. Making matters still worse, Allied intelligence efforts failed to recognize that armor units of a German *Waffen-SS* (*Schutzstaffel*) Panzer Corps were stationed near the drop zones. This meant that lightly armed British paratroops would face German tank units.

Despite these setbacks, a single British parachute battalion did fight its way to the Arnhem Bridge along the Rhine River. The 750 paratroops occupied several buildings on the southern side of the bridge. They repelled repeated attacks by German tanks and infantry that killed or wounded all but 100 British. They succumbed to the Germans on September 20 after four days of brutal combat. The remaining elements of the British 1st Airborne and recently dropped Polish 1st Independent Parachute Brigade continued to resist German counterattacks north of Arnhem. Meanwhile, the British XXX Corps never could relieve the British and Poles. Finally, on September 24, the few remaining unscathed paratroops and walking wounded were evacuated to safety. Some 8,000 British paratroops were killed, wounded, or captured. Neither American division suffered such severe losses. In the end, Operation MARKET GARDEN failed to reach the prize—establishing a bridgehead across the Rhine River. It would require several more months to liberate Arnhem.

Hell in the Hürtgen Forest and the Lorraine

As Field Marshal Montgomery attempted his drive into the Netherlands in the north in late September 1944, the U.S. 12th Army Group under Lieutenant General Omar Bradley inched toward the German border farther south. The overstretched Allied supply lines slowed their advance as the enemy resistance stiffened. Nevertheless, General Eisenhower ordered the U.S. 1st Army and 3rd Army (both major elements of 12th Army Group) to put pressure on the Germans in southern Belgium and in northeastern France.

Still farther to the south in Operation DRAGOON on August 15, some 200,000 American, British, Canadian, and Free French troops landed in France along the Mediterranean coast.

They moved north in hopes of breaching the fortified Siegfried Line guarding the German border in more places than the enemy could react to or defend at one time. The Allies pushed the German forces more than 200 miles north to the Vosges Mountains by mid-September. Once there, the Allied forces came under the newly organized 6th Army Group led by U.S. Army General Jacob L. Devers. The 6th then turned eastward in 1944 and advanced into Germany in 1945. Fighting could be fierce, as evinced by the 27,000 casualties suffered by the U.S. 3rd Infantry Division, which on paper included 16,000 officers and men. This figure was the worst among all American divisions in Europe. Even so, Operation DRAGOON made significant contributions in the European Theater because it attracted 300,000 German soldiers away from Montgomery and Bradley in the north. Of these, 7,000 were killed, 20,000 wounded, and 130,000 captured.

For the U.S. 1st Army to the south of Montgomery's 21st Army Group, putting pressure on the Germans in southern Belgium meant attacking through the Hürtgen Forest and into the city of Aachen in Germany proper. Lying just south of Aachen and straddling the Siegfried Line that extended north to south, the forest was a rugged area running 20 miles west to east and five miles north to south. Few roads or paths existed on the uneven ground. The fir trees not only limited movement by American vehicles but also obscured German defenders from American aerial reconnaissance and reduced the effectiveness of artillery fire and close air support. Adding to the problems, soldiers endured increasingly wet and cold weather as autumn turned to winter. On September 19, 1944, American units entered the woods in what became the longest and bloodiest battle in the European Theater.

From September 1944 to February 1945, division after division of the 1st Army entered the fray in the Hürtgen Forest. At times, the Americans outnumbered their German adversaries by a ratio of five to one. However, the Germans made the Americans pay for every inch of territory. After Americans attacked and gained ground, the enemy counterattacked and recaptured that ground. In all, eight U.S. Army divisions and support units totaling 120,000 soldiers saw action in this five-month bloodbath. Some 12,000 Americans died, 12,000 were wounded, and 9,000 more were incapacitated because of fatigue, pneumonia, trench foot, frostbite, or other noncombat maladies. The hardest hit, the U.S. 28th Infantry Division suffered a 50 percent casualty rate.

As Americans struggled through the Hürtgen Forest, other units of the 1st Army launched an assault on the city of Aachen in Germany. What had been expected to be a relatively quick victory turned into an urban battle lasting three weeks. The narrow streets and stone buildings gave the outnumbered defenders advantages against some 100,000 Americans. Bitter house-to-house fighting occurred in which every individual pocket of German resistance needed to be eliminated. Securing Aachen on October 21 represented an Allied psychological victory. It was not only the first German city captured by the Americans, but it had also been Charlemagne's ancient capital, putting the capital of the Holy Roman Empire—Germany's "First Reich"—in American hands.

Still further to the south of Hodges' U.S. 1st Army was Lieutenant George S. Patton's 3rd Army. During the fall of 1944, his units tried to secure the Lorraine Province in northeastern France in quick surges designed to overwhelm the German opposition. However, fuel shortages stalled his offensive along the Meuse River. Thereafter, the fortress city of Metz presented the most formidable barrier to Patton's drive toward the German border. The enemy defenses around Metz proved much more stubborn than anyone, including Patton, expected. Metz lay on the Moselle River about 30 miles to the north of Nancy. Several forts and observation posts connected by trenches and tunnels provided some 60,000 Germans with mutually supporting, interlocking positions. Aside from the difficult fighting situation for the Americans, the German resistance did not lessen, as the commanders of those positions could surrender only with Adolf Hitler's express permission.

Whole divisions of Patton's 3rd Army tried to cross the Moselle and subdue the fortifications around Metz in late September 1944. Frontal attacks failed, despite being supported by artillery and aerial bombardment. Instead of the sweeping movements that Patton had enjoyed since August and were the hallmark of the Second World War on the continent, the two sides settled into siege warfare. Reminiscent of the First World War, the combat proved to be bloody and slow because each German fort needed to be captured. Isolating and bypassing a fort was hardly ideal because its defenders could still disrupt American units moving deeper in the German lines. Wet and increasingly cold weather compounded the problems facing the Americans. The siege of Metz took three months, until November 22, 1944.

From the Battle of the Bulge to V-E Day, December 1944 to May 1945

As the fighting at Metz and Hürtgen Forest subsided by December 1944, the soldiers of the U.S. 12th Army Group paused for rest and refit. One of the coldest winters in decades stopped the American offensive along the German border. Forecasts for blizzards and frigid temperatures dashed all hopes of entering Germany before the thaw next spring. Instead, soldiers in the 28th, 99th, and 106th Infantry divisions and other assorted units in Hodges' 1st Army deployed along a 70-mile front in Belgium's Ardennes Forest. The 28th was barely at half-strength after weeks of heavy combat in the Hürtgen Forest, and the 99th and 106th were not yet battle-tested, having only recently landed on the continent. Behind them lay several other American units busily consolidating the recent American gains in the western half of the Ardennes. It looked like it might be a relatively quiet Christmas in this sector of the front lines. The American intelligence-gathering efforts, however, did not recognize a mobilization of German forces just beyond the front lines.

Allied assumptions that the German foe was bloodied, beaten, and in retreat pervaded the American forces from the lowest to the highest ranks. Such underestimations of enemy resolve and capability made it easier for the Germans to launch a massive surprise attack in mid-December 1944. For the Americans involved, this desperate month-long fight became known as the Battle of the Bulge.

The German plan called for an offensive through the seemingly impassable Ardennes Forest. Spearheaded by elite armor units, some 200,000 German soldiers and 1,500 tanks would overwhelm Hodges' 1st U.S. Army along a 70-mile front and drive more than 150 miles northwest into Belgium and on to Antwerp. This port city served as the major logistical center for ship-borne supplies being offloaded and transported to the Anglo-American forces that threatened the German homeland. Adolf Hitler hoped that his forces would destroy the 1st Army and then drive a wedge between Montgomery's 21st Army Group to the north and Patton's 3rd U.S. Army to the south. If successful, Hitler hoped that the British would make a separate peace with Germany, that the loss of supplies could stop the American offensive, and that Americans on the home front might lose heart and stop supporting the war effort.

Although Hitler's strategic goals for this surprise attack were delusional in their expectations, his plan did have historical precedents. Indeed, it resembled the successful German invasion of Belgium and France in 1940. Some senior generals did not support Hitler's plan, because they saw it as a pointless gamble with irreplaceable resources. Nevertheless, they were unwilling to challenge their *Fuehrer's* authority too vocally in the months after the nearly successful assassination plot led by Colonel Claus Stauffenberg. The remaining German generals feared vicious retribution such as execution or forced suicide if they appeared disloyal to Hitler.

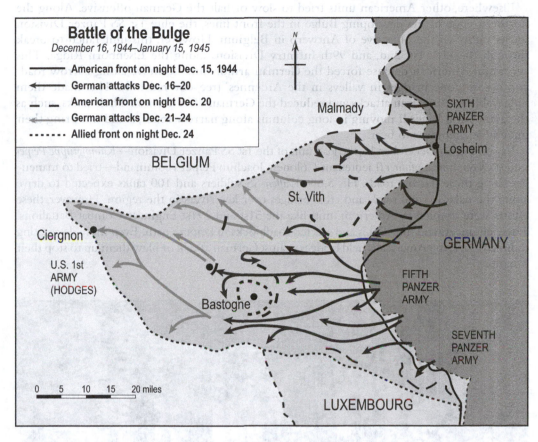

Map 12.5 Battle of the Bulge, December 16, 1944–January 15, 1945

In the early morning hours of December 16, 1944, the Germans emerged from the chilled fog, caught the 28th and 106th Divisions unawares, and overran many positions. American soldiers made desperate stands with only small arms against the enemy tanks. Within a matter of hours, thousands of hungry, tired, and cold American soldiers were killed, wounded, captured, or routed. The Germans in the southern and central sectors of the attacks opened a bulge that reached 70 miles into American-held territory.

American units made a stand in the village of Bastogne, which sat astride a crossroads that the Germans needed to seize quickly to maintain their momentum. They could afford neither the time nor the fuel to devote to besieging the town. American combat engineers held Bastogne until reinforced by the U.S. 101st Airborne Division and elements of the 10th Armor Division. On December 21, the Germans surrounded these American soldiers in the town. They launched repeated assaults on the American perimeter but failed to break through it. At one point, the German commanding general asked the American commander, Brigadier General Anthony McAuliffe, to surrender. McAuliffe's replied with one, now famous word: "Nuts." He and his soldiers held out until December 26. Their courageous defense of Bastogne cost the Germans critical fuel and time.

Elsewhere, other American units tried to slow or halt the German offensive. Along the northern edge of the developing Bulge in the front lines, the elite 1st *SS* Panzer Division set its sights on the objective of Antwerp in Belgium. However, this unit failed to break through the U.S. 1st, 2nd, and 99th Infantry Divisions along the Elsenborn Ridge. This successful American defense forced the German armor units to move along narrow roads and across stone bridges in valleys in the Ardennes' tree-covered hills. This made them vulnerable to American attacks and reduced the German effectiveness. Their tanks, such as the giant King Tiger II moving in long columns along narrow roads, could not bring their incredible firepower to bear.

Beginning on December 16, the lead unit of the 1st *SS* Panzer Division—*Kampfgruppe Peiper* under *Obersturmbannführer* (Lieutenant Colonel) Joachim Peiper's command—tried to maneuver along those narrow roads. His 5,800 *Waffen-SS* soldiers and 100 tanks expected to drive along the narrow rural roads and cross bridges over key rivers in the region. However, these efforts were stymied by American units like the 51st and 291st Engineer Combat Battalions. These engineers laid minefields and erected roadblocks in Peiper's path. Even more devastating to his advance, the Americans held bridges against German attack or blew them up to stop their progress.

Figure 12.2 U.S. Army Combat Engineers Wiring Trees for Demolition

American combat engineers wiring trees with dynamite that, when detonated, would make the trees fall in crisscross patterns and block roads to traffic. These obstacles, known as *abatis*, proved to be very effective in slowing the advance of German units during the Battle of the Bulge.

Source: U.S. Army Signal Corps Photograph, U.S. Army Engineer School History Office Archive

The most dramatic confrontation occurred on December 18 along Lienne Creek in Belgium. The American engineers blew up a bridge over this creek right in front of Peiper's eyes. It is said that the frustrated *SS* commander sat down, pounded his fist on his knee, and swore, *"Diese verdammten Pioniere! Diese verdammten Pioniere!"* In English, Peiper's words meant "Those damned engineers!" or more authentically "Those fucking engineers!" This bridge's destruction dashed Peiper's hopes for a breakout into open terrain. Only a few days later, he and his remaining 800 men retreated eastward on foot when his tanks ran out of fuel or were destroyed. The efforts by the American combat engineers and many thousands of soldiers helped seal the German defeat along the northern edge of the Battle of the Bulge.

Whereas some elements of General Hodges' 1st Army may have been slow to react on December 16, General George Patton's 3rd Army to the south reacted quickly to the German attack. He ordered three of his divisions (totaling nearly 50,000 men) to disengage from fighting in an east-west direction, turn to the north, move 100 miles, and attack the southern edge of the bulge by December 19—all during a blizzard with wind chill temperatures below zero. This was Patton's finest moment. His units relieved Bastogne on the day after Christmas. By the New Year, the American forces recovered from the shock of the German attack and launched their own counterattack that sent the enemy into retreat. The Battle of the Bulge lasted until January 15, 1945.

Bereft of any offensive capabilities, the once-mighty German Army withdrew inside its border, succumbing to the irresistible Anglo-American pressure from one side and the Soviet juggernaut from the other. In the west in early 1945, the Germans fought more delaying actions against the oncoming 73 Anglo-American divisions totaling four million soldiers. A large German force remained on the western side of the Rhine River facing Bradley's 12th Army Group. Hitler ordered his men to fight to the death rather than withdraw across the Rhine. In the ensuing battle, Americans destroyed this force, killing, wounding, or capturing some 400,000 German soldiers. By early March, the Anglo-American forces stood on the western bank of the Rhine from Kolbenz to Duisburg 100 miles downstream. That same month, the Anglo-American forces crossed the Rhine and entered Germany proper. Meanwhile, on the Eastern Front, Soviet forces prepared to make their final drive toward Berlin.

As the Allies moved farther into Germany, they stumbled onto camps filled with Jewish survivors of the Holocaust. American and British soldiers recoiled in horror when they found decayed remains of the dead and the emaciated bodies of the living in Dachau, Buchenwald, and Bergen-Belsen. These discoveries laid bare the fullest extent of the evils perpetuated by Adolf Hitler's Nazi regime. The slaughter of the Holocaust thus provided one of the strongest postwar justifications for the American participation in the Second World War.

The unrelenting tide of Allied victories raised hopes among American soldiers that the fighting in Europe would soon end in 1945. Sad news, however, spread through the ranks that President Franklin D. Roosevelt died on April 12. Through unknown to the Americans at home or abroad, his health had steadily deteriorated since mid-1944. Roosevelt's death ushered his Vice President Harry S. Truman into the office of President. Truman had the spent previous 10 years, from 1934 to 1944, representing Missouri in the United States Senate. Choosing Truman as a running mate in his unprecedented fourth 1944 election bid demonstrated Roosevelt's uncanny ability to choose the right people for key positions. He knew that Truman demonstrated political skill in the U.S. Senate, where he chaired a committee that investigated contractor mismanagement in defense spending for three years.

Now–President Truman assumed the nation's reins of leadership at a truly momentous time. The war in Europe was one month from its end, and the war in the Pacific saw the start of the campaign for Okinawa on April 1. However, he was not kept well informed. In fact, Truman had only talked privately with Roosevelt about strategy two times during the short months after being sworn in as Vice President on January 20, 1945. Neither the president nor his senior advisors briefed Truman about any major developments, especially the super-secret Manhattan Project that spent more than $2 billion on an immeasurably destructive weapon. He did not receive all the details until two weeks after Roosevelt's passing.

More immediately, Truman watched the death throes of Nazi Germany. The Anglo-American forces were less than 100 miles from the capital city of Berlin, but the western Allied leaders made the decision to allow the Soviets to seize Berlin, thus avoiding diplomatic friction. By April 24, the Soviets had surrounded the city of Berlin, cutting it off from any chance of relief by the dwindling German forces. Berlin was the scene of bitter house-to-house combat as the Soviets slowly tightened their grip on the city. On April 30, Adolf Hitler committed suicide rather than be captured by his enemy. Most resistance ceased in the coming weeks. Hitler's successor, Grand Admiral Karl Dönitz, tried to surrender solely to the Anglo-American forces. But, failing this, he surrendered on all fronts on May 7, 1945. This was V-E Day— Victory in Europe Day. The European portion of the Second World War was over. While a joyous occasion for Americans, their attention quickly turned to the other side of the world where fighting still raged.

Ominous Signs in the Pacific in 1945: *Kamikazes*, Iwo Jima, and Okinawa

During the final months of 1944, the Japanese recognized their situation was desperate. To stall the American onslaught, the Japanese began making massed *kamikaze* attacks to destroy American shipping. The word, translated as "divine wind," dated back to the thirteenth century when typhoons destroyed Mongolian warships sailing from the Asian mainland to invade the Japanese home islands. The Japanese had long interpreted those storms to be divine interventions that protected their home islands.

With the very real threat of American invasion came the need for a twentieth-century version of "divine wind" to protect Japan. Several thousand young Japanese men heeded the call to become *kamikaze* pilots in the Philippines campaign. They were inspired by loyalty to their nation, emperor, and ancestors to sacrifice their lives. After learning basic pilot skills, they crashed their airplanes into American vessels. Nearly 4,000 Japanese flew *kamikaze* missions. Of these, an estimated 600 pilots succeeded in sinking 30 U.S. Navy ships, damaging 350 ships, and killing or wounding at least 10,000 American sailors.

American servicemen of all ranks recognized that the Japanese willingness to die in the air, at sea, or on land meant the rules of conventional war did not apply to combat in the Pacific. Not only were the Japanese willing to fight to the death, but they also would kill American wounded or prisoners. These realities aroused fear and anxiety in every sailor, soldier, airman, and marine fighting in the battles for Iwo Jima and Okinawa in 1945.

Meanwhile, in the Central Pacific Theater in late 1944, a lull in fighting had occurred while MacArthur began his campaign for the Philippines. With his progress assured, the U.S. Navy's focus could return to securing the final two stepping stones toward the Japanese home islands in the new year. First came Iwo Jima. Capturing this island just 600 miles from Japan's coast

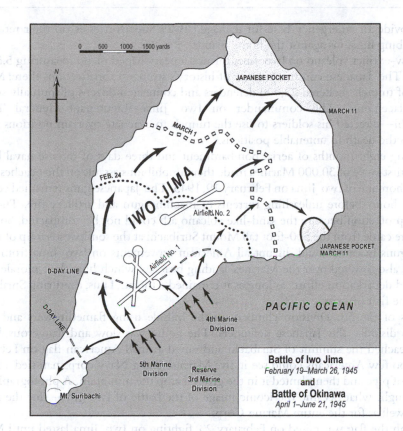

Map 12.6 Battle of Iwo Jima, February 19–March 26, 1945

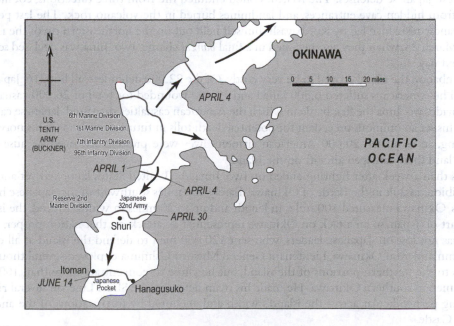

Map 12.7 Battle of Okinawa, April 1–June 21, 1945

would provide an emergency base for damaged B-29 Superfortresses on their return flights from bombing missions against the home islands.

The now-extinct volcano on Iwo Jima formed a pear-shaped island measuring 5.5 miles by 2.5 miles. The Japanese constructed one of history's strongest fortifications there: More than 20 miles of tunnels sheltered 22,000 defenders and connected dozens of mutually supporting gun emplacements. The commander on Iwo Jima—Lieutenant General Tadamichi Kuribayashi—directed his soldiers to use the tunnels to evacuate overrun positions instead of fighting to the death in untenable positions.

Following eight months of aerial bombardment and three days of intense naval bombardment, the first wave of 30,000 Marines made their amphibious assault on the beaches along the southern shoreline of Iwo Jima on February 19, 1945. The Japanese guns remained eerily silent for several hours before unleashing torrents of machine-gun and artillery fire. The Marines found no protection because the sand-like volcano ash could not be compacted. Some of the heaviest fire came from the 500-foot tall Mount Suribachi at the southwestern tip of the island. Japanese guns in caves could disrupt all American movements on Iwo Jima from this high ground. It also towered over the Marines' landing beaches, which hurt their morale as well as endangered debarkation efforts as long as it remained a threat. Thus, capturing Suribachi represented the first priority.

Marines of the 5th Division climbed up the hillside using flamethrowers and explosive charges to dislodge the Japanese defenders. The going was slow and dangerous, but a few Marines reached the summit of Suribachi and raised a small American flag on February 23. Because too few Americans could see it, five Marines and a Navy corpsman tied a larger flag to a piece of pipe and then planted it in the ground atop the mountain. A photograph and film footage caught what became the iconic image of the battle of Iwo Jima—for the American people as well as for the entire Marine Corps.

Although the flag was raised on February 23, fighting on Iwo Jima lasted until March 26. In those intervening weeks, a total of 70,000 Marines moved to the northeast through the strongest Japanese defenses. The Marines often endured fire from three directions, counterattacks from hidden cave entrances, and landmines buried in the volcano rock. The last pocket of Japanese resistance led by Kuribayashi himself held out on the northeastern tip of the island until March 25, when they also perished in a final *banzai* charge. Iwo Jima was declared secure the next day.

Combat on the island proved to be very costly. Of the 22,000 defenders, all but 216 Japanese died. The Americans suffered 6,800 killed and 19,200 wounded for total of 26,000 casualties. This made Iwo Jima the first battle in which the American casualties surpassed Japanese casualties. This set an ominous precedent for potential death tolls in future operations. This notwithstanding, an estimated 20,000 American airmen's lives were presumably saved because they could land their damaged aircraft on the island.

Less than a week after fighting ended on Iwo Jima, the United States launched yet another amphibious assault in the Battle of Okinawa. Barely 400 miles southwest of the Japanese home islands, Okinawa measured 100 miles in length and up to 20 miles in width. Indeed, the island was part of Japan, so an attack on Okinawa represented an attack on that nation proper. This fact was not lost on Japanese leaders, who sent 120,000 men to defend the island at all costs. As commander on Okinawa, Lieutenant General Mitsuru Ushijima deployed several thousand troops to the northern portions of the island, but he chose to concentrate more than 100,000 of his men in southern Okinawa. He made his main defensive the Shuri Line, on several ridges running perpendicular across the island's width and anchored by fortifications of the ancient Shuri Castle.

Box 12.2   Ernie Pyle Reports on the Greatest Generation

During the Second World War, civilians on the American home front learned about their loved ones serving in the military from letters, newsreels, and newspapers. Supporting this last effort was a journalist named Ernie Pyle. Before the conflict, he worked at every level, from editor of a college newspaper to managing editor of a major newspaper. But Pyle's real gift was writing in an intimate and readable style that painted word pictures of everyday life. After the attack on Pearl Harbor, he became a war correspondent—the Second World War's version of an embedded reporter. Pyle ignored stories about high-ranking officers and instead spotlighted the ordinary American fighting men in the field. Although he spent time on Navy ships and on Pacific islands, he favored the stories of soldiers fighting in Italy and Europe. Millions of Americans read Pyle's columns every week; and they earned him a Pulitzer Prize on June 6, 1944. He missed the award presentation in New York City because that was the D-Day invasion of Normandy. During the war, Pyle experienced several close calls while observing American troops in combat. This gave him the raw material to craft his well-written articles for civilians at home. In early 1945, Pyle left the European Theater to report on the Pacific War. Sadly on April 18 of that year, he was killed by a burst of Japanese machine fire on the island of Ie Shima off the coast of Okinawa.

The U.S. 7th and 96th Infantry Divisions and the 1st and 6th Marine Division made their landings on April 1, 1945. As on Iwo Jima, the Japanese did not contest this initial phase of the Battle of Okinawa. They chose to bide their time waiting for the Americans to walk into their mutually supporting positions with overlapping fields of fire. The Japanese had perfected this defense-in-depth. Hardly a shot was fired until the other American divisions moved closer to the Shuri Line. In May, a total of five American divisions fought in an area barely 20 square miles. Using tactics like those on Iwo Jima, Ushijima's men held their positions until the last moment, retreated through caves, and reappeared in the next line of defenses. Combat on Okinawa matched the savagery of combat on Iwo Jima and Peleliu, where progress was measured in yards.

Several hundred *Kamikaze* planes flew from Japan on suicide raids against American ships off the coast of Okinawa. The U.S. Navy put up torrents of antiaircraft fire and squadrons of fighters to try to stop the *Kamikaze* attacks, but they still sank or damaged many ships and killed or wounded 10,000 American sailors. These were the worst naval losses in the war.

For their part, the Americans on the ground made progress only by using flamethrowers and grenades as well as artillery bombardments of Japanese emplacements and aircraft flying close air support. The 7th Infantry Division captured the eastern section of the Shuri Line, and the 6th Marine Division seized the west in mid-May. These defeats caused the castle in the center of the line to fall to the 1st Marine Division by month's end. Approximately 45,000 surviving Japanese gradually withdrew to their other defensive lines farther south before final defeat on June 21, 1945.

The Battle of Okinawa cost the Japanese 100,000 lives of combatants, with fewer than 20,000 wounded and captured. Like Saipan, the civilians on Okinawa suffered 140,000 casualties. Some civilians committed mass suicide because they believed the Japanese government's propaganda that the Americans would brutalize them if taken alive. Of the 183,000 Americans on the island, more than 12,500 died and 40,000 were wounded in 82 days of combat operations. This amounted to a 29 percent casualty rate.

The losses on both sides made the potential invasion of Japan proper seem like a death sentence for the attacking forces. Nevertheless, in May, the American Joint Chiefs of Staff approved an amphibious assault on Japan's southernmost island of Kyushu. In this first phase of Operation DOWNFALL, some 14 American divisions (220,000 soldiers in combat units) would land in November 1945 and face an estimated 600,000 Japanese combatants. If the casualty rates on Okinawa or Iwo Jima were predictors of casualties on Kyushu, then a minimum of 20,000 dead and another 50,000 wounded American could be expected in the initial invasion.

Next, the second phase would entail an invasion of the main island of Honshu in March 1945. Another 25 American divisions (nearly 400,000 men) would make an amphibious assault near the capital of Tokyo. To put this into perspective, eight divisions made the assault on Normandy on D-Day in 1944. Against this massive force, the Japanese could muster at least one million service personnel and several million civilians on Honshu. They would fight to defend their capital and their emperor, so the likelihood of increased fanaticism had to be factored into both American and Japanese casualties. The cost of the invasion could surpass 130,000 American casualties. Ongoing operations against Japanese combatants and civilians and long-term occupation of Honshu could double or triple that initial death toll.

Such estimations were mere speculation because Operation DOWNFALL never occurred. However, one fact bore witness to the anticipated American losses: the U.S. military stockpiled 500,000 Purple Hearts so that every American casualty could be awarded this medal.

A Brave New Way of Warfare? The Atomic Bombs and V-J Day

Considering past casualty rates in the Pacific War and the anticipated rates in Operation DOWNFALL, recently sworn-in President Harry Truman needed to make a difficult decision during the summer of 1945. He had two choices: Should he order invasions of Japan later in 1945 and 1946, or should he use the atomic bombs against Japanese cities to force Japan's surrender as soon as possible?

One American atomic bomb was successfully tested in New Mexico on July 16, 1945. One day later, Truman met for the first time with the Soviet Union's Joseph Stalin at the Potsdam Conference in Germany. The three leaders of the Grand Alliance tried to decide the fates of a defeated Germany and a reestablished Poland. In addition, Truman told a nonplussed Stalin about the atomic bomb. The Soviet leader had already learned of the Manhattan Project through his spy network, but he probably could not grasp the incredible destructive power of the weapon.

Several other factors also affected Truman's choice to one degree or another. First, the American people were tiring of the war. After nearly four years of sacrifice and the recent defeat of Germany, they wanted to end of the conflict. Second, he experienced some of history's most horrific combat as an Army officer during the First World War. He had to expect that fighting in Japan would reach a similar scale. Third, Truman recognized that the U. S. military had spent $2 billion on developing the atomic bombs. This huge expenditure on a single weapons system equaled nearly one percent of the entire cost of American war effort—$300 billion. The expensive weapon was in his arsenal, so he needed to use it. Likewise, given wartime propaganda and this expense, the American people would have demanded that the atomic bombs be dropped. Fourth, Truman was mindful that the Soviet Union had turned its full attention toward East Asia where they massed their forces for an attack into Japanese-held

China. Using the atomic bombs against Japan would send a message to Stalin that the United States possessed a new weapon that changed the face of warfare. And fifth, racist views about the Japanese pervading American society doubtlessly made it easier for Truman to order that so many enemy soldiers and civilians be killed by the atomic bombs. Moreover, because fire-bombing Japanese cities had already killed hundreds of thousands of Japanese and damaged all but five major cities, killing tens of thousands more was not without precedent.

Taking all these factors into account, it made sense on utilitarian, practical, strategic, and dip-lomatic levels for Truman to use the atomic bombs. On August 6, 1945, the B-29 Superfortress *Enola Gay* dropped one bomb on the city of Hiroshima. It weighed nearly five tons, but its explosive power measured 13 kilotons, equating to 13,000 tons of conventional trinitrotoluene (TNT). The blast's shock wave and fireball devastated several square miles of the city, killed 70,000 Japanese, and injured another 80,000. Although shocked by the destruction wrought by the single bomb, Japan's leadership balked at surrendering and ending the Pacific War. Nationalistic pride together with pro-war factions in the government would not allow capitulation.

Japan's refusal to surrender left Truman with no viable alternative to dropping a second atomic bomb. The president believed that he needed to send a clear message to Japan: surrender now or risk a full-fledged invasion. Three days later on August 9, 1945, another B-29 dropped the second atomic bomb on Nagasaki. This bomb weighed just over five tons, but its explosive force equaled that of 21 kilotons of TNT. The blast killed 35,000 and injured 50,000 Japanese. Several hundred thousand more people would die over the decades because of complications caused by radiation emitted by both atomic bombs.

After seeing a second American super-weapon destroy another city, Emperor Hirohito real-ized his nation's situation was untenable. Thus, on August 15, he announced his decision to surrender in the best interest of preserving the Japanese nation and culture. This day of the cessation of hostilities in the Pacific War was "V-J" Day—Victory over Japan day. Because of the time difference between Japan and the continental United States, the day was observed on August 14 on the American home front. A little over two weeks later, the representatives of the Japanese government signed articles of surrender on the deck of battleship USS *Missouri* in Tokyo Bay. It was September 2, 1945.

Conclusion

From the American perspective, victory in the Second World War came at a cost of 400,000 dead and 800,000 wounded service personnel and very few civilian lives. These figures paled in comparison to 70 million combatant and civilian lives lost by the other belligerent nations, making this the bloodiest and most destructive conflict in human history.

Apart from decisive victories, strategic plans, innovative technologies, and courageous men and women in the armed services, two other key factors can be seen in the American victory: the commitment of the entire nation to the war effort, and the overwhelming industrial production of a global logistical system. If the Second World War represented the pinnacle of an American way of war, then certainly an American way of logistics was necessary to make possible the mobilization and ongoing support of the overwhelming force directed at the Axis powers. Military historian David E. Johnson labels this the American "Arsenal of Attrition."[3] This evocative phrase points to the ultimate impact of American industrial potential that not only equipped the U.S. military to fight the war but also helped keep the Allies in the war.

While the atomic bombs did hasten the end of the Second World War, they also heralded the beginning of new age of warfare. Truly, the weapons of mass destruction gave credence to the argument that the Second World War was a total war. So, too, did the German extermination of at least six million Jews and people in other groups during the Holocaust. After 1945, no more could nations expect to fight total wars in pursuit of ultimate goals without reaching nuclear war or committing genocide. The stakes were too high to risk another global war becoming a total war with total destruction. Thus, over the next 45 years, the United States fought a different sort of conflict—the Cold War.

Notes

1 E. B. Sledge, *With the Old Breed: At Peleliu and Okinawa* (Novato, CA: Presidio Press, 1981), pp. 159, 134.
2 "D-Day" has become synonymous with the landing on Normandy on June 6, 1944. However, the term referred to any such amphibious assault or landing in the Second World War. The term D-Day can be used as a generic term for the actual day of any amphibious landing in the European or Pacific theaters. The "D" stands for "day," so it could perhaps be written "Day-Day." In the same way, the exact time of an assault is known at "H-Hour," in which "H" stands for "hour."
3 See the wording in the title of chapter 3 in David E. Johnson, *Fast Tanks and Heavy Bombers: Innovation in the U.S. Army, 1917–1945* (Ithaca: Cornell University Press, 1917–1945).

Short Bibliography

Adams, Michael C. C. *The Best War Ever: America and World War II.* 2nd ed. Baltimore: The Johns Hopkins University Press, 2015.

Atkinson, Rick. *The Liberation Trilogy.* 3 vols. New York: Holt, 2002–2013.

Bailey, Beth, and David Farber. *The First Strange Place: Race and Sex in World War II Hawaii.* New York: The Free Press, 1992.

Burrell, Robert S. *The Ghosts of Iwo Jima.* College Station: Texas A&M University Press, 2006.

Crane, Conrad C. *American Airpower Strategy in World War II: Bombs, Cities, Civilians, and Oil.* Lawrence: University Press of Kansas, 2016.

D'este, Carlos. *Patton: A Genius for War.* New York: HarperCollins, 1995.

Dimbleby, Jonathan. *The Battle of the Atlantic: How the Allies Won the War.* New York: Oxford University Press, 2016.

Dolski, Michael. *D-Day Remembered: The Normandy Landings in American Collective Memory.* Knoxville: University of Tennessee Press, 2016.

Dower, John W. *War without Mercy: Race and Power in the Pacific War.* New York: Pantheon, 1986.

Ehlers, Robert S., Jr. *The Mediterranean Air War: Airpower and Allied Victory.* Lawrence: University Press of Kansas, 2015.

Frank, Richard B. *Guadalcanal: The Definitive Account of the Landmark Battle.* New York: Random House, 1990.

James, D. Clayton. *The Years of MacArthur, 1941–1945.* Boston: Houghton Mifflin, 1975.

Kennedy, David M. *Freedom from Fear: The American People in Depression and War, 1929–1945.* New York: Oxford University Press, 1999.

Koistinen, Paul A. C. *Arsenal of World War II: The Political Economy of American Warfare, 1940–1945.* Lawrence: University Press of Kansas, 2004.

MacDonald, Charles B. *Company Commander.* New York: Ballantine, 1968.

McManus, John C. *The Dead and Those About to Die: D-Day: The Big Red One at Omaha Beach.* New York: New American Books, 2015.

Meyer, Leisa D. *Creating G.I. Jane: Sexuality and Power in the Women's Army Corps during World War II.* New York: New York University Press, 1996.

Mierzejewski, Alfred C. *The Collapse of the German War Economy, 1944–1945: Allied Air Power and the Germany National Railway.* Chapel Hill: University of North Carolina Press, 1988.

Morison, Samuel Eliot. *History of United States Naval Operations in World War II.* 15 vols. Boston: Little, Brown, 1947–1962.

Pogue, Forrest C. *George C. Marshall.* 4 vols. New York: Viking, 1963–1987.

Potter, E. B. *Nimitz.* Annapolis: Naval Institute Press, 1976.

Ryan, Cornelius. *A Bridge Too Far.* New York: Simon & Schuster, 2974.

Schrijvers, Peter. *Bloody Pacific: American Soldiers at War with Japan.* 2nd ed. Basingstroke: United Kingdom, 2010.

Spector, Ronald. *Eagle against the Sun: The American War with Japan.* New York: Vintage, 1985.

Taaffe, Stephen R. *MacArthur's Jungle War: The 1944 New Guinea Campaign.* Lawrence: University Press of Kansas, 1998.

Takaki, Ronald. *Double Victory: A Multicultural History of America in World War II.* New York: Back Bay Books, 2001.

Ulbrich, David J. *Preparing for Victory: Thomas Holcomb and the Making of the Modern Marine Corps, 1936–1943.* Annapolis: Naval Institute Press, 2011.

Urwin, Gregory J. W. *Facing Fearful Odds: The Siege of Wake Island.* Lincoln: University of Nebraska Press, 1997.

U.S. Army Center of Military History. *The U.S. Army in World War II.* 78 vols. Washington: Office of the Chief of Military History, U.S. Army, 1947–1992.

U.S. Marine Corps. *History of the U.S. Marine Corps Operations in World War II.* 5 vols. Washington: Historical Branch, G-3 Division, Headquarters Marine Corps, 1958–1968.

Walker, J. Samuel. *Prompt and Utter Destruction: Truman and the Use of the Atomic Bombs against Japan.* Rev. ed. Chapel Hill: University of North Carolina Press, 2004.

Weigley, Russell F. *Eisenhower's Lieutenants: The Campaign of France and Germany, 1944–1945.* Bloomington: Indiana University Press, 1981.

Weinberg, Gerhard L. *A World at Arms: A Global History of World War II.* 2nd ed. Cambridge: Cambridge University, 2005.

TIMELINE

1947	1948	1948	1950–53	June 1950
National Defense Act	Women's Armed Forces Integrated Act	Executive Order 9981	The Korean War	North Korea invaded South Korea

Chapter 13

American National Security in the Early Cold War, 1945–1960

Following the end of the Second World War in 1945, the world looked to the future with hope for lasting peace. Only the United States and the Soviet Union rose from the rubble of history's most destructive conflict with preponderances of military and economic power. The common objective of defeating the Axis powers had sustained the Grand Alliance of the United States, the Soviet Union, and the United Kingdom throughout the war. However, with the old European power structure now swept from the continent, the Americans and Soviets eyed each other warily. A brief and tenuous honeymoon followed until 1947, when efforts to transcend differences, fears, and objectives between Washington and Moscow failed. Then the world plunged into the "Cold War." This confrontation pitted the democratic, capitalist United States against the totalitarian, communist Soviet Union, but it did not degenerate into a direct shooting war between the nations.

The United States would never return to isolationism. Instead, Americans attempted to restrain the spread of communism in the war-torn world and stop the extension of the Soviet Union's influence. A single thread of containment can be seen weaving its way through this chapter: Presidents Harry S. Truman and Dwight D. Eisenhower tried to contain Soviet and communist expansion, but they did so in different ways.

In this chapter, students will learn about:

- Starting the Cold War and establishing Truman's strategy of symmetric containment.
- Reorganizing the missions, structures, and social relations of the United States military.
- Fighting the Korean War as the first major proxy conflict between the superpowers.
- Eisenhower's "New Look" strategy and the evolution of asymmetric containment.

Peace in the Postwar World?

Thanks to efforts by the late President Franklin D. Roosevelt, delegations from several dozen nations met in San Francisco, California, during the summer of 1945. They wanted to form a new organization, the United Nations (U.N.). The Charter of the United Nations, as the resulting treaty is known, set up an organization that would ideally find peaceful ways to avoid another cataclysmic global war. Two legislative bodies comprised the U.N.: The larger General Assembly gave equal representation to each member nation in the world, and the smaller Security Council gave permanent seats to the five founding nations (United States, Soviet Union, France, United Kingdom, and China) and included several other rotating member states as eligible voters. The U.N. Security Council possessed the power to decide when peace was threatened; to determine the best reaction; and, if necessary, to direct the member states to use force. This capability harkened back to the concept of collective security enunciated in the League of Nations in 1920. Nevertheless, any permanent member could also veto decisions made by the Security Council.

Apart from establishing the U.N., the victorious Allies cooperated in other postwar efforts to seek justice for the victims of atrocities by the German and Japanese regimes. They set up military tribunals where those nations' military and political leaders faced charges of war crimes, crimes against humanity, and crimes against peace. The defendants found guilty faced execution or imprisonment.

Meanwhile, Allied forces settled into occupation duties in Germany and Austria. Their areas of responsibility had been sketched out at the Yalta Conference in February 1945 and at the Potsdam Conference in July 1945 as part of pragmatic agreements that helped secure ultimate victory in the Second World War. The Soviets kept the territories they captured from the Germans. Among these were satellite states like Poland and Romania and occupied zones such as what would become the German Democratic Republic (East Germany). These nations became known as the Eastern Bloc. The Americans, British, and reestablished French governments divided up the rest of the nation in what would become the Federal Republic of Germany (West Germany). The capital city of Berlin can be considered a microcosm of the nation's situation. Although 125 miles inside the Soviet zone, Berlin was also divided into four partitions with the Soviets controlling the eastern part of the city and the three other powers controlling the western part.

A line of political ideology thus demarcated the two Berlins, the two Germanys, and the two Europes. A speech by former British Prime Minister Winston Churchill encapsulated the suspicious attitude so prevalent in the United States. In 1946, speaking in Missouri, he coined the term "iron curtain" to describe the Soviet's totalitarian control that extended from the Baltic Sea in Northern Europe to the Mediterranean in the South. Churchill's speech gave rhetorical flair to American fears of communist and Soviet expansion.

In Asia, the American military assumed occupation duties to a much greater extent than in Europe. President Harry S. Truman demanded that the United States play the primary role in reconstructing a postwar Japan. The Soviets, for their part, entered the war against Japan in August 1945, which was too late to exert much influence in Japanese reconstruction. Governance of Japan fell under control of General Douglas MacArthur, who was named Supreme Commander, Allied Powers. The occupation of Japan by American forces began in August 1945 and lasted until April 1952, when they left and Japan gained independent nationhood. The United States also funded programs that stimulated growth in the nation's industries. In what may have been his greatest accomplishment, MacArthur formed a constitutional government based in Japan. Hirohito remained on the throne but ruled as a figurehead without divine status. In this way, Japan went from being a rogue nation to becoming an American ally. It is worth noting that the American effort to rebuild Japan, just as Germany, was also motivated by a belief that a prosperous Japan would be less susceptible to communist revolutionary influences.

The Start of the Cold War and the Advent of the Truman Doctrine

The end of the Second World War created an international environment that required a new military vocabulary and a new strategic tone. Only the United States and the Soviet Union emerged from the conflict as "superpowers." This term described these two nations as possessing military and economic capabilities so great that no other nations could directly challenge them. The postwar honeymoon between the United States and the Soviet Union lasted until 1947. By then, however, tensions between the superpowers erupted into a new type of conflict, the Cold War. Unlike "hot wars," cold wars are clashes of ideologies, symbols, and proxy fights between adversarial nations and their allies rather than formally declared "shooting" wars like the Second World War.

By 1949, both superpowers possessed atomic bombs in their arsenals. If a hot war should start between them, many contemporaries worried that use of these would be inevitable, resulting in the total destruction of both the United States and the Soviet Union. Later in the 1950s, the two nations developed infinitely more destructive nuclear weapons that raised the stakes of any potential shooting war. Because such outcomes were hardly desirable, the Americans and the Soviets directly confronted each other with words and combated each other indirectly in proxy wars between their respective allies. Proxy wars included the Korean War, where Americans fought North Koreans and Chinese, and later the Vietnam War, where Americans fought North Vietnamese and Viet Cong. These adversaries received money, equipment, and other support from the Soviet Union.

Throughout the Cold War, most American leaders and the American people assumed that all communists held similar goals that emanated from the Soviet Union. This single-minded lens through which Americans saw the world made their reactions seem myopic to observers in the twenty-first century. Even so, the Cold War was a zero-sum game for Americans living through it. Victory meant maintaining freedom and democracy, and defeat mean succumbing to communism and totalitarianism.

American fears appeared to be legitimate in Europe, where a devastated Germany, recovering France, and liberated Greece suffered from high unemployment and low industrial production. Such great instability made these nations' peoples susceptible to the siren song of communism, which promised economic equality, land redistribution, and guaranteed employment. The American conception of communism can also be compared to a virus that could infect desperate people with motivation to overthrow governments. Attempting to stop the spread of this virus, President Harry S. Truman used his economic and military aid to inoculate the peoples of Europe against communism as a part of a new American strategy known as "containment." This concept was articulated by George F. Kennan, an expert on the Soviet Union in the U.S. Department of State. In a seminal article in 1946, he argued that

> the main element of any United States policy toward the Soviet Union must be a longterm, patient but firm and vigilant containment of Russian expansive tendencies . . . . Soviet pressure against the free institutions of the Western world is something that can be contained by the adroit and vigilant application of counterforce at a series of constantly shifting geographical and political points, corresponding to the shifts and maneuvers of Soviet policy, but which cannot be charmed or talked out of existence.[1]

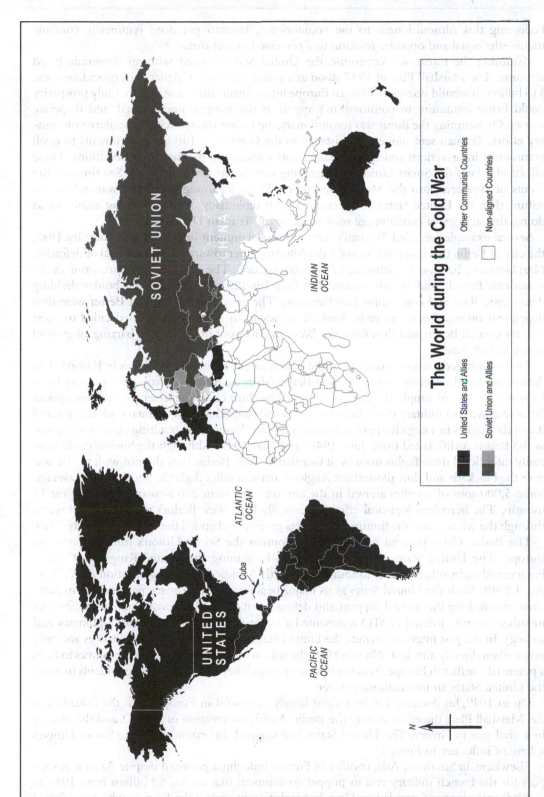

Map 13.1 The World During the Cold War

Following this admonishment to use counterforce, Truman practiced symmetric containment—the equal and opposite reaction to a perceived or real threat. [2]

Assuming the threat was economic, the United States reacted with an economic-based response. The Marshall Plan of 1947 stood as a prime example of Americans providing some $13 billion to rebuild war-torn Western Europe into a financially stable region. Only prosperity could bring immunity to communism's appeal to the hungry, unemployed, and desperate masses. Or, assuming the threat was revolutionary, the nation reacted with a counterrevolutionary effort. Truman sent monetary assistance to the Greek and Turkish governments to quell communist insurrections and helped bolster anti-communist regimes in both nations. These efforts also kept the Soviet Union from gaining easy access from the Black Sea through the Straits of Bosporus into the Mediterranean Sea. Lastly, assuming the threat was military in nature, then the United States could counter with diplomacy or force as a last resort. In so doing, this strategy of containment took shape in the Truman Doctrine.

Several examples revealed Truman's symmetric containment in Europe and Asia. By 1948, the city of Berlin that had once brought the Allies together toward a common goal of defeating Nazi Germany became a touchstone of immense friction. The city's western parts came under American, French, and British control, but they lay 125 miles behind the border dividing democratic West and communist East Germany. The people living in West Berlin were thus dependent on supplies to arrive by land, air, or water. In April, the Soviets decided to exert control over all Berlin, and thus force the Western Allies out of the city, by barring all ground access in late June.

This constituted a major challenge to the commitment of the United States in Europe. The Americans faced a decision point: Let West Berlin fall under Soviet control, apply military force to reopen access, or supply the city by aircraft. The third choice represented the best option, because it avoided military confrontation with locally superior Soviet military advantages, and it cast the Soviets in a negative light as besiegers of West Berlin. The resulting operation, known as the Berlin Airlift, lasted from June 1948 until May 1949. Although the Soviets could have easily interdicted these flights from West German to West Berlin, they did not wish to risk war over the blockade and thus allowed the Anglo-American relief flights to continue. On average, some 5,000 tons of supplies arrived in the city on more than 200 airplanes each day for 11 months. The herculean logistical effort successfully kept West Berlin's people fed and warm through the winter until the flummoxed Soviets gave up and ended the blockade in May 1949.

The Berlin Crisis pointed to the need to counter the Soviet Union's military power in Europe. The United States solved this problem by joining the United Kingdom, Canada, France, and eight other nations to found the North Atlantic Treaty Organization (NATO) in April 1949. With the United States as its major benefactor and primary partner, this military alliance called for the mutual support and defense to include, if necessary, military defense of member nations. Joining NATO represented a major departure in American diplomacy and strategy. In the past interwar periods, the United States remained aloof from alliances and only acted when directly attacked. Now in 1949, the nation committed its military resources to fight a potential conflict in Europe. Truman thus stepped well beyond all previous presidents to make the United States an international partner.

Up to 1949, his doctrine can be judged largely successful in Europe, with the initiation of the Marshall Plan, the effort during the Berlin Airlift, the creation of NATO, and the victory in a civil war in Greece. The United States had stopped the extension of the Soviet Union's sphere of influence in Europe.

Elsewhere, in Southeast Asia, conflict in French Indochina persisted despite American support for the French military and its puppet government that totaled $2 billion from 1946 to 1954. Revolutionary forces led by Ho Chi Minh fought against the French, who were forced to withdraw from French Indochina after their defeat at the Battle of Dien Bien Phu, also in 1954. Ho embraced communist goals like land redistribution and brutal retribution against his enemies, yet he and his Vietnamese followers also espoused the nationalistic object of independence. Regardless of this dual motivation, Truman and the later presidents could only see Ho's communist ideology as a serious threat to the entire region.

It was in China that President Truman and the United States failed to contain communist expansion. Following the defeat of Japan in 1945, the decades-long civil war resumed between Chiang Kai-Shek's nationalist government and Mao Zedong's communist revolutionary movement. Truman sent supplies and financial aid to Chiang, but Truman refused to commit American military forces because he did not want to start a wider war with the Soviet Union over American military intervention in China. Chiang's forces crumbled under the weight of battlefield defeats and internal corruption. By October 1949, Mao won the conflict, established the new People's Republic of China, and created one of history's most cruel regimes. Remnants of Chiang's followers fled to Taiwan, an island off the Chinese coast in the Pacific Ocean where he established the rival Republic of China. Even after he took power, Mao never forgot the assistance that the United States gave to his enemy, nor would he trust the Americans.

The loss of China to communism pointed to the need for a more consistent American strategy. At Truman's request, the "Report to the National Security Council—NSC-68" was completed in April 1950. The classified document came from the U.S. National Security Council (NSC), which was created in 1947. The NSC provided expert strategic and diplomatic advice to presidents. Its membership included the president, the vice president, and the secretaries of state, defense, and treasury. The general or admiral serving as chairman of the Joint Chiefs of Staff also acted as military advisor to the NSC.

NSC-68 effectively made the United States into a "national security state," where containment of communism stood as the top strategic priority. According to the report, communism imbued its followers with an ideology resembling religious faith, and the Soviet Union sought a global empire with revolution as the mean to achieve that goal. NSC-58 thus cast the Cold War as an apocalyptic struggle between good and evil, but the document also created a dilemma for Truman and every president who followed him: Could the United States fight a "limited war" with conventional forces to contain communism?

Social Changes in the U.S. Armed Forces, 1945–48

In addition to the sweeping changes in America's strategy and diplomacy, the U.S. military underwent similarly dramatic social transformations after the end of the Second World War. Some one million African Americans and 300,000 women had served in uniform during the conflict. Of these, all blacks served in segregated units with Caucasian senior officers. Women also faced limits in advancement, and they were expected to serve only for the duration of the conflict before leaving the military to return to civilian life. Both groups, however, gained senses of independence and pride from their wartime service. The critical contributions by women, African Americans, and other minorities likewise undermined many bigoted assumptions held by white civilians and service personnel alike.

Although aware of existing racism and sexism in America, President Harry Truman set about transforming the racial and gender policies of the U.S. military. In Congress, Republican Representative Margaret Chase Smith of Maine introduced legislation to grant regular status to women in the U.S. military. She faced opposition not only from men in the armed services and in Congress but also women in American society. They repeated many of the wartime worries that women's military service would subvert and muddle feminine gender roles deemed culturally acceptable. Only in times of great national need could women suspend their domestic responsibilities as nurturers and mothers. Peacetime duty, let alone integration, should not be options.

Representative Smith was hardly alone in her fight, however. She received help from the likes of General Dwight D. Eisenhower, General Omar N. Bradley, and recently appointed Secretary of Defense James Forrestal, all of whom offered supportive testimony before Congress. This coalition overcame opposition to win enough votes to pass the Women's Armed Service Integration Act. President Truman signed the legislation on June 12, 1948. This Act represented a major step toward gender equality because it gave regular status to women in the U.S. Army, Navy, Marine Corps, and newly established Air Force. Integration across gender lines, however, did not include women's service in combat ground units, on naval vessels, or in combat aircraft squadrons. Moreover, the percentage of females in uniform could not exceed two percent of total personnel, nor could flag ranks (general officers) be attained by women.

African Americans in uniform also faced uncertainty in the postwar era. They did not believe that they fought against the racism of Adolf Hitler's Nazi Germany only to come to home to continued segregation and discrimination. The African Americans realized that their wartime goal of "Double V"—double victory against racism abroad and at home—was only half fulfilled when the Second World War ended. Decorated African-American veterans were forced to sit at the backs of buses, use separate restrooms, endure racial epithets, and sometimes much worse at the hands of bigoted whites in the United States. Stories of racial harassment and violence directed against black veterans angered President Truman, so he helped African Americans and other minorities in uniform as a part of his larger effort to extend civil rights.

This was a brave step for Truman. Unlike the women's integration, he could not expect to pass a similar bill to end racist policies in the U.S. military. He did not have the votes in Congress because the most senior representatives and senators came from Southern states where antiblack racism affected voting rights and legal systems. They could block the president's legislation. Finding himself at an impasse in Congress, Truman exercised his other viable option by issuing an executive order. Such a directive carried the full force of law within the executive branch.

Acting in his role as commander-in-chief, Truman issued Executive Order 9881 on July 26, 1948. In an instant, he reversed the military's institutionalized policies of discrimination and segregation based on race, religion, or national origin. Ending such policies took many years because some racist civilian and military leaders tried to slow the process. The last all-black unit was desegregated in 1954, which was the same year that the U.S. Supreme Court's decision in *Brown v. Board of Education* banned segregation in American public schools. Nevertheless, vestiges of racism would remain entrenched in the military establishment and the entire nation for decades thereafter.

Postwar Demobilization, Military Unification, and Technological Transformation

Following the end of the Second World War, the U.S. military experienced dramatic demobilization. Its manpower and expenditures decreased from 12 million people and a $91 billion budget in 1945 to 1.6 million and a $10.3 billion budget in 1947. Similarly, severe demobilizations followed every past conflict in part because some Americans wished to return to prewar isolationism. Those in uniform also wanted to get back to their peacetime lives. Such was the American tradition of the citizen-soldier who served during a conflict's duration and returned home after its end. Lastly, most Americans and their elected officials could not tolerate continued expenditures for a massive national defense establishment in peacetime.

Too often, however, cuts in personnel were made without sufficient attention to expertise or experience. The more time overseas or in combat one possessed, the quicker that person would receive discharge papers. This left the U.S. military with the least-experienced and thus the least-prepared service personnel later in the 1940s. Steep budget reductions also plagued existing military units, leaving them understrength and unable to afford new equipment or adequate training. Consequently, combat readiness declined sharply among units and individuals alike.

For his part, President Harry Truman favored reductions in manpower and equipment. At the same time, he and other outward-looking Americans did recognize that the United States needed to retain sufficiently potent armed forces to present a credible deterrent to potential enemies such as the Soviet Union. This caused a conundrum: how to meet a serious threat with limited resources. Deterrence, for Truman and succeeding presidents, represented one viable means of containing Soviet expansion. The U.S. military needed to be strong enough to counter Soviet military threats and thereby discourage Soviet actions.

One major point of contention in demobilization occurred over how best to maintain that credible military deterrent. Lessons from the Second World War pointed to the need to find a realistic means of mobilizing the American people to fight in future conflicts. To give the nation a pool of trained men, Truman began working in late 1945 with Secretary of the Navy James Forrestal and Army Chief of Staff General George C. Marshall to try to create a Universal Military Training program. They argued that this provided an inexpensive alternative to a large, costly standing military. Universal Military Training also gave the nation the brute force to make good on its goals of deterrence and containment. However, these selling points fell on too many deaf ears in Congress and the American public. The nation had just endured war under conscription, so they refused to tolerate any required time in service.

Legislation for Universal Military Training foundered in Congress. This repudiation left the U.S. military with an existing program for mobilization. In time of war, the small regular military would initially be supplemented by the National Guard and Reserves. Additional manpower could be procured under the newly signed Selective Service Act of 1948, a law that required all American males 18 years old and older to register for service.

During the mobilization debate, another potentially major transformation of the U.S. military caused internal dissension. The U.S. Army's Chief of Staff General George C. Marshall and U.S. Army Air Force's General Henry Arnold pushed for a merger of the Army and the Navy into a single service. Then-Secretary of War Robert Patterson also favored folding all the branches into one service. Such a unified entity would, they hoped, be headed by a powerful civilian secretary and advised by a general staff. Marshall, Arnold, and President Truman saw "military unification" as the best means to centralize control of the entire military establishment. If adopted, this would have constituted the most sweeping structural reform in American military history.

The concept of unification dated back to the Second World War when American resources could not be balanced between entrenched interservice rivalries and competing strategic priorities. If unification occurred, the Army would benefit because it would resolve perennial problems of resource allocation with the Navy. The Army Air Force would likewise achieve independence as a service separate from the Army and thus enjoy equal footing with the Army and Navy.

However, Navy Secretary James Forrestal and Chief of Naval Operations Admiral Chester W. Nimitz resisted this push for unification because they believed it would minimize the sea service's autonomy and restrict development of naval aviation and naval atomic programs. The Marine Corps' Commandant General Alexander Vandegrift also opposed unification because he suspected the Corps would be marginalized as a shipboard security force. All sides made their cases in testimony in Congressional hearings, closed-door meetings, and public forums.

Several bills made their way through Congress only to be tabled or defeated. Finally, however, compromises resulted in the passage of the National Security Act of 1947. In some ways, this legislation included ground-breaking improvements that helped the nation's decision-making process. It created the National Security Council to be the president's highest-level advisory group and ended the unification crisis by creating a new Department of Defense. It could be considered a hybrid entity because it combined the existing War and Navy Departments. The 1947 Act, however, did not completely unify the military into a single department controlled by a single civilian secretary and a single general staff.

The new Secretary of Defense combined the Secretaries of War and the Navy into one cabinet-level post that coordinated American military efforts and allocated resources. But this new post did not exercise complete control of the department. Beneath the Secretary of Defense were three new civilian secretaries for the Departments of the Army, Navy, and Air Force that diluted the direct influence of the Secretary of Defense. The Joint Chiefs of Staff maintained its role as the body of senior military leaders. However, there was no chairman of the Joint Chiefs to coordinate their efforts. The 1947 Act gave the Air Force its own secretary and senior general on the Joint Chiefs of Staff, thereby granting the Air Force equality and autonomy with the Army and Navy. Lastly, the Act formalized the roles and missions of all four branches, including the U.S. Marine Corps.

Despite the structure put in place by the National Security Act of 1947, interservice antagonism increased because the Army, Navy, Air Force, and Marine Corps jockeyed for limited budget resources in an uncertain strategic environment. Control of atomic weapons stood as the greatest point of contention. The leaders of the Air Force and the Navy vied for control of the super-weapons as well as the vehicles to deliver them to targets. The Army's leadership, however, languished in a weak position, arguing that wars still required boots on the ground to defeat enemy forces and secure territory.

The new Department of Defense failed to alleviate the rivalry between the services. This issue came to a head in 1948 when the Air Force tried to monopolize control of the atomic weapons and their delivery systems. Secretary of Defense Louis A. Johnson sided with the Air Force because he believed strategic use of atomic weapons to be the best means of deterring and containing the Soviet Union's expansion. The U.S. Air Force helped its fight with the Navy for control of atomic weapons because it created the force structure necessary to support this mission in the Strategic Air Command (SAC).

Led by Lieutenant General Curtis E. LeMay beginning in 1948, SAC developed war plans for using atomic weapons and possessed the aircraft to deliver them to targets. He had long been a vocal advocate of strategic bombardment. During the last months of the Second World War, he commanded the Army Air Force in the Pacific theater when American aircraft firebombed many Japanese cities and eventually dropped the atomic bombs on Hiroshima and Nagasaki. LeMay's ardent belief that airpower represented the strategic panacea in modern warfare earned him the nickname "Bombs Away LeMay." He commanded SAC for the next nine years until 1957. Then, he became Vice Chief of Staff of the Air Force until 1961 and finally Chief of Staff from 1961 to 1965, thus dominating the service for two decades.

Secretary of Defense Johnson undercut the Navy by canceling construction plans for the new *United States*-class super-aircraft carriers, decreasing the Navy's active aircraft carrier force to only four such vessels and reducing the proportion of aircraft for those vessels. Johnson slashed expenditures for the Marine Corps' manpower and amphibious capabilities. The U.S. Army likewise experienced losses of funding that brought the number of active duty personnel to some 600,000 soldiers that year, in 1949. A year earlier, for example, Army Chief of Staff General Omar Bradley quipped that his service "could not fight its way out of a paper bag."[3]

Not only did Secretary Johnson sponsor the U.S. Air Force at the expense of its sister services but he and President Harry Truman also demanded that Army and Navy civilian and military leadership support their patronage of the Air Force. For his part, General Bradley did not publicly oppose his commander-in-chief or the defense secretary in 1949. He watched in silence as his Army was marginalized.

In October 1949, the Navy's leadership reacted to Secretary Johnson's unpopular decisions. Secretary of the Navy John Sullivan resigned his post in protest of the cuts, and senior admirals publicly confronted Secretary Johnson and President Truman by extension. They worried that such favoritism shown to the Air Force hurt their service's combat capabilities. In what became known as the "Revolt of the Admirals," the Chief of Naval Operations Admiral Louis Denfield and others testified before Congress that the Air Force's long-range strategic bombers were vulnerable to Soviet fighter attack, and that America's complete reliance on atomic weapons was neither realistic nor moral. In the aftermath, Admiral Denfield was dismissed for his criticisms of Johnson's decisions.

Despite the Navy's protests, the Air Force held onto primary responsibility for atomic weapons and assumed responsibility for long-range missile development. These roles cannot be underestimated. They effectively turned the SAC into a mini-Air-Force. Just as importantly, SAC's control of atomic (and later nuclear) weapons combined with American faith in the primacy of those weapons' destructive power to dominate strategic planning. The Soviet's acquisition of their own atomic weapons in 1949 helped solidify American reliance on these weapons.

Nevertheless, the Navy did stake some claim to developing naval aviation arms as a means of delivering atomic weapons on target. The sea service also expanded its research and development of a different application of atomic technology—the eventual launch of nuclear-powered submarines and surface warships allowed the Navy to make essential contributions to national defense. The new propulsion systems also speeded a captain named Hyman G. Rickover on his way to becoming the father of the nuclear Navy.

The U.S. Army, however, failed to overcome the focus on atomic weapons and other advanced technologies. Massed infantry and armor in ground operations were considered passé in the new age of fast strategic bombers carrying weapons of mass destruction. It would take an unexpected conflict in Korea in mid-1950 with equally unexpected conventional ground force requirements to allow the Army to reassert its place in the American military.

The Korean War: Invasion and Reaction, June–August 1950

From 1945 to 1950, President Harry S. Truman based his national security policies and strategies on symmetric containment—the attempt to stop communist or Soviet threats with equal and opposite reactions in perceived crisis areas. As Winston Churchill stated in 1946, an "iron curtain" separated Europe into two armed camps beholden to either the United States or the Soviet Union. Far away in northeastern Asia, a similar ideological contradiction physically divided the Korean peninsula at the 38th parallel, separating Soviet-supported North Korea from American-supported South Korea. The division was a legacy of the end of the Second World War after Japan surrendered control of Korea. After advancing south to that parallel by August 15, 1945, the Soviet Union installed a communist government led by dictator Kim Il-sung in the territory. Meanwhile, the United States supported Syngman Rhee's anticommunist government in the south. Both Kim and Rhee wished to eliminate the other's government and unify Korea under their respective rules. At the same time, each viciously purged threats inside their respective regimes.

Although relations between North and South Korea remained very tense after 1945, crises erupting in Europe and elsewhere in Asia took precedence in the minds of Truman and other American leaders. The biggest surprise and most pressing emergency to date in the Cold War demanded an immediate realignment of American focus, when, on a rainy Sunday morning, on June 25, 1950, more than 150,000 North Korean soldiers streamed cross the border into the south.[4] Though ordered by Kim Il-sung, the invasion began only after he received approval from the more-powerful communist leaders Mao Zedong and Joseph Stalin.

The North's invasion of South Korea caught U.S. military and civilian leadership off guard. The American military was not only unprepared for this crisis at the strategic and logical levels but it was likewise unable to react swiftly at the operational or tactical levels. President Truman and his senior advisors agreed that North Korea's act needed to be countered with military force, as outlined by George Kennan and in NSC-68. Indeed, Truman endorsed NSC-68 because of the North's attack.

On June 27, Truman received support in the form of United Nations Security Council Resolution 83 that labeled the North Korean invasion a "breach of peace" and called for military aid to be sent to South Korea. Thus, the conflict in Korea became an exercise in collective security, or euphemistically termed a "police action." Over time, a U.N. coalition of more than 20 nations sent aid to South Korea, but the United States shouldered most of the burden.

For his part, Truman authorized the commitment of American ground and air forces to combat operations in South Korea. However, he kept this conflict limited by not requesting a declaration of war by Congress. Truman also dispatched an aircraft carrier group from the Seventh Fleet to provide air and naval support. He gave control of all American and U.N. forces in the conflict to General Douglas MacArthur, who began rushing available units from Japan to Korea with orders to start counterattacking. Neither MacArthur nor his advisors, including his Chief of Staff Major General Edward M. Almond, realized the full extent of the North's invasion. A disconnect existed between the harsh realities on the Korean front lines and the optimistic perceptions in MacArthur's headquarters in Japan. His long-standing practice of surrounding himself with loyalists like Almond was proving costly. They either refused to recognize the desperation of the situation or declined to tell MacArthur the truth.

By early July, North Korean forces rapidly advanced southward, capturing the South's capital city of Seoul and the port city of Inchon on the peninsula's western coast. The few ill-prepared South Korean units failed to halt this overwhelming enemy onslaught. Most fled south toward an area around the port city of Pusan. Their nation appeared on the edge of collapse until American reinforcements began arriving on the first of July. However, these soldiers from the U.S. Eighth Army stationed in Japan were hardly combat-ready. Few had seen combat, and years of budget cuts reduced training to bare minimal levels. The soft living in Japan created a lax environment where physical fitness standards also declined. Making matters still worse, American weapons and equipment were often pulled from leftover Second World War stockpiles.

The first clash occurred on July 5 between some 5,000 men and 36 tanks of the North Korean Army and barely 525 American soldiers of Task Force Smith. The Americans tried to block the enemy advance long enough to buy time for the South Korean Army's retreat toward Pusan and the arrival of the Americans. Named for its commanding officer Lieutenant Colonel Charles B. Smith, the task force comprised elements of a battalion from the U.S. 24th Infantry Division. Each soldier arrived with only 120 rounds of ammunition and two days of rations. They also lacked sufficient artillery and antitank weapons.

Task Force Smith set up defensive positions straddling a main road near the village of Osan, just 20 miles south of Seoul. Although the Americans occupied some high ground that afforded

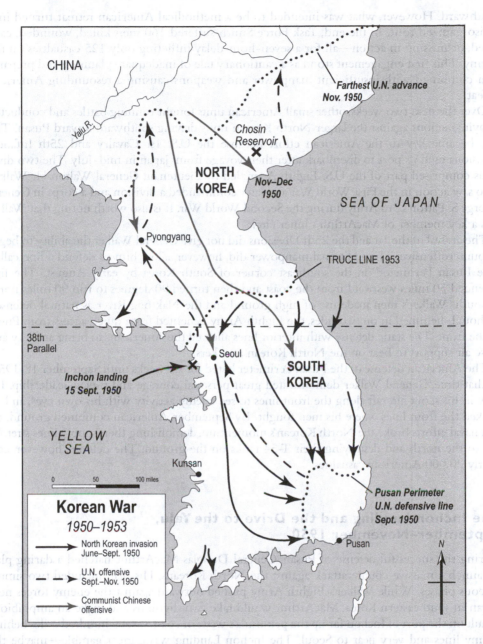

CHINA

Farthest U.N. advance
Nov. 1950

Yalu R.

Chosin
Reservoir   ✕

**NORTH
KOREA**   *Nov–Dec
1950*

SEA OF JAPAN

● Pyongyang

TRUCE LINE 1953

38th
Parallel

✕   ● Seoul

*Inchon landing
15 Sept. 1950*

**SOUTH
KOREA**

*YELLOW
SEA*

● Kunsan

0   50   100 miles

Korean War
1950–1953

→ North Korean invasion
June–Sept. 1950

⇢ U.N. offensive
Sept.–Nov. 1950

➡ Communist Chinese
offensive

*Pusan Perimeter
U.N. defensive line
Sept. 1950*

● Pusan

N

Map 13.2 The Korean War, 1950–1953

good visibility and overlapping fields of fire, their two-mile front was too long to defend against a determined assault. The North Koreans commenced their attack on the morning of July 5, spearheaded by their Russian-made T-34 tanks. The Americans repeatedly hit the tanks with artillery and rocket fire but with few appreciable results. The only true American advantage of air power was negated by the cloudy, rainy weather.

Task Force Smith took heavy casualties during the desperate fighting and failed to stem the enemy tide. Late that afternoon, Colonel Smith ordered his remaining men to withdraw southward. However, what was intended to be a methodical American retreat turned into a disorganized rout. In the end, Task Force Smith suffered 160 men killed, wounded, captured, or missing in action—all for a seven-hour delay inflicting only 125 casualties on the enemy. This first engagement stood as a cautionary tale of inadequate planning and preparation combined with insufficient manpower and weapons causing a resounding American defeat.

Over the next two weeks, other small American units fought running battles and conducted delaying actions against the larger North Korean units driving southward toward Pusan. The city became key to the American effort because the U.S. 1st Cavalry and 25th Infantry Divisions used its port to disembark after their voyage from Japan in mid-July. The two divisions comprised part of the U.S. Eighth Army led by Lieutenant General Walton H. Walker, who saw action in the First World War and later commanded a division and a corps in General George S. Patton's 3rd Army during the Second World War. It is also worth noting that Walker was a key member of MacArthur's inner circle.

The arrival of the 1st and the 25th Divisions did not give General Walker the ability to begin a counteroffensive. The additional manpower did, however, allow him to defend a line called "the Pusan Perimeter" in the southeast corner of South Korea by early August. The line extended 50 miles westward from the coast and then turned 90 degrees to run 90 miles north to south. Walker's men made use of high ground and the Naktong River as natural defenses. Although hemmed in on two sides, the Eighth Army benefited from quick access from Pusan to the front. The static defense with interior lines allowed the Americans to bring artillery and close air support to bear on the North Korean attackers.

The American defense of the Pusan Perimeter lasted for six weeks until September 18, 1950. In that time, General Walker demonstrated great personal courage and tireless leadership. He flew in his scout aircraft along the front lines to see enemy activity with his own eyes, and he walked the front lines where his men fought. By September, American combined ground, air, and naval efforts broke the North Korean's momentum, demolishing their supply lines stretching to the north and destroying their T-34 tanks on the ground. The defense, however, cost nearly 20,000 American casualties.

The Inchon Landing and the Drive to the Yalu, September–November 1950

During the successful defense of Pusan, General Douglas MacArthur hatched a daring plan to launch a massive counterattack against the North Koreans. His plan included two simultaneous phases. While Walker's Eighth Army pushed outward against the enemy forces near Pusan in southeastern Korea, MacArthur would take two divisions and make an amphibious assault on the port of Inchon far up the peninsula's western coast, several hundred miles behind enemy lines and very near to Seoul. The Inchon Landing was a great gamble—maybe the greatest in the general's career. If successful, this flanking maneuver against Inchon would allow the Americans to drive eastward across the Korean peninsula and cut off the North Korean supply lines.

Such a landing required that MacArthur cobble together troops and units to fill out the 7th Infantry Division and the 1st Marine Division. He placed these into X Corps under command of Major General Almond, who also retained his role as Chief of Staff of the Far East Command. This arrangement made command relations in Korea problematic. As a two-star general, Almond was junior to Lieutenant General Walker, but he also exercised greater authority as Chief of Staff to MacArthur.

This muddled chain of command hampered Walker's flexibility and violated the basic principle of unity of command. The American forces were divided into the X Corps and the Eighth Army with no operational coordination between them. For example, contentious planning among the Army, Navy, Air Force, and Marine Corps staffs plagued efforts to deal with enemy shore defenses, extreme tides, and coastal terrain obstacles. The 1st Marine Division's commander, Major General Oliver P. Smith, resented Major General Almond's condescending attitude toward him, nor did the experienced Smith appreciate the novice Almond's dismissive opinions about the ease of amphibious landings.

Despite all the personality, command, and logistical problems, the day of the Inchon amphibious assault finally came on September 15, 1950. American aerial and naval bombardments prepared the way for the landing forces, and they quickly overcame the challenges of defenses, tides, and terrain obstacles with minimal losses in men or equipment. After taking the North Koreans by surprise, American soldiers and Marines needed just two weeks to recapture Seoul. They then sat astride the major supply routes connecting the North Korean forces fighting in the south with their bases in the North proper. Meanwhile, Walker's Eighth Army broke out of the Pusan Perimeter to start driving the enemy toward Almond's X Corps. The North Koreans suffered tens of thousands of casualties before barely 30,000 survivors escaped across the 38th parallel. MacArthur's gamble succeeded beyond all expectations.

During the brief interlude in September while the U.N. and U.S. forces consolidated their gains, American leaders wondered about what to do next. Communism had been contained and the objective of liberating South Korea had been met in accordance with Truman's strategy of symmetric containment. But from the perspectives of President Truman and General MacArthur in the fall of 1950, the devastated North Korean military looked like an easy target, and with its final defeat, unification of both halves of Korea looked like a possibility. In this way, a nation could be reclaimed from communism.

The Chinese and Soviet governments warned that any intrusion by U.S. or U.N. forces beyond the 38th parallel could mean further escalation of the conflict. Fresh from his inspiring success at Inchon, MacArthur ignored these threats as mere bluffs. He received permission from Truman to proceed across the border into North Korea in late September, but the South Korean Army had to lead the way to make this seem like the South's unification effort, rather than an American-supported invasion. MacArthur's assurances notwithstanding, Truman still worried that this limited conflict in Korea might expand into a larger conflict with China or the Soviet Union.

Within a week after the South Koreans crossed the 38th parallel, the United Nations Security Council passed a resolution authorizing U.N. forces to follow them. MacArthur then ordered Almond's X Corps and Walker's Eighth Army to move northward. This thrust northward would turn out to reverse the American and South Korean fortunes. The North Korean Army's resistance collapsed under the weight of this pressure. On same day of October 19 when the enemy capital of Pyongyang was captured, President Truman met with General MacArthur on Wake Island in the Pacific Ocean to confer about future operations. The irrepressibly confident general assured his justifiably cautious commander-in-chief that further expansion in North Korea would not bring China into the war; but, if they did enter the conflict, then American airpower could devastate their ground forces.

The coalition of American, South Korean, and U.N. forces neared the Yalu River along the border with China in late November. Sporadic fighting broke out with Chinese forces. These engagements did not appear to be serious, nor did the Chinese commitment to be sustained. Indeed, some Americans, including MacArthur himself, expected that the conflict would end by Christmas of 1950.

The Surprise Chinese Offensive, November–December 1950

On November 25, the Chinese dashed American hopes for victory by launching a massive counterattack by the Peoples Liberation Army (PLA) across the Yalu River. The Chinese entered the conflict for several reasons, including the communist solidarity they felt with the North Koreans, the fact that a hostile Korea on their border could not be tolerated, and that the Soviet Union had offered support for this action. Some 300,000 soldiers of PLA sent Walton Walker's Eighth Army in northwest Korea and Edward Almond's X Corps in the northeast into full retreat. Just as the two American commanders had not cooperated in their previous advance, so too did they fail to coordinate their withdrawal. Without strong leaders and effective command and control, full U.S. Army divisions fled in disorder in the wake of the Chinese blitz. MacArthur's optimism regarding air power's ability to interdict enemy movement proved to be an empty and costly assumption.

The bitterly cold winter weather and the rugged terrain magnified the rapid advances by the Chinese. Few finished roads existed in the valleys and ravines of the mountains constituting 80 percent of the northern Korean peninsula. These factors slowed the retreat of the tens of thousands of U.S. and U.N. troops. Infantry tried to march on congested roads jammed with tanks, trucks, and vehicles prone to breakdowns in the frigid temperatures. The Chinese, on the contrary, traveled much lighter and traversed the hills and mountains. They could cover greater distances than the Americans.

In the west as part of the Battle of the Chongchon Valley, the U.S. 2nd Infantry Division tried to withdraw south of Pyongyang to safety on November 30. The Chinese meanwhile tried to surround the division and block its path toward the 38th parallel. The American withdrawal became a disorderly retreat as desperate soldiers fought their way along the narrow road through the mountains. Chinese poured machine-gun and mortar fire from high ground along what became be known as "the Gauntlet." Damaged American vehicles blocked parts of the road, and vehicles sometimes rolled over the bodies of soldiers lying in their paths. In less than one week, the beleaguered 2nd Division lost one-third of its manpower or 5,000 men. This made the division combat ineffective. The rest of the Eighth Army escaped the Chinese noose but not without losses in manpower, equipment, and morale.

To the east in the Battle of the Chosin Reservoir, some 70,000 fast-moving Chinese soldiers surprised and surrounded 30,000 U.S. and U.N. troops at this reservoir in a northeastern Korean valley. The Chinese controlled the high ground and blocked the escape route to the south. Most of the Americans came from the 1st Marine Division, which was augmented by several thousand American soldiers of the U.S. 7th Infantry Division and some British Royal Marines. Assessing his situation at Chosin beginning on November 27, U.S. Marine Major General Oliver P. Smith bluntly stated, "Retreat, hell! We're not retreating. We're just advancing in a different direction."

Two Marine regiments to the west of the reservoir broke through enemy lines with the help of close air support from American fighter-bombers. They linked up with the rest of the division holding the reservoir's southern tip in the town of Hagaru-ri. The fighting resulted in more than 4,000 Marine combat casualties. Several thousand more were incapacitated by frostbite and other deleterious effects of the frigid winter weather. By December 4, only 20,000 men remained from the original U.S. and U.N. force.

Once Major General Smith consolidated his forces, he turned his efforts toward making a larger break out toward the south. He declined to meet expectations of Major General Almond that he should destroy his heavy vehicles to speed his movement, or that reinforcements be dropped in by air. Instead, Smith ordered a fighting withdrawal down a narrow road toward the American-held port city of Hangnum. Smith's men defeated the Chinese blocking forces

Figure 13.1 Road Construction in the Mountains of Korea

U.S. Army engineers work to construct roads in remote and rugged terrain on the Korean Peninsula. On one side of the single-lane road stood steep hill, and the other side a cliff dropped off. The Chinese or North Koreans took advantage of these limited areas to place anti-vehicle mines with devastating effects. Similar scenarios also played out countless times in the rough terrain of Afghanistan in Operation ENDURING FREEDOM since 2001.

Source: U.S. Army Signal Corps Photograph, U.S. Army Engineer School History Office Archive

with combined arms operations utilizing infantry units, mobile artillery, and close air support. The 80-mile ordeal ended on December 11 when they arrived in Hangnum. Then Smith and his Marines left the city by ship four days later and sailed to Pusan.

The remaining U.S. and U.N. forces safely evacuated Hangnum on December 24, destroying the port after their withdrawal to keep the Chinese from using its facilities. Sadly, Walton Walker died in an automobile accident just one day before the evacuation was complete. His replacement, Lieutenant General Matthew B. Ridgway, soon arrived to take command of the U.S. Eighth Army. He had gained invaluable experience in the Second World War in an airborne division in Sicily and Normandy and then in the XVIII Airborne Corps during Operation MARKET GARDEN and the Battle of the Bulge. These taught him to be calm yet decisive under fire. Regardless, Ridgway would not be intimidated by MacArthur's imposing persona and soaring ego.

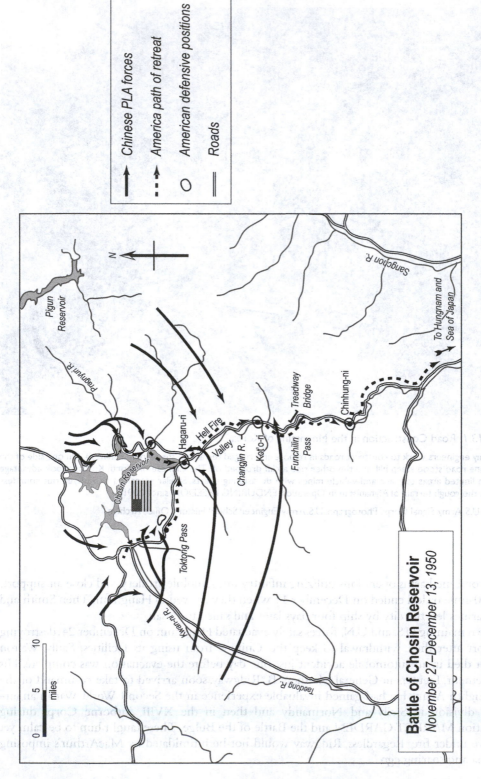

Battle of Chosin Reservoir
November 27–December 13, 1950

Map 13.3 Battle of the Chosin Reservoir, November 27–December 13, 1950

From War of Movement to War of Stalemate, January 1951–July 1953

By early 1951, the battered U.S. and U.N. forces retreated south of the 38th parallel with the Chinese in hot pursuit. Lieutenant General Ridgway inherited an Eighth Army with poor morale. To reverse this negative trend, he relieved subordinate commanders who did not attack the enemy at every opportunity. American units also began to make better use of terrain during flanking maneuvers. Because Ridgway knew that an effective logistical system raised combat effectiveness, he also supplied his troops with more food, mail, and winter clothing. Yes, the Eighth Army continued to withdraw, but Ridgeway wanted the Chinese to overstretch their own supplies, leaving them vulnerable to American air and ground attacks. He thus ordered American units fighting the Chinese to "Find them! Fix them! Fight them! Finish them!"

In February 1951, the U.S. 23rd Regimental Combat Team followed General Ridgway's guidance at the town of the Battle of Chipyong-ni, which lay just to the east of Seoul. He wanted the 23rd to stall the Chinese advance until other American units arrived and counterattacked. Some 25,000 Chinese soldiers made repeated attacks against only 4,500 American and French troops holding Chipyong-ni. But unlike their initial offensive 10 weeks earlier, the Chinese never overran the stubborn American defenses in the three-day battle. Timely aerial supply efforts replenished American food and ammunition. Effective close air support helped inflict 5,000 casualties on the enemy, while the 23rd suffered 350 casualties. As part of the 2nd Infantry Division, the 23rd also helped redeem the division's reputation after its costly losses in late 1950. This decisive victory broke the Chinese momentum. Indeed, the U.S. and U.N. forces launched additional counteroffensives that recaptured the city of Seoul and drove the enemy back to the 38th parallel.

While Ridgway's audacity helped reverse the tide in Korea, another event overshadowed his battlefield victories. The always-tense relationship between President Harry S. Truman and General Douglas MacArthur finally fell apart. The Truman-MacArthur Controversy dated back to the fall of 1950, when the general assured the president that the Chinese would not attack and, if they did, his forces would defeat them. When the Chinese made successful attacks in November, MacArthur's predictions were proven wrong. Nevertheless, he privately and publicly criticized Truman for favoring a limited Korean War—limited to conventional operations that would not spiral out of control into a global or atomic conflict.

The worst of several public statements came on April 5, when one of MacArthur's letters to Representative Joseph Martin (Republican, Massachusetts) was read aloud by Martin on the floor of the U.S. Congress. Knowing full well that his letter would be read, MacArthur called for a second front to be opened against China. In that there was "no substitute for victory" in Korea, MacArthur portrayed Truman's limited war as an unwinnable war. Open criticism of the president's policies was the final straw, and such insubordinate conduct led Truman to relieve the general on April 11, 1951. The president elevated Matthew Ridgway to command all U.N. forces in Korea, and also awarded him his fourth star. Additionally, Lieutenant General James Van Fleet replaced MacArthur's loyal subordinate Edward Almond as the new commander of the U.S. X Corps.

While this drama played out in the American high command, some 700,000 Chinese soldiers attacked along the entire front line. In the west, their progress slowed after defeats in the Battles of Imjin River and Kapyong and stopped just north of Seoul. In the east, South Korean and U.S. X Corps units bent but did not break under this extreme pressure. The Chinese lost an estimated 200,000 men in this spring offensive of 1951.

What had looked like a Soviet proxy victory over the United States in December 1950 soon turned into a bloody war of attrition from June 1951 to July 1953. Both sides entrenched near the 1950 border between North and South Korea, and fought over control of high ground that overlooked roads or valleys along the front lines. The fortifications resembled those of the First World War in complexity of design, as well as in effectiveness in stopping enemy assaults. Costly battles with descriptive names like Bloody Ridge, Heartbreak Ridge, Old Baldy, White Horse, Triangle Hill, Hill Eerie, and Porkchop Hill stretched from days into weeks, or even months. Thousands of American soldiers were killed and tens of thousands wounded in these blood-baths. The Chinese and North Koreans suffered still worse casualties. None resulted in war-winning victories; instead, they just added to the body counts in this war of attrition.

One other casualty, albeit a political one, of the Korean stalemate was President Harry S. Truman's reputation. His inability to achieve victory, the mounting American losses, and the endless negotiations did irreparable damage to his popularity. Not only did Truman face an endless war in Korea, he also encountered the rise of brazen political challenges at home. Beginning in early 1950, U.S. Senator Joseph McCarthy made vicious political attacks against Truman's administration for allegedly being soft on communism. The highly visible Republican from Wisconsin also leveled accusations that communists had infiltrated the federal govern-ment and subverted American policies, charges for which he never produced sufficient evi-dence. McCarthy gave his name to a brand of hysteria called "McCarthyism," which played on growing American fears of communist expansion, whether it was the loss of China earlier in 1949 or the stagnated conflict in Korea after 1951. McCarthy laid both these failures at Truman's feet.

The Election of Dwight D. Eisenhower and the Armistice in Korea

The low point in Harry Truman's popularity, and by extension that of the Democratic Party, came in the 1952 election. The Republicans seized on the perceived weaknesses to win a land-slide victory behind their presidential nominee—the highly respected Dwight D. Eisenhower. He relied on his military experience in the Second World War to present an image of solid and judicious leadership to the American people. He also made a pledge to travel to Korea. After the election, Eisenhower made good on this promise when he visited South Korea in late November 1952. This gesture was symbolic and substantive because it demonstrated the new American leader's commitment to ending the Korean War.

Once he became president in January 1953, Eisenhower added still more pressure to the negotiation process in Korea by threatening to use nuclear weapons if a settlement was not reached soon. Whether he would have gone to that next level is doubtful. Eisenhower, like Truman before him, feared escalation of a limited, regional conflict into a total, global war. Eisenhower's threat nonetheless carried weight in the eyes of the North Koreans, Chinese, and Soviets. This new president, after all, had made the fateful decision to launch the D-Day inva-sion back in 1944.

In March 1953, another significant change in Cold War leadership occurred when Joseph Stalin died. This left a power vacuum in Moscow that created ripple effects felt by North Korean and Chinese leaders. The Soviet government was unwilling to continue supporting their war efforts. The communist side thus lost some of its resolve in Korea.

While negotiations made halting progress in the spring of 1953, combat operations contin-ued at the front. Indeed, one of the war's bloodiest battles occurred during the last months of negotiations. From March 23 until July 16, Chinese and American forces clashed repeatedly in the Battle of Porkchop Hill. Named for its shape, this American outpost lay near the center of the front line. The U.S. 7th Infantry Division repelled three determined Chinese attacks on its defensive positions only with the help of concentrated artillery barrages. The Americans rained 77,000 artillery rounds down on the Chinese in a single day of combat. By July, when an armistice looked increasingly likely, the Americans abandoned their defenses on Porkchop Hill before the final Chinese assault, thus averting greater losses on both sides. Even so, the fighting cost 1,300 American casualties and 5,500 Chinese casualties.

Finally, on July 27, the U.N. and U.S. commander General Mark W. Clark and the Chinese and North Korean representatives signed an armistice at Panmunjom, a village in the front line. This truce established a demilitarized zone approximately 2.5 miles wide that ran near the 38th parallel across the east-west axis of the Korean peninsula. Since 1953, the United States has maintained units, including the 2nd Infantry Division, to guard the southern side of the Military Demarcation Line that divides the two independent Koreas.

The 37 months of conflict proved to be costly. In all, some 33,741 Americans were killed in action and 103,284 were wounded. An additional 2,835 Americans died from noncombat causes. Even today, the remains of approximately 8,000 have yet to be recovered for proper burial. The South Korean Army suffered nearly 600,000 casualties, while the U.N. forces endured some 15,000 casualties. The conflict also exacted a horrific toll on the civilian population of the South, a number that exceeded one million dead or missing.

The Korean War is sometimes portrayed as a tie or stalemate because the U.S. military made no territorial gains for all the sacrifices. It should be noted that American forces did not set out to conquer North Korea; instead, they fought to maintain the independence of South Korea as part of symmetric containment. The Korean War should thus be considered an American success.

Eisenhower's "New Look" and Asymmetric Containment Strategy

Just as Harry S. Truman had done, President Dwight D. Eisenhower tried to contain the expansion of communism and the Soviet Union in Korea and across the globe. However, the new president utilized different military means than his predecessor. Eisenhower believed that Truman's approach had failed because it was too predictable and too restrictive. The communist leaders in Moscow, Beijing, and elsewhere could anticipate what American reactions would be to their moves. At the same time, Eisenhower recognized that maintaining a sufficiently large American military to counter potential threats with equal and opposite countermeasures would be too draining on the American economy. Consequently, to regain the initiative yet reduce military expenditures, Eisenhower developed a strategy of asymmetric containment that he dubbed the "New Look." Putting his new strategy into effect required additional funding for new weapons technologies.

Apart from the perceived communist and Soviet threats abroad, Eisenhower faced a political faction that demanded a departure from the defeatist strategies of the Truman administration. Eisenhower's landslide victory in 1952 gave control of both the Senate and the House of Representatives to the Republican Party. As part of this shift in power, the rabidly anti-communist Joseph McCarthy assumed the chairmanship of the Senate Permanent Subcommittee on Investigations. He used this bully pulpit to try to expose communist conspirators in American society, the Eisenhower administration, and the U.S. Army. It was this third target that would be McCarthy's undoing. Televised hearings revealed his vitriolic attitude that, for many Americans, turned his crusade into a witch hunt. Not a single communist conspirator was convicted. By the end of 1954, McCarthy was censured by the Senate, and McCarthyism repudiated in most Americans' eyes.

After the Republican loss of the Senate majority in the 1954 midterm election, McCarthy lost his chairmanship. He faded from the political scene thereafter, but McCarthyism has lived on in the political fringes for decades. Every Cold War president feared being portrayed as passive or inactive in the face of the communist menace. All presidents until Jimmy Carter in 1977 have attempted to stop such expansion, either through symmetric containment like Truman or through asymmetric containment like his successor.

One of the pillars of Eisenhower's "New Look" can be seen in NSC 162/2, which was completed by the National Security Council and approved by the president in October 1953. This policy statement outlines possible American responses to Soviet or Chinese expansion. If incursions by these nations or their satellites occurred anywhere in the noncommunist world, then the United States could possibly react with nuclear strikes at the incursion point or against the source in the Soviet Union or China. Such threats of "massive retaliation," as it become known, gave Eisenhower flexibility and kept the Soviet or Chinese unsure about American reactions.

The first American tests of a new hydrogen bomb in late 1952 gave still more weight to this threat of all-out nuclear war. The terms "nuclear" or "thermonuclear" can be used interchangeably with "hydrogen" to describe the same weapons. All share the characteristic of producing immense amounts of energy through fusion reactions. A nuclear bomb's detonation could cause exponentially greater destruction than either atomic bomb dropped on Hiroshima and Nagasaki, both of which produced energy through fission reactions. The new nuclear bombs measured explosive power in megatons (millions of tons of TNT), as opposed to atomic bombs in kilotons (thousands of tons of TNT). Thus, a nuclear bomb could be 1,000 times more destructive or more than an atomic bomb.

With hydrogen bombs in the American arsenal, Eisenhower believed that he could deter Soviet or Chinese expansion, because massive retaliation and likely nuclear holocaust would not be worth risking by those two rational-thinking Cold War adversaries. The Soviet Union also developed its own nuclear weapons capabilities as a deterrent to perceived American expansion during the early 1950s.

The nuclear bomb's role in deterrence carried another fringe benefit for President Eisenhower, who wanted to reduce government expenditures on the military. The U.S. military expenditures had spiraled from $14.4 billion in 1950 to $43.4 billion in 1953 during the Korean War. Eisenhower believed that development of nuclear weapons as part of his New Look would be less expensive in the long term than maintaining a huge force of millions of American in uniform. He coined the term "more bang for the buck" to describe his frugal decision to increase the nuclear arsenal and add other new technologies. The Department of Defense expenditures fell to $30.4 billion in 1954 before gradually rising to $41.4 billion in 1960. Eisenhower's use of massive retaliation as a deterrent against the Soviet Union started a nuclear arms race with the Soviets that ultimately cost both nations increasingly more money. Thus, the president could not keep military spending as low as he had hoped.

Transformations in the U.S. Military in an Era of Reduced Budgets

Throughout this era of budgetary austerity, the four American military services resumed their peacetime struggle for appropriations and especially for the missions that justified those funds. The years 1953 and 1954 set the tone for the rest of the decade in terms of each service's attempt to carve a niche for itself in Eisenhower's overarching vision for American security. Eisenhower's first Secretary of Defense, Charles E. Wilson, supervised the process from 1953 until he resigned in 1957. Reminiscent of the late 1940s, each branch desperately attempted to hold or increase its piece of the budgetary pie throughout the 1950s.

During Secretary Wilson's tenure, the recently established U.S. Air Force increased its hold on the bulk of the Department of Defense's funds because it marketed its strategic bombing mission as essential to national security. Although the Air Force declined from 977,000 service personnel in 1953 to 815,000 in 1960, the losses in personnel are misleading. These reductions in manpower were less in relative and absolute numbers when compared to reductions in the Navy, Army, and Marine Corps. The Air Force's budgets hovered around 45 percent of annual military spending from 1952 through 1960. This amounted to $26.4 billion in 1952 during the Korean War, then a drop to $11.6 billion at the low point in 1955, and finally an increase to $19.2 billion in 1960. The outlays covered the costs of the Air Force's ongoing development of new aircraft and other equipment associated with the nuclear weapons and controlled by the SAC. In fact, under Curtis LeMay's leadership as its director until 1957 and then as Vice Chief of Staff of the Air Force, SAC received so much money that it could be considered to be a mini–Air Force.

The addition of the new B-52 "Stratofortress" to SAC's aircraft fleet in 1955 demonstrated how the Air Force leveraged resources to maintain its status in national defense. From 1945 to 1955, the United States had depended on propeller-driven, long-range strategic bombers to carry atomic and later nuclear bombs in potential conflicts. Jet propulsion, however, was the future of military aircraft—flying higher, faster, and farther.

In 1946, the Boeing Company won the bid to design and build a jet-propelled strategic bomber that combined extremely long range, heavy payload, and high ceiling at subsonic speeds. The resulting prototype YB-52 made its maiden flight six years later in 1952, and the finalized version of the B-52B entered service in early 1955. The massive Stratofortress boasted a combat range of 3,600 miles, a payload of 43,000 pounds of bombs, and a service ceiling of 47,000 feet. The advent of aerial refueling gave the B-52s a virtually unlimited range as well as the capability of hitting targets anywhere in the world. Its eight Pratt and Whitney J57-P-1W turbojets could cruise at 525 miles per hour. Originally designed to drop nuclear bombs on targets in Asia and Europe in the Cold War, the aircraft's heavy payload also made it an effective platform for conventional bombing missions against strategic and tactical targets.

The Air Force completed its move to jet propulsion later in the 1950s with the addition of aircraft like the F-102 "Delta Dagger" and F-104 "Starfighter." Their mission focused on intercepting and destroying enemy bombers. F-100 "Super Sabre" also came on line to fill the role of achieving air superiority against enemy aircraft. All three fighters could break the sound barrier.

During the 1950s, the U.S. Navy experienced budget cuts slightly deeper than the Air Force. Their survival relied on convincing arguments that their capabilities fit into Eisenhower's "New Look." In particular, aircraft carriers demonstrated their operational value by launching round-the-clock aerial missions against targets during the Korean War. Once the conflict ended, the Navy's contribution garnered support to spend $800 million on building the new super-carrier USS *Forrestal* and her three sister ships between 1954 and 1958. These new vessels measured 1,000 feet in length and displaced some 80,000 tons, making them the largest carriers built to date. Each held 85 planes, and some of these could carry nuclear bombs.

Nuclear capability took another form in the Navy beyond that of weapons systems. In the 1950s, a naval captain named Hyman G. Rickover helped develop nuclear power plants as a means of propulsion for warships. He argued that such a limitless energy source would allow submarines, for example, to remain submerged almost indefinitely. There would be no need to refuel the submarine's engines or recharge its batteries. This in turn reduced their vulnerability and increased their range.

Figure 13.2 Prototype of the YB-52 Side-by-Side With the B-17 and the B-29

In this 1952 photograph, the massive YB-52 (center) next to a Second World War-era B-17 "Flying Fortress" showed the relative size of the two bombers. The B-29 sits in the background. Once brought online in 1955, the B-52 "Stratofortress" became the primary strategic bomber for the U.S. Air Force. Continual improvements will keep these rugged and versatile aircraft flying through the 2040s, which will mean the B-52 will have seen active service for 90 years.

© Boeing

Box 13.1 Admiral Hyman G. Rickover: Father of the Nuclear Navy

In the twentieth century, there have been a few men who became synonymous with new military technologies. Among these were William "Billy" Mitchell who championed strategic airpower in the 1920s, and Curtis "Bombs Away" Lemay who did so for strategic airpower during the early Cold War. The U.S. Navy had such a figure in Hyman G. Rickover, who became synonymous with nuclear-powered warships during the Cold War.

Rickover spent his early naval career from 1918 until 1945 repairing damaged vessels, serving on submarines, and pursuing advanced education in engineering. However, because he never commanded ships in combat, his was hardly the glorified career path of someone who later attained four-star flag rank and remained in uniform for another four decades. After the Second World War ended, Hyman Rickover gained expertise in atomic and later nuclear energy. Then in 1949, he became director of the Naval Reactors Branch in the U.S. Navy's Bureau of Ships. In that role, Rickover supervised the design, construction, and launch of the world's first nuclear-powered submarine, the USS *Nautilus*, in 1954.

Figure 13.3 Hyman Rickover With Nuclear Submarine Model

In 1952, Captain Hyman G. Rickover uses a model to demonstrate how the first atomic-powered submarine worked.

© Bettmann/CORBIS

For the next three decades, he controlled ongoing development and expansion of the nuclear fleet totaling more than 200 nuclear-powered submarines and surface vessels. Rickover was the face of the nuclear navy, whether on the cover of *Time* magazine or in Congressional hearings. After an extraordinarily long 64-year career, Admiral Hyman G. Rickover retired in 1982 at the age of 82.

In 1954, the Navy launched the USS *Nautilus*, the first nuclear-powered submarine. Just four years later, the Norfolk Navy Yard in Virginia began work on a nuclear-powered super-carrier named the USS *Enterprise*. This mammoth warship's flight deck measured 1,123 feet in length, and it displaced nearly 95,000 tons. This carrier boasted unlimited range. The cost of the *Enterprise* exceeded $450 million.

As part of the Navy Department, the U.S. Marine Corps struggled to maintain its place in the American strategy during the 1950s. Although Marines proved themselves to be versatile fighters on the ground, in amphibious assaults, and in the air during the Korean War, the Marine Corps' manpower dropped from its peak of 249,000 Marines in 1953 to 170,000 in 1960. Other than a peacekeeping mission in Lebanon in the Middle East in 1958, they had few opportunities to demonstrate their combat effectiveness or tout their uniqueness in the American military establishment. The Corps also faced negative publicity when a tragic set of events and negligence in 1956 caused six deaths during basic training at Parris Island, North Carolina. This Ribbon Creek incident resulted in reforms that ended some harsh basic training activities.

Despite a lackluster decade, the Marine Corps did make significant strides in creating a new force structure that placed all necessary ground, amphibious, logistics, and aviation (rotary and fixed-wing) units under a single Marine commander. This combined arms force gave that commander the autonomy and flexibility to conduct battalion, brigade, or division-sized operations. This concept was formally recognized as the Marine Air-Ground Task Force in the early 1960s.

Like the Marine Corps, the Army emerged from the last two years of the Korean War having vindicated itself after the devastating defeats in 1950 and 1951. This conflict stood as a grim reminder that the United States needed to maintain forces capable of conducting large ground operations. Nevertheless, the Army endured the worst cuts among the four services following the Korean War. The Army went from 1.5 million soldiers and a $13 billion budget in 1953 to 850,000 soldiers and a $9 billion budget by the end of the decade. To put this in perspective, the $13 billion in 1953 amounted to 38 percent of total military expenditures and the $9 billion a mere 22 percent.

In the face of such deep cuts, the U.S. Army's leadership decided to reorient itself to the realities of the nuclear age. Beginning in 1954, the Army's new Chief of Staff General Matthew B. Ridgway modernized the division's force structure to match the combat expectations of a nuclear war. The unit's large command structures, complex supply networks, and slow movements made the division too vulnerable to attacks that would instantly incinerate several square miles of landscape. Ridgway therefore decided to make his divisions more nimble, flexible, and survivable on the new battlefield. Two years later in 1956, the reorganization of Army force structure resulted in the "Pentomic" Division.

This new unit constituted the most dramatic change in the divisional table of organization and equipment since the First World War. The Pentomic Division numbered 13,700 soldiers, as opposed to the old division's 16,000 soldiers. The term "Pentomic" referred to the new division's five Battle Groups of 1,400 men each. Commanded by colonels, each Battle Group consisted of four rifle companies, a mortar battery, and a headquarters company with signal and reconnaissance elements. The divisions also possessed a tank battalion and an artillery battalion with guns and rockets that fired conventional or nuclear shells. The soldiers maneuvered on battlefields in fast armored vehicles or through the air in helicopters. In theory, the mobile Battle Groups could scatter over a wide area to avoid destruction by enemy nuclear weapons, yet coordinate with other groups to launch their own attacks on enemy forces.

Although a creative solution in theory, the Pentomic Division did not work in practice. The tiny Battle Groups could not function autonomously without logistical support from the division, and as designed the division lacked the necessary resources to provide such support to its Battle Groups. In addition, the Battle Group was too small to fight as an independent unit that could fight on a conventional battlefield. Perhaps most significantly, the Pentomic Division's focus on nuclear weapons absorbed much of the Army's research and development money, so the Army failed to acquire new conventional weapons. By 1960, the Army began transitioning back to the old triangular division composed of three regiments and supported by substantial logistics and engineering elements.

Challenges to Eisenhower's Strategy of Containment, 1953–60

Despite possessing a significant advantage in nuclear weapons, President Dwight Eisenhower encountered challenges that could not be overcome by threatening massive retaliation. At the same time, the president would not commit the American military to ground operations because that could mean escalation into war with the Soviet Union or China. Consequently, Eisenhower turned to other means of maintaining American national security such as top secret covert operations. These activities sometimes violated democratic sensibilities, if not constitutional laws. When directed against communist or Soviet threats, such efforts were consistent with the president's asymmetric and pragmatic containment strategies.

Eisenhower relied heavily on the Central Intelligence Agency (CIA) to conduct covert operations. The National Security Act of 1947 created this agency as a successor to the Office of Strategic Services from the Second World War. Among its covert activities, the CIA gathered intelligence on security-related topics, groups, or individuals in nations across the globe. Subsequent presidential directives and legislation gave the CIA the authority to conduct covert operations to help achieve American objectives or thwart enemy objectives. Sometimes, these clandestine activities included support for assassination or *coup d'etat* attempts against foreign governments perceived to be dangerous to American security. The CIA also helped maintain governments friendly to American interests.

In 1953 and 1954, Eisenhower watched as anti-American and strongly nationalist governments took power in Iran and Guatemala. He directed the CIA to initiate covert operations to overthrow the sitting governments in both nations. In Iran, the threat was not communist in nature but economic. The CIA helped the British government overthrow a hostile Iranian government that, it was feared, would control the flow of petroleum, and withhold profits from a British oil company. Once the *coup d'etat* was successful, the pro-American and anti-communist Shah Mohammed Reza Pahlevi took power and ruled for the next 26 years. The CIA touted the successful *coup* in Iran as evidence of its effective covert operations.

In Guatemala, the threat of a Soviet foothold in Latin America and the Western Hemisphere scared Eisenhower. Although elected by the Guatemalan people, President Jacobo Árbenz did not maintain a democratic political system. He also undermined American commercial interests in the nation's banana production with policies that took land from the richest Guatemalans to give to the poorer farmers. This smacked of communist wealth redistribution to Eisenhower and his advisors. Making matters worse, Árbenz supposedly accepted military aid from the Soviet Union. If Guatemala succumbed to Soviet control, Eisenhower did not want nearby nations to fall to communism like dominos. Such losses carried a corresponding reduction in American credibility. These reasons prompted Eisenhower to direct the CIA to overthrow the Guatemalan government. The CIA spread anti-Árbenz propaganda throughout Guatemala and provided weapons and training to rebel forces to fight the government. This pressure proved too much for Árbenz who resigned and fled the country rather than face imprisonment or assassination.

Apart from CIA-driven covert operations in Iran and Guatemala, Eisenhower continued to provide support to allies struggling against communism. One prime example can be seen in his support of France's efforts to maintain its hold on French Indochina and particularly the eastern most area of Vietnam. The French military committed significant forces to fight against the rebellious Ho Chi Minh and his followers, known as the Viet Minh since 1946. The French wanted to keep Vietnam in its prewar empire. Like President Truman before him, Eisenhower worried that Ho's communist rhetoric might infect other nations in Southeast Asia. Also like Truman, however, Eisenhower failed to account for Ho's equally powerful nationalist message calling for Vietnamese liberation from the French Empire. Because he needed to contain communism, Eisenhower supplied the French with weapons and financial aid totaling more than $350 million.

By 1954, the French military had fought for eight years against the Viet Minh. The French employed conventional tactics with the military objective of establishing territorial control, yet they ignored the political goal of gaining the Vietnamese people's support for their empire. The French relied on the firepower of their artillery and protection of their armored vehicles. Even so, they never achieved a decisive battlefield victory against the Viet Minh, who countered the French advantage in firepower with guerilla tactics. The Viet Minh would suddenly appear, pour gunfire into French units, and then quickly fade back into the jungles before the French could react.

The French met their final defeat in the Battle of Dien Bien Phu in 1954. Some 50,000 Viet Minh surrounded a French base in a valley of the same name. The French suffered grievous casualties during daily barrages and frontal attacks by the Viet Minh. Not even French aerial resupply and reinforcement could stop the Viet Minh advance. French leaders appealed to President Eisenhower to commit American military force to their cause. Although the communist victory was inevitable because the French could not withstand the Viet Minh, Eisenhower decided to withhold American combat units from the fight. He believed that entering a conflict in Vietnam would require too large of a conventional commitment. After their defeat at Dien Bien Phu, the French military and colonial government left Vietnam later that year. Eight years of war had cost the French more than 100,000 soldiers killed in action.

Negotiations about the reality of a postcolonial Vietnam concluded that the nation should be divided into two halves: North Vietnam, officially named the Democratic Republic of Vietnam and led by Ho Chi Minh from 1954 until his death in 1969, and South Vietnam, officially named the Republic of Vietnam and led by a series of dictators supported by the United States. The peace negotiations also promised a popular election of a unified government in 1956. However, when no election occurred, Ho began to support another Viet Minh insurgency in South Vietnam, first with arms and later with North Vietnamese soldiers. He employed communist as well as nationalist rhetoric to recruit more guerilla fighters in the South with the goal of undermining and overthrowing the South Vietnamese government.

For Eisenhower, rebellion in South Vietnam equated to communist expansion. The United States propped up the government of President Ngo Dinh Diem in the South beginning in 1955. Diem was fiercely anti-communist, but he was also undemocratic. He ruthlessly retained control through imprisoning or executing his rivals, regardless of their ideologies. Still, from the American perspective, an anti-communist dictator was better than a communist government. From 1955 until the end of his presidency, Eisenhower sent financial aid, weapons, and military advisors to help South Vietnam stop the Viet Minh insurgents.

As part of the last type of support, several hundred American military personnel trained the South Vietnamese soldiers to use American weapons and tactics. Beginning in 1950 under President Truman, who had sent advisors to help the French, the Military Assistance Advisory Group supervised these activities. The American military advisors were not supposed to participate in combat operations, but some were killed during insurgent attacks. Even with this help, Diem's government could barely maintain power because the insurgency grew stronger and the Viet Minh more numerous. At the decade's end, the need for additional American support grew more urgent.

Eisenhower's Second Term: Setbacks and Losses, 1957–60

Dwight Eisenhower easily won reelection as president in 1956. In his calm and unassuming way, he demonstrated that he could be trusted to solve problems like ending the Korean War back in 1953. It appeared that the communists made no significant gains during this first term. Eisenhower's reelection efforts likewise benefited from a strong national economy, high living standard, and low unemployment rate. This apparent stability, however, belied the crises that he would face at home and abroad in the next four years.

Domestic problems in the United States intensified as the Civil Rights movement gained momentum. African Americans had long tried to overturn policies like segregation that promoted institutionalized racism in the civilian world. President Truman ended this policy in the military in 1948, but African-American civilians knew their separate schools, bus seats, diners, and restrooms were hardly equal to those of Caucasian Americans. Earlier in 1954, the U.S. Supreme Court handed down the landmark decision in *Brown v. Board of Education*. According to this ruling, all public schools in the United States needed to desegregate so blacks could attend classes alongside white students. Ending segregation, however, met with great opposition in Southern states.

President Eisenhower faced direct challenges to the federal government's authority in Arkansas in 1957. Despite the mandate from the Supreme Court, Governor Orval Faubus of Arkansas refused to desegregate all his state's schools. In fact, he ordered the Arkansas National Guard to block African-American students from entering an all-white school in the city of Little Rock. This act of defiance required Eisenhower's immediate and unambiguous action. He sent active duty soldiers to guarantee that those black students—the "Little Rock Nine"— could go to school without being harmed or stopped. The governor of Arkansas relented, and Arkansas schools desegregated.

Box 13.2   Civil Unrest and Forced Desegregation in Arkansas in 1957

In fall of 1957, tensions over desegregation came to a head in Little Rock, Arkansas, where nine black students tried to enter the all-white Central High School. On September 4, Governor Orval Faubus sent his state's National Guard to Little Rock ostensibly to prevent violence, but primarily to prevent black students from entering Central High School. The guardsmen turned the nine African-American students away from the school. When they tried again three weeks later, the ensuing race riot endangered the students and injured other African Americans. This made the purportedly egalitarian and democratic United States look hypocritical.

President Dwight D. Eisenhower could not tolerate this official act of defiance of the Supreme Court and the federal government, nor could he allow racially motivated violence to continue. On September 24, Eisenhower ordered soldiers from the U.S. Army's 101st Airborne Division to the city to escort the African-American students into Central High School. Eisenhower also called the Arkansas Guard into federal service, which effectively removed them from Governor Faubus' authority. Unable to resist such pressure from Eisenhower, Faubus relented, and the nine black students entered Central High School.

President Eisenhower utilized his prerogative as commander-in-chief to enforce the Supreme Court's decision and ensure compliance with desegregation. Given the fact that Faubus escalated the situation by calling out his state guard, it was also legitimate for Eisenhower to utilize the regular U.S. Army as a countermeasure.

The fall of 1957 also saw a major crisis in American security that came from the Soviet Union. On October 4, the Soviets launched a rocket that carried a satellite named *Sputnik* into orbit. Moving at 18,000 miles per hour, it orbited the earth every 92 minutes. This experiment captured the world's attention because *Sputnik* transmitted radio signals for 22 days. Those transmissions may have been merely a series of beeps monitored by radio operators, but they heralded a Soviet victory in the race into space. President Eisenhower was aware of Soviet efforts to launch its first satellite, but he did not anticipate the reactions of his fellow Americans. *Sputnik* marked the beginning of "the Missile Age."

Barely twice the size of a basketball, the 183-pound *Sputnik* did not directly threaten the United States. However, the Soviets could improve this technology to the point of placing nuclear bombs in intercontinental ballistic missiles (ICBMs) capable of striking targets anywhere in the United States in a matter of minutes. This new delivery system struck fear into every American and into those Americans in particular who had faith in U.S. technological superiority over Russia—from President Eisenhower in Washington to hometown neighbors. Indeed, in schools, children started practicing how to hide under their desks in the event of a nuclear attack. Some anxious Americans even constructed bomb shelters in their backyards in hopes of surviving nuclear strikes. The Soviets exploited *Sputnik* as propaganda to show the weakness and inferiority of the American capitalist system.

To close what was later termed as the "missile gap" between the superpowers, Eisenhower directed huge sums of money toward development of missile technology in civilian and military sectors. He wanted the United States to meet and surpass the Soviet Union. In 1958, the president established the National Air and Space Administration (NASA) to manage the space program. Its budget grew from $89 million in 1958 to $744 million in 1961. With unlimited support from Congress, NASA set about in the late 1950s to put Americans in space. Working with NASA and other agencies, the U.S. military launched several satellites beginning in 1958. In addition to the technological advances spurred by *Sputnik*, the missile gap pointed out the need for improved education in the United States. Eisenhower and Congress made technical training a top priority in the National Defense Education Act in 1958. Over the next two years, this legislation provided $400 million to American universities to provide fellowships and loans to students in sciences, mathematics, and engineering.

Still reeling from the hysteria over *Sputnik*, Eisenhower and the United States encountered another threat very close to home in 1959. In January, after six years of fighting, revolutionaries finally overthrew Cuba's government led by Fulgencio Batista. Like other dictators, Batista oppressed his people, yet his firm anti-communist stance and willing business partnerships garnered him American support. President Eisenhower believed his ouster to be a victory for communism. Once Batista's forces were defeated and he fled from Cuba, the charismatic revolutionary leader Fidel Castro assumed power in the new government. He brutally eliminated any potential competitors or remaining Batista supporters. Castro also nationalized the agricultural plantations and oil refineries owned by foreign, including American, corporations. The plantations were divided into cooperatives to be tended by Cuban farmers.

For most Americans, Castro's policies smacked of communism from the American perspective. Eisenhower first refused to acknowledge the legitimacy of Cuba's new government. He also began making secret plans for the CIA to support a counterrevolution to overthrow Castro and establish a new government more friendly to American interests. After all, Eisenhower needed to contain communist expansion, especially in Cuba just 90 miles south of Florida. Such American efforts and attitudes further alienated Castro, who turned to the Soviet Union for protection.

As if the loss of Cuba to communism was not bad enough, yet another setback took place in May 1960. The Soviet military shot down an American U-2 spy plane flying over Soviet Union territory and photographing Soviet ICBM bases. The U-2s flew surveillance missions at altitudes so high that Americans believed they would be invisible to radar detection and invulnerable to attack. Nevertheless, the Soviets did bring the spy plane down using a surface-to-air missile. They located the aircraft's wreckage and captured its American pilot. The U-2 incident caused great Eisenhower embarrassment and fueled tensions between the two superpowers. He was caught in the act of violating sovereign air space over another nation.

When he finally left office in January 1961, President Eisenhower bequeathed a nation facing many uncertainties to his successor John F. Kennedy. Problems simmered in Cuba and Vietnam, where communism made gains and threatened to expand. Because the late 1950s revealed flaws in Eisenhower's New Look, Kennedy would change American strategy and adopt his own approach to containing communist and Soviet expansion. Meanwhile, throughout the Eisenhower years, the U.S. military concentrated on developing technologically advanced weapons but relegated conventional forces to lower priorities. In an era of massive retaliation deterrence, and asymmetric containment of communism, the Navy and especially the Air Force enjoyed relatively generous funding for their missions to deliver nuclear weapons against enemy targets. Conversely, the Army and Marine Corps languished during the years of meager budgets that reduced their combat readiness.

Conclusion

In his farewell address on January 17, 1961, Eisenhower expressed a sense of foreboding about two threats to the United States. One was communism, which he believed to be "a hostile ideology global in scope, atheistic in character, ruthless in purpose, and insidious in method." The other threat was internal to the Unites States. Eisenhower explained that Americans "must guard against the acquisition of unwarranted influence, whether sought or unsought, by the military–industrial complex. The potential for the disastrous rise of misplaced power exists and will persist . . . . Only an alert and knowledgeable citizenry can compel the proper meshing of the huge industrial and military machinery of defense with our peaceful methods and goals, so that security and liberty may prosper together." His warnings about both threats would prove prophetic in the coming decades.

Notes

1 X, "The Sources of Soviet Conduct." *Foreign Affairs* 25 (July 1947): 575–76. ("X" was Kennan's pseudonym).
2 The concepts of "symmetric" and "asymmetric" containment are historical labels drawn from John Lewis Gaddis' seminal book *Strategies of Containment: A Critical Appraisal of Postwar American National Security* (New York: Oxford University Press, 1982).
3 Omar N. Bradley and Clay Blair, *A General's Life: An Autobiography* (New York: Simon and Schuster, 1983), p. 474.
4 June 24 in the continental United States due to the date change of the Sunday–Monday line.

Short Bibliography

Appleman, Roy E. *East of Chosin: Entrapment and Breakout in Korea, 1950*. College Station: Texas A&M University Press, 1990.

Bowie, Robert R., and Richard H. Immerman. *Waging Peace: How Eisenhower Shaped an Enduring Cold War Strategy*. New York: Oxford University Press, 1998.

Duncan, Francis. *Rickover and the Nuclear Navy: The Discipline of Technology*. Annapolis: Naval Institute Press, 1990.

Kaplan, Edward. *To Kill Nations: American Strategy in the Air-Atomic Age and the Rise of Mutually Assured Destruction*. Ithaca: Cornell University Press, 2015.

Linn, Brian McAllister. *Elvis' Army: Cold War GIs and the Atomic Battlefield*. Cambridge: Harvard University Press, 2016.

May, Elaine Tyler. *Homeward Bound: American Families in the Cold War Era*. New York: Basic Books, 1990.

McGregor, Morris J. *Integration of the Armed Forces, 1940–1965*. Washington: Center of Military History, 1982.

Millett, Allan R. *The War for Korea*. 2 vols. Lawrence: University Press of Kansas, 2005–2010.

Palmer, Michael A. *Origins of Maritime Strategy: The Development of American Naval Strategy, 1945–1955*. Annapolis: Naval Institute Press, 1988.

Sambaluk, Nicholas Michael. *The Outer Space Race: Eisenhower and the Quest for Aerospace Security*. Annapolis: Naval Institute Press, 2015.

Taaffe, Stephen R. *MacArthur's Korean War Generals*. Lawrence: University Press of Kansas, 2016.

Trauschweizer, Ingo. *The Cold War U.S. Army: Building Deterrence for Limited War*. Lawrence: University Press of Kansas, 2008.

1961	1961	1962	1965–73	November 14–17, 1965
Bay of Pigs	Berlin Crisis	Cuban Missile Crisis	Vietnam War	Battle of Ia Drang

TIMELINE

Chapter 14

Confrontations in the Cold War, 1960–1973

When John F. Kennedy became president in 1961, he inherited several serious Cold War challenges from Dwight D. Eisenhower. During the next 34 months, the United States encountered crises in the Caribbean, Central Europe, and Southeast Asia, where the Soviet Union asserted its influence. To meet these challenges, Kennedy embraced "Flexible Response" as his strategy of symmetric containment of communist expansion. Nevertheless, he failed to roll back this threat in Cuba and Vietnam.

After Kennedy's assassination in 1963, the new president, Lyndon B. Johnson, expanded on his predecessor's containment strategy by dramatically increasing the American commitment in South Vietnam. He sent as many as 543,000 American service personnel to that nation. Meanwhile, Johnson faced growing opposition from many antiwar groups on the home front. So great were these domestic pressures and so indecisive were American military efforts in the Vietnam War that Johnson lost hope for victory and decided against running for reelection in 1968. Republican candidate Richard M. Nixon won the presidential election that year. Between 1969 and 1973, he gradually withdrew the U.S. military from South Vietnam, which succumbed to North Vietnamese pressure and surrendered in 1975. This collective failure to roll back communist expansion constituted the first major defeat in American history.

In this chapter, students will learn about:

- Testing Kennedy's "Flexible Response" as the new strategy of symmetric containment of communism.
- Evolution of force structures, missions, and capabilities in the U.S. military.
- Tracking Johnson's expansion and the conduct of military operations in the Vietnam War.
- Explaining the American failure in the Vietnam War.

John F. Kennedy's "Flexible Response" and Symmetric Containment

On January 20, 1961, John F. Kennedy took the oath of office to become the youngest president in American history. His supreme confidence radiated throughout his inaugural address: "Let every nation know, whether it wishes us well or ill, that we shall pay any price, bear any burden, meet any hardship, support any friend, oppose any foe to assure the survival and the success of liberty." Beyond Kennedy's soaring oratory and infectious optimism, however, lay numerous threats to American interests as near as the Caribbean and as far away as Asia. The new president and his advisors decided that responding to communist and Soviet expansion required significant changes in the American military strategies and force structures.

Kennedy wanted more latitude to meet Soviet or communist challenges across a spectrum of American reactions, so he replaced Eisenhower's "New Look" with his own "Flexible Response." Against the threat of nuclear attack, the United States could counter with a nuclear arsenal equal to or greater than that of the Soviets. Against the threat of Soviet conventional warfare, the United States could counter with military forces capable of fighting and winning battles on the ground, in the air, or at sea. Against the threat of communist revolution, the United States could counter with American military personnel trained in "Counterinsurgency" tactics and with other military and financial aid to endangered nations. Kennedy wanted to react in opposite and proportionate ways to Soviet actions. He needed to control American reactions to avoid spiraling into nuclear war yet still demonstrate that the United States could make good on its commitments. Flexible Response thus shifted away from Eisenhower's asymmetric containment strategy toward a more symmetric strategy.

Eisenhower's small, lean American military needed to be expanded and restructured to fight in any possible conflict. The foundation for Kennedy's new military can be traced back to 1958, when the Department of Defense Reorganization Act was passed and signed into law. This sweeping legislation centralized authority under the office of the U.S. Secretary of Defense and the Joint Chiefs of Staff (JCS). Lines of authority ran from the JCS to the Defense Secretary and then directly to the president as commander-in-chief.

In the first month of his presidency, Kennedy chose Robert S. McNamara to become his Secretary of Defense. He wanted McNamara to consolidate the new military structure as outlined in the 1958 Act. Although he did allow for separate armed services with particular mission sets, McNamara believed that there should be a single defense policy and one unified national strategy. The new secretary exploited his office's greater influence to allocate money to the armed services and determine what activities, units, regions, and weapons systems received priority. If the Army, Air Force, Navy, or Marine Corps wanted to open new bases or develop new pieces of equipment, then that service needed to do cost-benefit assessments that measured the budgetary requirements against the potential capabilities. If the costs outweighed the benefits, then the proposal would not be funded.

As this process played out repeatedly, McNamara and his civilian advisors grew increasingly skeptical of military leaders' opinions. They worried that the different services' partisan interests ran contrary to proper business practices, if not Kennedy's strategic vision. Consequently, McNamara, Kennedy, and later President Lyndon B. Johnson promoted high-ranking military officers who would be loyal to them. In Johnson's case, their loyalty ensured that the military establishment would not challenge him or undermine his policies.

Box 14.1   Robert McNamara Biographical Sketch

The forty-five-year-old Robert F. McNamara brought wide-ranging managerial experiences to his new position as Secretary of Defense in 1961. He graduated from the University of California at Berkeley with an economics degree in 1937 and from Harvard Business School with a Masters of Business Administration. Then he worked at an accounting firm before returning to teach at Harvard. During the Second World War, McNamara served in the U.S. Army Air Force in the Office of Statistical Control where he analyzed the effectiveness of the strategic bombing campaign and monitored the efficiency levels of the squadrons executing that campaign. He rose to the rank of lieutenant colonel, but he never saw combat.

After the war ended, McNamara and several other bright young businessmen known as "Whiz Kids" went to work for Ford Motor Company. They helped to modernize and streamline the car manufacturer's operations by reforming administrative structure and controlling costs. McNamara rose through the ranks to become president of Ford in late 1960. He believed that solutions to problems could be found in numerical solutions in what is known as "systems analysis." This entails doing detailed cost-benefit analysis to determine the courses of action. For him, it was the process that solved problems.

McNamara was not President John F. Kennedy's first choice for Secretary of Defense in 1961. That person declined the offer from the president but recommended McNamara. Once in the position, he set about streamlining functions and organizational structures to maximize the efficiency of the Department of Defense. As his managerial style filtered down the ranks of the military, it pointed to the questions of whether men should best be led or managed on the battlefield as well as whether a military institution can be run like a corporation. The Vietnam War became the laboratory where these questions were answered.

McNamara advised Kennedy on the crises in Berlin and Cuba, and he laid the foundation for an expanding war in Vietnam. When Kennedy was assassinated, McNamara remained at the Defense Department under President Lyndon Baines Johnson. He helped to orchestrate the escalation of the Vietnam War to stop that domino from falling to communism. His dominant personality, arrogant attitude, and blind faith in systems analysis set him up for a fall from favor after the Tet Offensive. He simply could never divorce himself from the conventional war-making notion that victory was a mathematical equation of bombs and bullets versus time and lives.

Figure 14.1 Defense Secretary Robert McNamara, General Maxwell Taylor, and President John F. Kennedy Meeting on January 25, 1963

Secretary of Defense Robert F. McNamara (left) meeting with the Army's General Maxwell Taylor and President John F. Kennedy in the White House on January 25, 1963. They served on the Executive Committee of the National Security Council. This group gave the president intelligence briefings and provided a sounding board for his decisions.

Source: John F. Kennedy Library

Despite some bureaucratic obstacles and personality conflicts, three out of four services profited from Flexible Response as implemented by Defense Secretary McNamara. The U.S. Air Force's SAC nearly doubled its force from 600 ICBMs under Eisenhower to 1,000 under Kennedy. A new missile—LGM-30A Minuteman-I with a yield of approximately 1.2 megatons—came online in 1962. More advanced models were added to the American nuclear arsenal later that decade.

The Air Force's ICBMs comprised one-third of the nuclear triad, which it was hoped would provide a deterrent to the Soviet Union by making the superpowers' "mutual destruction" the only outcome of a nuclear war. Another third of the triad was the strategic bombing capability, centered on the B-52 "Stratofortress" with its long range and heavy bomb load. However, the Air Force saw its bomber force shrink despite the best efforts of General Curtis

E. LeMay, who commanded the SAC before being promoted to Air Force Chief of Staff in 1961. Using systems analysis, McNamara determined that several hundred nuclear missiles were more cost-effective than squadrons of bombers with significant overhead costs of maintenance and personnel. The missiles could also be placed on alert and launched in a matter of minutes, rather than the hours required for B-52s to scramble, get aloft, and fly thousands of miles to hit their targets.

The Navy also profited from Flexible Response because it increased the number of nuclear missile submarines to more than 40 vessels carrying 600 nuclear warheads. This force comprised the last third of the nuclear triad. The Navy likewise added nuclear-powered aircraft carriers to its surface fleet beginning with the USS *Enterprise* in 1962. This mammoth warship measured 1,123 feet with a 94,000-ton displacement. Its crew of 5,800 sailors supported up to 90 American aircraft of all types. The nuclear-powered carriers boasted virtually unlimited cruising range, mobility, and sustainability.

Throughout the 1950s and into the early 1960s, the Marine Corps experienced no improvements in budgets or manpower in part because the service played no part in the nuclear triad. Even so, the Marines adapted new technologies, such as the helicopter, to their time-honored mission of amphibious assault. They also formalized the Marine Air-Ground Task Force in 1962. This new force structure placed the command, ground combat, aviation, and logistics elements into a single organization that could take forms of battalion (Marine Expeditionary Unit) up to corps (Marine Expeditionary Corps) as needed.

Among the armed services, the Army experienced the greatest overall expansion under Flexible Response. After languishing throughout the Eisenhower years, the Army stood at 870,000 men and 14 divisions. But by 1962, growth in manpower and changes in force structure started to transform the Army into a service capable of fulfilling the missions of Flexible Response. The Army's strength increased to more than one million men with the activation of two more divisions.

The divisional structure also reverted from the 13,500-man Pentomic Division of the late 1950s back to the more potent 16,000-man Reorganization Objectives Army Division (ROAD) by 1961. These new divisions returned to the triangular organization with three combat brigades and included all necessary combat support and logistical support units. The changes allowed for independent maneuver and engagement with large enemy forces, just as had been seen in the Second World War and the Korean War. Under the ROAD reform, the Army could meet various conventional threats using infantry, mechanized armor, and airborne divisions. From the perspective of Robert McNamara, this new force structure made sense because it brought the divisions into line with Flexible Response.

Beyond altering its divisions, the Army augmented its unconventional warfare capabilities. Units fulfilling these missions can be traced to 1952 when the Army's Special Forces were part of the Psychological Warfare Division, and still earlier to the Office of Strategic Services during the Second World War. These highly skilled soldiers wearing distinctive green berets possessed knowledge of tactics, languages, and cultures that enabled them to conduct sabotage, surveillance, and other covert missions. In his first year as president, Kennedy decided to widen the Special Forces' roles to participate in larger operations and to train other soldiers in unconventional warfare. He added an additional 7,500 soldiers to the existing cadre of 1,500 in 1961. Special Forces units thereafter started deploying to Southeast Asia to train Laotian and South Vietnamese forces how to fight counterinsurgencies against communist guerilla forces "counterinsurgency." The Special Forces' skills and capabilities fit into Kennedy's desire for a military flexible enough to respond in unconventional operational environments. It is worth noting, however, that Kennedy's focus lay in the Caribbean and Europe during the first two years of his presidency.

The Bay of Pigs Fiasco and Another Berlin Crisis, 1961

After overthrowing Fulgencio Batista's authoritarian regime in Cuba in early 1959, Fidel Castro established himself as the nation's new leader. His sweeping reforms redistributed the arable land to the Cuban peasants and nationalized American-owned corporations. In the face of mounting American pressures, his revolution turned to communism and the Soviet Union. Having such a foe in the Western Hemisphere just 90 miles from the United States vexed Presidents Dwight D. Eisenhower and John F. Kennedy.

In the last year of his presidency, Eisenhower had laid the foundation for the CIA to act in Cuba to train, fund, and equip Cuban counterrevolutionaries. Then Eisenhower's secret plan called for them to invade the island, incite a popular uprising, overthrow Castro, and establish a government friendlier to American interests. The CIA succeeded in a similarly clandestine effort in Guatemala earlier in the 1950s. However, Eisenhower left office before he could put his plan into action.

Once Kennedy took office, he set the existing plan in motion, deciding that an amphibious assault would be made in the Bay of Pigs on the south-central coast of Cuba. During the early months of 1961, the CIA trained Cuban exiles in amphibious techniques and supplied them with landing craft and Second World War-era aircraft to suppress Castro's Cuban Air Force.

On the morning of April 17, some 1,400 counterrevolutionaries landed in the Bay of Pigs. The operation went awry from the start. CIA-backed aircraft failed to destroy the Cuban Air Force, which allowed the Cuban aircraft to target the landing forces and disrupted supply efforts. Deadly counterattacks by Castro's tanks and artillery also started soon thereafter. The anticipated assistance from the Cuban people never materialized because no anti-Castro uprising occurred. Despite the counterrevolutionaries' pleas for direct military intervention, President Kennedy did not consent to further American involvement. The counterrevolutionaries were killed, wounded, or taken prisoner by Castro's forces two days later on April 19, 1961.

The Bay of Pigs invasion failed because of poor planning, incompetent coordination, inadequate support, and overly optimistic assumptions on the part of the CIA. The fiasco undermined the credibility of the United States and President Kennedy in the world's eyes. Castro used the incident to stir up anti-American sentiment in Cuba, strengthen his hold on power, and arouse fears among other nations about American covert operations. In Moscow, the Soviet Union's Premier Nikita Khrushchev also exploited the failed invasion by promising to defend Cuba with his nation's nuclear missiles.

The young and still unproven American president needed to restore his reputation and American prestige. Later in 1961, Kennedy and Khrushchev met to try to settle disputes about control of Berlin, Germany. These centered on the prosperity of West Berlin and the ongoing deployment of American, British, and French forces in the city. Khrushchev attempted to press the issues by intimidation. He threatened to sign a separate treaty with the East Germans that would allow them to restrict air and ground access to West Berlin. This gave rise to the second Berlin crisis since 1948.

But Kennedy refused to withdraw American forces from Berlin. Instead, the president asked Congress for increased military spending, ordered the Army and the Marine Corps to prepare to deploy up to six divisions to Europe, and mobilized more than 150,000 National Guardsmen and Reservists. The additional manpower would give the United States the capability to back Kennedy's hard stance with Khrushchev.

As the two leaders jockeyed for advantage, thousands of East Berlin (and thus East German) residents fled into West Berlin in search of political freedom and economic opportunity in the democratic half of the city. Khrushchev and the East German leaders wished to maintain a tight rein against the movement of people to West Berlin. Too many of them fled to freedom and prosperity in the western portion of the city. To halt the exodus, on August 13, Khrushchev gave his consent to the East Germans to construct a 25-mile barrier that isolated West Berlin from the eastern part of the city and surrounding area. The wall rose almost overnight. Kennedy protested the division of the city and bolstered the American military presence in West Berlin, but he took no steps to demolish the wall. Khrushchev did not press the issue of a separate treaty, and the crisis subsided later in the fall of 1961. The premier did, however, leave the "Berlin Wall" in place, so he could claim a victory over Kennedy. Indeed, the wall became an enduring symbol of the Cold War—a literal "iron curtain" that divided Berlin, Germany, and Europe into the two halves for the next three decades. Even so, the Berlin Crisis was hardly the last, nor the most dangerous confrontation between Kennedy and Khrushchev.

Kennedy Versus Khrushchev in the Cuban Missile Crisis, October 1962

Throughout late 1961 and into 1962, relations between the United States and the Soviet Union remained tense. The American military efforts in Southeast Asia steadily increased as the conflict in Vietnam became a contest between American and Soviet proxies. Closer to home, the Soviets also began sending aid to Cuba to help Fidel Castro consolidate his hold on the nation, a move consistent with Khrushchev's declaration that he would support wars of national liberation. For Americans, this equated to Soviet support for any communist revolution.

By the fall of 1962, the situation in Cuba erupted into a dangerous confrontation between the superpowers over Soviet military activities on the island. On October 14, an American U-2 spy plane flying over Cuba captured high-resolution photographs of missile sites. The Soviets could use these to launch nuclear missiles with sufficient range to hit targets in much of the United States. This gave the Soviet first-strike capability to attack before the U.S. military could react, and the Soviets sought parity with the Americans who had placed missiles in Turkey to the south of their home country. Once Kennedy received confirmation about the missiles on October 15, he recognized that they made the United States vulnerable. Just as important was the damage to American credibility in the Western Hemisphere if such a threat could persist. Kennedy also needed to make up for his failure at the Bay of Pigs.

President Kennedy and his civilian advisors debated several options: inaction, diplomacy, blockade, air strike, or invasion. From the military's perspective, the JCS, and especially General Curtis LeMay believed that a massive air strike followed by full-scale invasion were the only realistic options. The JCS discounted possible escalation into direct conflict with the Soviets, but Kennedy was unconvinced. He worried that the Soviets would be compelled to react militarily if Cuba was attacked. Rejecting the invasion option based on counterarguments by McNamara and others, Kennedy decided on October 22 to initiate a quarantine of all weapons and equipment going to Cuba. A clever use of terminology lessened the perception that the Americans were reacting militarily. Indeed, though they are essentially similar, a "blockade" is an act of war, while "quarantine" is sufficiently innocuous sounding. Maintaining flexibility, the president kept open the option of air strikes by sending SAC's nuclear-capable B-52s on perpetual high alert. He prepared seven Army and Marine Corps divisions for an invasion of Cuba if necessary. Lastly, Kennedy moved American submarines armed with Polaris nuclear missiles within range of the Soviet Union. These decisions gave the United States not only coverage of Cuba but also leverage against the Soviets in ongoing negotiations. Moreover, Kennedy's decisions were also reminiscent of the Monroe Doctrine of 1823 in which the United States would not tolerate any interference by foreign powers in the Western Hemisphere.

Tensions between Kennedy and Khrushchev continued to rise at an alarming rate. Neither side was willing to stand down so easily, or appear weak in the eyes of the world. The American quarantine went into effect on October 25 as the U.S. Second Fleet took up station in the Caribbean. Some 180 American warships formed a line some 500 miles east of Cuba, where they intended to intercept Soviet vessels large enough to carry missiles. Those ships unwilling to halt would be sunk.

Although Khrushchev labeled it a "pirate action" and an "act of aggression," the quarantine forced the Soviet leader into informal and back-channel negotiations. He yielded to the pressure and backed down on October 26, assuring the president that Soviet missiles would be removed from Cuba if Kennedy promised there would no invasion of the island. The American president also agreed to withdraw American nuclear missiles from southern Italy and Turkey in exchange for the Soviet missiles leaving Cuba.

The Cuban Missile Crisis ended on October 28. The resolution made Khrushchev look weak and Kennedy look decisive. In hindsight, however, the victory is not so clear. Unbeknownst to the Americans, an invasion force landing on Cuba would likely have been met by Soviet tactical nuclear weapons also stationed on the island. Nevertheless, the efforts to avert nuclear war heralded other improvements in Soviet-American relations. In 1963, the two superpowers and the United Kingdom signed a Nuclear Test Ban Treaty that ended testing underwater, in the air, or in space.

More generally, Soviet-American relations moved more toward "détente"—a supposed relaxation of tensions and thawing of the Cold War—that lasted until 1979. Even so, the thawing of the Cold War did not end the threat of nuclear war, which still loomed large even during the height of the American commitment to defend South Vietnam. Meanwhile, very substantial segments of the U.S. military remained alert to a possible Soviet missile strike on American soil, and other forces stood guard in Western Europe against a possible Soviet invasion.

Growing Commitment in Vietnam: Advice, Training, and Support, 1961–63

Although crises in the Caribbean and Europe dominated news headlines during Kennedy's presidency, Southeast Asia also attracted American officials' attention. Communist *coup d'etats* against governments in Laos and South Vietnam loomed as possibilities. As originally posited by Dwight Eisenhower, if South Vietnam or Laos fell to communism, then Cambodia, Thailand, Malaysia, Indonesia, Burma, India, or the Philippines might also fall like dominos. Consistent with the goal of containment, Kennedy and the United States could not let this chain reaction occur.

Evidence of the amplified American presence in Southeast Asia can be seen in the increasing number of American military advisors sent to South Vietnam, from 900 men in 1961 to 16,000 in 1963. Additionally, Washington ordered the establishment of the U.S. Military Assistance Command, Vietnam (MACV) in 1962, replacing the Military Assistance Advisory Group (MAAG) that had existed since 1950. The senior American officer of MACV exercised joint command and control over ground and coastal naval assets in South Vietnam.

The increasing numbers of advisors coincided with the decline in viability of President Ngo Dinh Diem's South Vietnamese government. Firmly anti-communist but completely undemocratic in his rule, by the time Kennedy became president Diem held onto power through repressive programs designed to eliminate competitors and critics. Meanwhile, North Vietnamese-sponsored revolutionaries fought to overthrow the South Vietnamese president. Between 1946 and 1954, anti-French revolutionary forces had been called the "Viet Minh." However, by 1960, that organization was replaced by the National Liberation Front, which

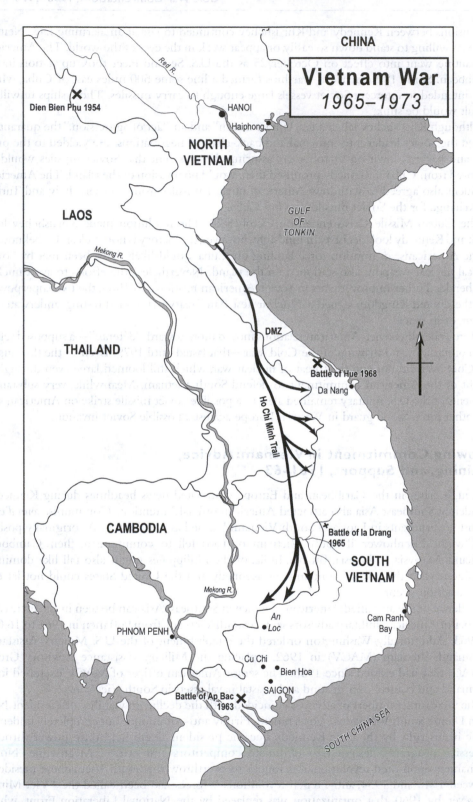

CHINA

Vietnam War
1965–1973

Red R.

✕
Dien Bien Phu 1954

HANOI

Haiphong

NORTH VIETNAM

LAOS

Mekong R.

GULF OF TONKIN

DMZ

THAILAND

✕
Battle of Hue 1968

Da Nang

Ho Chi Minh Trail

N

CAMBODIA

✕ Battle of Ia Drang 1965

SOUTH VIETNAM

Mekong R.

An
Loc

Cam Ranh
Bay

PHNOM PENH

Cu Chi

Bien Hoa

SAIGON

✕ Battle of Ap Bac
1963

SOUTH CHINA SEA

Map 14.1 The Vietnam War, 1961–1973

included communists, nationalists, and other groups in the South who opposed Diem's regime. More commonly, however, the South Vietnamese and Americans used the derogatory name "Viet Cong," translated to Vietnamese Communists, to describe their opponents, giving rise to the familiar "VC" moniker. Communist elements inside the NLF maintained connections to North Vietnam, and they primarily controlled the war effort against the American-supported South Vietnam.

Understanding the long conflict in Vietnam requires knowledge of that nation's geography, demographics, culture, and politics. Roughly the size of Italy, the narrow sliver of North and South Vietnam ran some 1,200 miles along the eastern coastline of Southeast Asia. Cambodia and Laos bordered the two Vietnams on the west, and China lay to the north. South Vietnam's topography varied from rice farms in low-lying land, rubber tree plantations in the Mekong River Delta, and jungle-covered hills and plateaus closer to the border with North Vietnam. Varying levels of humidity and temperatures ranged from 40 to 100 degrees Fahrenheit, depending upon elevation and season. South Vietnam received a significant amount of rainfall, especially during the monsoon season from May to November, turning roads into impassable morasses.

Approximately 80 percent of the 15 million people in South Vietnam lived at subsistence level as tenant farmers in close-knit families residing in hamlets, which were in turn grouped together as villages. Nearly all peasants were Buddhists, but the wealthy landholders tended to be French-educated Catholics with little in common with their poor countrymen. Although the South Vietnamese military consisted of some 250,000 soldiers serving in the Army of the Republic of Vietnam (ARVN), Diem's power depended mostly on the United States propping him up with financial and military assistance.

North Vietnam had a population of some 18 million, of whom hundreds of thousands of men and women served in the North Vietnamese Army (NVA). As the North's regular Army, these soldiers fell under command of General Giap, the talented leader who masterminded the defeat of the French forces at Dien Bien Phu in 1954. A student of military history, his tactical and strategic knowledge allowed him to notice weaknesses of the French, and later the Americans, that he could exploit. Giap coordinated efforts with as many as 300,000 Viet Cong fighters in the South and helped supply their guerilla war against Diem's government. Giap and his NVA soldiers shared the vision for a single communist nation as articulated by Ho Chi Minh, the president of North Vietnam. Thus, both communism and nationalism motivated Ho, Giap, and their followers—facts that American military and political leaders could never fully grasp.

Beginning in 1961, increasingly more Americans ventured into the unfamiliar physical environment in Vietnam and faced an equally unfamiliar enemy there. Apart from Marines who served in Latin America in the 1920s and 1930s, nearly all the senior U.S. military leaders had cut their teeth in combat in the Second World War and the Korean War. In these conventional conflicts, tactical victory meant controlling the battlefield at the end of an engagement. Operational victory could be achieved by stringing together a series of successful battles. On a higher level, strategic victory required that enemy forces be vanquished and enemy territory be occupied.

Fighting in Vietnam, however, did not align well with the recent experiences of the U.S. military. Holding territory or vanquishing enemy forces in set-piece battles were misapplied concepts in Southeast Asia. Serving as guerillas, or "insurgents" in 1960s parlance, the VC fighters would suddenly appear, ambush an American or ARVN unit, inflict casualties, and then retreat before any counterattack could take place. The VC fighters blended well into villages because they dressed, looked, and acted like presumably peaceful South Vietnamese peasants. Defeating this elusive enemy required new tactics and specialized training in counterinsurgency warfare.

As of 1962, the American military did have soldiers in Special Forces who learned, and in turn taught, these tactics to the ARVN soldiers. Indeed, President Kennedy embraced such intended roles for the Special Forces. He sent them to help the ARVN understand counterinsurgency tactics, utilize their superior firepower against the VC, and recruit anti-communist Vietnamese to serve. Like other American military advisors, the Special Forces accompanied the ARVN units on missions. However, the advisors could not participate in combat until 1962, when American advisors in Vietnam received permission to return hostile fire.

South Vietnam's Failed Programs, Battlefield Defeats, and a *Coup d'Etat*, 1963

Despite American material aid and training, the ARVN did not fare well in combat with the VC. One of the best early illustrations was the Battle of Ap Bac, which occurred in January 1963 in the Mekong Delta and pitted 300 VC fighters against 1,500 ARVN soldiers.

After locating a force suspected to include 120 VC fighters near the hamlet of Ap Bac, the ARVN planned to attack from three directions using infantry and Armored Personnel Carriers (APC). If necessary, troops could also be landed by helicopter, and airborne troops could be dropped by parachute. With numerically superior forces and a combined arms operational plan, the ARVN commanders and their American advisors believed that victory was assured.

On the morning of January 3, an unexpectedly large force of 300 VC fighters repulsed the ARVN's initial infantry assaults from the north and south, inflicting heavy casualties and pinning the surviving soldiers down in rice paddies. ARVN heli-borne reinforcements landing to the south took enemy fire from both hamlets and from the concealed positions between them. Inept South Vietnamese air strikes and artillery barrages did not quiet the VC. In the early afternoon, at the suggestion of the American military advisor to the ARVN commander, U.S. Army Lieutenant Colonel John Paul Vann, South Vietnamese APCs entered the fray. Armed with one machine gun and protecting 11 soldiers riding inside their armor-plated shells, the APCs attacked from the South, but the VC's intense fire halted their advance. Finally by late afternoon, Vann requested ARVN paratroopers drop behind the VC positions to block their escape. Even this maneuver could not be executed properly. Instead, they landed to the west on the wrong side of the enemy positions. Night fell before the paratroops could reach the enemy, and the remaining VC fighters retreated safely to the east across the rice paddies.

By the end of the Battle of Ap Bac, the ARVN suffered 180 casualties and the VC less than 60. Most of the VC fighters lived to fight another day. According to an aggravated Lieutenant Colonel Vann, the ARVN made "a miserable damn performance, just like it always is. These people won't listen. They make the same mistake repeatedly in the same way."[1] Several factors contributed to the ARVN's dismal showing: mistaken intelligence, ineffective coordination, low morale, and indecisive leadership. These problems dogged ARVN operations for the next 12 years.

American advice, training, and support to South Vietnam extended beyond combat operations to pacification efforts such as the strategic hamlet program. Because the VC relied heavily on local support, the ARVN attempted to pacify rural areas by isolating and protecting South Vietnamese peasants from interaction with the enemy. The strategic hamlet program called for ARVN units to search out and kill insurgents in villages and surrounding areas. While purging areas of VC influence, the ARVN moved the presumably neutral or friendly peasants from their old homes into new communities fortified with gun emplacements, barbed wire barriers, and other obstacles protecting their perimeters. In theory, these would keep the VC fighters from infiltrating the communities. By the end of 1963, millions of South Vietnamese peasants lived in several thousand fortified hamlets. The program failed to pacify the areas or the people living in them, however. Principally, corrupt South Vietnamese leaders failed to pay the peasants for their move, and inadequately defended hamlets fell to VC attacks. The ARVN units sometimes relocated the South Vietnamese by threat of force or even death. Such negative effects of the strategic hamlet program caused resentment among the peasants. Ripped from their ancestral lands, left destitute in their homes, and exploited in a corrupt system, many South Vietnamese otherwise unsympathetic to communism shifted their allegiance to the enemy's cause. The strategic hamlet program therefore proved to be an abject failure.

President Diem faced other internal problems after taking office in 1954. For example, he narrowly survived several assassination or *coup* attempts, in part because he retained American military and financial support that benefited the ARVN. But by the summer of 1963, President Kennedy's patience with Diem had waned to the point that he believed South Vietnam needed a different government. American leaders tried to convince Diem to leave office, but he refused. At the same time, the shrinking American support for the leader motivated several ARVN generals to oust him from power. Kennedy did not object to the plan. In fact, evidence points to the president and the CIA as having encouraged and sanctioned the *coup*.

On November 2, 1963, the generals succeeded in removing Diem from office. Token loyalist forces put up a fight in the capital city of Saigon, but quickly succumbed. Ngo Dinh Diem and his brother tried to escape from the city, but were captured and assassinated by junior officers in the ARVN. While the ouster of Diem came as no surprise to Kennedy, the details of his death stunned the American president. Regardless, Kennedy and his advisors needed to determine how best to deal with new South Vietnamese leaders.

The events in South Vietnam were, however, overshadowed by the assassination of President John F. Kennedy in Dallas, Texas, on November 22, 1963. His unfortunate death suddenly elevated Vice President Lyndon Baines Johnson to the presidency. Johnson had never received clear direction from Kennedy on how to proceed in South Vietnam, though. The trajectory of increasing commitment of American military and financial aid from 1961 to 1963 pointed to further escalation of American involvement. Nevertheless, while the American people mourned the loss of Kennedy, Johnson could not make any decisive moves in Southeast Asia for several months or maybe until the election in November 1964.

New President but Same Strategy: Lyndon Baines Johnson in Vietnam, 1964–65

Johnson brought the skills of a seasoned politician to the presidency, having served a dozen years in the House of Representatives and a dozen more in the Senate. In his first year as president, Johnson focused on solving domestic problems like poverty and discrimination. He had a vision for himself as a second Franklin Roosevelt initiating the second New Deal, which he called the "Great Society." He also pushed ground-breaking legislation such as the Civil Rights Act through Congress in 1964 and the Voting Rights Act in 1965, thereby guaranteeing liberties and suffrage to all American citizens.

Although concentrating on domestic issues, Johnson watched the conflict in South Vietnam with apprehension. In the wake of both Diem's and Kennedy's assassinations, the North Vietnamese took advantage of the turmoil by sending more arms to VC troops and preparing to deploy NVA forces to the South. It was clear to Johnson that, despite American efforts to train and advise the ARVN on counterinsurgency tactics, the VC had control over vast rural areas.

Throughout 1964, Johnson sent several thousand additional American service personnel to South Vietnam, raising the total to 25,000 by year's end. He also sent General William C. Westmoreland to become the commanding general of MACV on August 1, 1964. Earlier in his career, Westmoreland saw firsthand what superior American firepower and technology could do on battlefields, albeit leading units in conventional conflicts like the Second World War and the Korean War. From 1953 to 1963, he did tours on the Army staff at the Pentagon, served as Superintendent of the U.S. Military Academy, and commanded the 101st Airborne Division and then later the XVIII Airborne Corps.

Instead of attending the Army War College like so many senior officers, Westmoreland took an executive management course at the Harvard Business School in 1954. This meant he could speak the corporate language of Secretary of Defense Robert McNamara. Both men believed that winning war was a matter of directing the U.S. military's overwhelming amounts of man-power, bombs, shells, and bullets against an enemy as part of a bloody mathematical equation. Like McNamara, Westmoreland was loyal to their Commander-in-Chief, Lyndon Johnson, which in turn assured that Westmoreland would not be another upstart field commander like Douglas MacArthur was in the Korean War.

In the same week that Westmoreland assumed command of MACV, an incident occurred just off the coast of North Vietnam that provided President Johnson with a justification to escalate American involvement in Vietnam. On August 2, several North Vietnamese patrol boats launched torpedoes and fired shots at the destroyer USS *Maddox* in the Tonkin Gulf. The American vessel had sailed into waters claimed by North Vietnam to monitor radio traffic and radar use. This was hardly a new activity for American warships. In fact, the U.S. military conducted other covert operations in Northern territory as well. While North Vietnamese patrol boats would sometimes harass American ships, they had never fired on them until August 2. The *Maddox* evaded the attackers, returned fire, and damaged or sank the patrol boats. Another attack supposedly occurred on August 4, but insufficient evidence exists to prove what transpired. In the coming days, the veracity of the second attack did not matter because the incidents, while seemingly minor, took on much greater significance back in the United States.

Although both events remained clouded in controversy, President Johnson at the time believed the acts of aggression demanded immediate retaliation. On August 5, he ordered carrier-based aircraft to bomb several targets in North Vietnam. The same day, Johnson went to Congress to ask for more resources and greater latitude to stop communist expansion in Southeast Asia. After a brief debate, both houses of Congress approved his request by over-whelming margins.

Better known as the "Gulf of Tonkin Resolution," this measure gave the president the authority "to take all necessary steps, including the use of armed force, to assist" any allied Southeast Asian nation to defend itself. This resolution also permitted the president, "as Commander in Chief, to take all necessary measures to repel any armed attack against the forces of the United States and to prevent further aggression." The resolution amounted to a blank check for Johnson to act in South Vietnam and Southeast Asia as a whole. With a U.S. policy of escalation in the region, the Gulf of Tonkin Resolution did fit firmly into the American guiding strategy of the Cold War, the symmetric containment of communism.

Although Johnson had a mandate from Congress, he refrained from making noticeably greater American commitments in South Vietnam because he did not wish to endanger his chances in the November 1964 presidential election. He need not have worried, as he easily won the contest against the Republican Party's candidate, Barry Goldwater, who was an out-spoken conservative with unpopular stances on the conflict in Vietnam and on social programs supported by Johnson. Goldwater even suggested that the use of nuclear weapons might save South Vietnam and that Johnson's War on Poverty cost too much money. Such severe rhetoric allowed the sitting president to play the moderate in foreign policy and the progressive in domestic politics. On December 2, barely one month after the election, Johnson used his perceived mandate from the American people to authorize limited air strikes against targets in North Vietnam.

Escalation in Vietnam: Air War, Ground War, and the Draft, 1965

As 1965 began, the insurgent forces extended their control over more territory in South Vietnam. Johnson feared that the American ally might fall, yet he betrayed his unbridled contempt for the whole of Vietnam when he called it "a raggedy-ass little fourth rate country."[2] Such a racist attitude magnified the way that the American president and his advisors underestimated the enemy's battlefield capabilities and moral resolve. If the NVA and the VC were inferior in so many ways, then how could they stand up to the mighty United States?

In this context, President Johnson decided to take fuller advantage of his war-making powers. When the VC began attacking American bases in South Vietnam in February 1965, he decided to retaliate by ordering the U.S. Air Force to bomb targets in North Vietnam. Johnson believed strategic bombing could pressure the enemy into stopping its efforts in South Vietnam, boost morale in the ARVN, and destroy the North's industry and logistics. Operation ROLLING THUNDER started on March 2, 1965, and lasted more than three years, until late 1968.

The intensity of the American airstrikes slowly grew over those many months as part of the doctrine of "gradualism." This called for the U.S. Air Force and U.S. Navy to focus their overwhelming destructive capabilities against comparatively minor targets like power plants or storage facilities, while avoiding more significant ones. According to gradualism, this restraint would menace such key targets in the North as the capital of Hanoi and the major port of Haiphong in North Vietnam. If the United States could threaten to bomb these targets, officials thought, American diplomats could have more leverage in negotiations. Air power, however, did not convince the North Vietnamese to sue for peace in 1965, and thus, American aircraft began striking Hanoi and Haiphong Harbor the next year.

The first use of the American B-52s in South Vietnam occurred in April 1965. Although originally designed to make nuclear strikes against the Soviet Union, the Stratofortresses proved to be effective in dropping conventional ordnance on North Vietnamese targets. The bomber's long range also gave it extended loiter time that paid dividends in supporting American ground forces at the tactical level. As part of Operation ARC LIGHT, three of the massive aircraft would fly in tight formations at high altitudes. When receiving requests from embattled American ground units for direct support or when notified about enemy troop concentrations, three B-52s dropped 180,000 pounds of bombs that pulverized several square miles of territory. The ground shook from the explosive concussions, and survivors suffered ruptured eardrums, nose bleeds, and shell-shock.

In its 44 months, ROLLING THUNDER expended a staggering amount of American resources: some 300,000 sorties by American aircraft dropping nearly one million tons of bombs on enemy targets. This tonnage figure doubled the 500,000 tons of ordnance dropped in the entire Pacific Theater during the Second World War. The North Vietnamese reacted by creating a defensive network that relied on Soviet technology, particularly surface-to-air missiles, antiaircraft batteries, interceptor aircraft, and radar warning and tracking systems. The air defenses paid dividends for the North Vietnamese, as 180 American planes were shot down in 1965 alone.

Despite expanding the American commitment to South Vietnam, Johnson never stepped over the line from "limited war" to "total war." Understanding the volatility of international relations, he did not want to risk turning this regional proxy conflict into a global, nuclear conflict. Instead, the president wished to avoid any direct confrontations with the Soviet Union. Johnson could barely fight a limited war in Vietnam if he also hoped to achieve his domestic objectives. At home in the United States, Johnson preferred to educate, feed, and house the poor, and to send Americans to the moon, both of which required vast amounts of money.

It should also be noted that the United States had to sustain not only larger conventional force deployments to defend Western Europe against Soviet and Warsaw Pact invasions but also a potent nuclear arsenal capable of deterring the Soviet's nuclear forces. So in essence, President Johnson tried to fight one prolonged yet limited war in Vietnam while maintaining the necessary capabilities to fight two other conflicts—one conventional and the other nuclear.

Johnson's multiple strategic commitments and overstretched resources notwithstanding, two major turning points sparked the American escalation in South Vietnam. The first occurred when he ordered ground forces like the U.S. 3rd Marine Regiment and the U.S. Army's 173rd Airborne Brigade (Separate) to deploy to Vietnam in the spring of 1965. By year's end, more Marine units and the Army's 1st Infantry Division and the 1st Cavalry Division (Airmobile) also arrived in South Vietnam. These substantial American ground forces began combat and pacification operations within weeks after arriving in-country. They needed to overcome the dual challenge of finding and killing the VC while providing security and stability for the South Vietnamese civilian population.

The second turning point concerned American military manpower. Voluntary enlistments could not keep pace with the goal of putting 185,000 men in South Vietnam in 1965. The next two years saw troop levels reach 385,000 and then 485,000, respectively. When the Joint Chiefs of Staff proposed mobilizing the National Guard and the reserves, Johnson balked. He argued it would be obvious to the American people that Vietnam was not a limited war that required only finite resources. Instead, he made the fateful decision to rely more heavily on conscription, rather than voluntary service, to boost manpower levels. Draft inductions rose from 112,000 men in 1964 to their peak of 382,000 in 1966.

Box 14.2 The Draft and the Rotation System During the Vietnam War

Selective Service inductees came of out a larger pool of men aged 18 to 26 who were required to register in the Selective Service System. Beginning in 1963, married men were exempted from conscription. Then on August 26, 1965, Johnson changed the exemption to married men with children or those married before that day. College students could obtain deferments. Some men could be declined from the draft due to medical conditions like poor vision, moral issues like homosexuality, or other circumstances like pacifist religious beliefs. All other men were declared eligible and thus compelled to serve if receiving the draft notice. Conscription grew more unpopular as the Vietnam War lasted longer.

Many perceptions existed about conscription during the Vietnam War. Being drafted meant a higher probability of serving in front-line combat units and thus a greater risk being wounded or killed in Vietnam. Likewise, those drafted men tended to come from lower-income backgrounds and from minority groups. Others from middle-class or wealthier families found ways to defer military service, or they joined the reserves or the National Guard to reduce their chances of deployment to Vietnam. Selective service went through several reforms in attempting to reduce these disparities. Regardless, the public perceptions and statistical analyses have since been hotly debated by scholars.

After basic combat training and advanced individual training, the drafted and volunteer soldiers could serve a one-year tour of duty in South Vietnam. Marines only did a six-month tour but were encouraged to extend to a 13-month tour. Air Force pilots could finish tours in as quickly as seven months or completion of up to 100 missions, but flight crews stayed in Vietnam for nine to 12 months. U.S. Navy ships and the crews typically spent six to nine months on station near Vietnam. It should be noted that not all American volunteers or draftees went to Vietnam. Of the 1.7 million drafted and inducted from 1965 to 1973, approximately 40 percent deployed to South Vietnam.

Once "in county" as deploying to Vietnam was called, the soldiers and Marines were assigned as individuals to units permanently stationed in Vietnam. They found themselves as the "green" troops rotating into units to replacing departing or wounded. According to one participant, "We were not in Vietnam for ten years, but one year ten times." (Cited in David T. Courtwright, *Sky as Frontier: Adventure, Aviation, and Empire* [College Station: Texas A&M University Press, 2005, p. 210]). The recently arrived men or "grunts" may not have had friends or even acquaintances in their units, so they could only hope that strangers would teach them how to fight, act, and survive.

The rotation system degraded unit morale, cohesion, and combat effectiveness because the steady stream of incoming replacements and outgoing men endangered unit continuity of skills, tactics, and practices. The system also lent itself to American servicemen looking out for themselves as individuals, rather than seeing themselves as integral members of a group. The noncommissioned and commissioned officers may have perpetuated these attitudes because they also rotated in the same cycle and were susceptible to same challenges as the grunts. As the war dragged on and especially after the Tet Offensive in 1968, the morale problems of the rotation system grew more conspicuous.

Once in South Vietnam in 1965, the Marine units took up stations in the country's northernmost MACV's four corps-sized zones, near the border with North Vietnam. Marines faced constant threats from VC insurgents in the region and NVA soldiers crossing from north to south. Marine commanders experimented with ways to maximize protection of the local peasants with their overstretched manpower. The most promising solution came in the form of the Combined Action Program. Begun in August 1965, this program utilized rifle squads of 13 Marines to train South Vietnamese militiamen while also living in their villages and hamlets. This arrangement helped forge personal relationships with the people and allowed American units to gain their trust.

This pacification effort did have historical analogues. Although the Combined Action Program was pragmatic given the Marine Corps' finite resources in South Vietnam, the idea of Marines living, working, and fighting side-by-side with indigenous peoples was outlined in the Marine Corps' *Small Wars Manual* decades earlier in 1940. The Combined Action Program fit into two phases of the "inkspot" strategy. First, Americans would pacify a small area like a village by establishing stability and security there; then American and friendly villagers would expel VC fighters and extend safety over wider areas. The ink would thus spread outward.

Unlike the Marine Corps, the U.S. Army did not adopt approaches like the Combined Action Program. For one thing, this program could not be applied on a countrywide basis. Instead, General William Westmoreland favored large-scale operations designed to find and kill the VC and NVA forces. He believed that the United States could win the war by employing incredible firepower, exploiting superior technology, and ultimately bleeding the enemy to death by attrition. Defense Secretary Robert McNamara joined Westmoreland in seeing victory in Vietnam as a mathematical problem, balancing American casualties and time against payloads of bombs, numbers of bullets, and quantities of American ground troops. To help fight this war of attrition, Westmoreland used a new "Search and Destroy" strategy in which American units would lure the enemy into the open to be killed by coordinated artillery barrages and air raids. The major challenge came in combining search and destroy with special operations efforts. The U.S. military never figured out the proper way to do this in South Vietnam.

Because this strategy would be most effective if Americans could rapidly enter and exit areas, the helicopter proved to be the ideal vehicle for search and destroy missions. Unlike fixed-winged aircraft, which needed long runways to take off or land, helicopters could rise straight up into the air, hover, move laterally, or even fly backward. Such mobility gave helicopters distinct advantages in combat.

Among the helicopters available in the early 1960s, the UH-1 proved itself to be most ideal for military operations. Nicknamed the "Huey," this helicopter entered Army service in 1963. It had a crew of two men and could carry up to 12 passengers. The Huey possessed a range of 300 miles and reached a maximum speed of 125 miles per hour. Soldiers found that the UH-1 could play many roles, including command and control, supply and transport, observation and reconnaissance, close air support, and evacuation and rescue. All these capabilities came together in "Air Mobility" tactics, which in turn fulfilled the requirements in search and destroy. By June 1965, the newly designated 1st Cavalry Division (Airmobile) became the Army's first unit specifically designed to use helicopters. Just three months later, the 1st Cavalry deployed to South Vietnam.

Testing "Air Mobility" and "Search and Destroy" at Ia Drang, November 1965

In mid-November, General Westmoreland found a likely opportunity to test air mobility in the Ia Drang valley in South Vietnam's central highlands near the border with Cambodia. Some 3,000 NVA and VC combatants had taken up positions in caves in Chu Pong Massif (mountain). Just to their west in that valley was a clearing large enough for a helicopter landing zone (LZ). These factors set the stage for a clash between elements of the 1st Cavalry Division and the North Vietnamese. The ensuing Battle of Ia Drang included two distinct phases: The first

Figure 14.2 UH-1 "Huey" Helicopter Dropping Off Soldiers

Soldiers of the 1st Infantry Division jumping on a UH-1 "Huey" helicopter during an Air Mobility operation in South Vietnam in 1967. This tactic was key to the American military's Search and Destroy strategy.

© Robert R. McCormick Research Center

demonstrated the potential for helicopters and air mobility in combat, and the second revealed the vulnerability of American infantry on the ground.

The American plan called for 450 "sky troopers" of the 1st Battalion, 7th Regiment to ride in 16 Huey helicopters and land in a clearing code-named LZ X-ray. Once on the ground, the troopers would defend the LZ against enemy counterattacks. When the NVA and VC came out into the open, American military planners believed artillery fire and close air support would decimate them. Meanwhile, the Hueys would fly to the LZ to drop off supplies and evacuate wounded. Once the battle ended, the helicopters would extract the troopers from the area. During this fight, additional American troopers of the 2nd Battalion, 7th Regiment would land a few miles away and march to LZ X-ray to reinforce the 1st Battalion and help destroy the VC and NVA in the open. After the engagement, they would withdraw on foot to their original LZ.

Lieutenant Colonel Harold G. "Hal" Moore commanded 1st Battalion at Ia Drang. A combat veteran of the Korean War, he exercised decisive leadership in crises. Moore carefully studied North Vietnamese past and present tactics to better prepare his unit. Somewhat ominously, the 7th Cavalry was also the unit led by George Armstrong Custer at the disastrous Battle of the Little Bighorn in 1876. Moore hoped his troopers would not share the same fate nearly 90 years later.

The American troopers faced challenges from the moment they landed in the morning. The entire force of 450 men could not be carried to the LZ X-ray in a single trip by the 16 Hueys. It required five shuttle flights back and forth between the American base and the LZ, some 14 miles away and taking at least 30 minutes. Consequently, Lieutenant Colonel Moore had to establish his defensive perimeter with the first tiny contingent of 100 troopers. Fortunately, the enemy did not attack until early afternoon when 300 Americans were on the ground. These troopers succeeded in holding off assaults by a superior force of at least 1,000 NVA soldiers. Lieutenant Colonel Moore remained calm in the maelstrom, arranged his defenses as best he could, and called in fire support from nearby American artillery batteries.

Because the fighting turned the LZ "hot," the newly arrived helicopters ferrying additional men and ammunition came under enemy fire. The Hueys flew down to the clearing, hovered just above the ground while troopers jumped off, and then quickly rose back into the air. Although many helicopters took damage, their courageous pilots and crews kept returning to drop more men and evacuate the wounded. In this way, the remaining 150 troopers joined Moore's battalion by late afternoon. By nightfall of November 14, they repelled repeated NVA attacks from two directions and established a 360-degree perimeter around the LZ.

Early the next morning, a mass attack by the NVA and VC overran the southern edge of Moore's perimeter. Because such a large breach could cause the collapse of the entire American position, the radio call "Broken Arrow" went out over the airwaves. This signaled every available American aircraft to come the 1st Battalion's aid. Dozens of aircraft dropped their payloads on enemy combatants. Their bombs containing napalm killed or wounded many VC and NVA soldiers. The flammable napalm combined a thickening agent and gasoline to form a jellied substance. Once ignited, this burning mixture adhered to skin and other surfaces, and water could not quench napalm's flames. By late afternoon on November 15, the NVA and VC gains were reversed by the air strikes, and the perimeter was reestablished with help from newly arrived American reinforcements.

On the next day of the Battle of Ia Drang, the enemy forces made four more unsuccessful attacks. By the late afternoon, the NVA and the VC forces withdrew to their mountain caves, and the 1st Battalion left the LZ by helicopter. In all, Moore's unit lost 79 dead and 121

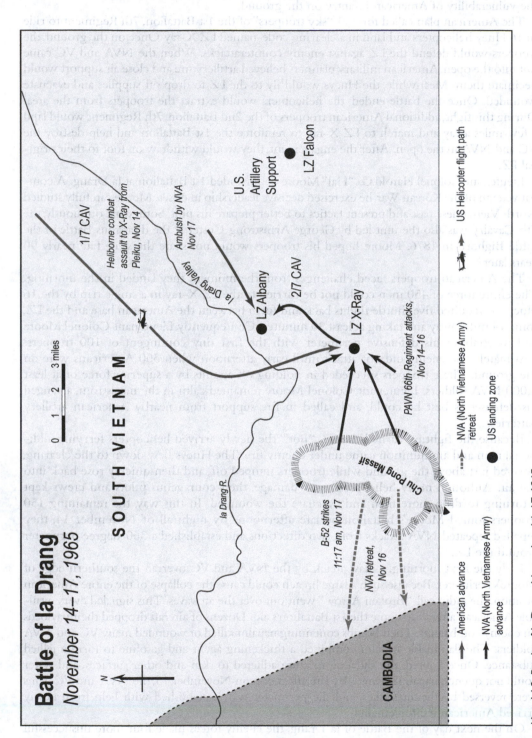

Map 14.2 Battle of Ia Drang, November 14–17, 1965

wounded out of 450 troopers. He did not suffer the same fate as Custer at the Little Bighorn because he enjoyed superior firepower provided by close air and artillery support as well as the lifeline provided by the helicopters. Even so, a 44 percent casualty rate represented a heavy price for a tactical experiment. Exact figures are not available for NVA and VC losses, but it is reasonable to put them at 1,000 or more dead.

Both sides claimed victory in this battle. For some Americans, the outcome validated their use of helicopters and air mobile tactics in search and destroy missions. The comparative casualty rates at the Battle of Ia Drang also fit into the systems analysis approach to warfare espoused by Defense Secretary McNamara and General Westmoreland. They predicted that the high body counts and favorable kill ratios of 10 enemy deaths to one American death would result in victory in a war of attrition.

It is interesting and bitterly ironic to note that the North Vietnamese also saw attrition as key to victory. On the political level, General Vo Nguyen Giap and Ho Chi Minh realized that inflicting casualties would wear down the American will to fight. They would willingly trade 10 North Vietnamese lives for one American life in this war with the United States, just as they had done against the French before them. On the tactical level, the North Vietnamese also recognized that helicopters were vulnerable to small arms fire when they slowed down to drop off soldiers. In the entire Vietnam War, the NVA and VC shot down 5,000 American helicopters.

The Battle of Ia Drang did not end, however, when the 1st Battalion lifted off of LZ X-ray on November 16, 1965. A completely different outcome happened to the 2nd Battalion that day as it marched several miles to a different LZ to be extracted by helicopter. En route, the 350 tired troopers formed a column some 550 yards long. Inadequate security and reconnaissance on the flanks left them vulnerable to ambush. Shortly after noon, more than 2,000 NVA soldiers sprang the trap, hitting the Americans with mortar fire and attacking on foot along the length of their column. Brutal close combat followed as small groups of American troops pulled together to defend tiny, isolated perimeters. Although timely support from American airpower and the arrival of a relief force saved the 2nd Battalion from complete annihilation, the NVA killed 155 and wounded 121 troopers. Their defeat was much closer to that of Custer at the Little Bighorn than Moore's 1st Battalion's experience.

Scenarios like the Battle of Ia Drang played out over and over again during the next seven years of the Vietnam War. In fact, this engagement's two phases can be considered as microcosms of ground combat: the U.S. military's employment of systems analysis and faith in firepower and technology versus the North Vietnamese use of military operations and political realities as weapons.

Looking for the "Light at the End of the Tunnel," 1966–67

As the first phase of their three-phase plan to win the war, General Westmoreland and Defense Secretary McNamara decided to "Americanize" the conflict by replacing the ineffective and unreliable ARVN with American combat units. The U.S. military could thus, the two men believed, take the war to the VC and NVA in the second phase. As the U.S. military ramped up operations in the air and on the ground in South Vietnam, the number of Americans sent to South Vietnam skyrocketed from 25,000 men to 184,000 by the end of 1965, and to 385,000 in 1966.

The manpower requirements for the Vietnam deployments meant that the U.S. Army and Marine Corps needed to grow. The Army went from 1.1 million soldiers in 1962 to 1.4 million in 1967, and the Marine Corps from 190,000 to 285,000 in the same five years. Many

American men volunteered for service in these early years, and personnel stationed in Europe and South Korea helped fill units in South Vietnam. These solutions, however, were not enough. The U.S. military also relied on the civilian draft to reach and maintain numbers: 382,010 men were inducted into service through Selective Service in 1966 and another 228,263 in 1967.

The ongoing expansion of American ground, air, and naval forces in Vietnam allowed Westmoreland to launch major offensives. Not only was his aggressive mind-set consistent with the Americanization process but the expansion also constituted the second phase of his plan to defeat the VC and NVA operating near the populated areas. Once the second phase was completed, the last of his three-phase plan would find and kill the remaining enemy combatants in the rural areas.

The second phase included actions like Operation CEDAR FALLS, which began on January 8, 1967. Some 30,000 American soldiers in the 1st Infantry Division, 25th Infantry Division, 173rd Airborne Brigade, and 11th Armored Cavalry Regiment attempted to expel the VC from a 60-square mile area north of Saigon called "the Iron Triangle." American units attacked from the east and blocked escape routes to the north and west. More than just finding and destroying the enemy, U.S. units deported South Vietnamese peasants suspected of sympathizing with the VC, destroyed their dwellings, and defoliated the jungle with chemicals sprayed by aircraft flying overhead. The Viet Cong reacted by withdrawing toward Cambodia and hiding in massive tunnel complexes rather than fighting in the open. Westmoreland judged CEDAR FALLS a success because they measured the pacified territory on a map against the relatively minor loss of 309 American casualties. However, the alienation of displaced South Vietnamese peasants, modest VC casualties, and the eventual reassertion of VC influence in the Iron Triangle hardly justified the entire effort.

Another example can be seen in Operation JUNCTION CITY, lasting from February 22 to May 14, 1967. During this 12-week period, four ARVN battalions, the 173rd Airborne Brigade, 196th Infantry Brigade, 11th Armored Cavalry Regiments, and elements of the 4th Infantry Division, totaling 25,000 men, moved into an area near the Cambodian border. They intended to drive the VC into unpopulated areas where they would fall victim to withering American firepower. In March, the largest air mobile assault in history took place when 240 helicopters offloaded American soldiers in one battle on a single day. After the operation ended in mid-May, Americans claimed to have inflicted 2,700 casualties on the VC against their own losses of 282 dead and 1,100 wounded.

Many other smaller engagements occurred in 1966 and 1967. These ranged from several thousand Americans fighting for hills or villages to several dozen soldiers in Long Range Reconnaissance Patrols setting ambushes for VC fighters. The Americans might momentarily clear the enemy from tracts of land. However, when their focus shifted elsewhere, the VC and NVA reclaimed control of that area. Although this cyclical process never ended, Westmoreland and McNamara could not divorce themselves from their faith in the search and destroy strategy. And they could not set aside their faith in American advanced technology and superior firepower. These fit too nicely in the systems analysis approach to war-making. Worse still, no subordinates could convince them otherwise.

Yet in hindsight what else were Westmoreland and McNamara to do? They needed a U.S. military—especially the Army—that could stop the Soviets in Europe in a conventional fight. So reorienting the Army's way of war-making too dramatically toward counterinsurgency would have undermined its combat effectiveness in Europe. So on some levels Westmoreland and McNamara found themselves in a catch-22. In addition to this no-win scenario, both were, as stated above, predisposed to fighting conventional warfare with body counts, kill ratios, superior firepower, and advanced technology.

In 1966 and 1967, popular support among the South Vietnamese civilians for their anti-communist government did not generate positive results because Americans disrupted or destroyed the livelihoods of so many. These actions by Americans failed to "win the hearts and minds" of the South Vietnamese. To reverse this negative trend, pacification programs were placed under the of a new organization called "Civil Operations and Revolutionary Development Support (CORDS)" in 1967. Under its auspices, the U.S. Army Special Forces, the CIA, and their South Vietnamese counterparts coordinated intelligence-gathering efforts. They tried to identify VC insurgents and find ways to destroy enemy communications and logistics. Sometimes the suspected VC sympathizers would be captured, interrogated, and even tortured until they revealed secret contacts, plans, or bases. In other cases, CORDS might authorize those suspected VC or sympathizers to be neutralized—a euphemistic term for assassination. These activities have since been labeled as terror tactics. Nevertheless, CORDS did help undermine and disrupt VC operations. As time went on, the NVA had to assume a greater role in the South as the VC's effectiveness declined.

By the end of 1967, American estimates of enemy body counts of 130,000 dwarfed the 11,000 American deaths, a kill ratio that seemed to reach a threshold of success of 10 dead enemy fighters for every single dead American serviceman. The war in Vietnam appeared to be going well. After-action reports and statistical studies bore out the American assumption that enough bullets, artillery shells, rockets, and bombs could bring the enemy to his knees.

So positive were these signs that during a press conference in November 1967, General William Westmoreland uttered the words "light at the end of the tunnel" to update the American people on progress in Vietnam. Elsewhere in Congressional hearings, the general testified that South Vietnam was almost secured against communism, and that American service personnel would soon come home. President Johnson shared Westmoreland's optimistic outlook. In fact, the president hoped that he might soon start withdrawing Americans from Vietnam within the next year.

On the home front, however, ominous signs revealed how years of conflict had caused anger and resentment among certain groups by late 1967. Earlier that decade, for example, most African Americans had supported the war effort, just as they had done throughout the twentieth century. But, disproportionately high percentages of African Americans being drafted and dying in Southeast Asia slowly aroused opposition to the war. Formerly pro-war leaders like Martin Luther King Jr. sided with radicals and militants like Stokely Carmichael. Increasingly, African Americans claimed that Vietnam "was a white man's war, but a black man's fight."

By 1967, these attitudes added to the simmering anger in African-American communities about racially charged issues. When riots erupted in cities across the United States, local authorities sometimes called in the National Guard to help restore order. Some blacks were killed in ensuing fighting in the streets, and many more were injured or arrested. The destruction wrought by the uprisings revealed an increasingly militant and desperate mood among some African Americans. Not all the civil rights activities degenerated into violence, however. Martin Luther King led 5,000 blacks in a peaceful antiwar march in Chicago in March 1967.

That decade also saw the growth of an increasingly vocal antiwar movement. Minor demonstrations started in 1964 when Congress passed the Gulf of Tonkin Resolution. The movement—or "loose coalition" might be a more descriptive term, in retrospect—gained momentum as more Americans fought and died in Vietnam in succeeding years. The draft proved to be a particularly contentious issue because the process seemingly too often selected poorer men and minority men to serve. A few thousand Americans eligible for the draft claimed conscientious objector status due to religious beliefs. Still more endured incarceration or fled to Canada rather than go to Vietnam. Meanwhile, men from middle-class or wealthy backgrounds possessed the wherewithal to attend college, defer military service, or avoid the draft altogether.

Although portrayed in the mid-1960s by the still largely pro-war American media as hippies and radicals, the antiwar movement attracted an ever-widening range of supporters. Civil rights activists and women's rights activists joined forces with religious leaders, teachers, attorneys, celebrities, students, and some veterans to oppose the war. It is also worth noting that some Americans opposing the war looked to self-interests like career goals or family plans. The Vietnam War protesters fed off the energy of the civil rights and women's rights movements, and those latter activists likewise drew energy from the antiwar movement. In addition to marches numbering in the hundreds of thousands of people, the antiwar movement's activities included burning draft cards, picketing government buildings, or occupying university buildings.

Despite the noisy protests against the Vietnam War, most American people continued to trust their civilian and military leaders in the closing months of 1967. If President Johnson and General Westmoreland correctly predicted victory in Vietnam, then domestic disturbances might have been minimized or ended in the coming years. But if not, then even more massive upheaval was sure to occur.

1968: The Tet Offensive

As the new year of 1968 began, it looked like the 485,000 American service personnel would succeed in winning the fight against communism in South Vietnam. American military leaders in Vietnam and political leaders in Washington, however, missed telltale signs that portended a much different future. They overestimated American progress and underestimated enemy tenacity.

One such indicator was the conspicuous increase in traffic moving on the Ho Chi Minh Trail. In mid-1967, approximately 500 trucks per month hauled tons of supplies several hundred miles through Laos and Cambodia to support the VC and NVA forces in the South. By December, this figure grew to 6,300 trucks. In addition, more than one million Vietnamese women pushed bicycles laden with supplies along the trail. Lastly, 80,000 NVA soldiers slipped into South Vietnam in 1967. General William Westmoreland and other American leaders ignored this dramatic upswing in movement on the Ho Chi Minh Trail in part because it did not fit into their assumptions about the "light at the end of the tunnel."

In the meantime, the South Vietnamese looked forward to the Tet holiday marking the Lunar New Year on January 30, 1968. The opposing forces had agreed to a cease-fire during the celebration. Unbeknownst to the Americans or ARVN, however, the VC and NVA planned a coordinated series of surprise attacks against dozens of major military bases and cities in the South. The leaders in Hanoi called this the "General Offensive, General Uprising," but it is remembered by Americans as the Tet Offensive. The North Vietnamese hoped that their attacks would create catastrophic shocks to the American and South Vietnamese military systems, rendering them incapable of reacting to so many threats at one time. Battlefield successes, communist planners hoped, would in turn incite the South Vietnamese peasants to overthrow their government.

On January 21, about a week before Tet started, the NVA assaulted the U.S. Marine base at Khe Sanh near the demilitarized zone, an intended feint that would divert American attention and resources from their efforts throughout the South. After surrounding the 6,000 Marines at Khe Sanh, some 17,000 NVA soldiers made repeated ground attacks and bombarded the base day and night with artillery in the surrounding hills. The Marines constructed fortifications that formed a perimeter around an airfield, which became the artery for aerial resupply from other American bases.

Shades of France's Indochina War began to appear, as the siege of Khe Sanh looked like a repeat of the debacle of Dien Bien Phu in 1954. Unlike the French defenders, however, the Marines enjoyed incredible amounts of close air and artillery support that kept the NVA at bay. Over the next 10 weeks, U.S. Air Force and Marine Corps aircraft flew 16,000 sorties and dropped 31,000 tons of bombs on areas outside the perimeter. American transport aircraft and helicopters supported the Marines on the ground with 19,000 tons of supplies by parachute drop or by landing and offloading cargo under enemy fire. Unlike Dien Bien Phu, too, the Marines held their ground until the siege lifted in April 1968. Only 205 defenders lost their lives in the fighting, while some 10,000 NVA soldiers died.

Nine days after the shooting started at Khe Sanh, another 85,000 NVA soldiers and VC fighters opened the main Tet Offensive on January 30, 1968. Ignoring the holiday cease-fire agreement, they struck more than 200 cities, towns, and bases across South Vietnam. They caught the unprepared Americans and South Vietnamese by surprise. In the capital city of Saigon, several NVA soldiers succeeded in breaching the U.S. Embassy's walls and occupying the compound before being killed by counterattacking Americans. It took several more days of bloody street fighting to root out and defeat the enemy in Saigon.

The Tet Offensive's bloodiest and longest fighting occurred in the city of Hue, which lay on the coast barely 30 miles south of the demilitarized zone. This major city possessed great symbolic and substantive importance. Once the imperial capital of Vietnam, Hue now served as a major base for American and ARVN logistics and military operations. Despite its significance, Hue was not heavily defended in early 1968, allowing the North Vietnamese to exploit this weakness and commit some 10,000 troops to capture and hold the city.

The initial North Vietnamese assaults on January 31 caught the American and ARVN units in Hue off guard. The enemy easily took control of the city, except for small pockets of ARVN and U.S. Marine resistance. The North Vietnamese raised their nation's flag over Hue's walled citadel that protected a palace complex. Ten days later on February 10, a counterattack against Hue came from American and ARVN units. They fought an enemy well entrenched in machine-gun bunkers and sniper positions, and who launched coordinated raids at night. The bitter combat raged block by block, house-to-house, leaving Hue in utter ruins. The combat in the citadel and imperial palace proved to be particularly vicious because of the risk of damage to the culturally and historically significant buildings. But, eventually, even these were targeted when enemy forces sheltered in them. Finally on February 29, Hue had been secured, and the ARVN hoisted their flag over the citadel. The month-long battle cost the North Vietnamese invaders at least 5,000 killed and thousands more wounded. The Americans suffered 1,800 casualties including 216 deaths, and the ARVN endured 2,600 casualties.

The main effort of the Tet Offensive ended in late February 1968. American and ARVN units won battlefield victories throughout South Vietnam, killing at least 45,000 VC and NVA combatants. They fought in the open using conventional tactics rather than the insurgent tactics of the past. This played into the hands of Westmoreland and the U.S. military, and left South Vietnamese communists vulnerable to massive American artillery and aerial firepower. The VC took so many casualties that it ceased to be a viable force in the future. Lastly, the North Vietnamese never incited a mass uprising of South Vietnamese people against their government.

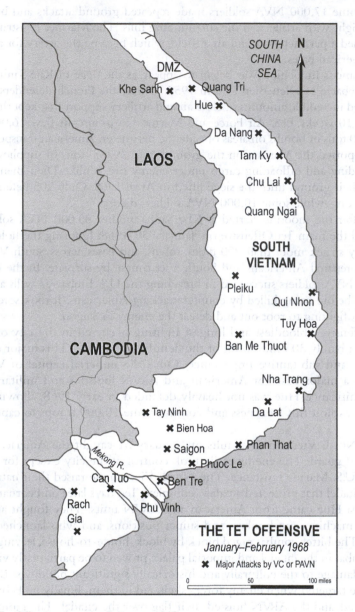

SOUTH
CHINA
SEA

N

DMZ

Khe Sanh ✕   ✕ Quang Tri

Hue ✕

LAOS

Da Nang ✕

Tam Ky ✕

Chu Lai ✕

Quang Ngai ✕

SOUTH
VIETNAM

Pleiku ✕

Qui Nhon ✕

Tuy Hoa ✕

CAMBODIA

Ban Me Thuot ✕

Nha Trang ✕

Tay Ninh ✕   Da Lat ✕

Bien Hoa ✕

Mekong R.   ✕ Saigon   ✕ Phan That

✕ Phuoc Le

Can Tuo   ✕ Ben Tre

Rach   Phu Vinh
Gia
✕

THE TET OFFENSIVE

January–February 1968

✕ Major Attacks by VC or PAVN

0   50   100 miles

Map 14.3 The Tet Offensive, January–February, 1968

Thus, the outcome of Tet should have been a prelude to defeating the communist insurgency at the tactical level in the South. But it was not.

Tet's Damaging Effects on American Public Opinion

Back on the home front in the United States, the Tet Offensive triggered a dramatic shift in public attitudes about the war. Televisions in living rooms across the United States showed the supposedly defeated VC and NVA launching surprise attacks on unsuspected and unprepared

American forces. No longer was there a military and government filter on what civilians' eyes would see, as in the Second World War. In 1968, after families sat down for dinner, images of American boys—color images, no less—came through, bloodied and often dead. It constituted a significant shift in the American consciousness. News programs listed the numbers of Americans killed and wounded, and news magazines displayed their photographs. Such portrayals of an audacious enemy exposed earlier statements about a "light at the end of the tunnel" as delusions, if not outright lies.

Confidence in President Lyndon Johnson and General William Westmoreland rapidly declined as the American casualty rate rose. In a broadcast on February 27, the highly respected CBS News anchorman Walter Cronkite lamented, "To say that we are closer to victory today is to believe, in the face of the evidence, the optimists who have been wrong in the past. To suggest we are on the edge of defeat is to yield to unreasonable pessimism. To say that we are mired in stalemate seems the only realistic, yet unsatisfactory, conclusion."[3] Cronkite's term "stalemate" did not equate to an American defeat, but his tone did capture the increasingly skeptical mood in the United States. This shifted the center of gravity on the home front.

For his part, Johnson could hardly believe the reports about Tet. He had accepted the optimistic conclusions drawn about kill ratios and body counts given to him by the U.S. military. As it turned out, those figures may have been inflated to ensure promotions for American commanders and ongoing support in Washington. Regardless of how accurate they were, the NVA and VC casualties failed to reduce the enemy's will to fight. Defense Secretary McNamara and Westmoreland hoped for victory through attrition, but by Tet it appeared the North Vietnamese were the ones winning the war of attrition. In the wake of Tet, a disgraced McNamara resigned his post in late February, and a discredited Westmoreland left Vietnam in June after completing his tour as commanding general of MACV.

As a result of the Tet Offensive, Johnson also faced an energized antiwar movement. Demonstrations occurred at more universities and cities across the United States. His loss of credibility spread to the Democratic Party where, despite being president, he faced serious primary opposition from antiwar Senators Eugene McCarthy and Robert Kennedy. McCarthy called for a slow withdrawal from Vietnam, while Kennedy demanded that American units immediately leave Vietnam. By the end of March, the public outcry and political pressure forced Johnson to make the agonizing decision to withdraw from the presidential election. His political career was yet another casualty of Vietnam.

Instead of running for reelection, Johnson wanted to focus all his time on the war. He sent reinforcements to South Vietnam bringing the total number of American service personnel to 536,000 men. At the same time, he decided to work for a negotiated peace in Vietnam, halting Operation ROLLING THUNDER's bombing raids in North Vietnam in hopes of bringing the enemy to the table. In fact, just before the presidential election in November 1968, Johnson ordered an end to all bombing in South Vietnam. None of these efforts helped end the conflict in Vietnam, however.

The political downfall of Lyndon Johnson was hardly the most tragic event in American history in 1968. In March of that year, several dozen American soldiers raped or massacred several hundred South Vietnamese women and children in the village of My Lai. Although not public knowledge that year, this incident revealed what could happen in units with poor leadership and moral bankruptcy within the ranks. At home, other tragedies occurred when two great leaders—Martin Luther King and Robert Kennedy—fell victim to assassins' bullets in April and June, respectively. Their tragic deaths roused more anger and frustration among African Americans. Race riots followed in more than 100 cities. Violence also erupted again in August when antiwar protesters clashed with police and National

Guardsmen in Chicago at the 1968 Democratic National Convention. While the fighting occurred in the streets, Vice President Hubert H. Humphrey accepted his party's presidential nomination.

The political damage to the Democratic Party in a year of riots and assassinations at home and military setbacks in Vietnam could not be undone. Humphrey lost in a close vote to the Republican candidate Richard M. Nixon in the election in November. As part of his campaign rhetoric, Nixon appealed to many voters by promising to restore order, discontinue the draft, and end the war in Vietnam. These three issues exploited all the Democratic Party's weaknesses. Although Nixon made assurances in his campaign, the war would drag on for another four years and just as many Americans would die in Nixon's war as Johnson's.

A New President and a New Strategy: Nixon and "Vietnamization"

When he became president in January 1969, Richard Nixon inherited a nation with deep internal divisions across racial and political lines. Neither consensus nor goodwill replaced the skepticism and cynicism so prevalent among many Americans. They had watched as trusted leaders assured them of victory in Vietnam only to have those predictions proven wrong in the Tet Offensive. The United States' inability to buttress South Vietnam against the communist onslaught pointed to American limitations. In sum, the United States government suffered from a loss in credibility at home and abroad.

Nixon adopted his own new approach to the conflict in Southeast Asia. Whereas Johnson pushed American forces into the front-line fight, Nixon reversed this emphasis with his "Vietnamization" in 1969. This entailed shifting the responsibility for combat operations to ARVN forces, while gradually withdrawing American service personnel from South Vietnam. The first 25,000 American troops returned to the United States in June 1969, and an average of 10,000 more departed every month thereafter for the next four years.

The remaining Americans helped train and advise the ARVN, while also providing combat units in selected operations. In the meantime, Nixon hoped to negotiate a peaceful resolution with the North Vietnamese government. Unfortunately, the North's political and military leaders understood that the Americans would have to eventually leave the South, and as such they did not see a brokered peace as necessary. Instead, the NVA continued combat operations in South Vietnam designed to undermine the Saigon government and dishearten American forces.

After succeeding General Westmoreland as the commander of MACV beginning in mid-1968, General Creighton W. Abrams took the leading role in Vietnamization. His style differed from that of his predecessor. Abrams never made sweepingly optimistic predictions about the war effort. Instead, he offered candid reports based on facts. He took up several major challenges during his next three years at MACV: Prepare the ARVN for independent combat operations, improve the political viability of the South Vietnamese government, manage the gradual withdrawal of American troops from South Vietnam, and maintain American morale amid rising drug abuse, disciplinary problems, and racial friction.

The last set of challenges proved to be the most difficult to overcome in the U.S. military. Drug use grew more acute as it became apparent to American service personnel that the war was not winnable, participation was not only dangerous but pointless, and support for the war effort at home declined. The most severe breakdowns in discipline can be seen in "fragging."

On a few rare occasions, enlisted men would throw fragmentation grenades into tents occupied by unpopular officers, killing or wounding them in the blast.

Racial problems also plagued the U.S. military. The racism inherent in the draft process and in the deployment process meant that a disproportionately high number of African Americans served in combat units in Vietnam. Once in military service, blacks could not expect the rapid promotions that some of their white counterparts received. The anger could boil over into protests or even violence, particularly on bases, where some Caucasian troops subjected African-American servicemen to slurs and other forms of harassment. Incidents occurred away from battlefields on posts and bases where most American servicemen spent their time in Vietnam. However, racial tensions were much less prevalent in units sent out to the field on combat missions. The fear of ambush, capture, and death brought American troops of all races and ethnicities together to fight their common North Vietnamese enemy rather than each other.

The futility of ongoing combat operations is represented in the Battle of Hamburger Hill in May 1969. American soldiers spent 10 days trying to wrest control of a mountain from the enemy in some of the most brutal fighting of the entire war. The Americans needed to neutralize NVA positions one by one in deliberate engagements that soldiers characterized as chewing up units like hamburger. Three weeks after securing the mountain, the Americans abandoned it because holding the position indefinitely was impractical. The pointless outcome pushed General Abrams to halt such large-scale search and destroy missions. Instead, he utilized American forces to guard the South Vietnamese borders or to carry out smaller unit patrol, sweep, and ambush missions.

Winless Fighting and Endless Negotiations, 1970–73

For many years, NVA and VC forces came across the Cambodian border to hit targets in South Vietnam and then retreat to safety in the neighboring nation. Although claiming neutrality in the conflict in Vietnam, the Cambodian government allowed the North Vietnamese to take refuge in this way. Unlike the communist forces, international neutrality laws hamstrung the United States and South Vietnam, making it difficult to violate Cambodia's neutral stance, even if it was a false pretense.

By March of 1970, however, the situation changed when an anti-communist faction overthrew the sitting government of Cambodia. The nation's new leader, Lon Nol, demanded that the NVA units leave Cambodia. Seeing the political change as a window of opportunity, President Richard Nixon directed the U.S. military to commence a joint operation with ARVN forces to venture into Cambodia and destroy the NVA bases. Nixon used the term "incursion" to distinguish this mission from an "invasion" because of the latter term's connotation of conquest. On April 29, approximately 20,000 American and South Vietnamese soldiers crossed into eastern Cambodia with mixed results. The NVA lost their supply depots near the border and needed at least one year to recoup those losses. Still, most enemy units merely moved farther west to safety. Two months later, at the end of June, the Americans returned to South Vietnam.

The incursion served as a litmus test of Nixon's policy of Vietnamization. The ARVN units performed well when fighting side by side with American counterparts, but their ability to do so independently remained in question. The same problems of ineffective leaders, unreliable units, and uneven performances that plagued the ARVN back in 1963 persisted into 1971. The best training and equipment the United States could provide had little bearing on whether ARVN units would falter in the face of NVA attacks.

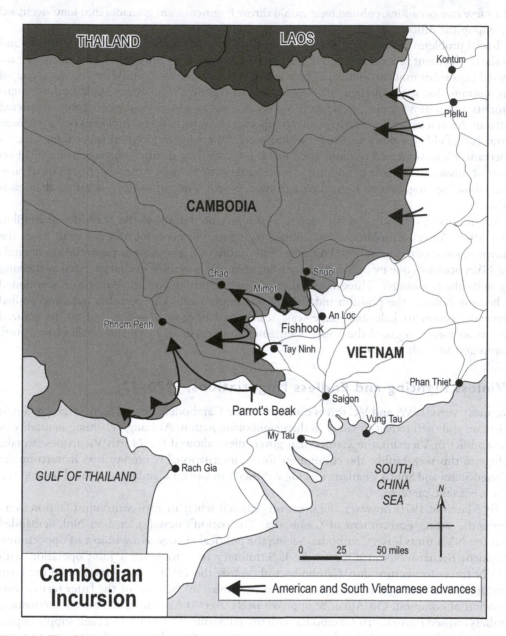

Map 14.4 The Cambodian Incursion, April–July 1970

Nowhere were the ARVN's flaws more conspicuous than in Operation LAM SON 719 in February and March of 1971. Much like in Cambodia prior to March 1970, the U.S. military could not legally cross into Laos; however, the South Vietnamese could. The operational plan called for 16,000 ARVN soldiers to move across the Laotian borders to achieve three goals: Cut the flow of supplies on the Ho Chi Minh Trail, test the capabilities of the

ARVN to fight on its own, and stop an impending NVA cross-border invasion before the dry season started.

Their initial advance made good progress in the first few days and threatened the Ho Chi Minh Trail's network of paths and roads. Then the North Vietnamese retaliated by sending more than 30,000 NVA soldiers to repel the ARVN attackers and force them to retreat into South Vietnam. Inclement weather, inadequate planning, and poor coordination further reduced ARVN effectiveness. Not even the massive firepower of American artillery and aircraft could turn the tide. The NVA exacted a high price of 7,500 casualties on the ARVN. Though the enemy lost 15,000 men, the Ho Chi Minh Trail remained safe. Operation LAM SON 719 demonstrated that the ARVN was not a viable fighting force and that Vietnamization was not a realistic policy.

Richard Nixon monitored events in South Vietnam and continued negotiations with North Vietnam. He sent Secretary of State Henry Kissinger to meet secretly with North Vietnamese counterparts and, on several occasions, to conduct peace talks to end the conflict. Nixon and Kissinger hoped to strike a balance between a complete American withdrawal and the North's ongoing presence in the South. This key point of contention affected the viability of the South Vietnamese government. If VC or NVA units remained in the South, then that nation could not maintain its independence.

Meanwhile, Nixon made good on his promise to bring service personnel back home. When he took office in 1969, the figure stood at 543,000 Americans in Vietnam. This dropped to 280,000 by 1971, and to 140,000 by 1972. Those hundreds of thousands of veterans returned to their country without the fanfare or appreciation enjoyed by veterans of earlier wars. Sometimes they walked through airport terminals to be jeered as "baby killers" or be spat upon by protesters, while many other soldiers immediately changed out of their uniforms and into civilian clothes in airport bathrooms to save themselves from their countrymen's heckling. Once in their civilian lives, the Vietnam veterans suffered from physical and psychological wounds of battle. It would take decades before these men, draftees and volunteers alike, could make peace with their past, if ever.

The news of the homecomings of so many Americans should have caused an upswing in public opinion regarding the Vietnam War, but this did not happen. Instead, polls showed a downward spiral in support for the war effort between 1970 and 1971. Making matters still worse, several tragic incidents and negative revelations came to light in the news media in those years. In 1970, an antiwar demonstration at Kent State University turned bloody when National Guardsmen opened fire and killed four protesters, while wounding nine. The next year saw the worst headlines. Almost all the American soldiers accused of committing the atrocities at My Lai escaped requisite punishment. Only the commanding officer was found guilty of murder and sentenced to life in prison. However, his punishment was later reduced to house arrest for less than four years. Before the dust settled on the My Lai trial, the *New York Times* published the so-called *Pentagon Papers* in June 1971. After being leaked to the media, these classified government documents revealed how, for many years, American military and political leaders deliberately misled the American people regarding the roles, purposes, and failures in the Vietnam War.

During 1971 and 1972, the North Vietnamese leaders kept careful watch on public opinion in the United States, American troop levels in South Vietnam, and the combat effectiveness of the ARVN. By 1972, all three appeared to be at their lowest ebb. The North Vietnamese sought a decisive victory that year. Beginning on March 30, in what was called the "Easter Offensive," more than 120,000 NVA soldiers came crashing through the demilitarized zone or across the Laotian and Cambodian borders into South Vietnam. The NVA chose this late March–early April period to use the cloud cover during monsoon season and thereby limit American close air support. The NVA experienced initial successes as they threw the ill-prepared ARVN forces into retreat and the civilian populace into chaos. Victory appeared to be close at hand.

Because only 103,000 American servicemen in support units and a few combat units remained in-country, the primary responsibility for repelling this invasion rested on the ARVN. As the NVA pushed farther into the South, the ARVN's resistance stiffened enough to stop the enemy advance in June and save their nation from defeat. The weather also cleared so that American air power could be directed against the NVA forces. Over the next two months in Operation LINEBACKER, the U.S. Air Force B-52 "Stratofortresses" and U.S. Navy planes flew more than 27,000 sorties that devastated NVA troop concentrations and demolished enemy supply lines to the South. Consequently, the enemy slowly retreated back to the North, having suffered some 100,000 casualties.

With the immediate threat to South Vietnam eliminated and North Vietnam weakened, Nixon halted Operation LINEBACKER in October 1972. He futilely hoped that the North Vietnamese would resume peace talks. Searching for a way to bring Hanoi to the negotiation table, Nixon ordered another round of bombing attacks in Operation LINEBACKER II on December 18. Nicknamed the "Christmas Bombings," these 11 days of raids constituted the most destructive conventional bombardment in history. The B-52s alone flew 740 sorties that delivered 15,000 tons of bombs against 32 military and industrial targets in North Vietnam, crippling the North's infrastructure.

Although the North Vietnamese succeeded in shooting down 18 B-52s, they grudgingly agreed to negotiations that resulted in the signing of the Paris Peace Accords on January 29, 1973. Excluding South Vietnam from the process, the American and North Vietnamese representatives agreed to the following stipulations: A cease-fire in place would occur between opposing forces; U.S. military forces would leave South Vietnam; American prisoners of war would be released; and the reunification of Vietnam would be achieved through democratic and peaceful processes. Back in the United States, President Richard Nixon praised this resolution as ending the war and bringing "Peace with Honor" to Vietnam and to Southeast Asia.

The Nixon-Ford Doctrine: Continued Détente and Deterrence

The Vietnam War put incredible stress on the American people on the home front as well as on their military and leaders. No longer could the United States easily occupy the moral high ground in its wars, and no more would Americans so willingly believe their leaders' justifications for wars. It was in this context that President Richard M. Nixon and his successor, Gerald R. Ford, tried to follow a strategy of asymmetric containment that did not necessarily counter threats with proportionate responses. The Nixon-Ford Doctrine looked more like that of Eisenhower in 1950s than it did the Kennedy–Johnson Doctrine in 1960s.

Whenever possible, Nixon and his principal advisor, Henry Kissinger, utilized diplomacy and deterrence rather than symmetric military force to contain communist or Soviet expansion. An experienced diplomat and expert on nuclear strategy, Kissinger served first as National Security Advisor and later as Secretary of State under Nixon and Ford. Both Kissinger and Nixon embraced political realism, an approach to international relations that assumed that nations act in their own self-interest to ensure national security and to attain, maintain, or expand power. In the early 1970s, political realism called for the United States to find advantages against the Soviet Union yet not achieve so much power that the Soviets would find themselves at a critical disadvantage.

The most significant instance of Nixon's diplomacy occurred in 1972 when he helped drive a wedge between China and the Soviet Union. Having watched the relationship between the two communist nations sour during the previous decades, Nixon saw an opening to normalize relations with China. Fear and suspicion dominated Sino-American relations. Nixon sent Kissinger to start secret talks with the Chinese government, and Nixon himself made the first official presidential visit to China in 1972, at which time he met with China's dictator Mao Zedong. Although nothing of substance involving national security was decided, Nixon gained extra leverage against the Soviet Union because reaching out to China created a tri-polar world that added China to the mix of the United States and the Soviet Union. Nixon and Kissinger also knew that the Soviets worried about increased Sino-American communications evolving into an alliance.

Such fears, for example, could be used to deter Soviet construction of additional nuclear weapons. During a visit to Moscow in 1972, Nixon forged two major settlements with Leonid Brezhnev, who deposed Nikita Khrushchev as the Soviet leader in 1964. They endorsed the Strategic Arms Limitations Talks (SALT I) Treaty that froze the numbers of certain nuclear missile systems and their launch sites at current levels. The Soviets also signed the Anti-Ballistic Missile (ABM) Treaty, which limited each nation's countermeasures to destroy incoming ICBMs and Submarine-Launched Ballistic Missiles (SLBM).

From Brezhnev's perspective, these treaties would keep the American offensive and defensive capabilities from surpassing the Soviet Union, and they meant that the Soviets did not need to exhaust their resources on constructing new launch sites or designing missile defense systems. Nixon's successor, Gerald Ford, continued negotiations for the follow-on SALT II Treaty. Their efforts to control nuclear arms helped extend détente between the two super-powers until 1979. In effect, the two presidents contained the expansion of Soviet nuclear capabilities.

Beyond their focus on nuclear weapons, Nixon realized that conventional threats in Europe had scarcely subsided during the years of U.S. involvement in Vietnam. Ford followed his lead. Indeed, the Soviets had taken advantage of America's focus on Southeast Asia to bolster their forces and those of their allies in the Warsaw Pact in the 1970s. They appeared poised to strike West Germany with numerically superior forces. Because any such attack represented a critical challenge for the United States and allied countries in NATO, the U.S. military needed to maintain readiness in Europe after the end of the Vietnam War. This focus resulted in several changes, including manpower mobilization, weapons development, and force structure, that dramatically transformed the military after1973.

Nevertheless, in the short term, the U.S. military suffered reductions in forces and severe declines in morale in the mid-1970s as a result of the drain on personnel and morale after Vietnam. Antiwar protests at home and atrocities like the My Lai massacre hurt the military's reputation. The defeat in the Vietnam War soured the American peoples' trust in government leadership. They could not forget General William Westmorland's unfulfilled promises of a "light at the end of the tunnel" in 1967, nor could they ignore President Nixon's thinly veiled assurances that "Peace with Honor" was anything other than defeat in 1973. Lastly, the Watergate scandal dominated news headlines, with charges that Nixon covered up criminal acts committed by his subordinates. This fallout deprived him of all political credibility and forced him to resign from the presidency in 1974. The new president, Gerald R. Ford, concentrated most of his energy on repairing the tainted image of his office. Despite his unenviable position as Nixon's successor, however, in his two years as president Ford did succeed in initiating several reforms in the U.S. military.

Conclusion

The last American combat units departed from South Vietnam on March 29, 1973. The conflict had left indelible impressions on the American psyche when the nation's military commitment to South Vietnam ended in defeat. The cry of "No more Vietnams" has echoed in the United States ever since. Despite the war's initial aims and the means expended to reach those goals, communism had not been contained. After 1973, President Nixon assured the South Vietnamese that the United States would come to their aid if attacked, but he could not make good on this pledge because his political fortunes declined in the wake of the Watergate scandal. The U.S. Congress also imposed stricter limits on presidential use of armed forces in the War Powers Resolution of 1974. After recovering from losses in 1973, North Vietnam launched a major attack and defeated the ARVN. The hapless South Vietnamese government surrendered in April 1975 in the final act of the Vietnam War. After a 30-year struggle to unify Vietnam, the North Vietnamese succeeded.

In the decade between 1964 and 1973, the United States sent some 3.4 million American service personnel to Southeast Asia. During the late 1960s, half a million of them were in-country. The Vietnam War dominated the lives of a generation of Americans, millions of whom not only served in uniform, but protested the conflict, or watched the conflict on television. In all, the United States lost 58,260 dead, of whom 61 percent were younger than 21 years old. Another 1,655 Americans are still missing in action. Among the 300,000 veterans wounded in combat, 75,000 suffered severe disabilities, 5,200 lost limbs, and 1,000 endured multiple amputations. Thousands of veterans also suffered the harmful effects of Agent Orange, a chemical sprayed on Vietnamese jungles to kill the vegetation. Even those American veterans with no physical injuries endured psychological injuries like post-traumatic stress disorder.

Notes

1   Cited in Neil Sheehan, *A Bright Shining Lie: John Paul Vann and America in Vietnam* (New York: Vintage, 1988), p. 277.
2   Cited in David Halberstam, *The Best and the Brightest* (New York: Penguin Books, 1983), p. 512.
3   Cited in Milton Bates, Lawrence Lichty, Paul Miles, Ronald H. Spector, and Marilyn Young, compilers, *Reporting Vietnam, Part 1: American Journalism 1959–1969* (New York: Library of America, 1998), pp. 581–82.

Short Bibliography

Burr, William, and Jeffrey P. Kimball. *Nixon's Nuclear Specter: The Secret Alert of 1969, Madman Diplomacy, and the Vietnam War.* Lawrence: University Press of Kansas, 2015.

Clodfelter, Mark. *The Limits of Air Power: The American Bombing of North Vietnam.* New York: Free Press, 1989.

Daddis, Gregory. *Westmoreland's War: Reassessing American Strategy in Vietnam.* New York: Oxford University Press, 2014.

DeBenedetti, Charles, and Charles Chatfield. *An American Ordeal: The Antiwar Movement of the Vietnam Era.* Syracuse, NY: Syracuse University Press, 1990.

Freedman, Lawrence. *Kennedy's Wars: Berlin, Cuba, Laos, and Vietnam.* New York: Oxford University Press, 2000.

Fursenko, Aleksandr, and Timothy Naftali. *"One Hell of a Gamble": The Secret History of the Cuban Missile Crisis.* New York: W.W. Norton, 1997.

Herring, George. *America's Longest War: The United States and Vietnam, 1950–1975.* 4th ed. Boston: McGraw-Hill, 2002.

Logevall, Fredrik. *The Embers of War: The Fall of an Empire and the Making of America's Vietnam.* New York: Random House, 2012.

McMaster, H. R. *Dereliction of Duty: Johnson, McNamara, the Joint Chiefs of Staff, and the Lies That Led to Vietnam.* New York: Harper Perennial, 1998.

Moore, Harold G., and Joseph Galloway. *We Were Soldiers Once . . . and Young.* New York: Random House, 1992.

Sheehan, Neil. *A Bright Shining Lie: John Paul Vann and America in Vietnam.* New York: Vintage, 1988.

Sorley, Lewis. *Westmoreland: The General Who Lost Vietnam.* Boston: Houghton Mifflin, 2011.

Tudda, Chris. *A Cold War Turning Point: Nixon and China 1969–1972.* Baton Rouge: Louisiana State University Press, 2012.

Westheider, James D. *Fighting of Two Fronts: African Americans and the Vietnam War.* New York: New York University Press, 1997.

Wyden, Peter. *The Bay of Pigs: The Untold Story.* New York: Simon & Schuster, 2979.

Chapter 15

From Cold War to *Pax Americana* to Uncertainty, 1973–2017

The Vietnam War cast a long shadow over the decades since 1973. Every president had to come to grips with the Vietnam experience, yet the ongoing threat of conflict with the Soviet Union or its satellites persisted. Richard M. Nixon and Gerald R. Ford tried to ease Cold War tensions and started to restructure the U.S. military's personnel policies, doctrines, and weapons systems based on lessons of Vietnam. In 1977, President Jimmy Carter unveiled a more cooperative, less antagonistic Cold War strategy. But within three years, America's enemies exploited and reversed the trend back to more confrontational policies. Then, the United States returned to a more aggressive Cold War strategy during Ronald W. Reagan's presidency from 1981 to 1989. He started a massive military expansion that surpassed the Soviet Union's ability to keep pace.

The disintegration of the Soviet Union ended the Cold War in 1991. During its final months, President George H. W. Bush sent the powerful American military to war in the Persian Gulf to halt aggression by Iraq and protect American interests. The American victory seemed to herald *Pax Americana* and a new era of global stability. Beginning in 1993, an optimistic President Bill Clinton cast the U.S. military in peacekeeping and peacemaking roles in regional conflicts. Whereas American involvement succeeded in some cases, it stimulated the growth of terrorism particularly in the Middle East.

On September 11, 2001, the hopes for global peace shattered when Islamic fundamentalists killed 3,000 people in terrorist attacks on American soil. President George W. Bush quickly retaliated by ordering an American-led coalition to invade Afghanistan because its government harbored the terrorists making the 9/11 attack. Two years later, Bush sent American forces into Iraq under the pretexts of destroying that nation's weapons of mass destruction and ousting its dictator, Saddam Hussein. Since 2001, more than 2.6 million American men and women have deployed to Afghanistan and Iraq to try to quell insurgencies and establish democratic systems. As of 2017, it remains in doubt if their sacrifices and investments will succeed in the long term.

Regardless, fighting these two wars has placed severe strains on Americans willingly to serve in the military and their families at home.

In this chapter, students will about:

- Recovering from Vietnam: The All-Volunteer Force, revised doctrines, and modernized weapons systems.
- Evolution of Cold War strategies in the Nixon-Ford, Carter, and Reagan Doctrines.
- Ending the Cold War and Fighting the Gulf War as the last acts of containment.
- *Pax Americana* and Clinton's new military interventionism.
- Entering the age of terror on September 11, 2001.
- Implementing the Bush Doctrine in Operations ENDURING FREEDOM and IRAQI FREEDOM.
- President Obama: Departing from Iraq, remaining in Afghanistan, and facing other threats in an uncertain future.
- Changing values in American society and its military.

Recovering From Vietnam: From Conscription to the All-Volunteer Force in 1973

Of all the services in the post-Vietnam era, the U.S. Army experienced the deepest cuts from its wartime peak of 1.6 million soldiers and 19 divisions in 1968 down to 785,000 soldiers and 13 divisions in 1975. The Marine Corps saw cutbacks from 300,000 men to less than 200,000 officers and enlisted personnel. The Air Force and the Navy dropped from 800,000 to 600,000 airmen and 700,000 to 535,000 sailors, respectively, in those years. Manpower hovered at these 1975 levels until 1990.

Beyond these reductions, the Vietnam War left the American military in a lower state of morale than in previous conflicts. Veterans did not enjoy the ticker-tape parades and cheering crowds of their fathers' homecomings in 1945. Many experienced indifferent reactions from the public upon their return. Other veterans told stories of being spat upon or called "baby killers" by angry antiwar protesters. Such episodes, even if rare, left lasting impressions in the collective veteran mind-set. Worse still, the veteran's memories of combat also haunted them for decades in nightmares, anxiety attacks, or other forms of post-traumatic stress disorder (PTSD).

Many caustic feelings about the Vietnam War centered on inadequacies and inequalities of the draft. President Nixon tried to alleviate these problems by switching from a conscripted to a volunteer military, thereby fulfilling a promise made in his 1968 campaign. This decision constituted a sea change in the military's primary means of mobilization since the Selective Service Act of 1917.

Nixon ordered several studies to determine how to entice high-quality recruits to volunteer for service. The military needed to overcome a poor public image caused by the negative stigma of Vietnam. Drug abuse, racial tensions, inadequate pay, poor discipline, and low morale also plagued the military. A fair question might have been: Why would young American men with intelligence, motivation, and potential want to volunteer for service in such a moribund institution? According to the studies, some difficulties could be solved by improving the quality of life in the military. Whether in the officer or enlisted ranks, service personnel needed to be paid sufficiently well to make their choice of military careers viable. They needed more comfortable housing on bases, higher allowances for off-base housing, improved health care for family members, moving expenses for frequent transfers, and expanded training and education opportunities. Nevertheless, the nagging problems of low morale, racial tensions, and poor discipline would take much longer to solve.

The end of the draft in July 1973 marked the dawn of the new All-Volunteer Force (AVF). The program got off to an inauspicious start because the Army failed to meet its recruitment quotas during that summer. The military filled some vacancies by raising the percentages of women recruits and opening more branches where they could serve. Part of the impetus for expanding female service opportunities came from the passage of the Equal Rights Amendment through Congress in 1972. Although never ratified, this legislation demonstrated significant support for women's rights as full-fledged citizens, which extended to military service where women eventually comprised more than 10 percent of the active force. For example, they entered the Army in such high numbers and filled so many military occupational specialties that the Army disestablished the Women's Army Corps in 1978. This decision opened noncombat branches to soldiers of either gender. Breaking gender barriers offered women avenues to promotion opportunities and advancement to ever higher ranks.

Several firsts for women occurred in the 1970s. Women became naval aviators and helicopter pilots in 1974. That same year, the Coast Guard Academy opened vacancies to women. The U.S. Military Academy accepted its first women in the fall of 1975. The Air Force designated women as pilots in 1977. By the end of the decade, female pilots flew missions for the SAC, and the Navy first assigned woman to sea duty on noncombat ships.

Despite these milestones, women still could not serve in ground combat units, fly combat missions, or sail on combat vessels. Sadly, they also faced challenges of sexual harassment or assault as well as institutionalized barriers to advancement. Although hard to measure, anecdotal evidence revealed that some women slowly gained respect from men with whom they served in the armed forces because of their diligence, discipline, and determination. The military also gradually instituted protections against abusive or discriminatory behavior directed at women.

Looking Toward the Next War: Doctrinal Reforms and Weapons Modernization

While the U.S. military shifted its focus toward conventional operations in Western Europe, the always-tense Middle East exploded into the 1973 Yom Kippur War. Fighting between Israel and neighboring Arab nations had occurred intermittently for the previous two decades. With support from the United States, the Israelis had held their own or soundly defeated their Arab adversaries.

On October 6 of that year, however, Egyptian and Syrian units launched two surprise attacks into Israeli-held territory along the Suez Canal to the south of Israel and the Golan Heights to the north. The Egyptians and Syrians used the Soviet-made T-62 and T-72 tanks. Both sides employed combined arms tactics with lethal results. The Israelis used shoulder-launched or vehicle-mounted antitank weapons that proved particularly effective in defensive stands for the Israeli forces. More than half the 5,200 tanks in the conflict were damaged or destroyed by those antitank weapons, enemy tank gunfire, or aircraft flying close air support missions. The conflict also proved that defenders could fend off numerically superior attackers. These realities were not lost on American strategists who saw the Soviet Union in Europe reemerging as the main threat to the United States. The revelations fostered major reforms in the U.S. Army in the decade after the Yom Kippur War.

The first reforms began in 1973, when the U.S. Army established the Training and Doctrine Command (TRADOC). This new organization absorbed training, doctrinal, and combat development tasks. The first two TRADOC commanders—Generals William E. DePuy and Donn A. Starry—recognized that the Army suffered from serious shortcomings in conventional capabilities. It had, after all, spent the last decade fighting insurgents in Vietnam.

For DePuy, the devastation of the Yom Kippur War repudiated any American expectations about achieving victory by fighting lengthy campaigns. Instead, he argued that the U.S. military must win the first battle of a conflict or risk never recovering or reinforcing for a second battle. DePuy believed this to be especially true in Europe where American and Soviet ground forces menaced one another. Like the Israelis, American units could stand and stop a numerically superior Soviet attack using antitank weapons and close air support. After three years of work, DePuy's new doctrine of "Active Defense" appeared in the 1976 edition of the Army's Field Manual 100–5 *Operations*.

After DePuy retired in 1977, General Starry assumed command of TRADOC and spent the next four years building on the foundation of Active Defense to create his doctrine of "AirLand Battle." He combined experience as an armor officer with the keen insights of a military intellectual. Starry wanted the Army to be able to take the offensive by executing "close," "deep," and "rear" operations against the Soviets. The first of these called for American forces to outmaneuver and overpower the enemy in "close" combat using combined air, artillery, armor, and infantry assets. In the second, American aircraft would strike enemy logistical targets "deep" behind the front lines, thus crippling Soviet supply lines feeding its combat units. The third would occur in the American "rear" area, where units, equipment, and weapons moved from the rear areas toward the front lines along efficient logistical system. Not incidentally, Starry's doctrine incorporated the best operational practices seen in the Allies' race across Europe in the fall of 1944. The AirLand Battle doctrine was published in the new Field Manual 100–5 *Operations* in 1982.

Generals DePuy and Starry not only supervised a golden age of Army doctrine between 1973 and 1981 but also restructured the Army's training system, drove the development of new weaponry, and helped mold the Army into a professional organization. To implement these changes, the Army needed well-trained and well-equipped soldiers. TRADOC expanded the existing education system for enlisted soldiers and officers alike so that they could acquire the skills and expertise appropriate to their ranks.

In addition to revising doctrine and education, TRADOC took the leading role in modernizing the Army's aging weapons and vehicles. Only then could the units fulfill the operational needs of Active Defense and AirLand Battle. TRADOC supervised the designing, contracting, and testing of the so-called "Big Five" advanced weapons systems. The M-1 "Abrams" tank and the M-2 "Bradley Fighting Vehicle" boasted better protective armor, higher speed, and more deadly firepower than their predecessors. Both the UH-60A "Black Hawk" multipurpose helicopter and the AH-64A "Apache" attack helicopter made substantial improvements in speed, payload, weaponry, and survivability over the Army's Vietnam-era helicopters. Lastly, the new MIM-104 "Patriot" surface-to-air missile offered greater mobility and better accuracy than did the older air defense missile systems. Although superior to their predecessors, the Big Five were criticized as too expensive and impractical to be fielded in large numbers. As will be seen, however, subsequent combat operations in the Persian Gulf War 1991 and other conflicts proved those naysayers to be wrong.

The U.S. Army was hardly alone in making significant changes in the post–Vietnam era. The Air Force developed better aircraft that made it the most potent air arm in the world by the late 1980s. Although strategic bombing remained the mainstay of Air Force budgets and missions, aerial combat in Vietnam showed the importance of the tactical level of air power. Most American pilots relied on air-to-air missiles to shoot down the Vietnamese enemy, and some fighters did not have cannons. Thus, if enemy aircraft got in too close, where missiles lost effectiveness, American pilots lacked the skills and the armament to win a dogfight.

American fighter or interceptor aircraft needed to be able to engage the enemy in close aerial combat as well as at long ranges beyond the horizon. A new generation of Air Force pilots, analysts, and engineers, dubbed the "Fighter Mafia," emerged at the cusp of the movement to introduce the improved aircraft designs. This group agitated for development of fighter aircraft capable of winning close-in dogfights.

Among the leading proponents for improved fighter aircraft and combat doctrine was an U.S. Air Force colonel named John Boyd. As a pilot, instructor, and theorist from 1946 to his death in 1997, Boyd helped to drive the development of innovative designs and doctrines. His persona was that of a brilliant maverick, though not as self-defeating as Billy Mitchell in the 1920s. Boyd created new operational mind-sets as seen in his "OODA Loop." He believed that organizations could successfully adapt to unfamiliar situations by following a process with several sequential steps: Observation to collect data, Orientation to analyze and synthesize that data to form a mental perspective, Decision to identify the best course of action given that mental perspective, and finally Action to implement the best decision. The OODA loop's influence extended well beyond Air Force cockpits and classrooms to influence American planning for Operation DESERT STORM in 1991 and the U.S. Marine Crops' maneuver warfare doctrine. (For

Figure 15.1 M1 Abrams Main Battle Tank and Apache Attack Helicopters

Two of the iconic weapons systems in the U.S. Army appear in this photograph of the M1 Abrams main battle tank and the Apache attack helicopters. They were part of the 1st Infantry Division deployed during the Persian Gulf War in 1991.

© Robert R. McCormick Research Center

a more detailed explanation of Boyd's wide-ranging theories and applications, see the essay in the online resources for Chapter 15.)

Boyd and the Fighter Mafia succeeded in bringing their goals to fruition in the F-15 "Eagle" and F-16 "Falcon," which entered service in 1976 and 1978, respectively. The twin-engine F-15 established itself as the Air Force's premier all-weather tactical fighter, with supersonic speeds exceeding Mach 2.5 (1,650 miles per hour) and armaments of one 20mm Gatling cannon and assorted combinations of missiles and bombs weighing up to 23,000 pounds. To put this in perspective, the F-15 carried more ordnance than the B-29 Superfortress of the Second World War era. The Eagle could also engage enemy aircraft at 50 miles with missiles or in close aerial combat with its gun.

Although the single-engine F-16 could not match the F-15's payload, the Falcon's sleek design gave it exceptional maneuverability and afforded unparalleled air superiority. The Falcon turned more tightly than the larger F-15 or comparable Soviet aircraft, giving the Falcon a distinct advantage in aerial combat. During the 1970s, the Navy also rolled out the new F-14 "Tomcat" and F/A-18 "Hornet," both of which enjoyed similar advantages in speed and maneuverability to the Air Force's fighters.

President Jimmy Carter and the Departure From Containment, 1977–80

In the presidential election of 1976, Jimmy Carter narrowly defeated Gerald Ford as much because of the backlash against Nixon's Watergate scandal as anything else. For his part, Carter took a different approach to presidential leadership at home and abroad. Once elected, he acted on his campaign promises to shift America's focus in diplomacy and military strategy to less belligerent stances. Moreover, he believed that American influence could best be employed in forging peaceful relations around the globe. Carter therefore departed from previous symmetric or asymmetric containment strategies in what might best be termed non-containment or non-interventionism. His presidency can be divided into two phases: 1977 through late 1979 was characterized by his attempts to recast the United States as peacemaker; the second phase ran to the end of his term in January 1981 and saw his efforts to reinvigorate the U.S. military. The changes in Carter's decisions regarding military matters in these two phases can be confusing.

As a promoter of human rights and self-determination in the mold of President Woodrow Wilson during the First World War era, Jimmy Carter stopped sending military and financial aid to Chile, El Salvador, Nicaragua, and Uganda because these nations oppressed their people. It did not matter that the authoritarian Chilean government, for example, held the line against communist expansion. Apart from his less-intrusive approach to foreign nations, Carter's sincere advocacy of human rights exposed many abuses in communist bloc nations, which in turn helped sow seeds for the relative peaceful disintegration of those totalitarian regimes more than a decade later when the Cold War ended.

Like Woodrow Wilson many decades before him, Carter's embraced self-determination as a means to change the relationship between the United States and its longtime client nation, Panama. Carter believed that ceding American control of the Panama Canal back to this nation represented a significant move toward Panamanian autonomy and sovereignty. He worked hard to obtain the necessary votes in the U.S. Senate in 1978 for two treaties that eventually ended American occupation of the Canal Zone in 1999.

In the larger Cold War context, Carter wanted to continue détente with the Soviet Union by negotiating arms reductions that he hoped would culminate in the SALT II Treaty. This move away from containment by threat or use of military force in the first three years of his presidency carried with it major reductions in defense spending. Carter stopped the development of the neutron bomb, a weapon that released more radiation than a nuclear bomb and thus caused more casualties but less physical destruction. He halted work on expensive new weapons systems such as the B-1 bomber program. Envisioned as a supersonic (faster than the speed of sound) strategic bomber, the B-1 would have replaced the older and slower B-52 bomber. Lastly, Carter cut the U.S. Navy's construction of new surface warships. He even announced plans for American units to leave South Korea, despite the ever-present threat of invasion by communist North Korea.

Although these decisions made Carter seem anti-military, he did maintain funding for several nuclear weapons systems, including the LGM-118A "Peacekeeper" ICBM and the UGM-96 "Trident I" SLBM. Both were multiple independently targetable reentry vehicles (MIRVs) that carried several nuclear warheads in each missile. After the MIRV-ed missiles reentered the earth's atmosphere, eight to 10 individual warheads could detach and destroy different targets. This maximized each missile's destructive capacity and hampered enemy tracking capabilities and defensive preparations.

Carter also pushed along construction of naval vessels and aircraft capable of launching or carrying nuclear weapons. The new *Ohio*-class nuclear submarines could unleash up to 24 MIRV-ed Trident missiles, giving a single submarine the ability to hit 192 enemy targets. The USS *Ohio* was commissioned in 1981, and 17 sister ships followed thereafter. Carter's interest in submarines started in part because he served aboard these vessels after graduating from the U.S. Naval Academy in 1946. Meanwhile, although top secret in 1978, the president also authorized the development of "stealth" aircraft that utilized advanced materials to make the them virtually invisible to enemy radar. Carter's choice to support nuclear capabilities yet block other weapons systems resembled Dwight D. Eisenhower's "More Bang for the Buck" approach of the 1950s. But this similarity can only be taken so far because, unlike Eisenhower, Carter eschewed the use of covert operations during most of this presidency.

Apart from decisions affecting the size and armament of the military, Carter pursued his main diplomatic goal of forging peaceful relations in war-torn areas. Nowhere was this effort more successful than in the Camp David Accords. During the fall of 1978, Carter brokered a peaceful settlement between Israel and Egypt over the Israeli's occupation of Egyptian territory following the Yom Kippur War. Signed in 1979, the Accords did not resolve Israeli-Palestinian problems, but Carter deserves credit for pushing an agreement that has stood the test of time. No major military conflict between Egypt and Israel has occurred since 1979.

Despite Jimmy Carter's best intentions in charting a less confrontational American course in the Cold War, two major international incidents exposed severe shortcomings in his approach. First, a revolution erupted in Iran in 1978 that toppled the pro-American, anti-communist government of the Shah Mohammad Reza Pahlavi. A radical new Islamic government that was hostile to the United States rose from the rubble. In November 1979, an angry Iranian mob forced their way into the American embassy in Tehran. They took the 52 American staff members hostage in November until January 1981.

Second, in December 1979, Soviet military forces invaded Afghanistan, presumably to prop up a communist government in that nation and fight against anti-communist Muslim insurgents. In the next months, more than 100,000 Soviet military personnel and thousands of tanks and helicopters entered the nation. They tried to quell several groups of rebellious insurgents known collectively as the *"Mujahideen,"* which translated as "those who engage in *jihad"* ("holy war").

In January 1980, Jimmy Carter reacted to the twin crises by announcing a reversal of his earlier military strategy and foreign policy. Nicknamed the "Carter Doctrine," the president started to use military force, if necessary, to protect America's interests in this oil-rich region against Soviet incursions or control. Carter also began increasing the defense budgets for new weapons systems. Later, in March, he ordered the activation of the Rapid Deployment Force (RDF), which could coordinate joint Army, Air Force, Navy, and Marine Corps operations in the Middle East.

Although designed to coordinate joint operations among all branches of the armed forces, the RDF was not sufficiently well-established to avert disaster in Operation EAGLE CLAW in April 1980. This mission to rescue the American hostages in Iran called for an American special operations unit, Delta Force, to infiltrate Iranian airspace by helicopter, land at a staging point, travel by truck to the American Embassy in Tehran, and extract the American hostages from Iran. The operation was aborted after weather problems, equipment malfunctions, and poor coordination that cost the lives of eight American service personnel. The failure of EAGLE CLAW caused Carter great embarrassment. This in turn added to his declining popularity with an American public already unhappy with the Russian invasion of Afghanistan and disheartened by a moribund economy at home.

Ronald Reagan and America's Resurgent Military Power, 1981–89

The presidential election of 1980 pitted a discredited Jimmy Carter against an optimistic Ronald W. Reagan. The challenger won that election in a landslide victory. Then, between 1981 and 1989, Reagan's foreign policy ended détente and directed the resurgence of American military power and reinvigoration of an anti-communist strategy. His approach to the Cold War differed from Carter's and from that of all previous presidents dating back to Truman. According to the *National Security Decision Directive 71* approved by Reagan in 1983, the United States would act "to contain and over time reverse Soviet expansionism." As such, the "Reagan Doctrine" combined symmetric containment that directly challenged the Soviet Union, asymmetric containment that fomented anti-communist revolutionary groups, and attempts to reclaim nations from communist control.

Reagan wanted the United States prepared to fight conventional and nuclear conflicts against the Soviet Union. These twin goals required larger budgets, newer doctrines, and more modern weaponry to meet threats across the globe. He used the adage "peace through strength" to encapsulate his view of military preparedness.

Reagan's budget requests for the Defense Department went to an amenable Congress, where they were not significantly altered or reduced until 1986, when Reagan faced a major scandal and the Republicans lost control of the U.S. Senate. The budgets increased almost eight percent every year before leveling off in the final years of his presidency. This amounted to approximately six percent of the annual gross domestic product (GDP) of the United States. The total Defense Department expenditures during the eight years of Reagan's presidency exceeded $2 trillion. Ultimately, the new president hoped to engage the Soviet Union in an arms race that would drive the Soviets into bankruptcy.

The U.S. Army directly benefited from Reagan's desire to prepare to fight a conventional war. If such a conflict started, it would occur in Europe, where it was thought massed Soviet ground forces in East Germany would sweep through the Fulda Gap into West Germany. Named for the East German border town of Fulda, invasion forces used this gap in the hilly countryside to move west or east for centuries. The Soviets recognized the potential to strike a decisive blow, and so, too, did strategic planners in the United States and NATO. They formulated a defensive plan consistent with AirLand Battle. If attacked through the Fulda Gap, some 80,000 American soldiers would fight delaying actions to break the Soviet momentum in "close" operations. This would buy time until American reinforcements cold arrive in "rear" operations, and until U.S. and NATO aircraft could cripple the Soviet logistical system in "deep" operations behind the front lines.

The U.S. Navy and Air Force also carved niches in Reagan's stronger military. Because the president wanted the Navy to return to unquestioned maritime supremacy, Secretary of the Navy John Lehman pressed to reach the plateau of 600 ships. During the Carter presidency, its strength remained between 530 and 540 ships. Lehman added more ballistic missile submarines, attack submarines, missiles cruisers, and supercarriers to the fleet. His Navy peaked at 594 ships, including 14 aircraft carriers and 102 submarines in 1987.

The Air Force enhanced its significant advantages in air power. Reagan restarted the construction of the B-1B supersonic strategic bombers, and he continued development of the so-called stealth bomber technology. Culminating in the B-2 "Spirit" in 1989, the specially designed aircraft's shape and advanced materials absorbed rather than reflected radar energy, making it invisible to enemy radar.

Beyond increases in ground, air, and naval forces, Reagan and his Secretary of Defense Caspar Weinberger worked to expand the United States' antiballistic missile capabilities. Reagan never liked the concept of "mutually assured destruction" because it was based on the fatalistic assumption that only fears of American-Soviet nuclear annihilation could deter nuclear war. Instead, he seized upon futuristic capabilities to destroy enemy ICBMs before they reentered the atmosphere. In a speech in 1983, Reagan introduced the Strategic Defense Initiative to the American people. Euphemistically labeled "Star Wars," this program stirred the imaginations of proponents and critics alike. That no viable surface-to-air missiles and orbiting laser technologies existed did not matter because the rhetoric of eliminating the Soviet's ICBM arsenal gave Reagan leverage against the Soviet's "evil empire."

The Reagan Doctrine in Action

Not content with developing new weapons systems, Reagan authorized military operations around the world. He wanted to stop the spread of communism, keep peace in war-torn regions, and respond to terrorist activities. Although he did attempt to intimidate the Soviets, he could likewise enter negotiations with them to achieve the larger goal of reducing the threat of nuclear war. These actions fit into the "Reagan Doctrine" and subsequently into the "Weinberger Doctrine."

By the late 1970s, several nations in Latin America experienced revolutions that replaced dictatorships with governments that either fell under Soviet influence or appeared at risk of doing so. Among these was the tiny Caribbean island of Grenada, where years of civil strife resulted in the rise of a communist government. The violence endangered Americans on the island, and worse still, Grenada's government built an airfield that could support communist subversion in the region. After hearing appeals from neighboring nations fearful of growing Soviet influence, Reagan ordered U.S. forces to invade Grenada, evacuate American citizens, and remove its government from power in Operation URGENT FURY. Some 7,600 American military personnel made airborne and amphibious assaults on Grenada on October 25, 1983. Though publicly declaring that they intended to rescue the Americans, their ulterior motivation centered on eliminating a potential communist threat. Although encountering stubborn defenses, they subdued the outnumbered Grenadians and Cubans two days later with low casualties. Reagan claimed a victory in the Cold War, but the operation revealed serious coordination and communication problems among Army, Navy, Air Force, and Marine Corps units. These needed to be resolved in future operations.

Elsewhere in 1983, Reagan utilized American forces in peacekeeping roles with less positive outcomes in Beirut, Lebanon. Located along the Mediterranean coast just north of Israel, this area saw incessant fighting between Israelis, Palestinians, and Lebanese. The U.S. Marines were deployed to Lebanon to help evacuate Americans beginning in the summer of 1982. They also hoped to establish some level of peaceful coexistence between the competing religious, ethnic, and political groups. The Marines' presence, however, caused friction with these groups and made them targets for attacks. Strict rules of engagement prohibited the Marines from protecting themselves. This dangerous situation resulted in a tragic incident that took place on October 23, 1983. At dawn on that Sunday, a radical Islamic terrorist drove a truck loaded with explosives into the Marine compound. The guards at the compound's gates did not have ammunition for their weapons and could not stop the vehicle. The truck crashed through barriers into the headquarters, where the detonation killed 241 Marines, soldiers, and sailors. These casualties and the situation that caused them showed the perils of Reagan's interventionist approach to foreign policy.

Experiences in Beirut and Grenada, as well as in Vietnam, spawned another statement of principles in the "Weinberger Doctrine." Its namesake, Defense Secretary Caspar Weinberger, argued in 1984 that there needed to be strict limitations and clear parameters for use of American military power. If criteria—vital national interests, wholehearted commitment, public support, last resort, likely victory, and clearly defined military and political objectives—were satisfied, then force could be used. These ideas set the tone for the rest of the Reagan years and foreshadowed subsequent presidential doctrines for the use of military power.

When Reagan perceived a serious threat to national interests, for example, he willingly authorized covert operations to hold the line against communist expansion and, where possible, reclaim nations from communist control. One of the largest of such efforts occurred in Afghanistan in a proxy war between the Soviet occupation forces and *Mujahideen* resistance fighters from 1979 to 1989. Using the CIA as a conduit, the United States funneled money and weapons to the Afghan resistance in what seemed to be an endless conflict. After suffering 65,000 casualties, however, the Soviets finally withdrew from Afghanistan in 1989. This year likewise marked the start of the Soviet Union's precipitous decline.

Among other external supporters of the Afghan resistance was the Saudi Arabian-born Osama bin Laden. He helped create an international organization that recruited and trained Arab Muslims to fight with the *Mujahideen*. After the Soviets left Afghanistan, bin Laden's organization evolved into the radical terrorist group Al-Qaeda, which targeted all "infidels."

Still another major American covert operation occurred in Nicaragua, where anti-communist *Contras* (counterrevolutionaries) tried to overthrow the *Sandinista*-run government. Previously, the *Sandinistas* had ousted an anti-communist dictatorship and assumed power in 1979 and seemed to be moving closer to becoming a Soviet satellite, especially after they joined the Cubans in supporting communist revolutionaries in neighboring El Salvador. In Reagan's mind, the new Nicaraguan government constituted a threat in Latin America. In 1982, he secretly authorized the CIA to finance, train, and arm the *Contras*. American support flowed into Nicaragua until 1985 when Congress cut off appropriations and forbade the CIA from funding the rebels. Despite these restrictions, the National Security Council, if not Reagan himself, utilized clandestine means to aid the *Contras* with profits from the illegal sale of weapons to Iran, the same Iranian regime that held American hostages and sponsored terrorist activities.

Meanwhile, Reagan won reelection in 1984 by an even greater landslide than in 1980. Within two years, however, public exposure of illegal covert activities ignited the Iran-Contra scandal. Highly publicized Congressional and criminal investigations led to indictments and convictions of several of Reagan's key advisors, who supervised the secret effort to subsidize the *Contras*. Although the president escaped direct blame and potential impeachment, his positive image lost some of its luster.

The year 1986 saw another development in the Department of Defense that dramatically changed the structure and the focus of the U.S. military. In October, Congress passed the Goldwater–Nichols Defense Reorganization Act, which expanded the influence of the chairman of the Joint Chiefs of Staff by giving him direct access to the president and the secretary of defense. The chairman also assumed a new position in the operational chain of command:

Theater commanders reported to the chairman, who then reported to the president. The 1986 Act made yet another significant change in the structure of operational forces. The theater commanders, regardless of branch, were given authority over all assets in their regions. In this way, for instance, President Jimmy Carter's Rapid Defense Force evolved into the U.S. Central Command (CENTCOM), which controlled all American military forces and operations in the Middle East.

As Reagan's second term ended, he enjoyed some remarkable successes. None was sweeter than the final thawing of the Cold War. Over time he slowly softened his previous anti-communist rhetoric about the Soviet Union as an "evil empire." Beginning in 1985, Reagan entered arms control negotiations with Mikhail Gorbachev, the new reform-minded Soviet leader. Reagan's ambitious military buildup helped drive an already crumbling Soviet Union into bankruptcy, but those same expenditures also ran the United States' national debt out of control. Regardless, the Soviets could not match the quality or the quantity of America's new weapons systems. This allowed Reagan to negotiate from a position of power. He and Gorbachev met four times between 1985 and 1988.

At their third summit, the two leaders signed the Intermediate-Range Nuclear Forces Treaty. This eliminated ground-launched ballistic and cruise missiles that could deliver nuclear warheads at medium ranges between 300 and 3,000 miles. Reagan also proposed the more sweeping Strategic Arms Reduction Treaty (START I) that, when signed in 1991, eventually reduced the two superpowers' nuclear arsenals by 30 percent in 2001.

George H. W. Bush's Challenges: Ending One War and Fighting Another War, 1989–93

Ronald Reagan left office before more dramatic events marking the end of the Cold War occurred. His successor, President George H. W. Bush, watched the last gasps of the Soviet Union and its allied Warsaw Pact nations. Peaceful demonstrations and free elections swept through East Germany, Hungary, Romania, and other Soviet bloc nations in 1989 in a revolutionary tide. The Cold War's most striking symbol—the Berlin Wall—came down on November 9 of that year amid the cheers of East and West Berliners. The two German states united into a single nation one year thereafter. Then on December 26, 1991, the Soviet Union dissolved, breaking into Russia and several other independent nations. This marked the final episode in the Cold War, and the beginning of a hopeful new age for many in the United States, Europe, and the world.

Even before the dissolution of the Soviet Union, President Bush began to reorient the United States' posture from anti-communism to self-preservation in a post-Cold War world. An example of this new focus can be seen in Operation JUST CAUSE in Panama. That nation's dictator, Manuel Noriega, sponsored the purchase and sale of illegal drugs in the United States. Bush could not let these activities continue, and he wanted to replace the hostile Noriega with a leader more malleable to American influence. A stable Panamanian government was especially important when that nation eventually assumed control of the Panama Canal. When diplomatic pressure and economic sanctions failed to stop Noriega's illegal activities, Bush ordered 26,000 American servicemen to remove the dictator from office. Although the resulting invasion succeeded with minimal loss of American life, some critics saw this coercive regime change as the United States flexing its imperialist muscles.

In retrospect, Operation JUST CAUSE exemplified the potential of careful planning, overwhelming force, and joint (among all armed forces) cooperation to achieve American goals under the new "Powell Doctrine." Named for General Colin Powell, who served as the Chairman of the Joint Chiefs of Staff under Bush, this doctrine governed where, when, why, how much, and how long the United States could use military force. By defining these parameters, Powell and Bush hoped to avoid more open-ended conflicts like the Vietnam War yet still fight short wars when and where American interests required action.

A much larger and more significant test of the Powell Doctrine emerged in 1990 during a crisis in the Middle East. The final months of the Cold War created great uncertainty because the Soviet Union no longer possessed the will or ability to influence the region as it had in the past, and the level of American action in the Middle East remained unclear. It was in this apparent power vacuum that Saddam Hussein, dictator of Iraq and head of the Ba'ath Party, decided to invade the tiny neighboring nation of Kuwait on August 2, 1990. Financial factors provided additional motivation for Hussein, who needed to repay large debts for its costly war with Iran in the 1980s. Indeed, the United States had supported Iraq in the conflict with Iran. Kuwait, however, made Iraq's predicament worse by overproducing oil and driving prices down, thereby depriving Iraq of its main source of income. From Saddam's perspective, the invasion represented both compensation for his nation's economic losses and proof of Iraq's increased status as a regional power.

Iraq possessed what was, on paper, one of the largest armed forces in the world, numbering more than one million men, 5,500 tanks, and 700 aircraft and helicopters. The Iraqis overran the Kuwaiti military in a matter of days. Once in control of the nation, the Iraqis pushed further south and established bases along the border with Saudi Arabia later in August. The United States and its many allies immediately condemned Iraq's invasion as a blatant act of aggression. Resolutions from the United Nation's Security Council called for economic sanctions against Iraq and a naval blockade to enforce those sanctions. On August 7, President George H. W. Bush answered the Saudi government's request for protection and ordered the start of Operation DESERT SHIELD.

American aircraft immediately began patrolling the area, and lead elements of the U.S. 82nd Airborne Division arrived on August 8 as the first American unit to take up defensive positions along the Saudi border. All American forces fell under control of General H. Norman Schwarzkopf, Jr., who commanded CENTCOM. Meanwhile, throughout the remainder of 1990, President Bush worked diligently to create a coalition of several dozen nations that provided varying levels of military assistance. At home, he called out the reserves and the National Guard to supplement the active duty units. The All-Volunteer Force mobilized for the coming war in good order.

Schwarzkopf created a multinational force capable of not merely defending Saudi Arabia but also, if necessary, driving Iraq out of Kuwait. By the end of October, some 210,000 American service personnel and 65,000 coalition troops stood online against the 400,000 Iraqi soldiers. On November 29, a decisive vote by the U.N. Security Council set a deadline of January 15, 1991, for Hussein to withdraw Iraqi forces from Kuwait or be expelled by force. Doubting American resolve and hoping to draw support from other Arab nations, he refused to comply.

In the weeks between the U.N. ultimatum and January 15, nearly 100,000 additional American combat troops reached the Middle East. All told, the potent ground force included the XVIII Airborne Corps and the VII Corps with a total of seven American divisions, two American armored cavalry regiments, a French division, and a British division. The coalition's Arab nations contributed several more divisions that, together with two U.S. Marine divisions and a brigade from a U.S. armored division, constituted a third corps-sized formation. In addition to ground forces, the U.S. Navy sent four aircraft carriers, two battleships, and several other warships to the Persian Gulf. The U.S. Air Force added a formidable array of several hundred fighter and bomber aircraft. By mid–January, the coalition boasted a total of 950,000 service personnel poised to drive Iraq out of Kuwait.

The January 15 deadline came and went, but the Iraqi regime refused to order its army to leave Kuwait. One day later, coalition forces unleashed a devastating air campaign as part of a larger offensive code-named Operation DESERT STORM. Over the next several weeks, the aircraft flew 100,000 sorties, dropping nearly 90,000 tons of bombs on Iraqi targets. The U.S. Navy launched hundreds of cruise missiles that destroyed Iraqi air defense sites and radar installations. These attacks demolished the Iraqi military's communications and logistics networks and isolated the units in Kuwait.

After five weeks of intense aerial bombardment, the American-led coalition forces crossed the Saudi border into Iraq and Kuwait on February 24, 1991. The ensuing ground campaign followed the detailed plans of Schwarzkopf and his staff. The Iraqis expected the main thrust to come north from the area of Saudi Arabia adjacent to Kuwait. The Iraqis constructed defensive barriers and concentrated their tanks and artillery along this 200-mile line at the Saudi border.

In arranging his forces, General Schwarzkopf placed the Marine and allied Arab units nearest to the Persian Gulf coastline, the U.S. VII Corps with its five divisions just to the west, and the U.S. XVIII Airborne Corps with its four divisions still further west in the desert. He stretched his force beyond the last Iraqi unit on the front line. This gave the XVIII's fast-moving air assault, airborne, armor cavalry, and light infantry units the opportunity to drive to the north far into the desert and then swing east toward Kuwait in an enormous flanking maneuver. Facing relatively light opposition, these units successfully cut off the Iraqi forces in Kuwait from their escape back to Iraq by February 27, 1991.

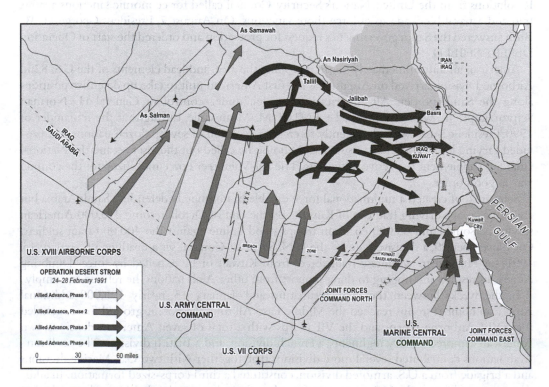

Map 15.1 The Persian Gulf War, February 1991

Meanwhile, on February 24, the coalition's U.S. Marine, coalition Arab, and VII Corps units began their methodical assault on the Iraqis' fortified positions. They quickly breached obstacles, sending the enemy into headlong retreat. The Marines and Arab forces moved directly north along the Persian Gulf coast toward the capital, Kuwait City. To their west, the armored units of the VII Corps pushed through the Iraqi defenses and swung eastward to help block their withdrawal to their home country. Along the way on February 27, the American forces won decisive victories like the Battle of Medina Ridge, where they destroyed 187 Iraqi tanks while enduring only four disabled American tanks. The Iraqis suffered such severe losses because the Americans possessed the M1 Abrams tank which, with its targeting systems, armor, and firepower, was far superior to the Iraqi's Soviet-built T-62 or T-72 tanks. Such victories finally put to rest criticisms regarding cost and combat effectiveness during the development of the Abrams back in the 1970s.

On the same day as Medina Ridge, the coalition forces entered Kuwait City, and a cease-fire was called the next day on February 28—just 100 hours after ground operations in DESERT STORM started. In this war, American losses amounted to only 148 combat deaths, but Iraqis lost approximately 20,000 soldiers killed and 50,000 wounded or captured. The supposedly formidable Iraqi military was effectively defanged for several years.

All branches of the American military executed AirLand Battle as outlined in the 1980s in FM 100–5 *Operations*. The air campaign fulfilled the requirements of "deep" operations by destroying Iraqi logistics and communications. The ground campaign followed the tenets of "close" operations by crushing the Iraqi units in fast-moving tank battles. Lastly, the coalition nations deployed and supplied their combat units per the expectations for "rear" operations. In sum, DESERT STORM equated to the conventional land campaign that the Americans expected to fight against the Soviets during the Cold War.

While appearing impressive on a map, however, the coalition's lopsided victory in the Persian Gulf War might have not have ended so well. General Schwarzkopf's risky three-pronged attack relied on surprise and technology, but it also benefited from incompetent Iraqi resistance and inferior enemy weapons. Inclement weather and sand storms partially negated the American advantages because these conditions slowed advances and caused mechanical problems. Finally, the coalition's logistical system may not have sustained more fighting because the initial campaign to liberate Kuwait stretched the American sealift and airlift capabilities to their breaking points.

After the cease-fire in late February, President George Bush faced a decision point. Should he push farther into Iraq and expel Saddam Hussein from power? Hussein and his Ba'ath Party kept tight reins on Muslim factions in Iraq, using brutal tactics of mass murders and imprisonments to stay in power. Hussein also remained a destabilizing force in the Middle East. Or, should Bush consolidate his gains and rebuild Kuwait? The coalition had demolished Iraq's armed forces. Iraq had to abide by limitations on weapons development and military operations as part of the surrender agreement. If Hussein refused, then force could be reapplied in the future.

As tempting as removing Hussein from power was, Bush chose the latter option for several reasons. First, the United States achieved the objective of liberating Kuwait mandated by the U.N. Security Council and coinciding with the Powell Doctrine. In this way, the Persian Gulf War could be said to fit into a Cold War-style model of symmetric containment. Next, an invasion of Iraq proper would have caused the collapse of the U.S.-Arab coalition and undermined American influence in the Middle East. Finally, many more American lives would have been lost during combat operations to defeat the Iraqi military and subsequent efforts in the reconstruction process. Indeed, such an effort could have evolved into a Vietnam-style quagmire, sucking resources, and taking lives in an endless, winless conflict. This final justification for stopping short of removing Hussein from power would prove eerily prophetic in view of the later events in Iraq after 2003.

Pax Americana and Bill Clinton's New Interventionism, 1993–2001

In the 1992 presidential election, the charismatic William Jefferson "Bill" Clinton defeated the incumbent George Bush in part because a maverick third-party candidate claimed nearly 19 percent of the popular vote. In January 1993, the new president unveiled an ambitious domestic agenda that included health care reform and budget-balancing legislation. On the foreign policy front, Clinton hoped to utilize American power to bring order and democracy to a world still in flux following the end of the Cold War. In so doing, perhaps the United States could create *Pax Americana*—American Peace.

In his first year in office, Clinton directed Secretary of Defense Les Aspin to review the priorities and missions of the U.S. military in hopes of maintaining sufficiently effective forces yet reducing expenditures by lowering personnel levels and closing bases. The review resulted in cuts in manpower. The Army experienced the most dramatic reduction from its Gulf War peak of 760,000 soldiers in 1991 to 480,000 in 1998. The leaner American military acquired lethal new technologies such as global positioning systems and laser-guided bombs. During the 1990s, new force structure designs called for smaller combat units with more speed and flexibility. The armed forces continued to develop joint capabilities that brought together Army, Air Force, Navy, and Marine Corps assets in unified commands.

In addition to reducing the American military and transforming its force structure, Clinton wanted to make good on his campaign promise to open the services to people of all sexual orientations. To date, the U.S. military had banned homosexuals and lesbians from serving in uniform. Supporting arguments centered on potentially detrimental effects to unit cohesion, discipline, and morale if service personnel engaged in open same-sex relations.

Opponents of the ban made various arguments, including that all Americans had obligations to serve as well as rights to exercise open association, engage in free speech, and receive due process in legal proceedings. They also believed that denial of these obligations and rights constituted discrimination. Nevertheless, Clinton encountered strong resistance in military circles, among conservative civilians, and in Congress, even from some of his fellow Democrats. Indeed, the public furor reached a fever pitch during the first year of his presidency.

Unable to overcome the opposition, Clinton issued Defense Directive 1304.26, known as the "Don't Ask, Don't Tell" (DADT) policy. It prohibited questions about sexual orientation yet permitted the U.S. military to pursue disciplinary action against anyone who claimed to be gay or who was caught participating in homosexual or lesbian acts. Such punishments were also on the books for heterosexual fraternization or adultery. This policy, however, could not protect secretly gay men and women in uniform from ongoing harassment or abuse. Although DADT failed to satisfy either side, it did move the U.S. military away from its complete prohibition of homosexuality.

Apart from the politicized debate that attracted so much attention in 1993, newly sworn-in President Clinton inherited the ongoing Operation RESTORE HOPE in Somalia. Located along the east African coast on the Red Sea and Indian Ocean, this nation had been wracked by years of civil war and mass starvation that caused at least 500,000 deaths. In late 1992, then-President George H. W. Bush deployed American units to ensure aid would help those in need. He also wanted to protect oil tankers sailing near the Somali coast. This sort of operation fit into Clinton's broader intentions to use American military strength to meet national security threats and to make peace, keep peace, and render humanitarian assistance.

During 1993 in Somalia, however, little progress could be made because of fighting among the warring factions and a lack of centralized authority in the relief effort. In May, the United Nations sent in peacekeeping units that included U.S. forces. These forces failed to ensure stability, even in the Somali capital of Mogadishu. After several attacks killed American soldiers, Clinton ordered elite American special operations units to locate and capture key Somali leaders.

On the afternoon of October 3, 1993, an American raid into Mogadishu went terribly wrong. While transporting special operations units into the city, several helicopters took ground fire from Somalis that forced them to crash-land, killing or wounding the Americans onboard. The remaining 90 Americans tried to rescue the survivors, but repeated attacks by 4,000 armed Somali militiamen forced them to fight for their own lives in defensive positions along the city streets. Finally, the next morning of October 4, an armored relief column evacuated the Americans from Mogadishu.

Poor coordination between U.S. and U.N. commanders combined with the televised spectacle of American soldiers' bodies being dragged through the streets to make this raid a disaster. Reeling from strong criticism mainly from Republicans, President Clinton ordered the withdrawal of U.S. forces from Somalia in 1994.

In some ways, the Somali fiasco understood as Bill Clinton's Bay of Pigs. Like the youthful John Kennedy in 1961, Clinton needed to redeem himself to be seen as a strong leader following the Mogadishu debacle. Nevertheless, he did not intervene in certain situations, such as stopping the genocide committed against ethnic minorities in Rwanda in Africa, where at least 500,000 people died during three months in 1994. It is likely that Clinton and his advisors feared any major American commitment might result in a repeat of Mogadishu.

The tragic events in Somalia and elsewhere pointed to the need for Clinton to define the extent of American military intervention in the post-Cold War world. He believed that the United States stood at a unique place in history. Never had any other nation wielded such a preponderance of military, diplomatic, and economic power, and never had there been so many opportunities to solve problems around the globe. The 1995 version of *A National Security Strategy for Engagement and Enlargement* listed the Clinton Administration's three "central goals" for the United States: "[S]ustain our security with military forces that are ready to fight," "bolster America's economic revitalization," and "promote democracy abroad."[1] All three goals were intertwined. American military force could help establish or maintain democratic governments. Then those stable democracies could engage in commerce with the United States. Lastly, commercial interaction could stimulate the American economy.

Later known as the "Clinton Doctrine," this strategy of American interventionism marked a conspicuous departure from the long-standing strategy of containment designed to maintain the *status quo* during the Cold War—a new American way of war. During the rest of Clinton's presidency, the U.S. military embarked on selective peacekeeping, humanitarian, and preemptive operations that fit into the goals of "engagement" and "enlargement."

Two prime examples of American peacekeeping efforts occurred first in Bosnia in 1995 and later in Kosovo in 1999. Both were provinces in the nation of Yugoslavia that had held various ethnic, religious, and national groups together under an authoritarian regime since the Second World War. This polyglot nation disintegrated when the Cold War ended in 1991. Thereafter, the states of Bosnia-Herzegovina (Bosnia), Slovenia, and Croatia declared independence. The latter two received recognition as sovereign nations. Bosnia did not achieve this status, however, because the neighboring Serbians tried to maintain control over other remnants of the former Yugoslavia to include Serbia proper, Montenegro, Kosovo, and Bosnia.

Beginning in 1992, Serbian military forces invaded Bosnia allegedly to protect the Serbian minority living there. The Serbian leader, Slobodan Miloševi , wished to absorb Bosnia into his nation, uniting all ethnic Serbs under one flag. To achieve this goal, the Serbians started ethnic cleansing programs to expel or exterminate all non-Serbian religious and ethnic groups. Rapes and murders occurred by the thousands, and millions of Bosnians were displaced from their homes in the ensuing three years of bloodshed. Such heinous war crimes drew condemnation from the United Nations, NATO, and the United States.

After some 8,000 Bosnia Muslims died in a massacre in July 1995, President Clinton agreed to NATO air strikes against Serbian forces. A counterattack by Bosnian Muslims and allied Croatians successfully reclaimed much territory from the Serbs. These concerted efforts brought Milošević into negotiations in December 1995 that subsequently ended the fighting. Some 20,000 American soldiers joined another 40,000 NATO soldiers in Bosnia to protect refugees from further harm, administer free elections of governments, and conduct searches with heavily armed patrols. Of these forces, the American component was essential to complete the missions. Even in 1999, some 6,000 American soldiers remained in Bosnia. These efforts could not ensure lasting peace among ethnic, religious, and national factions, however. The best outcome came from segregating Serbs, Croats, and Muslims into their own enclaves in Bosnia.

Although the U.S. and NATO presence stopped the Serbs from taking control of Bosnia, Slobodan Milošević did not stop the ethnic cleansing and genocide. In 1999, he directed his military to drive Albanian Muslims out of Kosovo, the southernmost province in Serbia. Following the pattern in Bosnia, Serbians conducted more mass executions and deportations in Kosovo. President Clinton believed that only force could stop these atrocities and relied on the U.S. Army's General Wesley K. Clark Jr. to take the lead in this intervention. In his role as supreme commander of NATO and American forces in Europe, Clark ordered an air campaign that killed 5,000 Serbian soldiers, crippled that nation's war-making capabilities, and pushed Milošević to withdraw his forces from Kosovo. On its face, this aerial bombardment proved successful and validated the Air Force's time-honored argument that airpower can win wars. However, aerial attacks did not always hit the right targets, as evinced by the accidental bombing of China's embassy in Belgrade, Serbia. Meanwhile, some 50,000 NATO ground troops, including 7,000 Americans, entered the beleaguered province on another peacekeeping mission. They gradually reduced the violence and restored order, but as in Bosnia, the best hope for lasting peace came in separating the opposing factions.

In addition to the peacekeeping operations in the former Yugoslavia, Clinton utilized the U.S. military in dozens of humanitarian operations in the United States and in South America, Europe, Asia, and Africa. These ranged from a few dozen to several thousand Americans participating in cleanup or relief efforts after natural or man-made disasters. These activities corresponded to Clinton's strategy of enlargement and enhancement. The United States could engender goodwill by perpetuating goodwill.

Amid peacekeeping and humanitarian operations, the U.S. military made several preemptive attacks against perceived threats to the new global peace. Throughout his presidency, for example, Clinton launched air strikes against targets when Iraq appeared to be rearming or violating the conditions of its surrender in 1991. Regardless, Clinton worried that Saddam Hussein might rebuild an army capable of disrupting the Middle East's balance of power or, worse still, that Iraq might develop chemical, biological, and nuclear weapons. Hussein set a precedent by using a weapon of mass destruction (WMD) in 1988 when his military killed at least 3,000 and injured another 7,000 people with poison gas. Hussein directed this attack against the Kurds, a rebellious ethnic minority living in northern Iraq. He was also suspected of developing more deadly WMDs, such as nuclear weapons. From 1993 until the end of Clinton's presidency, American aircraft attacks and cruise missiles frequently destroyed Iraqi military installations, suspected WMD facilities, and surface-to-air missile sites. The most effective of these strikes, Operation DESERT FOX, effectively ended Iraq's ability to produce WMDs and destabilized Hussein's ability to control his nation.

While Americans focused on threats in Iraq, other ominous signs pointed toward growing terrorist activities in the Middle East and in the United States proper. The end of the Cold War opened opportunities for many types of non-state violence that had previously been held in check by the two superpowers and their allies. For example, the *Mujahideen*, who had once fought the Soviets in Afghanistan in the 1980s, evolved into splinter groups such as Al-Qaeda in the 1990s. Meanwhile, a new and oppressive government known as the Taliban took power in Afghanistan and provided sanctuary to terrorist groups. Throughout the decade, radical Islamic terrorists targeted American civilians, service personnel, and embassies.

The two most conspicuous attacks formed bookends to Clinton's presidency. In 1993, a terrorist drove a truck containing explosives into the parking garage under one of the World Trade Center towers in New York City. The resulting explosion did not bring down the building as planned, but it did cause six deaths and several hundred injuries. Seven years later in the port city of Aden in Yemen, another terrorist piloted his boat alongside the guided missile destroyer USS *Cole*. The detonation of explosives onboard the boat left a 40-foot gash along the warship's waterline and killed or wounded 56 sailors. These attacks were linked directly to Al-Qaeda, and they demonstrated that no place was safe from acts of terrorism.

A New President Faces the 9/11 Attacks and an Era of Uncertainty

After a hotly contested victory in the 2000 election, the new President George W. Bush spent his first months in office focusing on domestic issues. Even so, he did stock his cabinet with several leaders with significant experience and expertise in foreign policy and military strategy. They fell into two camps. One group included Vice President Richard Cheney, Secretary of Defense Donald Rumsfeld, and Deputy Secretary of Defense Paul Wolfowitz. They believed in a "neoconservative" worldview that called for the United States to exert force to expand American influence and to stop potential challenges to that influence. Indeed, in some ways, Cheney and Rumsfeld implicitly embraced the Clinton Administration's goals of sustaining the U.S. military and promoting democracy as espoused in *A National Security Strategy for Engagement and Enlargement* in the mid-1990s.

The other group of Bush's advisors coalesced around the pragmatic Secretary of State Colin Powell. Like his "Powell Doctrine" years earlier in the Persian Gulf War, the retired-general-turned-diplomat continued to believe that carefully calculated applications of force represented the best options for military strategy and foreign policy in 2001. President Bush favored Powell's version of political realism for his election campaign platform and his first months in office.

Then, events on September 11, 2001, marked a major shift in American foreign policy and military strategy. On that clear and sunny Tuesday morning, Al-Qaeda terrorists hijacked four commercial passenger airliners. Following a plan masterminded by Osama bin Laden, they flew two aircraft into the twin towers of the World Trade Center in New York City, causing both 110-story skyscrapers to collapse in less than two hours. A third plane crashed into the Pentagon in Washington, D.C., damaging a large section of that building. Passengers overwhelmed hijackers in the fourth airliner and forced it to plummet to the ground and explode before the terrorists could crash into another building. In all, 2,996 people perished in the worst act of terrorism in American history. These attacks left an indelible mark on the psyche of President Bush, who then single-mindedly tried to bring the perpetrators to justice and stop future terrorist acts against the United States.

These attacks resulted in the "Bush Doctrine" and the "Global War on Terror." The president decided to retaliate against Al-Qaeda and the Taliban-controlled nation of Afghanistan that was supporting the group. Congress wholeheartedly backed Bush's decision three days after the attack in a Joint Resolution that gave the president almost unlimited authority to use force "to deter and prevent acts of international terrorism against the United States."

The president launched a retaliatory invasion into Afghanistan in October 2001 and later a preemptive invasion into Iraq in 2003. Both actions corresponded to the neoconservative advisors' sense of projecting American power across the globe. Cheney and Rumsfeld, for example, seemed to view the fight against terrorism as a zero-sum game not unlike the Cold War. Just as the world had once been divided into opponents or supporters of communism, so, too, was the world of the twenty-first century separated into opponents or supporters of terrorism. Sadly, this bifurcated model did not reflect the complex and fluid post–Cold War environment.

Combating terrorism posed serious challenges for the U.S. military. Even with the move toward lighter and more mobile forces in the late 1990s, American military units were ill-prepared to fight enemies such as Al-Qaeda that operated in decentralized cells. Because they were non-state actors, Al-Qaeda members could strike civilian or military targets with little or no warning. The "non-state actor" was a new name for groups such as guerrillas, partisans, and irregulars. National borders did not matter to them, and civilian immunity was ignored. Achieving victory in this nebulous conflict required adjustments in American strategy as well as force structure. Neither President Bush nor his neoconservative advisors, however, appeared cognizant of these distinctive problems of combating terrorism.

Immediate American Retaliation: Operation Enduring Freedom, 2001–03

Just four weeks after the 9/11 attacks, President Bush ordered the start of Operation ENDURING FREEDOM (OEF) on October 7, 2001. Backed by a coalition including NATO and other nations, the United States invaded Afghanistan to depose the oppressive Taliban government, destroy the Al-Qaeda presence, and install a more stable political system. The coalition forces encountered setbacks in dealing with the rugged terrain and inclement weather in Afghanistan. There could be no massive movement of tanks or ground units. Instead, the American-led coalition deployed smaller, more agile units together with helicopters and air assault tactics reminiscent of search and destroy missions in Vietnam.

The military portions of OEF can be divided into two phases, with the first lasting until December 2001. American and British forces used aircraft and cruise missiles to destroy Taliban and Al-Qaeda bases. Next, on the ground, American Special Forces units and some anti-Taliban Afghan fighters captured the city of Mazar-e Sharif near the northern border of Afghanistan. Meanwhile, British units secured the large airfield at Bagram, which in turn became the coalition's main base for logistical support and ongoing aerial operations. By early December, American, British, and friendly Afghan forces had secured the cities of Kabul, Kondoz, and Kandahar after bitter combat. The fall of Kandahar marked the end of the Taliban regime. These victories pushed the retreating Taliban and Al-Qaeda fighters farther into southern Afghanistan, or to the east toward Pakistan.

Running from December 2001 through March 2002, the second phase of OEF entailed consolidating gains in Afghanistan and completing operations to defeat the Taliban elsewhere in the country. The United States installed the previously exiled Hamid Karzai as the interim leader of Afghanistan, but he wielded only limited power outside the capital of Kabul. December also saw the initial efforts to create the Afghan National Army. The new NATO-led International Security Assistance Force (ISAF) initially trained and advised new Afghan units, but the ISAF eventually began to fight alongside them.

After losing control of Kandahar, some remnants of the Taliban and Al-Qaeda took refuge in the caves at Tora Bora in mountains near the Pakistani border. It also appeared likely that Osama bin Laden might be hiding in the area. Beginning on December 12, 2001, American, British, and German Special Forces units joined friendly Afghan forces in a methodical sweep through Tora Bora's extensive complex of caves. Although successful in killing some Al-Qaeda and Taliban fighters in the next five days, many enemy survivors escaped to safety in Pakistan.

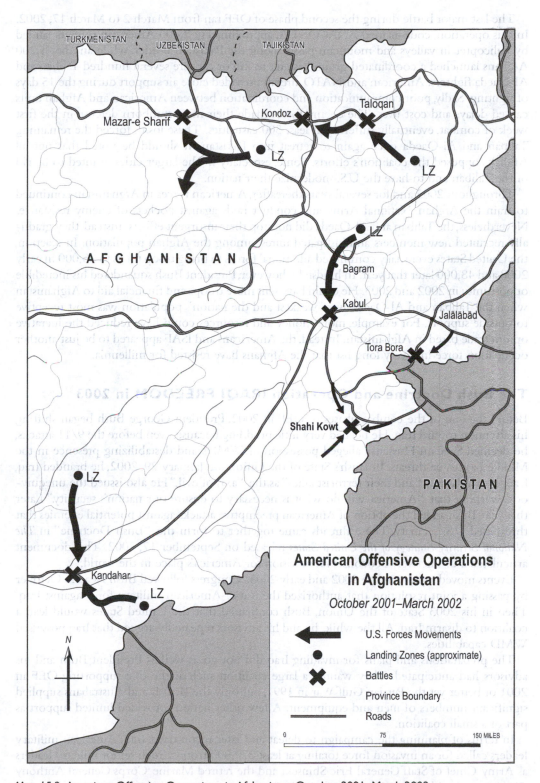

**American Offensive Operations
in Afghanistan**

October 2001–March 2002

← U.S. Forces Movements

● Landing Zones (approximate)

✕ Battles

Province Boundary

Roads

0   75   150 MILES

Map 15.2 American Offensive Operations in Afghanistan, October 2001–March 2002

The last major battle during the second phase of OEF ran from March 2 to March 17, 2002. In this operation, code-named ANACONDA, approximately 2,000 American soldiers landed by helicopter in valleys and mountain passes along the Pakistani border, while another 1,200 Afghans launched a coordinated ground assault to kill or capture several hundred Taliban and Al-Qaeda fighters. American and NATO aircraft provided close air support during the 15 days of fighting. Sadly, poor communication and coordination between American and Afghan units caused delays and cost lives. The enemy forces made their most stubborn defense in the first week of combat, eventually suffering at least 500 casualties. These losses forced the remaining Taliban and Al-Qaeda once again to retreat into Pakistan. It should be noted that not all Afghans opposed the coalition's efforts. Some, especially in the larger cities, wanted to be rid of the Taliban and to have the U.S. modernize their nation.

Throughout 2002 and for several years thereafter, American forces in Afghanistan continued to train the Afghan National Army and conduct raids against pockets of enemy resistance. Nevertheless, the Taliban and Al-Qaeda did not stop their insurgent efforts. Instead, they gradually recruited new members and instigated unrest among the Afghan population. In reaction, the United States eventually committed additional forces to bring troop totals to 25,000 in early 2008 and 48,000 later that year. In hindsight, however, President Bush squandered his incredible opportunity in 2002 and 2003. He could have sent more troops and financial aid to Afghanistan when the Taliban and Al-Qaeda were weakest and the nation's population was most receptive to outside support. For example, more money and resources could have reduced the lucrative opium trade based in Afghanistan. Instead, the Americans and ISAF appeared to be just another occupation force in a very long list that the Afghans have resisted for millennia.

The Bush Doctrine and Operation IRAQI FREEDOM in 2003

Before the end of the combat phases of OEF in 2002, President George Bush began shifting his attention toward Iraq. He needed very little prodding because, even before the 9/11 attacks, he deemed Saddam Hussein's alleged possession of WMDs and destabilizing presence in the Middle East to be threats. In Bush's State of the Union on January 29, 2002, he branded Iraq, Iran, North Korea, "and their terrorist allies" as the "axis of evil." He also issued the unequivocal warning that "America will do what is necessary to ensure our nation's security." Later that year, Bush added the option of American preemptive attacks against potential enemies that threatened U.S. security. These threads came together to form the "Bush Doctrine" in *The National Security Strategy of the United States* released on September 17, 2002. This document articulated a distinctively neoconservative vision for America's place in the world.

Events moved rapidly in late 2002 and early 2003. Congress followed Bush's lead in October by passing a joint resolution that authorized the use of American military force against Iraq. Then in his 2003 State of the Union, Bush confirmed that the United States would lead a coalition to disarm Iraq. All the while, he and his advisors repeatedly argued that Iraq possessed WMD capabilities.

The preparations and plans for invading Iraq did not go as well as President Bush and his advisors had anticipated. They wanted a large coalition such as the one supporting OEF in 2001 or better yet the Persian Gulf War in 1991, but only the British and Australians supplied significant numbers of men and equipment. A few other nations provided limited support as part of a small coalition.

In terms of planning the campaign to defeat and later reconstruct Iraq, American military leaders called for an invasion force totaling at least 270,000 troops. Such senior military leaders as Army Chief of Staff General Eric Shinseki and the retired Marine Corps General Anthony Zinni agreed with this estimate. In fact, Zinni went so far as to label an invasion of Iraq as a possible "Bay of Goats" in a sarcastic play on words referring to John F. Kennedy's failed Bay of Pigs invasion plan in 1961. No stranger to the Middle East, Zinni previously served as commanding general of CENTCOM from 1997 to 2000.

Despite compelling arguments, Defense Secretary Rumsfeld dismissed such high manpower requests because he believed that American airpower and superior weapons systems could overwhelm all Iraqi resistance. After all, these had worked 12 years earlier in the Persian Gulf War. Besides, the U.S. military has since developed even more effective weapons. Rumsfeld's inflexibility a bore striking resemblance to that of Robert McNamara during the Vietnam War.

Rumsfeld, Vice President Cheney, and other neoconservatives like Deputy Secretary Wolfowitz paid scant attention to the potential complications of reconstructing Iraq after the end of Hussein's regime. They optimistically believed that establishing a new peaceful and stable government would pose few serious problems. Moreover, they assumed that the Iraqi people would eagerly welcome the Americans, and they would rebuild their own government quickly.

With all the pieces in place, President Bush delivered an ultimatum to Saddam Hussein on March 17, 2003: The Iraqi dictator needed to leave his nation within 48 hours or risk facing the consequences. When Hussein did not comply, Bush ordered his CENTCOM commander, General Tommy Franks, to start Operation IRAQI FREEDOM (OIF) two days later. Combat operations began with an aerial "Shock and Awe" campaign against Iraqi military and political targets that left Iraq's senior leaders with little or no communications with units in the field. Then on March 21, some 122,000 American and 21,000 British and Australian ground troops left their bases in Kuwait to invade Iraq.

Major General Bufford Blount's 3rd Infantry Division spearheaded the American attack by charging out of Kuwait to the west into the desert before swinging north toward Iraq's capital city of Baghdad. After moving nearly 300 miles in three days, the division stopped long enough to surround the city of An Najaf. Laying just 100 miles from Baghdad, this city sat along the Tigris River and astride a major crossroads. Although delayed for three days by a massive sandstorm, the 3rd Division captured nearby bridges. After Major General David Petraeus and his 101st Airborne Division arrived on March 28 to finish the bloody task of securing An Najaf, the 3rd Division then continued its drive toward Baghdad. As it worked closer to the capital city, the 101st followed to consolidate the gains and protect supply lines.

Farther to the east, the other major American ground element—the 1st Marine Expeditionary Force—advanced northwest through Iraq on a major highway toward Baghdad. The aggressive Major General James "Mad Dog" Mattis commanded the 1st Marine Division, which was the key combat element of the 1st MEF. Just two days into the campaign on March 23, the Marines saw their first serious action at the city of An Nasiriyah, a major command post of the Iraqi Army and key crossing on the Euphrates River. The Marines captured two large bridges that were used to cross the river and continue their movement north. Even so, enemy forces needed to be cleared from An Nasiriyah. The Marines found themselves fighting not only regular Iraqi Army units but also armed Iraqi militia in civilian clothing. The ensuing battle lasted until March 29 but cost minimal American casualties. Once across the Euphrates, the Marines made rapid headway north until they reached the outskirts of Baghdad.

While the 1st Marine Expeditionary Force approached the eastern side of the capital city, elements of 3rd Infantry Division faced some of the war's most fierce combat in the Battle of Saddam International Airport on April 4, 2003. In a few hours, American units destroyed 30 Soviet-made T-72 tanks and killed several hundred Iraqi soldiers and militiamen before taking control of the airport. Thereafter, the attack on Baghdad began. On April 5 and again on April 7, the 3rd Division's armor units made "thunder runs" through the streets of the city. Columns of M1A1 Abrams tanks and Bradley Fighting Vehicles made quite a spectacle roaring through Baghdad and demolishing Iraq military vehicles. Thereafter, the 3rd Division entered in the

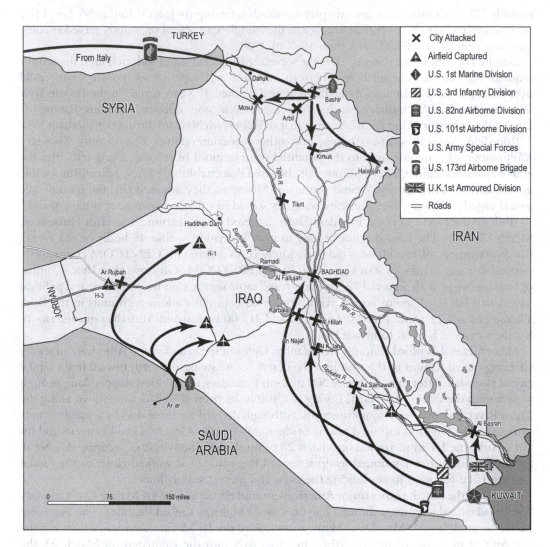

Map 15.3 American Offensive Operations in Iraq, March–May 2003

city en masse from the west, while the Marines swept in from the east. They quickly captured Saddam Hussein's palace and other government buildings. Although it required several more days to mop up resistance in the city, the Battle of Baghdad ended on April 9, 2003. The collapse of Hussein's regime ignited celebrations in the streets by some Iraqi civilians and looting by others.

Between March 17 and April 9, Americans experienced comparatively low casualties: 83 men killed in action, and 184 wounded in action. Iraqi losses were much worse, including 9,000 dead combatants and untold thousands of dead or wounded civilians caught in the crossfire. Despite the best American efforts, Saddam Hussein escaped before Baghdad fell. Over the next three weeks, Iraqi soldiers fled north of the capital, surrendered to coalition forces, or merely returned to their homes. Finally, while standing on the deck of the aircraft carrier USS *Abraham Lincoln* on May 1, 2003, an ebullient George Bush announced to the world that major combat operations had ceased in Iraq. Hanging overhead for all cameras to film, a massive banner read "Mission Accomplished." The United States had won the war, but could America win the peace that followed?

OIF: Nation-Building, the Insurgency, and the Surge, 2003–11

During the planning and preparations for OIF, senior American leaders such as Vice President Cheney, Secretary of Defense Rumsfeld, and Deputy Secretary of Defense Wolfowitz failed to anticipate the enormous commitment required to rebuild Iraq after the initial invasion. Several senior officers in the military also bore responsibility for problems. Whether from naïveté or hubris, they assumed that 25 million Iraqis would hail the Americans as liberators and willingly work to create a democracy to replace Hussein's oppressive regime.

Indeed, neoconservatives were so certain that stability would follow the American victory that prewar plans called for commanding officers of battalions and brigades to rotate out of their units in July 2003, barely four months after the start of hostilities. In hindsight, this decision caused serious problems because those commanding officers left their units just as they began to make contacts with Iraqis and learn about their areas of operations. With little understanding of these cultural or military contexts, the incoming commanders stumbled along trying to establish order. Meanwhile, the Iraqi insurgency gained more strength.

Apart from incorrect assumptions about the Iraqis' reception of the American troops, another set of unanticipated difficulties occurred in the U.S. military. The endless deployments took tolls on American service personnel and on the military's operational readiness. At any given time from 2003 until 2008, some 100,000 Americans served in Iraq and another 30,000 in Afghanistan. American units began rotations lasting 6–15 months. Then they returned to their home bases for a year of rest, and then they reset in preparation for yet another deployment. Even when soldiers or Marines transferred to new units, they could expect to spend another few months "down range," which was a euphemism for being deployed to Iraq and Afghanistan.

Box 15.1   All-Volunteer Force and the Modular Force at War, 2001–2017

Eleven years in Afghanistan and eight years in Iraq with at least 30,000 uniformed American personnel in each theater created challenges that reverberated from the corps-sized units down to the companies, and from tents outside Baghdad to households at Fort Knox, Kentucky, and everywhere in between. Meeting these challenges has pushed the U.S. military almost to the breaking point.

Some 2.5 million Americans did at least one tour of duty in OIF or OEF. Many served multiple tours in one or both theaters. Spending long periods in the combat zones and away from families put incredible stresses on even the most patriotic and loyal of American servicemen or servicewomen in the All-Volunteer Force. The concept of an AVF worked well enough in periods of relative peace in the 1980s and 1990s or during short conflicts like the Persian Gulf War in 1991. However, these ongoing projections of American force in OIF and OEF required a larger military. Calling the reserve and guard components to federal service represented one means of generating the necessary personnel. These men and women were volunteers who served one weekend per month and two weeks per year in their units. The operational tempo, however, required more manpower than the active, reserve, and guard components could meet.

At home, some Americans contemplated a reinstating of selective service to generate sufficient manpower. This did not occur, however, because too many other Americans remembered the acute problems of the draft in Vietnam. Wealthy or middle-class white men avoided the draft through deferments while lower-income Americans, especially minorities, got saddled with military service in disproportionate numbers in combat units.

Instead, the U.S. military sought to attract more volunteers and keep those already serving in uniform by extending lucrative incentives for enlistment and reenlistment. Appeals to patriotism occurred in the wake of the 9/11 attacks. The armed forces used such slogans as "There's strong and then there's Army Strong," "America's Navy: A Global Force for Peace," "It's not science fiction, it's what we do every day," and "The Few, the Proud, the Marines" to generate interest in enlisting or reenlisting.

The continuous streams of unit deployments in OIF or OEF also required a more flexible American military force structure. In the late 1990s, the U.S. Army's Chief of Staff General Eric K. Shinseki set in motion a major transformation of the traditional force structure built around the division. Numbering 16,000 men, these units included three maneuver brigade combat teams as well as assorted combat support and combat service support elements. The former included engineering or security units, and the latter included the transportation, medical, and other logistical units.

Shinseki believed the existing division was too large and unwieldy for the combat operations the Army was likely to undertake. They possessed the 70-ton M1A1 Abrams tank which, while lethal, was too bulky for urban warfare or mountain warfare. Instead, he wanted to replace the three brigades with four Stryker Brigade Combat Teams (SBCT). Numbering 3,000–4,000 soldiers and commanded by a colonel, the maneuver BCTs included two infantry battalions, one field artillery battalion, and requisite combat support and combat support units. The SBCT's primary vehicles would be the eight-wheeled "Stryker" armored personnel carriers that weighed 20 tons and offered more maneuverability on battlefields and better mobility in logistical terms than the Abrams. Shinseki wanted the SBCT to be deployable by air in a matter of days as opposed to weeks or months for full divisions.

Shinseki retired from the Army before he could complete his transformation efforts. His successor as Army Chief of Staff, General Peter Schoomaker, saw the process through to implementation. On his watch, the Army went from a division-centric to a BCT-centric force structure. This meant the BCT would be self-contained and capable of independent operations or mutual-supporting operations with other units. Schoomaker created infantry and armored (heavy) BCTs in addition to the SBCT. These "modular" BCTs could be tailored to fulfill any type of mission by adding and deleting units from its table of organization and equipment. Different types of BCTs could also be added to a divisional structure under overall command of a major general.

The new modular BCTs helped make the deployments of so many units in so many cycles over 16 years possible, though not without problems. For example, in a one-year deployment, there could be a National Guard infantry battalion from New York attached to a regular Army BCT normally under the 1st Infantry Division based at Fort Riley, Kansas, which in turn would be attached to the headquarters element of the 1st Armored Division based at Fort Bliss, Texas. All these might come under the XVIII Airborne Corps out of Fort Bragg. Matters would have been further complicated by the replacement of the BCT from the 1st Infantry Division with a brigade from the 1st Marine Division several months into the deployment. Each of these levels would have different specialties in infantry, armor, airborne, and amphibious operations. This fluid and confusing patchwork of units made developing coherent tactics, techniques, and procedures very difficult. This is to say nothing of struggles to maintain *esprit de corps* among unit personnel.

In late May 2003, President Bush appointed a American civilian named L. Paul Bremer III to administer the Coalition Provisional Authority in Iraq. In this role, Bremer became the *de facto* head of the new Iraqi state while he directed the reconstruction of Iraq. He found winning the peace to be unworkable. The Iraqi Shi'ites (55 percent), Iraqi Sunnites (30 percent), and the Kurdish Sunnites (15 percent) combined to form a powder keg of ethnic and religious divisions ready to explode. The Sunnites benefited from Saddam Hussein's family background. They enjoyed privileges and positions of authority in the regime run by his Ba'ath ruling party. Conversely, Hussein systematically oppressed the Shi'ites and Kurds. This led to ongoing sectarian violence after Hussein's rule ended in 2003 that hampered American efforts to establish political stability.

Bremer could never match stark military realities with viable political solutions in Iraq. Whether from ignorance, overconfidence, or neoconservative leanings, he supported two decisions that crippled long-term American chances of winning the peace. First, at Bremer's behest, the American occupation purged all Ba'ath Party members from their positions in the Iraqi government. For Bremer, this seemed like a rational decision because some party members served as instruments of death and suffering in Hussein's regime. Expelling all Ba'athists, however, meant that the Iraqi governmental infrastructure needed to be rebuilt from scratch without its most experienced administrators.

Second, Bremer disbanded the Iraqi Army. Once again on face value, this seemed like a prudent decision because too many Iraqi soldiers could exert undue pressure on the fledgling Iraqi government. Disbanding the Army, nevertheless, had the opposite effect. The former soldiers faced uncertain futures with no employment, and thus they became potential recruits for the growing anti-American insurgency. Despite the possibility for negative ramifications, however, Secretary Rumsfeld sanctioned and the high-ranking military leaders executed both of Bremer's fateful decisions. In fact, the official U.S. statements denied the existence of any Iraqi "insurgency" for many months even when evidence clearly demonstrated otherwise.

Some events seemed to validate the logic of Bremer and Rumsfeld. In December 2003, American soldiers captured Saddam Hussein, who had been in hiding since leaving Baghdad. He spent the next three years on trial before being hanged for committing war crimes, crimes against humanity, and genocide. Meanwhile, in January 2005, Iraq held its first competitive election. Three out of five Iraqi adults voted, because violence caused obstructions in a few provinces. Large groups of Sunnites either did not vote because they feared retribution or boycotted the election because they believed the process favored the Shi'ites.

Belying these otherwise encouraging events, many Iranians, Syrians, and Egyptians joined Iraqi insurgents to fight the Americans. They exploited the chaos of sectarian infighting between Sunnite and Shi'ite factions as well as the unpreparedness of the American and coalition forces for unconventional warfare. Making matters worse was the severe damage done to Iraq's infrastructure by the air and ground campaigns during the 2003 invasion. Electrical power, fresh water, and waste disposal only slowly came online in Baghdad and other cities.

Former Iraqi soldiers, Hussein loyalists, and foreign Islamic extremists gathered into small groups in Baghdad, Mosul, Tikrit, and Fallujah. They took up the title *"Jihadists"* to give themselves religious legitimacy inside Iraq and across the Middle East in their fight against, as they saw it, the American "infidels." Thus, religion and political factors became entangled motivations. Employing guerrilla tactics against coalition forces, the insurgents targeted buildings or convoys with suicide bombers, rockets, small arms fire, and improvised explosive devices (IED).

The last of these methods proved to be especially effective against the American units. In fact, they accounted for most the American casualties in OIF and OEF. Made of artillery shells, grenades, or other explosive materials, the IEDs were often homemade land mines or booby traps buried in dirt roads and beside paved roads. They might be triggered by vehicles rolling over pressure plates, or by insurgents remotely detonating them with cell phone signals. Combat stress among Americans rose to alarming levels because they felt helpless to stop these

surprise attacks. Try as they might, American and coalition forces could not consistently counter the IEDs. If Americans used minesweeping equipment that identified metallic objects, the
insurgents switched to nonmetallic materials. Combat engineers on route clearance missions
on roads in Iraq or Afghanistan faced situations akin to playing Russian roulette: Sooner or later
the IEDs, if not detected and neutralized, would cause American casualties. The U.S. forces also
attempted to disrupt the insurgent networks that funded, constructed, and distributed the IEDs
by tracking times, places, and types of devices as part of intelligence analysis.

The worst period of the Iraqi insurgency lasted from 2003 until 2007. During these years,
the coalition forces and the insurgents played a deadly game of hide and seek in Baghdad and
elsewhere. Apart from clearing roads of IEDs and other patrolling efforts, American units
conducted some major operations to rid the "Sunni Triangle" of its insurgents. The cities of
Baghdad in the southeast, Ramadi in the southwest, and Tikrit in the north formed the corners
of area. The city of Fallujah also lay along the southern edge of the triangle. The armed Sunnite
opposition established bases in these urban areas.

American units spent much of 2004 trying to clear insurgents from the Sunni Triangle.
During April, for example, elements of the 1st Marine Division tried to push the enemy out
of Fallujah. One month of hard combat, however, did not bring permanent victory. After the

Figure 15.2 An American Vehicle Disabled by an IED Detonation

Iraqi and Afghan insurgents emplaced thousands of IEDs from 2001 to the present. This unclassified photograph shows
how a detonation of this powerful device could damage the American "Buffalo" Mine Clearance Vehicle. IEDs also killed
or injured thousands of American service personnel in Afghanistan and Iraq since 2001.

Source: U.S. Army Engineer School History Office Archive

Marines withdrew, the insurgents regained control of the city until the Second Battle of Fallujah in late 2004. This time, a more powerful coalition force of 6,500 Marines and several thousand American, British, and Iraqi soldiers launched determined assaults against 3,000 Iraqi insurgents and newly arrived Al-Qaeda fighters defending Fallujah. Beginning on November 6, the battle raged for six long weeks in the most brutal combat experience in Iraq. As coalition units fought from house-to-house, they encountered booby traps and IEDs as well as enemy sniper, small arms, mortar, and rocket fire. Most of the fighting was over by November 16, yet the last insurgent resistance held out until late December. The coalition forces suffered 720 casualties, including 54 Americans killed and 425 wounded in action. Conversely, the enemy lost at least 1,200 killed and some 1,500 captured. Sadly, 800 Iraqi civilians also perished in the melee.

Just as in the Vietnam War, it was often hard to determine if Iraqi noncombatants were friends or foes. An Iraqi man might be seen talking nearby on a cell phone when an IED exploded. Did he detonate the device with his phone? Or was he only an innocent bystander? Noncombatant casualties mounted through years of insurgency. Estimates of dead and wounded among Iraqi civilians exceed 100,000 between the 2003 invasion and 2011 when American units departed Iraq. This figure, however, is likely too low. These losses marred efforts to win support for the new Iraqi government.

Some incidents caused more outrage among Iraqis. By early 2004, a scandal came to light at Abu Ghraib prison in Baghdad. U.S. Army reservists working as guards tortured and abused the Iraqi prisoners held there. The negative publicity about the heinous acts at Abu Ghraib added to an American image already battered by accusations of mistreatment of alleged terrorists detained at Guantanamo Navy Base in Cuba. Other stories surfaced about brutal interrogation tactics that occurred at CIA-run facilities in unnamed foreign countries.

More dispiriting developments occurred in Iraq from 2004 to 2006. The American dead numbered 849 killed in action in 2004, 846 in 2005, and 822 in 2006. Another 20,000 were wounded in ambushes or IED blasts. Despite this heavy price, efforts to quell the insurgency did not stop the violence against Americans or Iraqis. At least 100 IEDs were detonated in Iraq every day in 2006. Deadly sectarian violence persisted among the Sunnites and Shi'ites living in Baghdad and other cities. Each side armed their own militiamen in attempts to cleanse their neighborhoods of any opposing factions. It looked like the Americans could neither protect themselves nor the Iraqis; and the United States seemed to be hopelessly bogged down in another quagmire like Vietnam.

During the frustrations in 2006, a new U.S. strategy for the wars in Iraq and later Afghanistan slowly took shape. A group of military intellectuals and veteran officers gathered by Lieutenant General David H. Petraeus formulated a more viable counterinsurgency doctrine. As the new commanding general of the Combined Arms Command at Fort Leavenworth in Kansas, Petraeus was uniquely placed to put his experience in the field, his doctorate in international relations, and his creative problem-solving skills to use. He and his team compiled their ideas in Field Manual 3–24 *Counterinsurgency* in December 2006. It called for American combat troops to protect the Iraqis and to earn their trust by living, working, and fighting alongside them.

Petraeus' ideas appeared to be a new way of counterinsurgency warfare. They can be, however, traced in part to the Marine Corps' *Small Wars Manual* in 1940, to the Marine Corps' Combined Action Program during the Vietnam War, and to operations directed by Petraeus and other commanders earlier in OIF. One example can be seen in the U.S. Army's 1st Battalion, 35th Armored Regiment, Task Force Conqueror that deployed to Ramadi during the summer and fall of 2006. Lieutenant Colonel Tony Deane commanded this unit in what was then the most dangerous city in Iraq. He reached out to Sunnite sheikhs to forge partnerships with their tribes, who had grown hostile to Al-Qaeda because the terrorist group brutally mistreated their people. Among other positive outcomes was creation of an Iraqi police force and relative stability in Ramadi. Together, Deane's 1st Battalion and the tribes drove the Al-Qaeda forces out of the city and Anbar Province. Across the nation, other Iraqis rallied to fight Al-Qaeda in what became known as the "Anbar Awakening."

Then, in January of 2007, President Bush ordered the deployment of 20,000 additional troops to Iraq, raising the total strength to 170,000 later that year. As part of this "Surge," American units left the relative safety of their fortified bases to work closely with the Iraqi Army, provide protection for the Iraqi civilians, and direct overwhelming force against insurgents. Bush chose General Petraeus to lead the Surge as the new commander in Iraq. In this way, Petraeus executed the doctrine that he helped develop in the previous year. Meanwhile, American units not directly involved in combat conducted nation-building operations to help improve the Iraqi people's standard of living. These activities included constructing more roads, bridges, and government buildings.

Although the U.S. military suffered 909 deaths in 2007, the new American counterinsurgency strategy did achieve successes in training Iraq's Army, reducing sectarian violence, and curbing Al-Qaeda activities. A major change at the Department of Defense also facilitated these positive results: After the 2006 Congressional elections and just before the Surge began, President Bush replaced Defense Secretary Donald Rumsfeld with Robert M. Gates. The new secretary changed the neoconservative approach in Iraq and Afghanistan. Gates also ended the myopic culture in Rumsfeld's Defense Department, where little internal debate was tolerated.

After nearly 18 months of intensive combat operations in Iraq, the Surge ended in July 2008. Perhaps the most compelling evidence of its effects can be seen in the declining American deaths in subsequent years: 314 Americans were killed in action in 2008, 149 in 2009, 60 in 2010, and finally to the lowest total of 54 in 2011. In any event, the real measure of the Surge's success as well as that of OIF will take many years to determine.

Barack Obama: Continuity and Change in the U.S. Military, 2009–13

The start of a severe recession at home in the United States and ongoing problems in Afghanistan proved to be decisive factors in the 2008 American presidential election. The Democratic candidate Barack Obama won a convincing victory over his Republican rival, John McCain. Obama then spent his first term working toward several goals: withdrawing the U.S. military from Iraq, expanding the military commitment in Afghanistan, transforming social relations in the American military, utilizing advanced technology in operations, and embracing multilateral approaches to American military affairs and foreign policies. Because Barack Obama's presidency is so recent, the level of analysis cannot be as robust as it will be after more time has passed. Nevertheless, some observations can be made.

During his 2008 presidential campaign, Obama promised to bring American troops home from Iraq. Indeed, the Iraqi Parliament passed legislation in November 2008 that required American forces to withdraw by 2011. Shortly after taking office, Obama announced that the American military presence would drop from the current 150,000 troops to 50,000 in mid-2010. Obama directed the remaining American units to train Iraq's armed forces and continue nation-building efforts as part of Operation NEW DAWN, his new name for the American mission in Iraq.

The Iraqi military took on more responsibilities to maintain peace between the religious factions and continue the fight against the insurgents. Not unlike the way Richard Nixon extricated the United States from Vietnam, this process might best be termed as "Iraqization." A steady stream of Americans came home until the final unit left Iraqi soil on December 18,

2011. Although Iraq's efforts to maintain order were successful during the drawdown, its status as a stable and viable nation has since faced many problems.

Meanwhile, President Obama recognized that the decade-long attempts to modernize and democratize Afghanistan teetered on the edge complete failure. The Bush Administration never provided sufficient resources to OEF after launching OIF in 2003. The U.S. military and the ISAF could not pacify Afghanistan's rural or mountainous areas. Consequently, Obama expanded the commitment in this nation from 36,000 troops in 2009 to more than 100,000 in 2011. For the president, rescuing Afghanistan was necessary to save it from failure, maintain his own credibility as a leader, and reverse the growth of the Taliban and Al-Qaeda influence. Later in 2009, Obama set a date of mid-2011 to withdraw those troops. By then, it was hoped, the Afghan National Army could perform most of the combat operations against the insurgents.

Despite the additional American manpower, Afghanistan still could have fallen into irrevocable chaos in 2010. Insurgent attacks reached an all-time high of 1,500 incidents. The use of IEDs also rose dramatically, causing most combat-related Americans deaths. Within one year, these jumped from 303 in 2009 to 469 in 2010, and many thousands more were wounded during frequent IED strikes.

Obama turned to General David Petraeus in hopes that he could duplicate the successful Surge in Iraq by directing similarly aggressive counterinsurgency operations in Afghanistan. Between June 2010 and July of the next year, Petraeus put his doctrine into action by sending his troops out to live, work, and fight among the Afghan people. The American and ISAF forces also trained their Afghan counterparts so that, one day, they might act independently in combating insurgents. The cost of 418 American lives in 2011 reflected this greater commitment. That same year, President Obama set a deadline of 2014 for the complete American withdrawal from Afghanistan. However, only American combat operations had ceased by 2014. Even so, as of early 2017, nearly 10,000 American service personnel remained in Afghanistan to advise and train the Afghan military. In addition, U.S. Special Operations Forces and drones remain in country to fight the Taliban, Al-Qaeda, and other threats to Afghan stability and order.

Box 15.2   Changes in American Society and Reflections in the U.S. Military

In his first month as president, Barack Obama began working to repeal the "Don't Ask, Don't Tell" (DADT) policy of the U.S. military. He believed that this ban against military service by openly gay men and women denied them their rights as citizens. Arguments erupted on the airwaves, in Congress, and in courtrooms over the effects on unit cohesion, morale, and discipline if DADT was repealed and the ban against gays in the military was lifted. Those favoring the repeal gradually achieved a sufficient level of support to pass legislation ending DADT through Congress. Obama subsequently signed the legislation into law on December 22, 2010. Necessary changes in military legal procedures worked their way through channels over the next nine months until the Department of Defense ended DADT on September 20 of the next year. Since then, openly gay men and women have enlisted and reenlisted in the U.S. military, and a few same-sex marriages between service personnel have occurred on bases. Though opposition to the service of gays or bisexuals continues among social conservatives, the ban or DADT has not been reinstated.

More recently, at President Obama's behest, in June 2016 the Defense Department lifted its ban on transgender people serving in the military. The Defense Department's legal experts have also worked to revise the *Uniform Code of Military Justice* to account for the new sexual orientation by formulating procedures for handling abuse or other bad conduct. Other military organizations, such as the Army's TRADOC, developed and started implementing training and medical programs in line with more open policies. As of early 2017, estimates of transgender personnel run from 6,000 to 15,000 out of 1.3 million people serving in the U.S. military. Most people, however, have not yet self-identified as transgender. It is still uncertain what effects such inclusivity will have on the military's morale and unit cohesion in the long term.

Women have also made significant strides in breaking down institutional barriers, particularly regarding combat roles, long a divisive issue in military, political, and public circles. Although many military occupational specialties (MOS) have been opened to women for decades, the U.S. Army's combat arms and Special Forces units remained closed to them; the Air Force, Navy, and Marine Corps also had gender-based restrictions. The arguments opposing women in combat resembled those surrounding gays, invoking concerns about discipline, behavior, cohesion, and morale. Additional concerns centered on standards of physical strength which, if lowered to accommodate women, could result in reduced unit combat effectiveness as well as risk higher casualties.

All these factors notwithstanding, women did serve in combat zones, come under enemy fire, and return fire in Iraq and Afghanistan. In conflicts with no front lines, everyone outside secure bases became targets. Some female service personnel proved their mettle in combat. Military Police Sergeant Lee Ann Hester received the Silver Star for exceptional valor in close combat in 2005. She helped defend an American convoy during an ambush by insurgents. During the ensuing melee, Hester came under direct fire, attacked an enemy position, and killed at least three insurgents before the fighting ended.

Hester's example and other similar actions by female service personnel in Iraq and Afghanistan helped pave the way for President Obama and the Defense Department to end the ban on female combatants on January 24, 2013. This effectively opened almost every MOS to women, who then comprised 14 percent and 200,000 members of all branches of the U.S. military. Women started training in the combat arms, but they were not immediately assigned to combat units.

Higher up the military's chain of command, women enjoyed other firsts. In 2008 the first female officer—Ann E. Dunwoody—reached the rank of general, and assumed command of U.S. Army Materiel Command. Also significant was Michelle Howard's promotion to admiral and assignment as the Vice Chief of Naval Operations in 2014. As an African-American woman, her achievement broke barriers for her race as well as her gender. Two years later in 2016, Howard assumed her duties as the first African-American female to command U.S. Naval Forces Europe and U.S. Naval Forces Africa.

In recent years, women have made significant strides toward equity. Nevertheless, ongoing debates about their physical strength, let alone the incidents of sexual assault, harassment, and misconduct, continue to be very real issues that defy simplistic resolutions. Periodic investigations have revealed abuses endured by some women in uniform and perpetrated by some men serving with them as superiors, peers, or subordinates.

Obama's decisions regarding Iraq, Afghanistan, as well as social transformations in the armed forces showed his efforts to change the way the U.S. military functions as an institution and a policy instrument. These fit into an overarching "Obama Doctrine." Since taking office in 2009, he has utilized American force sparingly in many cases but not in others. The U.S. military left Iraq by the end of 2011 yet ramped up to meet threats in Afghanistan in 2010. Obama introduced negotiation and multilateralism as diplomatic options instead of the former-President Bush's penchants for confrontation and unilateralism. Obama dropped what he believed to be belligerent terminology in the "Global War on Terror" in favor of the less intrusive-sounding "Overseas Contingency Operations."

President Obama's *National Security Strategy* statement of May 2010 echoed in some ways President Clinton's *National Security Strategy for Engagement and Enlargement* of 15 years earlier. However, Obama downgraded traditional hard power approaches to American defense and foreign policy in favor of what was called "smart power." This tempered military force—to be used only when necessary—with soft power's reliance on negotiation, alliance, persuasion, and assistance. He also embraced multilateralism through organizations such as the United Nations, which he viewed as the arbiter of international disputes. Meanwhile the U.S. military began significant reductions in force after 2011.

Despite moving away from the "Bush Doctrine" in many areas, Obama expanded two types of military operations employed by his predecessor. First, Obama made much greater use of drones as part of operations by the Defense Department and the CIA. These remote-controlled, unmanned aviation vehicles can fly missions with minimal costs and negligible risks. Some, such as the MQ-1B "Predator," gather real-time intelligence or maximize strike opportunities because they loiter over targets for many hours. Drones are equipped with ultraviolet and infrared technology, so they can see anytime, day or night. Other drones, including the MQ-9 "Reaper," carry offensive munitions,

Figure 15.3 U.S. Air Force "Predator" Drone in Iraq

The U.S. Air Force's MQ-1B "Predator" Unmanned Aerial Vehicle (drone) takes off in support of Operation Iraqi Freedom in 2008. Using advanced capabilities, these drones provide close air combat support as well as intelligence, surveillance, and reconnaissance collection.

© U.S. Air Force/ Handout /Corbis

including the AGM-114 Hellfire air-to-surface missiles. These "hunter-killer" drones use laser-guidance systems to make precision strikes against personnel, vehicles, or buildings with little warning. With these characteristics, the U.S. military's drones perform the role for the American military that IEDs do for enemy insurgents: they are "force multipliers" in military terms.

Clandestine drone attacks have been credited with killing thousands of terrorists. Among the high-value individuals targeted by the drones were Anwar al-Awlaki in Yemen in 2011, Moktar Ali Zubeyr in Syria in 2014, and Mohammed Emwazi (infamously known as "Jihadi John") in Syria in 2015. Depending upon which source is used, these American attacks purportedly killed between 5,000 and 15,000 terrorists in the Middle East. Sadly, estimates of civilian deaths exceed the larger figure.

During Obama's two-term presidency, American drones made more than 550 strikes, or 10 times more than occurred in President Bush's eight years. The combined totals do not include drone strikes conducted during combat operations in Iraq or Afghanistan. For instance, more than 1,200 drones dropped ordnance on targets in Afghanistan from 2009 through 2012. It should be noted that these are only the attacks known through open sources. Many more drone strikes doubtless remain classified.

Second, Obama made frequent use of the Special Operations Forces like the 75th Ranger Regiment, Delta Force, and Navy SEAL (Sea, Air, Land) teams. These elite units infiltrate hostile territory, carry out precise tasks, and extricate themselves. The most publicized mission occurred on May 2, 2011, when SEAL Team Six killed Osama bin Laden. Efforts to find him had started right after the 9/11 attacks. It took nearly a decade before his location and identity could be confirmed with some certainty. The SEALs flew into Pakistan on advanced stealth helicopters, landed in bin Laden's compound, forced entry into his house, and killed him and several other family members and followers.

These units fall under the overall control the U.S. Special Operations Command. This organization has grown from 45,000 personnel in 2001 to 70,000 in 2017, while its budget increased even more dramatically, from $2.3 billion in 2001 to $6.6. billion in 2006 and finally to $10.8 billion in 2017. These rising numbers indicate how important the special operations and covert capabilities have become over time. In 2014 alone, President Obama deployed the Special Operations Forces on covert operations, military advising, security assistance, psychological operations, and other missions to 125 foreign nations.

Barack Obama and Uncertainties Facing the U.S. Military 2013–2017

After handily winning reelection in 2012, President Obama continued his preference for international cooperation through organizations such as the United Nations, rather than the American unilateralism practiced by his predecessor and the neoconservatives. Yet, Obama did not stop directing the U.S. military to conduct ongoing American drone strikes and covert operations.

Although allowing some closure because of the withdrawal from Iraq and assassination of Osama bin Laden, the year 2011 marked the start of several uncharted tests for Obama and the United States that became more challenging during his second term, from 2013 to 2017. Spontaneous popular uprisings and civil wars in the Middle East threatened to upset the region's delicate balance of power. Another test occurred as Iran came closer and closer to developing nuclear weapons. Elsewhere in East Asia and Eastern Europe, ominous signs could be seen in the rising ambitions of China and Russia. Meanwhile, American military units, albeit with fewer personnel, remained in Afghanistan, and the situation in Iraq remained dangerously fluid.

Back in December 2010, young people in Tunisia started popular demonstrations collectively known as the "Arab Spring." The protesters took to the streets to challenge their nation's authoritarian oppression, human rights violations, economic decline, high unemployment, and other serious problems; they saw little hope in the future. Tunisia's government was overthrown in 2011, and several attempts to form a more representative political system have followed.

Extensive use of social media fanned the flames of activism that eventually engulfed North Africa and then the Middle East. Over the next two years, similar protest movements toppled the governments of Libya, Egypt, and Yemen. However, when beset by these challenges to their power, the governments of Syria and Iraq fought to maintain control. In all these examples, bloody civil wars followed the Arab Spring. Meanwhile, President Obama looked on in ambivalence, wary of getting sucked into more Middle East conflicts yet also hopeful for some positive reforms.

The two most conspicuous conflicts occurred in Syria and Iraq. In early 2011, the Arab Spring protesters in Syria wanted the ouster of their nation's dictator, President Bashar al-Assad. Assad's security forces reacted with arrests and gunfire. This situation degenerated into the Syrian Civil War by July 2011. The rebels formed the Free Syrian Army (FSA) to overthrow Assad. In the six years of fighting that followed, as many as 500,000 Syrians have died and more than 6.5 million abandoned their homes; some 2.5 million of these fled the nation as refugees. As the horrific conflict drags on, these figures will rise.

President Obama reacted to the Syrian Civil War by condemning Assad. He also drew a "red line" that threatened harsh retaliation if Assad used chemical weapons. For his part, Assad took every possible measure to crush the FSA, including crossing that line and using chemical weapons in 2013. Obama demurred and did not respond with military force. Like so many Americans, he was reluctant to risk getting the United States directly involved into another conflict in the Middle East.

The Syrian Civil War grew more convoluted as the years dragged on. Saudi Arabia, Turkey, and Jordan eventually provided aid to FSA. Iran and Russia began supporting Assad in his bid to stay in power. Their assistance, including arms and money, helped him to crush the FSA. Elsewhere, the Kurds in Syria took up arms against Assad. However, the Kurdish involvement muddied the waters because Turkey started to fight the Kurds in addition to supporting the rebels against Assad. By 2013, the Syrian Civil War pitted the Sunnite nations supporting the rebels against Assad and several Shi'ite nations. Early the next year, a new group of Sunnite extremists—known as Islamic State of Iraq and Syria or ISIS—entered the fray and added more confusion because they attacked both rebels and Kurds but not Assad's forces.

During these same years, the hopes for a stable Iraqi state foundered as the nation plunged into its own civil war. Increasing violence by Al-Qaeda and sectarian Muslim factions undermined Iraq's already fragile political system. Those insurgents took advantage of the power vacuum left by the withdrawal of American forces in 2011. The infighting continued until 2013, when ISIS started fighting in Iraq and capturing large swaths of Iraqi territory.

ISIS has other names, including the Islamic State (IS), Islamic State of Iraq and the Levant (ISIL), or the Arabic acronym Daesh (al-**D**awla al-Islamiya fi Iraq wa al-**Sh**am). ISIS carved out a new state in parts of Syria and Iraq with Abu Bakr al-Baghdadi as its leader. The ideology of ISIS finds its roots in the radical Sunnite sect of Wahhabism that embraced exceptionally strict interpretations of sharia law. Nevertheless, ISIS spread across the entire region in part because of effective use of social media platforms for recruitment. Numbering between 30,000 and 200,000 men, ISIS fighters routinely execute Iraqis and Syrians. These include enemy combatants and civilians, such as more moderate Sunnites, Shi'ites, Kurds, Christians, and Yazidis. ISIS members have also used torture, sexual assault, and ethnic cleansing against opponents. This level of brutality proved to be too excessive even for Al-Qaeda, who joined the fight against

ISIS in 2015. In fact, Middle Eastern nations as disparate as Iran and Jordan have attacked ISIS because, according to Wahhabism, the Iranians and Jordanians are apostates with erroneous Islamic beliefs. This made ISIS a mutual enemy.

As early as 2013, President Obama sent aid to FSA in their fight against ISIS in Syria. He also deployed American military personnel to bolster the flagging Iraqi government. Drone strikes and covert operations increased. Although losing ground in Syria and Iraq in early 2017, ISIS continues to undermine peace efforts in the Middle East.

In addition to benefiting from the Arab Spring's consequences, President Obama helped craft an agreement in 2015 with Iran to regulate its development of nuclear weapons. Called the "Iran Deal," the Iranians agreed to inspections of their nuclear research sites by the International Atomic Energy Agency. In return, existing trade and financial sanctions against Iran were ended. If the Iranians were found to be procuring nuclear weapons, then more sanctions or worse repercussions could ensue. This agreement highlighted Obama's approach to foreign and military policy in that the United Nations, not the United States, received the reports on Iran. American detractors have panned the Iran Deal as appeasement of Iran, while Obama's supporters praise it as an example of multilateralism. Only time will tell which side's assertions are correct.

The Middle East was hardly the only region posing problems for President Obama and the United States. In East Asia and Eastern Europe, the resurgent Chinese and Russians started flexing their military muscles in the South China Sea and the Ukraine. Not only did the Chinese and Russians take advantage of perceived American weaknesses but they also hoped to bolster their respective governments' legitimacy and their people's pride at home, where their economies have stagnated. In addition, the volatile North Koreans frequently threaten armed conflict against the South Koreans the Japanese, or most recently the United States, which could completely destabilize the entire Pacific Rim.

This potential for conflict pushed Obama to reorient the U.S. military's focus in the "Pivot to the Pacific" strategy of 2012. The American military footprint in the western Pacific has grown larger as additional personnel and material moved into the region. The military has begun planning for offensive and defensive amphibious operations reminiscent of the Second World War. The scale has expanded since 1945, but not the principles. The American plans included a new concept called "Anti-Access/Anti-Denial" that updated amphibious doctrines, force structures, and specialized vessels for the twenty-first century, when adversaries possess high-speed aircraft, long-range missiles, or tactical nuclear weapons. It is no longer sufficient to control the air, ground, sea, and underwater spaces inside the horizon. Newer weapons systems require successful amphibious operations to establish supremacy over several hundred miles in all directions.

Box 15.3   Counting the Costs of the Wars in Iraq and Afghanistan, 2001–2017

More than 2.6 million Americans spent at least one tour of duty in Iraq and Afghanistan, and many did multiple tours. As of August 2017, the American death tolls in Iraq reached 4,497 personnel and in Afghanistan another 2,394. An additional 53,000 Americans were physically wounded during operations in the Middle East. Amputations and traumatic brain injuries rank among the most debilitating injuries. Lastly, there are untold hundreds of thousands of veterans suffering from invisible wounds of mind and spirit. In fact, it is estimated that one-third of all American veterans could be diagnosed with mental health conditions ranging from anxiety to PTSD.

These numbers point to the incredibly high financial and human costs of some 16 years of fighting. Approximately one-half of the 2.6 million veterans receive some type of disability benefit. For those with serious injuries and mental health conditions, the costs are much greater. The United States government is obligated to spend several hundred billion dollars to take care of these veterans over the next few decades. Even with the best management and more money, however, the federal and state veterans affairs programs face almost insurmountable tasks to provide care for the post-9/11 generation of veterans, let alone those from the Vietnam War.

Yet there are other second- or third-order human costs of the wars from 2001 to 2017. Most deployed veterans missed their children's first words or birthdays or graduations. Their spouses at home encountered daily challenges of being *de facto* single parents. After the joyous return of loved ones from Iraq or Afghanistan, many veterans and their families faced difficulties in readjusting to their changed lives. Too often, there is no way to recapture the pre-deployment normalcy. Some decide that divorces are the only options.

Although less visible to the public, additional costs can be seen in homelessness and suicide rates among veterans of Iraq and Afghanistan. As many as 50,000 of them are living on the streets. Some have lost their jobs. Others have succumbed to substance abuse. Many may also suffer with mental health conditions.

The most arresting statistics can be seen in veteran suicides. According to government studies, as many as 20 veterans take their own lives every day. That accounted for more than 7,000 suicides in 2014 alone. This single figure comes close to the total number of combat-related deaths of American service personnel during 16 years of conflict. Estimates point to 50,000 suicides since 2001. When comparing these statistics to civilian suicide rates, veterans are 21 percent more likely to commit suicide. In another tragic statistic, female veterans kill themselves six times (600 percent) more often than civilian women do. The ratio doubles for women ages 18–29, who take their own lives 12 times more often than civilians of the same age range do. Possible causes for these suicide include irrepressible feelings of hopelessness, shame, loneliness, or anxiety, as well as PTSD, Traumatic Brain Injury, and similar conditions. Assistance for veterans and their families can be found at these web pages of government and private organizations: www.mental health.va.gov/suicide_prevention/ and www.legion.org/suicideprevention.

Sources: U.S. Department of Defense: U.S. Casualty Status, 23 August 2017, www.defense.gov/casualty.pdf (accessed 24 August 2017); and U.S. Department of Veterans Affairs, "Suicide Among Veterans and Other Americans, 2001–14," 2 August 2016, www.mentalhealth.va.gov/docs/2016suicidedatareport. pdf (accessed 10 April 2017); and C.A. Hoffmire, et al., "Changes in Suicide Mortality for Veterans and Nonveterans by Gender and History of VHA Service Use, 2000–2010," *Psychiatric Services* 66 (September 2015): 959–65.

The year 2017 is too soon to offer any concrete conclusions about Barrack Obama's presidency and especially his second term. Even so, looking back to survey his eight years in office, certain patterns can be observed in his policies regarding the use of military force. Obama embraced the idea of an agile and lean American military that employs new weapons systems to achieve limited goals. He repeatedly used drones to attack terrorists and deployed Special Forces units to conduct clandestine operations. Thus, on one level, Obama's ways of war harkened back to the 1950s and the Eisenhower Doctrine embodied by the slogans "New Look" and "More Bang for the Buck." Both Presidents Dwight D. Eisenhower and Barrack Obama slashed military expenditures by reducing personnel levels. Both believe that the U.S. military should use advanced technology and covert action in pursuit of the nation's strategic objectives. Lastly, they willfully violated the sovereignty of other nations when they deemed it necessary to do so.

In other ways, however, Obama's military and foreign policies also resembled those of Jimmy Carter. Both presidents favored more international cooperation and softer diplomacy as replacements for unilateralism and belligerence. For his part, Obama appeared to waver in cases like his red line against Syria's use of chemical weapons in 2012 and later in his Iranian nuclear deal in 2015. Both Carter and Obama faced stubborn opposition in Congress, despite enjoying Democratic majorities during at least part of their respective presidencies. However, similarities between them cannot be taken much further because, whereas Carter eschewed covert operations, Obama has readily used drones and Special Forces throughout his presidency.

Writing from their perspectives as Irish scholars of international relations and history, David Fitzgerald and David Ryan believe that Barack Obama faced a "dilemma" in foreign policy and military affairs that resulted "from the fact that politically he must engage with the constraints of the US-centered" view of the world, "while simultaneously realizing, but finding it hard to maneuver outside it, that those beyond the US 'sphere of discourse'—allied or *not*—have a very different vision of the desired objectives."[2] This same dilemma plagued George W. Bush from 2001 to 2009, and it will confront the recently elected President Donald Trump in 2017 and beyond. In fact, the disconnect between what Americans want for other nations and what

Figure 15.4 U.S. Army Engineer Divers Rehabilitate a Pier After an Earthquake

Apart from combat operations, the U.S. military has committed significant resources to humanitarian efforts. In this photograph, a U.S. Army engineer diver rehabilitated a pier in the harbor of Port-au-Prince, Haiti. A major earthquake in January 2010 wrecked the pier, so that no humanitarian material could be offloaded. The divers spent 10 weeks to make the pier operational again and thus speed the relief shipments.

Source: U.S. Army Engineer School History Office Archive

those other nations' peoples actually want for themselves may be the quintessential dilemma encountered by every president from Theodore Roosevelt to Donald Trump.

Epilogue and Conclusion

What the American ways of war will look like in the future is uncertain. The unexpected election of Donald Trump as president in November 2016 makes forecasting still more difficult. The campaign against former Secretary of State Hillary Clinton saw Trump make bombastic statements regarding how, where, and why the United States might use military force to achieve national goals. After taking office in January 2017, Trump has defied orthodox thinking in foreign policy and military affairs circles. He seems to be neither an internationalist like Obama, nor a neoconservative like Rumsfeld. Instead, the mercurial President Trump wraps himself in isolationist rhetoric in one breath before touting his support for American military prowess in the next. During his first months in office in 2017, Trump has caused confusion in Europe and NATO, yet ordered missile attacks on Syria and increased troop deployments to the Middle East. His decisions do not necessarily match campaign statements in 2016. Thus, Trump's goals seem unknowable and appear subject to abrupt changes.

Even with so much uncertainty in 2017, it seems less likely that the United States will become involved in major conventional conflicts, because few potential adversaries could hope to match, let alone surpass, American firepower. Nevertheless, the U.S. military's personnel, vehicles, and weapons systems have endured so many operations years since 2001 that they now show the signs of severe attrition.

Because American forces are stretched very thinly, regional and nongovernmental threats are the greatest concerns. Problems in the Middle East, Africa, East Asia, and Eastern Europe will doubtlessly test President Trump's resolve, just as they did his predecessors. Foreign and military policy making in these regions will require American leadership capable of deftly balancing political, cultural, economic, diplomatic, and military considerations.

Inside the U.S. military, planners, doctrine writers, and research and development organizations will need to prepare for local insurgencies, seaborne piracy, terrorist attacks, and IED and WMD proliferation. Ideologies, whether religious or political, will continue to motivate people to fight. Such dangers as swarms of enemy drones attacking American warships or ground units will grow more real as nations and terrorist groups alike acquire more advanced drone technology. The new terrains of electronic warfare, cyberwarfare, and cyberterrorism are emerging as serious threats to American security. Computers run so much infrastructure that hacking, planting viruses, and emitting electromagnetic pulses could cripple America's communication networks or power grids. Conversely, the U.S. military needs to acquire capabilities to launch its own electronic and cyber operations against hostile nations or non-state actors.

Ultimately, the American military will adapt ways of war to counter new threats, just as it has done for centuries. These developments may include forward-looking technological, operational, or doctrinal innovations that meet dangers before they materialize. Some advances could be made on-the-fly during conflicts. Finally, as is sadly seen in the past, other adaptations could occur only as delayed American reactions to surprise attacks by seen or unseen foes.

Notes

1 White House Office, "National Security Strategy for Engagement and Enlargement," (February 1995), p. ii, www.au.af.mil//au//awc//awcgate//nss//nss-95.pdf (accessed 16 April 2017).
2 David Fitzgerald and David Ryan, *Obama, US Foreign Policy and the Dilemmas of Intervention* (Basingstroke, UK: Palgrave Pivot, 2014), 15.

Short Bibliography

Bailey, Beth. *America's Army: Making of the All-Volunteer Force.* Cambridge: Harvard University Press, 2009.

Bailey, Beth, and Richard H. Immerman, eds. *Understanding the U.S. Wars in Iraq and Afghanistan.* New York: New York University Press, 2015.

Black, Jeremy. *War in the Modern World, 1990–2014.* London and New York: Routledge, 2014.

Bolger, Daniel. *Why We Lost: A General's Inside Account of the Iraq and Afghanistan Wars.* New York: Houghton Mifflin Harcourt, 2014.

Bowden, Mark. *Black Hawk Down: A Story of Modern War.* New York: Atlantic Monthly, 1999.

Deane, Anthony E., and Douglas Niles. *Ramadi Declassified: A Roadmap to Peace in the Most Dangerous City in Iraq.* Bay Village, OH: Praetorian Books, 2016.

Echevarria, Antulio J., II. *Reconsidering the American Way of War: U.S. Military Practice from the Revolution to Afghanistan.* Washington: Georgetown University Press, 2014.

Evans, Ryan, editor-in-chief. *War on the Rocks* (blog). www.warontherocks.com.

Gordon, Michael R., and Bernard Trainor. *The Generals' War: The Inside Story of the Conflict in the Gulf.* Boston: Little, Brown, 1995.

Haynes, Peter D. *Toward a New Maritime Strategy: American Naval Thinking on the Post-Cold War Era.* Annapolis: Naval Institute Press, 2015.

Junger, Sebastien. *War.* New York: Twelve, 2010.

Kaplan, Fred. *The Insurgents: David Petraeus and the Plot to Change the American Way of War.* New York: Simon and Schuster, 2013.

Lambeth, Benjamin S. *The Transformation of American Air Power.* Ithaca: Cornell University Press, 2000.

Laslie, Brian D. *The Air Force Way of War: U.S. Tactics and Training After Vietnam.* Lexington: University of Kentucky Press, 2015.

Ricks, Thomas. *Fiasco: The American Military Adventure in Iraq, 2003 to 2005.* New York: Penguin Press, 2006.

Romaniuk, Scott N., and Francis Grice, eds. *The Future of US Warfare.* London and New York: Routledge, 2017.

Tangredi, Sam J. *Anti-Access Warfare: Countering A2/AD Strategies.* Annapolis: Naval Institute Press, 2013.

Trauschweizer, Ingo. *The Cold War U.S. Army: Building Deterrence for Limited War.* Lawrence: University Press of Kansas, 2008.

Woodward, Bob. *Obama's Wars.* New York: Simon & Schuster, 2010.

Index

Note: page numbers in *italics* refer to figures and maps